AMERICAN ERAS

DEVELOPMENT OF THE INDUSTRIAL UNITED STATES

1878 - 1899

AMERICAN ERAS

DEVELOPMENT OF THE INDUSTRIAL UNITED STATES

1878 - 1899

EDITED BY

VINCENT TOMPKINS

A MANLY, INC. BOOK

GALE

DETROIT   NEW YORK   TORONTO   LONDON

AMERICAN ERAS

DEVELOPMENT OF THE INDUSTRIAL UNITED STATES

1878 - 1899

Matthew J. Bruccoli and Richard Layman, *Editorial Directors*
Karen L. Rood, *Senior Editor*

Printed in the United States of America

The paper used in this publication meets the minimum requirements of American National Standard for Information Sciences-Permanence Paper for Printed Library Materials, ANSI Z39.48-1984. ∞™

Library of Congress Catalog Card Number 95-081586
ISBN 0-7876-1485-8

LIBRARY OF CONGRESS CATALOGING-IN PUBLICATION DATA

American Eras. Development of the Industrial United States, 1878-1899/
    edited by Vincent Tompkins
    P. Cm.
    Includes bibliographical references (p.) And Index.
    Printed in the United States of America
    1. United States—Civilization—1865-1918. I. Tompkins, Vincent.
E168.A5118 1997   97-3939 CIP\
973.8—dc21

CONTENTS

INTRODUCTION

The Gilded Age. In many ways the period from the end of Reconstruction in 1878 to the end of the nineteenth century was marked by excess and extremes. As the newly rich were building summer homes of monumental grandeur in Newport, Rhode Island, immigrants from Russia, Poland, Hungary, and Greece were crowding into dark and airless tenements in New York, Chicago, Milwaukee, and Detroit. Workers seeking better pay and shorter hours were engaged with the owners of railroads, mines, and factories in an intense struggle at a level of violence unimaginable a century later. As industrial expositions such as the World's Columbian Exposition in Chicago in 1893 celebrated the triumphs of modern technology, the American farmer suffered from drought and economic exploitation by the railroads and distant financiers whose fortunes seemed to increase even as the plight of the farmer worsened. While the standard of living for most Americans improved during the late nineteenth century, many noticed a stark contrast between wealth and poverty. As William Dean Howells, one of the era's great men of letters, wrote in *A Traveler from Altruria* (1894), "Accumulation rewarded its own with gains of twenty, of a hundred, of a thousand percent, and to satisfy its need, to produce the labor that operated its machines, there came into existence a hapless race of men who bred their kind for its service, and whose little ones were its prey, almost from their cradles." Henry George, a social critic whose writings criticized the powerful new business monopolies, fostered one of the protest movements of the era. In his widely read *Progress and Poverty* (1879) George wrote that the "association of progress with poverty is the great enigma of our times. So long as all the increased wealth which modern progress brings goes but to build up great fortunes, to increase luxury and make sharper the contrast between the House of Have and the House of Want, progress is not real and cannot be permanent."

The New American City. Nowhere were these contrasts so apparent as in the nation's cities, which absorbed the greatest share of a rapidly growing population and were home to the richest and the poorest of the nation's inhabitants. From 1880 to 1900 the U.S. population increased from 50,262,000 to 76,094,000. Some nine million were immigrants who arrived between 1881 and 1900 in one of the largest waves of immigration in American history. Earlier immigrant groups—British, German, Scandinavian—had often settled in rural areas, but the new immigrants of the 1880s and 1890s flocked to the cities, where wages were higher and where ethnic communities formed around parish churches, mutual-aid societies, and other social institutions capable of preserving some semblance of the life the immigrants had left behind. American cities grew at an astonishing rate. Migrants from rural areas and small towns combined with the new immigrants, mostly from southern and eastern Europe, to swell the ranks of American city dwellers. Chicago had 100,000 residents at the beginning of the Civil War and more than 1 million by the end of the century. During this same period New York City grew from 1.2 million to 3 million people. By 1890 immigrants accounted for 84 percent of the populations of Milwaukee and Detroit, 80 percent in New York, and 87 percent in Chicago. The growing pains that resulted from this rapid expansion were in plain view in almost every American city. Municipal services for delivering fresh water and for disposing of sewage were almost universally inadequate. Tenements, workers' cottages, and apartment buildings sprang up almost overnight, often without adequate zoning regulations and building codes. Tensions among various ethnic and racial groups over neighborhood turf sometimes erupted in violence that urban police forces were ill-equipped to contain. Corruption and inefficiency crippled municipal governments from Boston to San Francisco. For all of their shortcomings, however, the cities were vibrant and exciting, alive with opera houses, dance halls, theaters, department stores, art museums, and amusement parks that continued to lure newcomers for decades to come.

Weak Presidents. The story of the American federal government in the last two decades of the twentieth century is largely a tale of inaction and corruption. Few Americans today remember the names of U.S. presidents between Ulysses S. Grant and William McKinley; fewer still could list their accomplishments. For most of the period presidential candidates were chosen by party elders less for their leadership or charisma than for their suitability as symbols. During the 1870s and into the 1880s Republicans often nominated men who could point to their service in the Civil War, reminding voters that the Democrats had been the party of secession (a strategy known at the time as "waving the bloody shirt"). Until they nominated the electrifying orator William Jennings Bryan in 1896, Democrats tended to counter with equally respectable figures, including a war veteran of their own, whose positions differed only slightly from those of their Republican opponents. Once in office the presidents of the period had little influence over policy making, and much of their time was taken up with filling the thousands of positions in the federal bureaucracy with political allies. Most of the power in the federal government resided in Congress, where both houses seemed more intent on dispensing their own political favors than setting policy, and in the courts, which acted as a brake on reform impulses that threatened things as they were, overruling attempts by state governments to regulate railroad practices, blocking attempts to organize national unions of industrial workers, and upholding state laws establishing segregation in the South.

Strong Political Parties. Tariffs, land policy, currency, and railroads were perennial topics of oratory and debate, but on all but the tariff issue real differences between the parties were minor. Yet few institutions in the Gilded Age were as central to American culture as political parties. Organized along ethnic, racial, religious, occupational, and class lines, the parties gave the individual (male) citizen an important way of establishing a place in the community. Parties performed a practical function as well. As dispensers of patronage jobs and other forms of assistance, they were sometimes the only safety net for those living on the edge of poverty, and many happily traded their votes for the jobs or cash that the party political "machine" offered in return. By the end of the nineteenth century, however, the progressive movement had made some headway against the rule of bosses and political machines at the local level and against the power of courts and parties at the national level. The passage of laws setting standards for awarding federal jobs according to merit and providing for some government regulation of big business began to raise Americans' expectations about what government could and should accomplish.

The Age of Industry. While the national government remained a minor presence in the lives of most Americans, the industrial revolution was producing changes that affected nearly everyone. The growth of business and industry in the last two decades of the nineteenth century astounded, and often dismayed, contemporary observers, who marveled at the achievements of the new American industrial giants even while they lamented the passing of a simpler, and more egalitarian, agrarian society. The remarkable growth in the productivity of the American economy was built on a series of technological revolutions that began in the decades before and after the Civil War. A transportation revolution that had started with the construction of a network of canals in the 1810s

and 1820s accelerated rapidly with the spread of railroads, particularly in the 1860s, 1870s, and 1880s. Railroads made possible a truly national economy by speeding the flow of raw materials to manufacturers and allowing them, and farmers as well, to move their products quickly and efficiently to markets across the country. An accompanying revolution in communications was equally important to the foundation of a modern economy. It began with the invention of a practical telegraph in 1844 and continued with the completion of the first telegraph cable across the Atlantic in 1866 and the invention and application of the telephone in the 1870s. Other innovations transformed everything from office work to construction techniques: the open-hearth process for making steel in the 1860s, the typewriter (1868), the cash register (1879), electric light and power in the 1880s, and the adding machine (1891), for example. Such technological innovations were matched by equally important changes in the size and organization of business and the economy. Railroads were the pioneers. Their need for huge amounts of investment capital to construct new lines and to build cars and locomotives led to the centralization of financial markets on Wall Street in New York City. Railroads also experimented with new administrative structures that made jobs more specialized and created a new tier of middle managers. Though the Gilded Age is best known for its wealthy "robber barons" and "captains of industry"—men such as Andrew Carnegie, John D. Rockefeller, Jay Gould, Cornelius Vanderbilt, and J. P. Morgan—it was in fact an age in which ownership and management became distinct functions in the nation's largest corporations, with ownership spread among many stockholders and day-to-day operations in the hands of a new professional class.

The West. In 1890 the U.S. Census declared that "Up to and including 1880 the country had a frontier of settlement, but at present the unsettled area has been so broken into by isolated bodies of settlement that there can hardly be said to be a frontier line. In the discussion of its extent, its westward movement, etc., it can not, therefore, any longer have a place in the census reports." Three years later, in an address to the American Historical Association, whose members had gathered at the World's Columbian Exposition in Chicago, the historian Frederick Jackson Turner reflected on the significance of this pronouncement, arguing that America's character and its democratic institutions had been profoundly shaped by the nation's expansion from east to west across the continent. For Turner the frontier meant the boundary "between savagery and civilization," between settlements and "free land." In hindsight the story of the West during the 1880s and 1890s is a complex and tragic tale. Given the violence of the "Indian wars" of this period, no line between civilization and savagery can be drawn. Yet Turner was correct in identifying movement as one of the principal themes in American history. Historians estimate that the average westerner in the nineteenth century moved four to five times as an adult. Because so many occupations in the West—miner, logger, cowboy—were seasonal or temporary, much of the population was constantly on the move. For homesteaders, many of whom had been lured onto the western plains by railroads eager to increase their business, movement was often a necessity when drought or hard times struck. For Native Americans movement had many meanings. For some tribes it had been a way of life, a nomadic existence that was ended when a flood of white settlers poured into the West in the decades after the Civil War, forcing tribes onto government reservations where they were expected to settle down and farm the often infertile land. For others, such as the Nez Percé in the late 1870s, movement came as a desperate attempt to preserve their independence and way of life. As their great leader, Chief Joseph, said so eloquently, he sought the right to "be a free man—free to travel, free to stop, free to work, free to trade where I choose, free to choose my own teachers, free to follow the religion of my fathers, free to think and talk and act for myself." All too often, movement meant conflict between white settlers seeking a better life or quick riches and Native Americans hoping to protect their homelands and preserve their autonomy. From Little Bighorn in 1876 to Wounded Knee in 1890, episodes of violence punctuated western history in the late nineteenth century, and the myths they generated far outlived the census taker's frontier.

"Jim Crow." Like Chief Joseph, African Americans also longed for freedom in the late nineteenth century. They sought to maintain the rights guaranteed by the Thirteenth (1865), Fourteenth (1868), and Fifteenth (1870) Amendments to the Constitution, which abolished slavery, granted citizenship to former slaves, and extended voting rights to them, respectively. After the Compromise of 1877—in which southern Democrats helped Republican Rutherford B. Hayes win the presidency in return for his promise to remove the last remaining Federal troops from the South—the gains southern blacks had made in educational, political, and economic opportunities during Reconstruction were largely erased. Often members of the same elite social and economic class that had dominated southern politics before the Civil War, southern Democrats began a process of taking away African Americans' voting rights, trapping them in poverty and segregating them from white society. Most blacks made their livings as farmers in the rural South and found themselves trapped in a system of farm tenancy and sharecropping, whereby they rented land from white owners in return for a part of the profits they made from selling their crops. Borrowing against the estimated value of future crops to pay for food, rent, and other necessities, and owing money to landowners and merchants even when crops were poor or failed completely, created a cycle of indebtedness that was difficult to escape. Often the sharecroppers were charged inflated prices by landlords and local merchants.

Throughout the South, particularly in the 1890s, voting rights for blacks were stripped away—sometimes by threats and physical violence, other times by state laws establishing measures such as poll taxes that most blacks could not pay or literacy tests that registrars graded subjectively. Named after a character in a popular minstrel song, "Jim Crow" laws banished African Americans to separate schools and public accommodations. In 1896 the Supreme Court sanctioned this system of social segregation in its ruling in *Plessy* v. *Ferguson,* declaring that the Fourteenth Amendment "could not have been intended to abolish distinctions based on color, or to enforce social, as distinguished from political, equality, or a commingling of the two races upon terms unsatisfactory to either."

The Cross of Gold. The 1880s and 1890s were difficult times in rural America, as is apparent in the stream of migrants from rural counties to cities in search of work. In the South poor whites as well as blacks were caught in the sharecropping system. Many farmers who had been independent lost their land. A quarter of southern farmers were tenants in 1880; by 1900 that number had risen to one third. On the Great Plains, a cycle of boom and bust prevailed. Plentiful rainfall in the mid 1880s led to a fever of land speculation in parts of the West; farmland in parts of Kansas that had sold for $6.25 an acre in the 1860s was going for $270 an acre in 1887. Yet despite tremendous increases in productivity, western farmers, and those in the South as well, were hit hard by a long-term decline in the price of agricultural products, high interest rates for mortgages and other loans, and the power of the railroad owners and grain-elevator operators, without whom farmers could not get their crops to consumers. Nature seemed to conspire against them as well. Drought settled on the Plains in the late 1880s and lasted until the late 1890s. It was accompanied by plagues of locusts and chinch bugs. Some farmers responded by leaving the land, painting slogans such as "In God we trusted, in Kansas we busted" on their wagons. Others began to organize farmers' alliances. These groups, which began in Texas in the 1870s, spread quickly through the South and then the West, with the Southern Alliance claiming three million members by 1890. By 1892 the alliances had organized the People's Party—commonly known as the Populists—to push for electoral reforms, limits on power of the railroads and big business, and other measures that would ease the economic plight of farmers. Even as the depression of the 1890s drove farm prices down another 20 percent, the Populists gained strength. When the Democratic Party nominated William Jennings Bryan of Nebraska as its presidential candidate in 1896, the Populists decided to endorse him as well, largely because of his campaign against the gold standard, which many farmers believed was responsible for their difficulties because it restricted the money supply, keeping down the profits they made on their crops and keeping them in debt. Bryan won over

Democrats and Populists alike with a rousing speech to the Democratic National Convention, in which he warned advocates of the gold standard: "You shall not press down upon the brow of labor this crown of thorns, you shall not crucify mankind upon a cross of gold." Bryan's defeat at the polls that November ended the farmers' third-party campaign, but discontent in rural America continued to rock the political landscape into the twentieth century.

Work and Labor. For America's industrial workers the final quarter of the nineteenth century was a time of struggle, as years of steady work and good wages for skilled craftsmen could suddenly give way to months of unemployment. Though average wages rose during the period, industrial employers, themselves squeezed by artificially low prices created by the restricted money supply, routinely cut wages while trying to increase productivity. Skilled workers found themselves on the defensive as technological innovations and cheap immigrant labor threatened to make them obsolete and expendable. Attempts to form effective labor unions were countered by employer blacklists, armies of private detectives, and a judicial system more concerned with protecting the rights of property than the rights of labor. Labor organizations might have been more successful in countering the growing power of industrial corporations had they not been internally divided along ethnic and racial lines and between skilled and unskilled workers. Though efforts to form national industrial unions failed to achieve lasting success and stability, groups such as the Terrence Powderly's Knights of Labor and Eugene Debs's American Railway Union succeeded in establishing a clear agenda that focused on issues such as the eight-hour day, the right to organize and bargain collectively, improved workplace safety, and employer liability for workplace accidents. These issues formed the core principles for which working men and women fought well into the twentieth century.

Religion and American Life. At the end of Reconstruction the United States remained a predominantly Protestant nation, and among Protestant Americans there was widespread agreement on the literal truth of the Bible and the responsibility of Christians to spread the gospel among "heathen" peoples. Most public schools still relied on standard textbooks such as *McGuffey's Readers,* which championed the value of hard work, promised that virtue would be recognized and rewarded, and warned that those who broke the Sabbath or succumbed to the temptations of alcohol and other vices would be punished. The same Protestant morality dominated American colleges and universities. Most college presidents were ordained clergymen, and college curricula remained dedicated to these seemingly eternal truths. Yet during the 1870s and 1880s this comfortable consensus began to unravel. The massive immigration of Catholics and Jews set in motion a dramatic transformation of the American religious landscape. As Charles

Darwin's theory of evolution slowly gained acceptance with scientists and educators, a rift began to appear between liberal Protestants such as Henry Ward Beecher, who accepted evolution as the "record of the unfolding of *man* and of the race under the inspiration of God's nature," and conservative evangelicals such as the preacher Dwight L. Moody, who steadfastly condemned the theory of evolution as a blasphemous contradiction of holy Scripture. For Moody and other evangelical Protestants, evolution was only one of several temptations that threatened to undermine Christianity. The others included the theater, disregard of the Sabbath, and the Sunday newspaper. Despite these threats, however, religious faith remained—for Protestants, Catholics, Jews, and others—a vital element in American culture during the last quarter of the nineteenth century. Through the social-gospel and student-volunteer movements, as well as settlement houses and temperance crusades, religious ideals infused public life with a reform spirit that lasted well into the twentieth century.

From Highbrow to Lowbrow. The growing diversity of religious opinions in the late nineteenth century was paralleled by an astounding variety in American cultural life. By the 1880s and 1890s advances in technology had brought the illustrator's art within the reach of millions through mass-circulation magazines and some twelve thousand newspapers. The dime novel—which made Deadwood Dick and Horatio Alger Jr. household names—brought popular fiction to a broad reading public. The new railroads took traveling troupes of entertainers to small towns and rural villages that earlier had been isolated from all but the humblest cultural fare. This period was the heyday of the traveling circus, the Wild West show, and vaudeville theater. In urban areas the first amusement parks were beginning to appear, the most notable being Coney Island in New York, which by the end of the century was just a subway ride away from Manhattan. For those with more refined sensibilities there were other pleasures. Major American cities grew large enough to sustain opera companies and symphony orchestras and built elegant buildings to house them. In Chicago, Boston, and New York art museums became cathedrals of high culture and were gradually filled with the acquisitions of wealthy collectors and patrons. Readers who looked for more enduring works than the dime novels could enjoy fiction by an impressive array of talented American writers, including Henry James, William Dean Howells, Hamlin Garland, Sarah Orne Jewett, and the incomparable Mark Twain. Despite the scorn that later generations have heaped on the Victorian tastes and values of Americans in the late nineteenth century, this era was one of remarkable creativity in a truly democratic culture.

The Culture of Consumption. Americans at the end of the nineteenth century had many reasons to feel unsettled and uncertain. Confrontations between workers and employers seemed to threaten the social order. A nation that had created a mythic view of itself as uniformly Anglo-Saxon and Protestant was becoming increasingly diverse in race, religion, and culture. Distinctions between rich and poor challenged long-held notions of democracy and equality, and a nation that had been profoundly shaped by Thomas Jefferson's belief that "those who labour in the earth are the chosen people of God" was becoming a land of steelworkers, middle managers, doctors, lawyers, and social workers. At the end of the century uncertainties over these changes gave rise to two seemingly contradictory impulses. The first was the progressive movement, which aimed to bring rationality and efficiency to government, to curb the power of private in-

terests, and to restore the sense of community that seemed to have been lost. The other impulse was what historians now call a culture of consumption, centered on the belief that a sense of personal fulfillment and well-being could be created through the pleasures of purchase, acquisition, and display. The earlier Puritan ethic of hard work and self-denial was challenged by appeals to self-gratification that came from department-store windows, world's fairs, and the emerging advertising profession. It was as consumers that Americans found common ground, as older ways of defining themselves and their communities were eroded by the forces of modernity.

ACKNOWLEDGMENTS

This book was produced by Manly, Inc. Karen L. Rood and Anthony Scotti were the in-house editors.

Administrative support was provided by Ann M. Cheschi and Brenda A. Gillie.

Bookkeeper is Joyce Fowler.

Copyediting supervisor is Laurel M. Gladden Gillespie. The copyediting staff includes Phyllis A. Avant, Patricia Coate, Jeff Miller, William L. Thomas Jr., and Allison Trussell.

Laura Pleicones, L. Kay Webster, and Jane M. J. Williamson are editorial associates.

Layout and graphics supervisor is Pamela D. Norton.

Office manager is Kathy Lawler Merlette.

Photography editors are Julie E. Frick and Margaret Meriwether. Photographic copy work was performed by Joseph M. Bruccoli.

Production manager is Samuel W. Bruce.

Software specialist is Marie Parker.

Systems manager is Chris Elmore.

Typesetting supervisor is Kathleen M. Flanagan. The typesetting staff includes Stephanie L. Capes and Patricia Flanagan Salisbury.

Walter W. Ross, Steven Gross, and Mark McEwan did library research. They were assisted by the following librarians at the Thomas Cooper Library of the University of South Carolina: Linda Holderfield and the interlibrary-loan staff; reference-department head Virginia Weathers; reference librarians Marilee Birchfield, Stefanie Buck, Stefanie DuBose, Rebecca Feind, Karen Joseph, Donna Lehman, Charlene Loope, Anthony McKissick, Jean Rhyne, Kwamine Simpson, and Virginia Weathers; circulation-department head Caroline Taylor; and acquisitions-searching supervisor David Haggard.

AMERICAN
ERAS
1878–1899

WORLD EVENTS:

SELECTED OCCURRENCES OUTSIDE THE UNITED STATES

MAJOR POWERS AND LEADERS

Austria-Hungary — Emperor Francis Joseph 1 (1848–1916)

China — Emperor Tsai-t'ien (1875–1908), Empress Dowager Tz'u-hsi (regent, 1875–1889, 1898–1908)

France — Presidents Marie Edmé Patrice de MacMahon (1873–1879), Jules Grévy (1879–1887), Sadi Carnot (1887–1894), Jean-Paul-Pierre Casimir-Périer (1894–1895), Félix Faure (1895–1899), and Émile Loubet (1899–1906)

Germany — Emperors William I (1871–1888), Frederick III (1888), William II (1888–1918); Chancellors Otto von Bismarck (1871–1890), Leo von Caprivi (1890–1894), and Chlodwig Karl Victor, Prince of Hohenlohe-Schillingsfürst (1894–1900)

Great Britain (United Kingdom of Great Britain and Ireland) — Queen Victoria (1837–1901); Prime Ministers Benjamin Disraeli (1874–1880), William Ewart Gladstone (1880–1885, 1886, 1892–1894), Robert Gascoyne-Cecil, third Marquess of Salisbury (1885–1886, 1886–1892, 1895–1902), and Archibald Philip Primrose, fifth Earl of Rosebery (1894–1895)

Italy — Kings Victor Emmanuel II (1861–1878) and Umberto I (1878–1900)

Japan — Emperor Meiji (1867–1912)

The Ottoman Empire (Turkey) — Sultan Abdülhamid II (1876–1909)

Russia — Czars Alexander II (1855–1881), Alexander III (1881–1894), and Nicholas II (1894–1917)

MAJOR CONFLICTS

1877–1878—Russo-Turkish War

1878–1879—Second Afghan War between Great Britain and Afghanistan

1879—Zulu War against the British in South Africa

1879–1884—War of the Pacific (Chile versus Bolivia and Peru)

1883–1885—Nationalist uprising against Egyptian rule in Sudan

1884–1885—Tonkin War between France and China

1885—Serbo-Bulgarian War

1894–1895—Sino-Japanese War

1894–1895—French invasion of Madagascar

1895–1896—Italo-Ethiopian War

1896–1898—Egyptian reconquest of Sudan

1897—Greece vs. the Ottoman Empire

1898—Spanish-American War

1898—Great Britain and Egypt vs. Mahdi nationalists

1899–1900—Greece vs. the Ottoman Empire

1899–1902—Boer War

NEW NATIONS

1878—Montenegro, Romania, Serbia

1898—Cuba

1878

- British playwright William Schwenck Gilbert and British composer Arthur Seymour Sullivan complete *H. M. S. Pinafore,* their second popular comic opera.

- British novelist Thomas Hardy publishes *The Return of the Native.*

- German scientist Wilhelm Max Wundt (1832–1920) establishes the first laboratory devoted entirely to experimental psychology.

- French scientist Paul Bert conducts research on the deep-sea divers' disease known as "the bends," proving that the often fatal condition may be prevented by decreasing air pressure slowly and by degrees. The discovery makes the construction of bridges and underwater tunnels far less hazardous than in the past.

- A Belgian group headed by King Leopold II engages explorer Henry M. Stanley to establish trading stations in the Congo River region, a commission he carries out in 1879–1884.

7 Feb. Pius IX dies after the longest papacy in history, thirty-two years. He is succeeded by Leo XIII (1810–1893).

3 Mar. Russia dictates the Treaty of San Stefano, which marks its victory in Russo-Turkish War. The treaty recognizes the independence of Serbia, Montenegro, and Romania from the Ottoman Empire. Bulgaria is made an autonomous state within the empire with an agreement that Russian troops will remain there for two years.

11 May Radicals attempt to assassinate Emperor William I of Germany. Another such attempt is made on 2 June.

18 May Colombia grants a French company a nine-year concession to build a Panama Canal.

30 May Russia and Great Britain reach a secret agreement to divide up Bulgaria.

4 June Great Britain secretly agrees to defend Turkey against further incursions by Russia and others into Ottoman Empire territory in Asia Minor. In return British troops are allowed to occupy Cyprus.

13 June–
13 July At the Congress of Berlin, German chancellor Otto von Bismarck brokers a settlement of the differences among Russia, Great Britain, France, Italy, Turkey, and Austria-Hungary that have arisen in the aftermath of the Treaty of San Stefano and various secret agreements that have followed. The independence of Serbia, Montenegro, and Romania is reaffirmed, but Bulgaria is divided into three parts and given limited autonomy.

15 Aug. In Egypt Nubar Pasha forms a government with an Englishman as minister of finance and a Frenchman as minister of public works. The two European countries have extensive financial interest in Egypt because of the Suez Canal, which opened in 1869. Though still part of the crumbling Ottoman Empire, Egypt has had self-rule since 1805.

19 Oct. Germany passes the Anti-Socialist Law, which is renewed periodically until 1890. The law prohibits public meetings, publications, and collections involving Socialists or Communists, effectively driving the Socialists underground.

21 Oct. The Irish Home Rule Confederation, with Charles Stewart Parnell as president, is founded to campaign for independence from Great Britain.

20 Nov.	Reacting to Russian advances in central Asia, Great Britain invades Afghanistan to secure its frontier in India and puts Yakub Khan on the throne.

1879

- British novelist George Meredith publishes *The Egoist.*

- Russian novelist Fyodor Dostoyevsky publishes *The Brothers Karamazov.*

- Norwegian playwright Henrik Ibsen writes *A Doll's House.*

- The British defeat the Zulus in South Africa.

- After four years of fighting Egypt succeeds in cutting off Ethiopia from the sea.

24 Jan.	Samoa grants Germany use of the port of Apia and a naval base, in a treaty similar to one in which it gave the United States use of the harbor at Pago Pago in 1878.
18 Feb.	The Nubar government of Egypt fails after a demonstration by army officers thought to be backed by Khedive Ismail Pasha, who resents British and French involvement in the government of his country.
25 June	Under pressure from the British and French, the sultan of the Ottoman Empire deposes Khedive Ismail Pasha of Egypt. Tawfiq Pasha becomes khedive.
Sept.	Fighting flares up in Afghanistan after the murder of a British agent.
4 Sept.	The British and French ministers are reappointed to the Egyptian government with the condition that they cannot be removed without consent from Great Britain and France.
7 Oct.	Germany and Austria-Hungary sign a military alliance that remains in force until 1918.

1880

- France annexes Tahiti.

- French sculptor Auguste Rodin completes *The Thinker.*

- French fiction writer Emile Zola publishes his harshly naturalistic novel *Nana.*

- Russian composer Pyotr Tchaikovsky completes his *1812 Overture.*

- Two large corporations, the Barnato Mining Company and the De Beers Mining Corporation, are organized by British businessmen in South Africa to take advantage of the rich diamond mines in the region.

- Alarmed by Henry M. Stanley's activities on behalf of the Belgians in the Congo, the French send Savorgnan de Brazza to the region. He later makes treaties with tribal chiefs on the north side of the Congo, founds Brazzaville, and establishes a French protectorate there.

24 Mar.	Germany, Great Britain, and the United States sign an agreement recognizing Malietoa Talavou as king of Samoa and setting up an executive council with one representative from each of the three western nations.

June–Nov.	The Albanians prevent Montenegro from taking territory granted to Albania by the Treaty of Berlin. A meeting of the great powers gives Montenegro the Adriatic seaport of Dulcigno (present-day Ulcinj) instead. The Turks stage naval demonstrations in protest, but they back down after British threats to take over the customs house at Smyrna.
20 July	The British agree to recognize Russian-backed Ab-er-Rahman as ruler of Afghanistan.
22 Dec.	British novelist Mary Ann Evans (born in 1819), who wrote under the pseudonym George Eliot, dies.
31 Dec.	Boers (descendants of Dutch settlers in South Africa) in Transvaal declare a new republic, less than three years after their South African Republic was annexed by Great Britain.

1881

- Russian novelist Fyodor Dostoyevsky dies.

- New Zealand bars Chinese immigration.

- Led by Prime Minister William Ewart Gladstone, the British Parliament passes the Land Act, which creates a court to mediate between landowners and Irish tenants to fix fair land rents and grants tenants some security from being evicted without cause.

- Swiss fiction writer Johanna Spyri publishes *Heidi*.

- Norwegian playwright Henrik Ibsen writes *Ghosts*.

- British playwright William Schwenck Gilbert and British composer Arthur Seymour Sullivan complete their operetta *Patience*.

1 Feb.	Nationalist army officers rise up to protest foreign influences in the Egyptian government. A second nationalist revolt occurs on 9 September.
13 Mar.	Alexander II of Russia dies after his coach is bombed in Saint Petersburg. He had just signed an order that allows the orderly expression of dissenting opinion.
5 Apr.	To avoid war the British government recognizes the independence of the Boers' South African Republic under the nominal sovereignty of Great Britain.
30 Apr.–12 May	French troops invade Tunisia and make it a protectorate of France.
24 May	Great Britain, France, and Germany force Turkey to give up the parts of Thessaly and Epirus awarded to Greece by the Treaty of Berlin.
18 June	Russia, Germany, and Austria-Hungary form the secret Alliance of the Three Emperors, which remains in effect through 1887. They agree that if one of them goes to war with Turkey the others will remain neutral and that any further division of Turkish territory must meet with the approval of all three powers. Also, Austria-Hungary reserves the right to annex Bosnia and Herzegovina, and the three nations agree not to oppose the union of Bulgaria and Eastern Rumelia.

28 June	Austria-Hungary and Serbia sign a secret, ten-year treaty in which Serbia accepts much-needed financial help in return for promising not to make agreements with other foreign powers without approval from Austria-Hungary, which pledges to help Serbia in acquiring territory to the south of its borders. Although the Austrians recognize Milan as ruler of Serbia, the agreement essentially makes Serbia a protectorate of Austria-Hungary.
30 June	A major insurrection begins in Tunisia, forcing the French to launch military actions there, at the same time as it fights an uprising in neighboring Algeria, which has been part of France since 1848.
12 July	Faced with a continuing civil war in Samoa, the governments of Germany, Great Britain, and the United States recognize Malietoa Laupepa as king.

1882

- German scientist Robert Koch identifies the bacterium that causes tuberculosis.

- Writing under the pseudonym Carlo Collodi, Italian fiction writer Carlo Lorenzini publishes *The Adventures of Pinocchio*.

- Norwegian playwright Henrik Ibsen finishes *An Enemy of the People*.

- Russian composer Nikolay Rimsky-Korsakov completes the opera *Snow Maiden*.

- British playwright William Schwenck Gilbert and British composer Arthur Seymour Sullivan write *Iolanthe*.

- The Boers establish two states in Bechuanaland (Botswana).

- The French proclaim a protectorate over the northwestern part of the island of Madagascar.

5 Feb.	Under pressure from nationalists, Khedive Tawfiq Pasha of Egypt appoints a nationalist government.
6 May	Two high English officials are assassinated in Ireland by radicals, setting off a wave of terrorist attacks that includes the dynamiting of public buildings in England.
20 May	Italy, Germany, and Austria sign the Triple Alliance, pledging mutual assistance in case of attack by one of the other world powers. The alliance remains in effect until 1915.
25–28 May	With squadrons in the harbor at Alexandria the French and British successfully demand the resignation of the nationalist government in Egypt, but the khedive is unable to form a new government.
11 July	Supporting Khedive Tawfiq Pasha against nationalists forces, the British bombard Alexandria and send forces to protect the Suez Canal.
15 Sept.	The British occupy Cairo.

1883

- French Impressionist painter Edouard Manet dies.

- German scientist Robert Koch demonstrates that cholera is waterborne.

- British writer Robert Louis Stevenson publishes *Treasure Island.*

- German philosopher Friedrich Nietzsche publishes the first part of his best-known work, *Thus Spake Zarathustra.*

- Frenchman Paul Gauguin abandons his job as a stockbroker in order to become a full-time painter.

- French composer Leo Delibes finishes the opera *Lakme.*

- American-born British inventor Hiram Stevens Maxim invents the first fully automatic machine gun.

- William Siemens, the German-born British inventor, demonstrates his electric locomotive, the first vehicle of this kind, in northern Ireland.

- Swedish explorer Nils Adolf Erik Nordenskiold penetrates eighty-four miles into Greenland.

Feb.– Apr. The Germans establish a colony in South-West Africa, beginning their colonialism on that continent.

1 May The Egyptian government is reorganized, giving all real authority to the khedive and a British consul general. Under Consul General Sir Evelyn Baring, Earl of Cromer, British advisers are appointed for all important Egyptian officials.

1 June The government of Madagascar and the French go to war over the status of the island. The war continues inconclusively until December 1885.

8 June Tunisia and France sign the Convention of Marsa, giving France virtual control of the Tunisian government.

25 Aug. Faced with an uprising in Tonkin, the French force Emperor Tu Duc of Annam to sign the Treaty of Hué, recognizing the French protectorate over Cambodia and three kingdoms that correspond roughly to modern-day Vietnam: Tonkin, Annam, and Cochin China.

27 Aug. The small volcanic island of Krakatau in the East Indies erupts. Ash is thrown fifty miles into the air, and the sound is heard twenty-two hundred miles away in Australia. Areas near the volcano are in darkness for two and a half days, and the explosion sets off a tidal wave that drowns some thirty thousand people of Java and Sumatra.

30 Oct. Carol I of Romania, fearing that Russia intends to establish control of his country, arranges a secret alliance with Austria-Hungary, which remains in effect until 1916.

5 Nov. Sudanese religious leader Muhammad Ahmad, known as the Mahdi, defeats a British-led Egyptian force at the Battle of El Obeid in a vigorous revolt against Egyptian rule in Sudan.

1884

- Norwegian playwright Henrik Ibsen completes *The Wild Duck.*

- French composer Jules Massenet completes his opera *Manon.*

- British inventor Charles Algernon Parsons devises the first practical steam turbine, which can greatly increase the speed of steamships.

- Frenchman Louis Comte de Chardonnet invents rayon, the first artificial fiber.

- Russian-born French bacteriologist Ilya Ilich Mechnikov recognizes the role of white blood cells in fighting bacterial infections, a discovery that earns him a Nobel Prize in 1908.

- Great Britain annexes southeastern New Guinea while Germany takes control of the northeastern part of the island.

- Germany establishes protectorates over Togoland and the Cameroons in West Africa.

- Great Britain and France establish separate protectorates over parts of Somalia.

- The United States and Germany recognize the Belgian committee now known as the International Association of the Congo as a territorial power.

Jan.	The British force a reluctant Egyptian government to agree to evacuate Sudan, and Gen. Charles G. Gordon is sent to Khartoum to arrange the withdrawal of Egyptian troops and to negotiate a settlement with the Mahdi.
4 Apr.	The treaty ending the War of the Pacific, which has been raging since 1879, grants Chile an area of desert previously under the control of Bolivia and Peru. Chile declared war on its neighbors to obtain this land for its nitrates, which are used in fertilizers and explosives.
23 June	The Chinese defeat French forces at Baclé, beginning an undeclared war over Tonkin, which both China and France claim as a protectorate.
15 Nov.	Representatives of fourteen nations — including the United States, Great Britain, and Germany — arrive in Berlin for a conference on Africa, which continues until 26 February 1886. Agreeing to work for an end to the African slave trade, they declare complete freedom of commerce and navigation on the Congo, the Nile, and their tributaries. During this conference Britain, France, and Russia recognize the International Association of the Congo, which takes the name Independent State of the Congo.
Dec.	The British Parliament passes the Franchise Bill, which extends voting rights to nearly all males in Great Britain.

1885

- Austrian composer Johann Strauss completes the operetta *The Gypsy Baron*.

- British writer Walter Pater publishes the historical novel *Marius the Epicurean*.

- British novelist H. Rider Haggard publishes *King Solomon's Mines*.

- British poet and novelist Robert Louis Stevenson publishes *A Child's Garden of Verses*.

- French novelist Emile Zola publishes *Germinal*.

- German Carl Friedrich Benz builds the first working automobile powered by an internal-combustion engine. The car has three wheels.

- British explorer Richard Francis Burton begins translating *The Arabian Nights* into English, a task he completes in 1888.

- British playwright William Schwenck Gilbert and British composer Arthur Seymour Sullivan write their operetta *The Mikado.*

- *Liberty Enlightening the World* (better known as *The Statue of Liberty*), by French sculptor Frédéric Auguste Bartholdi, is presented to the United States.

- In West Africa, Spain establishes a protectorate over Rio de Oro and Spanish Guinea, and Great Britain proclaims a protectorate over the Niger River region.

- Having deprived the Boers of their states in Bechuanaland, Great Britain divides the entire territory into British Bechuanaland and the Bechuanaland Protectorate.

- Germany establishes a protectorate over German East Africa (now parts of Tanzania, Rwanda, and Burundi) and South-West Africa (now Namibia).

- Germany annexes the Marshall and Solomon Islands in the Pacific Ocean.

26 Jan.	Gen. Charles G. Gordon's proposal to make the Mahdi sultan of Sudan while maintaining a measure of Egyptian control over the nation has met with continued fighting and finally the massacre of Gordon and the garrison at Khartoum. Forces sent in August 1884 to relieve Gordon arrive too late to save him.
Apr.	An Anglo-Russian crisis occurs after Russian incursions into Afghanistan, and the British seize Port Hamilton on the coast of Korea in retaliation. The crisis is resolved by negotiation.
	King Leopold II of Belgium proclaims himself sovereign of the Independent State of the Congo, which becomes his personal possession, not a colony of Belgium.
8 Apr.	British Prime Minister William E. Gladstone puts forward the First Home Rule Bill, providing a measure of self-rule, but not complete independence, for Ireland. The bill is defeated in July, bringing down Gladstone's Liberal government.
7 May	The Canadian transcontinental railroad is completed. It opens to the public in May 1887.
9 June	In the Treaty of Tientsin, China recognizes the French protectorate of Tonkin in return for France's promise to respect China's southern borders.
21 June	The Mahdi dies in Sudan and is succeeded by Abdullah el Taashi.
30 July	Sudanese forces take complete control of Sudan. Skirmishes along the Sudan-Egypt border continue for the next ten years.
6 July	French scientist Louis Pasteur administers his rabies vaccine to a human for the first time.
1 Aug.	King Leopold II declares the neutrality of the Congo State.
18 Sept.	A rebellion breaks out in Eastern Rumelia, an autonomous province of the Ottoman Empire since 1878, led by individuals favoring a union with Bulgaria.

Oct.–Nov.	Reacting to Burmese violations of a treaty giving them rights to unrestricted trade in that country, the British launch the Third Burmese War, forcing King Thibaw into exile in India.
13 Nov.	Considering a Bulgarian takeover in Eastern Rumelia contrary to its interests in the Balkan region, Serbia declares war on Bulgaria. By the end of the month Bulgaria has invaded and totally defeated Serbia.
17 Dec.	In the treaty ending its war with Madagascar, France is given control of the island's foreign affairs but pledges not to interfere with domestic matters.
17 Dec.	Liberal Allan Octavian Hume convenes an "Indian National Congress," which becomes an annual event for discussing reforms in British colonial rule and measure for increasing Indian self-government. The meeting is usually considered the beginning of an upsurge in the Indian nationalist movement.

1886

- French sculptor Auguste Rodin completes *The Kiss*.

- British poet and fiction writer Robert Louis Stevenson publishes *Kidnapped* and *Dr. Jekyll and Mr. Hyde*.

- British novelist Thomas Hardy publishes *The Mayor of Casterbridge*.

- French chemist Henri Moissan isolates the element fluorine, for which he wins a Nobel Prize in 1906.

- French scientist Paul Héroult devises a practical method for the electrolytic production of aluminum, making this metal more plentiful and less expensive.

- Rich veins of gold are discovered in southern Transvaal.

1 Jan.	The British annex upper Burma; scattered guerrilla fighting continues until 1891.
3 Mar.	Austria-Hungary negotiates a peace settlement between Serbia and Bulgaria after forcing Bulgaria to withdraw from Serbian territory.
5 Apr.	Prince Alexander I of Bulgaria is named governor of Eastern Rumelia for a term of five years, essentially bringing about its annexation by Bulgaria.
20 June	The British and Dutch, who have argued over Borneo since 1881, agree to divide the island, with the Netherlands retaining the larger part.
24 July	China officially recognizes British control in Burma in return for the face-saving continuation of the tribute it has traditionally received from Burma.

1887

- Russian composer Nikolay Rimsky-Korsakov finishes *Capriccio Espagnol*.

- British novelist H. Rider Haggard publishes *She*.

- Italian composer Giuseppe Verdi writes his opera *Otello*.

- British novelist Arthur Conan Doyle introduces detective Sherlock Holmes, one of the most popular fictional characters of all time, in *A Study in Scarlet*.

- Great Britain celebrates Queen Victoria's "Golden Jubilee," in recognition of her fifty years as monarch.

- Polish Jew Ludwik Lejser Zamenhof, upset by the discrimination against Jews in Russia under the rule of Alexander III, devises an artificial language he calls Esperanto (one who hopes). Zamenhof hopes that it will be adopted as a universal language and lead to peace.

- German inventor Gottlieb Wilhelm Daimler builds the first four-wheeled automobile.

- Belgian biologist Joseph van Beneden shows that the number of chromosomes in the body cells of a particular species is always the same, except in sperm and egg cells, which contain only half the usual number.

- Austrian psychologist Sigmund Freud, following the example of fellow Austrian Josef Breuer and others, encourages psychologically disturbed patients to discuss their fantasies, sometimes with the aid of hypnosis.

- Great Britain and France agree to joint control of the New Hebrides.

- France combines Cochin China, Annam, Tonkin, and Cambodia into the united protectorate of Indo-China.

12 Feb. Great Britain and Italy sign the First Mediterranean Agreement, subsequently adhered to by Austria and Spain, establishing a basis for common action if France or Russia attempts to upset the status quo in the Mediterranean or North Africa.

18 June Russia and Germany sign the secret Reinsurance Treaty to replace the expired Alliance of Three Emperors among Russia, Germany, and Austria-Hungary, which Russia has refused to renew. Russia and Germany pledge that each will remain neutral if the other goes to war, except in cases when Germany invades France or Russia declares war on Austria. They also pledge to maintain the status quo in the Balkans, and Germany recognizes Russia's influence in Bulgaria. The treaty remains in effect until 18 June 1890.

21 June The British annex Zululand to keep the Boers of Transvaal from gaining a link to the sea.

24 July Germany sends troops to Samoa, deposing Malietoa Laupepa and proclaiming Tamasese king.

12 Dec. In the Second Mediterranean Agreement, Great Britain, Italy, and Austria agree that Turkey must be kept free of foreign domination and that the Turkish-controlled straits to the Black Sea must remain open.

1888

- Austrian composer Johann Strauss completes his *Emperor Waltz.*

- British author Oscar Wilde publishes the children's story *The Happy Prince.*

- Russian composer Pyotr Tchaikovsky writes his Fifth Symphony.

- Russian composer Nickolay Rimsky-Korsakov writes the symphonic suite *Scheherezade.*

- British inventor John Boyd Dunlop patents the pneumatic rubber tire, initially used for bicycles but later essential for automobiles, buses, and trucks.

- French scientist Henry Le Chatelier develops Le Chatelier's Principle, which predicts the nature of the change that will take place in an equilibrium when the conditions of that system are disarranged.

- German scientist Heinrich Rudolf Hertz discovers radio waves.

- Hungarian Samuel Teleki discovers Lake Rudolf in East Africa.

- The first Chinese railroad is built. It runs for eighty miles from Tangshan to Tientsin.

- Great Britain upholds the exclusion of Chinese immigration in Australia.

- The British establish a protectorate over the Cook Islands.

- The De Beers corporation, directed by Cecil Rhodes, gains a virtual monopoly on the South African diamond industry.

28 Jan.   Italy agrees to provide troops to Germany in the event of a Franco-German War.

13 May   Slaves in Brazil are emancipated.

4 Sept.   Mataafa leads a Samoan revolt in response to the German intervention of July 1887.

19 Oct.   Great Britain, France, Germany, Italy, Austria, Spain, the Netherlands, Russia, and Turkey sign the Suez Canal Convention, which declares the canal free and open to merchant and military vessels of all nations at all times, except when the government of Egypt deems a blockade necessary to its security.

29 Oct.   The British government gives the British South Africa Company, headed by Cecil Rhodes, nearly unlimited power to govern a large area north of Transvaal and west of Mozambique.

11 Dec.   The French colony of Gabon is united with the French Congo.

1889

- German philosopher Friedrich Nietzsche has a mental breakdown from which he never recovers.

- British playwright William Schwenck Gilbert and British composer Arthur Seymour Sullivan write their operetta *The Gondoliers*.

- French composer César Franck completes his Symphony in D Minor.

- Russian scientist Ivan Petrovich Pavlov studies the manner in which nerve action controls the flow of digestive juices in the stomach. In 1904 he wins a Nobel Prize for his work.

- Japanese bacteriologist Shibasaburo Kitasato isolates the bacterium that causes tetanus and also the one that causes anthrax.

	• British scientists Frederick Augustus Abel and James Dewar produce cordite, a mixture of nitroglycerin, nitrocellulose, and petroleum jelly that replaces gunpowder. The use of the new smokeless powder allows improved visibility on battlefields.
	• A Centennial Exposition in Paris celebrates the one hundredth anniversary of the French Revolution and features Alexandre-Gustave Eiffel's 984-foot-tall Eiffel Tower, the tallest man-made structure built to this time.
	• New Zealand adopts universal male suffrage.
30 Jan.	Grand Duke Rudolf, son of Francis Joseph I of Austria-Hungary, commits suicide with his mistress to avoid a marriage arranged by his father.
11 Feb.	Japan establishes a constitution after organizing a Western-style government modeled after that of Germany.
15–16 Mar.	A powerful hurricane hits the Pacific islands.
2 May	Menelik II of Ethiopia signs a treaty with Italy, which Italy interprets as establishing an Italian protectorate over Ethiopia.
31 May	Great Britain passes the Naval Defense Act, stipulating that the British navy must always be as powerful as the fleets of the next two strongest powers combined.
29 Apr.– 14 June	A conference among Germany, Great Britain, and the United States results in the Samoa Act, in which the three powers agree to restore Malietoa Laupepa to the throne and jointly supervise the government.

1890

	• French novelist Jacques Thibault, writing under the pseudonym Anatole France, publishes *Thais*.
	• British scholar James George Frazer publishes *The Golden Bough*, a study of ancient myths and rituals.
	• Norwegian playwright Henrik Ibsen writes *Hedda Gabler*.
	• British poet and fiction writer Rudyard Kipling publishes *The Light That Failed*.
	• Italian composer Pietro Mascagni writes his one-act opera *Cavelleria Rusticana*.
	• German scientist Emil Adolf von Behring discovers that it is possible to produce an immunity against tetanus by injecting an animal with a minute amount of blood serum from an animal infected with the disease.
	• Italy combines its holdings on the East African coast, where it has been establishing footholds since 1882, into the colony of Eritrea.
	• The French defeat the king of Dahomey in West Africa, forcing him to accept a French protectorate over his nation.
18 Mar.	Unhappy with his nation's policy toward Russia and hoping for closer relations with Austria and Great Britain, Emperor William II of Germany forces the resignation of Chancellor Otto von Bismarck, who has held the position for twenty-eight years.

1891

1 July	In an agreement with Great Britain, Germany gives up large colonial claims in East Africa in return for Helgoland, an island in the North Sea. Since the island is considered largely worthless, the agreement is seen as a German attempt to establish its friendly intentions toward the British.
2 July	An international conference in Belgium ends with the signing of the Brussels Act, which includes an agreement to systematically eliminate the slave trade worldwide.
3 July	King Leopold II gives Belgium the right to annex the Congo State after ten years.
17 July	Cecil Rhodes becomes prime minister of the British Cape Colony in South Africa.
29 July	Dutch painter Vincent Willem van Gogh, who has been living and working in France, shoots himself and dies.

- French poet Arthur Rimbaud dies.
- British author Thomas Hardy publishes *Tess of the D'Urbervilles*.
- British novelist George Du Maurier publishes *Peter Ibbetson*.
- French ballet composer Leo Delibes dies.
- German inventor Otto Lilienthal invents and flies the first hang glider that can bear the weight of a person for an extended period of time. He dies after a glider crash five years later.
- Construction begins on the Russian Trans-Siberian Railroad.

9 Feb.	King Menelik II of Ethiopia asserts that the treaty he signed with Italy on 2 May 1889 does not make his country an Italian protectorate.
15 May	Pope Leo XIII issues the encyclical *Rerum novarum*, which describes poor labor conditions as a moral problem in need of remedy.
	An uprising of Arab slave traders on the upper Congo and in the Tanganyika region is put down by Belgian troops over the next eleven months.
11 June	An Anglo-Portuguese Agreement ends a long territorial dispute in Africa, giving Portugal Angola and Mozambique and Great Britain Nyasaland (Malawi), which becomes the British Central African Protectorate in 1893.

1892

- British novelist J. M. Barrie publishes *The Little Minister*.
- Italian composer Ruggiero Leoncavallo writes the opera *Pagliacci*.
- Belgian-born French playwright Maurice Maeterlinck completes *Pelleas and Melisande,* often considered the first important Symbolist drama.
- British playwright Oscar Wilde writes *Lady Windermere's Fan*.
- Russian composer Pyotr Tchaikovsky writes the *Nutcracker Suite*.
- British novelist Israel Zangwill treats Jewish immigrant life in East London in *The Children of the Ghetto*.

- British poet and fiction writer Rudyard Kipling publishes *Barrack-Room Ballads.*

- Russian composer Sergey Vasilyevich Rachmaninoff writes his Prelude in C-sharp Minor.

- British scientist James Dewar invents the Dewar flask, a precursor of the thermos bottle.

- Russian scientist Dmitri Ivanovsky identifies the first known virus, the tobacco mosaic virus.

- German scientist Emil Adolf von Behring develops an antitoxin that produces immunity to diphtheria and helps to fight the disease if infection has already occurred. In 1901 he wins a Nobel Prize for this discovery.

- Abbas Hilmi II succeeds his father, Tawfiq Pasha, as khedive of Egypt.

- Dadabhair Naoroji becomes the first Indian to be elected to the British Parliament. He openly criticizes British policies in India.

- The French depose the king of Dahomey, sparking uprisings that continue into 1894.

- In East Africa the British begin the pacification of Nyasaland (Malawi), which continues until 1898.

- France continues its conquests on the upper Niger.

1893

- British playwright Arthur Wing Pinero writes *The Second Mrs. Tanqueray.*

- Russian composer Pyotr Tchaikovsky completes his Sixth Symphony, also known as the *Pathetique.* He dies later this year.

- Italian composer Giacomo Antonio Puccini completes his opera *Manon Lescaut.*

- Italian composer Giuseppe Verdi writes his opera *Falstaff.*

- The World Parliament of Religions is held in Chicago.

- Austrian novelist Arthur Schnitzler publishes *Anatol.*

- Bohemian composer Antonin Dvorák completes his *From the New World* symphony.

- German scientist Wilhelm Wien demonstrates that the higher the temperature of a substance, the shorter the wavelength of the radiation it produces. He wins a Nobel Prize in 1911 for this discovery, which lies behind Max Planck's groundbreaking work on developing the quantum theory in 1900.

- New Zealand grants woman suffrage.

- Laos becomes part of French Indo-China.

- Indian lawyer Mohandas K. Gandhi arrives in Natal, South Africa, to begin a protest against the mistreatment of Indian immigrants there by whites.

13 Feb.	Prime Minister William Ewart Gladstone of Great Britain introduces the Second Home Rule Bill in Parliament. Though the bill granting partial self-government for Ireland passes in the House of Commons on 1 September, it is overwhelmingly defeated in the House of Lords a week later.
27 Apr.	Universal male suffrage is established in Belgium. The Belgian government also begins plural voting, which gives the wealthy and other privileged classes of voters the right to vote more than once.
6 Aug.	A canal is cut through the isthmus that connects the Peloponnese peninsula to the rest of Greece.
10 Oct.	Prime Minister Eduard von Taaffe of Austria proposes a bill granting universal male suffrage. Its rejection on 19 October is followed by Taaffe's resignation.
13 Nov.	The British agree that the Transvaal should have Swaziland, but the Boers still lack access to the sea.
27 Dec.– 4 Jan.	France and Russia form an alliance, which remains in effect until 1915, promising to support one another militarily if either is attacked by Germany and its allies.

1894

- Under the pseudonym Anthony Hope, British novelist Anthony Hope Hawkins publishes his best-seller *The Prisoner of Zenda,* set in a fictional Balkan kingdom.

- French composer Claude Debussy completes his symphonic poem *Afternoon of a Faun.*

- British poet and novelist Rudyard Kipling publishes *The Jungle Book.*

- British novelist George Du Maurier publishes *Trilby,* introducing the fictional villain Svengali, whose name is still used to describe someone with evil intentions who manipulates another to do his bidding.

- British novelist Israel Zangwill publishes *The King of the Schnorrers.*

- British playwright Oscar Wilde writes *Salome.*

- British scientists John William Strutt, Baron Rayleigh, and William Ramsay discover argon, an inert gas. Both men win Nobel Prizes in 1904.

- In Java, Dutchman Eugene Dubois discovers a thigh bone, skullcap, and two teeth of a primitive hominid, which he names *Pithecanthropus erectus* (erect ape-man). Such hominids are later called *Homo erectus.*

- British archaeologist Arthur John Evans begins digs in Crete that establish the existence of an early Minoan civilization.

- South Australia grants women the right to vote. By 1909 all the other Australian states follow suit.

- The British win their third war against the Ashanti tribe of West Africa and establish a Gold Coast protectorate.

3 Mar. Prime Minister William Ewart Gladstone of Great Britain, upset by the failure of the Second Home Rule Bill and unwilling to go along with an increase in naval expenditures, retires from politics at age eighty-four.

15 Mar. An agreement between France and Germany leaves France free to advance through Sudan to the Nile. Subsequent maneuvers by the British and Belgians to stop the French fail because of objections from Germany.

18 June Great Britain announces that it has established a protectorate over Uganda in East Africa.

24 June President Sadi Carnot of the French Republic is assassinated by an Italian anarchist. He is succeeded by Jean-Paul-Pierre Casimir-Périer.

1 Aug. China and Japan go to war over Korea.

Sept. The French send Victor Liotard to establish posts in southwestern Sudan as part of a plan to occupy all of the region and to force the British to leave Egypt by threatening to interfere with the Nile water supply. Some in the French government hope to create a belt of French colonies from West Africa across the Nile and Ethiopia to French Somaliland.

25 Sept. The British annex Pondoland to the British Cape Colony, establishing a link to Natal.

15 Oct. Capt. Alfred Dreyfus, a French Jew assigned to the war ministry, is arrested and charged with treason on the basis of a document forged by Maj. Marie-Charles-Ferdinand-Walsin Esterhazy. Dreyfus is court-martialed, found guilty on 22 December, and deported to Devil's Island in French Guiana. Liberals and anticlerics charge that he had no motive for such treason and is being used as a scapegoat because he is a Jew.

12 Dec. After further friction between France and the government of Madagascar, which resents the imposition of a French protectorate over the island, France invades and completes its conquest of the island by 1 October 1895.

1895

- British novelist Thomas Hardy publishes *Jude the Obscure.*

- British playwright Oscar Wilde completes *The Importance of Being Ernest.*

- British science-fiction writer H. G. Wells publishes *The Time Machine.*

- British scientist William Ramsay is the first to detect the presence on Earth of the element helium, which was found thirty years earlier on the Sun.

- German scientist Wilhelm Conrad Rontgen discovers X rays, initiating what has been called a Second Scientific Revolution and winning a Nobel Prize in 1901 for this discovery.

- Native uprisings begin in Mozambique and last into 1899, hampering Portuguese efforts to develop the colony.

17 Jan. French President Jean-Paul-Pierre Casimir-Périer resigns because of the controversy generated by the Dreyfus Affair, which also affects the political fortunes of his successor, Félix Faure.

23 Jan. Norwegian Leonard Kristenson and the crew of his whaler become the first humans to stand on the land inside the Antarctic Circle.

24 Feb.	Cuban nationalists rise up against Spanish rule, putting in motion a series of events that culminates in the Spanish-American War of 1898.
Mar.	Italian forces enter Ethiopian territory, intending to establish control over the country.
17 Apr.	The Treaty of Shimonoseki ends the Sino-Japanese War. Under its provisions, China recognizes Korea's independence; gives Taiwan, the Pescadores Islands, and the Liaotung Peninsula to Japan; and pays Japan a large indemnity.
23 Apr.	Russia, France, and Germany force Japan to return the Liaotung Peninsula to China and accept a second large indemnity instead. The action is the beginning of a period of antagonism between Russia and Japan that leads to the outbreak of the Russo-Japanese War in 1904.
3 May	The British South Africa Company territory south of the Zambezi is named Rhodesia to honor Cecil Rhodes.
June	Germany opens the Kiel Canal, which cuts across the isthmus south of Denmark and allows easy access between the North and Baltic Seas.
11 June	The British annex Tongaland to block the Boers' last avenue of linking Transvaal to the sea through Swaziland.
Aug.	Turkish troops begin to massacre Armenian nationalists seeking independence from the Ottoman Empire.
Sept.	King Menelik II of Ethiopia declares war on Italy, whose troops have been advancing into his country.
8 Oct.	The queen of Korea is assassinated. Her murder is assumed to be associated with the rivalry between Russia and Japan for control in Korea.
17 Oct.	Under pressure from the major powers, the sultan of the Ottoman Empire agrees to some reforms for Armenia, but the massacre of Armenians continues.
11 Nov.	British Bechuanaland, which lies west of the South African Republic, is made part of the British Cape Colony.
29 Dec.	Leander Starr Jameson, administrator of the British South African Company territory and a close friend of Cecil Rhodes, leads five hundred horsemen in an illegal act of war, invading Boer territory in what has become known as the "Jameson raid." Rhodes and Jameson, along with British Colonial Secretary Joseph Chamberlain, believe incorrectly that British settlers in the territory will rise up to assist Jameson against the Boers. Jameson surrenders on 2 January 1896.

1896

- British novelist J. M. Barrie publishes *Sentimental Tommy* and turns to playwriting.

- Italian composer Giacomo Antonio Puccini completes the opera *La Bohème*.

- Polish novelist Henryk Sienkiewicz publishes *Quo Vadis?*

- Russian dramatist and fiction writer Anton Chekhov writes his play *The Seagull*.

- British poet A. E. Housman publishes *A Shropshire Lad*.

- French physicist Antoine-Henri Becquerel discovers that a uranium compound is the source of previously unexplained radiation. In 1903 he shares a Nobel Prize with Pierre and Marie Curie for his work on radiation.

- A group of young, liberal Turkish exiles, who become known as the "Young Turks," is founded to advocate reform and modernization of the Ottoman Empire.

- The first modern Olympic Games are held in Athens, Greece.

- Hungarian Jew Theodor Herzl publishes *The Jewish State,* calling for the reestablishment of the Jewish homeland, helping to begin what is later called the Zionist movement.

3 Jan. Attempting to show the British the foolishness of being isolated from Germany, William II sends a telegram to President Paul Kruger of the Boer South African Republic congratulating him on stopping the Jameson raid. The telegram infuriates British citizens, who clamor for an alliance *against* Germany rather than one with it, as William II has intended.

6 Jan. Because of his part in planning the Jameson raid, Cecil Rhodes is forced to resign as prime minister of the British Cape Colony.

15 Jan. After much friction between Great Britain and France in Southeast Asia, the two nations agree to guarantee jointly the independence of Siam (Thailand) so that it can serve as a buffer between the British in Burma and the French in Indo-China.

Feb. Greece foments an insurrection in Crete, hoping to annex the island, which is part of the Ottoman Empire. After intervention by the major powers the sultan agrees to give Crete partial autonomy.

Mar. Col. Georges Picquart, the new head of the French intelligence service, uncovers evidence that Maj. Ferdinand-Walsin Esterhazy has forged the letter that incriminated Capt. Alfred Dreyfus, but his superiors refuse to reopen the case and transfer Picquart to a post in Tunis.

1 Mar. Ethiopian forces win a decisive victory over the Italian invaders at the Battle of Adua, ending the war between Ethiopia and Italy.

13 Mar. Egyptian and British troops led by Gen. Horatio Herbert Kitchener begin the reconquest of Sudan to keep it from falling into French hands

17 Mar. Responding to the Jameson raid, the Boer governments of Transvaal and the Orange Free State form a military alliance.

3 June Russia and China sign a secret treaty that allows Russia to construct a railroad across Manchuria as a shortcut to Vladivostok.

6 Aug. France proclaims Madagascar a French colony.

26 Aug. Armenian revolutionaries seize the building that houses the Ottoman bank, inspiring other uprisings in the Ottoman capital and resulting in a three-day slaughter of thousands of innocent Armenians. Armenians continue to be killed until after June 1897, when the Armenian nationalist movement begins a gradual collapse.

26 Aug. Philippine insurrectionists led by Emilio Aguinaldo rise up against colonial government by Spain.

26 Sept.	The Transvaal passes the Aliens Expulsion Act, aimed particularly at British settlers, an act that Great Britain interprets as a threat to its sovereignty over the Boer state.
26 Oct.	Italy signs a treaty recognizing the independence of Ethiopia.

1897

- Great Britain celebrates Queen Victoria's "Diamond Jubilee," marking the sixtieth anniversary of her coronation.

- French composer Paul-Abraham Dukas writes *The Sorcerer's Apprentice.*

- British poet and fiction writer Rudyard Kipling publishes *Captains Courageous.*

- Russian playwright Anton Chekhov completes *Uncle Vanya.*

- French artist Henri Rousseau paints *The Sleeping Gypsy.*

- French playwright Edmond Rostand stages his *Cyrano de Bergerac.*

- The Moscow Art Theater is founded by Konstantin Stanislavsky, who has produced Chekhov's plays.

- British science-fiction writer H. G. Wells publishes *The Invisible Man.*

- Polish-born British novelist Joseph Conrad publishes *Nigger of the "Narcissus."*

- British novelist Bram Stoker publishes *Dracula.*

- German inventor Karl Ferdinand Braun invents the oscilloscope, a precursor of the television screen.

- British scientist Joseph John Thomson discovers the first subatomic particle. In 1906 he wins Nobel Prize for his discovery.

- British scientist Ronald Ross discovers the protozoan that causes malaria, which becomes the first infectious disease known to be caused by a nonbacterial agent. Ross, who also finds that the protozoan is carried by mosquitoes, is awarded a Nobel Prize in 1902 for his discoveries.

- British inventor Charles Algernon Parsons displays his steam-turbine engine at the Diamond Jubilee of Queen Victoria. During a review by the British navy, Parsons's steam-powered ship, the *Turbinia,* passes their ships at top speed, greatly enhancing the popularity of steam turbines among shipbuilders.

2 Feb.	The people of Crete again rebel against Ottoman control.
6 Feb.	Crete declares its union with Greece.
10 Feb.	Greek troops leave for Crete to defend it against an impending Ottoman attack.
20 Mar.	Ethiopia and France sign a treaty defining the frontier between Ethiopia and Somalia. The French hope to use Ethiopia as a base for an advance on the Nile.
17 Apr.	Greece declares war against the Ottoman Empire in spite of pressure from Russia and Austria-Hungary, which hope to avoid another Balkan crisis.
14 May	Great Britain and Ethiopia sign a treaty granting much of Somaliland to Ethiopia, but King Menelik II of Ethiopia refuses to surrender his claims on the Nile, as the British have hoped.

18 July The treaty ending the Greco-Turkish War leaves Crete under Turkish sovereignty, while granting Crete a modicum of self-government and installing an international force there to keep the peace. Prince George, a younger son of the king of Greece, is appointed high commissioner of the island.

Aug. Hungarian Jew Theodor Herzl organizes the first Zionist Congress in Basel, Switzerland.

Nov. Mathieu Dreyfus discovers independently that Maj. Ferdinand-Walsin Esterhazy has forged the letter that has incriminated his brother Capt. Alfred Dreyfus and demands that Esterhazy stand trial.

1898

- British playwright George Bernard Shaw satirizes conventional attitudes in three plays published this year: *Arms and the Man, Candida,* and *Mrs. Warren's Profession.*

- British science-fiction writer H. G. Wells publishes *The War of the Worlds.*

- British novelist Anthony Hope (Anthony Hope Hawkins) publishes *Rupert of Hentzau.*

- Italian electrical engineer Guglielmo Marconi is sending and receiving signals using radio waves over eighteen-mile distances. In 1900 he patents the earliest version of the radio.

- Danish inventor Valdemar Poulsen patents a method of wire recording.

- Polish-born French scientist Marie Curie and her husband, Pierre Curie, isolate polonium and radium, elements in uranium ore that are more radioactive than uranium and thorium. Marie Curie is awarded Nobel Prizes in both physics (1903, with her husband and A. H. Becquerel) and chemistry (1906).

- Russian physiologist Ivan Petrovich Pavlov begins studying conditioned reflexes, observing that if he rings a bell every time he feeds a dog, the dog's natural response to food — salivation — can eventually be provoked by ringing the bell alone.

- British scientists William Ramsay and Morris William Travers discover the elements neon, krypton, and xenon.

- Camillo Golgi describes cytoplasmic nerve cells of interlaced threads that become known as the "Golgi apparatus."

- The Social Democratic Party, led by Georgy Valentinovich Plekhanov, is founded in Russia.

11 Jan. Maj. Ferdinand-Walsin Esterhazy is tried and hastily acquitted. Debate over the Dreyfus Affair reaches a high point with Dreyfusards (liberals, anticlerics, Jews, intellectuals) expressing outrage at Esterhazy's almost immediate exoneration and anti-Dreyfusards (clerics, conservatives, militarists, and anti-Semites) continuing to assert that Capt. Alfred Dreyfus is guilty.

13 Jan. French novelist Emile Zola publishes *J'accuse,* an open letter to the president of the French republic denouncing the members of the general staff who condemned Dreyfus.

23 Feb.	Because of his accusations of individuals connected to the Dreyfus Affair, Zola is tried for libel and sentenced to a year in prison, but he escapes to England.
28 Mar.	The German legislature allocates funds for building a modern German navy, prompting the fear in Great Britain that Germany plans to challenge them on the seas.
1 May	During the Spanish-American War, the American fleet commanded by Commodore George Dewey destroys the Spanish ships in Manila bay.
22 June	Ethiopian and French forces reach the Nile, while other Ethiopian troops push north and south, expanding the boundaries of their country to those of present-day Ethiopia.
13 Aug.	American troops, assisted by Emilio Aguinaldo's guerrillas, take Manila during the Spanish-American War.
22 Aug.	After the death of King Malietoa Laupepa of Samoa, German warships land to support Mataafa. Backed by the Germans, he is elected king in November, but the British and Americans refuse to recognize him.
30 Aug.	French chief of intelligence Col. Hubert-Joseph Henry admits to forging documents used to implicate Capt. Alfred Dreyfus. He commits suicide in prison the next day.
2 Sept.	Gen. Horatio Herbert Kitchener's army defeats Sudanese troops at Omdurman and takes Khartoum.
10 Sept.	While traveling in Switzerland, Empress Elizabeth of Austria-Hungary is assassinated by an Italian anarchist.
17 Sept.	General Kitchener's troops in Sudan reach Fashoda and discover it has been occupied by the French, precipitating the Fashoda Crisis, the most serious threat to Anglo-French relations of the period. Finding itself unprepared for war with Great Britain, France orders the withdrawal of its troops on 3 November.
17 Nov.	Germany begins to plan a railroad from Berlin to Baghdad in Iraq, then part of the Ottoman Empire. Great Britain and Russia are worried by this obvious attempt to increase German influence in the Middle East.
21 Nov.	Trade between Italy and France is reestablished.

1899

•	British writer Rudyard Kipling writes "Recessional," a poem expressing the fear that Great Britain's status as a world power may decline.
Jan.	Following a brief civil war in Samoa, Mataafa sets up a provisional government.
19 Jan.	Egypt and Great Britain agree to establish and jointly administer Anglo-Egyptian Sudan.
15 Mar.	British and American warships bombard Apia in Samoa to protest the actions of Mataafa and the Germans.
21 Mar.	In an agreement with Great Britain, France relinquishes all claim to Egypt and the Nile Valley in exchange for territory in the Sahara Desert.

24 Mar.	British settlers in Transvaal send Queen Victoria of Great Britain a petition listing their grievances against the South African Republic.
13 May	A British-German-American commission meeting in Samoa abolishes the Samoan monarchy.
18 May– 29 July	At the First Hague Peace Conference delegates from twenty-six countries reach no agreement on methods of arms control and disarmament, but establish a permanent court for international arbitration to be headquartered at The Hague.
31 May– 5 June	President Marthinus Steyn of the Orange Free State hosts a conference between President Paul Kruger of the South African Republic and Sir Alfred Milner, British high commissioner in South Africa. The two sides fail to resolve their differences, and by September both sides are preparing for war.
Sept.	Somali chief Mohammed ben Abdullah, who becomes known as the "Mad Mullah," proclaims himself Mahdi and begins raiding British and Italian possessions in East Africa.
9 Sept.	Following the admissions of Col. Hubert Henry, Capt. Alfred Dreyfus is retried, again declared guilty, and given a reduced prison sentence of ten years. President Emile-François Loubet, the Dreyfusard who took office earlier this year, pardons Dreyfus on 19 September. The case is reopened on 12 July 1906, and Dreyfus is finally exonerated.
12 Oct.	The Boer War breaks out in South Africa, finally ending in total British victory in May 1902.
3 Oct.	A serious border dispute between Venezuela and British Guiana, which began in 1895, is finally settled. Great Britain obtains most of the territory in question, except for the mouth of the Orinoco River, which Venezuela retains.
14 Nov.– 2 Dec.	The United States, Great Britain, and Germany sign treaties dividing the Samoan Islands among themselves.

THE ARTS

by JESSICA DORMAN

CONTENTS

Sidebars and tables are listed in italics.

1878

Fiction Edward Eggleston, *Roxy;* Anna Katharine Green, *The Leavenworth Case;* Henry James, *The Europeans.*

Poetry Sidney Lanier, "The Marshes of Glynn"; John Greenleaf Whittier, *The Vision of Echard and Other Poems.*

Music "Carry Me Back to Old Virginny," by James A. Bland; "A Flower for Mother's Grave," by Harry Kennedy; "The Old Wooden Rocker," by Florence Harper; "The Skidmore Fancy Ball," music by David Braham, lyrics by Edward Harrigan; "Sweet Mary Ann," music by Braham, lyrics by Harrigan.

- A survey reveals that American theaters are fire hazards, citing flammable scenery and faulty floor planning as factors; one in four theaters burns down within four years of construction.

- Richard Morris Hunt, a favorite architect of the upper classes during the Gilded Age, begins work on the Vanderbilt mansion in New York City.

- Wild West exhibitions by equestrian daredevil W. F. Carver entrance eastern audiences.

12 June Poet and antislavery activist William Cullen Bryant dies in New York City.

1879

Fiction Hjalmar Hjorth Boyesen, *Falconberg;* George Washington Cable, *Old Creole Days;* William Dean Howells, *The Lady of the Aroostook;* Henry James, *Daisy Miller;* Frank R. Stockton, *Rudder Grange;* Albion W. Tourgée, *A Fool's Errand.*

Music "The Babies on Our Block," music by David Braham, lyrics by Edward Harrigan; "In the Evening by the Moonlight," by James A. Bland; "In the Morning by the Bright Light," by Bland; "Oh, Dem Golden Slippers," by Bland.

- The Chicago Art Institute opens, signaling a cultural renaissance for a city leveled by fire just eight years earlier.

- The first Madison Square Garden, a railroad station converted into an entertainment arena, opens on Twenty-sixth Street in Manhattan.

- Sculptor Daniel Chester French completes a bust of his Concord neighbor Ralph Waldo Emerson.

13 Jan. *The Mulligan Guards' Ball,* a farce by Edward Harrigan, opens at the Theatre Comique in New York City and runs through 24 May.

14 Apr. Walt Whitman delivers a lecture in New York City on the death of Abraham Lincoln. In 1865–1866 Whitman, who was deeply moved by the assassination of Lincoln, wrote two poems about the dead president: "When Lilacs Last in the Dooryard Bloom'd" and "O Captain! My Captain!"

30 Apr. Sarah Josepha Hale, author of "Mary Had a Little Lamb" and longtime editor of *Godey's Lady's Book,* dies in Philadelphia.

16 June *H. M. S. Pinafore,* the first Gilbert and Sullivan production to be staged in New York City, opens at the Bowery Theater.

1880

Fiction   Henry Adams, *Democracy;* Louisa May Alcott, *Jack and Jill: A Village Story;* Thomas Bailey Aldrich, *The Stillwater Tragedy;* George Washington Cable, *The Grandissimes;* Lucretia Peabody Hale, *The Peterkin Papers;* Marietta Holley (Josiah Allen's Wife), *My Wayward Pardner;* Harriet M. Lothrop (Margaret Sidney), *The Five Little Peppers and How They Grew;* Albion W. Tourgée, *Bricks Without Straw;* Lew Wallace, *Ben-Hur;* Constance Fenimore Woolson, *Rodman the Keeper: Southern Sketches.*

Poetry   Henry Wadsworth Longfellow, *Ultima Thule.*

Music   "A Bird from O'er the Sea," by C. A. White; "Cradle's Empty, Baby's Gone," by Harry Kennedy; "De Golden Wedding," by James A. Bland; "The Five-cent Shave," by Thomas Cannon; "The Full Moon Union," music by David Braham, lyrics by Edward Harrigan; "Hear Dem Bells," by D. S. McCosh; "Whist the Bogie Man," music by Braham, lyrics by Harrigan; "Why Did They Dig Ma's Grave So Deep?" by Joseph P. Skelly.

* Twenty-one-year-old Pauline Hopkins stars in the Boston premiere of her musical drama *Slaves Escape.*

* The Metropolitan Museum of Art in New York City, founded in 1870, moves to a new building in Central Park in uptown Manhattan.

* John Knowles Paine's Second Symphony premieres in Boston.

* Expatriate artist James McNeill Whistler paints *Venice: Nocturne in Blue and Silver.*

* Albert Pinkham Ryder summons up the otherworldly in his painting of *The Flying Dutchman.*

4 Feb.   Steele MacKaye's melodrama *Hazel Kirke* opens in New York at Madison Square Theater.

May   Francis F. Browne of Chicago publishes the first issue of *The Dial: A Monthly Review and Index of Current Literature,* which soon becomes well known for its intelligent reviews of the important books of the day. The magazine moves to New York in 1916 and becomes a champion of American and international modernist literature in 1920s, ceasing publication in 1929.

8 Nov.   French actress Sarah Bernhardt makes her New York debut at Booth's Theater.

1881

Fiction   George Washington Cable, *Madame Delphine;* Rose Terry Cooke, *Somebody's Neighbors;* John William De Forest, *The Bloody Chasm;* Joel Chandler Harris, *Uncle Remus: His Songs and His Sayings;* William Dean Howells, *Dr. Breen's Practice;* Henry James, *The Portrait of a Lady* and *Washington Square.*

Poetry   Ina Coolbrith, *A Perfect Day, and Other Poems;* John Greenleaf Whittier, *The King's Missive and Other Poems.*

Music   "Are You Going to the Ball This Evening?" by Joseph P. Skelly; "My Love's a Rover," by C. A. White; "Paddy Duffy's Cart," music by David Braham, lyrics by Edward Harrigan; "Peek-a-boo!" by William J. Scanlan; "Wait 'Till the Clouds Roll By," by Charles E. Pratt; "The Widow Nolan's Goat," music by Braham, lyrics by Harrigan.

- Boston publisher James R. Osgood withdraws from publication the so-called seventh edition of Walt Whitman's *Leaves of Grass* (actually the sixth edition) after the Boston district attorney declares the book obscene literature; the Philadelphia publisher Rees, Welch takes over the edition, selling two thousand copies in one week, partly because of the publicity generated by its having been banned in Boston.

- William Dean Howells resigns the editorship of *The Atlantic Monthly*.

- For the third consecutive year Mary Cassatt is the only American to show paintings with the French Impressionists in Paris; this year her paintings *The Cup of Tea* and *Mrs. Cassatt Reading to Her Grandchildren* are included in the exhibit.

- Edward MacDowell composes his *First Modern Suite* for piano.

- Hired by the Boston and Albany Railroad, architect Henry Hobson Richardson designs railroad stations in and around Boston.

June Roswell Smith, one of the founders of *Scribner's Magazine* in 1870, acquires nine-tenths of the stock in the magazine and subsequently changes its name to *The Century Illustrated Monthly Magazine*. In October Richard Watson Gilder becomes editor of the magazine, serving through 1909. During the 1880s and 1890s the magazine serializes fiction by the leading American realists, including Henry James and William Dean Howells.

1 June *The Professor*, the first play written by actor William Gillette, opens at Madison Square Theater in New York City.

1882

Fiction Samuel Langhorne Clemens (Mark Twain), *The Prince and the Pauper*; F. Marion Crawford, *Mr. Isaacs*; William Dean Howells, *A Modern Instance*; Elizabeth Stuart Phelps Ward, *Doctor Zay*; Constance Fenimore Woolson, *Anne*.

Poetry Ella Wheeler Wilcox, *Maurine and Other Poems*.

Music "Bring Back My Bonnie to Me," by Charles E. Pratt.

- Walt Whitman's autobiographical *Specimen Days and Collect*, notes and essays featuring his recollections of the Civil War, is published.

- Abraham Cahan, a Russian Jew, arrives in New York City, where he later becomes editor of the Yiddish-language *Jewish Daily Forward* and publishes fiction such as *Yekl: A Tale of the New York Ghetto* (1896) and *The Rise of David Levinsky* (1917).

- Publisher John W. Lovell launches the popular "Lovell's Library" and proceeds to publish a new book (priced at ten to twenty cents) every day.

- John Singer Sargent paints *The Daughters of Edward D. Boit*.

24 Mar. Poet Henry Wadsworth Longfellow, author of "Paul Revere's Ride" and "Hiawatha," dies in Cambridge, Massachusetts; he is subsequently the first American memorialized in the Poets' Corner at Westminster Abbey in London.

27 Apr. Transcendentalist essayist and poet Ralph Waldo Emerson dies in Concord, Massachusetts.

11 Dec. A performance of Gilbert and Sullivan's *Iolanthe* is lighted by 650 incandescent bulbs at the Bijou Theater — the first time such lighting has been used in American theater.

1883

Fiction Hjalmar Hjorth Boyesen, *A Daughter of the Philistines;* F. Marion Crawford, *Dr. Claudius;* Edward Eggleston, *The Hoosier School-Boy;* Mary Hallock Foote, *The Led-Horse Claim;* Joel Chandler Harris, *Nights with Uncle Remus;* E. W. Howe, *The Story of a Country Town;* George W. Peck, *Peck's Bad Boy and His Pa;* Howard Pyle, *The Merry Adventures of Robin Hood;* Constance Fenimore Woolson, *For the Major.*

Poetry James Whitcomb Riley, *The Old Swimmin' Hole and 'Leven More Poems;* John Greenleaf Whittier, *The Bay of Seven Islands and Other Poems;* Ella Wheeler Wilcox, *Poems of Passion.*

Music "Marguerite," by C. A. White; "My Dad's Dinner Pail," music by David Braham, lyrics by Edward Harrigan; "Strolling on the Brooklyn Bridge," music by Joseph P. Skelly, lyrics by George Cooper; "There Is a Tavern in the Town," author unknown; "When the Robins Nest Again," by Frank Howard.

- Samuel Langhorne Clemens (Mark Twain) recalls the river of his youth and young adulthood in *Life on the Mississippi.*

- Thomas Eakins paints *The Swimming Hole.*

- The Modern Language Association, a professional organization for teachers of literature and language, is founded.

- Benjamin Franklin Keith opens his first theater; by the time of his death in 1914 he owns some four hundred vaudeville theaters.

24 May The Brooklyn Bridge opens to traffic with President Chester A. Arthur presiding over the ceremonies.

4 July William Frederick Cody produces his first Buffalo Bill's Wild West Show, in North Platte, Nebraska.

22 Oct. The Metropolitan Opera House in New York City opens with a production of Charles Gounod's *Faust.*

1884

Fiction Katherine MacDowell (Sherwood Bonner), *Suwanee River Tales;* Alice Brown, *Stratford-by-the-Sea;* Samuel Langhorne Clemens (Mark Twain), *Adventures of Huckleberry Finn;* F. Marion Crawford, *A Roman Singer;* Joel Chandler Harris, *Mingo and Other Sketches in Black and White;* John Hay, *The Bread-Winners;* Helen Hunt Jackson, *Ramona;* Sarah Orne Jewett, *A Country Doctor;* Mary Noailles Murfree (Charles Egbert Craddock), *In the Tennessee Mountains;* Frank R. Stockton, *The Lady, or the Tiger? and Other Stories.*

Poetry Thomas Bailey Aldrich, *Mercedes, and Later Lyrics.*

Music "Always Take Mother's Advice," by Jennie Lindsay; "The Fountain in the Park," by Robert A. King; "White Wings," by Banks Winter.

- A statue of founder John Harvard, sculpted by Daniel Chester French, is placed in Harvard Yard at Harvard University in Cambridge, Massachusetts.

- Chicago-based architect William Jenney uses a steel frame in his ten-story Home Insurance Company building, the first full-scale use of steel skeletal construction.

- Artist Winslow Homer moves to Prout's Neck, on the Maine coast, and depicts a rescue at sea in *The Life Line;* despite frequent travel, Homer makes Maine his home base for the rest of his life.

- John Singer Sargent shocks high society and stodgy critics with his eroticized portrait *Madame X.*

12 Apr. Producer David Belasco's *May Blossom* opens in New York at the Madison Square Theater.

1885

Fiction George Washington Cable, *Dr. Sevier;* Rose Terry Cooke, *Root-Bound and Other Sketches;* F. Marion Crawford, *Zoroaster;* Marietta Holley (Josiah Allen's Wife), *Sweet Cicely;* Oliver Wendell Holmes, *A Mortal Antipathy;* William Dean Howells, *The Rise of Silas Lapham;* Thomas Allibone Janvier, *Color Studies;* Sarah Orne Jewett, *A Marsh Island;* Henry Francis Keenan, *The Money-Makers;* Mary Noailles Murfree (Charles Egbert Craddock), *The Prophet of the Great Smoky Mountains;* Edward Payson Roe, *Driven Back to Eden.*

Music "A Handful of Earth from My Dear Mother's Grave," by Joseph Murphy; "I Had $15 in My Inside Pocket," by Harry Kennedy; "Poverty's Tears Ebb and Flow," music by David Braham, lyrics by Edward Harrigan; "Sleep, Baby, Sleep (Irene's Lullaby)," by John J. Handley; "There's a Light in the Window," by Bobby Newcomb.

- Theater managers begin to fireproof their buildings with asbestos curtains.

- Architect Henry Hobson Richardson builds the Marshall Field Wholesale Store in Chicago, a model for practical yet vibrant urban design.

15 Feb. Leopold Damrosch, director of the Metropolitan Opera company, dies; he is succeeded by his son Walter.

21 Feb. After four and a half years of construction, a dedication ceremony marks the completion of the Washington Monument in Washington, D.C.

1886

Fiction Louisa May Alcott, *Jo's Boys;* Amelia E. Barr, *The Bow of Orange Ribbon;* Frances Hodgson Burnett, *Little Lord Fauntleroy;* Rose Terry Cooke, *The Sphinx's Children and Other People's;* William Dean Howells, *Indian Summer;* Henry James, *The Bostonians* and *The Princess Casamassima;* Sarah Orne Jewett, *A White Heron and Other Stories;* S. Weir Mitchell, *Roland Blake.*

Poetry John Greenleaf Whittier, *Saint Gregory's Guest and Recent Poems.*

Music "Johnny Get Your Gun," by Monroe H. Rosenfeld; "The Letter That Never Came," by Paul Dresser; "Maggie, The Cows Are in the Clover," by Al W. Filson; "Never Take No for an Answer," by J. F. Mitchell; "Remember, Boy, You're Irish," by William J. Scanlan; "Rock-a-Bye Baby," by Effie I. Canning.

- Denman Thompson's New England drama *The Old Homestead* is staged; it remains one of the most popular American plays for more than two decades.

- Thomas Eakins is forced out at the Pennsylvania Academy of Fine Arts after arguing that female students be allowed to study nude models.

- Louis Sullivan begins work on the Auditorium Building in Chicago; construction will extend over three years.

Jan.   William Dean Howells's first "Editor's Study" literary column is published in *Harper's Monthly.*

Mar.   Paul J. Schlicht of Rochester, New York, founds *Cosmopolitan Magazine,* which during the 1880s and 1890s publishes fiction and nonfiction by American realists such as William Dean Howells, Henry James, Mary E. Wilkins Freeman, Hamlin Garland, Sarah Orne Jewett, Theodore Dreiser, Harold Frederic, and Stephen Crane. Having moved to New York City in 1887, the magazine becomes a muckraking journal during the early years of the twentieth century, campaigning for social reform, and in the 1960s it becomes a popular magazine for career women.

27 Apr.   The eminent architect Henry Hobson Richardson dies at age forty-seven.

17 May   The Cincinnati Art Museum opens to the public.

28 Oct.   The Statue of Liberty is dedicated in New York Harbor with "Give me your tired, your poor, / Your huddled masses yearning to breathe free" — lines from Emma Lazarus's sonnet "The New Colossus" — engraved on its base.

1887

Fiction   Alice Brown, *Fools of Nature;* Palmer Cox, *The Brownies, Their Book;* Harold Frederic, *Seth's Brother's Wife;* Mary E. Wilkins Freeman, *A Humble Romance;* Alice French (Octave Thanet), *Knitters in the Sun;* Joel Chandler Harris, *Free Joe and Other Georgian Sketches;* Marietta Holley (Josiah Allen's Wife), *Samantha at Saratoga;* Joseph Kirkland, *Zury: The Meanest Man in Spring County;* Thomas Nelson Page, *In Ole Virginia;* Rowland Evans Robinson, *Uncle Lisha's Shop.*

Poetry   Madison Cawein, *Blooms of the Berry;* Lizette Woodworth Reese, *A Branch of May.*

Music   "Happy Birds," music by Edward Holst, lyrics by C. T. Steele; "I Owe $10 to O'Grady," by Harry Kennedy; "If the Waters Could Speak as They Flow," by Charles Graham; "The Outcast Unknown," by Paul Dresser.

- Sculptor Augustus Saint-Gaudens completes his *Lincoln* memorial for Lincoln Park in Chicago.

- Journalist-poet Eugene Field writes two of his most enduring poems, "Little Boy Blue" and "Wynken, Blynken, and Nod."

- Thomas Eakins completes his portrait of Walt Whitman.

- Arthur William Foote, a member of the so-called Boston Classicist school, composes *In the Mountains,* an overture.

- Ada Rehan, John Drew, and Mrs. George H. Gilbert star in actor-playwright Augustin Daly's hit comedy *The Railroad of Love.*

1888

Fiction Louisa May Alcott, *A Garland for Girls;* Edward Bellamy, *Looking Backward;* Margaret Deland, *John Ward, Preacher;* Edward Everett Hale, *Mr. Tangier's Vacations;* Grace King, *Monsieur Motte;* Joseph Kirkland, *The McVeys;* Amélie Rives, *The Quick or the Dead?*

Poetry Madison Cawein, *The Triumph of Music and Other Lyrics;* Walt Whitman, *November Boughs.*

Music "The Convict and the Bird," by Paul Dresser; "Drill, Ye Terriers, Drill," author unknown; "The Mottoes That Are Framed upon the Wall," music by W. S. Mullaly, lyrics by William Devere; "Oh, That We Two Were Maying," music by Ethelbert Nevin, lyrics by Charles Kingsley; "Where Did You Get that Hat?" by Joseph J. Sullivan; "The Whistling Coon," by Sam Devere; "With All Her Faults I Love Her Still," by Monroe H. Rosenfeld.

- After the publication of Edward Bellamy's utopian novel *Looking Backward,* many readers join Bellamy Clubs, dedicated to redistributing wealth and transforming society.

- George Eastman markets the first Kodak box camera, ushering in an era of popular photography.

- Arthur William Foote's acclaimed choral composition *The Wreck of the Hesperus* premieres in Boston.

- Construction begins on the Boston Public Library, an Italian Renaissance structure designed by the New York firm of McKim, Mead and White.

- Western landscape artist Albert Bierstadt paints *The Last of the Buffalo.*

6 Mar. Louisa May Alcott, author of *Little Women* (1868, 1869), dies in Boston; her father, Transcendentalist philosopher Bronson Alcott, precedes her in death by just two days.

14 Aug. Actor DeWolf Hopper recites Ernest Thayer's poem "Casey at the Bat" at Wallack's Theater in New York City.

1889

Fiction Jane Goodwin Austin, *Standish of Standish;* Mary Hartwell Catherwood, *The Romance of Dollard;* Samuel Langhorne Clemens (Mark Twain), *A Connecticut Yankee in King Arthur's Court;* Lafcadio Hearn, *Chita: A Memory of Last Island;* William Dean Howells, *Annie Kilburn;* Francis Hopkinson Smith, *A White Umbrella in Mexico;* Charles Dudley Warner, *A Little Journey in the World;* Constance Fenimore Woolson, *Jupiter Lights.*

- Thomas Eakins paints *The Agnew Clinic.*

- Thomas Edison, working with material developed by George Eastman, creates film for motion pictures.

- Americans dance the two-step to John Philip Sousa's first popular march, "The Washington Post March."

2 Feb. Frank A. Munsey publishes the first issue of *Munsey's Weekly,* an unapologetically "popular" magazine packed with accessible short fiction. Becoming a monthly in 1891, the magazine serializes fiction by popular romance writers such as F. Marion Crawford, H. Rider Haggard, and Anthony Hope.

12 July   Works by Edward MacDowell, Arthur William Foote, John Knowles Paine, and other composers are performed at the Paris Exposition, signaling the coming-of-age of American classical music.

1890

Fiction   Gertrude Atherton, *Los Cerritos;* Kate Chopin, *At Fault;* Ignatius Donnelly, *Caesar's Column;* William Dean Howells, *A Hazard of New Fortunes;* Henry James, *The Tragic Muse.*

Poetry   Thomas Bailey Aldrich, *Wyndham Towers;* Emily Dickinson, *Poems;* James Whitcomb Riley, *Rhymes of Childhood;* George Edward Woodberry, *The North Shore Watch.*

Music   "The Irish Jubilee," music by Charles B. Lawlor, lyrics by James Thornton; "Maggie Murphy's Home," music by David Braham, lyrics by Edward Harrigan; "Throw Him Down, McCloskey," by J. W. Kelly; "Thy Beaming Eyes," music by Edward MacDowell, lyrics by William Henry Gardner.

- The eleventh U.S. Census declares the American frontier closed; three years later, addressing the American Historical Association in Chicago, Frederick Jackson Turner examines "The Significance of the Frontier in American History."

- Impressionist Childe Hassam paints *Washington Arch in Spring.*

- Author Lafcadio Hearn moves to Japan; he will spend the rest of his life overseas, publishing *Glimpses of Unfamiliar Japan* in 1894 and *Out of the East* in 1895.

- McKim, Mead and White's new Madison Square Garden is completed in New York.

- Louis Sullivan designs the first American skyscraper, the Wainwright Building in Saint Louis.

9 July   Reginald De Koven's comic opera *Robin Hood* opens in Chicago; it includes the popular songs "Brown October Ale" and "Oh, Promise Me."

9 Dec.   Playwright James A. Herne's realistic drama *Margaret Fleming* opens in New York.

1891

Fiction   Jane Goodwin Austin, *Betty Alden: The First Born Daughter of the Pilgrims;* Ambrose Bierce, *Tales of Soldiers and Civilians;* Hjalmar Hjorth Boyesen, *The Mammon of Unrighteousness;* H. C. Bunner, *"Short Sixes";* Rose Terry Cooke, *Huckleberries Gathered from New England Hills;* Richard Harding Davis, *Gallegher and Other Stories;* Mary E. Wilkins Freeman, *A New England Nun;* Hamlin Garland, *Main-Travelled Roads;* Joseph Kirkland, *The Captain of Company K;* Mary Noailles Murfree (Charles Egbert Craddock), *In the "Strange People's" Country;* Francis Hopkinson Smith, *Colonel Carter of Cartersville.*

Poetry   Thomas Bailey Aldrich, *The Sisters' Tragedy with Other Poems;* Emily Dickinson, *Poems, Second Series;* Richard Hovey, *Launcelot and Guenevere: A Poem in Dramas;* Lizette Woodworth Reese, *A Handful of Lavender.*

Music "The Last of the Hogans," music by David Braham, lyrics by Edward Harrigan; "Molly O!" by William J. Scanlan; "The Pardon Came Too Late," by Paul Dresser; "The Picture That Is Turned toward the Wall," by Charles Graham; "Ta-ra-ra-boom-de-ré," by Henry J. Sayers.

- Sculptor John Quincy Adams Ward's memorial to Henry Ward Beecher is installed in Borough Hall, Brooklyn, four years after the death of the popular preacher.

- Theodore Thomas resigns as head of the New York Philharmonic to assume charge of the the Chicago Orchestra.

22 Feb. The melodrama *Mad Money* opens in New York; saloon keeper Steve Brodie, famous for having jumped off the Brooklyn Bridge in 1886, "re-creates" his jump on stage.

4 Apr. Acclaimed actor Edwin Booth, brother of Lincoln assassin John Wilkes Booth, makes his final appearance after more than four decades on the stage.

5 May Carnegie Hall opens in New York City.

1 July America's first international copyright law goes into effect.

28 Sept. Herman Melville, author of *Moby-Dick* (1851), dies in obscurity in New York City; his last completed work, *Billy Budd,* remains unpublished until 1924.

1892

Fiction Hjalmar Hjorth Boyesen, *The Golden Calf;* F. Marion Crawford, *Don Orsino;* Richard Harding Davis, *Van Bibber and Others;* Mary Hallock Foote, *The Chosen Valley;* Edward Everett Hale, *East and West;* Joel Chandler Harris, *Uncle Remus and His Friends;* Marietta Holley (Josiah Allen's Wife), *Samantha on the Race Problem;* William Dean Howells, *The Quality of Mercy;* Grace King, *Tales of Time and Place;* Thomas Nelson Page, *The Old South.*

Poetry Ambrose Bierce, *Black Beetles in Amber;* Madison Cawein, *Moods and Memories;* Paul Laurence Dunbar, *Oak and Ivy;* Walt Whitman, *Leaves of Grass* ("Death-bed" Edition).

Music "After the Ball," by Charles K. Harris; "The Bowery," music by Percy Gaunt, lyrics by Charles H. Hoyt; "Daddy Wouldn't Buy Me a Bow-Wow," by Joseph Tabrar; "Daisy Bell" (or "A Bicycle Built for Two"), by Harry Dacre; "Molly and I and the Baby," by Harry Kennedy; "Push Dem Clouds Away," by Gaunt.

- Stephen Crane leaves Syracuse University after one semester and begins chronicling slum life in New York City for city papers.

- Charles K. Harris composes "After the Ball," which later becomes the first song to sell five million copies in sheet music.

- Edward MacDowell completes his First Piano Sonata, the *Tragica.*

- Mary Cassatt is commissioned to paint *Modern Woman,* a mural for the Woman's Building at the 1893 World's Columbian Exposition in Chicago.

- Augustus Saint-Gaudens's sculpture *Diana* is placed atop the new Madison Square Garden in New York City.

- Daniel Burnham and John Wellborn Root's sixteen-story Monadnock Building is completed in Chicago; it is the tallest masonry building in the United States.

Jan.   Charlotte Perkins Gilman's short story "The Yellow Wall-Paper," describing a young woman's slide into mental illness, appears in *New England Magazine*.

26 Mar.   Walt Whitman dies in Camden, New Jersey.

27 Aug.   Fire destroys the interior of the New York Metropolitan Opera House.

Nov.   William Peterfield Trent founds *The Sewanee Review* at the University of the South in Sewanee, Tennessee. Primarily devoted to Southern literature and culture, it is the longest-running literary quarterly in the United States.

1893

Fiction   Ambrose Bierce, *Can Such Things Be?*; Hjalmar Hjorth Boyesen, *Social Strugglers*; Stephen Crane (Johnston Smith), *Maggie: A Girl of the Streets*; Alice French (Octave Thanet), *Stories of a Western Town*; Henry Blake Fuller, *The Cliff-Dwellers*; Hamlin Garland, *Prairie Folks*; Marietta Holley (Josiah Allen's Wife), *Samantha at the World's Fair*; Henry James, *The Real Thing and Other Tales*; Lew Wallace, *The Prince of India*.

Poetry   Richard Hovey, *Seaward: An Elegy on the Death of Thomas William Parsons*.

Music   "The Fatal Wedding," music by Gussie L. Davis, lyrics by H. W. Windom; "Little Alabama Coon," by Hattie Starr; "Say Au Revoir But Not Good-bye," by Harry Kennedy; "Two Little Girls in Blue," by Charles Graham.

- The "City Beautiful" movement gathers momentum as city planners tout the salutary powers of communal space; Kansas City responds with plans for an elaborate network of parks and public boulevards.

- Wellesley College professor Katherine Lee Bates writes "America the Beautiful"; in 1895 the poem is set to a tune known as "Materna."

- The newly completed seventeen-story Manhattan Life Insurance Building is the tallest building in New York City.

1 May   The World's Columbian Exposition opens in Chicago with sculptor Daniel Chester French's seventy-five-foot-tall *Statue of the Republic* casting its imposing shadow over the crowds of fair goers.

27 Nov.   The newly renovated Metropolitan Opera House in New York City reopens with a performance of *Faust*.

15 Dec.   The New York Philharmonic performs the world premiere of *From the New World*, Czech composer Antonin Dvorák's ninth symphony.

1894

Fiction   Thomas Bailey Aldrich, *Two Bites at a Cherry With Other Tales*; George Washington Cable, *John March, Southerner*; Kate Chopin, *Bayou Folk*; Samuel Langhorne Clemens (Mark Twain), *The Tragedy of Pudd'nhead Wilson and the Comedy of Those Extraordinary Twins*; Paul Leicester Ford, *The Honorable Peter Stirling and What People Thought of Him*; Mary E. Wilkins Freeman, *Pembroke*; William Dean Howells, *A Traveler from Altruria*; Brander Matthews, *Vignettes of Manhattan*; Margaret Marshall Saunders, *Beautiful Joe*; Harriet Prescott Spofford, *A Scarlet Poppy and Other Stories*.

Poetry   Bliss Carman and Richard Hovey, *Songs from Vagabondia;* Ina Coolbrith, *The Singer of the Sea;* George Santayana, *Sonnets and Other Verses.*

Music   "And Her Golden Hair Was Hanging Down Her Back," music by Felix McGlennon, lyrics by Monroe H. Rosenfeld; "I Don't Want to Play in Your Yard," music by H. W. Petrie, lyrics by Philip Wingate; "The Little Lost Child," music by Joseph W. Stern, lyrics by Edward B. Marks; "She May Have Seen Better Days," by James Thornton; "The Sidewalks of New York" (or "East Side, West Side"), by James W. Blake and Charles B. Lawlor.

* W. H. Donaldson of Cincinnati founds *Billboard* as an "amusement weekly" posting timetables and routes for circuses, carnivals, and vaudeville troupes as well as directories of people in the entertainment business; the magazine later changes its focus to the popular-music industry.

* Margaret Marshall Saunders's dog story *Beautiful Joe* is a best-seller, eventually selling more than a million copies.

* Louis Sullivan starts work on the Guaranty Building in Buffalo, New York, another skyscraper crafted according to his motto "form follows function."

25 Feb.   Steele MacKaye, playwright, producer, and founder of the American Academy of Dramatic Art, dies in Timpas, Colorado.

1895

Fiction   James Lane Allen, *A Kentucky Cardinal;* John Kendrick Bangs, *The Idiot;* Alice Brown, *Meadow-Grass: Tales of New England Life;* Robert W. Chambers, *The King in Yellow;* Stephen Crane, *The Red Badge of Courage;* Henry Blake Fuller, *With the Procession;* Hamlin Garland, *Rose of Dutcher's Coolly;* Edward Everett Hale, *If Jesus Came to Boston;* John Ames Mitchell, *Amos Judd;* Alice Moore Dunbar Nelson, *Violets and Other Tales;* Charles Dudley Warner, *The Golden House.*

Poetry   Thomas Bailey Aldrich, *Unguarded Gates and Other Poems;* Ina Coolbrith, *Songs from the Golden Gate;* Stephen Crane, *The Black Riders.*

Music   "The Band Played On," music by Charles B. Ward, lyrics by John E. Palmer; "Down in Poverty Row," music by Arthur Trevelyan, lyrics by Gussie L. Davis; "Just Tell Them That You Saw Me," by Paul Dresser; "My Best Girl's a New Yorker," by John Stromberg; "The Sunshine of Paradise Alley," music by John W. Bratton, lyrics by Walter H. Ford; "You've Been a Good Old Wagon, but You've Broken Down," by Ben R. Harney.

* Samuel Langhorne Clemens (Mark Twain) embarks on an international lecture trip in an effort to work his way out of debt.

* Stephen Crane's decidedly antiromantic Civil War novel, *The Red Badge of Courage,* becomes a best-seller.

20 Feb.   Frederick Douglass, abolitionist, former slave, and author of *The Narrative of the Life of Frederick Douglass* (1845), dies.

4 Sept.   *The Prisoner of Zenda,* a play based on a best-selling 1894 novel by Sir Anthony Hope Hawkins, opens at the Lyceum Theater in New York.

19 Nov.   Landscape architect Calvert Vaux, who designed Central Park in New York City with Frederick Law Olmsted, drowns in Gravesend Bay, off the coast of Long Island.

1896

Fiction   George Ade, *Artie: A Story of the Street and Town;* James Lane Allen, *Summer in Arcady;* John Kendrick Bangs, *A Houseboat on the Styx;* Abraham Cahan, *Yekl: A Tale of the New York Ghetto;* Samuel Langhorne Clemens (Mark Twain), *Personal Recollections of Joan of Arc* and *Tom Sawyer, Detective, and Other Tales;* Stephen Crane, *The Little Regiment and Other Episodes of the American Civil War;* John Fox Jr., *A Cumberland Vendetta and Other Stories;* Harold Frederic, *The Damnation of Theron Ware;* Sarah Orne Jewett, *The Country of the Pointed Firs;* Annie Fellows Johnston, *The Little Colonel;* William Gilbert Patten (Burt L. Standish), first novel in his Frank Merriwell series.

Poetry   Thomas Bailey Aldrich, *Judith and Holofernes;* Bliss Carman and Richard Hovey, *More Songs from Vagabondia;* Emily Dickinson, *Poems, Third Series;* Paul Laurence Dunbar, *Majors and Minors* and *Lyrics of Lowly Life;* Lizette Woodworth Reese, *A Quiet Road;* Edwin Arlington Robinson, *The Torrent and the Night Before.*

Music   "All Coons Look Alike to Me," by Ernest Hogan; "A Hot Time in the Old Town," music by Theodore M. Metz, lyrics by Joe Hayden; "In the Baggage Coach Ahead," by Gussie L. Davis; "Kentucky Babe," music by Adam Geibel, lyrics by Richard Henry Buck; "May Irwin's `Bully' Song," by Charles E. Trevathan; "Mister Johnson, Turn Me Loose," by Ben R. Harney; "Mother Was a Lady," music by Joseph W. Stern, lyrics by Edward B. Marks; "My Gal Is a High Born Lady," by Barney Fagan; "On the Benches in the Park," by James Thornton; "Sweet Rosie O'Grady," by Maude Nugent; "You're Not the Only Pebble on the Beach," music by Frederick J. Redcliffe (Stanley Carter), lyrics by Harry B. Berdan (Harry Braisted).

•   Louis Sullivan discusses the aesthetics of the skyscraper in "The Tall Office Building Artistically Considered."

•   After a lifetime of conflict with the arts establishment, Thomas Eakins is given a one-man show in Philadelphia.

15 Jan.   Matthew Brady, well known for his Civil War photography, dies in New York City.

23 Apr.   The first public motion-picture show, a pastiche of short scenes and skits, is screened at Koster and Bial's Music Hall in Manhattan.

5 Oct.   William Gillette's Civil War thriller *The Secret Service* opens at the Garrick Theatre in New York City with Gillette in the starring role.

1897

Fiction   James Lane Allen, *The Choir Invisible;* Alice Brown, *The Day of His Youth;* Mary Hartwell Catherwood, *The Spirit of an Illinois Town and The Little Renault;* Kate Chopin, *A Night in Acadie;* Richard Harding Davis, *Soldiers of Fortune;* Ellen Glasgow, *The Descendant;* Henry James, *The Spoils of Poynton* and *What Maisie Knew;* Richard Malcolm Johnston, *Old Times in Middle Georgia;* Alfred Henry Lewis, *Wolfville;* S. Weir Mitchell, *Hugh Wynne, Free Quaker;* Charles M. Sheldon, *In His Steps.*

Poetry   Edwin Arlington Robinson, *The Children of the Night.*

Music "Asleep in the Deep," music by Henry W. Petrie, lyrics by Arthur J. Lamb; "At a Georgia Camp Meeting," by Kerry Mills; "Break the News to Mother," by Charles K. Harris; "On the Banks of the Wabash, Far Away," music by Paul Dresser, lyrics by Dresser and Theodore Dreiser.

- John Philip Sousa composes "The Stars and Stripes Forever."

- Augustus Saint-Gaudens's memorial to Civil War commander Robert Gould Shaw is unveiled on the Boston Common.

- Construction begins on the New York Public Library, an impressive example of Beaux-Arts architecture designed by the New York firm of Carrère and Hastings.

- Author and illustrator Frederic Remington, well known for his depictions of the American West, publishes a collection of his *Drawings*.

- A patent for the player piano is granted to inventor Edwin S. Votey.

1898

Fiction Gertrude Atherton, *The Californians*; Stephen Crane, *The Open Boat and Other Tales of Adventure*; Paul Laurence Dunbar, *Folks from Dixie*; Finley Peter Dunne, *Mr. Dooley in Peace and War*; Ellen Glasgow, *Phases of an Inferior Planet*; Henry James, *The Two Magics: The Turn of the Screw, Covering End*; Mary Johnston, *Prisoners of Hope*; Charles Major, *When Knighthood Was in Flower*; Brander Matthews, *Outlines in Local Color*; S. Weir Mitchell, *The Adventures of François*; Frank Norris, *Moran of the Lady Letty*; Thomas Nelson Page, *Red Rock*; Francis Hopkinson Smith, *Caleb West*; Edward Noyes Westcott, *David Harum*.

Poetry Richard Hovey, *The Birth of Galahad* and *Along the Trail*; George Cabot Lodge, *The Song of the Wave and Other Poems*; Morris Rosenfeld, *Songs from the Ghetto*.

Music "Gold Will Buy Most Anything but a True Girl's Heart," music by Monroe H. Rosenfeld, lyrics by Charles E. Foreman; "Gypsy's Love Song," music by Victor Herbert, lyrics by Harry B. Smith; "I Guess I'll Have to Telegraph My Baby," by George M. Cohan; "Kiss Me, Honey, Do," music by John Stromberg, lyrics by Edgar Smith; "My Old New Hampshire Home," music by Harry von Tilzer, lyrics by Andrew B. Sterling; "The Rosary," music by Ethelbert Nevin, lyrics by Robert Cameron Rogers; "She Is More to Be Pitied Than Censured," by William B. Gray; "She Is the Belle of New York," music by Gustave Kerker, lyrics by Hugh Morton; "She Was Bred in Old Kentucky," music by Frederick J. Redcliffe (Stanley Carter), lyrics by Harry B. Berdan (Harry Braisted); "When You Were Sweet Sixteen," by James Thornton; "Zizzy, Ze Zum, Zum," music by Lyn Udall, lyrics by Karl Kennett.

- Connecticut native Charles Ives composes his First Symphony.

- Charles W. Chesnutt's short story "The Wife of His Youth," a dissection of intraracial prejudice, appears in *The Atlantic Monthly*.

4 Apr. Bob Cole and Billy Johnson's *A Trip to Coontown*, the first full-length musical written, performed, and produced by African Americans, premieres at the Third Avenue Theatre in New York City.

July *Clorindy, or The Origin of the Cakewalk*, a musical by Will Marion Cook and Paul Laurence Dunbar, opens in New York City.

7 Nov.   The great Austrian contralto Ernestine Schumann-Heink makes her American operatic debut, appearing in *Lohengrin* in Chicago.

1899

Fiction   Ambrose Bierce, *Fantastic Fables;* Alice Brown, *Tiverton Tales;* Charles W. Chesnutt, *The Conjure Woman* and *The Wife of His Youth and Other Stories of the Color Line;* Kate Chopin, *The Awakening;* Winston Churchill, *Richard Carvel;* Margaret Deland, *Old Chester Tales;* Paul Laurence Dunbar, *The Uncalled;* Paul Leicester Ford, *Janice Meredith;* Henry James, *The Awkward Age;* Alice Moore Dunbar Nelson, *The Goodness of St. Rocque and Other Stories;* Frank Norris, *McTeague;* Booth Tarkington, *The Gentleman from Indiana;* Edith Wharton, *The Greater Inclination.*

Poetry   L. Frank Baum, *Father Goose: His Book;* Stephen Crane, *War Is Kind;* Paul Laurence Dunbar, *Lyrics of the Hearthside;* Richard Hovey, *Taliesin: A Masque;* Edwin Markham, *The Man with the Hoe and Other Poems.*

Music   "The Curse of the Dreamer," by Paul Dresser; "Hello, Ma Baby," by Joe E. Howard and Ida Emerson; "I'd Leave My Happy Home for You," music by Harry von Tilzer, lyrics by Will A. Heelan; "The Moth and the Flame," music by Max S. Witt, lyrics by George Taggart; "My Wild Irish Rose," by Chauncey Olcott; "Stay in Your Own Back Yard," music by Lyn Udall, lyrics by Karl Kennett; "When Chloe Sings a Song," music by John Stromberg, lyrics by Edgar Smith.

- Two Revolutionary War novels, *Richard Carvel* by Winston Churchill and *Janice Meredith* by Paul Leicester Ford, are best-sellers.

- Winslow Homer captures the brute power of nature in his paintings *The Gulf Stream* and *After the Hurricane.*

15 Jan.   Edwin Markham's blank-verse poem "The Man with the Hoe" is published for the first time, in the *San Francisco Examiner,* and quickly becomes a labor standard; during Markham's lifetime the poem is published in more than ten thousand newspapers and magazines in more than forty languages.

18 July   Horatio Alger, author of popular "rags to riches" novels, dies.

18 Sept.   John Stark of Sedalia, Missouri, publishes Scott Joplin's "Maple Leaf Rag" and sets off a national craze for ragtime.

6 Nov.   Actor William Gillette creates his most memorable role, starring as the British sleuth in *Sherlock Holmes,* his adaptation of Arthur Conan Doyle's detective fiction. The production opens at the Garrick Theatre in New York City, is performed regularly in the United States and Great Britain until 1903, and is revived frequently, with Gillette playing the title for the last time in 1932.

OVERVIEW

A New World. "Consider that we shall be as a City upon a Hill, the eyes of all people are upon us," said John Winthrop, first governor of the Massachusetts Bay Colony. Winthrop spoke these words in a sermon he delivered on shipboard as he and his fellow Puritans crossed the Atlantic to the New World in 1630. Two and a half centuries later the "eyes of all people" gazed once more on America—specifically on Chicago, site of the spectacular World's Columbian Exposition of 1893. On the shores of Lake Michigan fair organizers had erected a White City, symbol of a gleaming past and a sparkling future. America in the late nineteenth century stood poised to enter a new era of world prominence, and it hoped to demonstrate its worthiness through its art. On both sides of the Atlantic many still considered the American arts second rate copies of European models. Yet some Americans were creating works that rivaled the Europeans' in style and sophistication. At the same time, in American music, art, literature, and architecture, new styles were emerging from uniquely New World roots, setting the stage for the international prominence of American arts and letters in the twentieth century.

Spectacle in Chicago. Visitors to the Chicago World's Fair witnessed the wealth—and variety—of American artistic genius. In the Woman's Building *Modern Woman*, a luminous mural by American Impressionist painter Mary Cassatt, depicted American women at work and play. Thomas Eakins, a pioneering realist from Philadelphia, displayed *The Gross Clinic* (1875) and *The Agnew Clinic* (1889), his defiantly unsentimental portraits of medical science. The Beaux-Arts exhibition buildings designed by McKim, Mead and White—the preeminent New York architectural firm—flashed their gleaming facades beneath the electric lights of the White City. Architect Louis Sullivan, the father of the skyscraper, lured visitors into the Transportation Building through a massive "Golden Doorway." Sullivan's building faced a large lagoon—one of many fairyland touches orchestrated by landscape architect Frederick Law Olmsted. Should a visitor tire of the fair and wander into the city proper, young musicians such as Scott Joplin and Otis Saunders waited in the entertainment districts, playing the syncopated strains of early ragtime.

Another Pageant. The aura of optimism and creative vitality projected by the World's Columbian Exposition could not dispel the darker currents astir in American society. North and south, east and west, American citizens faced the specter of financial ruin. During 1893 Americans experienced the most devastating depression to hit the nation to that time. As young Ray Stannard Baker walked the streets of Chicago as a reporter for the *Daily Record,* he passed tramps, starving urchins, and displaced families. Shaken, Baker watched the "bright banners, the music, and the tinsel" of the Columbian Exposition yield to "another pageant, sombre and threatening, that of the depression and panic of 1893–94."

The City. As Baker's observation suggests, the financial troubles of the 1890s brought into focus the "problem" of the American city. Once primarily an agricultural nation, the United States had increasingly acquired an urban cast. The percentage of Americans residing in cities of one hundred thousand or more skyrocketed over the second half of the nineteenth century: from one in twelve in 1860, to one in eight in 1880, to one in five by 1900. Cities large and small swallowed—metaphorically, if not literally—small towns and rural communities. Fiction, photographs, and architectural plans helped to record this urban transformation. When journalist Jacob Riis invaded the slums of New York City with his flash camera, the American public became alerted to, in Riis's words, "How the Other Half Lives." Novelists such as Stephen Crane, Henry Blake Fuller, Frank Norris, and Theodore Dreiser weighed the perils and prerequisites of city life. Frederick Law Olmsted—the mastermind behind Central Park in New York City in the 1860s and Boston's Emerald Necklace park system in the 1890s—heralded communal space as an antidote to urban pressure. Daniel Burnham, the Chicago-based architect who oversaw planning for the Columbian Exposition, helped spearhead a "City Beautiful" movement that, by the early twentieth century, had salvaged such decayed metropolitan areas as Washington, D.C. In time, a generation of city planners maintained, urban misery might give way to urban renewal.

A Melting Pot. In the minds of many Americans, the growth of the cities went hand-in-hand with another development: immigration. During the late nineteenth century there was an unprecedented influx of foreigners into the United States. Some twenty-five million newcomers, the majority from southern and eastern Europe, crossed the Atlantic between the end of the Civil War and the start of World War I. Less imposing in number but still forceful in presence were the approximately 110,000 Asian immigrants (mostly Chinese and Japanese) who crossed the Pacific during this same period. Immigrants to America were inspired by symbols as compelling as the Statue of Liberty (dedicated in New York Harbor in 1886) or by needs as mundane as shelter, sustenance, and employment. First- and second-generation Americans created some of the nation's most enduring cultural monuments of the 1880s and 1890s: German-born John Roebling and his son, Washington, built the Brooklyn Bridge; German-born Leopold Damrosch and his son Walter nursed the Metropolitan Opera House through its infancy. At the same time the theory that America could serve as a "melting pot"—assimilating individuals of all racial and ethnic origins—was examined, and challenged, by artists of many persuasions. As Russian-born Abraham Cahan observed in *Yekl: A Tale of the New York Ghetto* (1896), America in the 1890s had become home to "people with all sorts of antecedents, tastes, habits, inclinations, and speaking all sorts of subdialects of the same jargon, thrown pell mell into one social cauldron—a human hodgepodge with its component parts changed but not yet fused into one homogeneous whole."

European Allure. The influx of European immigrants to America was paralleled on a much smaller scale by an exodus of American artists to Europe. When American painter William Merritt Chase commented that he would "rather go to Europe than go to heaven," he spoke for an entire generation drawn to the educational and cultural offerings of the Old World. The painters Mary Cassatt, John Singer Sargent, and James McNeill Whistler, the sculptor Augustus Saint-Gaudens, and the novelist Henry James all spent substantial portions of their lives overseas—some settling permanently abroad, others shuttling back and forth between America and Europe. By the late nineteenth century a European education was nearly a necessity for ambitious American architects. Once a hobby for cultured gentlemen such as Thomas Jefferson and Charles Bulfinch or a trade passed from master to apprentice, architecture had become, by the 1890s, highly professionalized. Scores of Americans studied architecture at the Ecole des Beaux-Arts in Paris. For many artists Europe liberated creative potential. Thus, the Impressionist movement, initiated by French painters, inspired Americans such as Cassatt, John Twachtman, and Childe Hassam to break with tradition and experiment with color selection and brush technique. In other cases, however, European influences proved less beneficent.

Highbrow versus Lowbrow. America at midcentury, Henry James observed, had known "no State, in the

European sense of the word, and indeed barely a specific national name. No sovereign, no court, no personal loyalty, no aristocracy, no church, no clergy, no army, no diplomatic service, no country gentlemen, no palaces, no castles, nor manors, nor old country-houses, nor parsonages, nor thatched cottages, nor ivied ruins. . . ." In 1880, James added, the United States remained a site of "terrible denudation." Although James's commentary may be overstated, it voices the anti-American mindset of certain American apostles of high culture. As popular entertainments such as dime novels, pop music, vaudeville, and ragtime proliferated in the late nineteenth century, high culture retrenched. Some critics saw sympathy for popular forms as suspect. When the Paris-trained H. H. Richardson identified two staples of Americana—the grain elevator and the steamboat—as compelling architectural designs, his status as the premier American architect excused such eccentricity. But after Richardson's death in 1886, Beaux-Arts traditionalists attacked American eclecticism and launched a revival of neoclassic design. Indeed, across America, highbrow and lowbrow squared off in a struggle to define and control culture. Museum administrators wondered whether to welcome the "masses" to their temples of fine art while people's advocates argued for lower admission costs and Sunday hours. Genteel composers such as John Knowles Paine and Edward MacDowell composed classical works in the European mold while John Philip Sousa set America marching to the beat of "The Washington Post March" (1889) and "The Stars and Stripes Forever" (1897). Novels by highbrow and lowbrow writers alike were commonly serialized in American magazines before their publication in book form, offering American readers a wide choice of inexpensive fiction. "No literature, no novels, no museums, no pictures," James had complained. One critic's wasteland was another's land of plenty.

New Voices, Old Struggles. During the latter decades of the nineteenth century, "high" and "low" culture alike acquired a more multidimensional cast. New voices in literature and music included groups long excluded from the arts establishment: women, workers, and racial minorities. At midcentury female writers had flourished in the literary marketplace—Nathaniel Hawthorne, for one, groused about the "mob of scribbling women"—but nearly all were confined to the realm of sentimental literature. By the turn of the century women had expanded their literary sphere: Emily Dickinson with her stylistically innovative, emotionally compelling poetry (first published in 1890, four years after Dickinson's death); Charlotte Perkins Gilman with her economic treatises and feminist utopias; Kate Chopin with her realistic stories of Creole life; and Pauline Hopkins with her novels, plays, and essays on the subject of race. Hopkins was just one of many African Americans to break new ground in the arts. Black performers, long typecast by the popular formula of the minstrel show, gradually took to new stages. Ragtime—syncopated piano music rooted in the banjo picking of the minstrel show—made national figures of musicians such as Scott Joplin. Drawing on ragtime rhythms, the classically trained violinist Will Marion Cook composed and produced the hit all-black musical *Clorindy* (1898). Paul Laurence Dunbar, who wrote the lyrics for the show, went on to become one of the most popular American poets of his day.

Realism. Diversity enriched the American arts—and served as a reminder of the many perspectives bound up in the American experience. Post–Civil War America was a nation of many regions and many peoples, all struggling to define their roles in a newly reconstituted nation. In the search for self-definition many late-nineteenth-century artists rejected the romanticism of earlier periods, in which artists often glorified the grandeur of the American landscape and the heroism of its people. Instead of such romanticized views of American life artists of the late nineteenth century championed "realistic" representations of regional culture, contemporary social conditions, and individual consciousness, even when these accurate depictions of everyday life revealed hardship and injustice. Literary realism assumed several forms—ranging from the local-color sketches of Sarah Orne Jewett, Hamlin Garland, Joel Chandler Harris, and Helen Hunt Jackson, to the genteel representations of William Dean Howells, to the psychological probings of Henry James. Over time early practitioners of realism were eclipsed by a bolder breed employing literary naturalism to examine the hereditary, economic, and environmental forces acting on humankind. Many visual artists also took up the banner of realism. Painters such as

Winslow Homer and Thomas Eakins produced realistic works that repudiated the romanticism of the midcentury Hudson River School. In architecture Louis Sullivan's credo, "form follows function," challenged the neoclassic notions of those who designed banks and office buildings that looked like palaces and temples.

Liberty. In 1883 prominent American authors and visual artists were asked to donate token items such as letters, essays, and sketches to a raffle—the proceeds to be applied toward a pedestal for the Statue of Liberty. Samuel Langhorne Clemens (Mark Twain), the leading American humorist, responded to the request with a characteristic mix of levity and insight. "Suppose," he mused, "your statue represented [Liberty] old, bent, clothed in rags, downcast, shame-faced, with the insults and humiliation of 6,000 years, imploring a crust and an hour's rest for God's sake at our back door?—come, now you're shouting! That's the aspect of her which we need to be reminded of, lest we forget it—not this proposed one, where she's hearty and well-fed, and holds up her head and flourishes her hospitable schooner of flame, and appears to be inviting all the rest of the tramps to come over. O, go to—this is the very insolence of prosperity." As Clemens knew, lofty abstractions—Liberty, Justice, the American Dream—required more than faith to make them a reality. Late-nineteenth-century America was tested by depression and prosperity, by urban ills and urban energies, and by the manifold challenges of an increasingly diverse population. Their work reflecting the variety and vitality of contemporary life, American artists helped to shepherd the nation into the twentieth century.

TOPICS IN THE NEWS

AMERICAN IMPRESSIONISM IN ART

An Artist's Paradise. Europe beckoned to American artists of the late nineteenth century. The painter William Merritt Chase, originally from Indiana, proclaimed that he would "rather go to Europe than go to heaven"—a sentiment shared by many in his generation. The art studios of Munich, London, Antwerp, Rome, and above all Paris swarmed with young Americans during the latter decades of the century. Some Americans—the painters James McNeill Whistler in England, Mary Cassatt in France—settled overseas more or less

permanently. Others studied abroad and then returned to the United States to teach, to paint, and to plant European ideas in American soil. Of all the artistic movements to bloom in Europe during the 1870s and 1880s, none proved more hardy—or more readily exportable—than Impressionism.

The Many Facets of Impressionism. The Impressionist movement transformed painting in the late nineteenth century. Whether applied to a set of artists or to a set of artistic conventions, the term *impressionist* suggests both the "impression" of emotions felt by artist and audi-

Susan Comforting the Baby (circa 1881), by Mary Cassatt

ence and the "impression" of atmospheric effects (such as light, shade, and color). As a French critic explained in the 1870s, impressionists "render not a landscape but the sensation produced by the landscape." The year 1874—when Claude Monet exhibited *Impression: Sunrise,* a painting of the French seaport of Le Havre—is often identified as the birth point of the movement. Over the following decade, French artists such as Monet (1840–1926), Camille Pissarro (1830–1903), Edouard Manet (1832–1883), Edgar Degas (1834–1917), Paul Cézanne (1839–1906), and Pierre-Auguste Renoir (1841–1919) boldly explored the interplay of form and light. Strokes of color lit up their canvases. Many early critics considered the Impressionists' broad brush strokes a sign of laziness and technical incompetence ("the original pancake of visual imbecility," complained one observer at an Impressionist show). Others, however, yielded to the spell of what Whistler called "the poetry of sight."

American Interpretations. Prominent late-nineteenth-century American painters influenced, in varying degrees, by impressionistic technique include Chase (1849–1916), Whistler (1834–1903), Cassatt (1845–1926), Winslow Homer (1836–1910), Frank Duveneck (1848–1919), Theodore Robinson (1852–1896), John Twachtman (1853–1902), John Singer Sargent (1856–1925), Childe Hassam (1859–1935), Irving Wiles (1861–1948), and Cecilia Beaux (1863–1942). Born into a wealthy family in Philadelphia, Cassatt traveled widely in her youth. She settled in Paris in 1868, modeled occasionally for her

friend Degas, and produced affecting, unsentimental portraits of women and children at play and at work. A sampling of titles—*The Nurse* (1878), *Susan Comforting the Baby* (circa 1881), *Sewing Woman* (circa 1882), *Mother and Children* (1901)—suggests Cassatt's respect for the daily routine of women's lives. Sargent infused his portraits of the social elite — such as *The Daughters of Edward D. Boit* (1882), *Madame X* (1884), and *Mrs. Joshua Montgomery Sears* (1899)—with glamour, color, and a dash of what one critic called the "nervous tension of the age." Although best known as a portraitist, Sargent also painted landscapes. Both Twachtman and Hassam are remembered for their impressionistic renderings of American scenes. Twachtman, inspired by Monet's depictions of the French countryside around Giverny, purchased a country home in Greenwich, Connecticut, and painted the changing moods of New England. His *Winter* (circa 1898) shows a landscape blanketed in white, with just a hint of a red barn visible through the frost. "We must have snow and lots of it," Twachtman observed. "Everything is so quiet and the whole earth seems wrapped in a mantle." Hassam, a Boston native, resisted the term *impressionism,* which he took to mean "going straight to nature for inspiration, and not allowing tradition to dictate your brush." More than any other American artist, however, Hassam captured the essence of French Impressionism in his American themes. In paintings such as *At Gloucester* (1890), *Evening in New York* (circa 1890s), *New England Headlands* (1899), *Dewey Arch* (1900), and *Hollyhocks, Isles of Shoals*

(1902), Hassam created visual effects that one critic compared to "taking off a pair of black spectacles that one has been compelled to wear out of doors, and letting the full glory of nature's sunlight color pour in upon the retina."

Sources:

Richard McLanathan, *The American Tradition in the Arts* (New York: Harcourt, Brace & World, 1968);

Emily Ballew Neff and George T. M. Shackelford, *American Painters in the Age of Impressionism* (Houston: Museum of Fine Arts, 1994).

BANDS, ORCHESTRAS, AND TOURING TROUPES

Classical Models. Within the classical arena, the latter decades of the nineteenth century were a period during which there was little new in American music. The most respected American composers of the age—John Knowles Paine (1839–1906), Dudley Buck (1839–1909), Silas Gamaliel Pratt (1846–1916), Arthur W. Foote (1853–1937), Edward MacDowell (1860–1908), Horatio William Parker (1863–1919), and Mrs. H. H. A. Beach (1867–1944)—wrote well-received pieces that were derivative of European classical music, often from earlier periods. MacDowell's First Piano Sonata, known as the *Tragica,* typifies the genre: composed in 1891–1892, the *Tragica* was played frequently at concerts and parlor gatherings and inspired one leading critic to compare MacDowell to Ludwig van Beethoven (1770–1827). A century later MacDowell and his *Tragica* are all but forgotten by the music establishment. Yet even as MacDowell and his contemporaries busied themselves emulating European models, a vibrant musical culture emerged on native ground. Bands and orchestras—many of them touring troupes—brought this musical culture to American towns and cities, invigorating classical music with traditional American rhythms.

John Philip Sousa. Born into a lower-middle-class family in Washington, D.C., John Philip Sousa (1854–1932) grew up within the brassy orbit of marching-band music. Sousa's father, a trombonist, played in the U.S. Marine Band. Young John Philip once threatened to run away from home and join a circus band—but he soon relented and joined his father's troupe as a teenage apprentice. Trained in harmony, composition, and violin, Sousa began his formal career as a composer in the late 1870s. From 1880 through 1892 he served as director of the Marine Band, a position that gave him free rein to polish and perform his own compositions. Sousa's first big hit, "The Washington Post March" (1889), proved a perfect accompaniment for the two-step, a new dance that was taking the country by storm. Other popular Sousa marches include "Semper Fidelis" (1888), "The Thunderer" (1889), "The High School Cadets" (1890), "Manhattan Beach" (1893), and "The Stars and Stripes

John Philip Sousa in 1885, dressed in the uniform he wore as director of the U.S. Marine Corps Band

Forever" (1897). No Fourth of July celebration would be complete without the stirring tones of a Sousa march. Although Sousa also composed dances, operettas, and overtures, he is remembered as America's "March King."

The Band Phenomenon. The popularity of John Philip Sousa's music helped stimulate a band craze that lasted from the late 1880s into the early 1900s. One 1889 estimate placed the number of military bands in the United States at ten thousand. Nearly every town had a bandstand and a band of its own. Americans' romance with band music attracted bands from across the Atlantic. Big "business bands," many of them Italian in origin, invaded the United States in the 1890s. The Italian conductor Giuseppe Creatore, whose band toured the Midwest in 1899, transfixed one observer in Kansas City: "Now he leans over the row of music stands, he smiles the smile of a lover—pleading, supplicating, entreating, caressing—with outstretched hand, piercing the air with his baton, like a fencing master. Almost on his knees, he begs, he demands, he whirls around with waving arms. He laughs, he cries, he sings, he hisses through his clenched teeth."

Theodore Thomas. The audiences that flocked to big-band concerts also packed American symphony halls during the late nineteenth century. Among the musicians who helped to introduce symphonic music to main-

Snap the Whip (1872), by Winslow Homer

stream America was Theodore Thomas (1835–1905), a German-born violinist who made his mark as an orchestral conductor. Understanding that classical music remained something of a riddle to many of his listeners, Thomas endeavored to "sell" classical music to American audiences by including both familiar and unfamiliar pieces on a program—and by making sure that the "light" music featured musical themes that reappeared in the "serious" work. By such means, the unfamiliar was made familiar, the inaccessible accessible. As director of his own touring orchestra from 1862 through 1876, the New York Philharmonic from 1877 to 1891, and the Chicago Orchestra from 1891 to his death in 1905, Thomas brought symphonic music to the masses. Thomas's method of mixing musical styles persists in the programs of "Pops" orchestras across the country.

Sources:

Gilbert Chase, *America's Music: From the Pilgrims to the Present* (Urbana: University of Illinois Press, 1992);

John Tasker Howard, *Our American Music: Three Hundred Years of It* (New York: Crowell, 1946);

Joseph A. Mussulman, *Music in the Cultured Generation: A Social History of Music in America, 1870–1900* (Evanston, Ill.: Northwestern University Press, 1971).

BEYOND ROMANTICISM IN ART

Epic Landscapes. American painting at midcentury was dominated by the Hudson River School: Thomas Cole (1801–1848), Asher Durand (1796–1886), Frederic Church (1826–1900), and other artists whose epic landscapes reflected a young nation's sense of manifest destiny. The poet William Cullen Bryant (1794–1878)

gloried in the "scenes of wild grandeur" that Cole painted. The "mountaintops with their mighty growth of forest never touched by the axe," "banks of streams never deformed by culture," and "depths of skies bright with the hues of our own climate" were signs of paradise on earth. Over time, of course, the earthly Eden celebrated by the Hudson River painters gave way to the urban, industrial realities of the post–Civil War period. Two American artists who came of age in the late nineteenth century pioneered a realistic style of painting that more accurately represented a changed American "landscape."

Winslow Homer. At the start of the Civil War *Harper's Weekly* hired a young illustrator from Massachusetts to serve as its wartime artist-correspondent. In ink sketches and oil portraits Winslow Homer (1836–1910) captured the bleakness of the battlefield. At the end of the war Homer began to work primarily in oils and watercolors; he started out by painting the farms and fields of his native New England. Critics, accustomed to the romantic vision of the Hudson River School, struggled to comprehend Homer's perspective. "Mr. Homer goes in, as the phrase is, for perfect realism," commented novelist Henry James in 1875. "He not only has no imagination, but he contrives to elevate this rather blighting negative into a blooming and honorable positive." James took little pleasure in Homer's "barren plank fences," "glaring, bald, blue skies," "big, dreary, vacant lots of meadows," or "freckled, straight-haired Yankee urchins." Homer's "vigorous way of looking and seeing" made him "an almost distinguished painter," James admitted, but his work remained "damnably ugly." Over the years

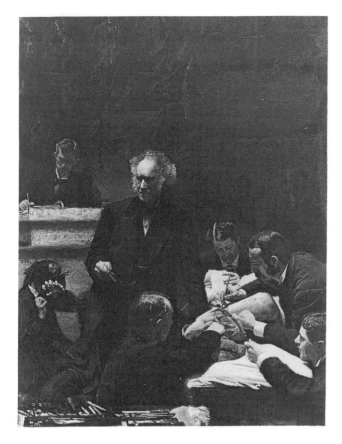

The Gross Clinic (1875), by Thomas Eakins

Homer's reputation improved, but never to the point of universal appeal. From the early 1880s Homer worked out of a studio at Prout's Neck, on the Maine coast. From this permanent base he remained a wanderer, visiting—and painting—in the Adirondacks, the Catskills, Virginia, Florida, England, Cuba, and the Bahamas. Sympathetic toward human frailty and ever-conscious of human dignity, Homer nonetheless avoided overt displays of sentiment. The individuals he painted— the schoolboys at play in *Snap the Whip* (1872), the clustered women and children in *Waiting for the Return of the Fishing Fleet* (1881), the lone hunter dwarfed by his surroundings in *Winter Coast* (1890), the fisherman awaiting death at sea in *The Gulf Stream* (1899)—are subject to the unyielding forces of time and of nature.

Thomas Eakins. If Homer was known for his revision of the American outdoors, his contemporary Thomas Eakins (1844–1916) was notorious for a different sort of realism. Following his graduation from high school, Eakins studied art and anatomy. After three and a half years of further training in Europe, Eakins returned to his hometown of Philadelphia. Eakins's early portraits of athletes—including *Max Schmitt in a Single Scull* (1871) and *Baseball Players Practicing* (1875)—explore the physical, functional aspects of the human body. With *The Gross Clinic* (1875) Eakins extended his anatomical studies in new directions. *The Gross Clinic* shows an op-

eration in progress: a surgeon explains procedure to an audience of medical students, and his assistants probe at the surgical incision while the patient's mother recoils in fear. Critics called Eakins a butcher; at the 1876 Centennial Exhibition in Philadelphia administrators buried *The Gross Clinic* in the medical (rather than arts) section. The Centennial did not mark Eakins's last conflict with a hostile arts establishment. A teacher since 1876 at the Pennsylvania Academy of the Fine Arts—and director of the academy school since 1882—Eakins was forced out in 1886 for insisting that female students study anatomy from nude models.

An Altered Tradition. Eakins did find a measure of acceptance in his lifetime. In major works such as *Crucifixion* (1880), *The Swimming Hole* (1883), *The Agnew Clinic* (1889), and *Salutat* (1898), he continued to probe physical form and function. In time he earned the respect of his peers. He won a gold medal at the 1893 World's Columbian Exposition, had a one-man exhibit in Philadelphia in 1896, and was elected in 1902 to the prestigious National Academy of Design. By the turn of the century the realism of Homer and Eakins had supplanted the romanticism of the Hudson River School. Artistic conventions continued to change. As the nineteenth century slipped into the twentieth, a coterie of experimental artists—George Inness (1825–1894), John La Farge (1835–1910), Ralph Albert Blakelock (1847–1919), and the visionary Albert Pinkham Ryder (1847–1917)—helped American art take its first steps toward the abstract, surrealistic forms of the future.

Sources:

Lloyd Goodrich, *Thomas Eakins,* 2 volumes (Cambridge, Mass. & London: Published for the National Gallery of Art, Washington, by Harvard University Press, 1982);

Jean Gould, *Winslow Homer: A Portrait* (New York: Dodd, Mead, 1962);

Gordon Hendricks, *The Life and Works of Thomas Eakins* (New York: Grossman, 1974);

Hendricks, *The Life and Works of Winslow Home* (New York: Abrams, 1979);

Donelson F. Hoopes, *Eakins: Watercolors* (New York: Watson-Guptill, 1981);

Richard McLanathan, *The American Tradition in the Arts* (New York: Harcourt, Brace & World, 1968);

Emily Ballew Neff and George T. M. Shackelford, *American Painters in the Age of Impressionism* (Houston: Museum of Fine Arts, 1994).

THE BIRTH OF THE SKYSCRAPER

An American Innovation. The skyscraper dominates today's city skyline. The most distinctive American contribution to world architecture, the skyscraper epitomizes the idealistic and material essence of the modern metropolis. Today's tallest building in the world rises some 1,535 feet above Shanghai, China. Other structures top 900 feet in Hong Kong, Japan, Kuala Lumpur, Singapore, Chicago, New York, Philadelphia, Atlanta, Dallas, Houston, Los Angeles, Seattle, and Toronto. The high-rise has become such a visual commonplace that it is easy to forget that, prior to 1883, the word *skyscraper* did not even exist.

During the 1890s American architects erected the first buildings ever to reach for the heavens, as they experimented with new materials and technologies that made their aspirations possible.

The Need for Height. The birth of the skyscraper represents a confluence of commercial necessity and technical innovation. At the end of the Civil War, the tallest buildings in cities such as New York and Chicago reached just four or five stories above street level. A decade later a handful of office buildings had attained a height of nine or ten stories. More than any other factor, the invention of the passenger elevator made this first skyward shift possible. Invented in the 1850s and integrated into commercial buildings during the 1860s and 1870s, the passenger elevator (steam-driven, in its earliest incarnations) made upper-story rental space commercially viable. Electric power, incandescent lighting, and the invention of the telephone—all innovations of the late 1870s and early 1880s—further transformed the capacity of commercial space and, not incidentally, drove up the price of urban real estate.

Solving a Structural Dilemma. The escalating cost of urban lots in the late nineteenth century made high-rise buildings an attractive option for developers. The Great Chicago Fire of 1871 forced architects to develop advanced fireproofing techniques. The only obstacle remaining between earth and sky was the structural dilemma of how buildings could be designed to support the weight of additional stories. During the 1870s builders employed "wall-bearing construction" to erect tall buildings that inevitably featured external walls built of stone or brick; these masonry walls supported the full weight of the building. Thicker and thicker walls, particularly at ground level, permitted taller buildings—but, beyond a certain point, this solution defeated the goal of commercial utility. Who would rent a ground-floor office with walls so thick that windows—if they existed at all—were reduced to the size of slots? Architects of the 1880s resolved the dilemma by switching primary support from the external to the internal walls. Skyscrapers constructed from the mid 1880s onward were invariably metal-framed, or "hung-masonry," buildings, freed from the constraints of gravity by the magic of skeletal construction, first with iron and later with steel.

An Aesthetically Pleasing Whole. The advent of metal-frame construction permitted the development of a tall-building aesthetic. The ten-story office buildings of the 1870s had simply been four-story structures stretched as tall as wall-bearing construction would permit: architects piled one floor on top of the next, block upon block. Louis Henri Sullivan (1856–1924), the architect invariably linked to the birth of the skyscraper, is remembered as a design pioneer. Sullivan essentially adapted a classical three-stage scheme to the high-rise building. His notion of a skyscraper comprised a base, a shaft, and a cap. The Wainwright Building in Saint Louis, designed by Sullivan

The Wainwright Building in Saint Louis as it appeared in 1925. Designed by architect Louis Sullivan in 1890, this office building is generally considered the first American skyscraper.

in 1890, is commonly identified as the first "true" American skyscraper (as opposed to the "tall office building" of the 1880s). Subsequent Sullivan designs—including the Schiller Building in Chicago (1891), the Union Trust Building in Saint Louis (1892), the Guaranty Building in Buffalo (1894), and the Bayard Building in New York (1897)—confirmed his reputation. Sullivan's slogan "form follows function" has encouraged many later critics to misidentify him as a bleak utilitarian. Yet any examination of Sullivan's work reveals that aesthetic as well as pragmatic factors affected the master's conception of the "functional." The twentieth-century city dweller has Sullivan to thank for the notion that a tall building should be inspirational as well as functional.

Sources:

William H. Jordy, *American Buildings and Their Architects: Progressive and Academic Ideals at the Turn of the Twentieth Century* (Garden City, N.Y.: Anchor/Doubleday, 1976);

Vincent Scully, *American Architecture and Urbanism,* revised edition (New York: Holt, 1988);

Robert Twombly, *Louis Sullivan: His Life and Work* (New York: Viking, 1986).

THE BROOKLYN BRIDGE

A Poem of Granite and Steel. Ever since its completion in 1883 the Brooklyn Bridge has fascinated the American public. Every feature of the built and natural

Ever since the first colonists arrived in the New World, Americans have enjoyed drinking beer. The North American colonies boasted a commercial brewery as early as 1612; by the time of the Revolution local breweries dotted the Northeast. Not until the 1870s, however, did large-scale brewing operations become feasible. Technological developments — steam heating, artificial refrigeration, and, by the 1890s, electricity to power compressors — finally permitted brewers to make beer year-round, even in the warmer regions of the country. The focal points of the industry shifted, too, with Cincinnati and Milwaukee becoming the nation's new brewing centers. The mammoth urban breweries that were constructed across the country during the 1870s, 1880s, and 1890s are compelling architectural legacies of the late nineteenth century. These structures loomed over downtown areas, dwarfing residential units and shops.

Many breweries built in the late nineteenth century displayed the eclectic detailing common to the High Victorian period. The imposing American Brewery in downtown Baltimore, built in the mid 1880s, was a five-story brick structure topped with a gabled tower. This architectural style —dubbed "Germanesque-Teutonic Pagoda" by somewhat baffled critics — was partially fanciful and partially functional. Large windows around the "pagoda" added a decorative touch to the facade but also exposed the ventilators integral to the brewing process. Although few of the great nineteenth-century breweries remain in operation, in their heyday these structures slaked the public's thirst not only for beer but also for architectural spectacle.

Source: Diane Maddex, ed., *Built in the U.S.A.: American Buildings from Airports to Zoos* (Washington, D.C.: Preservation Press, 1985).

---

landscape contributes to the spell: the intricate web of steel cables suggesting both delicacy and strength, the massive granite towers standing like twin Gothic gateways to Manhattan and Brooklyn, and the East River flowing dark and swift to the harbor below. A popular ballad of the 1880s, "The Highway in the Air," captured the romantic aura of the new bridge. Young New Yorkers of the late nineteenth century warbled:

> I firmly hope and trust, that the Highway in the air,
> Will unite the two cities by the sea,
> In interest and affection, and that the wedded pair,
> Will give a loving Brooklyn Bride to me.

More than a century later New Yorkers' romance with its "highway in the air" endures. Architectural critic Lewis Mumford once described the Brooklyn Bridge as a "poem of granite and steel." The bridge combines grace, power, and utility, remaining an architect's dream and an onlooker's delight.

History of the Suspension Bridge. Although the concept of a suspension bridge—a roadway suspended by ropes, chains, or cables—dates to antiquity, suspension designs did not figure prominently in modern bridge construction until the early nineteenth century. Several small suspension bridges, designed and patented by James Finley (1762–1828), appeared in America during the first decade of the century. More ambitious projects were mounted overseas in the following decades. In the early 1820s British engineer Thomas Telford (1757–1834) built a dramatic bridge over the Menai Strait in Wales, using metal chains as a suspension element.

During the same decade the Frenchman Marc Séguin (1786–1875) employed wire cables rather than chains in the bridge he built over the Rhône River. Séguin's use of cables later proved popular in America—which by the 1840s had begun a full-fledged love affair with the suspension bridge.

John Roebling's Vision. John Roebling (1806–1869) popularized the suspension bridge in the United States. Born in Mühlhausen, Germany, Roebling immigrated to Pennsylvania in 1831. During the middle decades of the century he cemented his reputation with a series of high-profile suspension projects. He rebuilt a collapsed bridge at Wheeling, West Virginia, and designed bridges at Pittsburgh, Niagara Falls, and Cincinnati. As early as 1857 Roebling proposed—to the great amusement of the New York press—that a bridge be built between Manhattan and Brooklyn. A decade later, after a particularly severe winter halted ferry traffic on the East River, the city agreed. The scale of Roebling's design matched that of the premier American metropolis. His plans called for twin granite towers, each 276 feet high, to stand at either shore, separated by a central span measuring 1,595 feet in length.

A Family's Tragedy and Triumph. Roebling did not live to see his masterpiece materialize. In 1869 his foot was crushed while he was surveying the building site. The wound became infected, and he died within weeks. His son, Washington Roebling (1837–1926), took charge of the project. Trained as a civil engineer, the younger Roebling was well-qualified to carry on his father's work. Tragedy continued to stalk the Roebling

The Brooklyn Bridge as it appeared from the Manhattan side shortly after it was opened to traffic on
24 May 1883

family. In the spring of 1872 Washington developed decompression sickness after working underwater in a pressurized chamber; he remained wheelchair-bound for the rest of his life. Despite his disability, Washington Roebling saw the project to completion, directing construction from his Brooklyn home with the aid of his wife, Emily. When the Brooklyn Bridge opened to traffic on 24 May 1883, it represented a triumph of the will of an extraordinary American family.

Sources:

Peter Conrad, *The Art of the City: Views and Versions of New York* (New York: Oxford University Press, 1984);

Alan Trachtenberg, *The Incorporation of America: Culture and Society in the Gilded Age* (New York: Hill & Wang, 1982).

THE CHICAGO STYLE OF ARCHITECTURE

A National Style. In H. H. Richardson (1838–1886) America recognized indisputable genius. But could any one architect, or any one architectural style, be singled out as quintessentially American? Throughout the 1880s a debate raged between those architects eager to identify a representative "American" style and those who believed that no single style could hope to represent the vitality—and diversity—of the nation. One critic suggested that his countrymen "aim to unite the quiet serenity shown in the Greek with the heaven-aspiring tendency of the Gothic. Aim to have the proportions as agreeable and the whole as harmonious as the Greek. As agreeable as the French. As vigorous as the English. As refined as the

Florentine. As systematic as the German. . . . and the time may come when foreigners will copy as eagerly from us as we now do from them." Champions of regional American architecture disagreed. Frederick Corser, a Minnesotan, fulminated against the American penchant for importing architectural styles from abroad. Good architecture, Corser insisted, answered a native population's "living needs." Corser counseled American architects to "adapt your buildings to the nature of things instead of trying to get up national styles or import the fashion of King this and Queen that."

Out of the Ashes. Chicago—the largest city in the fastest-growing region of the country—answered Corser's call for a vital indigenous architecture. In 1871 a devastating fire had nearly razed the downtown area of the city. When the smoke cleared, one in three buildings was burned beyond repair. Miraculously, over the following two decades, a bustling new city emerged from the ashes. The population of Chicago more than doubled between 1880 and 1890; buildings of seven, eight, nine, as many as twelve stories dotted the downtown area. By 1893, with visitors strolling the shores of Lake Michigan and marveling at the World's Columbian Exposition, Chicago had decisively entered the ranks of world-class cities. Boosters of Chicago rated their city above the aging metropolises of the East Coast. "How much do you suppose people in Iowa and Kansas and Minnesota think about Down East?" asks a character in Henry Blake Fuller's novel *The Cliff-Dwellers* (1893). "Not a great deal," the speaker continues, adding, "It's Chicago they're looking to. This town looms up before them and shuts out Boston and New York, and the whole seaboard from the sight and thoughts of the West and the Northwest and the New Northwest and the Far West and all the other Wests yet to be invented." Fuller's prose captures the spirit of a reborn city. With its lofty skyscrapers and imposing commercial buildings Chicago loomed literally as well as figuratively in the nation's imagination.

Developing the Loop. A trolley route encircling downtown Chicago gave rise to a nickname for the area: "The Loop." Among the architects who transformed the Loop in the aftermath of the Great Fire, the elder statesman was William Le Baron Jenney (1832–1907), a graduate of Yale who had continued his architectural studies in Paris. Jenney arrived in Chicago in 1867, following a five-year stint in the army engineer corps during the Civil War. Over the next decade Jenney's architectural office served as training ground for several architects whose names would be associated with the renaissance of Chicago: Daniel Burnham (1846–1912), William Holabird (1854–1923), Martin Roche (1853–1927), and Louis Henri Sullivan (1856–1924). Two other noted architects, Dankmar Adler (1844–1900) and John Wellborn Root (1850–1891), also migrated to Chicago and joined forces with Sullivan and Burnham, respectively. Working as collaborators and competitors, this band of architects transformed the Loop into a showcase commercial center.

Notable Buildings. Many post–Civil War commercial buildings in America were designed as virtual advertisements for an era of conspicuous consumption. Department stores assumed the form of palaces; so did insurance offices, banks, and stock-market buildings. Chicago rejected the gaudy. A commercial building should look like a commercial building: big, bold, and bluntly functional. Among the notable buildings developed in Chicago during the 1880s and 1890s are the Home Insurance Building (Jenney, 1884), the first American structure completely supported by a steel frame; the Rookery (Burnham and Root, 1885–1888), an expansive granite office building with an airy interior courtyard; the Tacoma Building (Holabird and Roche, 1886–1888), fourteen stories tall, with a frame constructed of riveted steel; the Monadnock Building (Burnham and Root, 1889–1892), sixteen stories tall and praised by Sullivan as "an amazing cliff of brickwork"; the Second Leiter Building (Jenney, 1889–1891), a latticework structure modeled on Richardson's Marshall Field store; and the Reliance Building (Burnham and Root, 1890–1895), with a steel skeleton enclosed in grayish terra-cotta.

Commercialism versus Classicism. Late-nineteenth-century Chicago harbored high-culture aspirations. The Art Institute was founded in 1879; the Chicago Symphony in 1891; and the University of Chicago in 1892. Still, commerce and industry were the city's life-

The Reliance Building in Chicago (1895), designed by architects Daniel Burnham and John Wellborn Root

blood—and the urban landscape reflected this exuberant materialism. The World's Columbian Exposition of 1893 could have served as a showcase for the city's distinctive commercial style. Instead, under Daniel Burnham's direction, the designers of the fairground looked backward rather than forward. In the words of one contributing architect, "It is the high function of architecture not only to adorn this triumph of materialism, but to condone, explain and supplement it, so that some elements of 'sweetness and light' may be brought forward to counterbalance the boastful Philistinism of our times." Indeed, in finished form, the fair blatantly repudiated the Loop. With its domes, statues, and ubiquitous white stucco, the White City wallowed in classical revival styling. Louis Sullivan was among those who considered the White City "an appalling calamity" that warped the course of American architecture. Not all was lost, how-

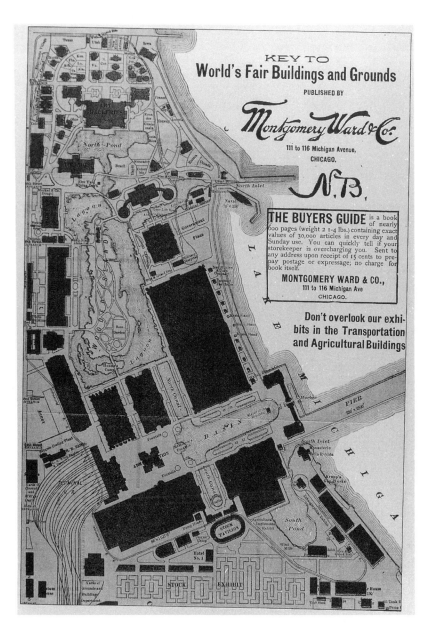

Map of the World's Columbian Exposition in Chicago, showing the boulevards, squares, and water features designed by Frederick Law Olmsted

ever, for the adherents of Chicago's "commercial style." Long after the crowds of 1893 had dispersed and the storybook fairgrounds had closed, the buildings of Chicago's Loop remained on exhibit and, more important, in use.

Sources:

William H. Jordy, *American Buildings and Their Architects: Progressive and Academic Ideals at the Turn of the Twentieth Century* (Garden City, N.Y.: Doubleday, 1972);

Alan Trachtenberg, *The Incorporation of America: Culture and Society in the Gilded Age* (New York: Hill & Wang, 1982).

CITY BEAUTIFUL: THE RISE OF URBAN PLANNING

A Changing Balance. At the start of the Civil War only one out of twelve Americans lived in a city of more than one hundred thousand inhabitants. By the start of the 1880s that figure stood at one in eight; by the turn of the century one in five. More American cities were big cities, and more Americans—many of them immigrants—called these cities home. Two-thirds of New England townships declined in population during the 1880s, even as the population of the region swelled by 20 percent. Similar demographics applied in the Midwest, as immigrants (from small towns, rural areas, and foreign lands) swelled urban populations. As cities expanded, so too did the communication, transportation, and economic channels connecting the metropolis to hinterland. It was the rare individual in the late nineteenth century whose way of life was not touched in some way by urbanization.

The Other Half. The depressions (or "panics") of the 1870s and 1890s devastated rural populations, as failures of railroads severely hampered the farmers' ability to get their crops to market. Still, no matter how shaky their financial status, residents of the small town and the countryside enjoyed one advantage over city dwellers: the relief of open space. While investigating urban living conditions, Danish-born journalist Jacob Riis (1849–1914) counted 522 people living in one acre in the Bowery district of New York City. Small rooms—measuring just thirteen feet square—housed as many as a dozen lodgers. Riis's epochal study of city life, *How the Other Half Lives* (1890), located a netherworld of poverty within walking distance of the poshest New York neighborhoods. Using photographs and text, Riis depicted an urban hell and entered a plea for urban reform. In many respects, Riis was a precursor of the "muckrakers" who transformed American journalism during the early years of the twentieth century. Riis considered it a journalist's duty to educate the public and to stimulate reaction and reform. "Long ago it was said that 'one half of the world does not know how the other half lives,'" Riis noted. "It did not know because it did not care. . . . Information on the subject has been accumulating rapidly since, and the whole world has had its hands full answering for its own ignorance." The essential optimism of Riis's vision dovetailed with that of the city planners who set out to remodel the American city in the 1890s.

Making the Cities Beautiful. Late-nineteenth-century reformers worked—with varying degrees of success—to revise tenement laws, construct affordable and sanitary housing, provide cultural and recreational opportunities for the poor, and eliminate graft from municipal government. Many reformers and social workers were associated with the settlement-house movement: residents of Hull House in Chicago or the Henry Street Settlement in New York lived by choice in poverty-stricken neighborhoods, the better to form meaningful bonds with the populations they intended to aid. While reformers worked through political and philanthropic channels, urban planners approached the question of urban renewal from an aesthetic perspective. Calibrating the salutary effect of urban oases (whether a park, a museum, or a railroad station) on urban dwellers, these landscape architects set out to transform the built environment.

Olmsted's Vision. Frederick Law Olmsted (1822–1903), arguably the most influential urban planner in the United States, worked to turn American cities green. European cities, Olmsted noted, gracefully integrated parks, grand avenues, and residential neighborhoods. American cities, on the other hand, had been built up, block by block, by profit-hungry developers. Olmsted believed that open space—scarce in American cities—could be an antidote to the pressures of urban existence. Public parks, he proclaimed in 1870, represented "the greatest possible contrast with the restraining and confining conditions of the town, which compel us to walk circumspectly, watchfully, jealously, which compel us to look closely upon others without sympathy." Along

with Calvert Vaux (1824–1895) Olmsted designed the gardens, ponds, meadows, and pathways that coalesced into New York's Central Park in the 1860s and 1870s. In 1893 he designed a fairyland of lagoons, squares, and boulevards for the World's Columbian Exposition in Chicago. During the same decade Olmsted completed the complex of parks and riverways that became Boston's "Emerald Necklace." The joggers, dog walkers, and rollerbladers who throng Central Park or Boston's Esplanade today validate Olmsted's vision of healthy communal living.

Reclaiming L'Enfant's Plan. The urban muddle of the late nineteenth century was particularly apparent in the premier "planned" American city: Washington, D.C. The Washington of the 1890s barely resembled the crisp grid of avenues and parks envisioned by planner Pierre-Charles L'Enfant (1754–1825) in the 1790s. The restoration of Washington to a closer approximation of L'Enfant's vision represents the crowning accomplishment of the "City Beautiful" movement in America. Daniel Burnham—head architect of the World's Columbian Exposition—served on a Senate Park Commission charged with resuscitating the nation's capital. From 1901 to 1908 Burnham oversaw the construction of monumental buildings along the major axes of the city, the sprucing up of the Mall, and the clearing of parkland along the Potomac. By the early twentieth century Washington had been transformed into a national showpiece. Burnham's theory of urban renewal—sketched out in later, largely unimplemented plans for San Francisco, Cleveland, and Chicago—emphasized the classical, the monumental, the orderly, and the beautiful. Yet his concept of the City Beautiful largely ignored the commercial vitality and (often healthy) disorder of the modern metropolis. American cities, from the late nineteenth century to the present, have stood witness to the ongoing interplay of chaos and order.

Sources:

Charles E. Beveridge, *Frederick Law Olmsted: Designing the American Landscape* (New York: Rizzoli, 1995);

Thomas S. Hines, *Burnham of Chicago, Architect and Planner* (New York: Oxford University Press, 1974);

Vincent Scully, *American Architecture and Urbanism*, revised edition (New York: Holt, 1988);

William H. Wilson, *The City Beautiful Movement* (Baltimore: Johns Hopkins University Press, 1989).

DIME NOVELS AND HISTORICAL ROMANCES

A Book for a Dime. During the 1880s and 1890s the American literati assumed the mantle of social reform and scientific inquiry. William Dean Howells defended the anarchists arrested in Chicago's Haymarket bombing. The normally aloof Henry James wrote two expressly "political" novels, *The Bostonians* (1886) and *The Princess Casamassima* (1886). And the young writers known as naturalists began to spin progressively darker and grimmer tales of urban malaise, social inequity, and

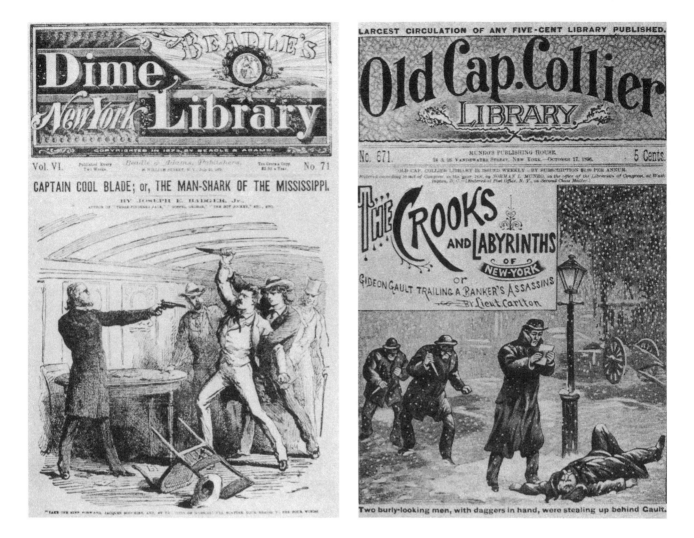

Covers for two of the many dime novels that were popular among American readers during the last four decades of the nineteenth century

individual pathology. The reading public clamored for a little escapism and found it in the dime novel. Before the Civil War American readers' morbid curiosity and sensual cravings had been satisfied by sensational "story papers" and pamphlet novels (the latter selling in twenty-five-cent installments). In 1860 the publishing firm of Beadle and Adams offered readers a new option—"A DOLLAR BOOK FOR A DIME!!"—and made money by providing the soldiers of the Union army with cheap reading matter. Within a few years competitors such as Frank Tousey, Norman Munro, and Street and Smith were also publishing dime novels, the literary phenomenon of the late nineteenth century.

Cheap Thrills. "It was her woman's destiny, not the more certain because of her savage origin," observes the narrator of *Malaeska: The Indian Wife of the White Hunter* (1860), a melodramatic thriller in which "woman's destiny" and "savage origin" guarantee a tragic death for the protagonist. Ann Sophia Stephens (1810–1886), the author of *Malaeska*, holds a place in history as the author of the first American dime novel. Published by Beadle and Adams as its first title, the book sold half a million

copies. Cheaply produced tales of romance, skulduggery, adventure, and mayhem, dime novels proliferated in the decades following the Civil War. Enterprising authors plumbed American history for romantic settings, eccentric characters, and melodramatic potential. Revolutionary and Civil War stories enjoyed a great vogue, as did tales of the Wild West. Quasi-historical novels regularly blurred the line between fiction and nonfiction, biography and hagiography. Thus E. Z. C. Judson (1823–1886), who wrote more than four hundred dime novels under the pen name Ned Buntline, elevated his friend William Cody from man to myth in a series of books about "Buffalo Bill." (Judson himself was a larger-than-life character who juggled careers as a trapper, soldier, journalist, and reactionary politician.) The most successful dime novelists worked endless variations on tried-and-true formulas: Horatio Alger Jr. (1832–1899) with his rags-to-riches stories, Laura Jean Libbey with her working-girl romances, and Edward Wheeler with his Deadwood Dick westerns.

In his groundbreaking study *Golden Multitudes* (1947) Frank Luther Mott defined a best-seller as a book whose yearly sales equaled at least 1 percent of the population of the continental United States during the decade in which it was published. In the following list of best-sellers the minimum sales figures were 375,000 for the 1870s, 500,000 for the 1880s, and 625,000 for the 1890s. Like the best-seller lists of today, Mott's nineteenth-century roster features its share of thrillers, romances, and animal stories. Yet the popularity of serious works by such eminent authors as Emile Zola, Gustave Flaubert, and Leo Tolstoy testifies to the broad sympathies of the nineteenth-century American reading public.

1878
Anna Katharine Green, *The Leavenworth Case*

1879
Henry George, *Progress and Poverty*

1880
Joel Chandler Harris, *Uncle Remus*
Margaret Sidney, *The Five Little Peppers and How They Grew*
Lew Wallace, *Ben-Hur*
Emile Zola, *Nana*

1881
Gustave Flaubert, *Madame Bovary*

1882
Ludovic Halévy, *L'Abbé Constantin*

1883
James Whitcomb Riley, *The Old Swimmin' Hole and 'Leven More Poems*
Hannah Whitall Smith, *The Christian's Secret of a Happy Life*
Mark Twain, *Life on the Mississippi*

1884
Johanna Spyri, *Heidi*
Robert Louis Stevenson, *Treasure Island*

1885
Robert Louis Stevenson, *A Child's Garden of Verse*
Mark Twain, *Adventures of Huckleberry Finn*

1886
Frances Hodgson Burnett, *Little Lord Fauntleroy*
H. Rider Haggard, *King Solomon's Mines*
Leo Tolstoy, *War and Peace*

1887
Marie Corelli, *Thelma*
H. Rider Haggard, *She*

1888
Edward Bellamy, *Looking Backward*
Hall Caine, *The Deemster*
Marie Corelli, *A Romance of Two Worlds*
A. C. Gunter, *Mr. Barnes of New York*
Mrs. Humphry Ward, *Robert Elsmere*

1889
Guy de Maupassant, *Stories*

1890
Arthur Conan Doyle, *The Sign of Four*
Arthur Conan Doyle, *A Study in Scarlet*
Rudyard Kipling, *Barrack Room Ballads*
Rudyard Kipling, *Plain Tales From the Hills*
Anna Sewell, *Black Beauty*

1891
J. M. Barrie, *The Little Minister*
Rudyard Kipling, *The Light That Failed*
Rudyard Kipling, *Mine Own People*

1892
J. M. Barrie, *A Window in Thrums*
Arthur Conan Doyle, *The Adventures of Sherlock Holmes*

1893
Sarah Grand, *The Heavenly Twins*
Robert Louis Stevenson, *Dr. Jekyll and Mr. Hyde*

1894
George du Maurier, *Trilby*
William H. Harvey, *Coin's Financial School*
Anthony Hope, *The Prisoner of Zenda*
Ian Maclaren, *Beside the Bonnie Brier Bush*
Margaret Marshall Saunders, *Beautiful Joe*

1895
Stephen Crane, *The Red Badge of Courage*
Opie Read, *The Jucklins*

1896
Henryk Sienkiewicz, *Quo Vadis*

1897
Charles M. Sheldon, *In His Steps*

1898
Ralph Connor, *Black Rock*
Edward Noyes Westcott, *David Harum*

1899
Winston Churchill, *Richard Carvel*
Paul Leicester Ford, *Janice Meredith*

Source: Frank Luther Mott, *Golden Multitudes: The Story of Best Sellers in the United States* (New York: Macmillan, 1947).

The Detective. The advent of detective fiction overlapped with the rise of the dime novel. Early detective stories by Edgar Allan Poe (1809–1849) were succeeded in the 1870s and 1880s by full-length detective novels such as *The Leavenworth Case* (1878) and *That Affair Next Door* (1897) by Anna Katharine Green (1846–1935). Nick Carter, surely the most ubiquitous detective of all time, appeared in more than one thousand dime novels (written over the years by dozens of authors). Over time pulp fiction usurped the place of the dime novel in the literary marketplace. Pulp magazines—named for the low-grade paper on which they were printed—entered mass circulation in the mid 1890s.

Romance, Royalty, and Revolution. A more respectable cousin of the dime novel—the historical romance — also enjoyed a vogue during the latter decades of the nineteenth century. Whether set in faraway lands or the mist-shrouded ground of early America, these works shared a predilection for simple plots, high romance, and moralistic conclusions. Where the utopian novel offered programmatic suggestions for change, historical fiction offered escapism, pure and simple. And whereas naturalists such as Frank Norris (1870–1902) and Stephen Crane (1871–1900) portrayed individuals as pawns of forces beyond their control, authors of historical fiction resurrected the notion of the invincible hero. Readers of late-nineteenth-century historical fiction enjoyed stories of kings and queens, knights and damsels, prophets and pilgrims, admirals and generals. The preeminent work in this mold, *Ben-Hur* (1880) by Lew Wallace (1827–1905), pitted its early Christian hero against the Romans in a chariot race. An Indiana author, Charles Major (1856–1913), who wrote under the pen name Sir Edwin Caskoden, selected sixteenth-century England as the setting for *When Knighthood Was in Flower* (1898), an immensely popular novel that chronicled the romance between a queen and a commoner. When American historical novelists turned their attention to war—as did F. Marion Crawford (1854–1909) with *Via Crucis* (1898), or Winston Churchill (1871–1947) with *Richard Carvel* (1899)—they invariably stressed romance over realism. The average reader preferred such fare to more-troubling books about the vicissitudes of life in war or in peace.

Sources:

Michael Denning, *Mechanical Accents: Dime Novels and Working-Class Culture* (London & New York: Verso, 1987);

Frank Luther Mott, *Golden Multitudes: The Story of Best Sellers in the United States* (New York: Macmillan, 1947).

FOUNDING THE METROPOLITAN OPERA

An Age of Opulence. The story of the Metropolitan Opera House in New York City unfolds amid privilege and desire. During the late nineteenth century a coterie of moneyed families, their fortunes swelled by post–Civil War speculation, set new standards for conspicuous consumption. Yet despite their cash and their flash, the nouveaux riches of New York remained excluded from the inner circles of the old Knickerbocker gentry. In the 1870s and early 1880s New York boasted an adequate opera house: the Academy of Music, founded in 1849 and located downtown on Fourteenth Street. Edith Wharton (1862–1937), novelist of New York manners, opened her *Age of Innocence* (1920) at the academy: "the world of fashion was still content to reassemble every winter in the shabby red and gold boxes of the sociable old Academy. Conservatives cherished it for being small and inconvenient, and thus keeping out the 'new people' whom New York was beginning to dread and yet be drawn to." The old families controlled the "sociable old Academy"; the "new people" angled for acceptance. One evening in 1880 the balance of social power shifted. German soprano Lilli Lehmann (1848–1929) recalled the fateful moment in her memoir, *My Path Through Life* (1914): "As one evening [at the Academy] one of the millionairesses did not receive the box in which she intended to shine because another woman had anticipated her, the husband of the former took prompt action and caused the Metropolitan Opera House to rise."

Under Construction. The snubbing of the "millionairess"—a Vanderbilt, as fate would have it—inflamed the "new money" set. These "upstarts" pooled their resources and designated a site for a new opera house on Broadway between Thirty-ninth and Fortieth Streets. Construction began in 1881 and proceeded slightly behind schedule. By spring 1883 the building was finished, and the choicest boxes were apportioned among the shareholders. On 22 October the Metropolitan staged its first opera: Charles Gounod's *Faust* (1859), featuring the soprano Christine Nilsson in the role of Margherita.

Rank and Ruckus. Architect Josiah Cleveland Cady (1837–1919) had designed several other New York landmarks, among them the Museum of Natural History. The Met, however, was Cady's only theater, and connoisseurs complained about poor acoustics and a small backstage area. More problematic than the architectural design, however, was the behavior of society patrons. For many people, the ritual of operagoing had next to nothing to do with music. With three full tiers of private boxes, the Met more than doubled the luxury capacity of the old Academy. All told, boxes accounted for nearly 25 percent of the three-thousand-odd seats at the Met. For many who owned or rented "box" seats, a night at the opera meant a chance to display one's wardrobe and chat with one's friends. Upper-class patrons ignored a notice posted in January 1891 by the Met's board of directors: "Many complaints having been made to the directors of the Opera House of the annoyance produced by the talking in the boxes during the performance, the Board requests that it be discontinued." A few people, of course, attended the Met to listen to opera. One middle-class

The Metropolitan Opera House in New York City as it appeared in 1913

music lover complained that the incessant chatter from the private boxes drowned out his favorite arias. A response in the New York press dismissed the complaint and confirmed the social order: "It is very certain that these magnificent music-dramas are only made possible for him by the more ornate portion of the community."

Experimentation. A parade of respected performers — including Lehmann, Marcella Sembrich, Italo Campanini, Adelina Patti, Etelka Gerster, Albert Niemann, Lillian Norton-Gower, Marianne Brandt, Max Alvary, and Julius Perotti—graced the Met stage during its first decade. Backstage, however, chaos reigned. Under the direction of the theatrical entrepreneur Henry E. Abbey (1846–1896), the Met lost some $600,000 during the 1883–1884 season. Under Abbey's replacement, Leopold Damrosch (1832–1885), the company performed only German opera. Critics raved but audiences dozed. Finley Peter Dunne (1867–1936), a leading humorist of the era, satirized the reputation of Germanic opera:

> "That's Wagner," she says. "'Tis th' music iv the future," she says. "Yes," says Donahue, "but I don't want me hell on earth. I can wait f'r it."

After Damrosch died in 1885, his son Walter (1862–1950) succeeded him and continued to stage German opera through the fall of 1891. At this juncture, however, Damrosch's contract expired, and the Met reverted to more crowd-friendly Italian and French fare. (The first Met performance of an American opera, Frederick Shepherd Converse's *The Pipe of Desire,* occurred in 1910.) By the turn of the century the Met had finally achieved a level of stability in its finances and artistic philosophy, but before it became a repository of "high culture," it had traversed some exceptionally low terrain.

Source:
Irving Kolodin, *The Story of the Metropolitan Opera Company, 1883–1950: A Candid History* (New York: Knopf, 1953).

FROM MINSTREL STAGE TO BROADWAY

The Minstrel Legacy. As early as the 1700s, white actors—their faces smeared with burnt cork—took to the stage in "blackface" to portray African Americans. By the 1830s such portrayals had evolved into a staple form of entertainment at the circus or between acts at the theater, with song and dance augmenting display. By the next decade the first full-length "minstrel shows" had taken shape. These extravaganzas, featuring broad comedy, elaborate dress, and plaintive singing, represented (or misrepresented) black folkways for white audiences. The sentimental plantation ballads of white composer Stephen Foster (1826–1864)—including "Old Folks at Home" (1851), "Massa's in de Cold Ground" (1852),

"My Old Kentucky Home" (1853), and "Old Black Joe" (1860)—helped make the minstrel show the dominant form of public entertainment in the United States at midcentury.

African American Variations. Success rendered the minstrel formula largely inviolable. Thus, when African American minstrels took to the stage in the post–Civil War period, they invariably "blacked up" and conformed to stereotypes (the childlike servant, the comic buffoon) created by the white minstrels who preceded them. Billy Kersands (1842–1915), a talented African American minstrel, became one of the highest-paid entertainers of the 1870s and 1880s. His singing and soft-shoe dancing, along with his talent for mimicry and physical comedy, enchanted audiences, white and black. Yet Kersands's clowning reinforced rather than repudiated minstrel stereotypes. In some cases, however, the minstrel show provided an arena in which African Americans could poke fun at white culture. Traditionally the minstrel show concluded with a "walk-around" or "cakewalk": a ritualized dance in which couples high-stepped and promenaded in the manner of—or in mockery of—plantation elite. As the critic Eric Sundquist points out, the cakewalk could represent not only "a burlesque of black freedom and cultural integrity" but also a turnabout "in which the racist appropriation of black life . . . gave way to an African American reversal of the stereotype." Without a doubt the minstrel tradition blunted the expressive range of African American entertainers. At the same time, minstrelry nurtured talents, opened doors, and spawned musical genres that flourished in the late nineteenth and early twentieth centuries.

Syncopated Rhythm. One mainstay of the minstrel show was the banjo, an instrument imported from Africa (where it was called the *banza, banjil, banjer,* and *banshaw* in various dialects). Most early banjos had four strings. By the mid nineteenth century, however, the typical North American banjo had sprouted a fifth string: shorter than the other four, and designed to be picked with the thumb. Interviewed in 1897, Kentucky-born pianist Ben Harney (1871–1938) theorized that the origins of ragtime music lay in this shortened fifth string. "The colored performer," Harney explained, "strumming in his own cajoling way, likes to throw in a note at random, and his thumb ranges over this for effect. When he takes up the piano, the desire for the same effect dominates him, being almost second nature, and he reaches for the open banjo-string note with his little finger." In ragtime, Harney continued, the pianist's left hand keeps time while the right hand—driven by the little finger—sends the tune spinning "off stride."

Ragtime Musicians. During the 1890s and the early years of the early twentieth century Saint Louis, New Orleans, Chicago, Memphis, Baltimore, Kansas City, and New York served as magnets for black ragtime composers such as Tom Turpin (1873–1922), Tony Jackson (1876–1921), Joe Jordan (1882–1971), and Euday Louis

Will Marion Cook, composer of the music for the 1898 hit musical *Clorindy* and other popular Broadway shows

Bowman (1887–1949). Scott Joplin (1868–1917), the king of ragtime pianists, came from a musical family: his father, a former slave, played the fiddle; his mother played the banjo and sang. As a young man Joplin set off to make a living as a roving pianist, playing in saloons and bordellos throughout the South and Midwest. The pianist Otis Saunders, whom Joplin met at the World's Columbian Exposition in Chicago in 1893, encouraged Joplin to transfer some of his compositions to paper. "Maple Leaf Rag," published in 1899, sold more than a million copies in sheet-music form; its success freed Joplin from the necessity of touring and allowed him to devote more time to teaching and composition. After the turn of the century Joplin's string of hits continued with rags such as "The Easy Winners" (1902), "The Entertainer" (1902), and "The Cascades" (1904).

The popularity of the minstrel show helped establish rigid conventions for public performance in the mid nineteenth century: white entertainers sampling "black" musical forms always performed in blackface. By the 1880s, however, the rules had begun to change. The agent of change was the banjo: a humble instrument of African origins that had served for decades as a mainstay of the minstrel show. Suddenly hordes of young white women began taking banjo lessons and — if they were brave — performing at private parties and soirees. College boys formed banjo clubs. "Extra-Fine" banjos retailed for upwards of $100. Although some enterprising folks performed works by Frédéric Chopin on their banjos, the banjo repertoire remained weighted toward "folk" music, much of it derived from the African American tradition. Once this banjo craze was underway, however, white performers no longer donned blackface to strum a banjo.

A two-page advertisement in the December 1893 issue of *Stewart's Banjo and Guitar Journal* illustrated the curious cultural status of the banjo. "Should you say `Banjo Concert' to your Grand-Father, he might have this picture in his mind's eye," announced a bold headline over a crude sketch of a banjo player with the stereotypical features of the minstrel: a corked face, gaudy striped shirt, and oversized shoes. "The banjo was once monopolized by the Negro minstrel performers, and hence it became associated with the black face, and was some times called the `Negro instrument,'" the advertisement continued. "The banjo of to-day is altogether another instrument. YOU WILL NOT see anything like the above at the great Banjo Concert, at the Academy of Music, Philadelphia, on Saturday Evening, January 13th, 1894." Clearly, racial prejudice helped "sell" events such as the Philadelphia Banjo Concert. Yet the "evolution" of the banjo also heralded a growing respect for African American musical contributions — and foreshadowed the vogue of ragtime, jazz, and other black-influenced genres of the late nineteenth and early twentieth centuries.

Source: Karen Linn, *That Half-Barbaric Twang: The Banjo in American Popular Culture* (Urbana: University of Illinois Press, 1991).

Show Business. The minstrel tradition and its ragtime offshoot served as a training ground for many of the greatest African American performers of the late nine-teenth century. Georgia-born Bob Cole (1868–1911) got his start in the minstrel theater of the 1890s. A songwriter—whose songs included the 1893 "Parthenia Takes a Likin' to a Coon" and "In Shin Bone Alley"—and performer, Cole broke with his white bosses in 1895 and formed his own theater company. With his collaborator, Billy Johnson, Cole produced the Off-Broadway show *A Trip to Coontown* in 1898; never before had African Americans written, performed, and produced a full-length musical. Sam Lucas (1840–1916), a cast member in *A Trip to Coontown*, had been active in minstrel theater since the late 1860s. The most famous black actor of his generation, Lucas helped usher in a new era when he starred as Uncle Tom in the 1915 silent-film version of *Uncle Tom's Cabin*. The conservatory-trained violinist Will Marion Cook (1869–1944) melded ragtime rhythms with classical phrasing in his hit musical *Clorindy, or The Origin of the Cakewalk*. Featuring the songs "Darktown is Out To-night," "Who Dat Say Chicken in Dis Crowd?," and "Hottest Coon in Dixie," *Clorindy* opened in July 1898 to rave reviews. Its cast of twenty-six African American singers and dancers wowed audiences at the open-air Casino Theater Roof Garden in New York City and won accolades for Cook and poet Paul Laurence Dunbar (1872–1906), who wrote the lyrics. An intense professional, Cook enjoyed continued success as a bandleader, a composer of popular songs, and a musical director of Broadway shows. Although he remained frustrated by the narrow range of options open to black musicians, Cook recognized that *Clorindy* was a breakthrough. "Negroes were at last on Broadway, and there to stay," Cook recalled. "Gone was the uff-dah of the minstrel! Gone the Massa Linkum stuff! We were artists and . . . nothing could stop us."

Sources:

Edward A. Berlin, *King of Ragtime: Scott Joplin and His Era* (New York: Oxford University Press, 1994);

Susan Curtis, *Dancing to a Black Man's Tune: A Life of Scott Joplin* (Columbia: University of Missouri Press, 1994);

Karen Linn, *That Half-Barbaric Twang: The Banjo in American Popular Culture* (Urbana: University of Illinois Press, 1991);

Thomas L. Morgan and William Barlow, *From Cakewalks to Concert Halls: An Illustrated History of African American Popular Music from 1895 to 1930* (Washington, D.C.: Elliott & Clark, 1992);

Eric Sundquist, *To Wake the Nations* (Cambridge, Mass.: Harvard University Press, 1993).

IN SEARCH OF UTOPIA: FICTION

The Utopian Tradition. During the 1880s and 1890s utopian literature enjoyed an American renaissance. Imaginary worlds (some of them appealing, some horrific) cropped up in novels such as Edward Bellamy's *Looking Backward* (1888), Ignatius Donnelly's *Caesar's Column* (1890), Henry Olerich's *A Cityless and Countryless World* (1893), King Gillette's *The Human Drift* (1894), and William Dean Howells's *A Traveler from Altruria* (1894). In appropriating the utopian form Ameri-

Novelists Edward Bellamy, who envisioned a utopia made possible by technology and a powerful government, and Ignatius Donnelly, who warned readers of the negative social consequences that such "advances" might create

can authors tapped a well-established tradition. The word *utopia*—a Greek term meaning either "no place" or "ideal place"—first entered the literary lexicon in 1516, when the British author Sir Thomas More (1477 or 1478–1535) published a political fantasy titled *Utopia*. Later British works in the utopian vein include Francis Bacon's *New Atlantis* (1627) and Samuel Butler's *Erewhon* (1872).

Beyond Escapism. Overwhelmed by rapid change—fast-growing cities, financial "panics," unprecedented industrial growth—Americans of the late nineteenth century were eager to imagine alternate worlds. Yet most literary utopias offered something more substantive than escapism. In these works attentive readers could find political advice and cultural commentary. Many authors employed utopian fiction to promote socialist, populist, or feminist viewpoints. The role of technology was another popular theme—not surprising, given the gradual eclipse of an agrarian way of life in America. Some utopian works, set in the near future, suggested that technology could liberate humankind from needless toil. Other works, however, held technology in low esteem—celebrating instead simple societies unspoiled by factories and machines.

Stranger in a Strange Land. By far the most influential of late-nineteenth-century utopian works was Bel-

lamy's *Looking Backward*, the story of a young man who falls asleep in Boston in 1887 and wakes up in the same city in the year 2000. As he explores his new surroundings, Bellamy's protagonist marvels at the miracles wrought by time, technology, and an all-powerful "state." In Bellamy's future wonderland the state regulates employment, community service, and the production and distribution of consumer goods. Crime, disease, and social injustice have been all but eradicated, and leisure time and cultural opportunities abound. "With a tear for the dark past, turn we then to the dazzling future, and, veiling our eyes, press forward," urges one citizen of the "new" world. "The long and weary winter of the race is ended. Its summer has begun. Humanity has burst the chrysalis. The heavens are before it." Bellamy's optimism proved infectious: with several million copies printed, *Looking Backward* became one of the best-selling novels of the nineteenth century. In the early 1890s thousands of readers formed "Bellamy clubs" and joined the short-lived Nationalist Party in an attempt to translate Bellamy's vision into national policy. The popularity of *Looking Backward* highlights the efficacy of narrative as political accessory. Bellamy's engaging story (complete with an across-the-centuries romance) made the notion of socialism palatable to the average American—something a dry political tract never could have accomplished. The novel inspired a host of "nationalist" clubs with thousands of members seeking a brighter future. Other influential utopian works of the period, such as Howells's *A Traveler from Altruria,* resembled *Looking Backward* in presenting a sugar-coated version of socialism.

A Dystopian Vision. Not all imaginary worlds were friendly. Dystopian literature—the word *dystopia* literally means "bad place"—inverts the utopian formula, conjuring up nightmare visions of political oppression and technology run amok. Many science-fiction novels of the twentieth century—among them Aldous Huxley's *Brave New World* (1932) and George Orwell's *1984* (1949)—fall into the dystopian tradition pioneered by writers such as Ignatius Donnelly, a Minnesotan active in late-nineteenth-century politics. In his novel *Caesar's Column,* set in 1988, Donnelly described a future in which the rich wallow in pleasure while the poor toil like slaves. Inevitably the poor turn on their oppressors and launch a bloodbath. Donnelly took part in the political movement known as Populism. Like other western and southern agrarians, he feared exploitation at the hands of American business and industrial interests. And, like Edward Bellamy before him, Donnelly knew how to combine literature and politics. *Caesar's Column* stood as both warning and promise: if pressed too hard, Donnelly warned, the American rural underclass might rise up in revolt.

Sources:

Ann J. Lane, Introduction to *Herland,* by Charlotte Perkins Gilman (New York: Pantheon, 1979);

Lewis Mumford, *The Story of Utopias* (New York: Boni & Liveright, 1922);

John L. Thomas, *Alternative America* (Cambridge, Mass.: Harvard University Press, 1983).

AN INTERNATIONALLY ACCLAIMED ARCHITECT: H. H. RICHARDSON

First Among His Peers. In 1885 the *American Architect and Building News* asked seventy-five American architects to identify the ten buildings they most admired in the United States. The poll yielded one clear favorite: Trinity Church, in Boston's Copley Square. Designed by the Louisiana-born and Paris-trained H. H. Richardson (1838–1886), Trinity received 84 percent of the first-place votes. Of the top ten vote getters, four other structures were Richardson creations: the city hall and the state capitol in Albany, New York, the Sever Hall classroom building at Harvard University, and the town hall in North Easton, Massachusetts. Richardson, just forty-seven years old at the time, stood without peer among American architects.

Parisian Training. Born in New Orleans, Henry Hobson Richardson grew up in a well-to-do plantation household. After graduating from Harvard University in 1859, Richardson went to Paris to commence his professional training at the Ecole des Beaux-Arts, headquarters of the Western architectural establishment. Rich-

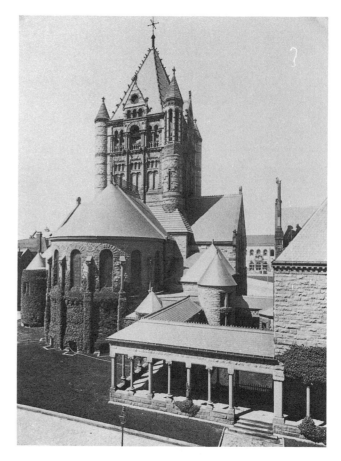

Trinity Church (1877) in Copley Square, Boston, designed by architect H. H. Richardson. In an 1885 poll of American architects this church was voted the most admired building in the United States.

ardson was only the second American student accepted to the Ecole; Richard Morris Hunt (1827–1895) had preceded him, in 1848. Richardson's funding from home lapsed in 1861, because of the Civil War. Although he had not yet completed his program of study, Richardson left school to work as an assistant at a Paris architectural firm. He remained there until the end of the Civil War in 1865, when he returned to the United States to begin his American career.

Concrete Shape and Color. Although his birth and education had fitted him for an aristocratic life—and although the industrial barons of the American Gilded Age richly rewarded those architects willing to subvert good taste to conspicuous display—Richardson scorned upper-class frippery. "It would not cost me a bit of trouble to build French buildings that should reach from here to Philadelphia," he observed on his return to America, "but that is not what I want to do." Richardson's earliest work borrowed from popular Gothic and Renaissance forms; by the 1870s, however, his work grew more innovative. In 1872 Richardson won the design competition for Trinity Church. He relocated his office from New York to Boston and began work on the building that established him as an American original. Completed in 1877, Trinity featured a cavernous inte-

The Ecole des Beaux-Arts in Paris, which taught the principles of classical architecture, served as the high temple of architectural studies in the nineteenth century. By the close of the century American architecture had become big business, and a Paris education had become a prerequisite for professional success. By the late 1880s young architects had begun to reject H. H. Richardson's Romanesque revivalism — with its bold displays and medieval echoes — and to edge toward the new "Academic" style that had come into vogue at the Ecole des Beaux-Arts. As the architect Joseph Wells (1853–1890) explained, "The classical ideal suggests clearness, simplicity, grandeur, order and philosophical calm — consequently it delights my soul. The medieval ideal suggests superstition, ignorance, vulgarity, restlessness, cruelty and religio — all of which fill my soul with horror and loathing." The typical Beaux-Arts building was monumental in scale, symmetrical in composition, and marked externally by statues, columns, and grand staircases. At its best the Beaux-Arts style lent dignity to turbulent, sprawling American cities. At its worst it institutionalized the excesses of the Gilded Age.

The East Coast emerged as the capital of Beaux-Arts classicism — and the New York architectural firm of McKim, Mead and White, founded in 1879, became the leading exponent of the style. With his partners William R. Mead (1846–1928) and Stanford White (1853–1906), Charles F. McKim (1847–1909), who had been Richardson's assistant during the early 1870s, chal-

lenged the Richardsonian aesthetic. In Boston, directly across from Richardson's Trinity Church in Copley Square, McKim, Mead and White built the Boston Public Library (1888–1895). Faced in gray stone and modeled on the palatial buildings of the Italian Renaissance, the library could not have presented a sharper contrast to the hulking, asymmetrical, multichromatic church across the way. In 1893 McKim, Mead and White helped transform the shores of Lake Michigan into a vision in white: their designs, along with those of Daniel Burnham and Richard Morris Hunt, established Beaux-Arts as the "official" style of the World's Columbian Exposition. Closer to home McKim, Mead and White designed the magisterial Penn-Station (1906–1910) in downtown Manhattan, where it joined other monuments to Beaux-Arts splendor: the Metropolitan Museum of Art (Hunt, 1880–1895), the New York Public Library (Carrère and Hastings, 1895–1902), and the Grand Central Terminal (Warren and Wetmore, 1903–1913). Critics have argued that Beaux-Arts structures — beautiful, grand, and somewhat off-putting — celebrate wealth not taste. Yet in their very majesty, these works also reflected the optimism of a new, Progressive Era.

Sources: David P. Handlin, *American Architecture* (London: Thames & Hudson, 1985);

Lewis Mumford, *Sticks and Stones: A Study of American Architecture and Civilization* (New York: Boni & Liveright, 1924);

rior space decorated by artist John La Farge (1835–1910). The church—set on a triangular lot on the edge of the new Back Bay of Boston—was large in mass and simple in proportion. Its rough granite facing, contrasting stone trim, and rounded arches resurfaced in future Richardson designs. Richardson liked to explain that the architect's work "is plastic work, and, like the sculptor's, cannot be fully judged except in concrete shape and color, amid actual lights and shadows and its own particular surroundings." The buildings that Richardson designed over the following decade—the town hall at North Easton (1879), perched on granite ledges; the Marshall Field Wholesale Store (1885), its multistory arcades reflecting the vitality of downtown Chicago—bespoke Richardson's sensitivity to the magic of "particular surroundings."

The Richardsonian Legacy. Richardson influenced

American architecture to such an extent that his name was adopted as an adjective. "Richardsonian" architecture was an interpretation of the Romanesque—a style first developed in western Europe around the year A.D. 1000 and marked by rounded arches, decorative arcades, and profuse ornamentation. Richardson's work differed from earlier Romanesque design in its deemphasis of ornament and its use of polychromatic wall design. (When the critic Lewis Mumford dubbed the 1880s and 1890s "the brown decades," he had in mind the russets, beiges, and auburns of Romanesque brickwork.) A romantic as well as a pragmatist, Richardson once identified "a grain elevator and the interior of a great river steamboat" as the most compelling of design projects. During his brief lifetime Richardson, who died in 1886 at age forty-seven, completed more than sixty major works and inspired legions of disciples. During the late 1880s and into the 1890s architectural firms in Boston, Detroit, and Chicago perpetuated the Richardsonian style—frequently, alas, rendering it earthbound in the process. Meanwhile, a cadre of New York–based architects spearheaded a classicist revival that repudiated the Richardsonian legacy, but in the century since his death Richardson has been recognized as an American original.

Sources:

John Burchard and Albert Bush-Brown, *The Architecture of America: A Social and Cultural History* (Boston: Little, Brown, 1961);

Leonard K. Eaton, *American Architecture Comes of Age: European Reaction to H. H. Richardson and Louis Sullivan* (Cambridge, Mass.: MIT Press, 1972);

William H. Jordy, *American Buildings and Their Architects: Progressive and Academic Ideals at the Turn of the Twentieth Century* (Garden City, N.Y.: Doubleday, 1972);

James O'Gorman, *H. H. Richardson: Architectural Forms for an American Society* (Chicago: University of Chicago Press, 1987).

INTERNATIONAL COPYRIGHT

The Question of Copyright. Among the original powers granted to Congress by the U.S. Constitution was the power "To promote the Progress of Science and useful Arts, by securing for limited Times to Authors and Inventors the exclusive Right to their respective Writings and Discoveries." In the century following ratification of the Constitution, hundreds of state and federal statutes defined and revised the terms and scope of copyright protection. By the late nineteenth century literary copyright ranked among the most hotly debated of legal issues. The question of international copyright—the rights of "alien" authors in America and American authors abroad—sparked controversy.

Legalized Piracy. Throughout the better part of the nineteenth century, no copyright provisions existed to protect foreign material. The legal loophole allowed American publishers to republish foreign fiction without paying royalties, so it was cheaper for American houses to publish works by foreign authors than to publish Americans' works. In the 1880s a book by a popular American writer—Cooper or Hawthorne, Longfellow or Whitman, for example—cost a dollar or more, while popular British writers such as Dickens and Scott were available in pirated editions for a quarter. A similar condition in England worked to the disadvantage of Americans published there. Henry Wadsworth Longfellow complained that though he had twenty-two publishers in England and Scotland, only four even took the trouble to send him a copy of their editions of the works, and he received almost no royalties on foreign sales. Such piracy flourished in the magazine industry: eager to control production costs, editors gleefully raided British periodicals. When Americans discussed the issue of international copyright, they frequently framed the debate in terms of the common good. In 1868 one commentator reminded authors "that they have a nobler calling than the professional man or the mechanic; that their aim should not merely be to make money." In opposing the free flow of literary goods, *"they also oppose the progress of popular knowledge."* Foremost among the American periodical pirates was *Harper's New Monthly Magazine,* founded in 1850 as a digest of prepublished material. *Harper's Monthly* declared its mission was to expose American readers to "an immense amount of useful and entertaining reading matter, to which, on account of the great number and expense of the books and periodicals in which it originally appears, they have hitherto had no access." The editor of another American literary digest (first called *The Pirate,* later *The Corsair*) celebrated "the privilege assured us by our piratical law of copyright," to " 'convey' to our columns, for the amusement of our readers, the cream and spirit of everything that ventures to light in England, France, and Germany."

A National Disgrace. Not all members of the literary community, however, smiled on the practice of piracy. As the nineteenth century progressed, prominent American literati noted that other nations had successfully negotiated copyright agreements. Why not the United States and its foreign partners, most notably Great Britain? "It is a disgrace," fumed the publisher George Haven Putnam, the American Champion of international copyright "that the two great English-speaking people, claiming to stand among the most enlightened of the community of nations, should be practically the only members of such community which have failed to arrive at an agreement in this all-important issue." In an age of imperialism, the issue of international copyright became a matter of national pride. Yet American public opinion, Putnam noted with dismay, lagged behind "the standard of international justice already attained by Tunis, Liberia, and Hayti."

A New Law. A series of bills designed to amend international copyright law languished in congressional committee during the 1860s, 1870s, and 1880s. By the end of this period, however, the tide had begun to turn. In 1888 Brander Matthews, professor of literature at Columbia University, remarked, "We now enjoy the privilege of piracy, as the dwellers on a rocky islet used to enjoy the privilege of wrecking—and we avail ourselves of this privilege only to the perdition of our own souls." On 4 March 1891, the Senate voted its approval of the International Copyright Bill passed by the House of Representatives the previous December. Signed into law by President Benjamin Harrison, international copyright went into effect on 1 July of 1891. At long last, foreign authors were granted the protection of American copyright law—as, under reciprocal agreement, American authors gained the protection of foreign law.

Sources:

Frederick Gerhard, *Will the People of the United States Be Benefited by an International Copyright Law, or Will Such a Law Be an Injury to Them?* (New York: Privately printed, 1868);

George Haven Putnam, ed., *The Question of Copyright* (New York: Putnam, 1891);

Philip Wittenberg, *The Protection and Marketing of Literary Property* (New York: Julian Messner, 1937);

James Playsted Wood, *Magazines in the United States,* second edition (New York: Ronald Press Co., 1956).

JAMES AND HOWELLS: TWO REALISTIC NOVELISTS

The Dangers of Fiction. In the early days of the American republic, critics considered fiction a swoon-inducing form that muddled the heads and the morals of readers (most of them susceptible young women). Many early novels did indeed focus on crime, intrigue, and illicit sexuality. A book peddler might advertise his wares with the cry "Seduction! Revolution! Murder!" William Hill Brown (1765–1793), whose *The Power of Sympathy* (1789) is generally considered the first American novel, admitted that "this species of writing hath not been received with universal approbation." Eager to win approval for his novel, Brown emphasized its positive qualities: "the dangerous Consequences of SEDUCTION are exposed, and the Advantages of FEMALE EDUCATION set forth and recommended." Although the novel form had eased into respectability by the 1870s—thanks to popular American authors such as James Fenimore Cooper (1789–1851), Nathaniel Hawthorne (1804–1864), and Harriet Beecher Stowe (1811–1896)—the taint of the past remained.

From Romance to Realism. As Henry James noted in 1884, "The old superstition about fiction being 'wicked' has doubtless died out, . . . but the spirit of it lingers in a certain oblique regard directed toward any story which does not more or less admit that it is only a joke." No longer "wicked," late-nineteenth-century fiction remained (in James's opinion) moralistic, melodramatic, and resolutely "make-believe"—despite the fact that, as James argued, "the only reason for the existence of a novel is that it does attempt to represent life." During the 1860s and 1870s a handful of American authors attempted to "represent life" realistically in fiction. Rebecca Harding Davis (1831–1910), author of *Life in the Iron Mills* (1861), declared it her mission "to dig into this commonplace, this vulgar American life, and see what is in it." Union army veteran John William De Forest (1826–1906) published *Miss Ravenel's Conversion from Secession to Loyalty* (1867), the first novel to offer a realistic assessment of the Civil War, and Edward Eggleston (1837–1902), an Indiana author, dissected the American heartland in *The Hoosier Schoolmaster* (1871). Not until the 1880s and 1890s, however, did "realism" become entrenched in American letters.

The Dean of American Letters. Ohio native William Dean Howells (1837–1920) moved to Boston in 1865, determined to crash the ranks of the American literary establishment. His arrival in Boston coincided with the final flush of New England literary glory. On earlier visits to Boston, Howells had been lucky enough to meet several of his literary idols, including Ralph Waldo Em-

A LITERARY COMBINATION.

Mr. H—w—lls: ARE YOU THE TALLEST NOW, MR. J—MES?
Mr. J—mes (not ignoring the question): BE SO UNCOMMONLY KIND, H—W—LLS, AS TO LET ME DOWN EASY;
IT MAY BE WE HAVE BOTH GOT TO GROW.

Cartoon in the 22 February 1883 issue of the humor magazine *Life* suggesting that neither Henry James nor William Dean Howell is as great a writer as the British novelist William Makepeace Thackeray, whose best-selling novel *Vanity Fair* (1848) had made him famous on both sides of the Atlantic

erson, Nathaniel Hawthorne, Oliver Wendell Holmes, and James Russell Lowell. Joining the staff of the preeminent American literary magazine, *The Atlantic Monthly,* in 1865, Howells was becoming a member of the club. He worked at *The Atlantic* for fifteen years, serving as editor-in-chief from 1871 to 1881. From his chair at *The Atlantic*—and later as a columnist for *Harper's Monthly* (1886–1892, 1900–1920)—Howells nurtured young talents such as Hamlin Garland, Stephen Crane, Charlotte Perkins Gilman, and Frank Norris. In his own fiction Howells pioneered the art of American realism. His novels include *A Modern Instance* (1882), which tackled the then-taboo subject of divorce; *The Rise of Silas Lapham* (1885), about an ethically tormented Boston businessman; and *A Hazard of New Fortunes* (1889), a tale of New York City (the novelist's home after 1888) that reflects Howells's increasingly liberal political viewpoint.

A Citizen of the World. Howells's brand of fiction had its detractors as well as its advocates. Some readers quite simply found realism dull. In one of the *Devil's Dictionary* entries that he began writing in 1881 the humorist Ambrose Bierce (1842–1914) defined *realism* as

Two popular authors of local-color fiction: New Englander Mary E. Wilkins Freedman and Tennessean Mary Noailles Murfree, who used the pen name Charles Egbert Craddock

"The art of depicting nature as it is seen by toads. The charm suffusing a landscape painted by a mole, or a story written by a measuring-worm." Henry James (1843–1916)—one of Howells's lifelong friends and one of the greatest prose stylists of the age—did his best to elevate the "charm" quotient of American realism. James grew up in a wealthy, cosmopolitan family. He spent his youth in New York, Newport, and Europe; studied for one academic year at Harvard Law School (1862–1863); and spent much of his adulthood overseas, eventually becoming a British citizen. Whereas Howells relied for effect on descriptions of external phenomena, James probed emotions and psyches. James described one critical scene in *The Portrait of a Lady* (1881)—a scene in which the heroine, Isabel Archer, meditates by a fireplace—as "a representation simply of her motionlessly *seeing,* and an attempt withal to make the mere still lucidity of her act as 'interesting' as the surprise of a caravan or the identification of a pirate." In early works such as *Roderick Hudson* (1876), *Daisy Miller* (1879), and *The Portrait of a Lady* James examined the effect of European society on the American character. During the mid 1880s James wrote two "political" novels: *The Bostonians* (1886), a critique of the women's movement, and *The Princess Casamassima* (1886), a critique of political anarchism. During the 1890s and into the early twentieth century, James's work became more dense and more explicitly concerned with minute shifts in mood and manner. *The Spoils of Poynton* (1897), *The Wings of the Dove*

(1902), *The Ambassadors* (1903), and *The Golden Bowl* (1904) are among his major works from this period. A relentless self-critic, James kept a series of notebooks and—in his final years—painstakingly revised nearly all of his published fiction for publication in the New York Edition (1907–1918) of his works. "Humanity is immense, and reality has a myriad forms," he once wrote; "the most one can affirm is that some of the flowers of fiction have the odor of it, and others have not."

Sources:

Cathy N. Davidson, *Revolution and the Word: The Rise of the Novel in America* (New York: Oxford University Press, 1986);

Amy Kaplan, *The Social Construction of American Realism* (Chicago: University of Chicago Press, 1988);

Eric Sundquist, ed., *American Realism: New Essays* (Baltimore: Johns Hopkins University Press, 1982).

LOCAL-COLOR FICTION

An American Palette. After the Civil War the United States was still a nation of disparate cultures—each region marked by distinctive customs, values, and economic conditions; each region struggling to find its niche in a newly reconstituted union. Nowhere was the nation's inherent diversity more evident than in its literature. The advent of literary realism in the late nineteenth century brought into focus the kaleidoscopic cast of American life. A group of realists known collectively as "local colorists" recorded the intonations and variations in American regional cultures. Perhaps the defining genre of the era, local-color fiction captured the dialects, the daily routines, the physical landscapes, and the emotional makeup of a multicultural nation.

Undermined by Sentiment? Local-color writers such as Sarah Orne Jewett (1849–1909), Joel Chandler Harris (1848–1908), and Helen Hunt Jackson (1830–1885) were among the most popular writers of their time. Yet the label "local colorist" has always suggested a writer of second-class stature. The pejorative note stems in part from the gender bias of literary critics. Although Harris and other male authors—including E. W. Howe (1853–1937), Thomas Nelson Page (1853–1922), and George Washington Cable (1844–1925)—contributed to the local-color phenomenon, a large number of local colorists were women. Many of their compositions were homely short stories, informed by folk wisdom and suffused with mundane domestic detail. Critics deemed the genre insufficiently bold and overly sentimental. Just as sentimental literature of the mid nineteenth century (another predominantly "female" genre) had been dismissed as pabulum for the masses, local-color literature was categorized as something less than "serious" art.

Of New England Nuns and Huckleberry Harvests. New England produced one of the more bountiful crops of local colorists. Sarah Orne Jewett, Mary E. Wilkins Freeman (1852–1930), and Rose Terry Cooke (1827–1892) were among the most prominent of this group. Jewett, whose byline appeared regularly in *The Atlantic Monthly*, is best known for *The Country of the Pointed Firs* (1896), a collection of sketches depicting women's lives unfolding in harmony with nature in a Maine coastal village. In the short stories collected as *A Humble Romance* (1887) and *A New England Nun* (1891) Freeman identified frugality and narrow-mindedness as the Puritan legacy in New England. Cooke, a Connecticut native, wrote sometimes humorous, often heartbreaking stories of rural life that were collected in *Somebody's Neighbors* (1881), *Root-Bound and Other Sketches* (1885), *The Sphinx's Children and Other People's* (1886), and *Huckleberries Gathered from New England Hills* (1891). Another New Englander by birth, Helen Hunt Jackson was a prolific author of travel literature, light verse, and local-color fiction. Jackson, who spent much of her adulthood in the West, is best known as the author of *Ramona* (1884), a California novel that was one of the earliest popular works to address the plight of Native Americans.

Other Regional Voices. Each region of the country produced its share of local colorists—some of whom celebrated the familiar, some of whom probed the darker recesses of everyday existence. Hamlin Garland (1860–1940), who grew up in Wisconsin, Iowa, and South Dakota, took as his subject the economic hardship—and cultural bleakness—of midwestern farm life. *Main-Travelled Roads* (1891), a collection of haunting short stories, and *Rose of Dutcher's Coolly* (1895), a novel set on a Dakota farm, are Garland's best-known works.

E. W. Howe, a Kansas newspaper editor, described a similarly inhospitable midwestern landscape in *The Story of a Country Town* (1883). Joel Chandler Harris, a journalist for the *Atlanta Constitution*, charmed millions with his "Uncle Remus" tales, the first of which was published in that newspaper in 1879. Drawing on African American narrative tradition, Harris, who was white, spun humorous tales that, beneath their folksy veneer, made a compelling case for tolerance across race and class lines. Two other celebrated Southern local colorists were Mary Noailles Murfree (1850–1922), who wrote about Tennessee mountain life under the pen name Charles Egbert Craddock, and Kate Chopin (1850–1904), who examined the influence of Creole and Cajun roots on New Orleans culture.

A Posthumous Renaissance. In recent years critics and readers have rediscovered local-color fiction. Now celebrated for their powers of observation and their narrative acuity, local colorists are enjoying a posthumous renaissance. Feminist scholars in particular have seized on this body of work as evidence that women's writing—and "popular" literature in general—has been undervalued by the literary establishment. Local-color fiction also functions as a repository of cultural data. As television, advertisements, and superhighways (both the information and the automotive variety) chisel away at regional differences, readers can thank yesterday's local colorists for helping preserve slices of regional life for posterity.

Sources:

Lawrence Buell, *New England Literary Culture: From Revolution through Renaissance* (Cambridge: Cambridge University Press, 1986);

Josephine Donovan, *New England Local Color Literature: A Woman's Tradition* (New York: Ungar, 1983);

Emily Toht, ed., *Regionalism and the Female Imagination* (New York: Human Sciences Press, 1985).

MUSEUMS FOR THE MASSES

High Culture. During the 1870s art became enshrined in the United States. Over the course of the decade grand art museums—hitherto a rarity in America—opened their doors. The Museum of Fine Arts in Boston opened in 1870. Philadelphia built its Museum of Art in 1876, the same year that it hosted the national Centennial Exposition. Chicago, bounding back from the Great Fire of 1871, established its Art Institute in 1879. And in 1880 the Metropolitan Museum of Art in New York, founded in 1870, moved into new, palatial headquarters. At long last major American cities boasted adequate facilities for the display of fine art. By any measure, however, these new museums reinforced the division between high and low culture—and high and low society. The museums owed their existence to the patronage of society's upper crust. Inside they were crammed with European masterworks; outside they resembled European palaces. Art—or so the evidence suggested—was meant to occupy an airy province.

The Cincinnati Art Museum and Academy, circa 1900

A Competing Model. Even as New York, Boston, Philadelphia, and Chicago built shrines to high culture, a broader definition of American art became current elsewhere. The notion of "useful" art animates the story of Cincinnati and its quest for an art museum. Prior to 1870 Cincinnati thrice had attempted to establish a permanent art gallery. Each attempt had failed because of lack of interest and lack of funds. In 1877, however, a new group of boosters emerged: the Woman's Art Museum Association (WAMA). Although most of the WAMA women hailed from the upper classes, the organization prided itself on democratic values. Taking the South Kensington Museum (later the Victoria and Albert Museum) in Great Britain as its model, the WAMA emphasized the links among art, industry, and civic life. A museum, the WAMA declared, ought "to educate and develop the genius of the masses." A museum should offer public classes (in design, painting, and the textile arts) in addition to displaying fine art. In 1880, after three years of vigorous promotional activity by WAMA, a local industrialist donated $150,000; the city picked a building site (Eden Park, an enclave overlooking the downtown area); and the WAMA and the newly formed Cincinnati Museum Association (CMA) set to work acquiring collections.

The Museum Opens. The Cincinnati Art Museum opened to the public on 17 May 1886. Both inside and out, the museum did the Queen City proud. The building itself was a handsome Romanesque structure designed by a disciple of H. H. Richardson, the preeminent American architect. The curators sought out rising American painters, a strategy that established Cincin-

nati, over the following decade, as a center of contemporary American art. Other collections—a bequest of American Indian artifacts, for instance—went unappreciated in the 1890s, but later cemented the reputation of the Cincinnati Art Museum.

Complications. Only two issues complicated Cincinnati's quest to establish a truly democratic institution: entrance fees and Sunday hours. Admission fees (twenty-five cents per visit at Cincinnati) kept museums financially solvent. Such fees, however, often proved prohibitively high for members of the working class. For most workers, Sunday remained the only "free" day of the week—and thus the only day available for attending museums, parks, or sporting events. Should a museum charge reduced rates on Sundays? If it did open on Sundays, would it violate the sanctity of the Sabbath? One museum official counseled in favor of Sunday openings; "A better behaved, more orderly lot of people have never been seen together in a public building," this official noted of museumgoers in Pennsylvania; "only *three men* were put out of the Museum for being rude to ladies." He added, "*if Grog Shops are open,* and people will go to the park on Sundays, it is better to give them *a refined and attractive* place to pass part of their afternoon, and thus avoid the temptation which strong drink offers to many."

A Refuge in Eden Park. Convinced that the American public deserved access to American art, the Cincinnati Museum resolved to stay open on Sundays and to charge a reduced admission fee of ten cents. Yet even the most "democratic" nineteenth-century art institutions were likely to remain top-down enterprises: opportunities for an urban elite to protect common folk from the

Stephen Crane, whose best-selling novel *The Red Badge of Courage* (1895) depicts the Civil War so realistically that some veterans believed they must have served with Crane, who was born six years after the war ended

evils of the "grog shop." Still Cincinnati's faith in "the genius of the masses" set an example for museums across the country. Drawn by the museum's compelling collections of American art, crowds still make the pilgrimage to Eden Park.

Sources:

Herbert and Marjorie Katz, *Museums, U.S.A.* (Garden City, N.Y.: Doubleday, 1965);

Robert C. Vitz, *The Queen and the Arts: Cultural Life in Nineteenth-Century Cincinnati* (Kent, Ohio: Kent State University Press, 1989).

NATURALISM IN FICTION

An Increasingly Urban Landscape. The late nineteenth century was a testing ground for such cherished American ideals as optimism, individualism, and the myth of the self-made man. Americans had long subscribed to an agrarian idyll: a belief that—in Thomas Jefferson's words—"cultivators of the earth" were "the most vigorous, the most independant [*sic*], the most virtuous" of citizens. Over the course of the nineteenth century, however, the face of the American landscape changed. In 1850 the population of New York City stood at just under 700,000; by 1900 it had risen to more than 3.4 million. The population of Chicago skyrocketed from approximately 30,000 to 1.7 million during this same period. Many of the new city dwellers were immigrants; many were all but incapacitated by poverty. Not until the

twentieth century did America's urban population equal its rural population, but by the end of the nineteenth century the cities and their ever-growing slums were already exerting a damping influence on the hopes of millions for a better life.

The Death of Free Will? As America grappled with change, so too did Europe. Everywhere, it seemed, evidence cropped up to suggest that external circumstance, rather than free will, determined the shape of an individual's life. Charles Darwin (1809–1882) sent shock waves through scientific and theological circles with his theories of evolution. Karl Marx (1818–1883) saw the relationship of labor and capital as the engine for inevitable change. The French authors Gustave Flaubert (1821–1880) and Emile Zola (1840–1902) adopted determinism as an artistic theory, crafting literary works that portrayed men and women buffeted by forces beyond their control. The objective style of Flaubert and Zola—labeled *naturalism*—was a valuable model for authors chronicling the dissolution of the American dream.

Stephen Crane's Dreamers. At the age of twenty a college dropout named Stephen Crane began observing slum life in the Bowery district of New York City. He worked as a newspaper "stringer" and submitted sketches of slum life to the *New York Tribune*. In 1893, using the pen name Johnston Smith, Crane published at his own

Charlotte Perkins Gilman (1860–1935) earned a reputation as one of the most provocative literary voices of her generation but not before being silenced by the medical prejudices of the day. A grandniece of Harriet Beecher Stowe, Charlotte married at the age of twenty-four, gave birth to a daughter, and shortly thereafter lapsed into depression — a condition often blamed, in the late nineteenth century, on women's intrinsic weakness. Placed under the care of the well-known physician S. Weir Mitchell (1829–1914), Gilman was sentenced to a "rest cure." Under this regimen, she was remanded to bed and prohibited from reading, writing, or communicating with the outside world.

Out of this experience Gilman crafted "The Yellow Wall-Paper" (1892), a classic story of gender relations and mental illness. Gilman's protagonist suffers from "a temporary nervous depression — a slight hysterical tendency." Her husband, John, a physician, prescribes a rest cure. From a bedroom with walls covered by yellow wallpaper, the woman looks out on a world deemed too taxing for her feminine constitution:

> Out of one window I can see the garden — those mysterious deep-shaded arbors, the riotous old-fashioned flowers, and bushes and gnarly trees

> . . . I always fancy I see people walking in these numerous paths and arbors, but John has cautioned me not to give

way to fancy in the least. He says that with my imaginative power and habit of story-making, a nervous weakness like mine is sure to lead to all manner of excited fancies, and that I ought to use my will and good sense to check the tendency. So I try.

Higher education and the professions began opening up to women in the late nineteenth century. As "The Yellow Wall-Paper" suggests, a backlash resulted. According to the medical establishment, intellectual activity threatened a woman's reproductive fitness, and "story-making" and "fancy" distracted women from domestic concerns. While many late-nineteenth-century women languished as chronic neurasthenics, Charlotte Perkins Gilman found solace and strength in art. She separated from her first husband, moved to the West Coast, became a lecturer on women's rights, and married her cousin George Houghton Gilman. In 1898 she published the treatise *Women and Economics,* a classic argument for women's financial independence. Gilman continued as a prolific writer of fiction and nonfiction well into the twentieth century. Among her works from this later period are a trilogy of feminist utopian novels — *Moving the Mountain* (1911), *Herland* (1915), and *With Her in Ourland* (1916) — about a fictional land inhabited only by women.

Source: Ann J. Lane, *To Herland and Beyond: The Life and Work of Charlotte Perkins Gilman* (New York: Pantheon, 1991).

---

expense *Maggie: A Girl of the Streets,* a grim story of a young woman drawn, by the promise of love, into prostitution. *Maggie* was largely ignored by the critics and the public, but *The Red Badge of Courage* (1895), the story of a young soldier immobilized by the horrors of the Civil War, made him famous. Crane's fiction made a case for the centrality—and the ineffectuality—of imagination. His characters strain after change and excitement. Thus, his short story "The Open Boat" (1898), in which shipwrecked sailors face death at sea, begins with mingled images of hope and desperation. "None of them knew the color of the sky," Crane wrote. "Their eyes glanced level, and were fastened upon the waves that swept toward them. These waves were of the hue of slate, save for the tops, which were of foaming white, and all of the men knew the colors of the sea." Experience, for Crane, is aestheticized—why else even notice "the colors of the sea"? Hope, however, is nullified by circumstance: the onrushing waves, the flying bullets, the city streets. Crane's characters (prostitutes, soldiers, and sailors alike) manufacture dreams from the landscape at hand,

and the landscape kills them as readily as if no dreams had been dreamt at all.

Pawns of Passion and Circumstance. Crane's writing exemplifies a basic tenet of naturalism: it depicts men and women as pawns of mighty "forces"—passions, addictions, economic systems, environmental phenomena—that work inexorably against individual expression. While Crane took slum life in New York as his earliest subject, his contemporary Frank Norris examined the underside of life in California. In *McTeague* (1899), the story of a physically imposing, slow-witted San Francisco dentist, Norris created a memorable naturalistic protagonist. McTeague's predisposition toward alcoholism triggers a slow descent into brutality:

> Below the fine fabric of all that was good in him, ran the foul stream of hereditary evil, like a sewer. The vices and sins of his father and of his father's father, to the third and fourth and five hundredth generation, tainted him. The evil of an entire race flowed in his veins. Why should it be? He did not desire it. Was he to blame?

Paul Dresser, whose "On the Banks of the Wabash" (1897) was one of the most popular songs of the 1890s

McTeague loses his dental practice, strangles his wife, flees San Francisco, and dies of dehydration in the middle of Death Valley during a vain and greedy search for gold. Norris's later naturalistic works include *The Octopus* (1901), *The Pit* (1903), and *Vandover and the Brute* (1914). In powerful (if occasionally awkward) prose Norris captured both the vitality and the desperation of human endeavor. The naturalistic mode pioneered by Crane and Norris was later adopted and refined by such early-twentieth-century American masters as Theodore Dreiser, Jack London, and John Dos Passos.

Sources:

Walter Benn Michaels, *The Gold Standard and the Logic of Naturalism* (Berkeley: University of California Press, 1987);

Alan Trachtenberg, *The Incorporation of America: Culture and Society in the Gilded Age* (New York: Hill & Wang, 1982).

POPULAR MUSIC

A Question of Taste. The distinction between "popular" and "serious" music—a distinction that Americans take for granted today—originated in the late nineteenth century. While it is impossible to pinpoint an exact moment at which highbrow and lowbrow diverged, it is pos-

sible to examine the forces and personalities that drove the popular-music industry in its early years.

The Industry. Lyricists, composers, and publishers flocked to Manhattan during the 1880s and 1890s, but not until the early twentieth century did music makers consolidate around Twenty-eighth Street—prompting one critic to dub the thoroughfare "Tin Pan Alley," after the tinny sound of music-room pianos. Decentralization characterized the music industry in the pre–Tin Pan Alley era. No self-respecting city of the 1880s lacked an "opera house" (or, by the 1890s, a "vaudeville theater") for the staging of light musicals. While public performance marked one facet of popular music culture, private performance marked another. Friends and family might gather in the parlor or around the kitchen table, armed with sheet music and determined to re-create the melodies of the music hall.

The Songs. The subjects of popular songs ran the gamut from the romantic to the political to the mundane. "Good-By old Stamp, Good-by" (1883) celebrated the government's decision to slash the cost of a first-class letter from three cents to two; "Gliding in the Rink" (1884) described the new fad of roller skating; "The Merry Singer" (1891) listed the merits of the Singer sewing machine; and "The Silver Knight of the West" (1896) celebrated the Populist idol and presidential candidate William Jennings Bryan. Many late-nineteenth-century "hits" relied for effect on emotional manipulation. In the words of Charles K. Harris (1865–1930), one of the most successful composers of the day,

sentiment plays a large part in our lives. The most hardened character or the most cynical individual will succumb to sentiment sometime or other. In all my ballads I have purposely injected goodly doses of sentiment, and invariably the whole country paused.

"After the Ball" (1892), a cautionary tale of love and jealousy, earned Harris more than $100,000 in royalties. "Break the News to Mother" (1897), another Harris tearjerker, enjoyed a tremendous vogue during the Spanish-American War.

The Composers. The men and women who crafted American hit songs were a motley bunch. Joseph P. Skelly (1850–1895), a plumber by trade and a drunk by habit, had a hit with "Why Did They Dig Ma's Grave So Deep?" (1880)—which includes the lines "Lonely she sits by the old kitchen grate, / Sighing for mother, but now 'tis too late." Harris was completely self-taught; Kerry Mills (1869–1948)—who wrote "At a Georgia Camp meeting" (1897) and "Meet Me in St. Louis, Louis" (1904)—boasted a conservatory background. Edward B. Marks (1865–1945) and Joseph W. Stern (1870–1934), who teamed up to compose a plaintive ballad titled "The Little Lost Child" in 1894, worked as button salesmen on the side. Chauncey Olcott (1858–1932), author of "My Wild Irish Rose" (1899), got his show business start in the 1870s, singing and

The American labor movement came of age in the late nineteenth century, expressing itself in song as well as deed. Labor ballads often addressed topical issues such as the Haymarket riot of 1886, the bloody Homestead steel strike of 1892, and the ongoing struggle for an eight-hour workday. Other labor songs were simple love ditties gussied up with a working-class twist. For example, "Factory Song," featuring the refrain "And somebody's name is Fred," charted the reveries of a lovestruck working girl. Working-class composers frequently set protest lyrics to popular melodies. Hence "Yankee Boodle," a diatribe against President Grover Cleveland, was sung to the tune of "Yankee Doodle."

Throughout the nineteenth century, factory hands and shop workers regularly toiled ten or more hours a day, six days a week, year in and year out. These conditions made the crusade for an eight-hour workday the centerpiece of the labor struggle and a popular subject for labor balladeers. T. C. Walsh of New York, a member of Local 96 of the United Brotherhood of Carpenters and Joiners, was inspired by the AFL battle for shorter hours to write the lyrics for "The Eight-Hour Day" (1890), which begins:

A glorious dawn o'er the land is breaking,
And from the sleep of serfdom waking;
    See the sons of toil arise.
Hearken to the song they're singing,
Through the welkin gladly winging,
Joy unto the weary bringing,
    On, still on, it flies.

        "Let scabs and cowards
        Do what they may,
        Eight hours, eight hours,
        Shall be our day."

Aloft our banner courts the sky,
The glorious day of freedom's nigh,
    From toiling long and late;
"Eight hours" shall be our working day,
"Eight hours" to sleep fatigue away,
"Eight hours" to seek in wisdom's ray,
    Improvement of our state.

        "Let scabs and cowards
        Do what they may,
        Eight hours, eight hours,
        Shall be our day."

Source: Philip S. Foner, *American Labor Songs of the Nineteenth Century* (Urbana, Chicago & London: University of Illinois Press, 1975).

---

waiting tables at a bar operated by his mother. Paul Dresser (1857–1906), whose hits included "The Outcast Unknown" (1894), "Just Tell Them That You Saw Me" (1895), "On the Banks of the Wabash" (1897), and "My Gal Sal" (1905), grew up in poverty. The brother of novelist Theodore Dreiser, Dresser "trained" for his career as a composer by singing with minstrel companies, performing stand-up comedy, and acting in popular melodramas.

Sources:

Lester S. Levy, *Grace Notes in American History* (Norman: University of Oklahoma Press, 1967);

Nicholas E. Tawa, *The Way to Tin Pan Alley: American Popular Song, 1866–1910* (New York: Schirmer, 1990).

POPULAR THEATER

Mass Appeal. William Shakespeare, predicted one critic in 1882, "is destined to become the Shakespeare of the college and university, and even more the Shakespeare of private and select culture. Nor will he ever be perfectly himself and perfectly at home anywhere else." Throughout much of the nineteenth century Shakespeare had belonged to every man, woman, and child—regardless of social class. Some theater companies presented "traditional" interpretations of the bard; others adapted his work to comic, even bawdy purposes. *Richard III* might be performed as *Bad Dicky, Romeo and Juliet* as *Roamy-E-Owe and Julie-Ate*. By the 1880s "high" and "low" drama began to diverge. "Why, I've played an act from *Hamlet,* one from *Black-Eyed Susan,* and sung 'A Yankee Ship and a Yankee Crew' and danced a hornpipe . . . all in one night. Is there any one you know of today who can do that?" asked the actor Edward L. Davenport (1815–1877), lamenting bygone times. In that pre-Hollywood era, however, theater was the crown jewel of American popular culture, and the New York stage—testing ground for new technologies and showcase for the world's leading actors—sparkled brightest of the bright.

The Production. Realistic settings and sensational effects made late-nineteenth-century theater a spectacle. When Lew Wallace's 1880 novel *Ben-Hur* was adapted for the stage in 1899, the chariot races, rigged on treadmills, thrilled New York audiences. Behind the spectacle of *Ben-Hur* and other theatrical extravaganzas hovered the guiding presence of astute producers and stage managers. David Belasco (1853–1931), perhaps the best-known producer of the period, was a San Francisco native whose spare-no-expenses style and passion for stage realism made him a leading force in the theater well into the twentieth century. Steele MacKaye (1842–1894)—like many of his colleagues, an actor and playwright as well as a producer—pioneered the use of overhead electric lighting on stage. Augustin Daly

William Gillette (center) in his popular Civil War spy drama, *Secret Service* (1896)

(1838–1899), whose theater was home to the most star-studded stock company in New York, made his name adapting European plays to American settings. Richard Mansfield (1854–1907) helped introduce American audiences to modern drama with his production of Bernard Shaw's *Arms and the Man* (1894).

The Farce. Twentieth-century critics often dismiss late-nineteenth-century theater as a muddle of old (melodramatic) and new (realistic) styles. If the theater of the 1880s and 1890s failed to generate a trademark style, it did not fail to entertain—and, occasionally, challenge—American audiences. Some playwrights merged old forms with new subjects. Thus, Bronson Howard (1842–1908) loosed the force of farce on the contemporary business world in *Young Mrs. Winthrop* (1882) and *The Henrietta* (1887). Other playwrights, such as Edward Harrigan (1845–1911), reveled in the raw power of burlesque. A composer of popular songs, sketches, and plays, Harrigan worked a cycle of farces around his ditty "The Mulligan Guard" (1873). Featuring Harrigan and his comedy-duo partner Tony Hart (1855–1891), *The Mulligan Guard's Picnic* (1878), *The Mulligan Guards' Ball* (1879), and similar follow-ups satirized the military mindset of post–Civil War America. Another prolific author of "light" drama, Charles Hale Hoyt (1860–1900), scored with *A Texas Steer* (1890), a political satire; *A Trip to Chinatown* (1891), a tale of ill-fated urban adventuring; and *A Temperance Town* (1892), a social farce. Perhaps the most popular actor of the era, William Gillette (1855–1937), was also the author of thirteen original plays. Gillette's most significant work, *The Secret Service* (1896), was a spy thriller set in Civil War times. The actor earned kudos, too, for his performance in *Sherlock Holmes* (1899), a reworking of the Arthur Conan Doyle detective stories. Another popular actor-producer, James O'Neill (1847–1920), father of playwright Eugene O'Neill (1888–1953), became so identified with the leading character in the melodrama *The Count of Monte Cristo,* which he produced for the first time in 1883, that audiences refused to accept him in any other role.

The Advent of Realism. American theater of the late nineteenth century had its serious side as well. The "forward-looking" realistic dramas staged in New York during the 1880s and 1890s inspired avant-garde playwrights of the early twentieth century but were not always welcomed by audiences accustomed to melodrama. After watching a performance of *Margaret Fleming* (1890) by James A. Herne (1839–1901), one critic noted with regret that the dialogue was conducted in "the colloquial English of the shops and streets and the kitchen fire-place" by characters representing "the everyday nonentities that some folks like to forget when they go to the theatre." Despite such criticism, Herne's realistic style took root and prospered. Among the popular plays written by Herne were *Shore Acres* (1892), set in Maine; *The Reverend Griffith Davenport* (1899), a Civil War drama about a liberal southern clergyman; and *Sag Harbor* (1899), written with David Belasco. Other notable social dramas—or "problem plays"—of the period include Steele MacKaye's *Paul Kauvar* (1887), a sympathetic study of anarchism inspired indirectly by the 1886 Haymarket bombing in Chicago; and *The District Attorney* (1895), a clever take on political corruption

Paul Laurence Dunbar, widely known in the 1890s as the "poet laureate of the Negro race"

written by Charles Klein (1867–1915) and Harrison Grey Fiske (1861–1942).

Sources:

Gerald Bordman, ed., *American Musical Theatre: A Chronicle* (New York: Oxford University Press, 1992);

John Gassner, ed., *Best Plays of the Early American Theatre* (New York: Crown, 1967);

Lawrence W. Levine, *Highbrow/Lowbrow: The Emergence of Cultural Hierarchy in America* (Cambridge, Mass.: Harvard University Press, 1988).

RACE AND ETHNICITY IN LITERATURE

The Melting Pot. "What then is the American, this new man?" asked Michel Guillaume Jean de Crèvecoeur (1735–1813), a French immigrant whose *Letters from an American Farmer* (1782), introduced American folk and folkways to curious readers on both sides of the Atlantic. "I could point out to you a family whose grandfather was an Englishman, whose wife was Dutch, whose son married a French woman, and whose present four sons have now four wives of different nations," Crèvecoeur observed. "Here individuals of all nations are melted into a new race of men, whose labours and posterity will one day cause great changes in the world." Crèvecoeur's imagery suggested a phrase, *melting pot,* that gradually passed into public parlance. Yet despite the ideal of the melting pot, barriers to assimilation remained. Racial and ethnic tensions ran particularly high in the United States during the late nineteenth century. Unprece-

dented levels of immigration, coupled with the recent upheavals of the Civil War and Reconstruction, fragmented American society. In the literature of the period many authors asked anew, "What then is the American?"

Crossing the Color Line. Charles W. Chesnutt (1858–1932), born in Cleveland to free black parents, devoted his career to issues of race and race relations. He published two collections of short stories, *The Conjure Woman* and *The Wife of His Youth and Other Stories of the Color Line,* in 1899, the same year in which his biography of the African American orator Frederick Douglass (1817–1895) appeared. In the title story of his second collection, first published in *The Atlantic Monthly* in 1898, Chesnutt tackled the thorny issue of intraracial prejudice. His protagonist, Ryder, an upper-class mulatto, makes plans to marry a light-skinned black woman. Yet he is haunted by the dark-skinned Liza Jane—the "wife of his youth" who reappears on the eve of his wedding. In this and other stories of racial identity Chesnutt questioned the moral foundation of the assimilationist "ideal." White writers also surveyed the "color line" dividing American society. In 1865 Albion W. Tourgée (1838–1905), fresh from service as an officer in the Union army, moved to North Carolina, where he practiced law and engaged in Reconstruction politics. In the opinion of his North Carolina neighbors, Tourgée was a *carpetbagger:* a term applied, with venom, to Northerners who came to the South after the close of the

Pauline Hopkins (1859–1930) was just twenty-one years old when, in 1880, her musical drama *Slaves Escape* premiered in Boston, with Hopkins herself singing a lead role. A romance of the Underground Railroad, in which a band of slaves flees a Mississippi plantation, Hopkins's musical combines dialect, humor, and pathos. She revised *Slaves Escape* slightly in later years, renaming the play *Peculiar Sam* (after its protagonist) to distinguish it from the popular William Wells Brown drama *The Escape.* The following excerpt, from the first act of *Peculiar Sam,* describes Sam's reaction to the news that his beloved Jinny ("the plantation nightingale") has been forced to marry the unscrupulous black overseer Jim.

MAMMY: *(breathing hard)* For de Lor's sake boy do you kno' what dey's gone an' done up to de big house? Dey's gone an married dat dear chile, dat lamb ob a Jinny, to dat rascal ob an oberseer Jim.

SAM: *(excited, grasps her arm)* Mammy, tell me agin! You don't mean it! Tell me dey haint done dat!

MAMMY: *(astonished)* Hey yar boy, lef' be my arm. You mean to scrunch me to a jelly? *(He drops her arm)* Yes, deys bring dat gal up like a lady; she neber done nuthin' but jes wait on Marse fambly an' now ole Marser's dead dey's gone an' married her, their way to Jim an' de gal can't bar de sight ob him. It's de meanes' thing I eber seed. . . .

SAM: *(sorrowfully)* Po' Jinny, po' little gal *(sings)*:

Ah! Jinny is a simple chile,
    Wif pretty shinin' curls,
An' white folks love her best, of all
    The young mulatto girls;
Tell her to wait a little while,
    Tell her in hope to wait,
For I will surely break the chain,
    That binds her to the gate.

Sam resolves to spirit Jinny, Mammy, and the rest of the plantation slaves to freedom on the Underground Railroad. After an occasionally comical journey (during which Sam disguises himself as a "gentleman overseer" and steals $100 from the slow-witted Jim), the band reaches freedom in Canada. As the final scene opens, years have passed: the former slaves are happily settled in their new lives, with Jinny a "singist" and Sam's sister Juno a "school marm." Sam has undergone the most radical transformation. Recently elected to the U.S. Congress, he returns to the family hearth to share the good news and claim his beloved Jinny:

PETE: Jes' tell us one thing cap'n, 'fore you goes eny farther, is you 'lected?

VIRGINIA: Yes, Sam do relieve our anxiety.

SAM: I think you may safely congratulate me, on a successful election. My friends in Cincinnati have stood by me nobly.

MAMMY: Praise de Lord! Chillern I hasn't nuthin' lef' to lib fer.

Hopkins's decision to contrast dialect and "proper" speech (the latter indicating Sam's "success" and Jinny's educated status) may strike today's readers as crude. At the time, however, the play's happy ending (complete with Sam and Jinny's linguistic transformation) spoke to many African Americans. The political experiment of Reconstruction had encouraged, if briefly, a belief in social and political integration. Not only might former slaves shed their chains, Hopkins suggested, they might also shed their slave dialect and gain a permanent place in the national power structure.

Source: Leo Hamalian and James V. Hatch, eds., *The Roots of African American Drama: An Anthology of Early Plays, 1858–1938* (Detroit: Wayne State University Press, 1991).

Civil War. Tourgée's southern sojourn—he returned north in 1878, following the demise of Reconstruction—provided him with abundant literary material. *Figs and Thistles* (1879) and *Toinette* (1874; revised as *A Royal Gentleman,* 1881) are tales of the Civil War era; his most notable works, *A Fool's Errand* (1879) and *Bricks Without Straw* (1880), are set in the South during Reconstruction. An outspoken advocate of African American civil rights, Tourgée emerged as one of the more sensitive writers on race relations during the period.

Taking the National Stage. A medley of African American voices achieved national prominence during the second half of the nineteenth century. William Wells Brown (1814–1884), born a slave in Kentucky, escaped to freedom and flourished as an abolitionist lecturer, practicing physician, and literary jack-of-all-trades. With *Clotel: or, The President's Daughter* (1853), Brown became the first African American to publish a novel in the United States. Brown was also an active presence in American theater through the turn of the century because of the lasting popularity of his antislavery dramas *Experience; or, How to Give a Northern Man a Backbone* (1856) and *The Escape* (1858). Brown's writing served as inspiration for Pauline Hopkins (1859–1930), a New England writer whose early plays *Aristocracy* (1877), *Wi-*

nona (1878), and *Slaves Escape* (1880) foreshadow her later work as editor of *Colored American* magazine and author of *Contending Forces* (1900), a politically charged sentimental novel. W. E. B. Du Bois (1868–1963), after earning his Ph.D. from Harvard in 1895, embarked on an illustrious career as an author, editor, and social reformer. Du Bois's sociological study *The Philadelphia Negro* (1899) was followed by his masterpiece, *The Souls of Black Folk* (1903)—and, in subsequent years, by an array of historical and literary treatments of race in America. Paul Laurence Dunbar (1872–1906), dubbed the "poet laureate of the Negro race," published his verse in popular collections such as *Lyrics of Lowly Life* (1896), *Lyrics of the Hearthside* (1899), *Lyrics of Love and Laughter* (1903), and *Lyrics of Sunshine and Shadow* (1905). Although best known for his poetry—which he read, to packed lecture halls in the United States and abroad—Dunbar also composed sentimental stories, novels, and plays before his death at age thirty-four.

A Nation of Immigrants. Questions of ethnic as well as racial identity engrossed American authors during the latter decades of the nineteenth century. Lafcadio Hearn (1850–1904), part Irish and part Greek, immigrated to the United States in his late teens and found work as a journalist first in Cincinnati and later in New Orleans. Hearn published books on Negro-French proverbs and Chinese legends before moving to Japan in 1890 and devoting the rest of his career to the study of Japanese culture. H. H. Boyesen (1848–1895), a native of Norway, arrived in America in 1869 to pursue an academic career. Boyesen's scholarly essays are largely forgotten, but his later novels—*The Mammon of Unrighteousness* (1891), *The Golden Calf* (1892), and *The Social Strugglers* (1893)—remain noteworthy examples of realistic fiction. Abraham Cahan (1860–1951), a Russian Jew who moved to the United States in 1882, captured the flavor of immigrant life in works of fiction such as *Yekl: A Tale of the New York Ghetto* (1896), *The Imported Bridegroom and Other Stories* (1898), and *The Rise of David Levinsky* (1917). Cahan wrote in Yiddish as well as English and served for decades as editor of the Yiddish-language *Jewish Daily Forward*. The Yiddish vaudeville theater also reflected the cross-ethnic influences discernible in Cahan's fiction: one popular play of 1895, by the Yiddish playwright H. I. Minikes, was titled *Tsvishn indianer* (Among the Indians). The literature of the late nineteenth century is consumed by issues of inclusion and exclusion. American novels, stories, poems, and plays reveal a multicultural, multiracial society both enriched by, and yet resistant to, the allure of the melting pot.

Sources:

Werner Sollors, *Beyond Ethnicity* (New York: Oxford University Press, 1986);

Eric Sundquist, *To Wake the Nations* (Cambridge, Mass.: Harvard University Press, 1993).

SCULPTURE

The Ideal Form. "Not a nude figure, I hope," comments a character in Nathaniel Hawthorne's *The Marble Faun* (1860). Hawthorne's novel, set in Rome, tracks a band of American artists abroad. As Hawthorne's sculptor, Kenyon, prepares to unveil a "figure," his friend Miriam observes, "Every young sculptor seems to think that he must give the world some specimen of indecorous womanhood, and call it Eve, Venus, a Nymph, or any name that may apologize for a lack of decent clothing." Miriam's teasing remarks shed light on the state of nineteenth-century American sculpture. At midcentury a marble nude titled *The Greek Slave* (circa 1843) enchanted the American art world. Hiram Powers (1805–1873), creator of *The Greek Slave,* had recently immigrated—like so many sculptors of his generation—to Italy, where he and compatriots such as Horatio Greenough (1805–1852) developed a taste for grandeur, classicism, and what Greenough called "colossal nudity"—ideals foisted, with varying degrees of success, on the American public. Powers's *Greek Slave,* lacking clothes but retaining a measure of chastity, found an adoring audience: "It is not her person but her spirit that stands exposed," Powers declared. Mid-nineteenth-century nudes idealized the female body, even as patriotic monuments—*Andrew Jackson* (1853), by Clark Mills (1815–1883) in Washington, D.C.; *Washington* (1856), by Henry Kirke Brown (1814–1886) in New York City; *Thomas Hart Benton* (1868), by Harriet Hosmer (1830–1908) in Saint Louis—idealized the male statesman. These ideals were modified, but seldom challenged outright, by the sculpture of succeeding generations.

Augustus Saint-Gaudens. Hosmer, Chauncey B. Ives (1810–1894), William Rimmer (1816–1879), Erastus Dow Palmer (1817–1904), and John Quincy Adams Ward (1830–1910) were among the prominent American sculptors of the late nineteenth and early twentieth centuries. The two dominant figures of the period, however, were younger artists: Augustus Saint-Gaudens (1848–1907) and Daniel Chester French (1850–1931). The historian Henry Adams (1838–1918) described his friend Saint-Gaudens as a cautious, observant, and oddly calm artist. "He never laid down the law, or affected the despot, or became brutalized . . . by the brutalities of his world," observed Adams. "He required no incense; he was no egoist; his simplicity of thought was excessive." Saint-Gaudens received a cosmopolitan education in New York, Paris, Florence, and Rome; early on he won the respect and patronage of older artists such as the painter John La Farge (1835–1910) and the sculptor J. Q. A. Ward. With his *Farragut* (1881) and *Sherman* (1903) monuments in New York, his *Lincoln* (1887) in Chicago, and his *Robert Gould Shaw* (1897) in Boston, Saint-Gaudens upheld the ideal of the American hero. Saint-Gaudens's work combines grace and vitality—qualities that harmonized with the spirit of the contemporary Beaux-Arts revival. The prestigious architec-

Monument to Admiral David Glasgow Farragut (1801–1870) in New York
City, sculpted by Augustus Saint-Gaudens in 1881

tural firm of McKim, Mead and White placed Saint-Gaudens's nude *Diana* atop their Madison Square Garden in 1892. The following year they transported *Diana* to Chicago to stand guard over the White City of the World's Columbian Exposition.

Daniel Chester French. French possessed neither the sophisticated gloss nor the cosmopolitan training of Saint-Gaudens. Born in Exeter, New Hampshire, French was largely self-trained as a sculptor. He received his first significant commission in 1873: the *Minute Man* in Concord, Massachusetts, designed to commemorate the centennial of the "shot heard 'round the world." President Ulysses S. Grant (1822–1885) attended the 1875 installation ceremony at the old North Bridge in Concord; Ralph Waldo Emerson (1803–1882) unveiled the statue. The *Minute Man* commission opened doors for the young New Englander. French sculpted a founder's statue—*John Harvard* (1884)—for the campus of Harvard University and a seventy-five-foot *Statue of the Republic* (1893) for the World's Columbian Exposition. French is best remembered for the pensive, thirty-foot-tall statue of Abraham Lincoln enshrined in 1922 in the

Lincoln Memorial in Washington, D.C. Although neither Saint-Gaudens nor French revolutionized American sculpture, each created monuments to the raw power of the sculpted form.

Sources:

Charles H. Caffin, *American Masters of Sculpture* (Garden City, N.Y.: Doubleday, Page, 1913);

Sylvia E. Crane, *White Silence: Greenough, Powers, and Crawford. American Sculptors in Nineteenth-Century Italy* (Coral Gables, Fla.: University of Miami Press, 1972);

Richard McLanathan, *The American Tradition in the Arts* (New York: Harcourt, Brace & World, 1968).

THE WEST LAUGHS LAST: HUMOR WRITERS

New Frontiers. In July 1893 at the World's Columbian Exposition in Chicago, the historian Frederick Jackson Turner (1861–1932) delivered an address on "The Significance of the Frontier in American History." "The true point of view in the history of this nation," Turner argued, "is not the Atlantic coast, it is the great West." Throughout the course of American history, the "West" had beckoned to explorers, settlers, and speculators, inspiring all with visions of untamed land and untapped resources. Turner's dismissal of "the Atlantic coast" turned traditional cultural valuations topsy-turvy. In literary circles, the "East" had always reigned supreme. New England monopolized the literary marketplace through the mid nineteenth century. New York, the center of commerce, began angling for position as the American cultural capital in the decades following the Civil War. Yet even as the frontier celebrated by Turner "closed," a new chapter in American literary history opened. When western writers began to speak out, in the 1880s and 1890s, they did so with a distinctive and compelling literary voice.

Self-Definition through Opposition. Telling tall tales or spinning gothic yarns, writers such as George Washington Harris (1814–1869), William Gilmore Simms (1806–1870), and Bret Harte (1836–1902) reminded readers that "civilization" as defined by New England literary tradition was no match for the brutality, diversity, and sheer exuberance of western life. From the start western literature was characterized by linguistic vitality. Slang and broad humor suffused the work of western writers, tickling readers while dismaying literary purists. Western writers experimented with form as well as with style. As William Dean Howells commented, "The West, when it began to put itself into literature, could do so without the sense of any older or politer world outside of it; whereas the East was always looking fearfully over its shoulder at Europe, and anxious to account for itself as well as represent itself."

Dissemination by the Press. The daily press played an invaluable role in defining the voice of the West. Columnists and contributors experimented with dialect and light verse; readers, many of them settled in sparsely populated regions, made newspapers their primary source of information and "culture." Journalist Eugene Field (1850–1895) wrote a humor column, "Sharps and Flats," for the *Chicago Daily News* during the 1880s and 1890s. Many of Field's poems—among them "Little Boy Blue" and "Wynken, Blynken, and Nod"—became national treasures. James Whitcomb Riley (1849–1916), a native of Indiana, wrote sentimental poems narrated in a distinctive Hoosier dialect for the *Indianapolis Journal*. William Sydney Porter (1862–1910), who became famous as O. Henry in the early years of the twentieth century, honed his storytelling skills with humorous pieces published in Texas newspapers during the mid 1890s.

America's Favorite Humorist. Of all the westerners to dabble in literary journalism, the most famous by far was Samuel Langhorne Clemens (1835–1910). Raised in the Mississippi River town of Hannibal, Missouri, Clemens adopted the pen name Mark Twain in 1863, after he started work at the Virginia City, Nevada, *Territorial Enterprise*. Over the following decades Clemens—a journeyman printer, riverboat pilot, itinerant traveler, lecturer, and writer— saw the "old southwest" of his youth

Western humor writer Bret Harte

"civilized" by new settlers and altered forever by the abolition of slavery. His writing combines hints of nostalgia with sharp political commentary on the economic and moral inequities that sustained a nonidyllic past. His travel narratives—*The Innocents Abroad* (1869), *"Roughing It"* (1872), and *A Tramp Abroad* (1880)—humorously depict the plight of "typical" Americans in unfamiliar territory. *The Prince and the Pauper* (1881) and *A Connecticut Yankee in King Arthur's Court* (1889) are historical fantasies set in England. Twain's masterpiece, *Adventures of Huckleberry Finn* (1884)—a sequel to his earlier boy's story, *The Adventures of Tom Sawyer* (1876)—combines nostalgic reveries and humorous sketches with a biting attack on the institution of slavery. A later work, *Pudd'nhead Wilson* (1894), skewers American attitudes toward race with its tale of two infants, one white and one black, swapped at birth. As his life progressed, Twain's outlook grew darker. Frequently in debt, deeply dismayed by the corruption of America's "Gilded Age," the preeminent American humorist went to his grave a pessimist.

Sources:

Christine Bold, *Selling the Wild West: Popular Western Fiction, 1860 to 1960* (Bloomington: Indiana University Press, 1987);

Michael Kowalewski, ed., *Reading the West: New Essays on the Literature of the American West* (New York: Cambridge University Press, 1996).

HEADLINE MAKERS

MARY CASSATT

1844-1926
ARTIST

A Taste of Europe. Born into a wealthy Pennsylvania family, Mary Stevenson Cassatt enlisted privilege in the service of artistic endeavor. She spent much of her adult life in France, where she was the only American artist who frequented the inner circles of the French Impressionists. The roots of Cassatt's success may be traced to a childhood rich in culture and creature comforts. Pittsburgh in the mid nineteenth century boasted no more solid citizens than the investment banker Robert Simpson Cassatt and his wife, Katherine Johnston Cassatt. Born on 22 May 1844, Mary Cassatt was one of five children; she had just turned seven when the family embarked on a four-year visit to Europe. On their return the Cassatts settled in Philadelphia—then the second-largest city in America. At age sixteen Mary enrolled at the Pennsylvania Academy of Art; six years later, having exhausted the academy's offerings, she ventured to Paris in the company of her friend and fellow art student Eliza Haldeman. As the prestigious Ecole des Beaux-Arts was closed to women, Cassatt was forced to pursue her studies in private lessons and in the artist colonies sprinkled across the French countryside.

The Young Artist. "Americans have a way of thinking work is nothing," Cassatt observed near the end of her career. "Come out and play they say." Blessed with money and leisure, Cassatt chose work over play. Having returned home in 1870, Cassatt moved with her family from Philadelphia to Altoona, Pennsylvania, where she struggled to maintain her artistic momentum away from the centers of cultural influence. New York galleries failed to sell her paintings, and a substantial collection of her early work, on display in a Chicago gallery, burned up in the Great Fire of 1871. That December twenty-seven-year-old Cassatt sailed again for Europe—and embarked on a period marked by both productivity and periodic self-doubt. In Italy, Spain, and France Cassatt acquired artistic technique by studying the old masters and mingling with the new. She developed a particular talent for painting women, both in portraits and the more informal "pictures" that she considered a higher form of art. In 1874 *Ida*, Cassatt's painting of a red-haired woman, so impressed Edgar Degas that he declared its unknown artist to be "someone who feels as I do." Although *Ida* had gained a spot in that year's Paris Salon—the "official" annual exhibition of fine art—Cassatt remained at odds with the art establishment, criticized for her "sloppy" brushwork and rambunctious use of color. Not until 1877, when Degas invited her to exhibit with the "Independents" (later known as the Impressionists), did Cassatt find a true home abroad.

Among the Impressionists. Impressionism liberated Cassatt from artistic convention. In early paintings Cassatt had strained for "mood" by draping sitters in exotic costumes or placing subjects in romantic settings. Now, however, Cassatt began to uncover "atmosphere" in the commonplace and to achieve fresh effects with experimental brush- and colorwork rather than artificial composition. Cassatt's parents and sister joined her overseas in 1877; her brother and his children visited often. Increasingly, Cassatt employed her relatives as models. Works such as *The Cup of Tea* or *Mrs. Cassatt Reading to Her Grandchildren,* both exhibited at the 1881 Impressionist show, stand as representative glimpses into the Cassatt family circle. Cassatt's many mother-and-child compositions of the 1880s and 1890s—among them, *Gardner Held by His Mother* (1888), *Mother's Goodnight Kiss* (1888), *At the Window* (1889), *Helene de Septeuil* (1889), *Baby on His Mother's Arm, Sucking His Finger* (1889), *Mother and Child* (1890), and *The Bath* (1890–1891)—depict a full range of domestic activity. Settled in Paris, surrounded by friends and family, Cassatt could half-jokingly describe her own domestic routine as "housekeeping, painting & oyster frying." Whatever her merits as housekeeper or cook, by the 1890s Cassatt's artistic talents had earned her the regard of her adopted land. "Mary is at work again, intent on fame & money she says, & counts on her fellow country men now that she has made a reputation here," Cassatt's mother commented in 1891. The following year Cassatt finally received a summons from the American art establishment.

A Modern Woman. In 1892 the organizers of the upcoming World's Columbian Exposition in Chicago commissioned Cassatt to paint a mural for the Woman's Building. Cassatt addressed her subject, *Modern Woman,* in three allegorical panels: "Young Girls Pursuing Fame," "Arts, Music, Dancing," and the centerpiece, "Young Women Plucking the Fruits of Knowledge or Science." The mural was abstract, symbolic, and, Cassatt hoped, "as bright, as gay, as amusing as possible." When a friend protested that Cassatt had depicted "woman apart from her relations to man," Cassatt countered that men were to be "painted in all their vigour on the walls of the other buildings." In her corner of the Woman's Building, the artist hoped to capture "the sweetness of childhood, the charm of womanhood." As she declared, "if I have not conveyed some sense of that charm, in one word if I have not been absolutely feminine, then I have failed." Like so many of the other artistic fancies on display in Chicago, Cassatt's mural was dismantled at the close of the fair in 1893 and subsequently lost.

Final Years. To the end Cassatt continued to paint women at work, at home, and at play. An advocate of women's rights, she held women responsible for their own advancement. "American women have been spoiled, treated and indulged like children," she observed late in life; "they must wake up to their duties." By 1915 eye trouble forced Cassatt to give painting. She remained a fixture of American expatriate society for another decade, dying at her country home outside Paris on 14 June 1926.

Sources:

Nancy Hale, *Mary Cassatt* (Garden City, N.Y.: Doubleday, 1975);

Nancy Mowll Mathews, *Mary Cassatt* (New York: Abrams, 1987);

Mathews, ed., *Cassatt and Her Circle: Selected Letters* (New York: Abbeville Press, 1984).

SAMUEL LANGHORNE CLEMENS

(MARK TWAIN)

1835–1910
NOVELIST

A Missouri Boyhood. In the autumn of 1835 Americans looked up and marveled as Halley's Comet—not due to reappear for another seventy-five years—illuminated the skies. On 30 November, as the comet passed overhead, a small-town lawyer, merchant, and real-estate developer named John Marshall Clemens welcomed a baby son into the world. John Clemens and his wife, Jane Lampton Clemens, had moved from place to place during the first twelve years of their marriage, settling in 1835 in the sleepy hamlet of Florida, Missouri. Young Samuel Langhorne Clemens joined a household that already included two older brothers, two older sisters, and a slave named Jenny. In 1839 the family moved thirty miles east to Hannibal, a bustling town of a thousand-odd residents. In this town perched on the banks of the Mississippi River, young Sam Clemens spent his childhood, absorbing the speech and spirit of antebellum life on the Mississippi.

The Young Journalist. The Clemens family suffered mixed fortunes during the future novelist's boyhood. A sister died in 1839; a brother died in 1842; and John Clemens died in 1847—a crushing financial blow for the family. To help support his mother and remaining siblings, Sam worked at a series of odd jobs. All the while he continued to explore the great Mississippi: swimming, fishing, and even, with friends, discovering the drowned body of a fugitive slave. In 1848 young Clemens became an apprentice at the office of the *Missouri Courier.* Three years later he joined the staff of his brother Orion's weekly, the *Western Union.* Journalism served as Clemens's introduction to a wider world. During the 1850s and into the 1860s he worked in various capacities for papers in Iowa, Pennsylvania, Ohio, and Nevada. During this same period he also worked as a riverboat pilot, a speculator, and a prospector. Clemens's early journalism anticipates his later work in many respects: it showcases his biting humor, his zest for travel, and his fondness for pseudonyms, including W. Epaminondas Adrastus Perkins, Thomas Jefferson Snodgrass, Josh, and finally, in 1863, Mark Twain. *The Innocents Abroad,* a humorous account of Clemens's 1867 travels in Europe and the Middle East, received excellent reviews when it was published in 1869 and became a best-seller. The following year the western author married an eastern heiress, Olivia Louise (Livy) Langdon of Elmira, New York.

During the 1870s and 1880s Clemens continued to craft a distinctive, multifaceted identity that combined the panache of the East with the vitality—and occasional rough edges—of the West. As Mark Twain, he became the preeminent American humorist of the late nineteenth century.

Literary Achievement. Twain's early works include *"Roughing It"* (1872), a western travelogue; *The Gilded Age* (1873), a satiric novel written with his friend Charles Dudley Warner (1829–1900); and *The Adventures of Tom Sawyer* (1876), another best-seller whose mischievous protagonist has charmed generations of young readers. He went on to write *A Tramp Abroad* (1880), further impressions of Europe gleaned during an 1878–1879 tour of the Continent; *The Prince and the Pauper* (1881), a historical fable set in sixteenth-century England; and *Life on the Mississippi* (1883), based on Clemens's experiences as a riverboat pilot. All the while, Clemens continued to travel, to publish sketches and stories in the popular press, and to cultivate prominent literary and political friends. One close friend, William Dean Howells, offered editorial advice as Clemens labored over drafts of a new novel. This book, originally conceived in 1876 as a sequel to *Tom Sawyer,* had languished for years as Twain tinkered with other writing projects. *Adventures of Huckleberry Finn,* finally published in 1884 in Great Britain and in the United States the following year, did indeed feature the scamp Tom Sawyer. But in Tom's friend Huck, Twain created a character who transcended the ranks of juvenile fiction. More worldly than Tom, and yet possessed of an essential idealism, Huck Finn is the quintessential American hero.

Huck Finn, American Iconoclast. Traveling down the Mississippi toward freedom on a raft, Huck and the fugitive slave Jim encounter an array of colorful characters during their quest for freedom. In a pivotal scene, when authorities post a large reward for Jim's return, Huck is forced to weigh "the law" against more complex standards of justice. "I see Jim before me all the time," Huck reflects: "in the day and in the night-time, sometimes moonlight, sometimes storms, and we a-floating along, talking and singing and laughing. But somehow I couldn't seem to strike no places to harden me against him, but only the other kind." Although he has already drafted a letter telling Jim's owner of the slave's whereabouts, Huck pauses before taking further action: "I was a-trembling, because I'd got to decide, forever, betwixt two things, and I knowed it. I studied a minute, sort of holding my breath, and then says to myself: 'All right, then, I'll *go* to hell.'" At this decisive moment—and again at the end of the book, when he determines to "light out for the territory" rather than be "sivilized" — Huck takes a stand as an American iconoclast, a self-willed outcast from proper society.

Adrift in America. The man who coined the phrase "The Gilded Age" found himself increasingly at odds with the acquisitive culture of late-nineteenth-century America. Throughout the 1890s Twain's reputation as a literary master grew, but debts—and doubts—accumulated. Darker overtones surface in Twain's later works such as *Pudd'nhead Wilson* (1894), a novel that comments on race, law, and humbug; "To the Person Sitting in Darkness," an essay denouncing American imperialism; and *The Mysterious Stranger* (begun in 1898, published posthumously in 1916), a meditation on the nature of evil. In an interview with *The New York Times* in 1905, Twain commented on the mixed blessings of literary fame: "My advice to the humorist who has been a slave to his reputation is never to be discouraged. I know it is painful to make an earnest statement of a heartfelt conviction and then observe the puzzled expression of the fatuous soul who is conscientiously searching his brain to see how he can possibly have failed to get the point of the joke. But say it again and maybe he'll understand you. No man need be a humorist all his life." Clemens's wife had died in the summer of 1904, and he spent his final years in restless transit from Connecticut to New York, Europe, and Bermuda. He lived to see Halley's Comet reappear in the heavens in early 1910; he died on 21 April at his home in Redding, Connecticut.

Sources:

Louis J. Budd, *Our Mark Twain* (Philadelphia: University of Pennsylvania Press, 1983);

Justin Kaplan, *Mr. Clemens and Mark Twain* (New York: Simon & Schuster, 1966).

SARAH ORNE JEWETT

1849-1909
NOVELIST

Inheritor of a Sentimental Mantle. When Harriet Beecher Stowe died in 1896 at the age of eighty-five, her twin daughters sent a photograph of their mother and a small, ornamental box in which the author of *Uncle Tom's Cabin* (1852) had stored her postage stamps to a woman whom their mother had considered a friend and a literary protegé: Sarah Orne Jewett. Although nearly half a century apart in age, the two authors were products and champions of New England domestic culture. Stowe and Jewett were also witnesses to the distinctive character of the northernmost state in the region. During the early 1850s Stowe had lived for a year in the coastal town of Brunswick, Maine, while her husband spent two terms as professor of theology at Bowdoin College. Stowe wrote *Uncle Tom's Cabin,* the novel that helped to launch the Civil War, in Brunswick, and her *The Pearl of Orr's Island* (1862) was based in large part on her memories of the rugged Maine seacoast. *The Pearl of Orr's Island* was an early, largely unheralded example of local-color fiction: a form of literature that aimed to represent, through close observation and muted sentiment, the patterns of regional life in America. In the 1890s, her own career in full ascent, Jewett identified "those delightful early chapters of *The Pearl of Orr's Island*" as a model for her own work. She praised Stowe for "writing about people of rustic life just as they were." The work of Sarah Orne Jewett, like that of Harriet Beecher Stowe before her, combines the most powerful elements of sentimental and realistic fiction in celebrating the lives of ordinary Americans.

Explorations. Born on 3 September 1849 in the southern Maine village of South Berwick, Sarah Orne was the middle child in a family of three daughters. As a young girl, she often joined her father, a doctor, on his rounds, and on her own she roamed the banks of the Piscataqua River, observing a natural landscape as varied as the social milieu she explored with her father. Jewett concluded her formal schooling in 1865 and began to devote more and more of her time to writing—first poetry, later fiction. An intimate knowledge of the New England culture and countryside animated Jewett's prose. In 1868, when she was nineteen, Jewett's short stories began appearing in the *Riverside Magazine for Young People, The Atlantic Monthly,* and other popular magazines. Jewett's breakthrough came in 1873, when *The Atlantic* published "The Shore House"—the first in a series of local-color sketches that showcased her distinctive style and subject matter.

Partnership. Although Jewett did most of her writing in Maine, she also became something of a habitué of Boston literary society. After the death in 1881 of editor and publisher James T. Fields—whose firm, Ticknor and Fields, published the works of such New England worthies as Nathaniel Hawthorne, Oliver Wendell Holmes, James Russell Lowell, and John Greenleaf Whittier—Jewett settled into the position of companion to Fields's widow, Annie Adams Fields. A cultural arbiter in her own right, Annie Fields (1834–1915) wrote poetry and presided over a literary salon, a regular, informal gathering of writers and critics. Jewett and Fields enjoyed an affectionate, intimate friendship, dividing their time together between Fields's home in Boston and Jewett's home in Maine.

A Professional Feminist. Jewett derived a sense of pride from her identity as a professional writer, which during the 1880s and 1890s developed hand-in-hand with a feminist sensibility. The protagonist of Jewett's novel *A Country Doctor* (1884) chooses a career in medicine over a woman's traditional "career" of marriage. Her later novels and short-story collections—including *A*

Marsh Island (1885), *A White Heron and Other Stories* (1886), and *The King of Folly Island and Other People* (1888)—explore the frustrations, desires, and achievements of New England women. The interlocking tales of Jewett's masterpiece, *The Country of the Pointed Firs* (1896), describe the rituals of a rural, female-centered world.

An Everyday Author. "How seldom a book comes that stirs the minds and hearts of the good men and women of such a village as this," Jewett once mused, apropos of her South Berwick neighbors; "the truth must be recognized that few books are written for and from their standpoint," she continued, venturing that "whoever adds to this department of literature will do an inestimable good, will see that a simple, helpful way of looking at life . . . in what we are pleased to call its *everyday* aspects must bring out the best sort of writing." Jewett knew, of course, that change was encroaching on her beloved Maine countryside. In the course of her lifetime, she saw South Berwick transformed from a sleepy village to a bustling vacation retreat. As one of the foremost American local-color writers, she helped to celebrate—and thereby preserve—the "everyday aspects" of a vibrant, vanishing culture.

Sources:

Paula Blanchard, *Sarah Orne Jewett: Her World and Her Work* (Reading, Mass.: Addison-Wesley, 1994);

Richard Cary, ed., *Sarah Orne Jewett Letters,* revised and enlarged edition (Waterville, Maine: Colby College Press, 1967);

Joan D. Hedrick, *Harriet Beecher Stowe: A Life* (New York: Oxford University Press, 1994).

LOUIS SULLIVAN

1856-1924
ARCHITECT

Rise and Fall. The life of Louis Henri Sullivan traces a simple arc: a dramatic ascent followed by an abrupt descent. Born in 1856, Sullivan spent his early years in Boston. From his parents—an Irish violinist and a Swiss pianist—he inherited artistic leanings. From his grandfather—the dominant presence in his childhood—he inherited the broadminded outlook of New England Transcendentalism. By the time he was thirteen Sullivan had already decided on architecture as a career. A series of short educational interludes followed: he studied in 1873 for a single term at the Massachusetts Institute of Technology; he apprenticed briefly under the architects Frank Furness (1839–1912) in Philadelphia and William Le Baron Jenney (1832–1907) in Chicago; in 1874 he went to Paris and enrolled at the Ecole des Beaux-Arts, the leading architectural institute of the western world. No fan of formal education—he once described his Parisian studio as a "damned pigsty"—Sullivan returned to Chicago in 1875 and in 1881 entered into partnership with Dankmar Adler (1844–1900). With his pioneering conception of the "tall office building," Sullivan succeeded H. H. Richardson (1838–1886) as the preeminent American architect. During the late 1880s and 1890s he helped transform America's urban landscape—and helped train a young architect named Frank Lloyd Wright (1867–1959). Yet the turn of the century heralded a turning point in Sullivan's fortunes. He began to drink too much and grew estranged from former colleagues. The stream of commissions dwindled precipitously. By the time of his death in 1924 Sullivan was mired in poverty and all but forgotten by the arbiters of architectural taste.

Form Follows Function. At the height of his career Sullivan reveled in the role of architectural philosopher. His slogan, "form follows function," stood as credo for a generation of architects who believed that natural laws—rather than abstract principles of beauty—ought to govern architectural design. The title of Sullivan's autobiography, *The Autobiography of an Idea* (1924), suggests the degree to which Sullivan, the man, and functionalism, the idea, overlap. In his autobiography Sullivan recalled the magic of discovering the form-to-function correlation in nature:

> Invariably, the form expressed the function, as, for instance, the oak tree expressed the function oak, the pine tree the function pine, and so on. . . . it was not simply a matter of form expressing function, but the vital idea was this: That the function *created* or organized its form. Discernment of this idea threw a vast light upon all things within the universe, and condensed with astounding impressiveness upon mankind, upon all civilizations, all institutions, every form and aspect of society, every mass-thought and mass-result, every individual thought and individual result.

Blueprint for a Skyscraper. Despite the seemingly prescriptive nature of his "form follows function" slogan, Sullivan was no ascetic. He considered beauty a "functional" element of any building. To the dismay of minimalists Sullivan regularly incorporated ornament in his architectural plans. His approach to skyscraper design best represents his essential philosophy. In an essay titled "The Tall Office Building Artistically Considered" (1896) Sullivan defined a skyscraper's function as lofti-

ness: a concept suffused with aesthetic potential. "It must be tall, every inch of it tall," he wrote. "The force and power of altitude must be in it, the glory and pride of exaltation must be in it." The problem of the skyscraper went beyond the utilitarian—how to fit the maximum number of stories on the minimal amount of land—and became a question of how to embody "loftiness" in design. As Sullivan saw it, the tall office building contained several functional components: a basement level; a ground floor with a grand entrance designed to lure the public into the building; a mezzanine level overlooking the banking or retail space below; an "indefinite number" of identical stories, each housing office space; and, an "attic" for storage and mechanical equipment. The trick was to mold these parts into a pleasing whole: "a proud and soaring thing, rising in sheer exultation that from bottom to top it is a unit without a single dissenting line."

Accomplishments. Sullivan centered his practice in Chicago—where his buildings include two that anticipate his successful skyscraper design: the Troescher Building (1884), with horizontal I-beams and resting directly on masonry piers, and the Walker Warehouse (1889), with vertical piers that are clearly defined as structural supports. He also imported his philosophy to cities across the nation. In Saint Louis he built the Wainwright Building (1890), a steel-framed structure commonly acknowledged as the first American skyscraper. In Buffalo he erected the Guaranty Building (1894–1895), a handsome structure faced in red terracotta. And in Manhattan he added the graceful Bayard Building (1897), his own favorite among all his tall buildings. Prior to the 1890s the concept of the urban "skyline" did not exist. Sullivan's lofty creations gave the modern American city its characteristic shape and character, form and function. "The skyscraper, in the dusk," wrote this architectural visionary, "is a shimmering verticality, a gossamer veil, a festive scene-drop hanging there against the black sky to dazzle, entertain, and amaze."

Sources:

William H. Jordy, *American Buildings and Their Architects: Progressive and Academic Ideals at the Turn of the Twentieth Century* (Garden City, N.Y.: Anchor/Doubleday, 1976);

Robert Twombly, *Louis Sullivan: His Life and Work* (New York: Viking, 1986).

PUBLICATIONS

William Malone Baskervill, *Southern Writers: Biographical and Critical Studies,* 2 volumes (Nashville, Tenn.: Publishing House of the M.E. Church, South, 1897, 1903)—an important book on the southern literary awakening of the 1850s, which contributed to a critical reassessment of southern writing;

John Bernard, *Retrospections of America, 1797–1811* (New York: Harper, 1887)—a British comedian's impressions of the American stage;

J. W. Buel, *The Magic City* (Saint Louis: Historical Publishing, 1894)—a portfolio of photographic views of the World's Columbian Exposition;

Mrs. J. T. Fields, *Life and Letters of Harriet Beecher Stowe* (Boston: Houghton, Mifflin, 1897)—a biography published just one year after the death of the author of *Uncle Tom's Cabin* (1852); written by Annie Adams Fields, widow of Stowe's sometime publisher James T. Fields;

Hamlin Garland, *Crumbling Idols: Twelve Essays Dealing Chiefly with Literature, Painting, and the Drama* (Chicago & Cambridge, Mass.: Stone & Kimball, 1894)—an attack on the conservative, eastern tradition in the arts by one of the midwestern, realist writers who became popular in the 1880s and 1890s;

Edwina Booth Grossman, *Edwin Booth: Recollections by His Daughter and Letters to Her and to His Friends* (New York: Century, 1894)—a collection of correspondence compiled by the daughter of the great tragic actor;

Sadakichi Hartmann, *Conversations with Walt Whitman* (New York: E. P. Coby, 1895)—memoirs of visits to Whitman made during 1884—1891 by a naturalized American poet and art critic, the son of a German father and Japanese mother;

Julian Hawthorne, *Nathaniel Hawthorne and His Wife,* 2 volumes (Boston: Houghton, Mifflin, 1884)—a biography of Hawthorne by his son, himself a prominent author and journalist;

William Dean Howells, *Criticism and Fiction* (New York: Harper, 1891)—a collection of essays by a prominent author and influential editor who champions realism in fiction and suggests that because in America there are "so few shadows and inequalities in our broader level of prosperity," American novelists "concern themselves with the more smiling aspects of life, which are the more American, and seek the universal in the individual rather than the social interests";

Howells, *My Literary Passions* (New York: Harper, 1895)—a literary memoir by the "Dean of American Realism";

Henry James, *The Art of Fiction* (Boston: Cupples, Upham, 1884)—published with an essay by British novelist Walter Besant, James's essay, which has been recognized as a major manifesto for realism, takes issue with Besant's claim that a novel should always have "a conscious moral purpose" and argues that the province of any artist should be "all feeling, all life, all observation" and that the novelist should "Try to be one of the people on whom nothing is lost";

James, *Hawthorne* (New York: Harper, 1879)—a biography of the author of *The Scarlet Letter* (1850), which serves as tribute to James's literary forebear as well as a forum for a Jamesian critique of nineteenth-century American society;

Noah Ludlow, *Dramatic Life as I Found It* (Saint Louis: G. I. Jones, 1880)—a memoir by a Shakespearean actor with descriptions of American drama in the West and the South;

Max Maretzek, *Sharps and Flats* (New York: American Musician Publishing, 1890)—a memoir by a nineteenth-century musical impresario;

Frederic E. McKay and Charles E. L. Wingate, eds., *Famous American Actors of To-Day* (New York: Crowell, 1896)—a directory of leading nineteenth-century thespians;

Harriet Monroe, *John Wellborn Root: A Study of His Life and Work* (Boston & New York: Houghton, Mifflin, 1896)—a biography of an influential Chicago architect by his sister-in-law, who later founded *Poetry: A Magazine of Verse* (1912–   );

George Santayana, *The Sense of Beauty* (New York: Scribners, 1896)—a groundbreaking study of aesthetics and the first philosophical treatise by a Spanish-born, American-educated philosopher-poet;

Montgomery Schuyler, *American Architecture* (New York: Harper, 1892)—studies of the Brooklyn Bridge, Gilded Age mansions, and the Chicago School by an outspoken architectural critic;

Horace E. Scudder, *Men and Letters* (Boston & New York: Houghton, Mifflin, 1887)—essays by the influential literary editor at Houghton, Mifflin, who went on to edit *The Atlantic Monthly* in 1890–1898;

Edmund Clarence Stedman, *Poets of America* (Boston & New York: Houghton, Mifflin, 1885)—an introduction to American verse by an influential New York-based poet and literary critic;

Stedman and Ellen M. Hutchinson, eds., *A Library of American Literature from the Earliest Settlement to the Present Time,* 11 volumes (New York: Charles L. Webster, 1888–1890)—an important collection that influenced the formation of the American literary canon for several generations;

Moses Coit Tyler, *A History of American Literature, 1607–1765,* 2 volumes (New York: Putnam, 1878)—a definitive survey of early American literature;

Mrs. Schuyler (Mariana Griswold) Van Rensselaer, *Henry Hobson Richardson and His Works* (Boston & New York: Houghton, Mifflin, 1888)—a tribute to the recently deceased architect, illustrated with architectural plans;

Barrett Wendell, *Cotton Mather: The Puritan Priest* (New York: Dodd, Mead, 1891)—the first major work by a longtime Harvard professor, this biography of a well-known Puritan writer helped to establish the legitimacy of American literature within the academy.

A nineteenth-century photograph of the Rookery in Central Park, Manhattan, designed by Frederick Law
Olmstead and Calvert Vaux

BUSINESS AND THE ECONOMY

by FREDERICK DALZELL

CONTENTS

Sidebars and tables are listed in italics.

1878

- Fifteen members of the Greenback Labor Party are elected to Congress. The party supports a stable federal currency and more silver coins, along with such popular labor positions as restricting Chinese immigration and legislating shorter working days.

- Frederick W. Taylor begins working for Midvale Steel Company in Philadelphia. By 1881 Taylor is conducting detailed time studies of work at the plant; two years later, Taylor has risen to chief engineer at the company.

- John "Bet-A-Million" Gates, who has already lost a fortune speculating in grain in Chicago, launches a barbed-wire business that will grow to become the American Steel & Wire Company in 1899.

28 Jan. The nation's first commercial telephone exchange begins operations in New Haven, Connecticut. It provides eight lines and serves twenty-one telephones.

1879

- Treasury Secretary John Sherman begins resumption of specie payments for greenbacks, under terms of legislation passed in 1875.

- Massachusetts adopts a ten-hour working day.

- The first American cash register is invented by James Rilty, a saloon keeper in Ohio, in an effort to reduce employee theft.

- The California Constitution bans the employment of Chinese workers.

- Cyrus McCormick, a farm-machinery manufacturer based in Chicago, incorporates his business as McCormick Harvesting Machine Company a company that pioneers new techniques including centralized management, franchised dealers, and distribution via a regional network of sales offices.

21 June Frank W. Woolworth opens the Great Five Cent Store in Utica, New York. Moving to Lancaster, Pennsylvania, several months later, he expands his line to include ten-cent offerings. By 1900 he is operating fifty-nine stores, with sales greater than $5 million, making his company the world's largest retailing business.

July The Tidewater Pipeline Company completes construction of an oil pipeline running from oil fields in Bradford to Williamsport, Pennsylvania, approximately one hundred miles.

18 July The Cincinnati soap and candle works owned by the Procter family develops a new soap, which it names "Ivory" (inspired by a verse from Psalms).

1880

- John Wanamaker's Philadelphia department store, the Grand Depot, hires a full-time advertising copywriter — a first in the United States.

Apr. George Pullman begins building a model industrial town outside of Chicago for the workers of his Pullman Palace Car Company.

1881

- Joseph Wharton, a merchant, donates $100,000 to the University of Pennsylvania to form the nation's first permanent school of business at the college level.

- Gustavus F. Swift, a Chicago meatpacker, hires Andrew J. Chase to design a refrigerated railroad car to carry his dressed beef to eastern cities. Other major meatpackers follow suit, including Philip D. Armour of Chicago and George H. Hammond of Detroit.

- William Filene starts a women's clothing store in Boston. In the next several decades, the store introduces bargain basement sales, as well as the progressive Cooperative Management Association.

- James Buchanan Duke shifts his manufacturing operations from chewing tobacco to cigarettes. Pressed by competitors, Duke automates production and advertises aggressively on a national scale.

- Ohio C. Barber, owner of the Barber Match Company, combines with three competitors to create the Diamond Match Company. The new company produces matches at a rate of two million a day and controls 85 percent of the national market.

- More than one hundred delegates from national unions meet in Pittsburgh to form the Federation of Organized Trades and Labor Unions, predecessor to the American Federation of Labor.

3 Mar. Congress authorizes a new federal agency to register trademarks.

1882

- Immigration to the United States reaches 789,000, the highest annual figure in the nineteenth century.

- Quaker Mill, owned by Henry P. Crowell in Ravenna, Ohio, develops the first continuous milling process.

- Dow, Jones & Company, a financial news service, is established, and within two years the firm is generating indexes for stock price averages.

2 Jan. John D. Rockefeller establishes the Standard Oil Trust as a means of bringing the forty separate enterprises that collectively comprise Standard Oil Company under more effective central control.

6 May Congress passes the Chinese Exclusion Act, banning the immigration of Chinese for ten years.

1883

- The state of New York passes legislation prohibiting the manufacture of cigars in tenement houses — one of the first governmental efforts to abolish sweatshops in the cities. The state supreme court strikes down the act.

Sept. The Knights of Labor elect Terence V. Powderly as their "Grand Master Workman," marking a period of national expansion for the organization.

18 Nov. American and Canadian railroads adopt standard time zones, standardizing clock and watch settings across the continent for the first time.

1884

- The Antimonopoly Party forms and advocates a graduated income tax and the regulation of trusts and monopolies.

- For the first time, the United States outstrips England in steel production.

May   Striking shop men of the Union Pacific Railroad join the Knights of Labor, beginning the latter organization's rise in national prominence and membership.

27 June   Congress creates the Bureau of Labor within the Department of Interior.

1885

- Chemist Robert F. Lazenby invents a new soft drink, calling it Dr. Pepper.

26 Feb.   Congress enacts the Contract Labor Law, or Foran Act, forbidding American companies from signing up cheap foreign workers with the promise of paying their passage to the United States.

Mar.   Workers of the Missouri Pacific Railroad strike against a wage cut. The walkout spreads throughout the southwestern railroad network, forcing Jay Gould to meet the strikers' demands.

1886

- Southern railroad lines — the last major set of railways to make the conversion — shift their tracks to the "standard" railroad gauge of 4 feet, 8 ½ inches.

- New York becomes the first state to set up a permanent agency to mediate labor disputes.

- In Atlanta, pharmacist John S. Pemberton devises a new medicinal drink that his bookkeeper Frank Robinson dubs Coca-Cola.

Mar.   Knights of Labor workers again strike against Jay Gould's Missouri Pacific Railroad. This time Gould resists, and by early May the strike collapses.

4 May   Strikers and political activists gather in Haymarket Square, Chicago, to protest the killing of a striker the day before by the police. At the gathering, a bomb is thrown, and the police respond by firing into the crowd. In an ensuing trial that attracts national headline attention, eight anarchist leaders are convicted of inciting the violence.

10 May   In *Santa Clara County Company* v. *Southern Pacific Railroad Company*, the U.S. Supreme Court rules that corporations enjoy the same rights under the Fourteenth Amendment as do natural persons. This ruling gives businesses more protection from state legislatures.

29 June   Congress approves the incorporation of trade unions.

25 Oct.   In *Wabash, St. Louis & Pacific Railway Company* v. *Illinois* the U.S. Supreme Court rules that states cannot regulate railroad rates for interstate traffic.

8 Dec.   The American Federation of Labor is established in Columbus, Ohio. It comprises twenty-five labor groups representing 150,000 members.

1887

- Richard W. Sears and Alvah C. Roebuck join forces to sell watches by mail.

4 Feb.	Congress passes the first Interstate Commerce Act to regulate big business. The law creates a five-member commission charged with supervising railroad freight rates to ensure that they are "reasonable and just."
2 Mar.	Congress enacts the Hatch Act, a law establishing an agricultural research and experiment station in each state with a land-grant college. By the end of the following year, forty-three stations are created.

1888

- Sears, Roebuck Company publishes its first mail-order catalogue.

- Quaker Mill joins with several competitors to form the American Cereal Company.

- Dow, Jones and Company begins publishing *The Wall Street Journal.*

- The Industrial Reform Party, Union Labor Party, and United Labor Party all nominate candidates for national offices.

Apr.	George Eastman of Rochester, New York, patents the Kodak, a small, standardized hand camera that is easy to produce and operate.
13 June	Congress creates the Department of Labor.

1889

- Steel magnate Andrew Carnegie publishes *Gospel of Wealth.*

- Isaac Merrit Singer begins selling electric sewing machines.

- George Eastman invents a celluloid-based roll film of high quality.

2 Mar.	Kansas passes an antitrust law, the first of its kind. Maine, Minnesota, and Tennessee follow suit in a few months.

1890

- For the first time in the national census, the value of the nation's manufacturing output equals that of its agricultural production. The United States is the top producer in the world of iron and steel, making 9.3 million tons.

- Backed by financing from the Vanderbilt family and J. P. Morgan, Henry Villard forms the Edison General Electric Company. The company controls the licensing of Thomas A. Edison's patents.

- The Procter & Gamble Company is formed and stumbles on a manufacturing process that makes Ivory Soap float. Soon the company is selling two hundred thousand bars a day, advertising nationally, and selling via a network of branch sales offices.

- The American Federation of Labor establishes the United Mine Workers.

- Herbert H. Dow starts Midland Chemical Company in Michigan.

- American Express offers the first traveler's checks, signaling the growing popularity of traveling by the middle class.

	Jan.	James Buchanan Duke combines with four other cigarette manufacturers to form the American Tobacco Company. By the end of the decade this company controls 62 percent of the nation's chewing tobacco market and 93 percent of the cigarette market.
	2 July	Congress enacts the Sherman Anti-Trust Act, prohibiting "every contract, combination in the form of trust or otherwise, or conspiracy, in restraint of trade or commerce among the several States."
	8 Aug.	Congress passes the Original Package Act, upholding the right of an individual state to regulate goods produced out of state.

1891

- Pemberton Chemical Company sells its operations to Asa Candler.

- Henry O. Havemayer creates the American Sugar Refining Company. By the time of Havemayer's death in 1907, his company controls half the sugar consumed in the United States.

24 Aug.	Thomas A. Edison files a patent for a motion picture camera.
29 Dec.	Edison files a patent for a wireless telegraph machine.

1892

- The Supreme Court of Ohio dissolves Standard Oil Trust within the borders of the state.

- Asa Candler registers the Coca-Cola trademark with the U.S. Patent Office and remarkets the medicine as a soda fountain drink.

- John Froelich builds the first self-propelled gasoline-powered tractor.

- Andrew Carnegie reorganizes his operations in Pittsburgh as Carnegie Steel, which becomes the world's largest steelmaking business with a capitalization of $25 million. Carnegie himself holds 55 percent of the company's stock.

- J. P. Morgan and Henry Villard form the General Electric Company, combining the facilities of Thomson-Houston, which manufactured arc lamps, and Edison General Electric, which specialized in incandescent lighting.

1 July   Workers at Carnegie's Homestead Steel Works go on strike, setting off a bitter, four-month struggle in which twenty strikers are killed and hundreds are fired.

1893

- Eugene V. Debs organizes the American Railway Union.

- In *United States* v. *Workmen's Amalgamated Council,* the U.S. Supreme Court holds that the Sherman Anti-Trust Act applies to unions.

21 Apr.   Financial panic erupts when American gold reserves fall below $100 million, setting off a national depression that lasts for four years. Hundreds of railroad companies, steel mills, and other businesses go under.

1894

- Over the course of the year, some 750,000 workers go on strike.

20 Apr.   The United Mine Workers Association (UMW) coordinates a national coal strike — the largest of its kind. Mine owners respond by hiring nonunion labor and marshaling police and state militia, eventually breaking the strike.

30 Apr.   Jacob S. Coxey, leading approximately four hundred people protesting unemployment and advocating public relief, reaches Washington, D.C. When the leaders of "Coxey's Army" are arrested the following day for violating local laws prohibiting parading on the Capitol grounds, the protest falls apart.

11 May   Workers of the Pullman Palace Car Company near Chicago go on strike. Many of the strikers are affiliated with the American Railway Union and manage to block much of the nation's rail traffic for several weeks. Federal troops and state militia break the strike by mid July.

28 June   Congress declares Labor Day a national holiday.

1895

- The Vanderbilt family builds The Breakers, a palatial "summer cottage" in Newport, Rhode Island, that costs $4 million.

- Businessmen found the National Association of Manufacturers.

21 Jan.   In *United States* v. *E. C. Knight Company* the U.S. Supreme Court holds that the Sherman Anti-Trust Act covers only monopolies in restraint of trade, not manufacturing.

27 May   In litigation stemming from the Pullman Strike, the U.S. Supreme Court sustains the use of court injunctions against strikers, including Eugene V. Debs.

1896

4 June   Henry Ford builds his first car, the Quadracycle.

8 July   William Jennings Bryan delivers his "Cross of Gold" speech to the Democratic National Convention, advocating free coinage of silver.

1897

- Seventy-five thousand UMW coal miners in Ohio, West Virginia, and Pennsylvania strike successfully for an eight-hour day, semimonthly pay, and the elimination of company stores.

- Midland Chemical Company becomes Dow Chemical Company, which develops and patents more than one hundred chemical processes.

- L. Frank Baum (writer of the Oz series of children's stories) publishes the first issue of *The Shop Window,* a "monthly journal of decorative art" on the design of department-store window displays.

1898

- The University of Chicago establishes a school of business, supported by John D. Rockefeller, to train professional business managers.

- L. Frank Baum founds the National Association of Window Trimmers.

7 Mar. In *Smyth* v. *Ames* the U.S. Supreme Court rules that railroads are entitled to "reasonable" returns on "the fair value of the property being used," a decision that invalidates a Nebraska statute setting rates for freight hauling.

1899

- The United Fruit Company is formed out of the Boston Fruit Company and several smaller entities. It amasses a fleet of refrigerated steamships, railroad facilities, and huge plantations in the Caribbean. By 1914 it has $73 million worth of investments in Central America.

- Thorstein Veblen publishes *The Theory of the Leisure Class,* an attack on the "conspicuous consumption" of the nation's business elite.

31 July Henry Ford incorporates the Detroit Automobile Company.

4 Dec. In *Addyston Pipe & Steel Company* v. *United States* the U.S. Supreme Court rules that negotiations between corporations to eliminate competition violate the Sherman Anti-Trust Act.

OVERVIEW

Change. The span between 1878 and 1899 represented a pivotal period for American businesses and the national economy. Over these two dozen years, millions of Americans found themselves caught up in massive, fundamental transformations. The process of industrialization, which had begun decades earlier, reached a dizzying pace as the century came to a close. As industrialization quickened, new kinds of businesses took hold in the economy—businesses that mass-produced and mass-distributed consumer goods on a scope unimagined by earlier entrepreneurs. This overhaul happened with astonishing speed, within the space of a single generation. It also propelled basic change in daily life: by the beginning of the twentieth century, new workplaces, stores, and products were changing how most Americans made their living, how they were paid, and where and what they bought with their earnings. In addition, overseas markets became more important in the 1890s, as did foreign (especially British) investments in American businesses.

Infrastructure. A key underlying condition for the growth of big business was the completion of a national rail network. Before 1878 railroads had begun to knit the Midwest and the Northeast together, and extended tentatively into other regions. Track construction accelerated from 1878 to 1890, spreading the possibility of reliable, speedy, and relatively inexpensive travel across the continent. Approximately 80,000 miles of railroad track had been laid by 1877; that figure more than doubled during the next dozen years to 163,596 miles of track in 1890. Rail transportation networks were still strongest in the Northeast and Midwest, but important trunk lines and capillary systems had been started in the South and to the West. Bridges spanned the major rivers, and all of the nation's major urban terminals were hooked into the network.

Railroads and the Growth of Business. The spread of a national rail network had important and far-reaching implications. Railroad growth directly spurred certain industries. The steel industry, for example, grew alongside the railroads: between 1881 and 1890 railroad owners purchased nearly fifteen million tons of rails, making them by far the steel mills' most important customers. In addition the railroads consumed billions of tons of iron, coal, lumber, and other materials. The railroads were also important as businesses in and of themselves; throughout the period they made up the country's biggest enterprise (either public or private). The largest lines maintained workforces that far outstripped any other private employer; in 1891 the Pennsylvania Railroad alone employed more than 110,000 workers. All told, the industry employed some 750,000 workers. The completion of a national network made it possible for businesses to ship goods much more efficiently, cheaply, and reliably within the country. Before the railroad, shippers depended on expensive, slow wagon travel over roads that became impassible in muddy and snowy periods or on barge and steamboat travel along rivers and canals that froze in the winter. Trains traveled on schedule, in all seasons and almost any weather, and they were capable of transporting bulky or heavy goods with relative ease and low expense. Producers and consumers could now reach each other across vast distances, across broad regions of the country. In this sense, the advent of mass production and mass consumption hinged directly on railroad expansion.

Immigration. The continued influx of immigrants also fed into economic transformation. The new arrivals swelled cities and provided labor and markets for businesses. However, the character of American immigration changed over the last decade of the 1800s. For example, immigrants before 1890 tended to come from northern and western Europe, from Germany and Ireland. In the 1890s newcomers began arriving in substantial numbers from southern and eastern Europe, Italy, Poland, and Russia. About half of the 3.7 million immigrants reaching the United States over this decade came from southeastern Europe. Most of these new arrivals made their way to industrial centers, factories, mining camps, and cities where they found economic opportunities in the burgeoning industrial expansion of the period. In 1900 about two-thirds of the "new immigrants" had located to the nation's largest cities, often crowded into slums and tenements, struggling at low-wage jobs to make new lives for themselves.

Urbanization. The last decades of the nineteenth century also witnessed an acceleration in the pace of urban growth. The majority of Americans continued to live in rural communities into the early twentieth century; however, not for much longer. By 1900 four out of every ten Americans lived in urban communities, and the nation's three largest cities each held populations of more than a million. Urban growth accompanied industrialization, and the largest cities clustered where industry grew most rapidly—in the Northeast and Midwest. Chicago became a metropolis, growing from 500,000 in 1880 to 1.7 million in 1900; Minneapolis (where much of the nation's flour-milling industry concentrated) grew from 47,000 to 203,000 over the same period; Buffalo climbed from 155,000 to 352,000. Smaller cities in every region also burgeoned. The steel town of Birmingham, Alabama, mushroomed from 3,000 to 26,000 over the 1870s and 1880s; Kansas City swelled from 3,200 to 38,000 over the same period; and Denver increased from 4,700 to 107,000. The urbanization of much of the nation's population grew out of, and in turn fed into, an equally far-reaching economic transformation. As social critic Henry J. Fletcher (who deplored the trend) observed in 1895 of Chicago, the metropolis "has swallowed the factories and workshops and work people of villages and minor cities within a radius of many hundred miles. Multitudes flock to the cities because the drift is that way." Industrial plants needed, and created, concentrations of workers in ever greater numbers. Meanwhile, as people congregated in urban communities and wage-earning jobs, they provided important mass markets for the new industrial economy.

The Ascendancy of Manufacturing. At its base, the new economy rested on industrial manufacturing. By 1899, 4.7 million wage earners were making their living in the nation's factories, producing goods with a total value of $11.4 billion. Industrialization, like urbanization, was most pronounced in the Northeast and Midwest, where factories produced more than 85 percent of the nation's total manufactured output. However, manufacturing established itself in several southern and western areas as well. Various specific industries drove this transformation, but to this generation of Americans steel represented the arrival of the United States as one of the world's leading industrial powers. In 1878 the nation's steel mills produced 820,000 short tons of raw steel and 2.1 million short tons of hot rolled iron and steel. (By the U.S. system of weights, a ton, or long ton, is 2,240 pounds; a short ton, which came into use in 1881, is 2,000 pounds.) By 1895 America had outstripped Britain to become the world's leading steel producer. Four years later production had climbed to nearly 12 million short tons of raw steel and 11.5 million short tons of hot rolled iron and steel. The number of workers in the steel industry, meanwhile, climbed from 130,000 in 1880 to 222,000 in 1900.

The Scale of Doing Business. Until 1880 the largest American factories employed several hundred people—enterprises that were typically capitalized at less than $1 million. (Capitalization is the amount of funding contributed to a business by the owner or stockholders.) Across the economic landscape, only the railroads were larger, with workforces in the thousands and capitalizations in the tens of millions of dollars. The new businesses that grew out of the late-nineteenth century landscape dwarfed their predecessors in scale. By 1890 Andrew Carnegie's steel plant at Homestead alone employed thousands of workers, while the largest railroad companies maintained workforces of more than one hundred thousand. The emergence of big business was closely connected to the establishment of new mechanisms of capital-building and investing and a domestic financial market that underwrote substantially more than the government and railroad securities had done previously. By 1900 John D. Rockefeller's Standard Oil Company of New Jersey was worth $300 million, and financial kingmakers like J. P. Morgan were overseeing unprecedented growth and consolidation in corporate, private investment markets.

Earning and Spending. Industrial growth distributed its benefits unevenly among Americans. According to a study conducted by the Illinois Bureau of Labor Statistics in 1883, coal miners in that state earned wages averaging $1.50 per day—when they were working, but employment was rarely steady. Meanwhile the miners reported varying costs for basic necessities. Rent on a two-room tenement for one miner's family (including a wife and five children) came to $6 per month, and the family's annual food bill (for bread, salt, meat, and coffee) cost $80. However, this family managed to grow some of its food; another miner estimated his family's food bill (for more elaborate fare, including steak, butter, and potatoes) at $90 per year. Workers in other industries had similar statistics. A railroad brakeman, for example, reported earning $360 per year; he, his wife, and eight children lived in a three-room house they rented for $5 per month, and subsisted on meals consisting chiefly of bread, syrup, and potatoes. Children, many of whom worked to help support their families, earned less: as a bobbin boy in a Pennsylvania textile mill in 1848, young Andrew Carnegie earned $1.20 per week. Meanwhile, participating in the new possibilities of mass consumption cost money that seems modest today but dug deeply into the wages of the working classes. The 1897 Sears, Roebuck Catalogue offered an ACME gasoline stove for $8.63; a man's suit ("Brown Twilled Melton Suit") for $4.85; a parlor organ for between $38.95 and $56 (a piano was more expensive at $125); a buggy for between $32.98 and $65; and a Colt revolver for between $10 and $12.

Working Hours and Conditions. Working hours and weeks were longer in the late nineteenth century than today. Most industrial workers and miners worked six days a week for between ten and twelve hours a day, and sometimes more. In fact, the implementation of ten- or eight-hour workdays became a major goal of labor, many times provoking bitter confrontations with employers. Meanwhile working conditions in jobs such as coal mining, meatpacking, and various other industries remained largely unregulated and frequently grueling and dangerous. No federal agencies or laws regulated workplaces, and effective state regulation varied, for the most part, from minimal to nonexistent.

Responses to the New Economy. Industrialization, mass production and distribution, and urbanization were revolutionary economic transformations. They represented radical innovations in American life, and Americans adjusted to them uneasily, often painfully. Many Americans became deeply disturbed by the growth of big business; the emergence of national-scale monopolies in a string of industries; the ostentatious wealth of robber barons; the escalating violence between laborers and factory owners; and the growing radicalism of workers as they organized into unions and political parties.

The Spread of the New Economy. The economic and social changes that marked this period traveled beyond the factory and the city. Ultimately, they reached out into the homes of virtually every American. In 1800, when most Americans lived on farms, their material and economic lives tended to focus on local, personal relationships. They usually did business on a small scale and dealt most often with local artisans, storekeepers, and merchants personally. Some money exchanged hands, but buying and selling just as often took place as face-to-face transactions involving credit or bartering goods and services within the locus of the town or county in which people resided. By 1900 this world was disappearing in all but the poorest and most remote sections of the country. The transformation, as dramatic as it was, occurred gradually: it was already under way before 1878, and it was not yet complete in 1899. However, it was a revolutionary change, and it hit much of mainstream America in the 1880s and 1890s.

TOPICS IN THE NEWS

AGRICULTURAL ECONOMY

Agriculture in an Industrial Economy. As the new industrial economy burgeoned, agricultural production also underwent profound changes. American farm output did not decline in the face of industrial growth; in fact, it grew at impressive rates over the last decades of the nineteenth century. New farmlands in the Dakotas, Nebraska, Kansas, and Colorado were linked by railroads and brought under cultivation. At the same time, farmers experienced fundamental, often unsettling, changes as they adapted to new conditions. By the late 1800s farm production was influenced by more impersonal market forces than ever before. Farmers depended heavily on banks for finance, railroads for shipping, and grain elevator operators for selling their crops. As a result, many farmers went into debt in the years after the Civil War. Whenever farm prices dropped, the financial pressures on farmers mounted steadily.

Wheat. Changes in the way wheat was shipped, stored, and sold typified the more general transformation in agriculture. Over the last decades of the nineteenth century two wheat processing centers emerged at the heart of a national network of distribution. In Minneapolis, Minnesota, a vast flour-milling industry developed and supplied new companies such as Pillsbury-Washburn. In Chicago, at the railroad hub that linked the farms of the West and Midwest to national markets, tens of thousands of carloads of wheat funneled through annually, each car carrying more than three hundred bushels. In 1890 alone, 150 million bushels of wheat moved through Chicago. To handle this volume, railroad companies and grain investors built huge grain elevators holding as many as five million bushels apiece; by 1888 Chicago grain elevators held thirty million bushels. Grain was divided and stored in the elevators by grade, the owner or agent receiving a receipt for this grain drawable from the elevators. These receipts were bought and sold, fueling a heated market in what were called grain futures. Other businessmen in the industry—millers, dealers, and exporters—relied on investments in grain futures to hedge against fluctuations in price and supply.

Meat. The production of meat underwent a parallel process of centralization. In 1881 the Chicago meatpacker East, Swift & Company made its first shipment of butchered meat in refrigerated railroad cars to the East Coast. In the process, the company redrew the map of meat production. Once the viability of

The changes that overtook agriculture over the last dozen or so years of the century were nearly as dramatic as those transforming industry. Farming still made up a substantial part of the economy, but one declining in relative importance. In 1870 just over half of the American workforce, 53 percent, made their living on farms. By 1890 the proportion had dropped to 42 percent. Still, agricultural production expanded, and the number of farms grew, from 4 million in 1877 to 4.5 million in 1890. At the same time, the farms mechanized; during this same period, the total value of American farm machinery climbed from $42 million to over $100 million. By 1890 more than nine hundred American companies were manufacturing agricultural machinery, producing more than $92 million worth of machines annually, including plows, harvesters, threshers, twine binders, dairy centrifuges, sprayers, pumps, and other implements. Mechanization affected all kinds of farms, but took root especially strongly in the upper Mississippi basin, on cereal farms in the northern plains. Here, over the late 1870s and 1880s new "bonanza" farms sprouted, spreading across thousands of acres each, marshaling heavy machinery and platoons of migratory workers — workforces of several hundred and more — to harvest their crops. These farms were not yet typical, but already they were signaling the direction American farming would take in the twentieth century.

Sources: John A. Garraty, *The New Commonwealth, 1877–1890* (New York: Harper & Row, 1968);

Fred A. Shannon, *The Farmer's Last Frontier: Agriculture, 1860–1897* (New York: Holt, Rinehart & Winston, 1945).

long-distance transportation had been demonstrated, meatpacking on a national, centrally controlled scale became possible. Other companies such as Oscar Meyer rapidly spread their operations to take advantage of the entrepreneurial possibilities, setting up processing plants, stockyards, feeding stations, and auction sites at key points in the country's new railroad network. Like the changes overhauling wheat farming, the revolution in meat production took farmers' markets out of local orbits and placed them in national as well as international hands.

Agrarian Protest. From the perspective of American farmers, these changes interposed a host of monopolistic middlemen between them and their markets. Railroads controlled shipments (without which crops or livestock were virtually worthless) and manipulated rates in ways that favored large shippers and penalized average farmers. Banks, mortgage associations, and other moneylenders demanded what farmers considered to be extortionate rates. Warehouse, elevator, and stockyard operators held broad leverage over how agricultural products were marketed and at what price. As a result, agrarian protest rose against eastern financial and business interests. This sentiment had been central in the organization of the Grange in 1867 and the farmers' alliances of the 1870s—efforts by farmers' collectives to control shipments, the marketing of crops, and the supply of seed and implements. These efforts continued in the 1880s as farm prices slowly declined. Farmers in the West, meanwhile, pressured their state legislatures to establish railroad regulations and the federal government to ease monetary policies by issuing greenbacks or coining silver currency. The Depression of 1893 made the farmers' plight especially acute, bringing many to ruin. Only the recovery of farm prices after 1897 brought relief.

Sources:
William Cronon, *Nature's Metropolis: Chicago and the Great West* (New York & London: Norton, 1991);

Fred A. Shannon, *The Farmer's Last Frontier: Agriculture, 1860–1897* (New York: Farrar & Rinehart, 1945).

THE DEPARTMENT STORE

Origins. By the end of the nineteenth century, the American economy was changing not only in its workshops and factories, but in the marketplace as well. Changes in how goods were distributed accompanied changes in how they were manufactured. The most visible and dramatic of these changes was the spread of department stores—sprawling retailing establishments that centralized much of the nation's retailing. They had already taken root in the largest cities by 1880: Lord and Taylor (1826), Macy's (1842), and Gimbel's (1842) in New York; Jordan Marsh in Boston (1841); Carson, Pirie, Scott (1854) and Marshall Field (1865) in Chicago; and Wanamaker's in Philadelphia (1861). These establishments offered urban customers wide assortments of goods and obtained their stocks via buyers who set up direct relationships between manufacturers and the stores. Meanwhile, beyond metropolitan boundaries, most Americans bought goods from small, local stores that sold limited selections of dry goods—stores supplied by larger wholesalers based in nearby cities. After 1880, as towns became small cities and cities became vast metropolises, department store retailing spread outward into the countryside.

Expanding Stocks. The mainstay of business for these stores was made up by clothing, dry goods, and household goods. As they grew they added new departments and took on what became a dazzling array of stock: men's and children's clothing, furs, carpets and rugs, upholstered goods, furniture, silverware, parasols and umbrellas, jewelry, hats, shoes, toys, books and stationery, china, glassware, crockery, flowers and feathers—whatever might sell. By selling at low prices and maintaining low profit margins, the stores (when

In the 1880s a movement arose that called for industrialization and outside investment in the South. The individual who became the most prominent spokesman of this movement was Henry W. Grady. The managing editor of the *Atlanta Constitution* between 1880 and 1889, Grady first gained national attention for his coverage of the August 1886 earthquake in Charleston, South Carolina. In December of the same year he was the main speaker at the New England Society of New York. The occasion was the society's annual dinner to commemorate the landing of the Pilgrims at Plymouth Rock. Grady's topic was "The New South," and his eloquent words became the most celebrated statement of the New South Creed. According to Grady, "The old South rested everything on slavery and agriculture, unconscious that these could neither give nor maintain healthy growth. The new South presents a perfect Democracy, the oligarchs leading in the popular movement — a social system compact and closely knitted, less splendid on the surface, but stronger at the core — a hundred farms for every plantation, fifty homes for every palace — and a diversified industry that meets the complex needs of this complex age."

Source: George Brown Tindall, *America: A Narrative History* (New York & London: Norton, 1984).

successful) kept a high volume of sales and a high turnover flow of business: profits were made by volume, rather than markup.

New Ways of Selling. Like the railroads and the largest manufacturing firms, department stores, too, expanded the scale of doing business, forming chains across the landscape, and they concentrated distribution by cutting out the mercantile middlemen—the wholesale "jobbers"—that had pinned together the earlier network of selling via local stores. More fundamentally, they promoted new habits of buying. Although they sold bolts of cloth, the new department stores offered ready-made clothing, factory-made, at prices and in assortments previously unknown. Unlike the country stores they replaced, the new retailers dealt in cash rather than trade or credit. Prices were no longer negotiated between storekeeper and customer; they were standardized and printed on tags on merchandise (a practice that made sense, given that these new stores, unlike their country cousins, deployed hundreds of salesclerks at a time). Most of the stores instituted money-back guarantees to dissatisfied customers. They also advertised more aggressively and enticingly, luring customers with handbills, printed cards, and newspaper and print ads that grandly extolled the virtues of stores' wares. Taken together, these developments helped to transform the consumer economy into a recognizably modern marketplace.

Montgomery Ward. A few pioneering businesses began retailing their goods through mail-order catalogues in the 1860s and 1870s, and the innovation caught on quickly. By 1874 Chicago retailer Montgomery Ward's catalogues had grown from one-page price lists to booklets seventy-two pages long that included woodcut illustrations. Business boomed, and Ward's catalogues grew accordingly; by the end of the decade they were more than five hundred pages long, offered more than twenty-four thousand different products, attracted some 750,000 letters from customers, and required three hundred clerks to manage. The 1896 edition featured the first live model—a little girl displaying a bonnet, apron, and dress. By 1900 the Ward catalogue weighed in at more than one thousand pages and generated between fifteen thousand and thirty-five thousand orders daily. Sewing machines, musical instruments, guns, farm equipment, bicycles, batteries, kitchen appliances, and ready-made clothing flowed out from the company into the countryside via this vehicle. Riding the profits of this wave of selling, Montgomery Ward in 1898 moved its operations to new quarters in Chicago covering an entire city block, surmounted by a tower twenty stories high, overseeing the flow of its goods.

Shop Windows. Along with long-distance mail-order outreach, the new department stores expanded their business by luring customers into the stores themselves using increasingly lavish window displays. It was between 1880 and 1900 that window trimming became a science and an art. Previously, merchants had paid little attention to their windows, perhaps piling up an ad hoc assortment of goods for sale, perhaps showing nothing at all. People such as writer and salesman L. Frank Baum ushered in a new style of in-store merchandising. As a young man on the rise Baum grew up the son of an industrialist and banker; as a young man he traveled as a salesman and thespian, writing, producing, and performing in theatrical tours through the Midwest. After trying to set up a store in Aberdeen, South Dakota, and going bust in 1891, he relocated to Chicago, where he vigorously promoted the power of shopwindows, as he put it, to "arouse in the observer the cupidity and longing to possess the goods." He founded a journal, *The Shop Window,* in 1897 and established the National Association of Window Trimmers the following year. With characteristic flair for theatrical flourish (and racial sentiments typical of his day), Baum urged shopkeepers to "Suggest the possibilities of color and sumptuous display that would delight the heart of an oriental." Baum's later career as a children's writer (he made a fortune and wider fame as author of *The Wizard of Oz*

The first Woolworth's store, which opened on 21 June 1879 in Lancaster, Pennsylvania

[1900] and various sequels) in many respects echoed his earlier one; he and those who followed his lead transformed downtown city streets into visions of artfully arrayed merchandise—a series of windows each (as Baum praised one display) a "peep into Elysium."

The Five-and-Ten Store. The new department stores grew as large as they did ultimately because they managed to sell not just luxury goods to the upper classes, but mass-produced goods to the masses. No business embodied this success better than Frank W. Woolworth's chain of five-and-ten stores. As a clerk at Moore & Smith's corner store in Watertown, New York, Woolworth in 1878 set up a "5-cent counter" offering what were then known as "Yankee Notions"—tin pans, washbasins, button hooks, dippers, and other small items that a collapsing wholesaler had unloaded cheaply. As Woolworth later recalled, "Like magic, the goods faded away." His initial effort to capitalize on this discovery—his first "Great 5-cent Store" in Utica—failed, but undeterred, Woolworth pulled up and moved to Lancaster, Pennsylvania, after a few months, adding a line of ten-cent offerings, and business thrived. Woolworth found he could buy goods cheaply if he bought in large lots, selling more cheaply than competitors and, over time, monopolizing the output of leading manufacturers. Among his early offerings were Christmas tree ornaments, novelties that the entrepreneur discovered while touring in Europe. By these methods he expanded rapidly into small cities: by the time he combined his chain with several others in 1911, he had established 319 Woolworth five-and-dimes across the nation and throughout the world (in England they were called "three and sixes").

The First Grocery Chains. The same period also witnessed the spread of grocery chains. One of the first, the Great Atlantic and Pacific Tea Company (founded in New York City by G. F. Gilman and G. Huntington Hartford, and later called A & P), already operated twenty-six stores by the time it added a grocery line to its tea business in 1865; by 1880 it ran more than one hundred stores. Competitors proliferated alongside: Grand Union in the 1870s, Kroger in the 1880s, and Jewel Tea in the 1890s. These stores were not yet the supermarkets they would become. They did not yet sell meat or produce; butchers and fruit and vegetable stands, respectively, sold these goods. In addition customers were still served by clerks who got the food off the shelves (Piggly-Wiggly would introduce self-service in 1916.) Still, the new grocery chains laid the foundation for the later supermarket chains, following other retailers as they spread out along regional and national transportation networks into the countryside.

Sears, Roebuck. What would become the most sprawling of the new emporiums—the largest retailer in the country, in fact, and the epitome of the new trends in retailing—began in 1886 when a railroad freight agent named Richard W. Sears bought a shipment of five hundred watches from a Chicago watchmaker for twelve dollars apiece and sold them up and down the railroad line for fourteen dollars apiece (many of them to station agent salesmen who, in turn, hawked them to customers for twenty dollars apiece). Sears founded the R. W. Sears

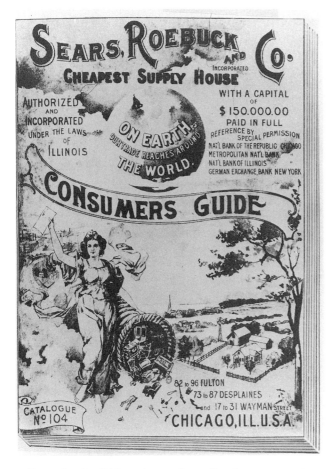

Cover for the 1894 catalogue of a mail-order company that revolutionized the way Americans shopped

Sources:

Robert Hendrickson, *The Grand Emporiums: The Illustrated History of America's Great Department Stores* (New York: Stein & Day, 1979);

William Leach, *Land of Desire: Merchants, Power, and the Rise of a New American Culture* (New York: Pantheon, 1993).

GOVERNMENT REGULATION OF BIG BUSINESS

The Challenge for Government. American journalist Henry Demarest Lloyd, writing in the *North American Review* in 1884, expressed a sentiment that was growing increasingly popular when he warned: "Society is letting these combinations [railroads] become institutions without compelling them to adjust their charges to the cost of production, which used to be the universal rule of price. Our laws and commissions to regulate the railroads are but toddling steps in a path in which we need to walk like men." Until the 1880s, individual states had taken care of business regulation. But as the scope of business grew national, the states lost control, and many began to look to the federal government to step into the economic arena. However, initial federal efforts were unsuccessful.

The *Wabash* Ruling. The first federal efforts focused on the railroads. Political support for effective regulation ran strong, because farmers and small-business people depended on railroads to transport their goods and felt helpless when shipping rates rose. By the late 1870s several states had tried to bring railroads under their regulation. Agricultural states had been especially aggressive, attempting to set rates in an effort to regulate the railroads' monopoly. However, the U.S. Supreme Court struck down these efforts in 1886 in *Wabash, St. Louis & Pacific Railway Company* v. *Illinois*, a ruling that prohibited the states from regulating commerce that either originated or ended beyond state lines. The *Wabash* decision raised the political stakes on the question of federal regulation of the railroads. Bills proposing federal regulation had already appeared before Congress; in 1883 Sen. Shelby M. Cullom from Illinois had introduced a bill setting up a federal commission that would establish guidelines governing the railroads. In the wake of the *Wabash* ruling, support for Cullom's proposal mounted rapidly and carried the bill through. In 1887 the Interstate Commerce Commission (ICC) was established—the federal government's first agency dedicated to the regulation of big business.

ICC. The ICC set a pattern that many later federal commissions would follow. The commission was made up of five members, appointed by the president and confirmed by the senate, serving for six-year terms. Thomas M. Cooley served as the first ICC chairman. The same act that established the ICC gave it a mandate by requiring that rates be "just and reasonable" and that railroads not favor some shippers over others. Nevertheless, after a promising beginning the ICC's effective regulatory power dwindled. A series of Supreme

Watch Company within a year and took on a partner named Alvah C. Roebuck shortly thereafter. Readily perceiving the possibilities of national marketing (he had, after all, worked for a railroad), Sears put together a small mail-order catalogue advertising his watches and, as he added to his line of goods, jewelry and diamonds. Sears, who wrote all the copy for his catalogue, pushed products with wide-open flamboyance and boosted sales by instituting installment payment plans and money-back guarantees. By September 1893 the business had taken form as Sears, Roebuck and Company, with a catalogue that had grown to 196 pages and sales of more than $400,000. Two years later, when the firm moved to Chicago, the catalogue's page count had climbed to 507 and its sales to $750,000: Sears was now proclaiming itself "The Cheapest Supply House on Earth." Like Montgomery Ward, Sears, Roebuck attracted the enmity of local rural merchants whose business it was swallowing; opponents dubbed the mail-order giant "Rears and Soreback" and "Shears and Rawbuck." Nevertheless the company continued to grow at a blistering pace: by 1899 it had expanded to twenty-four merchandising departments; the following year Sears, Roebuck surpassed Montgomery Ward with close to $11 million in sales.

STANDARD TIME

The new, railroad-driven economy brought many changes to everyday life, but perhaps the most fundamental one had to do with the very fabric of time. On Sunday, 13 November 1883, the nation went on "standard" time. Before this point, "noon" in any given locality had signified the moment when the sun stood highest in the sky, which meant that noon in Chicago was 11:50 A.M. in Saint Louis and 11:27 A.M. in Omaha. This arrangement suited the purposes of an earlier economy and society, when most business was conducted within local boundaries or on timetables that were necessarily flexible. However, railroads, which had to schedule complicated traffic along extended distances, needed a timekeeping system with fewer variations and clear precision. Thus the major railroad companies agreed to divide the country into four time zones and to set time within each to a standardized clock. In Chicago people moved their clocks back by nine minutes and thirty-three seconds to join Central Standard Time. It was a small adjustment, but one that powerfully demonstrated the extent to which the new economy was binding local communities more tightly together across vast distances. The change gradually took hold across the country, despite the fact that standard time was not written into law until the 1910s.

Source: William Cronon, *Nature's Metropolis: Chicago and the Great West* (New York: Norton, 1991).

terms as "monopolization" and "restraint of trade." As a result the federal government entered the twentieth century with only early, tentative instruments of business regulation.

Source:

Thomas K. McCraw, *Prophets of Regulation: Charles Francis Adams, Louis D. Brandeis, James M. Landis, Alfred E. Kahn* (Cambridge, Mass.: Harvard University Press, 1984).

THE HOMESTEAD STRIKE

The Seeds of Trouble. One of the most violent business-labor clashes of this turbulent period involved a company that typified the new industrial economy: Carnegie Steel, which by 1892 had risen to become the nation's largest steelmaker. Because of the prominence of its owner and because it was industries such as steel that were driving this new economy, the strike at Carnegie's Homestead steel plant in western Pennsylvania became an emblematic struggle of the age. Prior to the strike, Carnegie had publicly endorsed unionization and had settled earlier disputes with his workers on relatively generous terms. But the man he chose in 1889 to manage affairs at his Homestead mills, Henry C. Frick, was made of different stuff. As an operator of coal mines, Frick had established a reputation not only as a shrewd manager, but also as a tough union buster; in 1890 he had violently suppressed strikes at his coalfields. He came to Homestead, where twelve mills employed almost four thousand men, determined to dismantle the powerful leverage their union, the Amalgamated Association of Iron and Steel Workers, held over operations at the plant. Amalgamated was founded in 1876 and by 1891 had a membership of more than twenty-four thousand, making it the largest craft union in the nation at the time. However, it excluded unskilled workers and had failed to organize the larger steel plants. Homestead was the exception and, therefore, a test case for the union.

Preparations for Siege. Frick made his move in contract renewal negotiations in the spring of 1892, demanding wage reductions and announcing that the company would no longer bargain with Amalgamated. Meanwhile, Frick contracted with the Pinkerton Detective Agency for a force of armed guards. At the mills themselves, management dug in for a battle, ringing "Fort Frick," as the workers now named the plant, with watchtowers, gun slits, and a twelve-foot-high steel fence.

Battle. The strike began on 1 July 1892, after the union suspended work and Frick closed the mills and announced his plans to reopen using nonunion labor. Workers surrounded the plant with an armed picket line. Frick tried to bring in three hundred Pinkerton guards surreptitiously, on two barges and a towboat up the Monongahela River, but as the guards tried to disembark on 6 July, they confronted a mass of armed workers and their families. Gunfire broke out between the strikers

Court rulings restricted its authority, and by the late 1890s it could do little more than collect data.

Sherman Anti-Trust Act. In 1890, three years after the creation of the ICC, with public anxiety over the size and power of big business still running high, Congress took a further step into the regulatory arena, passing the Sherman Anti-Trust Act. This law banned "every contract, combination in the form of trust or otherwise, or conspiracy, in restraint of trade or commerce." Unlike the Interstate Commerce Act, however, the Sherman Act did not set up any new agency of enforcement; the government would rely on existing federal offices, notably the Department of Justice, to carry out its new policy. Over the next decade, amid sharp economic depression, attorneys general showed little stomach for battle with the largest trusts. Instead, the government took on loose cartels of small companies. A few more substantial cases went to court over the first twenty years, against railroad combinations and sugar, beef, oil, and meatpacking trusts. But rulings in these cases did not represent clear victories for the government. Confusion and indecision hovered over the legal meaning of such

Pennsylvania state militia arriving in Homestead to suppress the 1892 Carnegie steelworkers' strike

and the Pinkertons, who had been stranded on the riverbank. In the ensuing battle, seven guards and nine workers were killed; some of the wounded (twenty Pinkertons and forty strikers) later died. Securing assurances of safe passage from strike leader Hugh O'Donnell, the guards surrendered but had to make their way through an angry mob to escape.

Defeat. For a short time an uneasy peace hovered. On 10 July state militia arrived to enforce the peace. The strikers greeted the troops with a brass band and a formal welcoming committee, but Gov. Robert E. Pattison had sent the militia to enforce order on the company's terms, escorting strikebreakers to work and rounding up strike leaders to face indictments for murder, riot, and conspiracy. On 23 July, Alexander Berkman, an anarchist who became enraged by Frick's treatment of the Homestead strikers, shot the businessman twice in the neck while he sat in his Pittsburgh office. Although severely wounded, Frick survived and stubbornly refused to leave his office for treatment until the close of the workday. Meanwhile the strikers enlisted the support of Samuel Gompers and the American Federation of Labor, which tried to mobilize an effort to prevent the recruitment of strikebreakers, to organize a legal defense for the strikers facing trial, and to support the Homestead workers through sympathy strikes. Public opinion condemned Carnegie and Frick for their repressive measures, and a local jury quickly acquitted the three defendants brought to trial. Nevertheless, by

this point, the tide was turning against the strikers. Berkman's violent act discredited the labor movement. In addition Frick had the mills running on scab labor (nonunion workers) by September, and on 20 November, after four months, Amalgamated called off the strike. "Our victory is now complete and most gratifying," Frick cabled Carnegie in Scotland. "Do not think we will ever have any serious labor trouble again."

Source:

Leon Wolff, *Lockout, the Story of the Homestead Strike: A Study of Violence, Unionism, and the Carnegie Steel Empire* (New York: Longmans, Green, 1965).

LABOR

Big Labor? As businesses expanded and consolidated to secure advantages in the marketplace, workers tried to organize, and often succeeded, to exert leverage in the labor market. Changes in the workplace set imposing challenges for workers, who found themselves contending with increasingly large, concentrated, and distant employers. Periodic economic downturns also cut deeply into efforts to organize, as workers competed to survive. However, workers did organize and did take on management in often bitter efforts to secure or retain decent working conditions amid the dizzying process of industrial transformation.

Knights of Labor. The first organization to attempt to unite workers of all industries and occupations, the Knights of Labor grew from small beginnings: when it

A twelve-year-old boy pulling basting threads in a sweatshop, circa 1890

was founded in 1869 it was envisioned as a secret organization, something like a labor equivalent to freemasonry. It eventually shed its trappings of secrecy, and under the leadership of Terence V. Powderly, who was named "Grand Master Workman" in 1883, the Knights rapidly grew to become a major force in American business. The movement opened its ranks to skilled and unskilled workers alike, transcending earlier, single-craft-oriented trade unions. In addition it accepted women and African Americans, although the latter had to join segregated assemblies. Powderly set lofty goals for the Knights, envisioning ultimately the abolition of the wage system and its replacement with more-cooperative business structures. However, the Knights' more immediate goals reflected a concrete labor agenda: an eight-hour workday, the prohibition of child labor, and the improvement of workplace safety and conditions.

Triumph and Setbacks. After the Knights successfully organized a strike against one of Jay Gould's railroads in 1885, membership soared to more than seven hundred thousand by 1886, nearly 10 percent of the total industrial workforce, organized in some fifteen thousand local assemblies. However, momentum began to slip when a subsequent railroad strike collapsed the next year. Meanwhile, the Knights threw themselves into a national campaign to institute an eight-hour workday,

calling for a mass strike on 1 May 1886. More than three hundred thousand workers participated in the "Great Upheaval." Nonetheless the Knights lost a good deal of public support in the aftermath of these strikes, especially in the wake of events in Chicago, where the May Day strike led to a bombing in Haymarket Square in which seven policemen were killed. The city's civic leaders decried the radical ideas they detected at the root of the violence, tainting principles such as Powderly's critique of wage labor. Still, the Knights' biggest obstacle probably came from within the ranks, as skilled workers, disillusioned with the idea of joining forces with unskilled workers, peeled off to form craft unions. Membership dropped to one hundred thousand in 1890 and continued to fall off in the ensuing years. However, many of the goals of the Knights became central principles of other labor organizations that took up the struggle for better wages and working conditions.

American Federation of Labor. Meanwhile, efforts were under way to organize skilled labor within craft unions sustained by a national umbrella alliance. In 1881 a group of trade unionists convened to lay the foundation for a national federation of labor leaders. While the influence of the Knights of Labor remained strong, the federation languished, but in 1886, as the Knights' fortunes began to ebb, a second effort

Coxey's Army of unemployed workers in Washington, D.C., 1894

established the American Federation of Labor (AFL) at a convention held in Columbus, Ohio. Samuel Gompers of the Cigar Makers' Union became the federation's first president and held the office almost continuously up to his death in 1924. Unlike the Knights, the AFL was rooted in the craft union movement, and participating local unions retained complete autonomy. The federation thus gathered skilled workers, but not unskilled or semiskilled laborers. And unlike the Knights of Labor or the twentieth-century Industrial Workers of the World (Wobblies), the AFL eschewed radical or socialist politics, concentrating on improving labor conditions in individual crafts through union organization and contract negotiations.

Federation Fortunes. Like the Knights, the federation met with both setbacks and advances in its first few decades. AFL growth, which depended on the growth of participating trade unions, remained fitful into the late 1890s. Sporadic early victories on the issue of the eight-hour day were offset by more prominent setbacks in the Homestead Strike of 1892 and the Pullman Strike two years later. As of 1898 fewer than three hundred thousand workers were affiliated. However, after the 1893–1897 depression membership began to rise more rapidly. By the early twentieth century the federation had securely established itself as a national power.

Source:
Joshua Freeman and others, *Who Built America? Working People and the Nation's Economy, Politics, Culture and Society,* 2 volumes (New York: Pantheon, 1989–1992).

PANIC OF 1893

Crisis. The depression that occurred in the United States in 1893 was the worst in the nation's history. As the economy became more integrated and centralized, fewer businesses and workers operated outside the influence of national markets and were therefore more vulnerable to the effects of a national downturn. In April 1893 the U.S. Treasury's gold reserves fell below $100 million, setting off a financial panic as investors, fearing that the country would be forced to abandon the gold standard, scrambled to sell off assets and convert them to gold. This surge of selling rocked a market already unsettled by the spectacular failure of the Philadelphia and Reading Railroad in February; the collapse of the National Cordage Company on 4 May exacerbated the crisis. Banks everywhere began frantically calling in loans, and western and southern banks withdrew substantial deposits from New York banks. Bank failures spread rapidly; some six hundred occurred in the first months, especially in the South and West, rising to four thousand by the end of 1893. An estimated fourteen thousand businesses collapsed during the same period. The economy spent the next four years mired in the worst depression anyone had ever known. "The Americans are a people of magnificent achievements and of equally magnificent fiascoes," *Bankers' Magazine* of London declared as it surveyed the crisis across the Atlantic. "At present they are in the throes of a fiasco unprecedented even in their broad experience."

Governmental Response. Some fifty railroads went under in the chaos, and since this industry was one of the nation's largest and since it supported other industries, those failures rippled outwards; more than thirty steel companies collapsed in the wake of the railroad failures. The government, meanwhile, struggled to cope with the crisis, cutting off silver purchases to stem the outflow of its gold supply and in 1895 securing emergency loans in gold from Wall Street syndicates, including $65 million from John Pierpont Morgan and his associates. The bankers charged the government a hefty $7 million for this bailout—a price that angered many spectators. Popular sentiment mounted in opposition to the gold standard and in favor of the free and unlimited coinage of silver. Federal and state governments, in the meantime, with no sustained tradition of social welfare (which came only in the twentieth century), did little to alleviate the effects of the depression on the people.

Unrest. Among the working classes, layoffs and steep wage reductions threw families into desperate straits. As unemployment climbed to 20 percent in 1894, close to 2.5 million jobless men migrated in and out of cities looking for work. Chicago police stationed themselves at the railroad stations to keep tramps from coming into the city. Meanwhile, many of those who remained in the workforce were forced to take sharp pay cuts, provoking widespread labor unrest. By one count more than thirteen hundred strikes, involving 750,000 workers, hit the nation's factories and mines in 1894 alone, including violent confrontations between workers and authorities at Pullman in Illinois and between workers and authorities at coalfields from Appalachia to Idaho in response to a national strike by the United Mine Workers of America.

Coxey's Army. Impetus for direct federal relief for unemployed workers and their families came from a seemingly unlikely source: Jacob S. Coxey, an Ohio steel-mill owner, was forced in the financial panic to lay off forty of his quarry workers. Coxey proposed a federal public-works program, largely road construction, to provide jobs for the unemployed. He said it could be funded by issuing $500 million in paper money, which would also help the poor by increasing the amount of money in circulation. In order to drum up support for his "Good Roads Bill," Coxey announced he would "send a petition to Washington with boots on" and led an assemblage of displaced workers on foot from Massillon, Ohio, to the capital; he hoped to have 100,000 marchers. "Coxey's Army" started off on Easter Sunday 1894 with only about a hundred marchers (including Coxey's wife, Henrietta, and their son, whom they had named Legal Tender Coxey). By the time they reached Washington on 30 April, though, the pilgrimage had swelled to roughly four hundred, and thousands more had cheered them on as they passed through various towns. In fact, the protest had grown prominent enough to concern the federal government gravely; President Grover Cleveland announced he intended to use laws prohibiting parades on the Capitol grounds, and on 1 May he had Coxey and two of his lieutenants arrested.

WORKERS CRY OUT

A statement of the Pullman strikers, addressed to the American Railway Convention, 15 June 1894:

Rents all over the city in every quarter have fallen, in some cases to one-half. Residences, compared with which ours are hovels, can be had a few miles away at the prices we have been contributing to make a millionaire a billionaire. What we pay $15 for in Pullman is leased for $8 in Roseland; and remember that just as no man or woman of our 4,000 toilers has ever felt the friendly pressure of George M. Pullman's hand, so no man or woman of us all has ever owned or can ever hope to own one inch of George M. Pullman's land. Why, even the very streets are his. . . . Water which Pullman buys from the city at 8 cents a thousand gallons he retails to us at 500 percent advance and claims he is losing $400 a month on it. Gas which sells at 75 cents per thousand feet in Hyde Park, just north of us, he sells for $2.25. When we went to tell him our grievances, he said we were all his `children'. Pullman, both the man and the town, is an ulcer on the body politic. He owns the houses, the schoolhouses, and churches of God in the town he gave his once humble name.

Source: *United States Strike Commission Report.* Senate Executive Document No. 7 (53rd Congress, 3rd Session.) Washington: Government Printing Office, 1895.

"Insurrection" and Response. Dozens of demonstrations like Coxey's broke out during this turbulent period. As a "movement" these displays remained scattered and unorganized. But they excited considerable anxiety among conservatives nonetheless, especially when coupled with the attending wave of violent strikes. In fact, many conservative Americans came to fear that the unrest was becoming a general "insurrection." H. P. Robinson, editor of *Railroad Age,* wrote in January 1895: "It is probably safe to say that in no civilized country in this century, not actually in the throes of war or open insurrection, has society been so disorganized as it was in the United States during the first half of 1894; never was human life held so cheap; never did the constituted authorities appear so incompetent to enforce respect for the law." These sentiments strengthened the resolve of company managers and state, local, and federal authorities to meet the spreading strikes and protests violently, to maintain "order" in the midst of economic chaos.

Recovery. Recovery came slowly, but by the middle of 1897 signs began indicating that the economy was stabilizing. But the events of the previous four years had shaken the country. The economy had slipped into recession in 1873, 1884, and 1893, with this final depression being especially destructive. Meanwhile local, state, and federal authorities had proven inadequate to meet the economic turmoil that seemed to attend this new economy and its fluctuations.

Federal troops guarding the Pullman plant outside Chicago, 1894

Source:
Samuel Rezneck, *Business Depressions and Financial Panics* (New York: Greenwood Press, 1968).

THE PULLMAN STRIKE

Businessman. George Mortimer Pullman, the son of a farmer and carpenter born in upstate New York in 1831, was one of the most significant figures in American business history. He left school at age fourteen, working in a general store, and then as a carpenter. He moved to Chicago in 1859, where he found work in the burgeoning city. After a brief stint in Colorado he returned to Chicago in 1863 to begin building a new kind of sleeping car for railway travel, which he dubbed the "Pioneer." With a shrewd eye for promotion, Pullman lent his car to the federal government to bear the body of President Abraham Lincoln to Illinois for his funeral in 1865, a gimmick that attracted national publicity. Over the next several years he persuaded several railroads to accept his coaches (which were slightly wider than other railroad cars), and in 1867 he incorporated the Pullman Palace Car Company. Two years later Pullman expanded his industrial plant in the area of Lake Calumet, south of Chicago. In 1875 he added parlor cars to the company's line of offerings.

Product. For those who could afford to ride in them, Pullman's cars lent an air of gentility to railway travel. Curtains and carpets surrounded middle- and upper-class passengers with the comforts of home. "We know now that men will not climb in between the sheets of a Pullman sleeping-car bed with their boots on," a spokesman wrote in one of the company's promotional booklets, "and that they will not regard sleeping-car carpets and upholstery in the light of convenient cuspidors." The product was thus distinctly suited to its times, adapting upper-class amenities to the new railway-driven economy.

Town. To house workers at his thriving industrial plant, Pullman began construction of the town of Pullman in 1880. The businessman surveyed the land himself, working with landscape architect Nathan Barrett Berman to fashion a grid pattern wrapped around the factory and a town square. Other corporate/public buildings included a hotel, the Greenstone Church, an arcade market, a department store and shopping center for the workers, a library, and a savings bank—all of them owned by the company. The workers lived in brick row houses; larger houses closer to the center of town were reserved for engineers and foremen. The town was meant to be a model community, free of the slums, crime, and labor agitation that, in Pullman's view, were polluting the new industrial society. Plays at the Arcade Theater in Pullman were carefully chosen for moral influence by Pullman or his representatives. The town had no saloons, gambling houses, brothels, or dance halls—none of those establishments that, in regular working-class neighborhoods, undergirded working-class culture and entertainment. (Pullman considered these to be "baneful influences," and workers wanting a drink or a visit to a brothel had to go the neighboring town, Roseland.) Also there were no police stations, courts, or orphanages in Pullman.

Model Community. Pullman's vision of a benevolent, paternalistic industrial community gripped the imagination of middle-class America. The town became a popular sightseeing excursion for tourists visiting Chicago. In 1893, the year of the Columbian Exposition, some ten thousand foreign visitors made the trip, as did thousands of Americans. Pullman himself guided some of the tours of his industrial fiefdom. Much like Andrew Carnegie, Pullman considered the industrialist to be a social engineer. "The principle of my life," he declared, "has been that all wealth beyond one's need is held in trust for the benefit of all." His town and factory were meant to manifest this paternalistic vision.

Strike. Pullman's vision of benevolent industrial paternalism fell apart, however, with the advent of the 1893 depression. In 1894 he refused to lower rents despite wage cuts at his factory. Workers resolved to strike and put their grievances before the American Railway Union (ARU), which, under the leadership of Eugene V. Debs, was then emerging as a leader in the industrial union movement. Earlier in the year the ARU had won a strike against the Great Northern Railroad, and it promptly agreed to support the Pullman workers, calling for a nationwide strike and a boycott of Pullman's railroad cars and any trains pulling them. Rail traffic across the nation ground to a halt.

National Response. In the ensuing conflict the ARU set up command and control in a central committee headquartered in Chicago; pitted against the workers was the railroads' counterpart in the General Managers' Association, an organization that coordinated the twenty-six railroads arrayed against the union. Some 260,000 workers joined the strike, about half of them directly affiliated with the union. The conservative press portrayed Debs as a tyrant and the strike as a dangerous "insurrection." It looked even more like one when railroad managers got the federal and state governments to weigh in on their side. By attaching mail cars to trains carrying Pullman cars, the railroads gave Atty. Gen. Richard C. Olney the opportunity to call out the U.S. Army by arguing that the strike was interfering with the mail system. When troops marched into Chicago on 4 July, they confronted massed strikers in a melee that killed thirteen and wounded more than fifty. Resistance spread outward from Chicago; skirmishes between strikers and federal troops and state militia flared in twenty-six states, stretching from Maine to California. Casualties climbed to thirty-four. But by mid July the momentum behind the strike had collapsed. ARU leaders, including Debs, were arrested and charged with civil contempt. Critically, Samuel Gompers and the AFL leadership decided not to support the general strike and called on workers to return to their jobs.

End of Pullman. Despite crushing the strike, Pullman did not manage to sustain his vision of a model industrial community. Pullman died in 1897, and the following year a ruling by the Supreme Court of Illinois forced the company to sell the town property. Pullman would never be the same. Within a handful of years the Arcade

Theater closed, middle-class managers moved out of town, and in their wake saloons appeared.

Sources:

James Gilbert, *Perfect Cities: Chicago's Utopias of 1893* (Chicago: University of Chicago Press, 1991);

Almont Lindsey, *The Pullman Strike: The Story of a Unique Experiment and a Great Labor Upheaval* (Chicago: University of Chicago Press, 1942).

THE RAILROADS

Dynamics of Competition. In the late 1800s railroads were not like any other business. They required enormous outlays of capital to complete initial construction and consumed more money to keep trains running. In fact, a railroad's fixed costs ran high: no matter how much freight a railroad was shipping, it had to pay for track and engine maintenance, as well as salaries for thousands of workers, not to mention the costs of servicing the debt incurred to build the line in the first place. In other words, it cost nearly as much money to run empty trains as it did to run full ones. And no railroad could afford to shut down operations for any period of time. Therefore when a railroad faced competition for traffic, it usually became desperate and began to cut rates—either directly or by offering large shippers rebates. In fact, from a manager's point of view, it often made sense to charge shippers less than it actually cost the railroad to ship their goods, in order to attract or keep business from competitors. By the 1890s railroad competition had grown fierce indeed. Though farmers and small businessmen loudly accused the railroads of monopolizing transportation to markets, the railroads frequently found themselves locked into ruinous competition with each other.

Feverish Construction. Over the course of the 1880s new railroad construction occurred at a frantic pace. Approximately 71,000 miles of track were laid over the decade; in 1887 alone, 12,876 miles were built, more than any other year in the nation's history. By this point the railroad network in key regions was becoming overbuilt; financial speculation was driving construction, and competing lines were racing to put down track in order to lay claim to the best sites. Coupled with the fundamental operating dynamics of railroad finance, this reckless expansion set off major financial turmoil in the industry—turmoil that reverberated throughout the national economy. In the wake of the Panic of 1893, nearly two hundred railroads went into receivership, representing forty-one thousand miles of track and about $2.5 million of capital. By 1895 one-third of the nation's railroad mileage was in bankruptcy.

System Building. Meanwhile, beginning in the 1870s, two lines, the Pennsylvania Railroad and the Baltimore & Ohio Railroad, completed the country's first integrated systems—in each case connecting a web of small feeder lines with large trunk lines that ran for thousands of miles and linked cities in the Northeast and

Midwest, the heart of the nation's burgeoning industrial economy. Before this development, many had predicted that any railroad running more than five hundred miles would be too expensive to build and too complicated to run. However, the successful expansion of the Pennsylvania and the B & O signaled the future of the industry. Only the right conditions for consolidation were needed for other system builders to follow the example.

Gould. In the competitive chaos railroad managers struggled to make profits and gain control of the industry. In the 1880s they tried repeatedly to implement regional associations in efforts to set profitable rates and allocate traffic between competitors. However, these efforts lacked effective enforcement mechanisms and repeatedly broke down until a leading railroad magnate decided to voice his opinion. Jay Gould, who had driven much of the aggressive expansion of the previous decades, attended meetings of railroad investors convened by financier J. P. Morgan in 1888 and 1890. At these meetings he urged the formation of a central railroad cartel to set rates and distribute shipping among the various roads.

"Morganization." By 1890 many railroad owners and investors distrusted the financier who had driven so much of the competitive construction he now decried. Only Morgan held the financial prestige and credibility needed to pull off the ambitious task of reorganization. Therefore it was Morgan, with the millions of dollars of investment capital he and his affiliates controlled, who dominated the consolidation and reorganization of the nation's railroads, adopting a strategy that became known as "Morganization." Taking advantage of spreading railroad collapses, Morgan acquired bankrupted roads, infused them with enough new capital to survive, implemented strict cost cuts, and oversaw agreements with competing lines to reduce unnecessary competition. He then set up mechanisms to control the company—typically a voting trust of investors — for a period of years following reorganization to ensure that agreements were observed. Using variations of this essential formula, Morgan built the Southern railway system and reorganized and revitalized the Erie, Philadelphia & Reading, Northern Pacific, and other major lines. This consolidation of railroads during the 1890s moved the industry out of financial devastation and into the twentieth century.

Sources:

Vincent P. Carosso, *The Morgans: Private International Bankers, 1854–1913* (Cambridge, Mass.: Harvard University Press, 1987);

Albro Martin, *James J. Hill and the Opening of the Northwest* (New York: Oxford University Press, 1976).

THE RISE OF BIG BUSINESS

The New Scale of Business. There were large factories in the United States before 1880—businesses that were heavily capitalized, employing several thou-

Advertisements for new mass-produced goods in a late-1890s issue of *McClure's*

sand workers each. But over the next two decades an altogether new type of business, a new scale of doing business, swept over the American landscape. Once conditions were in place—including a nationally integrated railroad infrastructure, new technologies of mass production, and increasingly concentrated, urbanized markets—economic transformation happened with astonishing speed, over a dozen years or so, running from the late 1880s through the 1890s. In this short span, in a series of industries, new businesses were organized and old businesses reorganized to create enterprises that encompassed huge manufacturing plants spread over several geographic locations, coupled with nationalized systems of distribution and marketing. Big business thus joined mass production to mass distribution and in the process fostered mass consumption.

Mass Production. The industrial key to the rise of big business was the emergence of automated technologies of manufacturing, which appeared in dozens of industries in the 1870s and 1880s. Match production was one. After the Civil War, match-making machinery began replacing hand-production methods, and in the wake of this development the industry rapidly consolidated; by the early 1870s, four firms using various new machines pumped out 80 percent of the nation's total supply of matches. Then, in 1881, the four companies combined, merging the best attributes of their various machines, to form the Diamond Match Company. Within a decade, after additional modest improvements, the new giant's output had increased to the point that it could fill two million matchboxes a day, and do so with only seventy-five workers. Before the introduction of automated methods, this rate of production would have taken five hundred workers. The company also automated in-house manufacturing of boxes to package the matches. Diamond gradually consolidated its production in one giant plant at Barberville, Ohio. And as it grew it expanded vertically as well, putting together a national organization to coordinate the selling of its matches to wholesalers and eventually acquiring its own sawmills to ensure a steady supply of the raw materials. Thus the advent of mass production drove the industry toward monopoly and vertical integration.

Trend toward Monopoly. The story of automated production and corporate consolidation repeated itself in many other industries during this period. The tobacco industry, for example, underwent much of the same transformation in response to the invention of cigarette-making machinery by James Bonsack in 1882. At the time a skilled worker could roll by hand approximately 3,000 cigarettes a day. After a few years of tinkering, one of Bonsack's machines was churning out 120,000 cigarettes daily. North Carolina tobacco manufacturer James Buchanan Duke moved quickly to take advantage of this new technology, installing two Bonsack machines in 1884 and, once the machines had proven themselves, contracting with Bonsack the following year to lease his machinery to make all the cigarettes he produced. In this arrangement Duke secured a low lease rate from Bonsack, improving his competitive edge. Other major cigarette producers were forced to match Duke's moves to compete. Then in January 1890 the big players decided to merge and form the American Tobacco Company. The company dominated cigarette production, as well as plug tobacco and snuff.

Marketing the Cigarette. The deployment of machinery enabling the mass production of cigarettes and subsequent rise of Duke and the American Tobacco Company played a major role in making cigarettes a widespread commodity. Before 1880 most Americans who consumed tobacco did so in the form of cigars, pipes, chewing tobacco, or snuff. Once producers developed the capacity to produce in mass quantities,

they had to build up a base of consumers. Among his competitors, Duke proved especially assiduous on this front, designing packaging (Duke designed the familiar slide-and-shell box to protect cigarettes from being crushed during shipping) and creating brand names that he promoted in national advertising campaigns via cards, circulars, and handbills. In 1889, with sales of $4.5 million and profits near $400,000, Duke poured $800,000 into advertising costs, plastering his name on billboards, storefront windows, and the sides of barns across the country. These tactics pushed the cigarette market from 409 million in 1880 to 2.2 billion by the middle of the decade. Americans in large numbers learned to smoke cigarettes, first in urban markets (Duke moved to New York to coordinate his national growth) and gradually in the countryside as well.

Emergence of Brand Packaging. Flour milling illustrated a parallel trend in big business. Because flour was produced and consumed so widely, it resisted effective monopolization. And yet the industry underwent profound transformation that, in other respects, duplicated the rise of companies such as Diamond Matches and American Tobacco. In the early 1890s leading millers in Minneapolis and elsewhere weighed plans for merger, but the suggestion failed to attract support from all of the leading companies. Their efforts at monopoly blocked, two major millers combined to form the Pillsbury-Washburn Flour Company, which created in-firm organizations to handle the purchasing of unmilled wheat from farms throughout the West as well as the marketing of milled product. The company became the largest miller in the nation, operating a chain of grain elevators across the nation's wheat-growing regions. Unable to swallow up competitors altogether, Pillsbury-Washburn began packaging and advertising its wheat products as brands—Gold Medal Flour and Pillsbury Flour—in an effort to stay ahead of the competition and keep its product flowing smoothly into markets.

Breakfast Cereal. The same kinds of market imperatives drove the growth of another giant in the grain and cereal industry, Quaker Oats. This company had its roots in 1882, when oatmeal producer Henry P. Crowell built a new mill that highly automated the grading, cleaning, hulling, cutting, and packaging of oatmeal in a continuous process that amounted to a prototypical version of the modern assembly line. Like Duke, though, Crowell found he had to create a market to consume his product: Americans thought of oats as animal feed, rather than table fare. So in a campaign that paralleled Duke's, Crowell promoted his brand, Quaker Oats, using box top premiums and prizes, as well as rounding up testimonials and scientific endorsements encouraging the consumption of oat-based breakfast cereal. Meanwhile Crowell joined with several other major producers in 1888 to form the American Cereal Company, which would become Quaker Oats in 1901.

Oil well in Titusville, Pennsylvania

So men such as Crowell transformed the American breakfast table, creating a new association for the very word *cereal*.

Modern Consumer Economy. The arrival of big business had a broad and far-reaching impact on the American economy and on American society. These companies created new types of products, new ways to make money, and new kinds of workplaces. Perhaps most fundamentally, they transformed how Americans bought goods—they created new kinds of marketplaces and, so, new kinds of customers. These businesses depended on high volumes of production and steady rates of sale in order to operate at maximum efficiency. In their effort to craft national marketplaces for their product, they packaged their products in new ways that would be recognizable in an impersonal marketplace extending across the country and overseas. They advertised their products under brand names, and in the process they created new habits of consumption. Before 1880 few Americans smoked cigarettes or ate oats for breakfast cereal; other examples abound. George Eastman in 1887 invented a small, inexpensive hand-held camera that amateurs could use, and when he began mass-producing and marketing it the next year, families discovered that they could take their own pictures and portraits. Asa Candler bought a soft-drink formula from pharmacist John S. Pemberton in 1891 and patented Coca-Cola. William Wrigley Jr. first distributed chewing gum as a gimmick to promote his company's baking powder and soap; in 1899 he introduced a new flavor, spearmint, and pushed it with his customary vigor. ("Tell 'em quick and tell 'em often," was Wrigley's dictum.) Also by this time H. J. Heinz and Company had devised new canned foods; the Borden Milk Company condensed milk; and the Campbell Preserve Company condensed soup. By 1900 businesses had learned to stock and sell in a new consumer-oriented mass market in order to survive.

Source:

Alfred D. Chandler Jr., *The Visible Hand: The Managerial Revolution in American Business* (Cambridge, Mass.: Harvard University Press, 1977).

STANDARD OIL COMPANY

Background. In the 1850s a new industry emerged when refiners discovered that refined petroleum (which up until that point had been bought chiefly for its supposed medicinal properties) made an ideal fuel for lamps. (It would not become important for fueling engines until the twentieth century.) Production boomed; wells sprang up as large oil fields were discovered in Pennsylvania and the Midwest; and hundreds of small firms sprouted. In the decades after the Civil War this buzzing, frenetic activity formed the backdrop for the emergence of a new way of organizing business on an unprecedented large scale: the business trust. The instrument that devised this innovation was the Standard Oil Company, led by John D. Rockefeller.

Growth. Rockefeller had amassed effective control over oil refining in Cleveland in the late 1860s and early 1870s (Cleveland being an important refining region) by promising railroads a regular flow of business in return for lower shipping rates. His competitors, unable to obtain the same rates, found themselves faced with the choice of being ruined or agreeing to be absorbed by Standard Oil (via stock exchanges). Rockefeller's conquests, in turn, increased his leverage over the railroads and thereby magnified his advantages over remaining competitors. "If you don't sell your property," Rockefeller is reported to have warned one competitor, "it will be valueless because we have advantages of the railroads." By 1872 Standard Oil controlled more than a quarter of the total daily capacity of the industry.

Early Organization and Challenges. At this stage the "company" in fact consisted of many smaller companies that held stock in each other, often secretly. Meanwhile in the nation, the various remaining refiners engaged in intense, cutthroat competition over the 1870s, overproducing and slashing into profits. Rockefeller tried to protect Standard's position by promoting pools, or associations, among refiners: agreements to set prices, secure advantageous shipping rates, and allocate production quotas and profits. The most ambitious of these was the National Refiners Association, formed in August 1872. However, nonbinding agreements proved impossible to enforce and broke down repeatedly— "ropes of sand," Rockefeller called them. Moreover, Standard found itself fending off challenges from the railroads, from the oil producers supplying the refiners, and (as Rockefeller's tactics became more publicly known) from state and federal authorities. In 1879 a Pennsylvania grand jury indicted nine company officials for violating state antimonopoly laws.

Pipelines. The most serious challenge to Standard Oil came from the oil producers (at this stage the company did not actually drill for oil; it merely refined it). In 1879 an association of producers completed the Tidewater Pipeline, running from oil fields in Bradford to the Reading Railroad at Williamsport, Pennsylvania. This innovation demonstrated that crude oil could be shipped cheaply over long distances by pipeline—much more cheaply than by rail, in fact. Standard Oil quickly responded by beginning construction of its own network of pipelines. However, at this point Rockefeller and his associates found that they needed a more formal way to structure their business. Before Tidewater, Standard Oil had made good profits refining oil in Cleveland and other points and shipping it by rail. But the

cost-efficiency of pipeline transport made it imperative to ship crude oil to shipping points and refine it there. Standard Oil had already acquired refineries in New Jersey; now it would have to dismantle a good portion of its refining capacity in Cleveland and at other inland points and move operations closer to the ports. In order to accomplish this restructuring, the company needed to institute more centralized administrative machinery. Out of this challenge came the famous, and infamous, Standard Oil Trust.

The Trust. The Standard Oil Trust Agreement, signed by Rockefeller and associated investors on 2 January 1882, set up the trust as the central holding agency conglomerating forty companies. In effect this new corporate structure authorized a board of trustees to manage the properties of corporations joining the trust on behalf of their stockholders. This structure—the first of its kind—permitted the trust to work around state laws that might restrict operations in any single state while partially centralizing control over the various companies that Standard Oil comprised. To govern the trust, the agreement established an executive committee and vested it with broad administrative powers over Standard's various subsidiaries. The trustees promptly began reorganizing the business, moving the company's headquarters to New York and setting up several important new subsidiaries—the Standard Oil Company of New York and what would become the company's single most important individual company within the trust: the Standard Oil Company of New Jersey. By the mid 1880s the trust had moved into new headquarters at 26 Broadway in New York, manned by an extensive staff.

Expansion and Vertical Integration. Over the next few years the trust successfully concentrated refining in Cleveland (serving the domestic market), Philadelphia, and New York–New Jersey (where the company now located 45 percent of Standard's output). During the mid 1880s the company expanded its pipeline network and centralized its purchasing under a wholly owned subsidiary, the Joseph Seep Agency. By the end of the decade it was expanding its operations into crude-oil production and at the same time tightening its marketing procedures. In other words, in its first decade the trust systematically expanded Standard's scope of business, extending its control up and down the chain of oil extraction, manufacturing, and distribution. This vertical integration buttressed Standard's dominance of the industry. And during the same period, the company expanded overseas, setting up its first foreign affiliate—the Anglo-American Oil Company Limited of London—in 1888. By 1899 Standard Oil controlled 90 to 95 percent of the oil refined in the United States.

Federal Legislation. The 1890 Sherman Anti-Trust Act was aimed directly at the structure that Standard Oil had set up, and in its wake the company faced a major legal assault. Within two years the Ohio Supreme Court ordered the trust to divest itself of Standard Oil of Ohio, declaring in its ruling that "Monopolies have always been regarded as contrary to the spirit and policy of the common law. . . . A society in which a few men are the employers and the great body are merely employees or servants, is not the most desirable in a republic." Standard Oil responded by shifting the core holding company to Standard Oil of New Jersey (in that state laws governing business combinations were looser) and restructuring and enlarging its other companies. By 1899 "Jersey" had become the sole holding company for all Standard interests. Company assets by the turn of the century had reached $300 million. Growth continued into the first decade of the twentieth century, as did hostile governmental scrutiny.

Sources:

Allan Nevins, *Study in Power: John D. Rockefeller, Industrialist and Philanthropist*, 2 volumes (New York: Scribners, 1953);

Ida Tarbell, *The History of the Standard Oil Company* (New York: McClure, 1904);

Harold F. Williamson and Arnold R. Daum, *The American Petroleum Industry: The Age of Illumination, 1859–1899* (Evanston, Ill.: Northwestern University Press, 1959)

HEADLINE MAKERS

ANDREW CARNEGIE

1835-1919

STEELMAKER, PHILANTHROPIST

Career. Born in Dunfermline, Scotland, in 1835, Andrew Carnegie immigrated with his family to the United States and settled in 1848 in Pittsburgh. (His father was a skilled weaver who had fallen on hard times and decided to start anew in America.) In Pittsburgh young Carnegie worked in various mills and factories then secured a position as a telegraph operator for the Pennsylvania Railroad. He soon entered the hierarchy of railroad management and began to prosper; by the end of the Civil War he held investments in a range of businesses and had moved into the manufacture of bridges. In 1872 Carnegie entered the steel business, rising to dominate the industry by the end of the nineteenth century. In 1901 he retired, selling the Carnegie Steel Company (which produced a quarter of the nation's total steel output) to banker J. P. Morgan for nearly $500 million. At the time Morgan called him "the richest man in the world." He devoted the rest of his life to philanthropy, giving away a substantial portion of the wealth he had amassed.

A Plan for Success. Carnegie's steel mills grew to dominate the industry because Carnegie continuously and aggressively overhauled his production methods. He quickly adopted new technologies, becoming the first major steel producer in the United States. For example, he committed substantial capital in the Bessemer production process and employed a chemist at his blast furnaces. He was notoriously stingy in paying out dividends to his partners and filtered profits back into his company in the form of more modern equipment. As he stated in a private memorandum to himself: "Whatever I engage in I must push inordinantly."

Relationship with Workers. Carnegie also pushed his workers hard, operating his plants so as to maximize central control over production. Materials in the Carnegie mills moved smoothly along carefully designed paths, making production as efficient as possible: coal, for example, was carried on elevated trains. Carnegie also pioneered new accounting methods in his shops. Moreover, he was ruthless about wresting as much control as he could from skilled steelworkers who dominated traditional milling. He broke an attempt to unionize at his Homestead mill in 1892 with a lockout and a protracted, violent strike.

Company Structure. Carnegie's steel company demonstrated several important trends in American business. In financial and managerial terms, Carnegie Steel represented a transition from privately held businesses to corporations with ownership separate from management. The company was set up as a series of partnerships, with Carnegie himself holding a majority interest. Like modern corporate owners, Carnegie delegated the day-to-day management of his mills to reliable individuals, such as Henry C. Frick. The scope of Carnegie's operations, meanwhile, typified another business trend: as the business grew, Carnegie expanded his operations vertically. He purchased or leased iron ore fields in the Lake Superior regions and set up strategic business alliances with major coal mines in Connellsville, Pennsylvania, in order to ensure steady supplies of raw material. In addition he acquired control of railroads and steamship lines to transport his products. These moves were driven in part by his expansive business outlook, but they also stemmed from the way in which the mills themselves were set up: as processes became more automated and streamlined, the scale of production correspondingly increased. Carnegie came to depend on keeping his mills operating at high capacities in order to make profits and fuel further expansion.

Legacy. In the final analysis Carnegie's most enduring legacy was perhaps less tangible than the steel his mills produced or the fortune he earned and then distributed. It may have been his social philosophy, summed up in his essay "Wealth," originally appearing in the *North American Review* in 1889, a classic statement of industrial noblesse oblige in which the author charged the rich with making themselves into stewards of the commonwealth: "the man of wealth," he declared, must act as "trustee and agent for his poorer brethren, bringing to their service his superior wisdom, experience, and ability to administer, doing for them better than they would or could do for themselves."

Sources:

Andrew Carnegie, *The Gospel of Wealth, and Other Timely Essays* (New York: Century, 1900);

Joseph Frazier Wall, *Andrew Carnegie* (New York: Oxford University Press, 1970).

EUGENE V. DEBS

1855-1926
LABOR ORGANIZER

Early Life. Eugene V. Debs was born in 1855 and grew up in Terre Haute, Indiana, where his parents settled after emigrating from Alsace. He left school at age fifteen to work for the Terre Haute and Indianapolis Railroad. In 1875, some years after becoming a locomotive fireman for the railroad, Debs helped to organize a lodge of the Brotherhood of Locomotive Firemen. He was appointed secretary, beginning a rise through the various offices of the brotherhood that Debs combined with several local and state government positions as well as a job clerking for a wholesale grocery house.

Union. Debs's significance as a labor organizer stands in sharp contrast to his contemporary Samuel Gompers, president of the American Federation of Labor (AFL). While Gompers worked with skilled trade workers, Debs advocated united efforts by the skilled and unskilled and tied unionizing efforts to a comprehensive political agenda. In June 1893 Debs formed the American Railway Union and became its first president. American Railway, one of the new "industrial unions" open to both skilled and unskilled workers (though not to blacks) gained national prominence within the year when it won an important victory over the Great Northern Railroad; membership quickly swelled to more than 150,000. But the union's fortunes fell just as quickly, after Debs staked them on support for workers in the Pullman Strike (1894), coordinating a national boycott of trains pulling Pullman cars. For a time the ARU managed to paralyze rail traffic, earning notoriety for "King Debs." However, the AFL refused to join Debs's calls for a national sympathy strike, and the Pullman strike collapsed.

Socialism. In the aftermath Debs, who was indicted and jailed for his role in the strike, became both famous and infamous as a national labor hero. He made contact with prominent socialist spokesmen and joined the Populist political movement, backing the presidential campaign of William Jennings Bryan in 1896. As his political and economic philosophies evolved he began to espouse what he termed a "Cooperative Commonwealth," to be colonized by the unemployed in some western state. In 1897, as populism fell apart, Debs turned to outright socialism, declaring "The issue is Socialism versus Capitalism. I am for Socialism because I am for humanity." Following Debs's lead, the American Railway Union, by then much diminished, transformed itself into the Social Democracy of America. In 1900 Debs served as the Social Democratic Party's first presidential candidate. In 1905, after a second presidential candidacy, Debs helped to found the Industrial Workers of the World (IWW), though he later broke with the organization. During World War I Debs was jailed for opposing American intervention. He died in 1926, still espousing his socialist beliefs.

Sources:

Eugene V. Debs, *Walls and Bars* (Chicago: Socialist Party, 1927);

Nick Salvatore, *Eugene V. Debs: Citizen and Socialist* (Champaign: University of Illinois Press, 1982).

JAY GOULD

1836-1892
SPECULATOR, RAILROAD MAGNATE

Robber Baron. The financial practices attending the construction of railroads in the late nineteenth century gave the industry a bad name. A small group of extremely wealthy entrepreneurs became known as robber barons because of their aggressive and frequently dishonest business practices. Cornelius Vanderbilt, James Fisk, and others built immense personal fortunes through railroad promotion and consolidation. However, the prince of the robber barons was Jay Gould. He was born in 1836 and raised on a farm in upstate New York. As a young man he briefly operated a tannery. In 1859, at the age of twenty-three, he moved to New York City, where he set himself up as a leather goods merchant. During the Civil War he began speculating in the securities of small railroads and quickly grew wealthy. Gould developed the fine art of buying rundown railroads, making improvements, and selling out at a profit, meanwhile using corporate money for personal speculation and bribes.

Consolidation. In 1867 he and fellow speculators Daniel Drew and Fisk fought Vanderbilt for financial control of the Erie Railroad—a battle that became notorious as Gould and his partners issued millions of dollars worth of fraudulent stock and paid thousands of dollars more in bribes to judges and legislators. Gould's syndicate got the Erie, and he immediately moved to consolidate the line by leasing or buying up the smaller western lines that fed into it—a strategy that set off a general wave of consolidation among railroad companies. In October 1869 Gould teamed up again with Fisk in a spectacular, unsuccessful attempt to corner the gold market. Meanwhile, Gould continued with his railroad speculations, by 1875 acquiring financial control over the transcontinental Union Pacific—and so putting himself in position to begin building the first national integrated railroad system. By 1881 Gould controlled a railroad empire that stretched across the continent, spanning Boston, New York, Toledo, Chicago, Saint Louis, Kansas City, Omaha, and Denver.

Impact. Gould proved to be a better speculator than he was a railroad manager, and over the next few years he scaled back his holdings to concentrate on building a southwest regional system. Still, Gould's maneuvers had a far-reaching impact on the railroad industry as a whole, for his aggressive challenges to other lines forced more conservative investors such as William Vanderbilt to build systems of their own to protect their original holdings. Thus Gould helped to fuel the frenzy of railroad construction in the 1880s and 1890s that drove many railroads under and consolidated the survivors into trunk-and-feeder networks spanning broad regions. In addition to his railroad holdings, Gould amassed a controlling stake in Western Union Telegraph, which he acquired by manipulating the telegraph subsidies of his railroads. He also controlled New York City's elevated railroad system by 1886. He died in 1892, just before the national depression brought on, in large part, by railroads' overextension.

Source:
Julius Grodinsky, *Jay Gould: His Business Career* (Philadelphia: University of Pennsylvania Press, 1957).

JOHN PIERPONT MORGAN

1837-1913
BANKER

A Knack for Banking. John Pierpont Morgan was born into a prosperous mercantile-banking family in 1837 and was raised in Hartford, Boston, and London. After a formal education that began in New England schools and continued in Switzerland and Germany, Morgan was placed by his father in an affiliated firm, where he rose from junior clerk to a position brokering sugar in Cuba and Louisiana. In 1860 he returned to New York and opened his own office, handling much the same kind of business his father did, namely, managing American investments for English clients and trading in foreign exchange. During the Civil War years Morgan speculated in various kinds of financial investments, as well as foreign exchange and gold, and counseled English investors about conditions in the American market. Morgan also brokered some important railroad offerings and played a prominent role in the refinancing of the federal government's Civil War debt in the late 1860s and 1870s. In 1873, when Jay Cooke's firm went bankrupt amid a general financial panic, Morgan's firm became the nation's preeminent dealer in government bonds.

Wheeling and Dealing. In 1879 Morgan turned his focus to railroad finance, overseeing much of the consolidation then transforming that industry. Two dramatic negotiations—the first helping William Vanderbilt to quietly unload his huge personal holdings in railroad stock, the second handling $40 million in stock issued by the financially troubled Northern Pacific Railroad (in which Jay Cooke had invested heavily and disastrously)—buttressed Morgan's reputation and demonstrated the feasibility of selling large stock offerings via underwriting syndicates. Over the next few decades Morgan played a critical role in raising the huge sums of capital needed to build the major railroad systems of the period. From 1885 to 1890, in an effort to curb destructive competition, he convened a series of meetings to organize leading railroad companies into voluntary associations. When these broke down, Morgan shifted to system building, taking advantage of the Panic of 1893 to reorganize many of the largest systems and bring them under the control of boards of directors, or of voting trusts, that he and his associates closely controlled. By 1900 he had amassed financial control over the largest railroad empire in the country.

Not Enough. Still, Morgan did not achieve much mainstream public notice before the "gold crisis" of the mid 1890s, when he organized a syndicate to stem the outflow of gold from the U.S. Treasury. The terms of this assistance, when they became known, outraged the public and helped to bring down the presidential administration of Grover Cleveland in 1896. Morgan refused to divulge his profits to a congressional committee investigating the affair. Beginning the 1890s, meanwhile, Morgan expanded the scope of his financial activities beyond government securities and railroads. In 1892 he managed the formation of General Electric; in 1898 the Federal Steel Company; in 1901 U.S. Steel (capitalized at $1.4 billion); and in 1902 the International Harvester Company. Well before his death in 1913 he had become the most important financier in the country—a key conduit for moving European capital into U.S. investments—and a major figure in the rise of big business.

Sources:

Lewis Corey, *The House of Morgan: A Social Biography of the Masters of Money* (New York: G. Howard Watt, 1930);

Herbert L. Satterlee, *J. Pierpont Morgan: An Intimate Portrait* (New York: Macmillan, 1939).

JOHN DAVIDSON ROCKEFELLER

1839-1937
INDUSTRIALIST, PHILANTHROPIST

Beginnings. One of the most notorious robber barons of the late nineteenth century was born in 1839, the son of a merchant and patent-medicine salesman, in the Finger Lakes region of New York. In 1853 he moved with his family to Cleveland and entered business in 1856, at the age of sixteen, as a bookkeeper with a Cleveland mercantile firm Hewitt & Tuttle. Here Rockefeller first displayed the conservative, meticulous business instincts that would govern the rest of his career. After a few years he broke off and formed a wholesale grocery business of his own with a partner, Maurice B. Clark. Business boomed during the Civil War years, and the partners expanded into oil refining in 1863 under the name of Andrews, Clark & Company (Rockefeller preferring to keep his name out of the public eye). This business started as a sideline, but in 1865 Rockefeller bought out Clark and shifted his focus exclusively to the refinery. In 1869 Rockefeller consolidated the several partnerships by which he ran the business, forming the Standard Oil Company. By this point Rockefeller dominated refining in the Cleveland region; in coming years he expanded his domination on a national and a global scale and, in the process, made himself an infamous figure in the public mind.

Notoriety. Rockefeller tried to keep the growth of Standard Oil quiet, but as the business grew his tactics began attracting negative publicity. The first serious attack came in 1879, in an investigation by the New York state legislature into Standard Oil's dealings with the railroads. The investigation's findings became notorious when they were published in an article by Henry Demarest Lloyd in the *Atlantic Monthly* in 1881. Thereafter, independent refiners and producers kept steady pressure on Rockefeller. As his company fended off more or less continuous assaults from state and federal agencies, both the man and his business himself became notorious as embodiments of the trends transforming the American economy.

Retirement. Rockefeller retired from daily management of Standard in 1896, at the age of fifty-six, with a personal fortune that climbed (as his company continued to grow) to an estimated $900 million in 1913. Even before he retired he had already begun donating substantial sums to charitable causes; in 1891 he hired Frederick T. Gates to manage his philanthropic ventures, and by 1892 he had given more than $1 million to colleges (notably the University of Chicago, which was founded on Rockefeller money), libraries, hospitals, and other institutions. In 1913 he founded the Rockefeller Foundation. He died in 1937.

Source:

Allan Nevins, *Study in Power: John D. Rockefeller, Industrialist and Philanthropist*, 2 volumes (New York: Scribners, 1953).

PUBLICATIONS

Charles Francis Adams, *Railroads: Their Origin and Problems* (New York: Putnam, 1878)—the author draws on his experience as chairman of the Massachusetts Board of Railroad Commissioners to make broad policy recommendations about regulating the industry;

Edward Bellamy, *Looking Backward, 2000–1887* (Boston: Ticknor, 1888)—a best-selling novel in which the protagonist falls asleep for more than one hundred years, awakening in the year 2000 to a utopian society in which class and poverty have been wiped out and state control has replaced private ownership of land and industry;

Andrew Carnegie, *The Gospel of Wealth* (London: F. C. Hagen, 1889)—this book originally appeared as an essay titled "Wealth" in the *North American Review* (1889). Carnegie's social philosophy held that in a free society, an unregulated market would direct wealth to the people of the best ability. Carnegie also espoused the idea that the wealthy should consider their property as a trust to be managed for the public good;

Henry George, *Progress and Poverty* (San Francisco: W. M. Hinton, 1879)—a hugely popular tract in which George argued that private ownership of land had generated high levels of inequality and corruption. In order to correct the situation he advocated a "single tax" system to do away with land ownership;

George, *Social Problems* (Chicago & New York: Belford, Clarke, 1883)—a series of essays that warned of the social dangers attending the growing disparity between the wealthy and poor in the United States;

Henry Demarest Lloyd, *A Strike of Millionaires against Miners* (Chicago: Belford, Clarke, 1890)—Lloyd had already established himself as a prominent social critic in 1881 in "Story of a Great Monopoly," which had exposed the rise of the Standard Oil Company. This follow-up carried on the theme, calling out for social justice;

Lloyd, *Wealth against Commonwealth* (New York: Harper, 1894)—one of the most important works of the period, this book was a ringing indictment of the "monopoly" as socially dangerous and fundamentally un-American, singling out Standard Oil as a chief offender.

George McNeill, ed., *The Labor Movement: The Problem of To-day* (Boston: A. M. Bridgman, 1887)—the author argues that extremes of wealth and poverty were destabilizing American ideals and institutions of government and that the "wage-system of labor" would ultimately subvert "the republican system of government";

John Swinton, *Striking for Life* (Philadelphia: A. R. Keller, 1894)—a tract of labor activism, deploring the "aristocratic" concentration of wealth, the plight of indigent immigrants, and the disappearance of open western lands;

Thorstein Veblen, *The Theory of the Leisure Class* (New York, Macmillan, 1899)—an analysis of the spending habits of the middle and upper classes in American society in which Veblen pioneered the idea of "conspicuous consumption." Veblen argued that the economy's price system was structurally flawed and advocated instead what he called a "technocracy," in which engineers would rationalize production and distribution.

A railroad depot at the turn of the century

COMMUNICATIONS

by   NANCY E. BERNHARD

CONTENTS

Sidebars and tables are listed in italics.

1878

- E. W. Scripps founds the *Cleveland Penny Press,* which becomes the parent paper of a successful newspaper chain.

- Joseph Pulitzer purchases the bankrupt *Saint Louis Dispatch* and merges it with the *Saint Louis Westliche Post.*

1879

- The Heintzemann Press is founded in Boston by Carl Heintzemann. It raises the standards for schoolbooks in America and publishes popular literature at low prices.

1880

- The foreign-language press in the United States includes 641 German (80 dailies), 49 Scandinavian, 41 French, 26 Spanish, 13 Bohemian, 5 Welsh, and 4 Italian papers. Over the next twenty years the proportion printed in Eastern European languages will increase rapidly.

- William Rockhill Nelson, a promoter of community works, buys the *Kansas City Star.* It reaches a circulation of 170,000 before his death in 1915.

- The Thorne type-composing and -distributing machine is patented, introducing the first step in automated typesetting. Pressing a key brings a letter to an assembly place from a revolving cylinder, and the assembled type is justified by hand.

- The *New York Daily Graphic* prints the first quality halftone reproduction of a photograph — "Shantytown," depicting upper Fifth Avenue.

- Lew Wallace's novel *Ben-Hur: A Tale of Christ* becomes one of the best-selling books of the next few years. By 1888 it sells 290,000 copies.

1881

- The first halftone plates for letterpress printing are developed independently by Frederick E. Ives of Philadelphia and George Meisenbach of Munich. Ives's halftones began to appear in *Harper's Magazine* in 1884.

- Railroad magnate and former Civil War correspondent Henry Villard buys the *New York Evening Post* and *The Nation,* establishing an editorial triumvirate of E. L. Godkin, Carl Schurz, and Horace White.

15 Jan. The biweekly literary magazine *The Critic* is founded in New York.

29 Oct. Led by James Albert Wales, defectors from the humor magazine *Puck* found its competitor, *The Judge.*

1882

- R. Hoe and Company build their first double supplement press, which prints 24,000 copies an hour of a 4-, 6-, 8-, 10-, or 12-page paper. It is promptly purchased by James Gordon Bennett Jr. for the *New York Herald.*

- Harrison Gray Otis joins the *Los Angeles Times,* founded in 1881 by a group of printers. By 1886 he gains control of the paper and becomes notorious among printers for reducing their wages. Within four years circulation is up to 7,300.

- The United Press is founded by a splinter group from the Associated Press.

- *Printer and Publisher,* a periodical for journalists, is founded in Indianapolis. It adopts the title *National Printer-Journalist* in 1893.

- Albert Pulitzer, brother of Joseph, founds the *New York Morning Journal,* but after the price increases to two cents a copy circulation drops. Pulitzer sells the paper to John R. McLean in 1894, who in turn sells it to William Randolph Hearst the next year.

14 July The American Medical Association begins publishing the *Journal of the American Medical Association.*

Dec. The most popular children's magazine of its day, *The Golden Argosy, Freighted With Treasures for Boys and Girls* is founded by Frank A. Munsey Jr. The title is shortened to *The Golden Argosy* in 1886, and two years later it becomes an adult magazine.

1883

- The humor magazine *Life* is founded in New York by John Ames Mitchell.

- In New York City Irving Bacheller founds the first literary syndicate, supplying articles and short stories to newspapers.

- Theodore Low De Vinne, the outstanding American scholar-printer of the late nineteenth century, founds T. L. De Vinne and Company in New York. De Vinne was famous for his typography, wood engravings, experiments with coated papers, and writings on the history and practice of printing.

- Joseph Pulitzer buys the *New York World* for $346,000.

9 Feb. *Science* is founded in Cambridge, Massachusetts, by Alexander Graham Bell.

Dec. The *Ladies' Home Journal* is founded in Philadelphia by Cyrus H. K. Curtis and his wife Louisa Knapp.

1884

- S. S. McClure founds the McClure Newspaper Syndicate in New York. The syndicate makes the writings of famous writers such as William Dean Howells, Sir Arthur Conan Doyle, Jack London, and Rudyard Kipling available to small papers at low cost.

- The *Pittsburgh Evening Penny Press* is founded.

- T. Thomas Fortune founds the *New York Freeman,* later the *New York Age.*

25 Nov. The *Philadelphia Weekly Tribune* is founded by Christopher James Perry Sr. to fight racial discrimination. During its long history it also criticizes affluent African Americans for not doing enough to help impoverished blacks.

1885

- Ottmar Mergenthaler, a German living in the United States, patents the Linotype automatic typesetting machine, and by the following year it is in use at the *New York Tribune.* By 1890 a vastly improved model is in use throughout the United States and Europe.

- Ben Perley Moore of the *Boston Journal,* the dean of the capital Press Corps, founds the Washington Gridiron Club to allow journalists and politicians to meet in informal circumstances.

- A trade association for small dailies and weeklies, the National Editorial Association, is formed by B. B. Herbert of the *Red Wing Daily Republican* in Minnesota.

3 March The U.S. Post Office inaugurates special-delivery service.

1 Oct. The *Dallas Morning News* is founded.

1886

- The United States Type Founders Association appoints a committee to consider the mathematical systematization of all type bodies. They create the point system, dividing the pica into twelve equal parts. Great Britain adopts the system in 1898.

- The American Newspaper Publishers Association is founded by *Detroit Evening News* advertising manager William Brearly as a trade association for daily newspapers. It concerns itself with government mail rates, labor relations, new printing methods, and price control.

March *Cosmopolitan Magazine* is founded in Rochester, New York, by Paul J. Schlicht. Part family monthly and general literary magazine, the publication passes through the hands of several owners, and in 1889 becomes one of the most successful magazines in the country.

28 Oct. The Statue of Liberty arrives in New York Harbor, where it is greeted by a flotilla of boats — a welcome inspired by the *New York World.* The last $100,000 needed to bring the statue from France is raised by contributions from the readers of Pulitzer's paper.

1887

- The *New York Sun* inaugurates an evening edition.

- Circulation of the *New York Sunday World* surpasses a quarter million.

- The first long-distance telephone line in the United States is completed; it links New York and Boston.

- Robert Miehle invents the Miehle printing machine, which is manufactured in Chicago by S. K. White. It is the first in a class of modern "two-revolution" presses, in which the print bed moves neatly and precisely under a continuously revolving paper cylinder. It remains in use for many decades.

- The United Typothetae of America, an organization of master printers, is founded to fight the International Typographical Union movement for a nine-hour workday. Its first president is Theodore Low De Vinne.

Jan.   *Scribner's Magazine* is founded in New York as a high-quality literary magazine affiliated with Charles Scribner's Sons publishing house.

1888

- Twenty-three-year-old Arthur Brisbane becomes the *New York Sun* correspondent in London just as the Jack the Ripper murders commence. The intellectual Brisbane, later one of the most famous journalists in the world, surprises his editors by covering the grisly crimes in vivid detail.

- George Eastman introduces the Kodak, a square box camera that uses roll film. After taking all the pictures on the roll the customer mails the whole Kodak camera to the factory and receives in return pictures and a reloaded camera.

28 April   *Collier's Once a Week,* an illustrated general interest magazine, is founded in New York by P. F. Collier. The name changes to *Collier's Weekly* in 1895.

Oct.   *National Geographic Magazine* is founded in Washington, D.C., by Gardiner Greene Hubbard as the publication of the nonprofit National Geographic Society.

1889

- The *New York Sunday World* begins publishing a comic section.

- Edward W. Bok becomes editor of the *Ladies' Home Journal,* and circulation soon reaches half a million at an annual subscription price of one dollar.

- The first formal newspaper chain, the Scripps-McRae League of Newspapers, is founded to publish inexpensive, well-edited papers in small but growing industrial cities.

- Charles W. Dow founds the *Wall Street Journal,* an afternoon financial newspaper, in New York City.

2 Feb.   Frank A. Munsey founds the general-interest magazine *Munsey's Weekly,* which will reach an unprecedented circulation of 650,000 by the turn of the century.

Dec.   *Scribner's Magazine* publishes Jacob Riis's "How the Other Half Lives," an article with photographs depicting terrible conditions on the Lower East Side of New York City. In 1890 it becomes his best-known book.

- Benjamin Orange Flower founds *The Arena* in Boston as a monthly periodical advocating social reform and the benefits of religion.

1890

- Illiteracy is estimated at 13.3 percent of the U.S. population, a decrease of 3.7 percent since 1880.

- Jacob Riis joins the staff of the *New York Evening Sun.*

- The *New York Herald* earns $1 million in a year from advertising and subscriptions.

- The *Emporia Gazette* is founded in Kansas. In 1895 it is purchased by William Allen White, perhaps the most influential small-town publisher and editor in American history.

25 Jan.   Reporter Elizabeth Cochrane (Nellie Bly) arrives in New York after circling the globe in just seventy-two days.

10 Dec.   The World Building opens on Park Row in New York City.

1891

29 Dec.   Thomas Edison receives an early patent for a wireless telegraph.

1892

- Jacob Riis publishes his book *The Children of the Poor.*

1893

- The *New York Sunday World* installs color presses to print its Sunday supplements.

June   S. S. McClure founds *McClure's Magazine* to showcase the best material from his newspaper syndicate. It becomes the pacesetter of the ten-cent periodicals.

1894

- William Randolph Hearst's *San Francisco Examiner* publishes a series of stories on "Little Jim," the crippled son of a prostitute. The articles help increase circulation and induce readers to contribute $20,000 toward the erection of a hospital for handicapped children. One contemporary calls Hearst "a clever amateur."

1895

- Hearst buys the *New York Morning Journal* for $180,000.

- The Paige Compositor, which sets type and justifies the lines, is tested at the *Chicago Herald,* where thirty Linotype machines are already in use. James W. Paige of Rochester, New York, has produced the most sophisticated mechanism to that time, but when the competing Linotype technology is introduced he loses the support of his financiers, including Samuel Langhorne Clemens, who invested the first royalties from *Huckleberry Finn.* The project loses a total of $800,000.

- Stephen Crane's novel of the Civil War, *The Red Badge of Courage,* becomes a best-seller. In 1896 it ranks eighth on the top ten list of popular books.

1896

- Adolph S. Ochs buys *The New York Times.*

- The most popular cartoon comic in New York is "Hogan's Alley" which appears in Pulitzer's *World* and features the Yellow Kid, the ringleader of a group of tenement-district urchins who lampoon upper-class society.

Jan.   William Randolph Hearst, having recently purchased the *New York Morning Journal*, conducts a raid on the staff of the *New York Sunday World* and entices them with promises of large salaries. Everyone except one secretary leaves Pulitzer's paper for its new rival.

8 Feb.   The *New York World* announces it will cut its price in half, to one penny, in order to compete with its new rival, the *Journal*.

Nov.   The *New York World* and the *New York Journal* each sell 1.5 million copies on the day following the McKinley-Bryan presidential election.

1897

• Cyrus H. K. Curtis revives the *Saturday Evening Post*.

• Stephen H. Horgan of the *New York Tribune* runs a halftone on a rotary press, making possible the widespread use of photographs in newspapers.

• Experiments in Rural Free Delivery are initiated by the federal post office.

• The Yiddish-language *Vorwärts*, or *Jewish Daily Forward*, is founded in New York City by the Jewish Socialist Press Federation. Its circulation peaks in 1923 at 250,000 readers.

12 Apr.   The *New York Journal* becomes the first daily paper to be printed in two colors.

1898

9 Feb.   Hearst's *Journal* publishes a private letter written by Dupuy de Lôme, Spanish ambassador to the United States. The letter refers to President William McKinley as "weak and a bidder for the admiration of the crowd." This incident along with the explosion of the USS *Maine* six days later, influences the U.S. decision to declare war on Spain.

1899

• E. L. Godkin retires from the *New York Evening Post* and *The Nation*.

• John Wanamaker and Robert C. Ogden found *Everybody's Magazine* in New York City. It costs ten cents a copy and consists of serials, short stories, articles, and poems, with illustrations that had already appeared in the *Royal Magazine* (London).

OVERVIEW

Communications Links. A revolution in transportation and communications accompanied ever-growing industrialization of the United States that followed the Civil War. A national system of railroads, a rapid all-weather transportation so vital to the emergence of modern business, completed during the last two decades of the nineteenth century also provided the routes for telegraph and telephone lines. In fact many of the first telegraph companies were subsidiaries of railroads, providing crucial information on the location and progress of trains. The railroads also made possible a vastly expanded postal system and transformed the economies of rural life. Furthermore, improvements in transportation helped create two monopoly enterprises, Western Union Telegraph Company (1866) and American Telephone and Telegraph (1885), that greatly facilitated the modernization of American business by providing quick and efficient means of exchanging information.

Urban Culture. Between 1877 and 1899 a racially, ethnically, and religiously mixed urban society developed in the United States, standing in sharp contrast to the more homogenous, rural, small-town American culture of the early nineteenth century. Industrial growth lured rural Americans to the cities, and unprecedented emigration from southern and eastern Europe transformed the ethnic and religious makeup of the American population. The concentration of people in cities created markets for goods and amusements. New technologies brought about cheap manufacturing, wide distribution of products, and fast communication. Indeed traditional modes of communication were transformed. Paperboys delivered newspapers to doorsteps or cried the headlines on busy city sidewalks. Nearly every urban street corner had a small wooden newsstand. Meanwhile the change in communications also affected rural areas where most Americans still lived. During the late nineteenth century farmers acquired something that many city dwellers had already taken for granted—free delivery of the mail. A revamped postal system made possible mail subscriptions of journals and magazines. In 1883 the U.S. Post Office reduced the rate on first-class mail from three cents to two cents for each half ounce.

Technological Horizons. A host of new technologies in the printing industry sped and amplified the written word. Innovations in typesetting, printing, and distribution made it possible to print millions of copies of daily newspapers for the ever-growing urban populations. The spread of both the telegraph and the telephone aided the speedy gathering of news and began to alter the traditional role of the newspaper as the first source for news. Advances in color printing brought about the invention of the glossy illustrated magazine, which created markets of readers among women and children. As Americans increasingly perceived the family as a haven from the tumult of modern life, a host of new publications guided husbands and wives in the creation of the perfect modern home.

The New Journalism. In the last decades of the nineteenth century American newspapers evolved from a partisan forum for expressing political opinion to a source of news, stories, and entertainment. Many major papers severed their ties to political parties and causes, and while still retaining their political slants, took on a more businesslike independence. Journalism became recognized as a legitimate profession, no longer as a means to aggrandize politicians. The Associated Press (1848) and its splinter group, the United Press (1882), engaged in cooperative news gathering while associations such as the McClure Newspaper Syndicate (1884) supplied articles and short stories to newspapers. The "New Journalism" of publisher Joseph Pulitzer claimed to serve the democratic masses. The average American city dweller, interested in the latest gossip, controversies, and sports scores, found his or her way of life described and enlivened in the pages of the urban daily. Battles with Indians, the arrival of the Statue of Liberty in the United States (1886), reporter Nellie Bly's exploits around the world (1890), and the conflict with Spain (1898), are just some of the stories that enthralled readers. Meanwhile the greatest news story of the day—the emergence of city life—was given riveting expression in the New Journalism.

The Seamy Side. The loosening of social boundaries that inevitably accompanied the new urban lifestyle also brought with it an increased tolerance for sensational stories about the seamy side of life. In part a business strategy to sell more copies, in part a defiant intoxication with shocking facts, modern sensationalism was born in the last decade of the nineteenth century. The combination of titillating revelation, pseudoscience, and horror-show aesthetics so familiar to twentieth-century tabloid readers made its debut in the circulation wars of the 1890s in New York. Printers tested a new fast-drying ink on the nightdress of a jug-eared cartoon character named the Yellow Kid who became the emblem of the sensationalistic "Yellow Journalism." The Yellow Kid appeared in Pulitzer's *New York World* and provided witty

commentary on political and social issues of the day. But while Pulitzer's *World* and William Randolph Hearst's *Journal* descended to new depths in creating astonishing headlines, these papers also printed serious stories about politics and life on the streets. Like the nation it served, the journalism of the last decades of the nineteenth century was big, vibrant, and always reinventing itself.

TOPICS IN THE NEWS

ADVERTISING GETS RESPECTABLE

The Early Agencies. Unlike contemporary advertising agencies, which work for advertisers, most agencies of the 1870s worked for publishers or acted as independent brokers between advertisers and the media. A typical agency employed a staff of five: the principal, whose name the agency bore; an estimate man who dealt with rates and expenses; a bookkeeper; a clerk; and an office boy. There were no such things as copywriters, marketing departments, or account executives. Most newspapers derived less than a third of their income from advertising. In 1870 the total revenue from newspaper advertising amounted to $16 million; by 1900 it had grown to $95 million.

A Shadowy Business. Advertising was not regulated by the government, nor did it have a voluntary code of ethics. Publishers routinely lied about the circulations of their newspapers and magazines in order to charge higher advertising rates. Advertisements made claims that often bore little resemblance to the truth and offered outrageous enticements. Claims for gold mines, oil wells, cure-alls, and foolproof investment opportunities regularly appeared in all manner of publications, and the public had not developed the innate skepticism shared by many consumers a century later.

Patent Medicines. The most heavily advertised commodities of the 1880s and 1890s were nonprescription medicinal "cures" for everything from lethargy to cancer. One patent medicine purveyor bragged, "I can advertise *dish water*, and sell it, just as well as an article of merit. It is all in the advertising." Some of the concoctions were harmless, while others contained addictive proportions of opium, morphine, or alcohol. By the turn of the century the annual revenue in this industry reached $75 million each year. The most heavily advertised product of

the 1880s was St. Jacob's Oil, a so-called all-purpose cure. It was initially called Keller's Roman Liniment, supposedly because it was the secret behind the success of Caesar's legions, but the public did not buy it. The name was changed to St. Jacob's Oil, and the manufacturer claimed that it was made by monks in the Black Forest of Germany. It sold well, but the manufacturer stopped advertising, and the public stopped buying it. Meanwhile Drake's Plantation Bitters cured a variety of ailments and were advertised on the sides of barns, houses, and rocks along the train route from New York City to Philadelphia. The cryptic slogan "S.T. 1860X" accompanied the advertisements. Dr. J. H. Drake insisted the slogan was meaningless, but one cynical observer claimed it meant "Started Trade in 1860 with Ten Dollars Capital."

Growth and Reform. Slowly the advertising industry began to reform and regulate itself. Publishers swore to the accuracy of their circulation figures; national campaigns were conducted on behalf of reputable products; advertising became more honest. Francis Wayland Ayer, a Baptist Sunday-school superintendent, started a Philadelphia advertising firm in 1869 and counteracted the image of the advertising agent as con man. His "open contract" became the norm for the advertising business by clearly stating the exact financial terms between publisher and advertiser. At the same time, the explosion in manufacturing capacity after the Civil War helped businessmen see the profitability of increasing knowledge and demand among potential consumers. The first products that manufacturers marketed in this way were small household products that they wanted consumers to buy repeatedly, such as soap. These industries became the heaviest advertisers, later even spawning their own broadcasting genre, the radio and television soap opera.

THE THENUZ HOAX

During the Spanish-American War the rivalry between the *New York World* and the *New York Journal* spawned one of the best-known practical jokes in the annals of journalism. The *World* had six correspondents covering Cuba while its rival the *Journal* had more than two dozen. As was standard practice, each paper copied stories from the other. Arthur Brisbane, editor of the *Journal*, became so angry at the *World* that he devised a plan to embarrass the competition. He planted a story in his paper detailing the death of an Austrian artillery officer, Col. Reflipe W. Thenuz, serving under the Spanish officer Colonel Ordonez (odor-nose). A few days later — after the same report appeared in the *World* — the *Journal* reported that Reflipe W. Thenuz was an anagram of sorts for "We pilfer the news." To add insult to injury, the *Journal* sarcastically announced that it would solicit artists' designs for a Thenuz monument, and for days afterward the *Journal* printed letters from "readers" denouncing Pulitzer's staff as plagiarists.

Source: Joyce Milton, *The Yellow Kids: Foreign Correspondents in the Heyday of Yellow Journalism* (New York: Harper & Row, 1989).

The First Copywriter. In 1874 John Wanamaker, who had started a dry-goods store in Philadelphia after the Civil War, announced a fixed-price policy and a money-back guarantee. His business boomed, and in 1880 he hired an employee whose sole responsibility would be writing advertisements, the first copywriter. John E. Powers, who deliberately cultivated an air of mystery about himself, was not well known or well liked, but he became the most influential advertising man of his day. He first convinced Wanamaker to change the name of his Grand Depot store, since Americans always mispronounced *depot*. Powers's advertisements were full of understatement and near deprecation of the goods. In the "great, rough, unhandsome store," prices were "pretty apt to be below the market," for goods that "look better than they are, but worth a quarter, we guess." The public loved this peculiar style, and sales volume doubled within a few years. Powers's relationship with Wanamaker was a rocky one: he was fired in 1883, rehired the next year, and then fired for good in 1886.

Magazines Open Up. The polite magazines of the late nineteenth century accepted only a few advertisements for the back of each issue. It took another advertising pioneer, J. Walter Thompson, to change the minds of editors. He helped put advertisements between the covers of thirty-five publications, including *The Atlantic Monthly*, *The Century*, *Harper's*, *Lippincott's*, *Godey's*, *Peterson's*, and *North American Review*. When the *Ladies' Home Journal* and *The Saturday Evening Post* grew

popular, their publisher, Cyrus H. K. Curtis, was determined to keep them—including the content of their bountiful advertising—respectable and serious. By the end of the nineteenth century, advertising was a $500-million-a-year business and constituted 3.2 percent of the gross national product. The largest agency employed more than 160 people, and the potential growth of the business had not yet been glimpsed.

Sources:

Stephen Fox, *The Mirror Makers: A History of American Advertising and Its Creators* (New York: Morrow, 1984);

Jackson Lears, *Fables of Abundance: A Cultural History of Advertising in America* (New York: Basic Books, 1994).

AMERICAN CORRESPONDENTS COVER THE SPANISH-AMERICAN WAR

Myth and Legend. Two stories, neither of them true, color popular conceptions about reporters in the Spanish-American War of 1898. The first story concerns a telegram William Randolph Hearst allegedly sent to Frederic Remington, who was waiting in Havana to illustrate a war that was not happening. Hearst's cable—"You furnish the pictures, and I'll furnish the war"—suggests that the excesses of yellow journalism caused the war. Hearst's *New York Journal* agitated for American intervention in the Cuban uprising against the Spanish colonial government there and helped to fan the flames of belligerent sentiment. Desire to help the Cuban underdog, the search for overseas markets, and patriotism helped bring on the war. A second story maintains that Sylvester Scovel, the daring correspondent for Joseph Pulitzer's *New York World*, punched the American commander in Cuba, Maj. Gen. William Rufus Shafter, during the ceremony marking Spain's surrender. This story supports a countermyth to the one about Hearst, that the press worked against the government in the war. In fact Scovel hit Shafter only after the general struck him first. Moreover, Scovel spent much of the war working for the U.S. Navy as a spy and courier.

With the Insurgents. In 1895, after deciding that selling insurance was boring, Sylvester Scovel of Pittsburgh went to New York City and asked if the *New York Herald* would be interested in dispatches from Cuba. (An insurgency under Gen. Máximo Gómez was massing against the Spanish imperial government.) He was hired on the spot. While in Cuba Scovel attached himself to Gómez's forces, and for three months he sent dispatches to New York, unsure if any of them arrived. He was arrested while trying to bluff his way into Havana, and the regular *Herald* correspondent there denied any knowledge of him. But the correspondent for the rival *World*, Dr. William Shaw Bowen, went to see Scovel while he was incarcerated in Morro Castle. He was so impressed by the articulate young man that he obtained his release and proposed to hire Scovel for the *World*. When the *World* published an interview Scovel had with Gómez, the Spanish military governor, Valeriano Weyler, offered a $5,000 reward for the reporter, dead or alive. At the time Scovel

Nellie Bly, who traveled around the world in 1889–1890 on a tour sponsored by Joseph Pulitzer's *New York World*

was secretly in New York getting treatment for an infected gunshot wound to his leg, and Pulitzer warned him not to conduct himself as a partisan in the conflict.

All-Star Lineup. In 1896 a variety of correspondents covered the insurgency, many of them from the terrace of the Inglaterra Hotel. Joseph Pulitzer, concerned at the backlash against nonsensical reports coming from Havana, hired the famous, egotistical war correspondent James Creelman. During his long professional career Creelman conducted interviews with the Sioux leader Sitting Bull, Pope Leo XIII, and King George of Greece. Meanwhile, as the circulation war between Pulitzer and Hearst escalated, Hearst hired the world's most famous war correspondent, Richard Harding Davis, who had previously covered the coronation of Czar Nicholas II of Russia for the *Journal.* In addition, the sickly and young Stephen Crane, author of *The Red Badge of Courage* (1895), covered the conflict for the *World.* However, he did not reach Cuba until 1898 and then quickly became ill with malaria. When he filed a story with the *Journal*

for a fellow correspondent who had been wounded, the *World* fired Crane.

The Cuban Joan of Arc. Early in 1897 George Eugene Bryson of the *Journal* learned that Evangelina Cosio y Cisneros, a seventeen-year-old great-niece of the president of the provisional republic, was being held prisoner in a notorious jail, the Casa de Recojidas. When Hearst learned of her situation he printed front-page pleas for aid to the "Cuban Joan of Arc" and "girl martyr." James Creelman, now with the *Journal,* enlisted two hundred stringers, or occasional contributors to the paper, to collect signatures and letters of appeal from American citizens, including President William McKinley's mother and Mrs. Jefferson Davis. After many bribes to prison officials, the correspondents finally organized a jailbreak and took "Miss Cisneros" to New York. There the *Journal* covered her first elevator ride and a shopping trip and sponsored a speaking tour before losing interest in her.

Remember the *Maine*. In early 1898 President McKinley dispatched the USS *Maine,* a second-class battleship, to Havana. It was anchored near shore for three weeks, until 15 February, when a massive explosion sent it to the bottom of Havana Harbor. Two hundred sixty men of a crew of 354 were killed. No one knew what caused the explosion. Intelligent observers realized Spain had nothing to gain by blowing up the ship. (The U.S. Navy later theorized that a fire in a coal bunker onboard ship was the most reasonable explanation.) Nevertheless, many assumed that war with Spain had become inevitable, and indeed the nation moved closer to it. Hearst's *Journal* began a memorial fund for the dead. President McKinley asked Congress to declare war on Easter Sunday, 9 April 1898. It was not clear what the United States would do with Cuba once Spain had been defeated.

Enterprise. Two hundred correspondents covered the war, twenty-five of them employed by Hearst. Publishers spent unprecedented sums to scoop each other's stories. Cable costs to transmit a single story to New York sometimes reached $8,000. The Associated Press ran a fleet of boats that routinely crossed the lines under fire to find cable stations. Correspondents inflated their copy to match the growing headlines at home. Stephen Crane covered the famous charge up San Juan Hill by Theodore Roosevelt's Rough Riders as a blaze of glory. Most papers applauded the imperialistic impulse that sent the navy to Cuba and sent troops to suppress the Philippine insurgency of 1899 to 1902. After the Twentieth Kansas swept through a town of seventeen thousand in the Philippines leaving not a single survivor, Hearts's *Journal* proclaimed the righteousness of American expansionism: "The weak must go to the wall and stay there. . . . We'll rule Asia as we rule at home. We shall establish in Asia a branch agent of the true American movement towards liberty."

SCOVEL TAMES THE KLONDIKE

Recently married to *New York World* correspondent Sylvester "Harry" Scovel, young and demure Frances Scovel of Saint Louis planned to accompany her husband only as far as Chicago, from where he would depart to cover the Klondike gold rush in the summer of 1897. However, after meeting a frail and sickly woman in Chicago planning to go to the Klondike with her own husband, Fran Scovel announced, "If she goes, I can go too." Horrified to learn that women prospectors wore men's overalls, she assembled an outfit that combined knickerbockers with a short, full skirt. Arriving in Skagway, Alaska, the Scovels pitched a tent, and Fran proceeded to cook for the first time in her life, with less than exemplary results.

Harry Scovel hired Billy Saportas as agent for the *World*. After discovering that a bottleneck in the trail was keeping most people out of the mountains, Scovel charged a large amount of dynamite to the *World* and widened the trail. Fran and their horses almost fell off the muddy path, but her husband was proud of her fortitude and boasted, "She is no ordinary woman."

After Harry was suddenly called back to New York, he rushed off without saying good-bye to Fran, leaving a note telling Saportas to get her on board the boat to Seattle. When she reached Seattle Fran found a packet of lengthy, guilt-ridden love letters from her husband. In 1898, undaunted by her adventures in the Klondike, Fran followed Harry to Cuba, where he had become ill while covering the rebellion against Spain. Risking yellow fever and malaria, Fran managed to get him to a suitable hospital.

Harry died of complications from surgery in 1905, and Fran became the society columnist for the *Saint Louis Post-Dispatch*. After corresponding for years with Billy Saportas, who had joined the army, she married him in 1917. Fran Scovel lived to be ninety and died in 1959.

Source: Joyce Milton, *The Yellow Kids: Foreign Correspondents in the Heyday of Yellow Journalism* (New York: Harper & Row, 1989).

Amateur Spies. Throughout the war Sylvester Scovel and other members of the press corps provided intelligence to American commanders about the location of Spanish ships and troops. Yet the correspondents drew fierce criticism from military authorities for endangering American troops and violating censorship in pursuit of sensational stories. Scovel even carried messages back and forth to General Gómez, who feared that America's intention was not to grant Cuba its independence but to annex it as a colony. On the whole, leading correspondents such as Creelman and Davis added glory to a conflict that had few clear outcomes.

Sources:

Phillip Knightley, *The First Casualty: From the Crimea to Vietnam, the War Correspondent as Hero, Propagandist, and Myth Maker* (New York: Harcourt Brace Jovanovich, 1975);

Sidney Kobre, *The Yellow Press and Gilded Age Journalism* (Tallahassee: Florida State University Press, 1964);

Joyce Milton, *The Yellow Kids: Foreign Correspondents in the Heyday of Yellow Journalism* (New York: Harper & Row, 1989);

W. A. Swanberg, *Citizen Hearst* (New York: Scribners, 1961).

BREAKING DOWN BARRIERS

Nellie Bly. Born Elizabeth Jane Cochran (later spelled Cochrane) on 5 May 1864 in western Pennsylvania, Nellie Bly became a journalist to help support her family after her father died. In 1885 she wrote an anonymous response to a *Pittsburgh Dispatch* article about why women should stay home and not seek work or the vote. Editor George Madden ran an advertisement for the author to come forward and was so impressed with the pretty, well-spoken twenty-year-old that he offered her a job as a reporter for five dollars a week. Bly took her pen name from a popular song by Stephen Foster. She wrote about the conditions in the tenements and factories, gaining a prized invitation to join the Pittsburgh Press Club. However, more than anything else she yearned to travel.

Mexico, the Madhouse, and Phileas Fogg. Traveling to Mexico in 1886 with her mother as chaperone, Bly talked with all manner of Mexicans, from the elite to the poorest peasants. Her stories on the living conditions of the poor and the shortcomings of Mexican democracy almost got her arrested, but she escaped back over the border with her notes in her petticoats, pretending to be a niece of President Porfirio Díaz. Her book *Six Months in Mexico* (1888) brought her enough acclaim that she felt ready to tackle New York. When she arrived in the city Bly repeatedly tried to see Joseph Pulitzer. One day after waiting several hours to see him, she finally forced her way into his office and persuaded him to break his own rule against hiring female reporters. Bly's willingness to take great personal risks to get a story fueled the competition among New York papers and inaugurated a new kind of celebrity journalism. In 1887 she gained immediate notoriety by feigning madness to get herself committed to the mental hospital on Blackwell's Island. Her exposé of the conditions there precipitated a wave of reform. Next she got herself arrested and exposed the squalid conditions in the jails. At another time she went behind the scenes at Buffalo Bill's Wild West Show. Nothing, however, could duplicate her 1889–1890 trip around the world to beat the record set by Phileas Fogg, the adventurer of Jules Verne's novel *Around the World In Eighty Days* (1873). With a small satchel and a practical blue broadcloth dress, she sailed for England on a German steamer on 14 November 1889.

Headlines Galore. Pulitzer's *World* trumpeted her projected route of New York to London, then Calais, Brindisi, Port Said, Ismailia, Suez, Aden, Ceylon, Penang, Singapore, Hong Kong, Yokohama, San Francisco, and back to New York. A telegram from Verne greeted Bly in Southampton and she met the writer at Amiens, France, where he exclaimed that she was "a mere baby." Bly described appalling poverty in Brindisi, Italy; went bicycling in Colombo, Ceylon; visited a Hindu temple in Penang, Malaya; rode in a ricksha and bought a monkey in Singapore; and reached Hong Kong two days ahead of schedule. She celebrated Christmas with the American consul in Canton.

Breaking the Record. Meanwhile speculations ran rampant in New York, fueled by the *World* article "Nellie Bly Guessing Match," offering a trip to Europe to the reader who most closely guessed the time of her return. A stormy Pacific crossing slowed Bly's progress, and when a smallpox rumor threatened to keep her quarantined onboard ship in San Francisco Bay, she jumped into a nearby tugboat. A special *World* train sped her east, and she arrived in Jersey City on 25 January 1890, seventy-two days, six hours, eleven minutes, and fourteen seconds after she began.

Rapid Exit. In 1895, after a few more years of reporting in New York, Bly met the millionaire Robert Livingston Seaman, an industrialist and senior director of the Merchants' Exchange Bank of New York. The two had met in Chicago and were married within two weeks, despite the forty years difference in their ages. Bly left journalism for high society and luxurious travel. Seaman died nine years later, and Bly attempted to take over Seaman's Iron Clad Manufacturing Company, but employees swindled her into bankruptcy.

Return to Journalism. Bly opened the door for other women in journalism. When the American battleship *Maine* sank in Havana Harbor in 1898, Fanny B. Ward of the *New Orleans Times-Picayune* was there, one of the first American correspondents on the scene. It was, however, still the highest compliment a woman reporter could receive to be told, "You write like a man." Twenty years after she had left journalism Bly returned to writing because she once again needed to support herself. Her column on child welfare appeared in Hearst's *Evening Journal*. She died after a bout with pneumonia on 27 January 1922.

Sources:

Brooke Kroeger, *Nellie Bly: Daredevil, Reporter, Feminist* (New York: Times Books, 1994);

Madelon Golden Schlipp and Sharon M. Murphy, *Great Women of the Press* (Carbondale: Southern Illinois University Press, 1983).

THE LADIES' HOME JOURNAL AND PRACTICAL HOUSEKEEPER

The Curtises Try Something New. Cyrus H. K. Curtis, a publisher from Portland, Maine, and his progressive Boston-born wife, Louisa Knapp Curtis, moved to

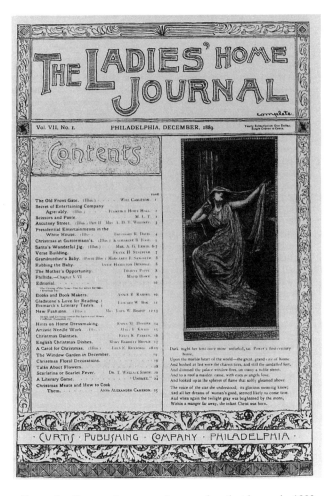

Cover for the popular woman's magazine that began in 1883 as a supplement to Cyrus H. K. and Louisa Knapp Curtis's *Tribune and the Farmer*

Philadelphia in 1876 because it was cheaper to publish their newspaper, the *People's Ledger*, there. The newspaper field was crowded in Phildelphia, and the *People's Ledger* failed. For the next three years they struggled with various other publications until they borrowed $2,000 from a relative and founded the *Tribune and the Farmer*. Cyrus edited the newspaper while Louisa acted as business manager. In the summer of 1883 Cyrus proposed a "Women and Home" department to fill some vacant space in the paper. Louisa wrote the material, and the column ran regularly thereafter. It stimulated a great deal of reader interest and advertising, and consequently the Curtises decided to publish a monthly women's supplement to the weekly *Tribune*. The *Ladies' Journal*, the first issue of that supplement, appeared in December 1883; all subsequent issues used the title *Ladies' Home Journal and Practical Housekeeper*. It soon surpassed the original publication in circulation and advertising revenue, capitalizing on the rising interest in reading among middle-class women. By October 1884 Curtis and his wife had sold the *Tribune* and established the *Ladies' Home Journal* as an independent monthly.

Ottmar Mergenthaler's original linotype machine, which he invented in 1884

Circulation Drives. Curtis was a master at increasing his lists of subscribers. He offered four subscriptions for one dollar, creating "clubs" in which his readers acted as his sales force. By the end of 1884 the *Ladies' Home Journal*'s circulation was 100,000. Curtis also tried to improve its quality by printing the work of well-known female fiction writers. Marion Harland's short story helped increase the list of subscribers to 270,000 by spring 1886. Louisa May Alcott refused to write a column for the *Ladies' Home Journal* until Curtis offered to pay $100 to her favorite charity. In 1887 Curtis vowed to reach a million subscribers and took a big gamble to reach it. He raised the subscription price of the *Ladies' Home Journal* to one dollar a year, expanded the magazine to thirty-two pages, added a cover, and brought in the advertising needed to sustain it. In 1889 membership reached more than 400,000 subscribers. Two years later the Curtis Publishing Company issued stock and was capitalized at $500,000.

The Formula. The *Ladies' Home Journal* remains to this day the prototype for women's magazines. Heavy with advertising and advice on homemaking, cooking, fashion, and children, it also included information on family relationships. In 1889 Curtis hired a previously unknown Dutch-born editor named Edward W. Bok. A peculiar man who seemed to have little affinity to women except his mother, Bok nonetheless developed the *Ladies' Home Journal* into a remarkably successful enter-

prise. He made readers feel that the magazine was a trusted friend and inaugurated columns such as "Side Talks with Girls" and even "Side Talks with Boys." He brought in well-known authors such as Rudyard Kipling and later secured a monthly column from Theodore Roosevelt, "The President," which Roosevelt dictated from his barber's chair. In 1895 he began publishing house plans and sheet music for John Philip Sousa marches among other popular songs. The famous architect Stanford White said that Bok had influenced American domestic architecture for the better more than any other man of his generation. Bok married the Curtises' only child, their daughter, Mary Louise. In 1900 the circulation of the *Ladies' Home Journal* topped 800,000 and three years later it finally reached 1,000,000.

Guide and Friend. The *Ladies' Home Journal* also published occasional features on timely topics in politics and business, usually in the form of profiles of famous women of the day. The topics of poverty, temperance, and the vote for women did get covered, if not extensively. The periodical took on the role as surrogate friend and occasional mother for many women. For females on remote farms or in the frontier areas of the West, it was a welcome companion. Yet its main audience was middle-class women in towns and cities with populations of more than ten thousand. Curtis studied the neighborhoods where these women lived and promulgated a picture of the successful domestic woman, a different picture from the submissive, pious "flower" peddled to earlier generations. According to the *Ladies' Home Journal* prized female attributes included intelligence, physical fitness and health, economic self-reliance, and the careful choice of a husband. While laden with contemporary notions of what was appropriate for each sex, the magazine brooked no tolerance of the notion that women were less capable than men. As a result the *Ladies' Home Journal* became the best-selling magazine of its time, an arbiter of taste in the emerging nationwide culture.

Sources:

Helen Damon-Moore, *Magazines for the Millions: Gender and Commerce in the* Ladies' Home Journal *and the* Saturday Evening Post *1880-1910* (Albany: State University of New York Press, 1994);

John Tebbel, *The American Magazine: A Compact History* (New York: Hawthorn Books, 1969).

MECHANICAL REVOLUTIONS

More and Better. As the population of the United States grew, newspaper circulation skyrocketed in the 1880s and 1890s, and technological innovations kept pace. Improved printing methods made possible an increase in newspaper and magazine distribution without increasing costs. The availability of these new processes allowed publishers to promote their papers with the knowledge that their presses could keep up with demand. Advertisers also bought more space, knowing that many readers would see their skillfully printed advertisements.

THE TYPEWRITER

The first known writing machine dates to England in 1714. William Austin Burt received the first American patent for a "typographer" in 1829. Over the next forty years some twenty different typewriting inventions appeared in the United States as well as Britain and France, but the first practical manual typewriter did not appear until 1868, when Christopher Latham Sholes, a former editor of the *Milwaukee Sentinel*, patented his invention. He sold his plan to arms manufacturer E. Remington and Sons in 1873. Three years later Remington introduced its Model I to the public at the Philadelphia Centennial Exposition. In 1878 it was upgraded to print both upper- and lower-case letters. This early Remington version sat on a sewing-machine stand and had a carriage return operated by a treadle. The first market for the machine was among writers, editors, and clergymen. Samuel Langhorne Clemens's *The Adventures of Tom Sawyer* (1876) is supposedly the first book to have been printed from a typewritten draft.

While the machine's utility was obvious, many people had doubts that the business world would ever adopt such an impersonal mode of communication. The Associated Press adopted the typewriter in 1885, but many of its journalists still wrote their copy in longhand. Sears, Roebuck and Company continued to send handwritten letters to its rural customers well into the twentieth century. Moreover, the typewriter cost as much as $125, a price few consumers could afford. By 1878 Remington had sold a total of only four thousand machines. New innovations made the typewriter cheaper as well as more reliable and efficient, and within ten years sales increased to fifteen hundred per month. In 1893 the type basket was placed in front of the platen, or roller, and in 1896 the automatic ribbon-reverse appeared. The typewriter brought women into the commercial workplace in greater numbers because its operation was considered a respectable occupation. By the end of the century the typewriter could be found in the majority of offices.

Sources: Daniel Boorstin, *The Americans: The Democratic Experience* (New York: Random House, 1973);

Richard N. Current, *The Typewriter and the Men Who Made It* (Urbana: University of Illinois Press, 1954).

Finally, a fall in the price of newsprint helped large-scale printing to remain cheap.

The Greatest Innovation. In the history of printing no innovation rivals the 1884 introduction of the Linotype machine. For more than four hundred years typesetting had remained the same—full pages of type had to be set manually, letter by letter, with individual precast type pieces. The Linotype allowed typesetters to create mechanically one line of type at a time.

Inventor. Ottmar Mergenthaler (1854–1899), a German living in the United States, patented his invention in 1885 after spending a year improving the original version. With a Linotype the typesetter used a device similar to a typewriter with ninety keys. By pushing a key a letter or punctuation mark (called matrices) could be put into place. After a line was finished a quick-cooling molten alloy was poured over the casts; once cooled it formed a complete line of type (called a slug). The Linotype also automatically justified text by inserting spaces between words and making each line the same width.

Change. The Linotype was an immediate success and revolutionized the printing industry. It allowed typesetters to set more than five thousand pieces of type per hour as opposed to fifteen hundred by hand. The machine required only one operator and allowed daily newspapers to shorten the time between receiving a story and getting it to the street. *The New York Times* became the first publication to use it in 1886, and by 1899 three thousand were in use worldwide. Magazines and books were typeset on the Linotype machine. It was supplanted only in the late twentieth century by electronic composition.

Speed and Color. By 1890 most papers began printing with stereotype plates, which not only sped up the printing process but allowed the breaking of columns for illustrations, headlines, and advertisements. Unlike a type-revolving press, the Hoe press could print forty-eight thousand twelve-page papers in an hour, allowing publishers to keep up with circulations of approximately half a million. New color presses, used to print the Sunday supplements, also came into use in the early 1890s. In 1893 the *New York World* became one of the first newspapers to use a color press.

The Halftone. In the 1880s most American newspapers illustrated their stories with engravings printed from zinc plates or woodblocks. The demand for artists was short-lived, however, because Frederick E. Ives was at work developing a process to prepare photographs for printing. Ives, who had been made the head of the photographic laboratory at Cornell University in 1876, when he was twenty, had his first success with a halftone in 1878. By 1886 he had perfected a commercial process. A photoengraving, or halftone, was made from an image photographed through a screen and then etched so that the details of the image were reproduced in dots. If the dots were close together, the image would be dark; the farther apart they were, the lighter the image would become. In 1897 Stephen H. Horgan of the *New York Tribune*, who had actually printed the first quality halftone,

Postage stamps for first-class, foreign, and special-delivery mail (1890–1893)

"Shantytown," in the *New York Daily Graphic* in 1880, contrived how to use halftones on rotary presses.

Labor. By the 1890s some of the larger urban newspapers employed more than one thousand people on their printing, editorial, and advertising staffs. Technological developments brought with them increased labor specialization and greater demands from workers. Beginning in 1881 the American Federation of Labor organized printers, pressmen, and engravers in unions that pressed for better wages, improved working conditions, and shorter hours. Between 1886 and 1901 the International Typographical Union split by specialty into four different unions, reducing the danger of plantwide strikes. Also, in 1899 the American Newspaper Publishers Association worked with the printers' unions to establish arbitration procedures to reduce the likelihood of strikes.

Sources:

W. Turner Berry and H. Edmund Poole, *Annals of Printing* (London: Blandford Press, 1966);

Sidney Kobre, *The Yellow Press and Gilded Age Journalism* (Tallahassee: Florida State University Press, 1964);

Michael Emery and Edwin Emery, *The Press and America: An Interpretive History of the Mass Media,* 7th edition, revised and expanded (Englewood Cliffs, N.J.: Prentice Hall, 1992).

THE NEW YORK TIMES

The Scourge of Tweed. In the early 1870s the Republican-oriented *New-York Times* exposed the rampant graft and corruption of the New York municipal government under Democratic leader William Marcy "Boss" Tweed. In the 1880s it uncovered abuses in the postal system, got the scoop on financier Jay Gould's corrupt attempts to control the Manhattan Elevated Railway, and published seething editorials against trusts and labor unions alike. The *Times* finally abandoned its strictly pro-Republican stance during the presidential election of 1884 because the Republican candidate, James G. Blaine, had been associated with various corrupt acts. The paper then began to establish a reputation for political independence.

Outstripped by the *World*. In the 1880s the growing popularity of the *New York World*, particularly its colorful Sunday edition, outpaced the *Times* in advertising and circulation. The *Times* temporarily reduced its price from three cents to two cents in 1883, but the construction of a new building undertaken in 1888 reduced profits dramatically. The Panic of 1893 nearly destroyed the paper, as circulation fell from a high of thirty-six thousand to nine thousand. The paper clearly needed a new approach and sound new management. In 1896 the thirty-eight-year-old publisher of the *Chattanooga Times*, Adolph S. Ochs, was offered $50,000 to become manager of *The New-York Times*. Ochs submitted a counterproposal, offering to invest $75,000 of his own money on the condition that, if successful at reviving the paper, he would receive a majority of stock and, hence, win control of the paper and its company. He ran the paper at a profit for three consecutive years, and the stock was duly delivered to him.

An Alternative to Yellow Journalism. While taking his cue from Pulitzer in actively pursuing readers, Ochs maintained the dignity and respectability of the *Times*. He employed bold headlines and offered juicy stories but emphasized strict factuality and decency. When searching for a new motto, he considered "It Does Not Soil the Breakfast Cloth" before settling on "All the News That's Fit to Print." Stressing the paper's utility to businessmen and society in general, Ochs set out to make the *Times* the newspaper of record. On 19 August 1896 he published a declaration of principle, which read in part: "It will be my earnest aim that the New-York Times give the news, all the news, in concise and attractive form, in language that is parliamentary in good society, and give it as early, if not earlier, than it can be learned through any other reliable medium; to give the news impartially, without fear or favor, regardless of any party, sect or interest involved; to make the columns of the New-York Times a forum for the consideration of all questions of public importance, and to that end to invite intelligent discussion from all shades of opinion."

AWFUL PAY, WORSE CONDITIONS

During the late nineteenth century most American newspaper reporters worked up to sixteen hours a day for just twenty to thirty dollars a week. Some beginning journalists earned as little as eight dollars, and other reporters were paid only by the number of lines they got into the paper. There was no reporters' union, and many continued to be paid according to the same wage scale they had worked for during the Civil War. Reporters sometimes banded together to cover the city, but publishers such as Joseph Pulitzer and James Gordon Bennett Jr. frowned on such cooperation. They instituted a spy system, kept benefits at a minimum, and limited story space, thus fueling sensationalism as reporters competed to get their stories in the paper.

One exception was Arthur Brisbane, whom Hearst lured to his paper with a salary of two-thirds what Pulitzer paid him, but with the promise of a $1,000 raise for every ten thousand copies the *Evening Journal* gained in circulation. At the height of the Spanish-American War, the paper sold almost two million copies in a single day, and Brisbane boasted it could have sold more but the printers ran out of paper. Because of the bonus clause in his contract his salary for the year topped $140,000.

Source: Michael Emery and Edwin Emery, *The Press and America: An Interpretive History of the Mass Media*, 7th edition, revised and expanded (Englewood Cliffs, N.J.: Prentice Hall, 1992);

Joyce Milton, *The Yellow Kids: Foreign Correspondents in the Heyday of Yellow Journalism* (New York: Harper & Row, 1989).

The Paper of Business. Businessmen and financiers found *The New York Times* indispensable (the hyphen was dropped in December 1896). Ochs printed the names of out-of-town buyers visiting New York, listed daily real-estate transactions, and published extensive market reports. Readers also appreciated the broad and detailed coverage of government news plus the Sunday book reviews. Despite its increased popularity with the businessmen, however, the *Times* had a circulation of only twenty-five thousand in 1898. Ochs took another risk and cut the price of the paper from three cents to one penny. Within a year sales jumped to seventy-five thousand and by 1901 passed one hundred thousand. Ochs's formula for straight news and useful information, not to mention his overall control, carried the paper into the twentieth century as the leading source of information in the nation.

Source:
Meyer Berger, *The Story of* The New York Times *1851–1951* (New York: Simon & Schuster, 1951).

REPORTING THE INDIAN WARS

Only the Brave Need Apply. After the Civil War the conflict between white frontiersmen and the Plains Indians changed from a guerrilla conflict to an all-out war fought between various western tribes and the U.S. Army. Lasting from 1866 until 1891, the Indian wars provided fresh opportunities to practice the reporting techniques developed during the Civil War. Aside from courage, a correspondent needed a good horse, a weapon, and a reliable courier to carry dispatches to a town with a telegraph office. Many times journalists had to fight as a matter of survival.

Could Anyone Expect Less? The first phase of the wars, lasting until 1878, was fought on the open plains. As Gen. Philip Sheridan stated: "We took away their country and their means of support, broke up their mode of living, their habits of life, introduced disease and decay among them, and it was for this and against this that they made war. Could anyone expect less?" The second phase came after the government set aside reservations for the Native Americans. Plains Indians did not adapt well to reservation life, and the government did not provide enough food. Efforts to leave the reservations became commonplace. The plains were irredeemably transformed in the fifteen years after the first railroad was completed through the Indian hunting grounds in 1860. Railroad towns grew up, and mining settlements followed. The endless prairie had become home to the whites.

Breakouts and Cleanups. After Gen. George Armstrong Custer and five entire companies of his regiment were killed at the Little Big Horn by the Sioux and Cheyenne (25 June 1876), the U.S. Army increased its efforts and eventually succeeded in breaking Indian resistance on the Great Plains. Correspondents covering the campaigns against the Nez Percé (1877), Bannock (1878), Northern Cheyenne (1878–1879), Ute (1879–1880), Apache (1885–1886), and Sioux (1890–1891) received better treatment from the army. When he went to cover the Third Cavalry in 1879, veteran Indian-war reporter John Finerty of the *Chicago Times* was assigned an old trooper to take care of his horse. The cavalryman rode behind him as if Finerty were an officer. His dispatches from the Apache campaign were among the last straightforward reports to come out of the western war. The so-called New Journalism had taken hold in New York, and the competition for circulation made later stories exaggerated, rumor based, and often outright false.

Half-Truths and Embroidery. Coverage of the Sioux confrontation with the Seventh Cavalry in 1890 played on fears of a widespread Indian uprising all across the West, when in fact quashing of the Sioux uprising signaled the end of the Indian wars. More than twenty correspondents covered the events, including the illustrator Frederic Remington for *Harper's Weekly*, but only three actually wit-

Central operating department of the New York office of the Western Union Telegraph Company, circa 1880

nessed the killing of Sitting Bull and the infamous massacre of the Sioux at Wounded Knee. Some were experienced reporters while others had never seen a battle or submitted a story before. Most filed reports based on embroidered accounts from scouts and camp followers. The Indian agency trading post and Findlay's Hotel at Pine Ridge, South Dakota, became maelstroms of gossip and half-truths. Reporters amused themselves by collectively composing their own newspapers, such as the *Badlands Budget* and a parody dime novel called *Short Bull, the Brigand of the Bad Lands*. While the typical reader got a good picture of government mismanagement, the Indian point of view was absent from all coverage of the wars. In fact, coverage of the Wounded Knee massacre provided a dress rehearsal for the excesses and half-truths of Spanish-American War reporting.

Sources:

Oliver Knight, *Following the Indian Wars: The Story of the Newspaper Correspondents Among the Indian Campaigners* (Norman: University of Oklahoma Press, 1960);

George R. Kolbenschlag, *A Whirlwind Passes: News Correspondents and the Sioux Indian Disturbances of 1890–1891* (Vermillion: University of South Dakota Press, 1990).

RURAL FREE DELIVERY

Mail. In 1847 railroads carried only about 10 percent of the U.S. mail while the remainder was transported by steamboat, by stagecoach, and on horseback. In 1855 the railroads began using special mail cars and central distribution points. By the 1870s the U.S. Postal Service was the largest and one of the best in the world even though it was irregularly administered.

Urban Free Delivery. Before 1825 there was no home delivery service. In that year the postmaster general was authorized to begin delivery in cities with populations of more than ten thousand. A carrier was not paid a salary and depended on collecting a one- or two-cent fee from the recipient, an awkward arrangement for everyone involved. This system lasted until 1863, when in the midst of the Civil War, Congress deemed that the carriers should be paid by the government. Other reforms soon followed. In 1879 Congress passed the Postal Act, which clearly defined what constituted second-class matter—newspapers, magazines, and journals. Six years later postal officials authorized a one-cent-a-pound rate for such material. In the late 1870s and early 1880s stamps cost two cents for first-class domestic letters, five cents for foreign letters, and ten cents for special delivery.

The Trip to Town. Until the 1890s more than 75 percent of Americans lived in rural areas or small towns, and for these people collecting the mail often took a half-day trip to the nearest post office. Youngsters were sometimes recruited to collect and deliver the mail. After home delivery had become a fixture in the cities, rural Americans began to think about the advantages of such service.

Political Hay. As early as 1879 small-town journalist John Stahl advocated rural free delivery, or RFD. In 1891, two years after his appointment by Republican president Benjamin Harrison, Postmaster General John Wanamaker, a self-made department-store magnate, began to champion RFD. Opponents believed that it was a ploy to win votes, and even farm journals pointed out the high costs of such a vast undertaking. Wanamaker's fellow Republicans said it smacked of socialism, a charge fueled when the rural Populist movement embraced RFD as consonant with its demands for a postal savings bank and government ownership of telegraph and telephone lines.

Pro and Con. Newspapers supported RFD as a means of expanding distribution, and many farm families were excited at the prospect of receiving world news, weather forecasts, and market prices on a daily basis. The National Grange endorsed RFD in 1891, and many farmers' alliances passed resolutions supporting it. With the help of Congressman James O'Donnell, a Republican from Michigan and a newspaperman, Wanamaker drafted a bill to send to the Congress. They asked for $6 million, but Congress voted a mere $10,000 for experimentation. Georgia Populist Tom Watson supported RFD, and in the presidential campaign of 1892 the Republicans endorsed it. After Democrat Grover Cleveland was elected, he appointed his crony Wilson Bissell to the office of postmaster general. Bissell quickly pronounced that RFD would bankrupt the nation, ignored the $10,000 already appropriated, and declined to discuss the issue further.

A Political Football. During the 1890s the farmers' list of grievances with the federal government was a long one, and the mail-delivery system was to them plain evidence of discrimination in favor of the privileged few: bankers, manufacturers, and city dwellers. In fact some urban businessmen had their mail delivered not just once but twice a day. In 1895 Congress directed Bissell to spend $20,000 on a feasibility study and to report during the next session on extending postal service throughout the country. Bissell refused to do so and then resigned. Cleveland replaced him with the well-loved William L. Wilson of West Virginia, a former Confederate soldier, university president, and congressman. The 1896 postal appropriation amounted to $40,000, and experiments were finally conducted. That year farmers hung their hopes on presidential candidate William Jennings Bryan, a Populist who had captured the Democratic nomination with his legendary "Cross of Gold" speech opposing the gold standard as contrary to the interests of the common man. Bryan was defeated, and the farmers had to wait another six years for the beginning of gradual implementation of RFD nationwide.

Sources:

Alfred D. Chandler Jr., *The Visible Hand: The Managerial Revolution in American Business* (Cambridge, Mass.: Harvard University Press, 1977);

Wayne E. Fuller, *RFD: The Changing Face of Rural America* (Bloomington: Indiana University Press, 1964).

THE TELEGRAPH

Hoopla. When the telegraph came into widespread use in the mid nineteenth century, predictions about its effects on society were mixed. Editor James Gordon Bennett of the *New York Herald* wrote that the paper that published news it received by telegraph was "such a specimen of journalism as has never before been equaled, from the creation of the world up to this morning, in the history of mankind. It . . . is enough to . . . bring us actually to believe that either the end of the world or the beginning of the millennium is at hand." In contrast, his contemporary Henry David Thoreau, contemplating the profusion of insignificant news made possible by the miraculous technology, wrote: "We are in great haste to construct a magnetic telegraph from Maine to Texas; but Maine and Texas, it may be, have nothing to communicate. . . . We are eager to tunnel under the Atlantic and bring the Old World some weeks nearer to the New, but perchance the first news that will leak through into the broad, American ear will be that Princess Adelaide has

THE DAILY GRAPHIC

In 1872 David Croly of New York launched the first pictorial daily newspaper. The *Daily Graphic* ran eight pages, three and one-half of which were covered with illustrations. The rest consisted of short news items. Since the halftone process that allowed mechanical reproduction of photographs had not yet been invented, *Daily Graphic* illustrators had to make engraved copies of photographs. On 4 March 1880 the art editor of the *Daily Graphic*, Stephen H. Horgan, made history by printing the first legible halftone. "Shantytown" was a picture of the impoverished upper Fifth Avenue. The newspaper also printed explicit pictures of crime scenes, including the murderer William Foster on the gallows. Samuel Langhorne Clemens thought that the *Daily Graphic* was a "marvelous paper" and wrote in appreciation: "I don't care much about reading (unless it be some tranquilizing tract or other), but I do like to look at pictures, and the illustrated weeklies do not come to me as often as I need them."

Nevertheless the paper had a brief life span of only sixteen years. Its circulation never exceeded ten thousand. In 1884 the *New York World* began printing illustration, and for five years the *Daily Graphic* fought a losing battle against the competition. Financial mismanagement and poor investments also hastened the demise of the paper. However, it left a lasting impact on journalism by proving the value of pictures to news coverage.

Source: Sidney Kobre, *The Yellow Press and Gilded Age Journalism* (Tallahassee: Florida State University Press, 1964).

the whooping cough." The question of whether the telegraph would be an actual improvement or a diversion from more consequential matters was quickly forgotten as the technology spread along burgeoning railroad lines. Small-town papers were revolutionized, and formed press associations to share the costs of the dispatches.

Thoroughly Modern Business. In 1866 the three largest telegraph companies in the country merged to form Western Union. It was the first modern nationwide business enterprise in the United States, and it enjoyed a powerful advantage over potential competitors. Railroad magnate and financier Jay Gould mounted the only real challenge to Western Union. In the late 1870s he began to organize the telegraph subsidiaries of railroad companies under his control. After acquiring the Union Pacific Railroad, Gould canceled its contract with Western Union and began to use the services of the Atlantic and Pacific Telegraph Company. In 1879 he created the American Union Telegraph Company, which soon monopo-

Hattie E. Bolster, Frank Drew, and Lizzie Hunt, the regular operators of the Lynn, Massachusetts, telephone exchange
in 1896. Female telephone operators were often called
"Hello Girls."

lized telegraph service in the southwestern United States. After Western Union stock plunged in 1881, Gould became its largest stockholder.

Press Associations. As early as 1848 a group of seven New York daily newspapers formed the Associated Press (AP) to take advantage of the new telegraphic technology and to cooperate in news gathering. In 1875 the wire between New York and Washington transmitted more than twenty thousand words a day. Between 1880 and 1900 the miles of telegraph lines covering the United States quadrupled, and AP wire service extended to Chicago, New Orleans, Minneapolis, and Denver. Other cities received news reports through express messengers or regular mail delivery. During this time the AP moved to consolidate its control over which newspapers benefited from their wire service. In conjunction with Western Union it provided member papers with special treatment and rates. The AP also prohibited its members from using any other news service. By 1880 only 50 percent of the morning dailies and 25 percent of the evening papers had access to AP service. The only serious com-

petitor was the United Press (not the twentieth-century wire service of the same name), founded in 1882. It went bankrupt in 1897 and merged with the AP.

Objectivity. The wire service soon became the primary source of national news. Its dispatches were collected from hundreds of contributors around the country, who were independent from political parties and local institutions. Reporters for the services were told to send "bare matters of fact" because the AP client papers represented the entire spectrum of political allegiance and interest. News was a "salable commodity" like any other. Wire service coverage thus produced impersonal, national, standardized news. For this reason historians have called it the originator of the journalistic notion of objectivity, as well as a powerful force for the creation of a national American consciousness that replaced earlier, regional identities.

Sources:

Menahem Blondheim, *News Over the Wires: The Telegraph and the Flow of Public Information in America, 1844–1897* (Cambridge, Mass.: Harvard University Press, 1994);

Alfred D. Chandler Jr., *The Visible Hand: The Managerial Revolution in American Business* (Cambridge, Mass.: Harvard University Press, 1977);

Mitchell Stephens, *A History of News: From the Drum to the Satellite* (New York: Viking, 1988).

THE TELEPHONE

Simultaneous Invention. In the mid 1870s at least three men were working independently toward electrical transmission of the human voice: Elisha Gray, a telegraph superintendent for Western Electric in Chicago; Alexander Graham Bell, a speech teacher for the deaf in Boston; and Thomas Alva Edison, a freelance inventor in Menlo Park, New Jersey. Amos Dolbeare, a professor at Tufts University, was another early telephone innovator. Bell applied for a patent on his invention on 14 February 1876, the same day that Gray registered his work on such a device. Bell's patent, issued on 7 March, became one of the most profitable and contested patents of the nineteenth century. On 10 March the first spoken words traveled over a wire when Bell said to his assistant, "Mr. Watson, come here, I want you." Over the next several months professors at Brown University worked to make Bell's invention smaller and more practical, and in July 1877 the Bell Telephone Company was formed.

Competition. Western Union quickly hired Edison to build an improved telephone that would avoid infringements on the Bell patents. Edison's improvements were actually more important to the modern telephone than Bell's original device. Western Union also bought Gray's and Dolbeare's patents—but overextended in railroad purchases to keep its telegraph business competitive and fearful of legal battles over the patents—the company agreed in 1879 to sell the patent rights to its instrument to Bell Telephone. Western Union subsequently found to its chagrin that the telephone competed with the telegraph.

Long Distance. At first the telephone was used only for local calls. A brilliant operations director for the Bell Company, Theodore N. Vail, who earlier had revamped the U.S. Postal Service, insisted that Bell retain the rights to develop long-distance service. Western Union had offered to end the telephone-patent war in exchange for entry into the long-distance field. Vail wanted to do more research and to expand Bell facilities, but conservative investors in the company resisted. Only when he threatened to resign in 1885 did they allow him to go ahead with building a long-distance subsidiary, the American Telephone and Telegraph Company (AT&T). He built the first long-distance lines from New York to Albany and to Boston in 1887. New lines began to open steadily thereafter—between New York and Chicago (1892), Boston and Chicago (1893), New York and Saint Louis (1896), and New York and Omaha (1897). By 1899 the net worth of AT&T was approximately $120 million, and it controlled forty-

One of these Kids given with Every Puzzle.

HULLY GEE!!
I HUNG DE TIRENTS

SAY, DE FREE CUBA PUZZLE IS ALL RITE, ME AN LIZ DONE IT SEE!

The Trade Supplied by the New England News Co., Boston, Mass.
Price 10c.   Sold Everywhere

Advertisement featuring the Yellow Kid, the popular cartoon character Richard F. Outcault created for Pulitzer's *World*

nine licensed subsidiaries, in essence monopolizing U.S. long-distance service.

Spread. By 1880 there was already one telephone for every one thousand people in the United States. Doctors estimated that they saved thousands of lives every year because they were summoned by telephone to treat emergencies. Newspapermen complained that news traveled so quickly over the telephone that morning papers would become obsolete. By 1900 there was one telephone for every one hundred people, and the device was considered an everyday convenience by more than a million Americans.

Sources:
John Brooks, *Telephone: The First Hundred Years* (New York: Harper & Row, 1976);

During the late nineteenth century nearly every city street corner had a newsstand. Pedestrians could find not only newspapers but a variety of magazines at these locations. The magazines, many of which are still published, addressed a variety of interests and were reasonably priced. The following magazines were among the most popular.

	Founded	Cost
Humor		
Puck	1877	10 cents
The Judge	1881	10 cents
Life	1883	10 cents
Home & Fashion		
Ladies' Home Journal	1883	6 cents
Good Housekeeping	1885	10 cents
Juvenile		
The Golden Argosy	1882	10 cents
General		
Cosmopolitan Magazine	1886	10 cents
Collier's Once a Week	1888	7 cents
Everybody's Magazine	1899	10 cents
The Saturday Evening Post	1821	5 cents
Munsey's Weekly	1889	10 cents
McClure's Magazine	1893	10 cents
Scribner's Magazine	1887	25 cents
Atlantic Monthly	1857	35 cents
Harper's Monthly	1850	25 cents
Harper's Weekly	1857	35 cents
Century Magazine	1870	35 cents

Source: Frank Luther Mott, *A History of American Magazines*, 5 volumes (Cambridge, Mass.: Harvard University Press, 1930–1968).

Alfred D. Chandler Jr., *The Visible Hand: The Managerial Revolution in American Business* (Cambridge, Mass.: Harvard University Press, 1977).

TEN-CENT MAGAZINES

A Pricing Revolution. In June 1893, to compete with popular monthly periodicals such as *Munsey's,* which was founded as a weekly in 1889 and became a monthly in 1891, and *Cosmopolitan,* founded in 1886, S. S. McClure founded a new monthly, *McClure's,* and set the price at ten cents, forcing its rivals to lower their prices to match. (Many weeklies cost thirty-five cents.) Over the next ten years other new magazines that sold for ten or fifteen cents appeared, and by 1903 they represented about 85 percent of the total magazine circulation in America. At the turn of the century the most profitable magazines

were *McClure's, Munsey's, Argosy,* and *Cosmopolitan.* While some tried lowering their prices even further, only *The Saturday Evening Post,* a weekly revived in 1897 by Cyrus H. K. Curtis, prospered at a nickel.

A Market Revolution. The new monthly magazines took advantage of improved printing technologies to publish many pleasing illustrations. Their contents varied, but they paid particular attention to contemporary social problems and reform movements. The sons and daughters of the working and middle classes took up the habit of reading as never before, and a national market for mass-circulation magazines was created. In 1865 there were 700 periodicals in the United States; in 1880 there were 2,400; and in 1885 there were 3,300.

Competition with Newspapers. The growth of the national advertising industry fueled the explosion of mass-circulation magazines, which competed with newspapers for advertising. In response newspaper owners formed the International Circulation Managers Association in 1898 and the Newspaper Advertising Executives Association in 1900 to fight for their share of the market. To survive, magazines such as *Atlantic, Scribner's,* and *Century* had to follow the new publications in their coverage of social issues. Although they were outstripped in circulation, these older, elite periodicals retained their prestige and influence. General weeklies such as *Harper's* and *Leslie's Illustrated* and humor weeklies such as *Life, Puck,* and *The Judge,* also had to compete for readers and advertising revenue.

The Seedbed of Muckraking. Ten-cent magazines were usually well written. Julian Hawthorne's coverage of the Spanish-American War in *Cosmopolitan* was popular among many readers. *McClure's* published fiction by Robert Louis Stevenson, Rudyard Kipling, Sir Arthur Conan Doyle, Edward Everett Hale, Joel Chandler Harris, Thomas Hardy, Stephen Crane, and O. Henry (William Sydney Porter), whose first story was submitted from the Federal Penitentiary at Columbus, Ohio. Ida M. Tarbell's serialized profiles of Napoleon in 1894 and Abraham Lincoln in 1895 each doubled the circulation of *McClure's.* In 1898–1899, after the Spanish-American War, McClure serialized Adm. Alfred Thayer Mahan's "The War on the Sea and Its Lessons," which dominated American military planning for decades. As the century turned, the formula for activist social writing that spurred government reforms had been set in place, and the ten-cent magazine became the engine for the most vigorous reformist period in the history of American journalism, that of the muckrakers.

Sources:

Louis Filler, *The Muckrakers* (University Park: Pennsylvania State University Press, 1968);

John Tebbel, *The American Magazine: A Compact History* (New York: Hawthorn Books, 1969).

YELLOW JOURNALISM AND THE CIRCULATION WAR OF 1896

Sunday *World*. During the 1880s the Sunday edition of Joseph Pulitzer's *World* increasingly became a collection of features, advertising, and drawings; each issue had forty-four to fifty-two pages. Circulation passed 250,000 in 1887. The young editor was Morrill Goddard, who had a talent for the feature angle on the news. He not only embellished facts but virtually created the pseudoscience articles featured in later tabloids, thus increasing the popularity of the *World*.

Yellow Ink. In 1893 Pulitzer installed color presses to print the Sunday supplements, and Goddard used them to expand the comics section, which had been inaugurated in 1889. The most popular cartoon, drawn by Richard Outcault, was "Hogan's Alley," which depicted life in the tenements of New York, through the eyes of "The Kid," a jug-eared, bucktoothed toddler in a dirty nightdress. The usual yellow ink gave the pressmen a headache because it took so long to dry, and when they finally formulated a quick-drying shade, they tried it out on the expanse of the boy's dress. The Yellow Kid was born and in the process heralded a new era of journalism.

Hearst Arrives. In 1895 William Randolph Hearst bought the ailing *New York Journal* for $180,000 and immediately tried to buy the staff that had made the Sunday *World* such a success. Hearst's business cards, bearing the words "Call me," mysteriously turned up on the desks of Goddard and his staff. Goddard met Hearst in the bar of the Hoffman House, where the publisher handed him an envelope containing $15,000, an instant bonus if he would agree to come over to the *Journal*. "But I need my writers and artists," the editor gasped. "All right," agreed Hearst. "Let's take the whole staff." Goddard spent the afternoon depositing the money in various banks, in case Hearst changed his mind. The *World* topped Hearst's offer, but Hearst raised his by another 25 percent. Just one secretary remained at the *World*.

Two Kids. Pulitzer hired the brilliant, young Arthur Brisbane to replace Goddard, and Brisbane soon drove the circulation of the *World* past six hundred thousand. To replace Outcault, who had also gone over to the *Jour-*nal, Brisbane hired George I. Luks to continue "Hogan's Alley." Both papers used the image of the Yellow Kid in their promotions, and he became the indelible symbol for the sensationalistic journalism both papers practiced in their escalating rivalry, thus the term "yellow journalism." Outcault came to loathe his creation so much that he later cried: "When I die don't wear yellow crepe, don't let them put the Yellow Kid on my tombstone, and don't let the Yellow Kid himself come to my funeral. Make him stay over on the east side, where he belongs." In 1897 Brisbane also defected to Hearst and became editor of the *Evening Journal*.

Wars. In 1896 the circulation of the *Journal* topped 150,000 at the price of a penny, so Pulitzer cut his two-cent price in half. Meanwhile Hearst, as the owner of several silver mines, backed William Jennings Bryan's fight against the gold standard and gained notoriety in the conservative East. His headlines grew steadily more outrageous, promising miracle cures, immortality, the truth about monsters and dragons, and the secret lives of criminals. Like Pulitzer, Hearst crusaded against political corruption, but he promised to do more than just print words. He carried headlines that boasted of "Journalism that Acts; Men of Action in All Walks of Life Heartily Endorse the Journal's Fight in Behalf of the People." Hearst installed his own color presses, and his Sunday supplement, eventually titled *American Weekly*, gained the largest circulation in the country and maintained it for decades.

Parity. Circulation figures for the *Journal* and the *World* hovered around the half million mark in 1896 and 1897. On the day following the presidential election in 1896 each paper sold an astonishing 1.5 million copies. The two titan publishers had set the tone for urban journalism for years to come.

Sources:

Sidney Kobre, *The Yellow Press and Gilded Age Journalism* (Tallahassee: Florida State University Press, 1964);

Joyce Milton, *The Yellow Kids: Foreign Correspondents in the Heyday of Yellow Journalism* (New York: Harper & Row, 1989);

W. A. Swanberg, *Citizen Hearst* (New York: Scribners, 1961).

HEADLINE MAKERS

MARY L. BOOTH

1831-1889
MAGAZINE EDITOR

Self-Educated. Born in Millville (later Yaphank), Long Island, New York, Mary Booth was an exceptional reader with a remarkable aptitude in French. She reputedly read the Bible at age five and at seven read the works of Jean Racine in the original. She moved at eighteen to Manhattan and found work as a vest maker, writing articles for literary and educational journals at night. *The New York Times* soon hired her to cover education and women on a piece-rate basis. Starting in 1856 she translated books from French into English, especially abolitionist tracts; eventually she would translate nearly forty volumes. In 1859 she wrote the first complete *History of the City of New York* from its Dutch settlement to its role as a financial capital.

Harper's Bazar. In 1867 publisher Fletcher Harper decided to start *Harper's Bazar*, a new periodical to act as a family-oriented counterpart to his successful *Harper's Weekly*. (It became *Harper's Bazar* in 1929.) It would carry serials and humor like its progenitor but dispense with politics in favor of fashion and home features. Unlike most American fashion magazines, which printed European designs a year or more after their introduction on the Continent, the new magazine would show dresses at the same time that women in Paris and Berlin saw them. Booth was reluctant to accept the position of editor when Harper offered it to her in 1867, but she took it nonetheless and soon showed her remarkable aptitude for the position. Working throughout her twenty-two years as editor without a typewriter or a secretary, Booth built up great personal power. After its first six weeks, *Harper's Bazar* reached a circulation of one hundred thousand.

Convention. Booth targeted Protestant middle-class women who aspired to improve themselves and their families. She offered advice on household management, decorating, food, etiquette, and health. Sub-

titled *A Repository of Fashion, Pleasure, and Instruction*, *Harper's Bazar* aimed to combine the practical and the beautiful. While Boot advocated woman suffrage, she refused to allow the slightest discussion of the topic in the magazine. Writing to one of her contributors, she said: "It surely involves no sacrifice of principle to be silent on a topic specially adapted to aggressive reform journals in writing for a paper with a wholly different purpose, especially as there is so much else to be said therein of the most vital importance to women that you will find noble work to do." According to Booth, the *Bazar* was not the place for political agitation.

Leading by Example. Booth believed that the obstacles to women's political equality would fall away naturally as women proved themselves capable of surviving in a male-dominated world. She had a reputation as a shrewd businesswoman as well as a skilled editor; yet she never acted in an unladylike manner. Sarah Bolton, author of *Successful Women* (1888), wrote of her: "To show other women that a woman may have consummate bility, and yet be gentle and refined and warm-hearted, . . . and that if one woman can stand at the head of a great journal it must be logically true that other trained women may come to stand at the head of the business they select—these, too, are public lessons of a life and a character worthy of study by our noblest girls." Booth died suddenly in 1889 of a heart ailment, a few weeks short of her fifty-eighth birthday.

Sources:

Maurine H. Beasley, "Mary L. Booth," in *American Magazine Journalists, 1850–1900*, edited by Sam G. Riley, *Dictionary of Literary Biography*, volume 79 (Detroit: Gale Research, 1989);

CHARLES A. DANA

1819-1897
NEWSPAPER EDITOR

Brook Farm. Born in Hinsdale, New Hampshire, Charles A. Dana grew up in western New York and learned business at an early age clerking at his uncle's store in Buffalo. In his spare time he studied Latin and Greek. He entered Harvard in September 1839, but his poor eyesight and tight finances prevented his completion of a degree. In September 1841 he joined the group at Brook Farm in West Roxbury, Massachusetts, a utopian community established by Rev. George Ripley and other Transcendentalists as a testing ground for their ideas about cooperative, democratic living in an environment that encouraged intellectual growth. Other residents at Brook Farm included the novelists Nathaniel Hawthorne and Louisa May Alcott; poet-essayist Ralph Waldo Emerson; literary critic Sarah Margaret Fuller, Marchesa D'Ossoli; and Unitarian minister William Henry Channing. In 1842 Dana also became acquainted with Horace Greeley, the legendary founder and editor of the *New York Tribune,* who often visited Brook Farm. Dana remained with the community for five years and taught Greek and German as well as writing articles for its newspapers, the *Dial* and *Harbinger.*

Blue Ribbon Apprenticeship. In 1846 Dana worked for a Boston paper before becoming city editor of the *New York Tribune* early the next year. He then took leave to observe the revolutions in Europe firsthand and rejoined the *Tribune* in early 1849. Dana was in charge at the *Tribune* whenever Greeley traveled, but friction between the two developed over style and issues. The final split occurred over Southern secession, with Greeley willing to have the South secede if that meant peace would be maintained, while Dana refused to tolerate the idea of a divided Union. In 1864 Dana sold his considerable interest in the paper and joined the Lincoln administration as second assistant secretary of war.

The *Sun*. In late 1867 Dana had enough financial backing to purchase the *New York Sun* for $175,000. Its circulation at the time was only forty-three thousand. Dana's creed for the paper was fierce independence, conciseness, and clarity. He kept stories short and limited the paper to four packed pages. Dana set the price of the *Sun* at two cents a copy in order to compete with the *New York World.* He also gave the "human interest story" new form by presenting a chronological narrative rather than a summation of facts. He was willing to print stories about sex and crime, news that other papers avoided. To fulfill his goal of vivid, terse stories, Dana assembled a remarkable staff of writers, including Julian Ralph, David Graham Phillips, Will Irwin, and Samuel Hopkins Adams. The *Sun* was known as a newspaperman's paper and became the classroom for many of the great journalists of the next half-century.

Color. The editorial page of the *Sun* was the wittiest and most colorful of all the New York papers. Its writers coined such phrases as "To the victor belongs the spoils," and "No King, No Clown, To rule this Town." It uncovered many scandals in government, and was among the first to devote portions of the paper to women's interests and sports. In 1887 Dana launched an evening edition of the *Sun* and hired the writers Amos J. Cummings, Arthur Brisbane (son of Albert Brisbane, a Brook Farm

alumnus), Richard Harding Davis, and the outstanding police reporter Jacob Riis. In stark contrast to the slim daily edition, the fat Sunday edition of the *Sun*—full of pictures and stories about cowboys, alligators, sea captains, and the inner workings of machines, plus book reviews and fashion news—set the standard for Sunday editions for the next century.

A Crisp Legacy. In his twenty-nine years as editor of the *Sun,* Dana provided a bridge from the journalism of the penny press to the New Journalism of Pulitzer and Hearst. Dana died in October 1897 of cirrhosis of the liver. While other papers published lengthy obituaries, at Dana's own direction the *Sun* acknowledged his passing with two brief lines atop its editorial column:

Charles Anderson Dana, Editor of
The *Sun,* died yesterday afternoon.

At the time of Dana's death the *Sun* had a circulation of 120,000, with the Sunday edition at 150,000.

Sources:

Sidney Kobre, *The Yellow Press and Gilded Age Journalism* (Tallahassee: Florida State University Press, 1964);

Janet E. Steele, *The Sun Shines for All: Journalism and Ideology in the Life of Charles A. Dana* (Syracuse, N.Y.: Syracuse University Press, 1993).

T. THOMAS FORTUNE

1856-1928
NEWSPAPER EDITOR

Printer, Page, and Postal Agent. Born in Marianna, Florida, to slave parents, T. Thomas Fortune had African, Irish, and American Indian ancestry. He went to the first school for black children opened in town after the Civil War, and, after constantly peering through the window of the print shop at the local paper, he was offered the chance to "stick type" into words. The family moved to Jacksonville after it was threatened by the Ku Klux Klan, and Fortune went to Tallahassee as a page in the state senate to help with family expenses. He studied at the Stanton Institute and became an expert typesetter at the *Jacksonville Daily Union.* Through the efforts of a local congressman, the seventeen-year-old Fortune was given the job of postal agent on a railway line. He then became a customs inspector in Delaware and stayed there long enough to save the money needed to enroll in Howard University in 1874.

Journalism. While in Washington Fortune worked as a messenger at the U.S. Treasury Department and for the *People's Advocate,* a black weekly, and took law classes at night. He met Frederick Douglass and married a childhood acquaintance, Carrie Smiley. The couple returned to Jacksonville for the birth of their first child, and Fortune worked as a schoolteacher and printer, but he decided that his family's future would be brighter in the less segregated North. After working for a white-owned religious newspaper in New York City in 1881, Fortune took over a struggling weekly black tabloid that he renamed the *Globe*. There he developed his straightforward editorial style, taking as his model former *New York Sun* editor and reformer John Swinton, who had started *John Swinton's Paper*. The *Globe* contained no skimpy "filler" stories, relying on writers all over the United States, including a boy in Great Barrington, Massachusetts, W. E. B. Du Bois, who would later become a founding member of the National Association for the Advancement of Colored People.

Economic and Legal Injustice. While keeping his commitment to oppose racial discrimination in the forefront, Fortune argued that monopolistic capitalism exploited working-class blacks and whites alike. The debt peonage of Southern sharecropping was the worst instance of racial-economic injustice, and he argued that the solution would be found in cooperation between blacks and whites. Fortune also wrote about the legal injustices facing blacks, saying, "There is no law in the United States for the Negro." He also encouraged civil disobedience in the absence of justice: "If it is necessary for colored men to turn themselves into outlaws to assert their manhood and their citizenship, let them do it."

Causes. Fortune closed the *Globe* in 1884 rather than turn it into an official voice of the Republican Party like most black newspapers of the day. Two weeks later he started the fiercely independent *New York Freeman*, which advocated Prohibition and other social reforms. He temporarily turned over the paper to his brother and another journalist in 1887, and they renamed it the *New York Age*. Fortune then wrote for the *New York Sun* before returning to the *Age* in 1889. Two years previously he started a movement to form an Afro-American League that was the precursor to the NAACP and the Urban League. The Afro-American League became dominated by the supporters of Booker T. Washington, who advocated vocational training and upward economic mobility—rather than political activism—to desegregate the South. Despite his initial militant stance, Fortune moved closer to the Washington camp as the century closed.

Unhappy Times. The *Age,* while popular, never provided Fortune with an adequate income, and he was eventually forced to sell it. For a time he became a derelict, begging money from friends and living in parks. In the final years of his life he recovered his stability and edited the *Negro World,* a publication of Marcus Garvey's back-to-Africa movement, although he never fully subscribed to Garvey's ideology. Hailed as the "Dean of Negro Journalism," Fortune wrote editorials for the paper until his death in 1928 at age seventy-one.

Sources:

Maurine H. Beasley, "Thomas Fortune," in *American Newspaper Journalists, 1873–1900,* edited by Perry J. Ashley, *Dictionary of Literary Biography,* volume 23 (Detroit: Gale Research, 1983);

Emma Lou Thornbrough, *T. Thomas Fortune: Militant Journalist* (Chicago: University of Chicago Press, 1972);

E. L. GODKIN

1831-1902
EDITOR

Restless. Born in Moyne, Ireland, E. L. Godkin was perhaps the foremost editorial voice of post–Civil War America. He abandoned the study of law at the Middle Temple, London, to work in a publishing house, and his interest in the struggles of the people of Hungary led to the publication of his first book, *The History of Hungary and the Magyars* (1853). In 1856 he immigrated to New York, hoping to fulfill his long dream of starting a journal of his own. Two years later he married an American woman.

The Nation. In 1865 Philadelphia philanthropist and abolitionist James McKim helped Godkin to amass $100,000 from forty stockholders to capitalize his magazine, *The Nation.* Godkin wanted to write about politics and economics more accurately than the daily press and to advocate "whatever in legislation or manners seems likely to promote a more equal distribution of the fruits of progress and civilization." Many stories in the publication emphasized the condition of blacks, the educational system, and the arts. *The Nation* reached a circulation of ten thousand, chiefly among the clergy, educators, and journalists. When the stockholders attempted to tell Godkin how to run *The Nation,* he reorganized it, and for fifteen years he and a handful of assistants produced the magazine.

An Unusual Political Blend. Godkin subscribed vehemently to the John Stuart Mill school of economic thought, which maintained government should never interfere with the workings of the economy. This fervent belief in economic laissez-faire, however, existed alongside popular hatred for trusts, or business monopolies. Although Godkin had little sympathy for labor's political causes, he did believe that the government should take a larger role in social matters, such as racial equity and woman suffrage. He also supported public education and civil-service reform. Alongside his complex views, Godkin had a notably compact and precise editorial style, full of wit and irony, and he was at his best when attacking corrupt institutions.

Enter Villard. In 1881, exhausted by years of editing *The Nation* alone, Godkin sold the paper to railroad magnate and Civil War correspondent Henry Villard. At the same time Villard bought the *New York Evening Post*, which had been founded by Alexander Hamilton in 1801. Along with Horace White and Carl Schurz, Villard edited the *Post*, and *The Nation* became a monthly supplement to the paper. Within two years Godkin became the chief editor of the *Post*.

Against Corruption. Godkin was most famous for his stand on the election of 1884 and uncovering the corruption of the Tammany Hall political machine in New York City. He labeled the 1884 Republican presidential nominee, James G. Blaine, unacceptably corrupt, even though Godkin himself was a Republican. In a famous piece that became known as the "deadly parallel" column, Godkin contrasted Blaine's campaign promises of clean government to his long history of friendship with business magnates and special interests. In 1890 Godkin launched a spirited investigation of municipal politics in New York, including a widely reprinted series of biographies of members of the Democratic Party Executive Committee. Two of these men immediately sued Godkin for libel, but a grand jury dismissed the charges within days.

Legacy. Perhaps Godkin's most enduring legacy is as a critic of the sensationalism that overtook daily journalism during the last decades of his career. He was a persistent voice against such "yellow journalism," calling newspapers that engaged in it "the common sewer for public and private immorality," emphasizing "the weakness of our poor humanity." Godkin retired from the *Post* in 1899, and after a series of strokes he died in 1902.

Sources:

William M. Armstrong, *E. L. Godkin: A Biography* (Albany: State University of New York Press, 1978);

JOSEPH PULITZER

1847-1911

EDITOR AND PUBLISHER

Recruited to America. Born in Hungary to a prosperous family, Joseph Pulitzer ran away from home at age eighteen to embark on a military career. After the Austrian army and the French Foreign Legion both rejected him because of his poor eyesight, he signed up with an agent of the Union army of the United States recruiting in Europe in late 1864. At the end of the Civil War he found himself penniless in New York City and worked at a series of miserable jobs. By 1868, however, he had become a citizen and was hired as a reporter for the leading German-language daily in the nation, Carl Schurz's *St. Louis Westliche Post*. Pulitzer soon became a top newsman and bought a share of the paper. He was then elected to the Missouri State Assembly and campaigned for the publisher Horace Greeley, who was a presidential candidate in 1872. He left newspapering for a time to return to Europe and marry, but soon returned to the United States and gained membership in the Washington, D.C., bar in 1874.

Papers. In 1878 Pulitzer bought the bankrupt *St. Louis Dispatch*, merged it with the *Post*, and created one of the great newspapers in the United States, the *Post-Dispatch*. Driven by insatiable curiosity and boundless energy, Pulitzer remade American journalism in the last twenty years of the nineteenth century. Claiming to be the champion of the people against injustice and ill-gotten power, he published a statement of policy that read in part: "The *Post and Dispatch* will serve no party but the people; be no organ of Republicanism but the organ of truth; will follow no causes but its conclusions; will not support the 'Administration,' but criticize it; will oppose all frauds and shams wherever and whatever they are; will advocate principles and ideas rather than prejudices and partisanship." At the same time the paper carried on high-minded crusades against monopolistic power, it also printed sensational stories about adultery and scandal. Furthermore, exaggeration and half-truths also appeared in Pulitzer's paper.

New York, New Journalism. Although he was a physical wreck from years of hard work, when Pulitzer heard in 1883 that the *New York World* was for sale, he bought it and quickly turned it into a successful paper. His formula for the New Journalism included sensational headlines and self-promotion. He maintained a strong news department and published an unparalleled editorial page. The *World* advocated taxes on luxuries, profits, and the wealthy, as well as railing against corruption in government. Those who were suspicious of wealth flocked to the paper, and those who approved of chasing profits disdained it. The *World* presented news in sensational form; when a heat wave took a terrible toll on children in the slums of New York, the headline in the *World* read: "How Babies Are Baked."

Success. Within one year Pulitzer's Sunday-edition circulation reached approximately ninety-five thousand, and by 1887 it increased to a quarter of a million. By paying close attention to the fact that four out of five New Yorkers were first- or second-generation Americans and by providing coverage of political figures along with entertainment, Pulitzer captured the public's imagination. He talked directly to his readers without being condescending. Over the years the worst sensationalism disappeared from the *World*, while its commitment to the well-written human-interest story never dissipated.

Later Years. Pulitzer added an *Evening World* in 1887, and three years later he opened a new building on Park Row, at the time the tallest building in New York City. Pulitzer retired in 1890 but continued to monitor the progress of his papers, summoning editors to his various homes or to his yacht. Among the editors who worked at the *World* were some of the best in the business, including John A. Cockerill, William Merrill, S. S. Carvalho, George Harvey, Frank I. Cobb, Morrill Goddard, and Arthur Brisbane. In his retirement Pulitzer supported the progressive spirit of reform and muckraking in journalism. He also endowed the Columbia School of Journalism and the Pulitzer Prizes. Chronic illness plagued Pulitzer in his remaining years. He died in October 1911 at age sixty-four aboard his yacht in Charleston Harbor, South Carolina.

Source:
W. A. Swanberg, *Pulitzer* (New York: Scribners, 1967).

JACOB RIIS

1848-1914
REPORTER AND PHOTOGRAPHER

Firsthand Experience. Born in Ribe, Denmark, Jacob Riis immigrated to New York in May 1870 at a time when the United States was in an economic slump. Although he could speak and read English and had served as an apprentice carpenter in Copenhagen, he found it difficult to find work. He tried mining in Pennsylvania, and after nearly starving to death he returned to New York, where he lived in crowded lodgings run by the police. These early experiences of poverty made a powerful impression on the young man that he carried with him for the rest of his life.

Reporter. Riis found work with a Long Island newspaper in 1873 and soon bought and sold a small paper in Brooklyn. He traveled back to Denmark where he married a childhood sweetheart in 1876. Returning to New York, he found work in 1878 at the *New York Tribune* for twenty-five dollars a week. Assigned to the police beat, cranking out stories in the little press room at 301 Mulberry Street, Riis found his calling. The building was surrounded by tenements, and Riis was able to translate the

miserable scenes there into human-interest stories that did not blame the victims for their own distress. Infused with the desire to help, he wrote stories that were alive with both suffering and hope.

Reformer. Riis frequently accompanied members of the Drexel Committee, appointed in 1884 to look into dangerous conditions in the tenements. The city passed the Small Park Act of 1887 to tear buildings down and make parks, but after city politics blocked any serious action, Riis began photographing overcrowded tenement rooms and delivering the pictures to the board of health. He brought unceasing publicity to the plight of the poor on the Lower East Side of New York, crusading for school playgrounds, better working conditions, and restrictions on the sale of liquor. His "How the Other Half Lives," printed with his photographs in the December 1889 issue of *Scribner's*, was published as a book the following year. In a culture that was still oriented around the printed word, Riis showed the power of the documentary photograph in shaping public opinion. Not only did *How the Other Half Lives* cause significant public outcry, it brought Riis to the attention of up-and-coming reform politician Theodore Roosevelt. Riis became Roosevelt's good friend and later his biographer.

Successes. In 1890 Riis applied for a position with the *Evening Sun*. Although editor Charles A. Dana was cynical about effecting reform, he nevertheless paid Riis fifty dollars a week and provided him with an assistant. In 1891 Riis wrote his biggest story, an exposé on the impurities, including raw sewage, in New York's Croton Reservoir. As a result of his investigations and pressure from the board of health, New York City bought the properties surrounding its water supply. In 1892 Riis published *The Children of the Poor*, a vivid description of how poverty affected the lives of young urban dwellers. He continued his attacks on corruption in the police department, and in 1894 a commission was appointed to investigate it. When Roosevelt was appointed president of the police commission in 1895, Riis took him on a tour of the worst crime- and poverty-stricken areas of New York City. Roosevelt spent $10,000 for new shelters and closed the horrific police lodgings. A park was constructed on the site of the Mulberry Bend slum in 1895.

Early Muckraker. Riis temporarily left newspaper work in 1899 to travel around the country lecturing about urban reform. He was a forerunner of the muckrakers, a group of journalists who wrote about civic corruption, corporate greed, and national apathy. Despite all the time he spent in the netherworlds of cities, Riis never became disillusioned nor did he lose his hope for reform. He died at the age of sixty-five after years of heart disease on 26 May 1914.

Sources:
Sidney Kobre, *The Yellow Press and Gilded Age Journalism* (Tallahassee: Florida State University, 1964);

James B. Lane, *Jacob A. Riis and the American City* (Port Washington, N.Y.: Kennikat Press, 1974);

Edith Patterson Meyer, *"Not Charity but Justice": The Story of Jacob A. Riis* (New York: Vanguard, 1974).

PUBLICATIONS

Hubert Howe Bancroft, *Literary Industries: A Memoir* (New York: Harper, 1891);—the autobiography of the author, published also as volume 34 of his *History of the Pacific States of North America;*

Arthur Brisbane, "The Modern Newspaper in War Time," *Cosmopolitan,* 25 (September 1898): 541–557—the editor of Pulitzer's *World* gives his opinion on the subject in the wake of the Spanish-American War;

W. M. Cornell, *Life and Public Career of Honorable Horace Greeley* (Boston: Lothrop, 1882)—a popular biography of a famous journalist and political leader;

G. S. Merriam, *Life and Times of Samuel Bowles* (New York: Century, 1885)—a biography of the editor who made the Springfield *Republican* eminent among newspapers of the day; this Massachusetts newspaper was known for its accurate news coverage;

S. N. D. North, *History and Present Condition of the Newspaper and Periodical Press of the United States* (Washington, D.C.: U.S. Government Printing Office, 1884)—a detailed history of American newspapers from 1639 to 1880 with statistical tables, catalogue of periodical publications, and a listing of newspapers in the possession of the American Antiquarian Society;

Harry Thurston Peck, "A Great National Newspaper," *Cosmopolitan,* 24 (December 1897): 209–220—Peck was a noted educator and author who served as the literary editor of the *New York Commercial Advertiser* (1897–1901);

Katherine Abbott Sanborn, *Our Early Newspaper Wits* (Boston: Case, Lockwood, & Brainerd, 1898)—Sanborn wrote on a variety of subjects; some of her other works include *Grandma's Garden, with Many Original Poems* (1883), *The Wit of Women* (1885), and *The Vanity and Insanity of Genius* (1886);

Charles Dudley Warner, *The American Newspaper* (Boston: Osgood, 1881)—an essay read before the Social Science Association at Saratoga Springs, New York, on 6 September 1881.

Contemporary illustration of Alexander Graham Bell demonstrating the telephone to a group of scientists in 1887

EDUCATION

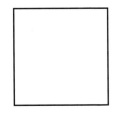

by   HARRIETT WILLIAMS

CONTENTS

Sidebars and tables are listed in italics.

1878

- The first reported Boys' Club for elimination of "tenement gangs" is organized in New York.

- An elementary school that provides manual as well as intellectual training is opened in New York.

1879

- Calvin Woodward establishes a branch of the Carlisle Indian School, a manual training school, in Saint Louis, Missouri.

- The Boston Cooking School, a "private cookery school for women," is opened.

1880

- The professional journal *Education* is founded as one of the earliest publications for disseminating the theories and methods of teaching.

- The first regularly admitted women students to the Massachusetts Institute of Technology are graduated.

- The Saint Louis Manual Training School, the first public high school with industrial training facilities, opens.

1881

- The Blair Bill, the first legislation designed to establish federal aid for education, is introduced in Congress but fails to pass.

- Booker T. Washington founds Tuskegee Institute, an agricultural and industrial training school for African Americans, in Alabama.

1882

- The Slater Fund, a northern private charitable organization, is established to send funds to the South for improving Negro education.

- Congressional appropriations lead to the establishment of off-reservation Indian boarding schools in several states.

- Yale's annual report by President Noah Porter suggests that American universities must offer moral and intellectual training, with the professors standing in loco parentis (literally, in the place of parents) to assure that students learn.

1883

- North Carolina's legislature rules that counties can raise taxes locally and divide those funds as taxpayers see fit between two separate, racially divided school systems.

- Col. Francis Parker assumes the presidency of Cook County (Chicago) Normal School.

1884

- The National Education Association officially recognizes a separate kindergarten category for its members.
- The journal *Popular Education* is founded.
- The Industrial Education Association is founded in New York City.

1885

- The Hatch Act establishes agricultural "experimental stations" in connection with land-grant colleges.
- Charles William Eliot, the president of Harvard University, presents an argument to the Nineteenth Century Club on the value of the elective curriculum.
- James McCosh, the president of Princeton University, refutes Eliot's argument to the Nineteenth Century Club.
- Mother Mary Regis Casserly opens a Catholic female tuition academy in Cambridge, Massachusetts, which serves as a normal school for nuns.
- Ten women in the United States hold earned doctorates.
- The public schools in Boston include cooking as a regular part of the curriculum.
- Bryn Mawr, a Quaker women's college dedicated to providing females with an intellectual experience comparable to that of any exclusively male college, is founded; Harvard president Charles William Eliot predicts its failure.

1886

- A Mississippi law is passed that allows state funds to be diverted from Negro to white schools through differentials in teacher salaries.

1887

- Students in the San Francisco elementary schools are classified into separate grades for the first time.
- Mother Katharine Mary Drexel establishes a boarding school for the Pueblo Indians in Santa Fe, New Mexico Territory.
- G. Stanley Hall, a psychologist and philosopher, founds the *American Journal of Psychology*.
- American millionaire Jonas Gilman Clark establishes Clark University in Worcester, Massachusetts, as a new center for research in the United States. G. Stanley Hall becomes its first president.

- Most public elementary schools include cooking and sewing as regular subjects in the curriculum for girls.

1889

- Charles de Garmo publishes the first American textbook based on Herbartian ideals, or the concept that teaching must be based on understanding the psychology of the learner.

- Jane Addams opens Hull-House, a Chicago settlement house that serves as an educational laboratory for teaching adults and immigrants.

- Julia Richmond is the first woman and the first Jew to be appointed a district superintendent of schools in New York City.

- No southern state has a compulsory school attendance law.

1890

- The second Morrill Act establishes a continuing federal grant to each state for an agricultural college.

- The number of public high schools reporting to the Bureau of Education is 2,771, with a total enrollment of 202,963.

- The Wisconsin Supreme Court in *Weiss* v. *District Board* prohibits religious instruction in public schools.

- The Mississippi Constitutional Convention gives local school boards almost complete control in apportioning state school moneys; this state ruling overrides the Peabody Fund's principle of equal distribution of support to white and black schools.

- Woodrow Wilson, who had earned a law degree and a doctorate in history, is named professor of jurisprudence and political economy at Princeton.

- William James publishes *The Principles of Psychology,* a book that marks the beginning of a direct attack on prior educational psychology.

- One of the earliest textbooks on the administration of schools, a 148-page volume called *School Supervision,* is published by a professor at the University of Iowa.

- The Teachers' College of New York formally affiliates with Columbia University.

- The average school year in the United States is 135 days.

- The annual expenditure for each child in average daily attendance in public schools in the United States is seventeen dollars.

- Three-tenths of 1 percent (.003) of the total population of the United States is enrolled in high school.

- Fifteen percent of the adult native white population and almost two-thirds of the black population are illiterate.

1891

- The journal *Educational Review* is founded.

- Salaries of Negro teachers in all southern states show a sharp decline.

- Stanford University, named after Leland Stanford Jr., opens in California.

- An average of 68 percent of the total receipts for public schools in the United States is derived from local sources; the rest is from state funds.

1892

- The Committee of Ten of the National Education Association investigates high school and college curricula. The committee establishes nine courses of study for college preparatory secondary curriculum so that colleges can begin to standardize entrance requirements.

- Charles Kendall Adams assumes the presidency of the University of Wisconsin. Under his leadership the university serves as a model for other state universities wishing to expand.

- The University of Chicago, soon recognized as an innovative model in higher education, is established with a large grant from John D. Rockefeller.

- Professor Frank McMurray of the Teachers' College, Columbia University, makes the first of his many appearances before the National Education Association to defend the efficacy of Herbartian methods.

- Yale and the University of Pennsylvania open some of their graduate departments to women.

1893

- At the American Historical Association conference in Chicago, Frederick Jackson Turner delivers an address titled "The Significance of the Frontier in American History." Turner's "frontier thesis" maintains that westward expansion has shaped the American character and helps explain national development.

1894

- Martha Carey Thomas is selected as president of Bryn Mawr College and begins dispelling doubts about women's intellectual capacities.

- Several states pass legislation to require manual training in the high school curriculum.

- Nineteen states still do not have compulsory school attendance laws.

1895

- Booker T. Washington makes an address at the Cotton States and International Exposition in Atlanta supporting the vocational education of African Americans.

- The first vacation school for urban children is established in Boston.

- The establishment of the National Herbart Society for the Scientific Study of Education marks an important development in educational theory and psychology.

- There are approximately 80,662 students enrolled in 398 private commercial and business colleges in the country.

1896

- The U. S. Supreme Court rules in *Plessy* v. *Ferguson* that states have the right to separate the races in public facilities, including schools.

- An article in *Educational Review* claims that vacation camps for "tenement lads may result more decisively in the formation of good character than all the school experiences of the rest of the year in town."

- Only 220 of 432 institutions of higher education offer courses in the science of education.

- John Dewey opens an experimental elementary school at the University of Chicago.

1897

- The Teachers' College of Columbia University offers more courses (sixteen) in education as a special study than any other American college or university.

- The number of pupils attending elementary schools is more than fifteen million.

- The age of compulsory attendance in states with attendance laws ranges from eight to fourteen.

- The percentage of girls in high schools in the country is 57.64.

- Nearly one-third of students who attend colleges and universities are women.

- A total of 1,583 women are enrolled in medical schools and 131 in law schools.

- The average annual per capita expenditure for public education is $2.62 in the country at large; in southern states the average ranges from 50¢ to 90¢.

1898

- Chicago establishes a model system of vocational schools for the urban poor with a curriculum designed by John Dewey, which includes nature study, gymnastics, music, and games.

- Only three states issue teaching credentials at the state level; elsewhere the credentials are issued locally.

1899

- The term "home economics" is coined at a summer conference in Lake Placid, New York, designed for educators to discuss ways of improving home life in modern society.

- Publication of University of Chicago professor John Dewey's *School and Society* marks the beginning of the Progressive education movement.

- The College Entrance Examination Board is founded by the Middle States Education Association to assess students' preparation for college work.

- Large retail operations such as the Daniels & Fisher stores in Denver and John Wanamaker's in Philadelphia begin operating mandatory on-the-job schools for employees under the age of eighteen.

- William James's book *Talks to Teachers* is published and assures teachers that knowledge of psychology will aid them in the classroom.

- The Chicago mayor's commission on school management publishes a set of principles to be used by city school superintendents; it is used by teachers of administration for decades.

OVERVIEW

Changing Economy, Changing Schools. The period from 1878 to 1899 was marked by major changes in the American way of life. In the early 1870s the United States was predominantly a nation of farmers, with 83.9 percent of the population living in rural areas or small towns of fewer than eight thousand inhabitants. Immigration and industrialization changed this picture of American life. In 1882 a record number of European immigrants further swelled the ranks of city dwellers. By the 1890s many rural Americans had begun drifting into the cities and nearly one-third of the population was classified as urban. Americans living in this increasingly industrial world were convinced that their era was a bridge between a traditional agrarian America of independent yeomen and a future dependent on cooperative activities in large-scale industries and vast urban areas, a change much like the one Great Britain had experienced a generation earlier. The changes from small-scale to large-scale industrial production, from domestic to factory organization, and from hand- to power-driven machine manufacturing were accompanied by fundamental changes in society. Instead of every man working independently for himself to scratch out a living, the new image of America was of a corporate state in which each worker was to do a specialized task in cooperation with the entire social system. Even in the Midwest where agriculture was still the heart of the economy, improvements in transportation and farm machinery turned farming into a much more sophisticated business. The South, however, was not experiencing this industrial expansion. As Reconstruction — that "hideous orgy of anarchy, violence, and unrestrained corruption" — came to an end with the withdrawal of federal troops in 1877, the afflictions of poverty, racial enmity, and resentment of northerners stunted any significant economic development until the early years of the twentieth century. Elsewhere in the United States, however, the rapidly increasing complexity of economic and social conditions called for significant changes in schooling.

Influences from Europe. Americans soon realized that the schools that had served the populace in the mid nineteenth century were not sufficient for the new era of industrial expansion. During the last two decades of the nineteenth century, therefore, significant reforms were introduced. Improvements came as a result of the scientific study of the elementary, secondary, and college curricula, and of the methods of teaching and learning. The impetus for these early reforms was from European educators, since there were no graduate programs of education in the United States to inspire American thinkers and practitioners. More than any other educational reformer, Johann Heinrich Pestalozz, who conducted experimental schools in Switzerland, laid the foundation for the modern elementary school and helped to reform elementary school practice. Pestalozzi, a strong advocate of universal education, insisted that teachers use the environment and experience of the child as the most valuable means and material of his or her instruction. The curriculum he advocated valued observation and investigation over memorizing, and thinking over reciting. These principles, popularized by American educators who traveled to Switzerland or who read reports in the earliest educational journals, had a wide influence on industrial education and the teaching of arithmetic, geography, reading, and elementary science.

Changing Education for Young Children. European influences that helped to change elementary school educational theory and practice came from two of Pestalozzi's disciples, Johann Friedrich Herbart and Friedrich Wilhelm August Froebel. Herbart maintained that interest was the most important element in good teaching, and he elaborated a five-step formal teaching method that emphasized student interest, the adaptation of instruction to the past experiences of the pupil, and the unification of the subjects. In the United States a fervid enthusiasm for Herbartian principles developed during the late 1880s and the 1890s. Many American converts wrote articles for teachers and lectured to educators, slowly dispensing the reformist theories throughout this country. In 1892 the publication of Illinois Normal School professor Charles McMurray's "how-to" book on Herbartian principles called *The General Method* popularized the ideas so widely that significant changes began to appear in elementary schools nationwide. Another enthusiastic follower of Pestalozzi, Froebel, directly contributed one of the most important reforms of the late nineteenth century—the kindergarten. Froebel, who emphasized the importance of social development and self-expression in education, inspired the earliest and most influential American educational reformers, Col. Francis Parker and John Dewey.

The High Schools. The American high school was born in the nineteenth century, and although there were high schools as early as the 1820s and 1830s, these schools existed primarily for a small segment of the population. At the end of the century adolescents and their families faced the unsettling consequences of the early commercial and industrial revolution, urban growth, and immigration — all of which rendered familiar strategies for personal mobility obsolete. In response, political activists and school reformers redefined the educational experiences of high school students, investing more money and reshaping existing secondary schools to confront the dilemmas of this new age. By the 1880s, especially in the Northeast, the free public high school was no longer an anomaly. Social reformers had eliminated most alternative forms of secondary instruction, such as tuition academies, seminaries, and other private institutions. Without a national ministry of education to dictate policy and implement reform, Americans built high schools through local initiative. Educators and activists shared ideas across state boundaries about how to create, shape, and administer high schools, producing some common features to educational systems across the nation. However, high schools still varied enormously in the nineteenth century. Most pupils studied what was called "the higher branches" in modest, ungraded country schools; others in more elaborate "union graded" schools in villages and towns; and a privileged minority in ostentatious architectural facilities that conservatives called "palaces" in many American cities.

Questioning the Collegiate Curriculum. Colleges, too, were struggling to adjust to the changing social and economic conditions of the industrial age. Defining what a liberal arts education should be had been problematic since, earlier in the century, the classical curriculum of Greek, Latin, mathematics, philosophy, science, and English had come under attack by both faculty and students. In the 1860s and 1870s scientific studies of evolution, beginning with Charles Darwin's *On the Origin of Species* (1859), further strained the limits of the traditional course of study as the range of courses gradually became wider and wider. Innovative educators intent upon establishing a more modern college education had to define what criteria would mark educated men and, since they were entering higher education in significant numbers for the first time, women. At major American colleges and universities both monumental and incremental changes in the curriculum were effected during the late 1880s and 1890s. Under Charles William Eliot's leadership, Harvard's approach was the most radical, allowing students to choose all of their courses

under an elective system. Few other universities went that far, but Stanford, Columbia, and Cornell came close.

The Rise of the Research University. Institutions of higher learning grew rapidly in number, endowment, and quality of instruction, but one of the most significant changes in the colleges was American scholars' attempts to increase the world's store of knowledge. In order to accomplish this new mission, it became necessary to provide the opportunities for postgraduate instruction in this country that had been available only in Europe, most notably Germany. During the 1880s more than two thousand Americans studied in German universities, twice as many as in the preceding ten years. When these young scholars returned home with their doctorates they were determined to provide opportunities for, as historian Arthur M. Schlesinger said, "the truth born of knowledge, for the eagerness to learn to do a few things supremely well instead of many things well enough, and perhaps an unconscious withdrawal from the soliciting materialism which characterized the ethics of the great captains of industry." For the first time in the American economy, the broad diffusion of worldly goods made it possible for middle-class young men to take advantage of opportunities for advanced studies that previously had been restricted to the wealthy few. The returning American scholars made their influence felt in many universities. At Johns Hopkins University, which had opened in Baltimore in 1876 primarily for graduate study, nearly every faculty member had a doctorate from Germany. In 1878 only four hundred Americans pursued nonprofessional graduate study; by 1898 nearly four thousand doctorates were awarded. By the end of the 1880s the University of Chicago, Harvard, and Yale all enrolled more graduate students than Johns Hopkins. It was no longer necessary for talented students to seek graduate training in Europe, for America offered rich opportunities at many different institutions of higher learning.

Technical and Professional Schools. By the 1890s most Americans realized that many new types of schools—trade, manual training, technical, commercial, corporate, agricultural, and evening schools—had to be developed to provide adequate vocational preparation for the new realities of industrialization. After 1880 immigration to the northern and midwestern United States from southern and eastern Europe and from the American South rose significantly. The percentage of illiteracy among these new immigrants, combined with the policy of labor unions' limiting the number of apprentices they would train, created a need for industrial training for adults. In 1885 a state law was passed by New Jersey providing subsidies to encourage cities to offer manual training in their courses, and three years later manual training became a part of the course in the elementary schools of Boston and New York. The trend toward more vocational study influenced higher education as well. Noteworthy higher institutions that combined serious study of industrial subjects with liberal arts courses include Tuskegee Institute (1881), Pratt Institute in Brooklyn (1887), Drexel Institute of Philadelphia (1891), and Armour Institute of Technology in Chicago (1893). A system of commercial education was begun in the 1880s, and the Wharton School in Philadelphia (1892) served as an important model for other business institutions. Schools for education in high technology also opened to serve an increasingly industrial society. Although the Massachusetts Institute of Technology had been opened in 1865, its enrollment and stature grew significantly during this era, and the Georgia School of Technology (1888), the Polytechnic Institute of Brooklyn (reorganized in 1889), and the Carnegie Institute (1895) gave future engineers and scientists more options for higher education.

The Feminization of Education. The period following Reconstruction was marked by women becoming schoolteachers in greater numbers. Hundreds of black and thousands of northern white women had been drawn into the desolate rural areas of the South during Reconstruction. Additionally, accelerated immigration and the settlement of the West created a demand for more schoolteachers. Since few women were able to afford a full liberal arts education, more and more female students demanded intermediate institutions offering vocational or professional training. The founding in 1884 of the exclusively white Mississippi State Normal and Industrial School initiated a pattern soon followed by Georgia, North Carolina, South Carolina, Oklahoma, and Texas. These schools offered a briefer and less expensive course of study than did colleges. By 1890 more girls than boys were being graduated from high schools, and this credential alone allowed students to begin teaching school. Communities unwilling to overtax themselves to support education soon came to appreciate the fact that these women worked at lower wages than their male counterparts. In 1880, for example, male teachers worked for an average monthly wage of $42.68; women teachers made $33.95 for the same jobs. Although Americans in the latter part of the nineteenth century demanded more and better schools, they were not eager to pay teachers for their expanded roles. For both men and women, the average monthly salaries for teaching more and more of America's students increased by only $11 between 1870 and 1908. Despite some financial setbacks for teachers, the period from 1878 to 1899 saw a revival of public interest in education for all citizens. By the late 1890s the forces of change were at work, and American education was at the beginning of a period of fundamental reform.

TOPICS IN THE NEWS

AMERICAN COLLEGES DEVELOP RESEARCH ROLES

Johns Hopkins University. In 1876 Johns Hopkins University opened in Baltimore with a mission different from that of any other American university. Under the leadership of President Daniel Coit Gilman, Johns Hopkins provided extensive nonprofessional graduate study similar to that available at German universities. Nearly all of the fifty-three faculty members had doctorates from institutions in Berlin, Heidelberg, Jena, and Halle, and this new center of graduate learning soon attracted scores of scholars whose work would spread the new ideals of study to other institutions in the United States. Among them were Josiah Royce and John Dewey in philosophy and psychology, Henry C. Adams and John Commons in political economy, J. Franklin Jameson and Woodrow Wilson (who later became president of the United States) in history and political science, and Edmund B. Wilson and E. G. Conklin in biology.

The Model Becomes Popular. Many eastern institutions, spurred by the success at Johns Hopkins, began to build their graduate programs. Soon a significant number of state universities also built graduate facilities, their interest in research usually spreading outward from their departments of agriculture. Fellowships, or small stipends for financial support of graduate research, became increasingly more available, and soon the numbers of scholars pursuing doctorates soared from four hundred in 1878 to nearly five thousand in 1898.

Johns Hopkins University, the first American university to offer research-oriented graduate programs

Expansion. Three universities emulating the Johns Hopkins model were soon founded: Clark University, Worcester, Massachusetts, in 1887, supported by a million-dollar gift from Jonas Gilman Clark; Catholic University of America, Washington, D.C., in 1889; and the University of Chicago in 1892, backed by the Rockefeller family. Clark University, headed by G. Stanley Hall, formerly a Johns Hopkins professor, specialized in the study of psychology and a few closely related subjects. Registration at Clark University consisted of giving one's name and address to an assigned thesis professor. There were no class lists, no grades; professors lectured whenever they chose, and students graduated whenever they successfully wrote and defended a thesis. Clark and the other new universities soon became quite competitive. With the monetary support of the Rockefellers, President William Rainey Harper of the University of Chicago was able to offer professors salaries twice as high as those at Clark. Hall, frustrated with a University of Chicago raid on his highly select faculty, characterized Rainey's courtship of his professors as "comparable to anything that the worst trust had ever attempted against its competitors." The location of the University of Chicago in a great and growing city was also an important factor in its success, and except for several large state universities, most progressive centers for research were located in or near urban areas. Near the end of the nineteenth century, for example, both Columbia University and New York University, crowded beyond capacity, were forced to move to larger, much more

expensive New York City sites as their graduate programs expanded.

Sources:
Arthur Schlesinger, *The Rise of the City: 1878–1898* (New York: Macmillan, 1933), pp. 202–246;

Laurence R. Veysey, *The Emergence of the American University* (Chicago: University of Chicago Press, 1965), pp. 125–158.

ASSIMILATION AND FEDERAL INDIAN EDUCATION

The Mission Schools. Prior to the 1870s the federal government had largely neglected Indian education, with Congress allocating no more than $130,000 annually to "civilize" the Native Americans. However, mission schools had long been established by dedicated Catholic and Episcopal educators. William Chapman, director of the Episcopal school on the Standing Rock Reservation, South Dakota, maintained that church training was infinitely better for the "naturally devout" Indian children than government education. Only a small fraction of the Indian population was served by these missionaries, but tribal leaders were unanimous in their support for the mission schools.

Remolding Indian Values. Although missionaries and some reformers were convinced that Indians could be "civilized," many whites believed that Indians were incapable of progress. Despite this prevailing sentiment, the federal government in 1879 began a plan to remold Indian culture, or what was referred to in documents of the day as "remolding his system of values." Congress implemented a policy of total

Three boys from the Pueblo tribe — Watte, Keise-te-Wa, and He-Li-te — at home (left) and after they enrolled at the Carlisle Industrial School (right), where they became Sheldon Jackson, Harvey Townsend, and John Shields

assimilation of Native Americans into mainstream society, expressing faith that Indians who were properly educated could adopt the norms and values of the dominant white culture. American leaders of the post-Reconstruction era were so sure of the supremacy of their ideals and dreams that they dismissed any other cultural values as inferior. Armed with nearly evangelistic fervor for reforming Indians, federally funded educators set to work.

Off-Reservation Boarding Schools. Richard Henry Pratt, a U.S. Army captain, founded Carlisle Indian School in 1879. This large industrial training institute, housed in a deserted army barracks in Carlisle, Pennsylvania, served as a model for the twenty-five other boarding schools that opened by the turn of the century. Captain Pratt's "acculturation policy" called for cutting the students' hair, changing their names, and teaching them new sports and new manners. Congress hailed the success of Carlisle by appropriating large sums for expansion of Pratt's model, and industrial training schools were founded away from reservations at sites such as Forest Grove, Oregon (1880); Albuquerque (1884); Chilocco, Oklahoma (1884); Santa Fe (1890 — later renamed the Institute of American Indian Arts); and Phoenix (1890). Despite the rapid expansion of the industrial boarding schools, many reformers criticized the programs. Ironically, their

objections were not to the assimilationist nature of the training. Instead, opponents argued that the schools trained too few youths at too great an expense. Their greatest objection, however, was that far too many of the Indians who attended the schools failed to maintain their new white identity after graduation; as critics claimed, these students "returned to the blanket."

Reservation Day Schools. Indian students educated at the boarding schools faced significant problems upon returning to the reservations. They were often ridiculed by their peers who had not left home, and more important, their industrial training was of little use on reservations in remote rural locations. These educated youth, therefore, became the first victims of the "either/or" policy of assimilation as their training forced them to choose either the culture of the white man or the culture of the Indian—there was no compromise. Critics of the off-reservation boarding schools succeeded in establishing reservation boarding and day schools near the end of the century. These schools were not only much cheaper to run, but they were also more acceptable to parents, who resented having their children forcibly removed to fill the quotas of off-reservation schools. Although these schools were closer to home and allowed more contact with family, the federally funded programs maintained the same assimilationist philosophy as the off-reservation schools, and some parents believed that

Boys in a manual-training class at a New York City public school, 1890s (photograph by Jacob Riis)

education such as this "represented the most dangerous of all attacks on basic Indian values, the one most likely to succeed in the end because it is aimed at children."

Sources:
Margaret Szasz, *Education and the American Indian* (Albuquerque: University of New Mexico Press, 1974), pp. 8–13;

Robert M. Utley, *The Last Days of the Sioux Nation* (New Haven: Yale University Press, 1963), p. 37.

CITY SCHOOLS, COUNTRY SCHOOLS

The Urban Environment. The growth of American cities dramatically affected American education during the last three decades of the nineteenth century. While children in the country continued to live in the age-old close-to-nature manner, city children were growing up in a largely new environment. An investigation conducted by G. Stanley Hall, then a lecturer in

Students at a one-room sod schoolhouse in Cummings Park, Nebraska, 1887

psychology at Harvard, showed that more than half the children entering Boston's primary schools in 1880 had never seen a plow or spade, a robin, squirrel, snail, or sheep; they had never observed peaches on a tree or growing grain and could not distinguish an oak tree from a willow or poplar. In place of these traditional experiences, the city youth were more familiar with images such as paved streets, telegraph poles, and pictures of prizefighters that came in cigarette packs. American children learning to read had completely different life experiences.

Wealthy City Schools. Urban schools tended to be much better than rural schools. The concentration of wealth and population in urban centers, combined with the stronger impetus toward reforms in teaching and learning, insured higher salaries for teachers, longer school terms, better buildings, and superior organization and methods of instruction. Some city schools became the center for new ideas that by the turn of the century would be known as "progressive education." Saint Louis schools, for example, under the superintendency of William T. Harris, introduced reforms such as public kindergartens and new elementary and high school courses in sewing, cooking, commercial subjects, and the manual arts. As the curriculum multiplied, it became necessary to add a fourth year to the high school, and by 1890 most city high schools offered four-year courses. According to census figures of 1890 large cities compiled a better record of literacy, with the American-born children of European immigrants doing better at reading and writing than the white children of native parentage. Analysts of the day attributed this superiority primarily to the fact that the children of immigrants were concentrated in the cities.

The traditional, time-tested way of examining pupils' knowledge of complicated grammar, vocabulary, selected prose, and facts from all the branches of study was predicated on the assumption, common among educators and the public alike, that memorizing and reciting difficult material strengthened the mind and demonstrated intellectual progress. Accordingly, more than half the average high-school student's time was spent in recitations: a time for the individual simply to say aloud what he or she had memorized from texts and from lectures. Students made anywhere from three to seven daily recitations, often in separate examining rooms. This didactic method of education was prevalent in all parts of the country, even though many theorists agreed with the Maine principal who claimed that "cramming is confused with education and the knowledge so gained soon forgotten, vanishing like Hamlet's ghosts at the approach of dawn." What mattered was contained in textbooks, stored in one's mind, and recited to teachers. Bestowing prizes on students who excelled at competitive recitation was a standard practice. In 1880 John Swett, a principal in San Francisco, admitted that "prizes and gifts are often abused as classroom stimulants," and therefore the wise teacher should "check the spirit of reckless ambition in the wild race for prizes and honors." Despite his condemnation, the majority of educators and citizens of the late nineteenth century believed that because youth "preferred play over study," the only way to force them to learn was through enforced recitations and/or the incentive of prizes.

Source: William J. Reese, *The Origins of the American High School* (New Haven: Yale University Press, 1995), pp. 133–138.

Rural Struggles. In rural districts the educational picture was much bleaker. Ungraded schools were still the rule, with a single schoolmaster shepherding pupils of all ages and degrees of advancement while disciplining unruly students. The school year was much shorter than in urban areas as well. In 1891 the typical city session lasted from 180 to 200 as compared to 70 to 150 days in the country. In the northern and western United States the rural school situation was the subject of constant recommendation by state commissioners of instruction. However, the division of meager resources among many small, independent school districts guaranteed that the rural schools would never flourish financially. In 1882 the state of Massachusetts abolished the district system, and schools began to be consolidated, with children transported by wagons to a centrally located, graded school. Before 1898 Ohio, New York, and New Jersey had also begun to consolidate small rural schools. However, in most other states—and especially in all areas of the South—rural conservatism was slow to yield to reform and the country schools remained in unsatisfactory condition.

Sources:

Ellwood Patterson Cubberley, *Public Education in the United States: A Study and Interpretation of American Educational History* (Boston & New York: Houghton Mifflin, 1919), pp. 252–253;

Arthur Schlesinger, *The Rise of the City: 1878–1898* (New York: Macmillan, 1933), pp. 160–201.

EDUCATING WOMEN

Inroads. During the last quarter of the nineteenth century, women made a significant push into higher education. The popularization of schooling for everyone, evident in the growth of common schools, high schools, and colleges, meant that more women and men had access to education. The Civil War had initiated new opportunities as well, since women had to assume places in schools as teachers when men went away to war. Furthermore, because so many men had died during the war, a large proportion of women could not expect to marry, and these women sought opportunities to support themselves. As immigration to the United States accelerated and the expansion west continued, both urban and rural areas required more schoolteachers. In addition, advocacy for female education had political dimensions; some of the same reformers who had previously backed abolitionism supported the collegiate education of women.

Need for Jobs. Since very few women could afford a full liberal arts education, advocates of female education also favored intermediate institutions offering vocational or professional training. Significantly, by 1890 more girls than boys were being graduated from high school. Economist Susan Carter attributes this trend to the fact that high school attendance gave women access to better jobs, especially teaching. Young women teachers could go right into the grammar school classroom after graduation. Normal schools, which provided a briefer and less expensive preparation for teaching the higher grades than did college, expanded significantly during the 1880s. Several female medical colleges opening at this time did not require collegiate education for admission.

Choices. Men still outnumbered women in the colleges, but as more women finished high school, they slowly made inroads into higher education. Many types of collegiate institutions grew: the private women's college, the religiously oriented coeducational college, the secular coeducational college, and the public single-sex vocational institution. Four private women's colleges, which became nationally known institutions, opened during the postwar decades: Vassar in 1865, Wellesley and Smith Colleges in 1875, and Bryn Mawr in 1885. The trustees of the latter school agreed with its

Students in the Fay House library at Radcliffe College, 1897

ambitious president, Martha Carey Thomas, that the emphasis of Bryn Mawr should be academic. Thomas, an early graduate of Cornell, resolved to make her college the equal of the best men's colleges. In the South several seminaries gradually became serious academic colleges in the 1880s; the Woman's College of Baltimore (known as Goucher), Mary Baldwin in Virginia, and Agnes Scott in Georgia are notable examples. Several prestigious colleges accommodated women by opening a female annex: Harvard chartered Radcliffe in 1894 as a degree-granting institution offering the equivalent of a Harvard degree, and Barnard College was opened as an adjunct of Columbia University in 1889.

Coeducation. Economy necessitated coeducation in areas other than the South, where tradition held firm and women seeking an education were relegated to women's schools. Most state institutions discovered that they could not delay the admission of women. The female presence was not a legal requirement under the Morrill Land Grant Act, but the act did not specifically exclude women. That act, first signed by President Abraham Lincoln in 1862, made public lands available to states to endow colleges for instruction in agriculture and the mechanical arts. The second Morrill Act of 1890, which required federal allocations to be "fairly divided between Negroes and Whites," enlarged college rolls. By the 1890s most land-grant colleges as well as state institutions outside the South were coed, and two major

universities opened that admitted female students from the start. In 1892 both Stanford and the University of Chicago actively recruited women as undergraduates, graduate students, and faculty members. Between 1870 and 1900 the number of women enrolled in institutions of higher learning increased nearly eightfold, from eleven thousand to eighty-five thousand. The number of women as a percentage of all students rose from 21 percent to at least 35 percent during these thirty years, and by 1900 there were more than twice as many women in coeducational institutions as in the separate women's colleges.

Sources:

Christie Anne Farnham, *The Education of the Southern Belle* (New York: New York University Press, 1994), pp. 181–186;

Barbara Miller Solomon, *In the Company of Educated Women* (New Haven: Yale University Press, 1985), pp. 43–61;

Charles Franklin Thwing, *A History of Education in the United States Since the Civil War* (Boston: Houghton Mifflin, 1910), pp. 125–162.

EXPANDING EDUCATIONAL OPPORTUNITIES FOR THE MASSES

The Kindergarten Movement. The period of 1878–1899 was marked by a tremendous growth in the types and numbers of educational institutions available to the public, ranging from nursery schools to new high schools. For the youngest learners, determined women

In the 1870s some scientists developed theories that endangered the progress of female higher education. Darwinian evolution relegated women to a permanently inferior condition, both physically and mentally. However, the most famous attack came from retired Harvard Medical School professor Dr. Edward Clarke's *Sex in Education* (1873), case studies of seven Vassar students. Clarke concluded that if women used up their "limited energy" on studying, they would endanger their "female apparatus." A girl could study and learn, he believed, only by risking "neuralgia, uterine disease, hysteria, and other derangements of the nervous system." This medical verdict confirmed folk wisdom that the female brain and body simply could not survive "book learning." The book went through seventeen printings and was widely discussed by the educated public. As a result, many women doctors and social scientists began studies that could possibly refute Clarke's findings. Dr. Mary Jacobi's essay "The Question of Rest for Women During Menstruation," which won the Boylston Prize at Harvard in 1876, was one of the many articles published disputing Clarke's conclusions. By 1885 the excitement over Clarke's book had largely subsided and a survey of coeducational institutions emphasized the positive effects of coeducation on both females and males.

Source: Barbara Miller Solomon, *In the Company of Educated Women* (New Haven: Yale University Press, 1985), pp. 54–57.

educators worked during the 1880s and 1890s to establish kindergartens and to effect a revolutionary change in attitudes toward young children. Elizabeth Palmer Peabody, the daughter of two teachers at Phillips Andover Academy and the sister-in-law of the writer Nathaniel Hawthorne, led a campaign to popularize the kinds of kindergartens she had discovered while traveling in Germany to observe the work of innovator Friedrich Wilhelm August Froebel. The schools were based on the concept of play and exploration. The children were provided with malleable equipment, such as Peg-Boards, perforated cards for wool embroidery, and soft balls. The walls were covered with pictures appealing to children, and the kindergartners played games and sang songs. This "play school" approach was contrary to the typical schoolroom of the day where children were expected to sit in rows and recite memorized facts.

Kindergartens Move West. Peabody, who personally financed thirty-one kindergartens in New England, established a training facility to provide instructors who understood Froebel's educational theory and practice. Her lectures in the Midwest inspired Susan Blow in Saint Louis, who convinced the superintendent of schools, Dr. William T. Harris, to start the first public kindergarten in the United States. By 1880 fifty-eight public kindergartens had been established in the Saint Louis schools. In 1888 Dr. William Hailmann of the LaPorte, Indiana, public schools established public kindergartens there; his wife, Eudora, ran a training school for kindergarten and primary-school teachers from 1885 to 1894. The movement for free kindergartens was also quite active in the West, where San Francisco was an influential center of training under the financial support of Phoebe Hearst, the mother of William Randolph Hearst. By the end of the century a significant number of communities became convinced of the benefits of early childhood education, and kindergartens gradually became part of the public education system.

Elementary Schools. The larger percentage of children entering the public primary schools during this period had little time for play or exploration. Their primary curriculum consisted mainly of the study of words for the purposes of learning reading and spelling. The mathematics by which their minds were to be trained had little relation to the kind of arithmetic needed in the world. The study of grammar did little to improve use of the language but "did much to prevent development of an appreciation of literature," as a teacher of the day put it. Of the fifteen million students in average daily attendance during the year 1897, the typical elementary school student attended a one-room school and was taught by a young woman who had little if any training beyond the elementary subjects herself and who was paid a total income of less than $300. There were compulsory attendance laws in thirty states, in one territory, and in the District of Columbia. The usual age of compulsory attendance was from eight to fourteen.

Corporate Schooling for Young Workers. Some of the burgeoning industries of the late nineteenth century discovered that their young, elementary school–educated workforce needed further education. Many corporations developed full-fledged schooling programs for employees. These programs, in turn, became models for the public school since the factory system made direct demands on the schools to produce workers with the correct social attitudes and skills. During the 1890s the National Cash Register Company, Heinz, Sherwin Williams, and the major railroad companies organized libraries for their workers and provided classes as well. The large retail houses, notably John Wanamaker's store in Philadelphia and E. A. Filene's of Boston, organized a corps of teachers who taught mandatory classes for all workers younger than the age of eighteen during the early morning hours when business was slow. At Wanamaker's, a teacher went through the daily newspaper explaining current events and answering

Students attending a night class for working children at a lodging house on Seventh Avenue in New York City, circa 1890 (photograph by Jacob Riis)

questions. Filene's offered employees courses in psychology, geography, health, science, and mathematics.

Secondary Education. A remarkable increase in the number of facilities and in the variety of subjects and curricula available to students occurred during the last decade of the nineteenth century. In 1890 there were a total of 4,158 secondary schools (of which 2,526 were public) in the United States. By 1900 the number had nearly doubled to 7,983, and of those, 6,005 were public schools. Most secondary schools in 1890 were still selective; only the best and brightest went beyond grammar schooling. The high school curriculum was largely academic, its program limited to English, foreign languages, mathematics, natural sciences, and history. These studies were organized into the following curricula: the Classical course, the Latin-Scientific course, the Modern Language course, and the English course. Only a few of the larger, urban high schools offered some clerical courses in 1890. However, the group attending high school by the turn of the century was much more heterogeneous in capacities and in economic and social status. To meet their needs, and the needs of an increasingly industrial society, many high schools by 1899 had introduced agriculture, home economics, and vocational studies in general. Greek, astronomy, and geology had all but disappeared from the curriculum by this time. City administrators, convinced that expanding secondary schooling would promote democratic progress, erected expensive and elaborate public buildings to house their new high schools. Called "palaces of extravagances" by their critics, these solid forms presented an image of propriety and order that middle-class citizens found extremely attractive, especially when they were located in otherwise chaotic cities.

Sources:

I. L. Kandel, ed., *Twenty-Five Years of American Education* (Freeport, N.Y.: Books for Libraries Press, 1966), pp. 225–271;

William J. Reese, *The Origins of the American High School* (New Haven: Yale University Press, 1995), pp. 80–103;

Agnes Snyder, *Dauntless Women in Childhood Education* (Washington, D.C.: Association for Childhood Education International, 1972), pp. 31–48, 59, 105;

Joel H. Spring, *Education and the Rise of the Corporate State* (Boston: Beacon, 1972), pp. 44–53.

INDUSTRIAL TRAINING FOR AFRICAN AMERICANS

"The Head, the Hand, the Heart." Hampton Normal and Industrial Institute was the first of the Negro training schools founded by northern philanthropy on the principle that "no education is complete which does not train the hand to work." At Hampton, established in 1868 and located in Virginia, founder Gen. Samuel Armstrong of the Freedmen's Bureau popularized a practical curriculum — industrial and agricultural education — for both former slaves and American Indians. Armstrong's aim was to "train selected youth

Public attention was turned to the problems of urban tenement living in 1890 when New York reporter Jacob Riis published *How the Other Half Lives*. Riis motivated significant reform movements when he wrote about the premature deaths of children doomed by the unsanitary conditions of the slums. His description of "little coffins stacked mountain-high on the deck of the Charity Commissioners' boat when it makes its semi-weekly trips to the city cemetery" riveted the reading public. Warning that the "rescue of children is the key to the problem of city poverty," Riis insisted that the slums must be fought with "sunlight and flowers and play, which their child hearts crave, if their eyes have never seen them." Vacation schools for poor urban children were a partial answer to Riis's call. The first was established in Boston in 1885, followed by New York in 1894 and Cleveland and Brooklyn in 1897. In 1898 Chicago established what would become a model vacation school system. Chicago's program, designed by John Dewey, included excursions to the country, drawing and painting from nature, music, gymnastics and games, sewing, and manual training. When the first Chicago children got off the railroad at the end of the line, they crawled on their hands and knees to feel the "ill-smelling and dusty chickweed" of the country soil for the first time. Vacation schools were popular with citizens of all political persuasions: some approved the moral rightness of rescuing children from the "vast human pig sties" that were the slums; others felt their value was in "leaving no boy or girl with unoccupied time, free to roam the streets with no friendly hand to guide them, save that of the police."

Sources: Jacob A. Riis, *How the Other Half Lives* (New York: Harper, 1890), pp. 33, 166–167;

Joel H. Spring, *Education and the Rise of the Corporate State* (Boston: Beacon, 1972), pp. 62–68.

who should go out and teach and lead their people," and his school provided experimental stations for agriculture, a building for domestic science study, and a trade school administered by the Worcester School of Technology. The innovative approach of combining traditional learning with trade education to "showcase the possibilities of the Negro race" attracted significant attention in the late 1870s. It was not unusual for several hundred northern tourists a day to visit the school, which was located in an area where only fifteen years earlier it had been illegal to teach a black person to read. Among the teachers working at Hampton were graduates of several of the most prestigious schools of the day, including Smith, Wellesley, Bryn Mawr, Williams, Amherst, and Yale.

Tuskegee Institute. Booker T. Washington, perhaps Hampton's most famous graduate, helped popularize the agricultural/industrial curriculum by establishing a second training school at Tuskegee, Alabama, in 1881. Washington, who credited Hampton as having "advanced my literary education, trained me to continuous and intelligent work with my hands, and awakened in me genuine respect for labor," was recommended for the position by his mentor, General Armstrong. In Macon County, Alabama, a part of the Black Belt (named for its rich soil), the area was populated by forty-five hundred whites and three times as many blacks. Washington said he created a curriculum at Tuskegee "adjusted to the actual needs of the people rather than to their theoretical needs," a course of study that would demand that all students, no matter how well-to-do their parents may be, learn a trade as well as reading, writing, and arithmetic. This requirement originally raised a storm of protest, but soon thirty-six industries were offered at Tuskegee and a steady stream of students poured in not only from the Alabama Black Belt but from Georgia, South Carolina, Florida, Mississippi, and Louisiana.

Critics. A significant number of African American intellectuals from the North strenuously objected to the type of education offered by industrial/agricultural institutes such as Hampton and Tuskegee. W. E. B. Du Bois, a prominent educator, argued publicly as early as the late 1890s that his race must be educated "to be what we can be, not what somebody else wants us to be." Calling the Hampton curriculum "educational heresy," Du Bois insisted that "necessary as it is to earn a living, it is more necessary and important to earn a life." Du Bois contrasted the aim of higher education—the development of power—with that of the aim of industrial training—the development of manual skills. He began a public debate over the propriety of segregated education with Washington that raged for several decades — Du Bois's eloquent and bitter rhetoric contrasting dramatically with Washington's polite persuasion. Washington had the support of powerful white philanthropists such as George Foster Peabody and Wallace Buttrick, who believed that industrial training was the appropriate form of schooling to assist in bringing racial order, political stability, and material prosperity to the South. Therefore, Washington's vision for industrial and agricultural education, supported by both southern white legislators and the financially influential philanthropists, was fully realized at Tuskegee during the 1890s.

Sources:
Harry S. Ashmore, *The Negro and the Schools* (Chapel Hill: University of North Carolina Press, 1954), pp. 13–29;

W. E. B. Du Bois, *The Education of Black People* (Amherst: University of Massachusetts Press, 1973), pp. 5–13;

Edgar W. Knight, *Public Education in the South* (Boston: Ginn, 1922), pp. 420–435;

Truman Pierce, *White and Negro Schools in the South: An Analysis of Biracial Education* (Englewood Cliffs, N.J.: Prentice-Hall, 1955), pp. 17–43.

PUBLIC EDUCATION IN THE SOUTH

Power Shift. The electoral campaigns of 1874–1876 returned the southern states to the control of the Democratic Party. The leadership was much the same as it had been prior to Reconstruction — primarily members of the elite classes who had never been sympathetic to public education. However, during Reconstruction people in the South had embraced the idea of public education, so in order to be elected the Democrats had to include maintenance of public schools, one system for each race, in their political platforms. The schools may have been maintained, but they did not prosper during the last twenty-five years of the century. Enrollments grew by more than 150 percent while educational revenues, derived primarily from taxes on property that had lost most of its value during the Civil War, plummeted. True values of property in the South averaged less than one-third of those of the North or Midwest. Post-Reconstruction legislatures made it difficult to improve education because they refused to permit local taxes for schools and so only a limited rate of taxation at the state level was available to support the two separate school systems.

Teaching Conditions. Every facet of education in the South suffered terribly during this period. Fewer than 5 percent of the teachers had college training; more than 60 percent had no definite professional training of any kind. Although the average annual salary for female teachers during the 1870–1900 period was about $300, average salaries in the South for the same period actually dropped from $175 to $159. Not only were salaries low, but in some cases the payment of them was uncertain. In South Carolina in the 1880s teachers routinely received vouchers on payday instead of a check. It was considered a progressive step when teachers were paid (much later) the face value of those vouchers rather than a reduced amount.

A Failing System. While illiteracy ranged from 30 to 45 percent of the total population (three times that of other areas of the country), only one pupil out of ten who enrolled in school reached the fifth grade and only one in seventy reached the eighth grade. Poorly equipped teachers worked with almost no supervision, merely "keeping school," as it was referred to at the time. Each small, isolated school was left to itself as county superintendents' jobs routinely went to incompetents as reward for political service; no qualifications were legally prescribed for any positions. The state superintendent in South Carolina in 1900 reported that "Each district has

CHAUTAUQUA

The Chautauqua movement originated from a Methodist camp meeting at Chautauqua Lake, New York, under the leadership of Bishop J. H. Vincent in 1874. Chautauqua outdoor summer meetings usually featured educational and inspirational lectures to educate adults. These meetings soon became widely popular all over the United States. A description of the movement's philosophy from an 1886 publication defines its lofty goals:

Chautauqua pleads for a universal education; for plans of reading and study; for all legitimate enticements and incitements to ambition; for all necessary adaptations as to time and topics; for ideal associations which shall at once excite the imagination and set the heart aglow. Chautauqua stretches over the land a magnificent temple, broad as the continent, lofty as the heavens, into which homes, churches, schools, and shops may build themselves into a splendid university in which people of all ages and conditions may be enrolled as students. . . . Show people that the mind reaches its maturity long after the school days end, and that some of the best intellectual and literary labor is performed in and beyond middle life.

Source: Theodore Morrison, *Chautauqua: A Center for Education, Religion, and the Arts in America* (Chicago & London: University of Chicago Press, 1974).

as poor schools as its people will tolerate, and in some districts anything will be tolerated." Rural schoolhouses in the South during the 1880s and 1890s were valued at less than $100 each.

Meager Reform Efforts. Northern philanthropists did not abandon their antebellum efforts in the South. George Foster Peabody, whose Peabody Fund remained active throughout the century, donated "one million dollars to be held in trust to promote intellectual, moral or industrial education in the most destitute portions of the United States." A major accomplishment of this endowment was the establishment of the Nashville, Tennessee, Normal College in 1875 (the school became the George Peabody College for Teachers in 1909). By 1897 more than $365,000 had been given in scholarships to southern teachers for training. In the late 1890s some reforms stirred in the public sector. The economy of the South grew: production of cotton increased; industrial investments multiplied; and railroad building expanded. The increase in wealth during this decade was nearly 50 percent. A foundation of substantial increases in school revenues and a new attitude toward the importance of education was present at the close of the century. However, the South entered the twentieth century with public school systems that were inferior to those in the rest of the United States, and the question of segregated Negro

OPPORTUNITY

Peter H. Clark, an educator and political activist in Cincinnati, devoted his life to expanding opportunities for African Americans to study "the higher branches," as the secondary school curriculum was called. Every pupil who attended any secondary school during the 1870s and 1880s was regarded as exceptional — someone whose claim to respect rested upon individual achievement, not birthright. Clark, whose grandfather was reportedly the explorer William Clark (he had sired several children with his black mistress), established Gaines High School for the "aristocracy of talent" among his city's black population. In the late 1870s Clark claimed to have boosted the school's academic quality to match its white competitors. By 1879 about 4 percent of blacks enrolled in the Cincinnati system were studying at Gaines, a percentage similar to the number of whites in secondary schools. However, this experiment with a black-controlled high school was not representative of other northern systems. The tiny percentage of African American youth in the North who attended secondary schools had to rely on their own efforts or upon the kindness of strangers, such as white philanthropists, missionaries, or sympathetic school board members.

Source: William J. Reese, *The Origins of the American High School* (New Haven: Yale University Press, 1995), pp. 233–235.

public schools was settled by a "separate but equal" doctrine that in reality meant only separate. In many parts of the South, public education as late as 1900 suffered in comparison with conditions of 1860.

Sources:
Harry S. Ashmore, *The Negro and the Schools* (Chapel Hill: University of North Carolina Press, 1954), pp. 12–52;

Edgar W. Knight, *Public Education in the South* (Boston: Ginn, 1922), pp. 422–450;

Truman Pierce, *White and Negro Schools in the South: An Analysis of Biracial Education* (Englewood Cliffs, N.J.: Prentice-Hall, 1955), pp. 17–42;

PUBLIC EDUCATION OF AFRICAN AMERICANS

Post-Reconstruction Efforts. During the 1870s and 1880s the majority of African Americans were still living in the South. By 1877, when the last remaining federal troops were withdrawn to end the Reconstruction period officially, the rudiments of the public education system in the South had been established with traditions that kept it segregated for nearly a century. The principle of universal education, which had been written into Reconstruction-era state constitutions, survived when southern whites returned to power, but everywhere in the South the laws were changed to provide that the races be educated separately. The separation of races had been fostered by the philanthropic organizations that had assumed primary responsibility for educational efforts. The Peabody Fund, for example, which began helping both blacks and whites as early as 1867, had benefactors whose position was that separate schools for the races were desirable. Most blacks were much more concerned with equal opportunity than with mixed schools, so Reconstruction governments had made no efforts to integrate the emerging public schools. When southerners returned to power, they faced dire poverty made worse by burdensome taxes on agricultural land that was barely producing, and they had vivid memories of graft and misappropriation of funds in government. Most leaders, who evidenced serious resentment and prejudice toward both northerners and African Americans, felt that education for black citizens was a responsibility of the federal government and of private philanthropy rather than a local burden.

Taxes and Educational Equity. When southern Democrats returned to power, they cut back property taxes dramatically, even though the school-age population was increasing rapidly. From 1875 to 1895 school enrollment in the South increased by more than two million pupils, or more than 150 percent. As black political power disappeared, it was inevitable that funds were diverted from blacks to whites. The schools were supported by state school funds, which were distributed on a per capita basis. This per capita distribution meant that considerably more money was allotted to black schools in "black" counties (the counties across the South with traditionally large numbers of black agricultural workers, exemplified by the Delta area in Mississippi). In "white" counties schools for whites received the greater apportionment of money. Such a situation was intolerable for the old planter classes who found themselves in the minority of the population of the "black" counties. These powerful property owners soon began passing laws that had the effect of diverting per capita spending to white schools. One way this shifting of moneys was accomplished was by state examinations for teachers, with salaries based upon the kind of teaching certificates granted. A wide range of salaries was possible even for the same certificate. Examining officers could give African American teachers lower salaries than were paid to whites with the same certificate. However, in counties where the black population was small, there was little money to divert. The result in these counties was a general antagonism to "Negro education" of any sort. The differential in expenditures became more marked as the century drew to a close, especially after the Supreme Court's *Plessy* v. *Ferguson* (1896) ruling sanctioned separate schools for the races.

Sources:

Harry S. Ashmore, *The Negro and the Schools* (Chapel Hill: University of North Carolina Press, 1954), pp. 13–29;

W. E. B. Du Bois, *The Education of Black People* (Amherst: University of Massachusetts Press, 1973), pp. 5–13;

Edgar W. Knight, *Public Education in the South* (Boston: Ginn, 1922), pp. 420–435;

Truman Pierce, *White and Negro Schools in the South: An Analysis of Biracial Education* (Englewood Cliffs, N.J.: Prentice-Hall, 1955), pp. 17–43.

PUBLIC SCHOOL TEXTBOOKS

"Storehouses of Knowledge." Nineteenth-century educators believed that textbooks were the "great storehouses of knowledge, and he who has the habit of using them intelligently has the key to all human knowledge." Technological innovations had led to cheaper, mass-produced print, and textbooks—from grammar to Latin to algebra—helped define acceptable knowledge and shape instruction. Textbooks presumably democratized information, making specialized learning available to everyone. William T. Harris, a staunch friend of the high school and later U.S. commissioner of education (1889–1906), defended these books in 1880 against charges that they promoted "lifeless instruction" since most class work consisted of memorization of the text contents. Standard texts, he argued, enabled "the bright pupil, even under the worst methods of instruction, to participate in the recorded experience and wisdom of mankind," and they also helped "even the dull and stupid, to some extent."

Voices of Authority. The most famous authors of high school textbooks were usually New England–born, Protestant, white men who had attended college or other higher schools. Many taught in prominent northern academies or colleges. The scientist Alonzo Gray taught at Phillips Andover in Massachusetts. Emma Willard, founder of the Troy Female Seminary in New York, wrote a popular history and a geography text. John Hart, the author of prominent English-language readers and literature texts, was a principal at Philadelphia's prestigious Central High School and later a professor at Princeton. Like many other textbook writers, he was an ordained minister whose faith was inextricable from his didactic voice. Books by these authors held common (and generally conservative) cultural views toward mankind, gender relations, nature, capital, labor, and America's destiny. These voices of authority taught talented youth common intellectual and moral precepts. Whether in chemistry or natural philosophy classes, students learned that the power of God was all important. Zoological classification named man "the lord of the Animal Kingdom . . . and man alone is created in the image of God." The Almighty demanded hard work and productivity through math problems that linked learning and life, as texts showed that those who were "shiftless" ended up poor. Grammar lessons promoted prevailing ideas about society and bourgeois

African American students at a segregated school in South Carolina, circa 1890

taste. Because textbooks were so ideologically selective, resentful southerners warned kinsmen to "beware of Yankee books."

Science, Math, and Values. The school curriculum was dependent on what textbooks were widely available: mathematics, the sciences, English, history, moral philosophy and such practical classes as mensuration (the study of measurement), and astronomy. Science was central to secondary instruction, and larger schools offered physics, physiology, chemistry, botany, and sometimes geology and zoology. The laws of science helped legitimize a society whose economic system favored growth and man's dominion over nature. High school chemistry texts, for example, promised practical education that would reveal the workings of a "beneficent God who always blessed a productive people." In 1884 the Woman's Christian Temperance Union officially endorsed a version of a physiology text by Dorman Steele that drew upon chemistry to attack alcohol, tobacco, and drug abuse. The God-given laws of science protected youth, Steele promised, but only if students mastered chemistry. He explained that alcohol was a stimulant, not a depressant (an incorrect, if widely held, view), and allowed "the animal instincts to assume the mastery of man." The association between textbook knowledge and respectable behavior was clear. Educators argued that science also trained the mind, taught logic and reason, and sharpened the powers of observation. Many educational writers in the late 1800s embraced the importance of mathematics as providential. Mathematics was integral to the curriculum because it "contributed to the spread of Christian, republican, civilized views about man and society." A nation enjoying geographical expansion needed mathematics to help build better roads, survey land, construct homes, and otherwise enhance commerce and human enterprise. "In the mines of the West, they will need geometry to aid them in mining and smelting," one textbook of the 1880s warned. These textbooks of the nineteenth century became as familiar and as influential as William McGuffey's *Eclectic Readers* (1836–1837) had been to the multitudes in the grammar schools.

Source:
William J. Reese, *The Origins of the American High School* (New Haven: Yale University Press, 1995), pp. 103–122.

TEACHERS AND TEACHING

Status of Teachers. Teachers were not universally held in high esteem during the last quarter of the nineteenth century. As one governor of South Carolina asked during this time in an address to the legislature, "Who are the teachers of our free schools? Are they men to whom we can commit with confidence the great business of education?" He then answered, claiming they were "grossly incompetent, but with the poor pay allowed them, we cannot reasonably calculate upon a better state of things." The status of teachers varied from state to state, but their professional status was suppressed because of poor pay in all areas of the United States. Salaries even in top school districts such as Bridgeport, Connecticut, in the late 1870s were $1,800 for male principals and $700 for the rare female teachers who served as principals.

Gender Gaps. The average male teacher in the United States made $800, while the average female elementary teacher made $300 to $400 per year. Nearly all teachers of younger children were women, with the grammar and high schools under the supervision of a male principal. The earliest secondary schools employed men at first, but by the 1880s women teachers had become more prevalent in public high schools. Chicago reported that its public high school system employed twenty women and sixteen men; Boston, forty women and thirty-five men. A male teacher-superintendent usually headed the schools and hired women instructors. In an age that characterized girls and boys as different elements in God's plan, differences in salaries based on gender seemed normal. However, some citizens argued that the elementary school teachers deserved more money since they taught more pupils. The commissioner of education in Ohio complained in 1878 that high school instructors constituted a minority of the teaching force but consumed disproportionate funds. In that state only 711 of the total of 23,003 teachers taught high school, but they consumed more than $436,000 of the $5 million expended for salaries.

Qualifications to Teach. The old theory that almost anyone could teach almost any school subject served to retard the growth of uniform certification practices. The licensing of teachers was a local function, and the fitness of candidates for teaching positions was generally determined in a haphazard fashion. College degrees ensured advantages, but most teachers attended normal schools rather than colleges. Even in an urban district such as Chicago in 1878, only 50 percent of the men and 10 percent of the women teachers had even attended college. Superintendents were often much more concerned with morality than education when hiring teachers. Even though urban schools were becoming more and more bureaucratic, the public still expected teachers to be Christian and of "high toned and refined" character. In a typical contract, a teacher was asked to keep the following promises in regard to conduct: "I promise to abstain from all dancing, immodest dressing, and any other conduct unbecoming a teacher and a lady. I promise not to go out with any young men except to do Sunday-school work." In one North Carolina district a man who had difficulty establishing his moral credentials because of notorious bad habits finally found employment when a friend gave him a "certificate of good moral character during school hours."

Sources:
Arthur T. Hadley, *The Education of the American Citizen* (Freeport, N.Y.: Books for Libraries Press, 1901), p. 53;

Edgar W. Knight, *Education in the United States* (New York: Greenwood Press, 1951), pp. 334–358;

William J. Reese, *The Origins of the American High School* (New Haven: Yale University Press, 1995), pp. 122–127.

HEADLINE MAKERS

FELIX ADLER

1851-1933

FOUNDER OF THE ETHICAL CULTURE SCHOOL

A Tradition of Philanthropy. Felix Adler, the son of a rabbi at Manhattan's Temple Emanu-El, grew up accompanying his mother as she visited and helped impoverished New York families. As a young professor of religious history and literature at Cornell University, however, he came to believe that private charity alone could not alleviate the position of the "perishing classes" driven to mob action by starvation and idleness. Adler believed that philanthropy had to "penetrate to the root itself and help the poor to help themselves." The depression of 1873 and the bloody riots that were its urban aftermath convinced Adler that "It is necessary to resort to radical measures, if we wish to help the poor. Education is the only accepted means of doing this, and therefore, all who have given the subject of human misery careful thought unite in the opinion that education—the best and most thorough education—is what we preeminently need."

Free Kindergarten. Adler founded the Ethical Culture Society in 1876, a movement devoted to the belief that man must develop morally and aesthetically as well as logically if he is to be truly educated. In 1878, at age twenty-seven, he and his friend Alfred Wolff distributed handbills through New York's poorest areas announcing the opening of a free kindergarten, the first in the city. Eight children appeared on opening day at the converted dance hall on West Sixty-fourth Street that housed the school. Soon eighty children were enrolled under the tutelage of Miss Fanny Schwedler, the school's original teacher. The kindergarten's staff provided a full-service philanthropic institution—washing, feeding, often clothing the children. Their mothers were also helped. The kindergarten worked closely with the district nursing service and a volunteer "ladies committee" in meeting home problems.

The Workingman's School. In 1880 Adler established the Workingman's School in New York, an institution to model innovative techniques far superior to what he called the "revolting" practices of the day. Adler condemned the "common schools," saying they were organized as a "combination of the cotton mill and railroad with the model State-prison. . . . From one point of view the children are regarded as automatons; from another, as India rubber bags; from a third, as so much raw material. They must move in step, and exactly alike." Adler was determined that this new institution should have meaning and interest at its center. The "ethical ideal of progress" was to pervade every course of study. History, for example, was to be taught as the sweep of civilization's advance in the "direction of democracy, liberty, equality, and fraternity," not the serving up of "dry facts hardly connected among themselves." Science was to be the study of the facts of nature through firsthand contact whenever possible. The reading tastes of the students were to be "watchfully cultivated" and composition "taught as art" with "little pieces complete in meaning" produced regularly in both narrative and descriptive formats. Students were encouraged to observe, to reason independently, and to refer, whenever possible, to original writings as support for their reasoning. The school flourished, and in the 1890s its name was changed to the Ethical Culture School and it was moved to a site on Central Park West, where a special laboratory, food study, and cooking were introduced. On 27 December 1891 a reporter from the *New York Tribune* wrote, "Eureka! I have found it at last! A school where children actually like to go. A school where the shiftless boy with the good memory does not stand higher than the painstaking boy who may possess ten times his mental powers. . . . A school which teaches the eye and the ear and educates the fingers while it is expanding the brain." The opportunities at Adler's school, including classes small enough to encourage individuality, stood in strong contrast to the meager opportunities and huge classes of the city schools in the 1880s.

Effects. In 1888 Adler helped organize a society for the scientific study of children, a group that became the Child Study Association in 1907. Furthermore, Adler's school became a model for other schools. In the 1890s the American education establishment felt the stirring of the "New Education," a movement based on the idea of "correlating studies around a central core," usually history, literature, or nature study. Along with the "cores" came an injunction to relate the subjects of the curriculum, to make them meaningful. Students would be taught in a manner that interested them, because the subject matter's significance would be clear. The Ethical Culture School served as an example of how this theory could be translated into action. Although Col. Francis Parker and John Dewey are perhaps better known as the founding fathers of progressive education in America, Felix Adler's contribution was to illustrate how a school could provide a cooperative social enterprise in connection with an ethical end in education.

Sources:

Felix Adler, *Creed and Deed* (New York: Putnam, 1877), p. 63;

Robert Holmes Beck, *American Progressive Education: 1875–1930* (Ann Arbor, Mich.: University Microfilms, 1965), pp. 16–51.

MOTHER MARY REGIS CASSERLY

1843-1917
FOUNDER OF THE CONGREGATION OF THE SISTERS OF ST. JOSEPH

The Challenge of Faith. Annie Casserly, a native of Ireland, immigrated with her family to America when she was nine. She was enrolled in St. Joseph Female Academy, a school conducted by Sisters of St. Joseph, in Flushing, New York. The motherhouse and novitiate of the order were located near the academy, and Annie Casserly grew up observing the life and work of these sisters, most of whom served as teachers in parochial schools all across New England. Immediately after she graduated, she received the habit of the community and took the religious name Sister Mary Regis. She accepted a position teaching at a newly formed parochial school in the Jamaica Plain section of Boston, where in 1873 the two hundred children who applied for admission represented 15 percent of the local school district enrollment. A significant challenge for teaching sisters in the 1870s and 1880s was that parochial schools had to be "free," since parishioners could rarely afford tuition. Sister Mary Regis agreed that the sisters would use the church basement as a schoolhouse and accept only a small stipend to cover living expenses. Poor and working-class parents expressed their appreciation for the efforts of the sisters by unwavering support and contributions in kind.

Mainstream Opposition. Under the leadership of Mother Mary Regis, the community of sisters rebutted every stereotype about the intellectual capacities and ambitions of the poor and insisted that the professional work of the sisters on their behalf be of high quality and publicly acknowledged. Nineteenth-century Protestants continued to view the development of Catholic schools as a serious threat to social harmony, to developing public schools, and to the rapid assimilation of immigrants flooding Boston and environs. The mere hint that a Catholic school was planned for a community unleashed a storm of controversy. A typical protest in 1884 was that of the Stoughton (Mass.) school committee, who deemed a proposed parochial school as "abhorrent to all true Americans."

Increasing Prestige. Mother Mary Regis fought to incorporate Catholic schools into local communities. From the time of her arrival in Boston, she determined that schools under her direction would resemble local public schools in all essentials. She prohibited the practices reminiscent of European convent schools, and although daily lessons in religion and moral values were offered, the curriculum, textbooks, and school calendars and teaching methods conformed to public school practice. This step deterred charges that children attending parochial schools lagged behind their public school counterparts in academic progress and social integration. At the same time, she favored innovative teaching practices such as field trips and integration of art and music into the academic curriculum. Although there were few formal requirements for public school teaching, by the 1880s the normal school movement had strengthened teacher preparation in New England. Mother Mary Regis demanded that sisters have professional development opportunities as well. In 1885 she opened a female tuition academy in Cambridge in order to advance the training of the sisters as well as the education of young girls. Wealthy patrons' tuition was steered to support central community needs, especially the higher education of the teaching sisters.

Lasting Influence. During her seventeen years as superior general of the community, Mother Mary Regis opened six parochial schools, an academy, a specialized program for the education of the deaf, and numerous programs for professional development for the sisters, including enrollment at Harvard University's Summer School. She did far more than administer a large nonprofit corporation and supervise a network of schools in an era when few women held such posts. She shaped public opinion so significantly that parochial schools, once reviled, became an accepted part of the definition of free education. Her work in the New England area advanced the integration of an outsider, working-class community into mainstream society.

Sources:

Mary Oates, "Organized Volunteerism: The Catholic Sisters in Massachusetts, 1870–1940," *American Quarterly*, 30 (Winter 1978): 652–680;

Maxine Seller, *Women Educators in the United States, 1820–1993* (Westport, Conn.: Greenwood Press, 1994), pp. 95–102.

CHARLES WILLIAM ELIOT

1834-1926
PRESIDENT OF HARVARD UNIVERSITY

Early Interest in Science. A graduate of the Boston Latin School, Eliot entered Harvard University at age fifteen. Unique experiences in Josiah Cooke's laboratory interested Eliot in laboratory techniques in teaching chemistry. He tutored in mathematics at Harvard in 1854 and four years later became the first assistant professor of mathematics and chemistry. Eliot distinguished himself as a teacher by using the laboratory method in his classroom and giving Harvard's first written examinations instead of the traditional oral tests. Denied tenure at Harvard, he taught chemistry at the Massachusetts Institute of Technology, studied education in Europe, and published two widely read articles on "The New Education" in *The Atlantic Monthly* in 1869. Partially because of the public regard he earned from these writings, he was selected that year as the twenty-second president of Harvard University, a position he would hold until 1909.

Tenure at Harvard. During his forty-year tenure at Harvard, he raised entrance requirements, organized Harvard's specialty schools under the collegiate system, and turned the institution into a major university. His reforms strengthened the schools of law and medicine, and the theological program was broadened from training for the Unitarian ministry to one that served many denominations. Eliot opposed coeducation but agreed in the late 1870s to a "Harvard Annex," a system of professors who offered instruction to selected women who were not allowed to earn degrees. In 1894 Harvard chartered Radcliffe College as a degree-granting institution. This model of the coordinate women's college offering an "equivalent" degree was widely adopted: Barnard College of Columbia University and Sophie Newcomb College of Tulane University are two notable affiliate schools.

The Elective System. Eliot's primary influence on education was his establishment of the elective system at Harvard, a reform followed throughout American higher education. Defining what liberal arts education should be became a problematic issue for educators in the last thirty years of the nineteenth century. Eliot's curricular reforms were radical: in the year 1884–1885 the freshmen of Harvard College took seven out of sixteen classes as required courses, but for the remainder of their college career, with the exception of a few exercises in English

composition, they took elective courses. Under Eliot's leadership Harvard provided a groundbreaking curricular model for twentieth-century education by allowing students to choose from a widening range of subjects that became part of a greatly enlarged liberal arts study.

Other Influences. Eliot's forty annual reports as Harvard president were landmark documents in the history of American higher education. The fifty-volume "five-foot bookshelf" of Harvard Classics and Junior Classics that he edited gave much of the American public an opportunity for self-education. As the chairman of the National Education Association's Committee of Ten, he wrote the committee report in 1892 that set the curricular pattern for the American high school. As a result of that report, the study of foreign languages and mathematics was introduced in the seventh grade, a curricular change that led to the subsequent development of the junior high school. Eliot was awarded the first gold medal of the American Academy of Arts and Sciences in 1915 and the Roosevelt Medal for distinguished service in 1924.

Source:
Edward Howe Cotton, *The Life of Charles W. Eliot* (Boston: Small, Maynard, 1926).

GRANVILLE STANLEY HALL

1844-1924
PRESIDENT OF CLARK UNIVERSITY

Science and Education. Granville Stanley Hall was graduated from Williams College in Williamstown, Massachusetts, and received a Ph.D. from Harvard University in 1878. He studied theology and philosophy in Germany and reported the Franco-Prussian War for American newspapers from 1868 to 1871. After teaching at Antioch College in Ohio and at Harvard, he returned to Germany to study physics, physiology, and experimental psychology. In 1882 he was granted $1,000 to establish a psychological laboratory at Johns Hopkins University, where he pursued his research in experimental psychology and trained men who would become eminent scholars, including James Cattell and John Dewey. Hall's research into the psychology of learning contributed significantly to the growing debate over the differences between schooling and education. His research, which focused carefully on childhood and adolescent psychology and the accumulation of life data, helped put the study of education on a firm scientific basis.

Educator and Philosopher. Hall's reputation as an educational philosopher grew during the 1880s. In

1889 he became president and professor of psychology at Clark University in Worcester, Massachusetts, positions he maintained until his retirement in 1920. Hall became an inspiring speaker and writer as well as a respected psychological researcher, and he was instrumental in making Americans familiar with the pathbreaking psychological work of Sigmund Freud. One of his contemporaries hailed him as one of the few "great personalities" of the day. Hall's influence was not only on "American education, but also for American life," an admirer claimed, citing as evidence Hall's claim that "The best of all uses of public benefactions is not for charity to the poor . . . beneficent as these are, but rather for affording the very best opportunities for the highest possible training of the very best minds in universities, because in training these the whole work of church, state, school, and charity is raised to a higher level, and in this service all other causes are best advanced."

Source:

Charles Franklin Thwing, *A History of Education in the United States Since the Civil War* (Boston: Houghton Mifflin, 1910), pp. 66, 180, 325.

WILLIAM TORREY HARRIS

1835-1909

U.S. COMMISSIONER OF EDUCATION

Advocate of Universal Education. The educator William Torrey Harris was graduated from Yale in 1855 and began teaching in Saint Louis in 1857. As a teacher, principal, superintendent, and eventually U.S. commissioner of education, Harris recognized that all children must be educated. "Education must relate first to citizenship," he wrote in 1898. He claimed that especially in the industrial age, citizens had to "maintain mobility, for with the great inventions of our age, we find ourselves all living in a borderland." Education, he argued, was the only way to "give people the power to climb up to better paid and more useful industries out of lives of drudgery." Despite his advocacy of lifelong education, he counted the school as only one of several important educational institutions, the others being the church and family.

Economy in Education. Harris was the reformer of the schools in Saint Louis, establishing the first free public kindergarten under the direction of Susan Blow, as well as advocating serious public health initiatives such as school-based vaccinations and a board of health closely allied with the board of education. However, he was keenly aware of economy in government. He advocated forty to sixty children in a classroom and employed women exclusively as educators in the

elementary grades. He acknowledged that women not only used milder forms of discipline but also worked for lower wages.

Harris's Influence. Harris's success in establishing excellent schools in Saint Louis, from the innovative public kindergarten through a much visited high school, served as a model for other educators. During his tenure as the U.S. commissioner of education (1889–1906) he participated in the National Education Association's Committee of Ten's Committee of Ten, a group appointed to determine the ideal national secondary school curriculum. Although Harris strongly believed that schools should teach material that is applicable to a student's life, he resisted demands for trade and vocational education, espousing instead studies of classics and a rigorous academic preparation for college. He also raised standards of teacher preparation and oversaw the standardization of the academic calendar for most public schools at seven months in 1889.

Source:

I. L. Kandel, ed., *Twenty-Five Years of American Education* (Freeport, N.Y.: Books for Libraries Press, 1966), p. 64.

COL. FRANCIS WAYLAND PARKER

1837-1902

FATHER OF AMERICAN EDUCATIONAL REFORM

From the War to the Schools. Francis Wayland Parker, who had risen to the rank of colonel in the Union army during the Civil War, began his influential career in education as a strict conformist to the schooling practices of the postwar era. He knew how to drill and discipline, and as principal of North Grammar School in Manchester, New Hampshire, he "had everything in good shape." As he relates in his autobiography, "I had battalion drill and marching, and everything went like clockwork. I ranked my scholars, changing their places from week to week." However, when he organized a normal school (a secondary school that provided for teacher training) in Dayton, Ohio, he ran into a wall of opposition from the teachers already in service. When an aunt died and left him $5,000, he left to study in Germany, determined to educate himself better in modern teaching methods. There he studied Friedrich Wilhelm August Froebel and Johann Friedrich Herbart, two pedagogical reformers whose ideas were sweeping Europe, and he returned to the United States a man convinced that "there was a great deal better way of teaching than anything I had done. Of course I had a great deal of enthusiasm and a great desire to work out the plan and see what I could do."

The "Quincy Experiment." When he returned to the United States in 1875 as superintendent of the Quincy, Massachusetts, schools, he instituted reforms that would become a model for twentieth-century educational practices. The prevailing paradigm for schooling was imitation and memory, each child drilling on identical materials so as to reach a norm in his absorption of the facts or to be punished with dunce cap or rod. Parker rejected these notions and in his five-year tenure at Quincy experimented with allowing children to learn "much as they learned to skate." The methods of instruction were "rational": he banned drill-rote methods of instruction, introduced the "phonetic" method of teaching reading, and "changed arithmetic, geography, and history not a little." Copybooks, along with traditional rewards and punishments, were altogether discarded. By 1880 these modest reforms, which have come to be called the "Quincy Experiment," had attracted some thirty thousand visitors to Quincy. Parker, one of America's best-known educators of the day, briefly supervised the Boston schools and then left to become the head of the Cook County Normal School (soon to become the Chicago Normal School) in Engelwood, Illinois.

The Artist Teacher. The staff that Colonel Parker assembled in Illinois was a living illustration of his ideal of the "artist teacher," a person skilled and trained in the science of education — a "genuine leader of little feet." The teachers whom Parker aggressively recruited were among the best in the nation, including Professor H. H. Straight, a student of the great Harvard naturalist Louis Agassiz; the mathematician William Speer; Dr. William Jackman, later dean of Chicago University's School of Education; and the artist Josephine Look. Parker was willing to pay whatever was necessary to get outstanding staff. When he offered Jackman a $3,000 salary, $1,200 more than the school board had allotted, the board demanded to know where the additional funds would be found. Parker responded, "Getting the money is your job. You sent me to get the best man capable of training teachers to teach science. I expect you to be grateful to me that I persuaded Dr. Jackman to come." This approach made him many enemies on the board, and from 1890 to 1898 both the financial and philosophical struggles were incessant, but Parker prevailed.

Lasting Influences. Parker built the Normal School into an institution that attracted international attention. G. Stanley Hall, the psychologist, claimed that he had to "come here every year to set my educational watch." The school developed a museum and a library, began manual training in 1883, and, most important, modeled a curriculum that would influence American educators for the next century. Parker suggested in an essay on the Chicago Normal School that "there are but two all-embracing subjects of study, nature and man." The studies of nature constituted the "central subjects" of his program: geography, geology, mineralogy, botany,

zoology, anthropology, and ethnology. However the curriculum was not divided up among these sciences in the traditional course of study; rather they were considered to be artificial distinctions that an adult made of a child's spontaneous study. Teachers needed to begin with the interests of the child, using these interests in the environment to instruct in all of the sciences. Parker believed that the techniques of written English — grammar, spelling, and punctuation — should be gained largely through the presentation of daily opportunities for writing correlated with other subject matter and much creative work.

Parker's Legacy. In 1897 John Dewey visited the Chicago Normal School, bringing the manuscript of "My Pedagogic Creed" to read to the faculty. Parker said of the essay, "This is what I have been struggling all my life to put into action." After Parker's death in 1902, Dewey, his friend and admirer, suggested that Parker had touched many with a "truer perception of the ideals and calling of the teacher." Although Parker died before the progressive school movement had national prominence, at least twelve of the outstanding progressive schools in the United States were founded by members of his faculty or the graduates of schools directly guided by his educational principles.

Source:

Francis Parker, "An Account of the Work of the Cook County and Chicago Normal School from 1883–1899," *Elementary School Teacher and Course of Study*, 2 (June 1902): 767.

ELLEN SWALLOW RICHARDS

1842-1911
FOUNDER OF THE HOME ECONOMICS MOVEMENT

Scientific Inquiry. Ellen Swallow was born in 1842 in Dunstable, Massachusetts, the daughter of two schoolteachers. Not until 1868, at age twenty-five, did Swallow go off to Vassar, one of the few options for women wishing to attend college in the East. Vassar was becoming an important center for women's education in the sciences during this time, and when Swallow was graduated in 1870, she was determined to continue her pursuit of scientific inquiry. Although there were no careers available to women in the sciences in the late nineteenth century, she was admitted as a special student and the first woman in the new Massachusetts Institute of Technology (MIT), then only five years old. She received a bachelor of science degree from MIT and then did graduate study there in chemistry for an additional two years. She married a young member of the MIT faculty, metallurgical engineer Robert Hallowell Richards, and they worked together experimenting with various ways to transform metal compounds. Her work was rewarded by her election to the American Institute of Mining and Metallurgical Engineers as its first woman member.

Scientific Education for Women. By the 1880s Ellen Richards became increasingly interested in the education of women in science and scientific issues. She organized a science section of the Society to Encourage Studies at Home, and she arranged to establish a Woman's Laboratory at MIT. When MIT established a chemical laboratory to study problems in sanitation in 1885, Richards was named as assistant there, primarily because she had published a manual on the chemistry of cooking and cleaning in 1882. She was soon named a faculty member at MIT, where she worked on a wide range of projects in sanitation engineering and taught courses in analysis of environmental problems to a generation of students who went on to careers in public sanitation.

The Home Economics Movement. Ellen Richards's principal contribution to American life was her introduction of the home economics movement. She was greatly concerned about the squalid conditions in the nation's urban slums, and she reasoned that the principles of sanitation and other household arts should be taught in the public schools. She helped establish a series of classes in housekeeping at the Women's Educational and Industrial Union in Boston, and in 1893 she ran a kitchen as an exhibit in the Chicago World's Fair featuring detailed information about the nutritional values of different foods. In 1899 she helped organize a series of annual summer conferences in Lake Placid, New York, aimed at improving home life in modern society. It was at these meetings that the term "home economics" was coined and the essential ideas of the home economics movement were developed. After the turn of the century Richards became president of the newly formed American Home Economics Association and then published a widely used textbook on home economics and sanitary science. In her opinion, everyone needed to become something of a sanitation engineer if society were to contend successfully with the mounting problems of waste and unhealthful living. Her work gave impetus to the home economics movement that was soon instituted in high schools across the country.

Source:
Maxine Seller, *Women Educators in the United States: 1820–1993* (Westport, Conn.: Greenwood Press, 1994), pp. 413–419.

PUBLICATIONS

Felix Adler, *Child Labor and Education* (Philadelphia: Burns Weston, 1899)—an exposé of the effects of child labor on education;

Adler, *Creed and Deed: A Series of Educational Discourses* (New York: Putnam, 1877)—philosophical treatises on the form of the "new ideal" of education, Spinoza, Judaism, and Christianity;

Association of Collegiate Alumnae, *A Preliminary Statistical Study of Certain Women College Graduates: Dealing with the Health, Marriage, Children, Occupations of Women Graduating Between 1869 and 1898 and Their Sisters and Brothers* (Bryn Mawr, Pa.: Bryn Mawr College, 1900)—a research study refuting the contention that higher education adversely affected the health of women;

D. P. Baldwin, "The Defense of Free High Schools," *Indiana School Journal*, 24 (July 1879): 294—an argument for establishing taxpayer-funded secondary schools;

John Dewey, *The School and Society* (Chicago: University of Chicago Press, 1899)—Dewey's seminal work on the schools and social progress, the life of the child, and the psychology of elementary education;

Eliza Duffey, *No Sex in Education; Or, An Equal Chance for Both Girls and Boys* (Philadelphia: Stoddart, 1879)—contains the views of various thinkers upon the matters treated in Edward Clarke's work *Sex in Education* (1877);

Charles William Eliot, *Educational Reform: Essays and Addresses* (Boston: Small, Maynard, 1898)—opinions from Harvard's president on higher education reform;

Granville Stanley Hall, *The Contents of Children's Minds* (New York: Kellogg, 1893)—a study of the psychological underpinnings of early learning;

Hall, *Hints Toward a Select and Descriptive Bibliography of Education* (Boston: Heath, 1886)—a compilation of influential writings in the field;

William Torrey Harris, *Introduction to the Study of Philosophy* (New York: Harper, 1889)—an introduction geared toward teachers;

Harris, *Psychologic Foundations of Education* (Boston: Heath, 1898)—an analysis of how psychology and learning are interrelated;

Henry Kiddle and Alexander Schem, eds., *The Cyclopedia of Education: A Dictionary of Information for the Use of Teachers, School Officers, Parents, and Others* (New York: E. Steiger, 1877)—dictionary of education terms;

George H. Martin, *The Evolution of the Massachusetts Public School System* (New York: D. Appleton, 1894)—a history of one of America's first education systems;

National Herbart Society (later the National Society for the Study of Education), *Yearbooks*, 1887–1896—a collection of articles on Herbartian theories of education;

Frank Parsons, *Our Country's Need* (Boston: Arena, 1894)—an argument for more widespread secondary education;

John D. Philbrick, *City School Systems in the United States* (Washington, D.C.: U.S. Bureau of Education, 1885)—statistical abstracts of city schools;

Ellen Swallow Richards, *The Chemistry of Cooking and Cleaning* (Boston: Whicomb & Barrows, 1886)—a scientific analysis of home economy;

Richards, *Domestic Economy as a Factor in Public Education* (New York: New York College, 1889)—an argument for the teaching of the science of home economy;

Jacob Riis, *How the Other Half Lives* (New York: Harper, 1890)—a sociological study of the tenements of New York.

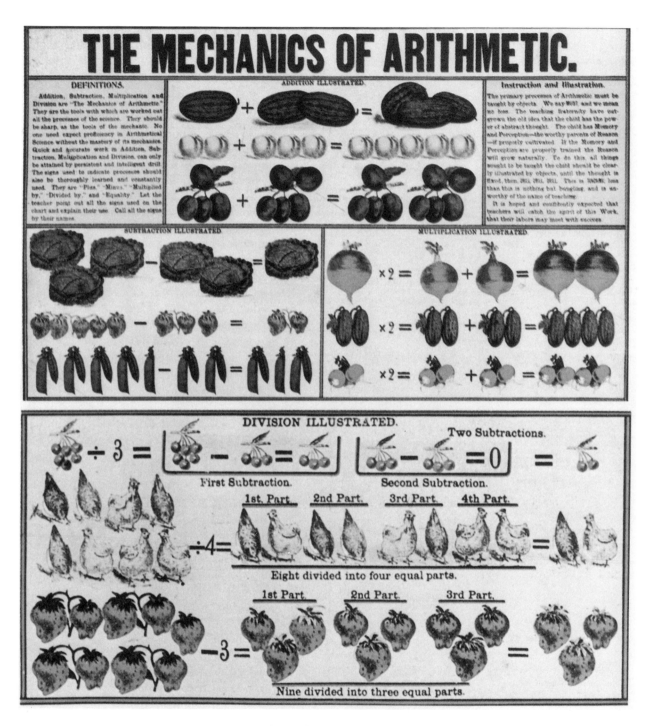

An elementary-school arithmetic poster published in 1894

GOVERNMENT AND POLITICS

by RODNEY P. CARLISLE AND JANE GERHARD

CONTENTS

Sidebars and tables are listed in italics.

1878

10 Jan. Sen. Aaron A. Sargent (R–Cal.) introduces a woman suffrage amendment in the Senate, where it is defeated by a vote of 16–34.

22 Feb. The Greenback Labor Party meets in Toledo and nominates candidates for the November elections, in which the party wins more than one million votes.

11 July President Rutherford B. Hayes asks for the resignation of fellow Republican (and future president) Chester A. Arthur, collector of the Port of New York, because of his corrupt practice of distributing federal jobs to loyal Republican Party members.

5 Nov. Democrats gain control of both houses of Congress for the first time since 1858. In the Forty-sixth Congress the House of Representatives has 149 Democrats, 130 Republicans, and 14 Greenback Laborites; the Senate has 42 Democrats, 33 Republicans, and one Greenback Laborite.

1879

• In the "Kansas Exodus" tens of thousands of African Americans, led by Benjamin "Pap" Singleton, migrate from the South to Kansas to escape the growing number of legal restrictions placed by southern state governments on former slaves.

15 Feb. Congress gives women the right to practice law before the Supreme Court.

1880

2–8 June At the Republican National Convention fights between the Stalwart faction, which supports the party-patronage system, and the Half Breeds, who favor reform, result in a compromise ticket of James A. Garfield, a Half Breed, for president and Chester A. Arthur, a Stalwart, for vice president.

22–24 June At their national convention the Democrats nominate Winfield Scott Hancock to run for president and William H. English for vice president.

2 Nov. Garfield defeats Hancock in a close presidential election, winning by an electoral vote of 214–155 and a popular vote of 4,446,158 (48.27 percent) to 4,444,260 (48.25 percent). The Greenback Labor candidate, James B. Weaver, gets 305,997 votes. Democrats lose their majority in the House, where Republicans outnumber them by 147–135 (plus 11 from minor parties), and the two major parties are tied in the Senate, 37–37 (plus 1 from a minor party).

17 Nov. The United States and China sign a treaty that allows the United States to "regulate, limit, and suspend" Chinese immigration, but not to ban it outright.

1881

• The federal government has doubled in size from fifty thousand employees in 1871 to one hundred thousand in 1881.

2 July President Garfield is shot by disappointed officeseeker Charles J. Guiteau, who claims he was attempting to ensure that Vice President Arthur, a Stalwart who favors the spoils system, would become president.

1882

19 Sept. President James Garfield dies of complications from the wounds he sustained in July and is succeeded by Vice President Arthur, who surprises his supporters by allying himself with proponents of a merit system for civil-service appointments.

6 May Congress passes the Chinese Exclusion Act, suspending Chinese immigration to the United States for ten years.

3 Aug. Congress passes a law that imposes a head tax of fifty cents on each new immigrant and excludes people who are insane, mentally retarded, or likely to become public charges.

7 Nov. In congressional elections Democrats regain a majority in the House of Representatives, outnumbering Republicans by 197–118 (plus 10 from minor parties), while Republicans win a 38–36 majority in the Senate (plus 2 from minor parties).

1883

16 Jan. Congress passes the Pendleton Civil Service Reform Act, an attempt to depoliticize appointments of federal employees engaged in governmental operations. Signed into law by President Arthur, the act establishes a Civil Service Commission and specifies rules for a merit system based on competitive examinations.

3 Mar. Congress authorizes the building of three steel cruisers as part of the movement to establish a modern navy.

1884

3–6 June At the Republican National Convention James G. Blaine is nominated for the presidency with Gen. John A. Logan as his running mate.

8–11 July At their convention Democrats nominate Grover Cleveland and Thomas A. Hendricks to head their national ticket.

6 Oct. As part of the movement to reform the U.S. Navy, the Naval War College is established at Newport, Rhode Island.

4 Nov. Cleveland is elected president in an extremely close election, defeating Blaine by a popular vote of 4,874,621 (48.5 percent) to 4,848,936 (48.25 percent) and an electoral vote of 219–182. Protest movements represented by the Greenback Labor Party and the Prohibition Party win more than 300,000 votes (3.21 percent). The Democrats keep their majority in the House (183–140 plus 2 from minor parties), and the Republicans control the Senate (38–36 plus 2 from minor parties).

1885

25 Feb. Congress prohibits the fencing of public land in the West, and on 7 August President Cleveland backs the act by ordering the removal of all illegal enclosures.

3 Mar. The U.S. Post Office begins special-delivery service.

1886

19 Jan.   Congress passes a Presidential Succession Act. If both the president and vice president are unable to serve, they are succeeded by members of the cabinet in the order that their departments were created.

3 May   At the McCormick Harvester plant outside Chicago police fire into a crowd of striking workers, killing one and wounding others.

4 May   At a protest rally in Haymarket Square, Chicago, one policeman is killed and seventy-six others are wounded (six fatally) by a bomb allegedly thrown by anarchist strikers. As a result, eight radical labor leaders are arrested; seven are sentenced to death; and four are eventually hanged.

25 Oct.   In *Wabash, St. Louis & Pacific Railway* v. *Illinois* the Supreme Court rules that only the federal government, not the individual states, may regulate interstate railway rates.

2 Nov.   In the congressional elections Republicans lose four seats in the Senate but hold their majority over the Democrats by 39–37. In the House, Democrats lose ground but keep a majority of 169–152 (plus 4 from minor parties).

1887

•   Henry Bowers forms the American Protective Association, an anti-Catholic, nativist organization centered in the Midwest.

•   American settlers in Hawaii force King Kalakaua to establish a constitutional government.

20 Jan.   The Senate approves a treaty giving the United States the exclusive right to establish a naval base at Pearl Harbor in Hawaii.

4 Feb.   Congress passes the Interstate Commerce Act establishing the Interstate Commerce Commission, the first national regulatory commission, in an attempt to curb price fixing and other abuses by interstate railroads.

8 Feb.   Congress passes the Dawes Act, which provides for the division of tribal lands among individual Native Americans and the sale of "surplus" land to non-Indians.

1888

5 June   The Democrats nominate President Cleveland to run for a second term, with Allen G. Thurman as his running mate.

13 June   Congress creates a Department of Labor, without cabinet-level status.

25 June   The Republicans nominate Benjamin Harrison and Levi P. Morton to head their national ticket.

6 Nov.   Harrison narrowly defeats President Cleveland, by an electoral vote of 233–168. Although Harrison wins the election in the Electoral College, Cleveland receives more popular votes, 5,534,488 (48.62 percent), than Harrison, who garners 5,443,892 (47.82 percent). Minor-party candidates from the Union Labor and the Prohibition parties win nearly 400,000 votes, preventing either major party from gaining a clear majority. In Congress Republicans gain control of the House of Representatives by 166–159 and maintain their 39–37 majority in the Senate.

1889

11 Feb.	Congress raises the Department of Agriculture to cabinet status.I
2 Nov.	North Dakota and South Dakota become states, followed by Montana on the eighth and Washington on 11 November.

1890

14 Apr.	At a conference that began in Washington, D.C., on 2 October 1889, Western Hemisphere nations form the Pan-American Union.
27 June	Congress passes the Dependent Pension Act granting a pension to any Union army veteran of the Civil War who had served ninety days and was unable to support himself by manual labor, causing pension roles to swell from 490,000 in 1889 to 966,000 in 1893 and the cost of pensions to increase from $89 million to $175 million during the same period.
2 July	Congress passes the Sherman Anti-Trust Act, which authorizes the federal government to initiate court proceedings to dissolve trusts or contracts in restraint of trade, in an attempt to limit or prevent business monopolies.
3 July	Idaho becomes a state, followed by Wyoming on 10 July.
1 Oct.	The Republican majority in Congress passes the McKinley Tariff, raising duties on imported goods and turning the popular vote in the 1890 elections for the House of Representatives to the Democrats.
4 Nov.	Republicans gain eight seats in the Senate for a 47–39 majority (plus 12 from minor parties), but they drop seventy-eight seats in the House, giving the Democrats a hefty 235–88 majority (plus 9 from ninor parties).

1891

•	After succeeding her brother to the Hawaiian throne Queen Liliuokalani issues an edict revoking the constitution of 1887 and assuming autocratic powers, thus taking power away from the pro-American annexation faction, which has dominated Hawaiian politics since the establishment of a constitutional government in 1887. American settlers form a revolutionary committee.
4 Mar.	Congress passes the International Copyright Act, granting British, French, Belgian, and Swiss writers copyright protection in the United States.
19 May	The national Populist Party is founded in Cincinnati.

1892

7–11 June	At their national convention Republicans nominate President Benjamin Harrison for reelection with Whitelaw Reid as his running mate.
21–23 June	The Democrats nominate former president Grover Cleveland to run for a second term with Adlai Ewing Stevenson as his running mate.
4 July	The Populist Party nominates James B. Weaver for president and James G. Field for vice president. They run on a reform platform that calls for increased silver coinage, a federal income tax, and national ownership of railroads.

8 Nov.   Former president Grover Cleveland defeats incumbent Benjamin Harrison by more than 370,000 votes, becoming the only president to serve two nonconsecutive terms. Cleveland wins 46.05 percent of the popular vote to 42.96 percent for Harrison and wins in the electoral by a margin of 277–145. Weaver, the Populist candidate, wins 8.5 percent of the popular vote and 22 votes in the Electoral College. The Democrats win a majority in the Senate (44–38 and 3 from minor parties) and maintain control of the House (218–127 and 11 from minor parties).

1893

17 Jan.   Queen Liliuokalani of Hawaii abdicates the day after U.S. Marines land to back a rebellion led by proannexation American settlers.

1 Feb.   Hawaii is proclaimed a U.S. protectorate with Sanford B. Dole as president of the provisional government.

1894

•   The Immigration Restriction League is founded, expressing Americans' fears that their culture and way of life are threatened by the high numbers of immigrants entering the United States.

1 May   Jacob S. Coxey and two lieutenants are arrested in Washington, D.C., for trespassing on the Capitol lawn. The arrest breaks up Coxey's "bonus" army of some four hundred veterans, who have marched across the country to bring attention to the plight of unemployed veterans.

11 May   A violent strike begins at the Pullman railroad plant outside Chicago.

26 June   Supporting the Pullman strikers, the American Railway Union strikes against most railroads. President Cleveland sends in federal troops to break up the strike, which is led by Eugene V. Debs, who is arrested and imprisoned for violating a court injunction prohibiting workers from interfering with the delivery of the mail. The strike finally ends on 3 August.

4 July   The Republic of Hawaii is proclaimed, and the government is recognized as a foreign power by President Cleveland on 7 August.

27 Aug.   Congress passes the Wilson-Gorman Tariff Act, which lowers the tariff rate; many see it as a victory for Democratic reductionism and a blow against Republican protectionism. Attached to the act is a graduated income tax, which the Supreme Court declares unconstitutional in 1895.

6 Nov.   In congressional elections Republicans regain control in the Senate (43–39 and 6 from minor parties) and the House (244–105 and 7 from minor parties).

12 June   President Cleveland calls on Americans to avoid giving aid to Cuban rebels who have risen up against the colonial government of Spain.

1895

1896

16–18 June	At their national convention the Republicans nominate William McKinley and Garret A. Hobart to head their national ticket.
7–11 July	At the Democratic National Convention, after delivering his "Cross of Gold" speech advocating the free coinage of silver, William Jennings Bryan wins the nomination of his party for the presidency. Arthur Sewall is nominated for vice president.
22 July	The Populists nominate Bryan for president with Thomas E. Watson of Georgia as his running mate.
3 Nov.	McKinley is elected president, defeating Bryan by a popular vote of 7,108,480 (51.01 percent) to 6,511,495 (46.73 percent) and an electoral vote of 271–176. Republicans maintain their control of the House (204–113 and 40 from minor parties) and Senate (47–34 and 7 from minor parties).

1897

7 July	Congress passes the Dingley Tariff Act, raising import duties to a new high averaging 57 percent.

1898

15 Feb.	The U.S. battleship *Maine* explodes in the harbor at Havana, Cuba.
20 Apr.	Congress adopts a joint resolution recognizing Cuban independence and authorizing the president to use military force if it is necessary to force Spain to withdraw from Cuba.
24 Apr.	Spain declares war on the United States.
25 Apr.	Congress passes an official declaration of war on Spain, effective 21 April.
1 May	In the Battle of Manila Bay Adm. George Dewey defeats the Spanish Pacific fleet without losing a man.
1 July	American forces in Cuba defeat the Spanish at El Caney and San Juan Hill.
3 July	Adm. William T. Sampson defeats Spanish fleet off Santiago, Cuba.
7 July	Recognizing the strategic military value of its naval base at Pearl Harbor, Congress approves the annexation of Hawaii by joint resolution.
17 July	Spanish troops in Cuba surrender to the United States.
13 Aug.	American troops take Manila, completing the invasion of the Philippines.
8 Nov.	In congressional elections Republicans maintain control of the House (185–163 and 9 from minor parties) and the Senate (53–26 and 8 from minor parties).
10 Dec.	A treaty ending the Spanish-American War is signed in Paris.

1899

- The expansion of the federal government makes it one of the leading U.S. employers, reaching close to 250,000 by 1899.

- Secretary of State John Hay convinces Great Britain, France, Russia, Germany, Italy, and Japan to agree reluctantly to an "Open Door" policy in regard to trade with China rather than erecting prohibitive trade barriers to other nations.

9 Jan.   Congress ratifies the treaty with Spain, which is signed by President McKinley on 10 February. The United States acquires Puerto Rico and Guam, and Spain grants independence to Cuba. The United States buys Spanish holdings in the Philippines, gaining virtual control over the islands.

OVERVIEW

Ushering in the Gilded Age. In 1876, as the United States celebrated the centennial of its independence, one of the most disputed and corrupt presidential elections in American history spelled the end of the Reconstruction era and the beginning of a new period of American history. After the Civil War, Congress stationed federal troops in the states of the former Confederacy with the intention of ensuring the rights of African Americans. In reality these troops did little for most former slaves. Instead they served mainly to keep power in the hands of Republicans loyal to the federal government and away from Democrats who had supported the Confederacy. By 1876 federal troops remained in only three southern states—Florida, South Carolina, and Louisiana—representing the vestiges of federal Reconstruction policies.

The Hayes-Tilden Controversy. In the 1876 presidential election Republican Rutherford B. Hayes won 4,034,311 votes (47.95 percent) while his Democratic opponent, Samuel J. Tilden, earned 4,288,546 (50.97 percent). Under the Constitution, however, the president is selected by presidential electors from each state, not by popular votes. In Florida, South Carolina, and Louisiana enough of the electoral votes were in dispute to keep the election undecided. After much political maneuvering, these three states, and Oregon—with a total of twenty-two votes—each sent two sets of returns and left the decision of which votes to count up to Congress, where the Democrats controlled the House of Representatives and the Republicans controlled the Senate.

The Compromise of 1877. The dispute was resolved by the so-called Compromise of 1877, by which a joint committee of Congress turned the problem over to a special electoral commission made up of five senators, five congressmen, and five Supreme Court justices. The group was carefully selected to include seven Republicans, seven Democrats, and one independent, David Davis, who was one of the Supreme Court justices. At the last minute, however, Davis could not serve on the commission and he was replaced by a Republican. When the commission announced its decisions, the voting fell along party lines: eight in favor of seating all the Republican electors, and seven in favor of seating all the Democratic electors. Democrats in the House of Representa-

tives made it clear that they would accept the recommendations of the commission only if they received certain concessions, the chief one being that if they agreed not to block Hayes's election, he would remove the last federal troops from the southern states. The withdrawal of the last federal troops in April 1878 marked the end of Reconstruction and the beginning of what has become known as the Gilded Age, an era in which political corruption, the spoils system, and back-room deals contributed to a weak federal government largely incapable of meeting the needs of a complex, industrialized society.

Redefining Government. Most Americans in the late nineteenth century believed that the federal government should limit its activities to delivering the mail, collecting tariffs, providing patronage, guarding the coasts, fighting Indians, and preserving civic order. Yet the rapid growth of large, national corporations raised a host of new concerns about the role of government in overseeing business and industry. Factory workers called for a shorter workday, safety standards for the work-place, and regulations to protect working women and children. Farmers asked for laws to prevent them from being exploited by the railroads that carried their crops to market and by bankers who lent them money. Politicians and businessmen asked if the government should protect average citizens by regulating businesses or if it should allow big business to shape the national economy. In general the vision of what the federal government might do for its citizens was limited by the tradition of laissez-faire, allowing events to follow their own course without government interference—until the end of the period when an economic crisis forced the federal government to take action.

Congressional Power. The U.S. government in the late nineteenth century was smaller and weaker than the federal government in the twentieth century. Congress overshadowed the presidency in authority and power. With its growing number of specialized committees Congress was the place where politicians hammered out federal policy amid a riot of local, state, and special interests. At the same time Democrats and Republicans were beginning to debate and rework the distinction between local and national.

The Courts. With a relatively weak executive branch, the court system often had a disproportionately large role in setting policy. For example, during the 1870s states attempted to regulate railroad rates, but in 1886 the Supreme Court declared these state laws unconstitutional, ruling that the railways were a form of interstate commerce and, as such, fell under federal jurisdiction. The courts also refused to strike down the "Jim Crow" laws that southern states passed to legalize segregation, failing to protect the civil rights of African Americans and ultimately adopting a "separate but equal" doctrine that allowed segregation to continue well into the twentieth century.

Political Parties. Between 1878 and 1900 the Republican and Democratic parties also helped to fill the vacuum created by a weak executive branch. Republicans saw themselves as the party of Abraham Lincoln, representing hardworking, churchgoing, liberty-loving Americans and committed to the gold standard and high tariffs, while Democrats wanted lower tariffs and a gold- and silver-backed currency. Party affiliations were more the product of ethnic, racial, religious, and regional identity than a result of ideological differences. As the 1880s progressed Republicans spent less and less time "waving the bloody shirt," realizing that continuing to blame the South for the Civil War would not win them votes. The Democratic Party was an amalgamation of diverse groups. Immigrants and newcomers often found their first allies in the urban Democratic boss and his "machine," whose operatives gave jobs and aid in exchange for votes. Southern, or "Bourbon," Democrats remained hostile to Reconstruction policies and to government intervention.

The Monetary System. A chaotic monetary and banking system presented ongoing problems. The supply of money in the United States did not grow as fast as the national economy, causing deflation: that is, prices of goods fell, and the value, or buying power, of the dollar increased. As deflation continued unchecked, wealthy people got richer, while working people got poorer. Debtors, farmers, and working people fought for some system that would increase the money supply and relieve pressures on them. Many argued for the abandonment of the single gold standard as the backing for all currency in favor of a silver and gold standard. Positions on silver versus gold shaped the politics of the period, especially in the 1890s.

Tariffs. The primary means of raising funds for the federal government was levying tariffs on foreign goods. Tariffs, or taxes on imports, were also a way for the federal government to protect domestic products from foreign competition. By scheduling high tariffs on particular categories of imported manufactured goods and agricultural products, the government could shelter American manufacturers and farmers. For example, tariffs on textiles allowed eastern manufacturers to keep the prices of their goods artificially high instead of making them competitive on the world market. If the tax was extremely high, it prevented or severely limited the sales of imported items on the American market and discouraged foreign manufacturers from selling in the United States. While such high tariffs protected some American manufacturers, they hurt others and the American consumer. For example, California clothes sellers had to pay high prices for textiles manufactured in New York and Philadelphia because import duties increased the price of cheaper imported cloth from England to such an extent that buying it was prohibitive. Ultimately the consumer had to pay high prices for clothing. Tariffs became controversial as they drove up the prices of many products and decreased the selection of consumer goods on the American market.

The Spoils System. The daily operations of government remained mired in traditional partisan competition for the benefits and resources of office holding. The press and politicians labeled the various practices of the era: the distribution of government positions by the victorious party was called the *spoils system;* tariff protection through bargaining (and later the practice of any sort of vote trading through which politicians secure the passage of legislation in their own interests) became known as *logrolling;* lucrative government contracts or appropriations were called *pork barrel;* cash given to politicians by contractors was labeled *boodle;* and extreme patriotism or chauvinism, typically in support of aggressive overseas expansion, was *jingoism.* They also had frequent cause to use the old term *gerrymandering* to refer to the establishment of new, oddly shaped voting districts to favor the election of a candidate from a specific party.

Reforming Politics. Reformers fought to replace the spoils system by establishing a merit system for civil-service appointments that would rid government bureaucracy of warping partisan influences. They sought to end logrolling as a means of determining import duties by calling for a neutral tariff commission; they proposed competitive bidding to end pork barrel and boodle; and they hoped gerrymandering could be replaced with fair political reapportionment. Every president or political leader who fought for civil-service reforms had the difficult and paradoxical task of convincing the beneficiaries of the status quo to change a process by which they had benefited. Politicians who voted for change turned their backs on the system that had backed them; politicians committed to maintaining the status quo turned their backs on a growing number of voters who supported reform and modernization.

Movements for Change. During the 1880s and 1890s many Americans joined political organizations to express their discontent with politics as usual. Feeling increasingly alienated from the new style of corporate business and national marketing, farmers—who suffered from falling prices throughout the 1880s and were particularly hard hit by the economic depression of 1894—flocked to the populist movement, particularly in the South and the

West. Organized labor gained momentum in the 1880s and 1890s with the rise of the Knights of Labor, the eight-hour workday movement, and various protests by industrial workers over wages and conditions. While Congress and the courts remained skeptical of the labor movement, workers agitated for and sometimes won improvements in working conditions, hours, and wages. By the turn of the century reformers had set out to clean up city, state, and national governments. Progressivism, a broad-based, loosely knit coalition of reformers, hoped to make the government more effective in protecting children, female workers, immigrants, and laborers in general. Populism, organized labor, and progressivism made the 1890s a period of rethinking the social contract between government and the public.

An International Presence. By the last two decades of the nineteenth century many Americans were advocating a greater international role for the United States, specifically in the Pacific in regard to Hawaii and Samoa and in the Caribbean, where the struggle of Cuban rebels against colonial Spanish rule attracted American sympathy. A movement to modernize and professionalize the American military, particularly the navy, resulted in a more powerful navy with a new fleet of steel ships. Naval actions proved decisive in the short Spanish-American War of 1898. The United States annexed Hawaii and extended its influence in the Caribbean and in the Pacific, gaining Puerto Rico and Guam through the treaty with Spain that ended the war. The United States also gained virtual possession of the Philippines and heavy influence over the government of a newly independent Cuba.

Political Rights for Women and Minorities. African Americans and women fought for an increased voice in their political destinies, laying the basis for reforms finally achieved in the twentieth century. African Americans found themselves with few allies in the post-Reconstruction era, as Bourbon Democrats reasserted control over the South and a new generation of eastern and midwestern politicians, less committed to the struggles of the Civil War, took the reins of power. Although the Fifteenth Amendment (1870) gave male African Americans the right to vote, they were systematically denied that right in southern states by a series of state laws instituting measures such as literacy tests and poll taxes as well as by outright harassment and violence. White women's suffrage activism gained strength in these years, as women active in temperance, progressivism, higher education, and city government called for the right to vote as a first step in achieving political equality with men. African American suffragists linked the struggle for women's suffrage with African Americans' civil rights and called for their white sisters and for black communities to support them. The battle for woman suffrage would not end until the ratification of the Nineteenth Amendment in 1920.

Rewriting the Rules. Battles over political rights for African Americans and women, over political reform, tariffs, money policy, and the role of the United States in Asia and Latin America were the chief concerns of the federal government for the last quarter of the nineteenth century, laying the groundwork for measures that decisively shaped American government and politics in the twentieth century.

TOPICS IN THE NEWS

AMERICAN GOVERNMENT IN THE GILDED AGE

The Presidency. Presidents in the post–Civil War era were less powerful than presidents of the twentieth century. Until the presidency of Theodore Roosevelt in 1901–1909, the president was more involved in party politics and patronage than in making and enforcing public policy. He also had little influence over appropriations and expenditures. Governmental bureaus and departments were much more attuned to Congress—specifically to the powerful House Appropriations Committee—than to the White House. The chief responsibility of the president in these years was patronage, or the filling of federal positions. Patronage took enormous amounts of time, and the president had little staff to help him make appointments to as many as one hundred thousand positions. President James A. Garfield, a Republican, complained in 1881 that "All these years I have been dealing with ideas, . . . and here I am considering all day whether A or B should be appointed to this or that office." Democrat Grover Cleveland, who served as president in 1885–1889 and 1893–1897, attempted to strengthen the presidency, believing that the most important goal he could achieve was to assert the "entire independence" of the executive from the legislative branch; yet faced with a Republican Senate and armed only with the power to veto their legislation, he was largely unsuccessful.

Congress. Part of the reason for the power Congress enjoyed in the late nineteenth century was the rapid increase in the amount of business that came before it. From 1871 to 1881, 37,409 public and private bills were introduced in the Congress; the number nearly doubled between 1881 and 1891 and reached 81,060 in 1900. Such a tremendous workload forced Congress to regulate its procedures and organization. The committee structure of both the House and Senate expanded during these years. By 1892 there were forty-four standing committees in the Senate and fifty in the House.

The House of Representatives. Much of the business in the House fell increasingly under the control of key committees and the powerful Speaker of the House. Democrat John G. Carlisle of Virginia, who was speaker in 1883–1889, and Republican Thomas B. Reed of

---

BOODLE

During the second half of the nineteenth century urban politics ran on extensive systems of "boodle," or kickbacks. Politicians needed cash for their political campaigns — to pay for advertising and printing costs, to pay to get voters to the polling places, and to distribute favors to those who worked for their reelection. The paychecks of mayors and other city officials were never high enough to take care of all these expenses, but there was another source of ready money. When the city awarded contracts for public improvements such as water and sewer systems, bridges, highways, gas and trolley lines, parks, and public buildings, contractors earned large profits. In fact, such a contract represented hundreds of thousands, often millions, of dollars for the company that submitted the winning bid. For such a construction firm or utility company it was a small cost to include an under-the-table cash payment of a few thousand dollars to elected officials to ensure that the firm would get a contract and at favorable terms. Such payments became known as "boodle."

Maine, speaker in 1889–1891 and 1895–1899, made themselves and the chairmen of the powerful committees on Appropriations and Ways and Means a majority on the Rules Committee, creating "a masterful steering committee" to solve procedural problems and control the flow of legislation. The speaker himself had the power to block bills he did not like. In 1887 a congressman paraded in front of Speaker Carlisle for three hours hoping to be recognized so that he might introduce a bill; finally in frustration he tore the bill into pieces. Despite the volume of business before it, the House was also more casual than it became in the twentieth century. Members frequently left the floor to meet in a bar tucked away in a corner of the Capitol, aptly named The Hole in the Wall, where liquor was served at all hours, until it closed in 1903.

The White House draped in mourning after President James A. Garfield died from gunshot wounds inflicted by a deranged office seeker, September 1881

The Senate. During the mid 1880s future president Woodrow Wilson described the Senate as "a small, select, and leisurely House of Representatives," but by the 1890s a forceful Senate leadership had imposed new procedures similar to those followed in the House. Republicans William B. Allison of Iowa, Nelson W. Aldrich of Rhode Island, Mark Hanna of Ohio, and John Spooner of Wisconsin as well as Democrat Arthur P. Gorman of Maryland brought an unprecedented procedural discipline to the Senate. Until the ratification of the Seventeenth Amendment in 1913, senators were chosen by state legislatures rather than by popular elections. The procedure made senators more beholden to political parties and special interests than to the public, and in 1893, 1894, 1898, 1900, and 1902 the House passed amendments providing for the direct election of senators. Each time, the Senate refused to act on the amendment, earning a reputation for being an exclusive "millionaires' club."

Federal Bureaucracy. The modern apparatus of departments, commissions, and bureaus took shape during these years as the daily management of a rapidly expanding economy grew more complex. New agencies included the Department of Labor (1880), the Civil Service Commission (1883), and the Interstate Commerce Commission (1887); the Department of Agriculture, established in 1862, was raised to cabinet status (1889). The largest federal department was the Interior Department, comprising more than twenty agencies, including the Bureaus of Education, Pensions, Indian Affairs, the Census, the Land Office, and the Geological Survey. After the passage of the Pension Act of 1890, which made pensions available to every disabled Union army veteran who had served at least ninety days and to their widows and dependents, the Pension Bureau became one of the larg-

est agencies, employing sixty thousand men and women by the late 1890s. The Treasury Department, another massive and important department, grew from 4,000 employees in 1873 to nearly 25,000 in 1900. The Post Office Department, which employed more than 56,000 people (about 56 percent of the federal work force) in 1881, grew to nearly 137,000 (about 57 percent) by 1901.

Sources:

Richard Hofstadter, *The Age of Reform: From Bryan to F.D.R.* (New York: Knopf, 1955);

Morton Keller, *Affairs of State: Public Life in Late Nineteenth Century America* (Cambridge, Mass.: Harvard University Press, 1977);

David J. Rothman, *Politics and Power: The United States Senate, 1869–1901* (Cambridge, Mass.: Harvard University Press, 1966).

AMERICAN PARTY POLITICS

The Two-Party System. During the 1880s and 1890s the two-party system functioned as the electoral counterpart to the government. For all but two years during these decades the Republican Party controlled the Senate, and for twelve years the party held the White House. The Democratic Party controlled the House of Representatives for about half the period. While both parties held national conventions every four years, they operated predominantly as state and regional organizations that existed in a web of obligation and reward between the party and local citizens and businessmen. Party platforms in these years took positions on national concerns such as temperance and tariffs, but they also addressed local and regional issues of concern to specific constituencies.

The Major Parties. Both the Democratic and Republican Parties were vast coalitions of individuals with differing viewpoints who came together for the purpose of fielding national candidates who could win elections.

New Yorkers at Madison Square on election night 1888 celebrating the news that Republican presidential candidate Benjamin Harrison has won their state (illustration by Charles Graham for *Harper's Weekly*)

Only on the tariff question—where the Republicans favored high, protective tariffs and the Democrats favored low tariffs to keep down consumer costs—did the two parties take distinctly different stands on the issues of the day. Except for the two nonconsecutive terms of Grover Cleveland, the Republicans controlled the presidency from 1861 to 1913, but popular support for the two parties was actually about even: between 1872 and 1896 no elected president won a majority of the popular vote, and vote totals for the two major-party candidates were extremely close.

The Republicans. Known as the Grand Old Party, or GOP, the Republicans were typically Protestants from old-time Yankee families, usually of British descent or from other established American stock. Home to free soilers, former members of the Whig Party, and abolitionists before the Civil War, the GOP continued to attract reformers in the 1880s and 1890s while also drawing anti-Catholic, anti-immigrant nativists, skilled workers, and farmers from the Northeast and Midwest. In the late nineteenth century the party found itself undergoing transformation to adapt to the needs of a changing society. The party was traditionally made up, in the words of Massachusetts Republican senator George Hoar, of "the men who do the work of piety and charity in our churches, the men who administer our school systems, the men who own and till their own farms, the men who

perform the skilled labor in the shops." The issue facing the GOP was how to adapt the party's individualistic ideals with an increasingly polyglot, urban, industrial society. They responded by calling themselves the party of prosperity as well as piety. During the 1870s and into the 1880s Republicans continued to "wave the bloody shirt," a reminder that it was the Democrats who had led the South into rebellion and ignited the Civil War. Republicans maintained their support for the ideal of equal rights, but in the 1880s they began to realize that their "bloody shirt" strategy was no longer effective; voters wanted to put the war behind them, and a new generation of politicians no longer identified with the factional divisions of the Civil War and Reconstruction era.

The Democrats. As the party of Abraham Lincoln and abolitionism, the Republicans had a reputation for morality while the wide-ranging Democrats, with their tolerance for diverse opinions, were known as supporters of individual liberty. In contrast to the Republican "insiders," the Democrats were a party of "outsiders," including immigrants, Catholics, Jews, southern whites, and a host of freethinkers. The southern "Bourbon" Democrats refused to accept the lessons of Reconstruction. After 1878 they gained political control in the southern states, undoing the attempts of Reconstruction Republicans to establish and ensure equal rights for African Americans. Their rhetoric of Jeffersonian Democ-

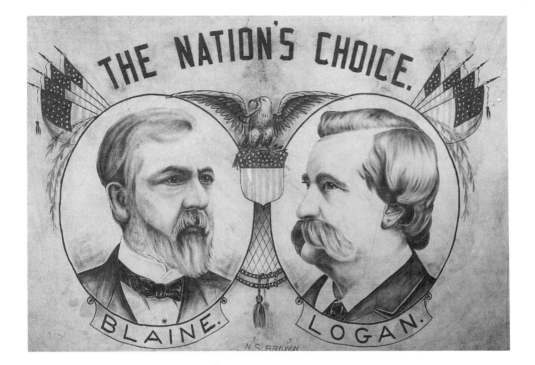

Campaign posters from the 1884 presidential election: (top) Republicans James G. Blaine of Maine and John A. Logan of Illinois; (bottom) Democrats Grover Cleveland of New York and Thomas A. Hendricks of Indiana

STALWARTS, HALF BREEDS, AND MUGWUMPS: A GLOSSARY

The Republican Party was anything but unified in the last third of the nineteenth century. It was established in 1854 by a confederation of old-line political groups, and having provided the winning presidential candidate six times successively beginning in 1860, it continued as a party of headstrong factions, whose divisions were clearly drawn and who had the illusion of arguing among themselves to determine who should lead the country.

The Stalwarts were the old guard, those whose loyalties stemmed from the origins of the Republican Party. Their leader in the 1870s was Ulysses S. Grant, and Stalwarts enthusiastically supported his unsuccessful bid for a third term as president in 1880. Grant, who led Union forces during the Civil War and served as president in 1869–1877, stood as a living symbol of the traditional values they held dear. The geographical base of the Stalwarts was in the Northeast, where congressional seats were safe from the Reconstruction politics that created a volatile electorate impatient with national politicians. They were especially strong in New York State, where Sen. Roscoe Conkling kept a firm grip on the awarding of federal patronage. The foundation of the Stalwart philosophy was that the Civil War had been a victory for the Union, and that the principles of the prewar Union should prevail. They had no interest in concessions to the South in the name of national unity.

The Half Breeds, led by the charismatic James G. Blaine of Maine and Ohioan William McKinley, were liberal, practical-minded Republicans who came to prominence in the 1870s believing that the Republican Party had to reach out to disaffected Democrats to maintain its supremacy. They favored accommodation in the South and union on shared principles above all. The Half Breeds shaped a future-minded party that sought to embrace factions rather than to stifle them.

The Mugwumps were Republican dissenters, who emerged in the election of 1884. They were bitterly opposed to the Republican Party the Half Breeds had wrought. In the attempt to broaden the Republican base, the liberal arm of the party had drifted from accommodation to outright corruption, the Mugwumps argued. The Mugwumps stood for ending excessive political patronage through civil-service reform. Though they thrived on factionalism, they thought that when interest groups made their point they should disband. The Mugwumps' name was said to be an Indian term for pompous people. In the 1884 presidential campaign between Blaine and Grover Cleveland, the Blaine supporters called renegade Republicans Mugwumps, meaning, it was said, that they were educated beyond their intelligence. Party regulars also joked that the Mugwumps had their "mugs" on one side of the fence and their "wumps" on the other.

---

racy, free trade, limited government, and personal freedom (including opposition to temperance) met with sympathy in some quarters of the North and appealed to many reformers nationwide. As memories of the Civil War and Reconstruction faded, a new generation of politicians from the North and Midwest were less and less interested in old political divisions and more interested in business and financial issues. New Yorker Grover Cleveland, a reform Democrat, embodied the Bourbon Democrats' philosophy. During his two nonconsecutive terms as president, he opposed high tariffs and soft money, vetoed Republican pension bills, and tried to support a vision of business unhampered by federal intervention.

Campaigns. Politics had become a national pastime by the 1890s. Campaigners distributed colorful banners, hats, flags, and buttons, and plastered the candidates' faces on playing cards, leaflets, and pamphlets. The Democratic donkey and the Republican elephant could be seen everywhere. Party operatives combed streets, saloons, and neighborhoods drumming up votes for their candidates. In the 1880s and 1890s voter participation

reached an all-time high, with 70–80 percent of those eligible to vote doing so.

Urban Political Machines. Powerful city bosses and their political "machines" linked the national party to the local level. The Democratic Party incorporated thousands of new immigrants into its urban operations, providing networks through which supporters could find work, loans, and companionship. For many newcomers urban machines provided a way to participate not only in politics but in a neighborhood-based community. Bosses depended on their people for votes and rewarded them for their efforts. Urban machines looked out for working-class families, helping them to achieve the same benefits enjoyed by the middle class, such as the new city services of water, sewerage, and electricity. Although the notorious Democratic boss William Marcy Tweed (1823–1878) was sent to prison in 1872 for plundering the New York City treasury, the Tammany Hall men's political club he had created continued to dominate the Democratic nominating process and distributed municipal jobs to loyal voters and party workers. A similar system of payoffs and rewards to local Democratic loyalists operated in Chicago. During the 1880s Chris Buckley, the "Blind Boss" of San Francisco, was said to stand at polling places with the pockets of his overcoat filled with quarter-eagle gold coins (each worth $2.50). As he shook the hand of each man who had voted for him, he slipped his loyal supporter a coin. Voter fraud was not just an urban phenomenon. In 1888 West Virginians cast 159,440 votes in the presidential election, while the state had only 147,408 eligible voters, and Grover Cleveland won the state by a margin of only 506 votes.

Sources:

Michael McGerr, *The Decline of Popular Politics: The American North, 1865–1928* (New York: Oxford University Press, 1986);

H. Wayne Morgan, *From Hayes to McKinley: National Party Politics, 1877–1896* (Syracuse, N.Y.: Syracuse University Press, 1969);

Paul Kleppner, *The Third Electoral System, 1853–1892: Parties, Voters, and Political Culture* (Chapel Hill: University of North Carolina Press, 1979).

AMERICAN POLITICS: REFORMING THE SPOILS SYSTEM

The Spoils System. In 1881 more than 50 percent of all federal jobs were patronage positions. As control of the presidency shifted from one major party to the other in 1885, 1889, 1893, and 1897, dramatic turnovers occurred in personnel. Post Office positions were considered excellent rewards for party loyalists, and the department became notorious for its high numbers of underworked administrators. After he took office for his first term in 1885, President Cleveland, the first Democratic president since James Buchanan left office in 1861, replaced nearly forty thousand postmasters. This system of rewards was costly, created chaos and inefficiencies, and became the focus of critics who saw patronage as an abuse of power. As governing the nation became increasing complex and the amount of work multiplied, members of both parties saw the need for a class of civil-service workers who would not be dependent on party patronage for their jobs and would remain in their positions regardless of party turnovers.

Civil-Service Reform. Educated and well-to-do Americans pointed to corruption in the spoils system and called for civil-service reform, but others complained that the true motive of these individuals was to weaken the urban bosses, who had taken power away from the upper- and middle-class Anglo-Saxon Protestants who had once dominated city, state, and national politics and placed it in the hands of immigrants, Catholics, and the working class. Changing the spoils system proved difficult. Congress was reluctant to take away a valuable tool for garnering voter support. Attempts at reform took place during the presidencies of Ulysses S. Grant (1869–1877) and Rutherford B. Hayes (1877–1881), but the entrenched patronage system remained largely intact.

The Pendleton Act. Following the assassination of President Garfield by a frustrated office seeker, a group of concerned citizens—including professors, newspaper editors, lawyers, and ministers—organized the Civil Service Reform Association in 1882 and won the support of the Democratic senator George H. Pendleton of Ohio. The Pendleton Civil Service Reform Act was passed on 16 January 1883. The act authorized the president to appoint a three-person Civil Service Commission, which established a system of standards for federal jobs and opened a competitive application process for hiring. The act also barred political candidates from soliciting campaign contributions from federal workers. The new system covered about 14 percent of government appointments at first and about 40 percent by 1900. While patronage did not disappear altogether, reforms helped to establish a professional identity for government workers akin to those of doctors and lawyers. There emerged a class of federal employees who attempted with varying degrees of success to remain above the fray of party politics.

Stalwarts versus Mugwumps. Republican "Stalwarts" who relied on the spoils systems for support were outraged by the reform attempts of first the "Half Breeds" and later the "Mugwumps" in their party. Stalwarts accused Mugwumps of wanting government jobs to go to college-educated relatives who could pass the new civil-service tests. At their 1884 national convention the Republicans nominated James G. Blaine, a Half Breed whose reputation had been damaged eight years earlier by allegations that he had taken bribes from the railroads. As his running mate, the Republicans had chosen Sen. John A. Logan, a Stalwart. After the Democrats responded by nominating Grover Cleveland, a reform candidate with a reputation for honesty, the Mugwumps bolted their own party to support him, and Cleveland won the election.

Sources:

Ari Hoogenboom, *Outlawing the Spoils: A History of the Civil Service Reform Movement, 1865–1883* (Urbana: University of Illinois Press, 1961);

Gerald W. McFarland, *Mugwumps, Morals, and Politics, 1844–1928* (Amherst: University of Massachusetts Press, 1975).

AMERICAN POLITICS SOUTHERN STYLE

Southern Polling Practices. While corrupt, party machines served the important function of integrating newcomers and the urban poor into politics. Southern blacks, predominantly former slaves, had few allies in the post-Reconstruction period to help them become full participants in the political system. Ratified in 1870, the Fifteenth Amendment granted African American males the right to vote, a privilege they exercised freely throughout the Reconstruction period, electing large numbers of African Americans to local, state, and national offices, including seats in both houses of Congress. Between 1866 and 1876 fifteen African Americans served in the House of Representatives. After Reconstruction ended in 1878, the number of African American congressmen declined, but a few continued to be reelected, including John Roy Lynch, a former slave, who served as the speaker of the

Democratic playing cards from the 1888 presidential campaign with President Cleveland as king, his wife, Frances, as queen, and vice-presidential candidate Allen G. Thurman of Ohio as jack

Mississippi House of Representatives and as a Republican congressman from 1873 to 1883.

Disfranchising African Americans. In the 1880s a rising tide of racism and the growing presence of Populism and other forms of political unrest in the South made conservative white southerners fearful that poor whites and African Americans might join forces and upset Democratic rule in the region. Using threats and violence, fraudulent vote counts, literacy tests, poll taxes, and separate ballots and ballot boxes for state and federal elections, as well as by holding periodic voter registrations at places inaccessible to African Americans, southern states created major roadblocks to blacks' participation in the electoral process, denying the vote outright to the vast majority. The Democratic Party of South Carolina, for example, enacted a rule in 1894 that stated, "every Negro applying to vote in a Democratic primary election, must produce a written statement of ten reputable white men" who could swear the applicant voted Democratic in previous elections. The consequence of

such practices was a dramatic decline in southern voting. The southern turnout in presidential elections went from 64 percent of eligible voters in 1880 to 43 percent in 1900.

The Federal Elections Act. In an effort to ensure that more African Americans could vote and to clean up corrupt polling practices, Congress debated the Federal Elections Act of 1889–1890. The key element of the bill was a provision that allowed federal circuit courts, not the state, to oversee congressional elections if one hundred or more voters in a district requested it. In such cases federal marshals would supervise the balloting and vote counting. The bill was the Republicans' last effort to reinstate gains that had been won in the Civil War but had quickly evaporated in the wake of Reconstruction. The pervasive racist belief that African Americans were not intellectually capable to participate in politics and a widespread indifference to the dilemma of southern blacks blocked passage of the bill.

The Kansas Exodus. After the abolition of slavery southern plantation owners continued to need cheap labor to work their land. Under various systems of sharecropping and farm tenancy, former slaves worked plots of land either for a share of the crop they raised or for rent. With crop prices in a long-term decline and with control of the contracts in the landowners' hands, sharecroppers and tenants found themselves poorer and more in debt with each passing year. Poverty combined with the growing threat of racially motivated lynching and the curtailment of their legal rights to convince some African Americans to seek better lives outside the South, and many headed to the newly opened land of the Midwest. Their first large post–Civil War "exodus" was to rural Kansas. Led by former slave Benjamin "Pap" Singleton, who was proud to be called the "Moses of the Colored Exodus," this migration attracted national attention. Singleton, who had escaped and settled in Detroit before the Civil War, moved to Tennessee after the war and began to preach self-help to former slaves. Between 1876 and 1879 he personally led as many as seven thousand people to settle in Kansas.

Migration Fever. Throughout 1879 a migration fever swept through the South, and thousands of African Americans set out for Kansas, many traveling by steamboat up the Mississippi to Saint Louis, and by rail the rest of the way. Democrats in Congress saw the exodus as a plot by the GOP to pack the developing state with black, Republican voters. In Kansas African American farmers found a degree of the autonomy and civil rights that had eluded them in the South.

Sources:

Edward L. Ayers, *The Promise of the New South: Life After Reconstruction* (New York: Oxford University Press, 1992);

Morton Keller, *Affairs of State: Public Life in Late Nineteenth Century America* (Cambridge, Mass.: Harvard University Press, 1977);

C. Vann Woodward, *Origins of the New South, 1877–1913* (Baton Rouge: Louisiana State University Press, 1971);

Woodward, *The Strange Career of Jim Crow* (New York: Oxford University Press, 1955).

DOMESTIC CONCERNS: MONETARY REFORM

Declining Prices. Throughout the post–Civil War era heated political fights over whether paper money should be backed by silver and gold or gold alone and how much currency should be available reflected deep social divisions among Americans, pitting easterners against westerners, farmers against businessmen, and the poor against the wealthy. This debate was accompanied by a long, steady decline in prices. In general, wholesale and retail prices in the United States fell from a high-water mark at the end of the Civil War to a low point in the 1890s. As a result the value of a dollar increased; in 1892 it could buy twice what it could in 1866. Americans who had money could buy more for less, but for anyone with goods to sell this downward trend constituted a crisis.

Farmers. Farmers were particularly hard hit by the long-term price decline. While they had fixed mortgages and other debts to pay on their land, buildings, and equipment, the amount of revenue farmers earned from their crops declined with each year. During this period a farmer who had to make loan payments of $500 a year might have his annual income from the sale of his crops decrease from $1,000 to $700. Bad crops and poor weather often made conditions worse, and many farmers went bankrupt during the 1880s.

Hard versus Soft Money. The decline in prices was driven in part by the rapid growth of the American population and the national output of products without a corresponding increase in the supply of money. During the Civil War the government had issued "greenbacks," paper currency that could not be exchanged for gold or silver. This increased money supply caused inflation, and the government intended to retire the greenbacks from circulation. A postwar depression, however, resulted in a division of opinion on the paper-money issue. During the late 1860s and throughout the 1870s "hard money" advocates argued that withdrawing all paper money or limiting the supply and backing it with gold or silver would keep the value of the dollar high. "Soft money" advocates, or "greenbackers"—including the Greenback-Labor Party—argued that increasing the amount of inconvertible money in circulation helped farmers pay their debts, keeping them solvent and spurring economic growth. After President Ulysses S. Grant successfully vetoed an 1874 bill that would have increased the supply of paper money, Congress passed the Specie Reduction Act of 1875, which reduced the paper-money supply to $300 million and authorized the redemption of paper money for gold, effective 1 January 1879.

Gold versus Silver. After the passage of the Specie Reduction Act, advocates of increasing the money supply turned their focus to advocating the coinage of silver money. The Coinage Act of 1873 had removed the silver dollar from coinage and established a single gold standard, angering silver miners in the West, especially after new discoveries in the mid 1870s resulted in an increased production of silver. Supported by these silverites as well as farm and labor groups, the Bland-Allison Act of 1878 restored the silver dollar as legal tender, instructing the secretary of the treasury to buy between $2 million and $4 million in silver every month. Because the secretary acted conservatively, the results were not inflationary, but neither did they increase the money supply sufficiently to please free-silver advocates.

The Sherman Silver Purchase Act. In 1890 politicians struck a compromise between backers of the gold standard and those advocating a silver and gold standard, or "bimetallism." The Sherman Silver Purchase Act of 1890 directed the treasury to purchase 4.5 million ounces of silver each month, the same amount being produced by western silver mines. The Treasury Department would then issue notes equal in value to the costs of these

Among the most memorable lines in American political oratory are the last two sentences of William Jennings Bryan's speech during the platform debate at the 1896 Democratic National Convention: "You shall not press down upon the brow of labor this crown of thorns. You shall not crucify mankind on a cross of gold." By the time he reached these lines Bryan, who had a well-deserved reputation as a spellbinding orator, had gained the rapt attention of all the delegates with many other quotable lines. Beginning with the theme that the monetary issue had divided the East from the West, rich from poor, and big businessman from storekeeper, farmer, and laborer. Bryan responded to claims that unlimited coinage of gold and silver was bad for the country because it was bad for business, appealing to the sentiments of people for whom the bloody divisions of the Civil War were still recent history:

In this contest brother has been arrayed against brother and father against father. The warmest ties of love and acquaintance and association have been disregarded. Old leaders have been cast aside when they have refused to give expression to the sentiments of those whom they would lead, and new leaders have sprung up to give direction to his cause of truth. . . .

. . . When you come before us and tell us that we shall dis-turb your business interests, we reply that you have disturbed our business interests by your course. We say to you that you have made too limited in its application the definition of a business man. The man who is employed for wages is as much a business man as is his employer. The attorney in a country town is as much a business man as the corporation counsel in a great metropolis. The merchant at the cross-roads store is as much a business man as the merchant of New York. The farmer who goes forth in the morning and toils all day, begins in the spring and toils all summer, and by the application of brain and muscle to the natural resources of this country creates wealth, is as much a business man as the man who goes upon the board of trade and bets upon the price of grain.

The miners who go a thousand feet into the earth or climb two thousand feet upon the cliffs and bring forth from their hiding-places the precious metals to be poured into the channels of trade are as much business men as the few financial magnates who, in a back-room, corner the money of the world.

We come to speak for this broader class of business men. Ah, my friends, we say not one word against those who live upon the Atlantic coast; but those hardy pioneers who braved all the dangers of the wilderness, who have made the desert to bloom as the rose — those pioneers away out there, rearing their children near to nature's heart, where they can mingle their voices with the voices of the birds — out there where they have erected school-houses for the education of their young, and churches were they praise their Creator, and cemeteries where sleep the ashes of their dead — are as deserving of the consideration of this party as any people in this country. . . .

There are two ideas of government. There are those who believe that if you legislate to make the well-to-do prosperous that their prosperity will leak through on those below. The democratic idea has been that if you legislate to make the masses prosperous, their prosperity will find its way up through every class and rest upon it. You come to us and tell us that the great cities are in favor of the gold standard. I tell you that the great cities rest upon these broad and fertile prairies. Burn down your cities and leave our farms and your cities will spring up again as if by magic. But destroy our farms and the grass will grow in the streets of every city in the country.

Source: *The Speeches of William Jennings Bryan,* 2 volumes (New York: Funk & Wagnalls, 1913).

purchases, redeemable in gold or silver. The compromise was based on the agreement that Republican members of Congress would support the Sherman Silver Act in return for Democratic support of the McKinley Tariff, which established the highest duties to date on imported manufactured goods. The "Million Dollar Congress" angered reformers, farmers, and workers, who gained little from the compromise.

Political Divisions over Money. Gold-standard advocates, mostly members of the business community, argued that the introduction of silver damaged the economy. In November 1890 the failure of Baring Bros., a British banking house, caused British investors to sell U.S. securities, causing a drain on American gold reserves. This event—coupled with a decrease in revenues because of the McKinley Tariff and a sharp decrease in government funds because the Pension Act of 1890 vastly increased the number of Civil War veterans who were eligible for pensions—caused the U.S. gold reserve to decline below $100 million by 21 April 1893, bringing on the Panic of 1893. Facing an economy in ruins, President Cleveland called a secret session of Congress for August 1893 and urged the repeal of the Sherman Silver Purchase Act. Only a gold standard, he insisted, could pull the country out of economic depression. Cleveland won repeal after a bitter battle that divided the Democrats, causing severe damage politically for him and his supporters.

Bryan versus McKinley. At the 1896 Democratic Convention "Silver Democrats" won the upper hand, securing the nomination of free-silver advocate William Jennings Bryan. Republicans, committed to gold, linked their future to hard money and William McKinley of Ohio, who won the election. A general upturn in prices in the late 1890s lessened the drive for monetary reform. The increased minting of coins and the discovery of gold

Democrats parading in support of their 1892 candidates for president and vice president, Grover Cleveland and Adlai Stevenson (grandfather of the Democrats' presidential candidate in 1952 and 1956)

in Alaska contributed to an easing of the money-supply crisis. The United States did not abandon the gold standard until 1933, in the midst of the Great Depression.

Sources:

Milton Friedman and Jacobson Schwartz, *A Monetary History of the United States, 1867–1960* (Princeton, N.J.: Princeton University Press, 1963);

Walter T. K. Nugent, *Money and American Society, 1865–1880* (New York: Free Press, 1968);

Irwin Unger, *The Greenback Era: A Social and Political History of American Finance, 1865–1879* (Princeton, N.J.: Princeton University Press, 1964).

DOMESTIC CONCERNS: REGULATING COMMERCE

Railroad Regulation. The establishment of a transnational railroad system after the Civil War dramatically changed the nature of industry and, as a result, of government. Railroads reshaped regional alliances, stimulated businesses, and increasingly tied the country together in one national market. At the same time the structure of the railroad industry left customers vulnerable to unethical business practices, leading many to call for government oversight of the railroads.

Unfair Pricing. Competition proved difficult to sustain in the railroad industry. Larger lines drove smaller ones out of business by undercutting their rates. Once a larger company had taken over a smaller company's routes, it raised prices to finance other acquisitions.

When a single railroad company controlled a route, the company could charge whatever it chose for transporting freight and passengers. These prices were not only inflated but often whimsical and unfair. Companies often discounted the rates for passenger seats and freight space just before a train left the station. The railroads also regularly gave free rail passes to legislators and politicians. Many feared the special treatment legislators enjoyed blinded them to corruption of the railroad industry.

The Interstate Commerce Act. Lack of regulation especially hurt farmers who relied on the railroad to carry their crops to urban markets. In 1867 they had banded together to found the Patrons of Husbandry, better known as the Grange, and in the 1870s they convinced five states to pass so-called Granger laws regulating railroad rates. The railroads affected by the laws challenged them in a case that went to the Supreme Court, which upheld the laws in *Munn* v. *Illinois*. In 1886, however, the court reversed itself, overturning the state laws by ruling in *Wabash, St. Louis & Pacific Railway* v. *Illinois* that railroads were a form of interstate commerce and as such were subject to federal regulation only. In 1878 the House had passed a bill calling for such federal legislation, but it died in the Senate. After the *Wabash* decision, Congress—backed by President Grover Cleveland, who supported federal railroad regulation—passed one of the most important legislative measures of the era, the Interstate Commerce Act of 1887. This act created the first federal regulatory agency, a five-person Interstate Commerce Commission to oversee passenger and freight charges on any railroad that operated in more than one state. The commission was also authorized to hear public testimony on violations, to examine company records, and in general to oversee law enforcement as it applied to railroads. Many railroad companies welcomed federal oversight to stop cutthroat competition and to end rebates and discounts. While a series of Supreme Court cases in the late 1890s undercut the powers of the Interstate Commerce Commission, it provided the basis for federal regulation of commerce in the twentieth century.

Sources:

Morton Keller, *Affairs of State: Public Life in Late Nineteenth Century America* (Cambridge, Mass.: Harvard University Press, 1977);

Page Smith, *The Rise of Industrial America: A People's History of the Post-Reconstruction Era* (New York: McGraw-Hill, 1984).

FINANCING THE FEDERAL GOVERNMENT

Tariffs. During the Civil War the federal government had levied an income tax, which had accounted for about 20 percent of its revenues. With various domestic manufacturers' and sales taxes adding another 23 percent, internal revenues exceeded tariffs, or taxes on imported goods, as a source of federal funds. After the war most domestic taxes were phased out, and the income tax expired in 1872. The primary means of financing the federal government became tariffs. American producers and manufacturers had long relied on the government to use tariffs as a way to block foreign competition with their products on the domestic market. For example, Louisiana beet growers, Pennsylvania iron and steel manufacturers, West Virginia coal-mine owners, and Ohio and Texas wool growers all feared that low-priced imports would drive them out of the American market. High tariffs imposed on such foreign goods priced them above domestic products. Yet other industries—including iron manufacturers who required foreign ore and Chicago meatpackers who bought foreign salt—depended on foreign imports for their daily operations and advocated lowering tariffs to keep down their production costs. Farmers and cattlemen with large foreign markets also favored low tariffs as a means of encouraging foreign countries to lower their customs duties on American products. As a result of competing business interests, the major tariff legislation passed during the 1880s and 1890s was the culmination of intense negotiation by politicians who traded votes in exchange for guarantees of support for their own tariff requests, and the resulting laws were filled with hundreds of adjustments and exceptions for special interests. As one commentator said of the 1883 tariff, "Its general character cannot be easily described; in truth, it can hardly be said to have any general character."

Tariff Politics. The tariff question was one of the few issues on which the two major parties took distinctly dif-

A McKinley soap doll from the 1896 Republican presidential campaign

ferent positions. Republicans favored protectionism and Democrats backed reductionism. The Democrats called their unsuccessful Mills Tariff Bill of 1888 and their successful Wilson-Gorman Tariff Act of 1894 examples of their promise to reduce tariffs, while the Republicans viewed the McKinley Tariff Act of 1890 and the Dingley Tariff Act of 1897 as triumphs of Republican protectionism.

Regional Differences. Protectionist tariffs hurt consumers because without foreign competition the selection of goods on the market was limited and American producers and manufacturers kept prices artificially high. Yet workers in industrial states often favored protectionist tariffs because high profits for manufacturers meant more factory jobs. For consumers in the West and South, which had fewer factories, the favoring of manufacturers over fair pricing seemed unfair and abusive at a time when the incomes for farmers and ranchers were severely reduced.

Sources:

John A. Garraty, *The New Commonwealth, 1877–1898* (New York: Harper & Row, 1968);

Morton Keller, *Affairs of State: Public Life in Late Nineteenth Century America* (Cambridge, Mass.: Harvard University Press, 1977);

Page Smith, *The Rise of Industrial America: A People's History of the Post-Reconstruction Era* (New York: McGraw-Hill, 1984).

Grover Cleveland was an unlikely ladies' man. Weighing nearly three hundred pounds, he was described by his physician as very corpulent, with a short, thick neck, and by one biographer as having hanging jowls and a walrus mustache that he began wearing in his early thirties. He assumed the presidency at the age of forty-seven as a bachelor with a reputation as a man who enjoyed a good cigar, a stout drink, and a pretty lady. As a young man in Buffalo, where he worked as a lawyer, Cleveland did much of his politicking in the neighborhood bars, where beer cost a nickel a stein and lunch was free to drinkers; in the evenings he frequented the beer gardens, which offered a pleasant atmosphere and free-spirited camaraderie.

Among Cleveland's lady friends in Buffalo was Mrs. Maria Crofts Halpin. When she told Cleveland in 1870 that she was pregnant with their child, he responded by offering her seclusion during her pregnancy and financial support. He is said to have refused to marry her because he suspected she had other male companions and that the baby might not be his. His successful campaign that year for Erie County sheriff may have also affected his decision. When her son was born, Cleveland had him placed in an orphanage and later arranged for a friend to rear him, to the consternation of Mrs. Halpin, who apparently had little say in the matter.

In 1874 Cleveland's friend and former law partner Oscar Folsom died, naming Cleveland as executor of his estate and guardian of his daughter, Frances. Cleveland looked after her diligently and watched her grow with increasing affection. By the time he was elected president in 1884, Frances Folsom was an attractive young lady and the apple of her guardian's eye. He married her in 1886, the year she graduated from college. She was twenty-two; he was forty-nine. Theirs was the first wedding to take place in the White House, and Cleveland was the first serving president to take the vows of matrimony. Frances Cleveland was an immediate hit in Washington. The president's associates appreciated her domesticating influence on her sometimes gruff and unceremonious husband. The birth of the Cleveland's daughter, baby Ruth, after his first term had expired and he lost his bid for reelection, further softened Cleveland's image and helped him in his successful campaign for reelection to the presidency in 1892. However, not even the birth of the Cleveland's second daughter, Esther, in 1893, the first baby born in the White House, and another daughter in 1895, when the president was fifty-eight, was enough to save Cleveland from the political effects of the Panic of 1893. Cleveland left office for good in 1896 and turned his attentions to his family. The Clevelands had two more children, both boys, after his second term.

GOVERNMENT AND LABOR

Labor Protests. Throughout the post–Civil War era, critics of monopolies and industrial capitalism protested the growing impersonality of the factory system and the long hours and grueling conditions workers endured for little pay. The membership of the largest workers' organization, the Knights of Labor, founded in 1869, reached a high point during the 1880s, with about seven hundred thousand members in 1886. The Knights of Labor opposed the traditional wage system, favoring alternatives such as worker cooperatives in which there would be no employers or employees, and laborers would control the production and distribution of the products they made. Many Americans viewed unions and other labor organizations as radical, fearing that they preached class warfare and called for too much governmental control over industry. Both houses of Congress, the presidents, and the courts objected to labor organizing and resisted any shift in power away from employers to workers. Those who controlled the two major parties at state and federal levels resisted any efforts to regulate hours, working conditions, or wages, arguing that the private contract between worker and employer could not be violated.

The Eight-Hours League. The campaign for a shorter workday gained momentum during the 1880s. The Eight-Hours League advocated a "natural" rhythm of eight hours for work, eight for sleep, and eight for leisure, a dramatic challenge to the typical twelve-hour workday and six-day workweek. League members boycotted products made in shops with workdays of more than eight hours and attended social events supporting the eight-hour movement. During the first week of May 1886, more than 190,000 workers nationwide walked off their jobs to protest long hours, winning shorter workdays for more than 150,000 workers. Among them were workers at the McCormick Harvester plant south of Chicago, where violence erupted on 3 May, with police firing into a crowd of workers, killing one man and seriously wounding others. The shorter-hours campaign ended in tragedy on 4 May 1886 at Haymarket Square in Chicago. At a mass demonstration called to protest the

Workers in New York City demonstrating in favor of an eight-hour workday, 1880s

events at the Harvester plant and to support the eight-hour day, a bomb killed a policeman and wounded seventy-six others (six of whom later died from their injuries), and the Chicago police retaliated by starting to shoot into the crowd, killing one demonstrator and wounding at least twelve others, some of whom died soon after. The incident was widely described by newspapers as the first stirrings of a violent revolution by radical workers. After a dramatic, closely watched trial of eight anarchists, during which the prosecution produced no evidence linking the defendants to the riot, the court sentenced seven of the anarchists to death and one of them to fifteen years in prison. Four were hanged in 1887; one committed suicide; and three lingered in jail until Illinois governor John Peter Altgeld pardoned them in 1893.

Aftermath. The Haymarket incident, the trial, and the controversy surrounding Altgeld's pardon brought to national attention the deep division of opinions on labor issues and the widening gaps between rich and poor, capitalist and worker. Labor supporters claimed that cities across the country used the Haymarket affair as an excuse to shut down workers' legitimate expressions of their political will. Conservatives, on the other hand, saw the incident and the response of the Chicago police as necessary to ensure law and order. Employers associations shared information and resources in an attempt to rid their factories of troublesome union organizers. As the Knights of Labor went into decline as a result of these tactics, a rival trade organization, the American

Federation of Labor (AFL), founded in December 1886 with Samuel Gompers as president, made significant gains in membership, especially after the economic depression of 1893. Unlike the Knights of Labor, the AFL organized only skilled workers and had a more cautious and conservative set of goals.

Government Response. During the 1890s state and federal governments increasingly responded to strikes by securing court injunctions against them and employing troops. The state militia ended the bloody strike at the Carnegie steel plant in Homestead, Pennsylvania, in 1892, and that same year federal troops were sent to enforce martial law during the silver strike at the Coeur d'Alene mines in Idaho. President Grover Cleveland ordered federal troops to restore order during the Pullman strike of 1894, and Eugene V. Debs and other strike leaders were imprisoned.

Sources:

Leon Fink, *Working Men's Democracy: The Knights of Labor and American Politics* (Urbana: University of Illinois Press, 1983);

David Montgomery, *The Fall of the House of Labor: The Workplace, the State, and American Labor Activism, 1865–1925* (Cambridge & New York: Cambridge University Press, 1987).

INDIAN POLICY

Ending Native American Sovereignty. Before the Civil War the federal government had typically negotiated treaties with various tribes, as though they were foreign "nations," but in its General Appropriations Act of 1871 the House of Representatives specified: "hereafter

Alice Fletcher (far left), agent for the Bureau of Indian Affairs, signing up members of the Nez Percé tribe for allotments of land on their reservation in Lapwai, Idaho, circa 1890

no Indian tribe or nation within the territory of the United States shall be acknowledged or recognized as an independent nation, tribe, or power, with whom the United States may contract by treaty." The act facilitated a paternalistic approach to Native Americans designed to force them to give up their nomadic ways and to settle on isolated reservations, where they were expected to learn farming and take up "civilized" ways of life. The Bureau of Indian Affairs, one of the largest divisions of the huge Interior Department, also established special boarding schools that removed young Native Americans from their tribes, preventing them from learning their own religions and traditions while teaching them the ways of white society.

Federal Paternalism. Despite these assimilationist measures Native Americans were not treated as full-fledged citizens of the United States. In *Elk* v. *Wilkins* (1884) the Supreme Court ruled that the Fourteenth Amendment (1868), which specifies that any person born or naturalized in the United States is a citizen, did not apply to Native Americans. They ruled that an Indian who left the reservation was not eligible to vote because he had not been naturalized, but since reservations were within the territory of the United States, Native Americans were not eligible for naturalization procedures. Thus, the only way they could become citizens was through congressional acts extending citizenship to individual persons or tribes. (All Native Americans were finally granted full citizenship in 1924.) The ruling perpetuated the definition of Native Americans as wards of the federal government who were incapable of handling their own affairs.

The Land Squeeze. After the Civil War and the completion of the first transnational railroad link in 1869, railroads brought more settlers to the mountain states and the Great Plains. As available western lands were occupied by white ranchers, homesteaders, and miners, new federal policies forced Native Americans from lands that were theirs by tradition or treaty and onto reservations., There they often starved and faced mistreatment and even death at the hands of government troops as well as white settlers. During the 1870s several Indian groups resisted relocation to reservations and the white takeover of lands. While a final bloody massacre occurred at Wounded Knee Creek in South Dakota in 1890, by 1878 the so-called Indian wars were largely over. (See *Lifestyles and Social Trends*.)

The Dawes Act. In 1887 Congress passed the Dawes Severalty Act, ostensibly "to fit the Indian for civilization and absorb him into it" by dividing the lands on each reservation, which were held in common by a tribe, into homesteads for individuals or nuclear families. The act also stipulated that any surplus land could be sold to whites. Over the next decade enactment of the Dawes Act not only stripped western tribes of large portions of their lands but also decimated the internal structures of tribes. With only small allocations of land many could not support themselves. Within twenty years two-thirds of Indian land had been sold to whites, and much tribal culture and tradition was lost.

Sources:

Daniel Boorstin, *The Americans: The Democratic Experience* (New York: Random House, 1973);

Frederick E. Hoxie, *A Final Promise: The Campaign to Assimilate the Indians, 1880–1920* (Lincoln: University of Nebraska Press, 1984);

Patricia Nelson Limerick, *The Legacy of Conquest: The Unbroken Past of the American West* (New York: Norton, 1987).

INTERNATIONAL AFFAIRS: HAWAII AND THE SPANISH-AMERICAN WAR

Naval Expansion. In 1880 international experts ranked the U.S. Navy twelfth in the world, sounding a wake up call for the government. The following year a naval advisory board recommended the construction of a new fleet of steel-bottomed ships. In 1883, during the administration of Chester Arthur (1881–1885), Congress approved funding for a shipbuilding program, and the following year the U.S. Naval War College was founded in Newport, Rhode Island, to provide naval officers with postgraduate training in international law, history, and technical subjects useful as the navy was modernized. During Grover Cleveland's first term (1885–1889), Undersecretary of the Navy William Whitney reorganized naval administration to make it more modern and efficient. He coordinated the work of the various bureaus involved in purchasing materials and equipment, destroyed antiquated ships, and oversaw the construction of the new fleet. When Whitney left office in 1889, he had begun building or had authorized twenty-two steel ships that became the nucleus of the modern navy. The New Navy program continued after Whitney's departure. By 1900 the fleet was ranked third in the world, behind only those of Great Britain and Germany.

Good Policy, Good Politics. The New Navy policies received warm support from businessmen, politicians, and from many within the navy. By insisting that armor plates for the new ships be made in the United States, the navy directly supported the expansion of the American steel industry, bringing new jobs to American shipyards and making millionaires of steel producers. Because it stimulated the economy and strengthened the position of the United States on the world stage, the New Navy also enjoyed bipartisan political support. During the 1890s the building of an effective fleet provided Presidents Benjamin Harrison, Grover Cleveland, and William McKinley with a powerful international bargaining tool. Backed by sea power, the United States was able to convince other world powers to consider its positions on affairs in Latin America and the Pacific.

Hawaii. The New Navy enabled the United States to assume a larger role in international affairs. The debate over annexing the Hawaiian Islands served as a rehearsal for later disagreements over what that role should be, sparking controversy over whether the United States should seek to acquire overseas territory like the great colonial empires of Europe. Americans, mainly farmers and missionaries, had settled among native Hawaiian tribes in the early nineteenth century. By the 1880s descendants of these white settlers owned large sugar plantations and cattle farms and exerted considerable power. In 1887 they forced King Kalakaua to install a democratic government and adopt a liberal constitution. Since 1875 sugar planters in Hawaii had been protected by an arrangement that freed them from custom duties on sugar imports to the United States in exchange for a promise that no Hawaiian territory would be given or leased to a nation other than the United States. This reciprocal trade agreement was renewed in 1884, but Congress did not approve it until 1887, when Hawaii gave the United States the right to build a naval base at Pearl Harbor. Under the McKinley Tariff of 1890, however, Hawaiian sugar growers lost their trade advantage. All sugar imports to the United States were given duty-free status, and planters in the United States were paid a bounty of two cents a pound for their sugar. Hawaiian sugar planters lost some $12 million. Amid growing discontent with U.S. involvement in Hawaiian affairs, Queen Liliuokalani succeeded her brother on the throne in 1891, revoking the liberal constitution and assuming autocratic powers. In January 1893, with the help of U.S. Marines from the naval cruiser *Boston,* Americans in Hawaii led by Sanford B. Dole overthrew the Hawaiian government and asked to be annexed by the United States, in large part because they hoped to profit from the two-cents-per-pound bounty for domestic sugar.

The Annexation Battle. The landing of the marines had been authorized by John L. Stevens, the U.S. minister to Hawaii, who favored the annexation of Hawaii by the United States. Without authorization from the U.S. State Department, Stevens recognized the new government and proclaimed Hawaii a U.S. protectorate. A treaty of annexation was drawn up, and just weeks before Republican Benjamin Harrison left office on 4 March 1893, it was sent to the Senate, where Democrats blocked its ratification. After Democrat Grover Cleveland began his second term as president, he withdrew the treaty from consideration by the Senate, and sent former congressman James H. Blount, a liberal Republican from Georgia, to investigate the situation in Hawaii, where he withdrew the marines. After Blount reported that Stevens had acted improperly and that, except for the sugar growers, most Hawaiians opposed annexation, Cleveland denounced the American rebels, and although he recognized Dole's provisional government, he attempted to restore the queen to the throne with the provision that she pardon the rebels and reinstate the constitution of 1887. Despite the queen's agreement to these conditions, Dole's provisional government remained in power, arguing that it had been recognized by the United States, which did not have the right to interfere in Hawaiian internal affairs. Unwilling to use force to reinstate Queen Liliuokalani, an angry Cleveland refused to resubmit the annexation treaty to the Senate. On 4 July 1894 the provisional government proclaimed the Republic of Hawaii, which the United States formally recognized the following month. The new Hawaiian constitution had a provision welcoming annexation by the United States, which Cleveland blocked for the remainder of his tenure in of-

The wreck of the *Maine* in the harbor at Havana, Cuba, 1898

fice. For several years Hawaiian annexation remained a heavily partisan issue, with Republicans favoring it and Democrats opposing. Cleveland's successor, Republican William McKinley, sent a new annexation treaty to the Senate in June 1897, but Democrats and anti-imperialist Republicans managed to delay ratification. Finally, on 7 July 1898, recognizing the strategic importance of Pearl Harbor during the naval war with Spain in the Pacific, both houses of Congress ratified the Hawaiian annexation by joint resolution, a procedure that required only a simple majority of the votes cast rather than the two-thirds vote required for passage in the Senate.

The Spanish-American War. Most Spanish colonies in South and Central America had won their independence by the mid 1820s, but with its strong naval force Spain continued to hold its territory in the Caribbean. By 1896 the Cubans' call for freedom had led the Spanish to establish a ruthless military regime, which attempted to prevent Cubans from joining rebel forces at night by gathering many of them behind Spanish lines in detention centers called *reconcentrados,* a term translated in the American press as "concentration camps."

Fanning the Flames. American sympathy for the Cuban rebels was fueled by press coverage of the conflict in U.S. newspapers. Led by Joseph Pulitzer's *New York World* and William Randolph Hearst's *New York Journal*—which were engaged in a major circulation war—American newspapers tried to outdo each other with gruesome and heart-wrenching stories of Spanish torture and mistreatment of captured prisoners. Although President Cleveland tried to maintain neutrality, offering to help Spain bring about peace through instituting Cuban home rule, Spain refused the offer. In November 1896 Republican William McKinley was elected president on a platform that endorsed Cuban independence, and by 1898 pressure had mounted for the United States to side actively with the rebels and to demand Cuba's independence from Spain. Though many American business leaders opposed intervention, $50 million in U.S. investments in Cuban mining and sugar created another incentive to bring an end to Spanish rule.

War. In a show of naval force President McKinley ordered the U.S. battleship *Maine* to visit Havana, Cuba. On 15 February 1898, while in the harbor, the ship exploded and sank. Many suspected sabotage, although later accounts suggest that the explosion was accidental. Urged on by widespread cries of "Remember the Maine!," McKinley demanded that Spain make a truce with Cuban rebels. Spain agreed, but the United States prepared for war, and on 20 April, at the request of President McKinley, Congress recognized Cuban independence and authorized the use of military force if Spain did not agree to withdraw by the twenty-third. On 22 April McKinley ordered a partial blockade of Cuban ports, prompting Spain to declare war on 24 April. The next day the United States declared war on Spain, retroactive to 21 April. After a brief series of military engagements, the United States defeated Spain. Commodore George Dewey led the Pacific naval squadron to victory over the Spanish fleet in the Battle of Manila Bay on 1 May 1898, winning a promotion to admiral and the adulation of the American people. Victories on 1 July at El Caney and San Juan Hill in Cuba, where American troops included Col. Theodore Roosevelt's famous "Rough Riders," were followed by a naval victory off Santiago on 3 July that spelled defeat for Spain, which surrendered on 17 July. In the peace treaty signed on 10 December, Spain sold its territory in the Philippines to the United States for $20 million, renounced all claims to Cuba, and ceded Guam and Puerto Rico to the United States as indemnity for the costs of the war.

Lt. Col. Theodore Roosevelt (center) with some of his "Rough Riders" after the Battle of San Juan Hill, July 1898

The Legacy of the War. The brief Spanish-American War justified the massive, ongoing program of naval modernization and expansion. Its outcome raised the key question of how the United States was to deal with its newly acquired overseas empire, which also included uninhabited Wake Island, claimed by the United States in 1898 as a military outpost, and some of the Samoan Islands, partitioned by the United States and Germany in 1899. On the eve of the twentieth century the United States found itself deeply involved in the difficult international politics of the Caribbean and the Philippines, no longer insulated from the conflicts and tensions of the rest of the world.

Political Divides. Politicians split over what to do with the new territories. "Jingoists" argued that as a great nation, the United States should have an empire like those of the major nations of western Europe, which were competing fiercely for control of raw materials, markets, and military outposts around the globe. Many Americans believed that the "Anglo-Saxon race" was destined by God and nature to govern "inferior" peoples such as Cubans, Puerto Ricans, Filipinos, and Polynesians. Anti-imperialists, many of whom were old enough to remember the Civil War, argued that as a democracy, the United States should not possess a colonial empire. Sharing the jingoists' unenlightened racial views, many

anti-imperialists also pointed out that if the new possessions became U.S. territories, with the promise that they could eventually become states, the nation would be admitting as citizens millions of Spanish-speaking peoples, many of African-Latin and Asian ancestry.

The Compromise. President McKinley, who was standing for reelection in 1900, found himself torn between the two positions. He and Congress eventually settled on a series of compromises. They reaffirmed the independence of Cuba, but with a provision that the United States could intervene to maintain democratic government in the new country. Many Cubans found the provision insulting to their capability for self-government. To make such intervention possible and to ensure the sea lanes past Cuba, the United States claimed a large military reservation on the southeastern end of the Island at Guantánamo Bay. Puerto Rico, Guam, and American Samoa were made U.S. territories, while a U.S. civil government was set up in the Philippines, with the commitment to grant independence when the United States believed the Filipinos were "ready" for self-government. (The Philippines did not achieve full independence until 1946.) Like most compromises, these settlements satisfied no one. From 1899 through 1902 a brutal guerrilla war continued between U.S. troops and insurgents in the Philippines, with scattered resistance until 1906. By the turn of the century the United States, long an advocate of democratic self-government, found itself in control of an empire.

Sources:

Ernest R. May, *Imperial Democracy: The Emergence of America as a Great Power* (New York: Harcourt, Brace & World, 1961);

H. Wayne Morgan, *America's Road to Empire: The War with Spain and Overseas Expansion* (New York: Wiley, 1965);

Thomas J. Osborne, *"Empire Can Wait": American Opposition to Hawaiian Annexation, 1893–1898* (Kent, Ohio: Kent State University Press, 1981);

William Adam Russ Jr., *The Hawaiian Republic, 1894–98, and Its Struggle to Win Annexation* (Selinsgrove, Pa.: Susquehanna University Press, 1961);

David F. Trask, *The War with Spain in 1898* (New York: Macmillan / London: Collier Macmillan, 1898).

MOVEMENTS FOR CHANGE: NATIONALISTS AND SINGLE TAXERS

Opposing Big Money. The rapid growth of monopolies, first in the railroads and then in basic industries such as oil refining and steel production, came as a shock to many Americans. As monopolies drove out small business by undercutting their prices, a deep-rooted suspicion of the concentration of wealth and power spread among American middle-class voters and consumers. During the 1880s and 1890s reformers offered a range of new solutions to the problem of rapid industrialization, hoping to restore a more harmonious balance between city and country, employers and employees, large and small businesses. Many hoped to distribute the nation's expanding wealth more fairly and to dilute the concen-

By most any account the White House was in a disgraceful state of disrepair at the end of the nineteenth century. The budget for maintenance of the president's residence was appropriated by Congress, and testy legislators used that power to keep the chief executive humble. Presidents who protested ran the risk of seeming, in the electorate's judgment, to have misplaced priorities. People may have thought that palaces were for kings, but the official presidential residence fell so far short of palatial splendor that some presidents were ashamed to entertain foreign heads of state there.

The White House, which seemed spacious in Jefferson's day, was uncomfortably cramped during the presidencies of Garfield, Cleveland, Harrison, and McKinley. Because the space was available years earlier, an array of bureaucratic offices had moved into the White House, with little regard for the president's privacy or safety. Areas formerly reserved for guests were turned into offices. Because of its heavy use, the building required a high level of maintenance, which was neglected. The plumbing was archaic by post–Civil War standards; the ceilings sagged; and the walls reportedly creaked eerily, perhaps the result of the refurbishing that took place after the building was burned during the War of 1812. The house was also damp and drafty, causing illness and even deaths of some pre–Civil

War presidents, in the view of Theodore Roosevelt, who insisted on remodeling after he took office in 1901.

Frances Cleveland complained about the dreariness of the presidential living quarters during her husband's first term; in 1886, his second year in office, she had married President Cleveland in the Blue Room, which had been substantially spruced up for the occasion. At the time there was a single telephone in the White House and a staff of seven, of whom five were assigned to help the first lady with the taxing responsibilities of entertaining a parade of dignitaries. Caroline Harrison, whose husband was chief executive between Cleveland's two terms in office, complained more effectively. She got Congress to grant funds for interior renovations, including repair of hazardous wiring, and she had a telephone switchboard installed. She also got authorization to have an exterminator deal with the rats that infested the building. When Cleveland was elected to a second term in 1892, the living quarters were too cramped for his growing family. Mrs. Cleveland redecorated the Red Room and had the living quarters painted and newly wallpapered. Still, she was more comfortable elsewhere, and the Clevelands lived in their own home, except when official duties required the president's presence on Pennsylvania Avenue.

---

tration of power in the hands of a few corporations. Two of these reform movements came from individuals whose best-selling books galvanized readers across the country.

Henry George and the Single Tax. In 1871 Californian Henry George, a newspaperman and printer, published *Our Land and Land Policy,* a pamphlet in which he set out his doctrine of a single tax. George argued that land values rose not solely because owners made improvements on their land but also because population growth increased the demand for it. The amount of land could not be added to, and as more people competed to own a fixed amount of land, its value rose. George reasoned that a single tax on the increased land value, taxing what he called the "unearned increment," would benefit society as a whole by sharply reducing the disparity between the wealthy and poor. George elaborated on his single tax in his best-selling book *Progress and Poverty* (1879). Soon, Single-Tax Clubs were established across the United States, attracting reform-minded individuals who believed the single tax alone could restore a more egalitarian society. George himself twice ran unsuccessfully for mayor of New York City, dying in 1897 during his second attempt.

Edward Bellamy's Nationalist Vision. New Englander Edward Bellamy offered another solution to the problem of economic disparity. Bellamy believed that the process of forming monopolies was a natural one and would lead to an efficient, single corporate enterprise that could be operated in the national interest by the government. In 1888 Bellamy published a utopian novel, *Looking Backward, 2000–1887,* in which Julian West falls asleep in 1887 and wakes up in the year 2000 to discover that a new, just society has fully done away with the social and economic inequities of late-nineteenth-century industrialism. In the year 2000 all businesses have been consolidated into a single enterprise operated by the government, and everyone finds suitable employment in the "Industrial Army." Furthermore, every citizen accepts responsibility for his or her fellow citizens in "mutual obligation of citizen to nation, and nation to citizen." *Looking Backward* became a best-seller, selling more than three hundred thousand copies within the first two years of its publication. In 1890 more than five hundred thousand Americans nationwide, including many leading reformers, belonged to "Nationalist Clubs." Though the Nationalist and Single-Tax move-

The White House kitchen, circa 1890

ments faltered, their existence revealed Americans' anxiety about the emerging industrial economy and the growing energies of political reform.

Source:
John L. Thomas, *Alternative America: Henry George, Edward Bellamy, Henry Demorest Lloyd, and the Adversary Tradition* (Cambridge, Mass.: Harvard University Press, 1983).

MOVEMENTS FOR CHANGE: POPULISM AND PROGRESSIVISM

Populists. The spirit of protest —whether generated by radicals and labor unionists, by critics such as George and Bellamy, or by farmers reeling from low prices—animated third-party politics in the 1880s and 1890s. During the 1880s diverse agrarian organizations such as the Farmers' Union, the Texas State Alliance, and the National Colored Farmer's Alliance joined forces to form two large national organizations: the Southern Alliance and the National Farmers Alliance of the Northwest. These groups singled out several enemies, including the "Eastern money interests" that controlled monetary supply and policy, the network of middlemen who moved crops from field to market, the large railroad companies whose influence over the agricultural economy and national politics was widespread, industrial monopolies, and supporters of the gold standard. Eager for a solution to the many problems faced by farmers in the 1880s and 1890s, the alliances supported a broad program of political, economic, and monetary reform.

The People's Party. The genesis of the People's Party, or Populists, came in December 1889, when representatives of the two farmers alliances and labor groups met in Saint Louis with members of the Grange—a militant group that had been forming farm cooperatives and fighting for government regulation of the rates charged farmers by railroads and warehouses—and members of the Greenback Party, founded in 1875 by Grangers and others favoring the circulation of more paper money and opposing a return to the gold standard. The Greenback Party had unsuccessfully fielded presidential candidates in the 1876, 1880, and 1884 elections and had had some success in the congressional elections of 1878, but it had become largely defunct after 1884. The People's Party combined agrarian and labor protests and the farming interests of the South and West against the rich and more politically powerful East. The first statewide People's Party was formed in Kansas, and more soon followed. On 19 May 1891 at a gathering in Cincinnati more than fourteen hundred delegates from thirty-two states formed the national People's Party.

The Populist Platform. The Populists called for many of the reforms demanded by farm and labor interests, including increased coinage of silver money, a national currency, governmental regulation or ownership of all transportation and communication lines, a graduated income tax, lower tariffs on manufactured goods, a postal savings bank, direct elections of U.S. senators, adoption of the secret ballot, the establishment of the initiative and the referendum (measures that allowed the introduction and passage of laws by direct vote of the people), prohibition of foreign ownership of land, a shorter workweek, and restrictions on immigration. One of the Populists' more radical proposals was Southern Alliance leader Charles W. Macunis's "sub-treasury system," a plan that called for government warehouses where farmers could deposit their crops and receive credit—in the form of greenbacks—until the crops were sold.

Setting a National Agenda. The Populist Party proved to be an important force in national politics, with impressive showings in the 1892 and 1894 elections, and the party succeeded in bringing the issues of money supply, labor and farm grievances, anxiety about monopolies (particularly the railroads), and the unfair effects of the tariff to the national stage. Many Americans were frightened by the Populist alliance between farmers and laborers, seeing their ideas as radical and potentially dangerous for the country. While the Populist Party went down to defeat in the 1896 presidential election, when they endorsed the Democrats' free-silver candidate, William Jennings Bryan, many of their proposals were taken over by progressive candidates in other parties, and the Populist movement continued to animate national politics until World War I.

Progressivism. By the end of the nineteenth century reformers in both major political parties were calling themselves "progressives" to indicate their commitment to a just and equitable society. These reformers were spurred on by accounts of urban blight written by reporters such as Jacob Riis, by political orators such as Populist and Democrat Williams Jennings Bryan, and by grassroots organizations such as the Nationalist Clubs and the Single-Tax Clubs. Furthermore, constant agitation over the limited money supply, poor working conditions, the discriminatory tariff, and the restriction of women from voting, led many reform-minded citizens and politicians to search for new ways to address problems spawned by rapid urbanization and industrialization. Rather than a single party, progressivism was a loose coalition of reform groups and impulses that shaped national and local politics well into the twentieth century.

Cleaning up Corruption. Progressivism developed from a wide variety of pressures for modernizing society and for cleaning up corruption on local, state, and national levels. Moral reformers attacked the spoils system, political corruption, boodle, and the power of saloons. Many of these reformers worked at the municipal level, and helped to elect reform mayors and city councils in small and large cities. Other groups sought to establish a more sound political democracy, advocating direct election of senators, a secret ballot, and votes for women. Still others hoped to modernize government by bringing the navy and military up to date and by building a stronger federal government that could regulate corporations and the economy. Many hoped to take what they saw as the short-sighted, narrow-minded focus of partisan politics out of important national policy issues such as the money supply and tariffs and to create a governing class that would watch out for national rather than local and party-based allegiances.

Working within the Two-Party System. Progressive reformers continued build a political power base through elections. As with the Greenback Labor Party, the Populists, Henry George, and the prohibition movements, progressives attempted to gain control of political parties and to win elections on the state and national levels. Unlike earlier reformers, however, progressives worked within the Democratic and Republican Parties, lining up behind whichever candidate endorsed the reforms they supported.

Sources:

Lawrence Goodwyn, *The Populist Movement: A Short History of the Agrarian Revolt in America* (New York: Oxford University Press, 1978);

Steven Hahn, *The Roots of Southern Populism: Yeoman Farmers and the Transformation of the Georgia Up Country, 1850–1890* (New York: Oxford University Press, 1983);

Richard Hofstadter, *The Age of Reform: From Bryan to F.D.R.* (New York: Knopf, 1955);

Morton Keller, *Affairs of State: Public Life in Late Nineteenth Century America* (Cambridge, Mass.: Harvard University Press, 1977).

MOVEMENTS FOR CHANGE: TEMPERANCE AND PROHIBITION

Temperance and the Prohibition Party. Alcohol use and abuse had long been a key issue for reformers when antiliquor activists turned to presidential politics to end what they saw as the degenerative effect of alcohol on the family and the moral fiber of the country. The Prohibition Party, formed in 1869, was a well-organized, vocal organization that had run candidates in every presidential election since 1872, reaching the peak of its influence in 1892. Unlike the Greenback and Populist Parties, the Prohibition Party did not work through coalitions. Although it also supported woman suffrage, prison reform, and the prohibition of gambling, the party focused on a single issue and pursued the dominant strategy of achieving the prohibition of alcohol by fielding a successful presidential candidate. Although no Prohibition presidential candidate was ever elected, they often received enough votes to influence the outcomes of the close presidential elections of the 1880s and 1890s. In these close contests Prohibitionists most often hurt Republicans more than Democrats.

The Anti-Saloon League. Some temperance supporters did not share in the presidential orientation of the Prohibition Party. In 1895 these reformers, many of them middle-class women, formed the Anti-Saloon League, which focused its campaigns on the disastrous effects of alcohol on families and the growing influence of corrupt politicians in urban political machines. Building on state prohibition successes in New England and the Midwest, the Anti-Saloon League worked for passage of a constitutional amendment that would prohibit the manufacture and sale of alcoholic beverages nationwide. This movement eventually succeeded with the passage of the Eighteenth Amendment in 1919.

A Broad Movement for Reform. The Anti-Saloon League attracted support from middle-class professional men and women who believed that widespread emigration from Ireland, Germany, and later Central Europe, was changing the political and social landscape of the country. Municipal political machines that relied on the

Uncle Sam wearing a crown of thorns, an editorial cartoonist's response to William Jennings Bryan's famous "Cross of Gold" speech at the 1896 Democratic National Convention

votes of recently naturalized immigrants and the poor often used saloons as informal gathering halls. Saloon keepers played key roles in the political machine, often by distributing "the spoils"—or jobs—awarded to loyal supporters and by overseeing the fraudulent voting system that ensured the "right" people won local elections. For these reasons, the Anti-Saloon movement drew support from a much wider array of people than the largely one-issue Prohibition Party.

Sources:

Ruth Bordin, *Woman and Temperance: The Quest for Power and Liberty, 1873–1900* (New Brunswick, N.J.: Rutgers University Press, 1990);

Norman H. Clark, *Deliver Us From Evil: An Interpretation of American Prohibition* (New York: Norton, 1976);

Robert H. Wiebe, *The Search for Order, 1877–1920* (New York: Hill & Wang, 1967).

PRESIDENTIAL ELECTIONS

Close Elections. Between the disputed presidential election of 1876 and the dramatic contest of 1896, presidential elections were close contests in which minor-party candidates drew enough votes away from the Republicans and Democrats to ensure that neither major party candidate won a majority of the popular vote. The two major parties did all they could—legally and illegally—to ensure their own candidate's victory. Presidential elections in the 1880s were battles over political patronage, with little disagreement over issues between the two major parties.

Third Parties. The issues-oriented politics of the 1880s came from a series of third parties that gained national followings with single-issue campaigns that pulled votes away from the major party candidates. The 1880 and 1884 elections marked the gradual decline of the Greenback-Labor Party, which favored increasing the supply of paper money and opposed a return to the gold standard. The party had its strongest showing in the 1878 congressional elections, winning more than one million votes and fourteen seats in the House of Representatives. In 1880 its presidential candidate, James B. Weaver, garnered more than three hundred thousand votes (3.32 percent). After Greenback-Laborite Benjamin Franklin Butler won just over 175,000 votes (1.7 percent) in 1884, the party became largely defunct, with some members later joining the Populist Party. In 1885 Adin Thayer concluded that "the result of the election settles the question that one of the two great parties will continue to control the government, and that there will be no new national party for a generation to come that will have any considerable influence in politics." The next third party to gain a national voice was the single-issue Prohibition Party. In 1884 Prohibition candidate John P. St. John of Kansas received nearly 150,000 votes (1.47 percent) in a close election in which Democrat Grover Cleveland defeated Republican James G. Blaine in the popular voting by less than twenty-six thousand votes. In 1888 Prohibition candidate Clinton Fisk received nearly 250,000 votes (2.19 percent), and in 1892 Prohibitionist John Bidwell won more than 270,000 votes (2.25 percent). The party exerted strong pressure on Republican platforms and candidates throughout the Midwest and found supporters among churchgoing rural areas in the North and among middle-class southerners who feared the effects of liquor on blacks and poor whites. Prohibition was too narrow an issue to carry the country, but the Populists absorbed many of the concerns of the Prohibition Party in the 1890s.

The People's Party, or Populists. In July 1892 the first formal Populist national convention brought together an impressive group of speakers, including Ignatius Donnelly of Minnesota, Jeremiah "Sockless Jerry" Simpson of Kansas, and Tom Watson of Georgia. As their presidential candidate the convention nominated James B. Weaver of Iowa, who had run for president of the Greenback ticket in 1880, and for his running mate they chose James G. Field of Virginia, a former Confederate general. This ticket earned more than one million popular votes (8.5 percent) of the roughly twelve million cast in the 1892 presidential election and won five states outright for a total of twenty-two electoral votes. The Populists also did well in the 1894 congressional elections. Support for the party faded after the 1896 presidential election, in which the Populists backed Democratic candidate William Jennings Bryan, but much of their platform was co-opted by the Democrats.

An Italian brass band from Buffalo, New York, visiting Republican presidential candidate William McKinley at home in Canton, Ohio, during his 1896 "front-porch campaign"

The Election of 1880. With President Hayes keeping a promise to serve only one term, the Republicans were divided over the presidential nomination, with various factions supporting former president Ulysses S. Grant, Sen. James G. Blaine of Maine, and Treasury Secretary John Sherman of Ohio. On the thirty-fourth ballot, however, a darkhorse candidate emerged: Sherman's campaign manager, James A. Garfield, former speaker of the House and senator-elect from Ohio. Despite his protests that he was not a candidate, Garfield, who had a distinguished military record as brigadier general in the Union army, won the nomination on the thirty-sixth ballot. Chester A. Arthur of New York was chosen as Garfield's running mate on the first ballot. To prevent the Republicans from "waving the bloody shirt" at them as the party of southern whites and Confederate sympathizers, the Democrats turned to another distinguished Union general, Winfield Scott Hancock. His only real opposition came from supporters of the 1876 Democratic standard-bearer, Samuel J. Tilden of New York, who announced after the first ballot that he was not a candidate. Hancock won the nomination easily on the third ballot, and Rep. William H. English of Indiana was the Democrats unanimous choice for the second spot on the ticket. In the November election Garfield narrowly edged out Hancock in the popular voting, garnering 4,446,158 votes (48.27 percent) to 4,444,260 (48.25 percent) for Hancock. Yet Garfield swept the heavily populated northeastern and midwestern states, winning in the electoral college by a margin of 214–155.

The Election of 1884. After the assassination of President Garfield in 1881, Vice President Arthur became president. His efforts to reform the civil-service system had earned him the enmity of the Stalwarts in his party. Republicans turned to James G. Blaine, who had served as Speaker of the House and secretary of state under Garfield and Harrison. As the "plumed knight" of reform and a leader among the Half Breeds in 1876, he had been a presidential contender until charges that he had taken bribes from the railroads destroyed his chances for the presidential nomination. Yet despite the allegations against him, he had remained popular in his party. After Blaine defeated Arthur on the fourth ballot, the party nominated Stalwart John A. Logan, a senator from Illinois, for the vice presidency. The Democrats nominated a reform candidate, Gov. Grover Cleveland of New York, who arrived at the convention as the front-runner and won on the third ballot. The party nominated Sen. Thomas A. Hendricks of Indiana for his running mate. The ensuing presidential campaign was one of the dirtiest in American history. Democratic newspapers reprinted the old charges against Blaine, as well as new letters with more embarrassing disclosures. The Republican press responded by revealing that as a young bachelor Cleveland had fathered an illegitimate child. Cleveland admitted paternity. As Democrats chanted "Blaine, Blaine, James G. Blaine, the continental liar from the state of Maine," Republicans responded with "Ma, Ma, where's my pa?" (After Cleveland won the election, Democrats gleefully added: "Gone to the White House, ha, ha, ha.") Blaine was also hurt when a visitor to his New York headquarters, the Reverend Samuel D. Burchard, referred to the Democrats as the party of "rum, Romanism, and rebellion." Blaine, who heard the remark, did not repudiate it, severely damaging his chances with Irish Americans, whose vote he had been courting. The various charges and countercharges hurt Blaine more than Cleveland, as disillusioned Republican Mugwumps defected to the Democratic camp. Cleveland defeated Blaine by fewer than twenty-six thousand popular votes (48.5 percent to 48.25 percent) and thirty-seven electoral votes (219–182), becoming the first Democratic president since before the Civil War.

The Election of 1888. The Democrats renominated incumbent president Grover Cleveland by acclamation and easily agreed on former senator Allen G. Thurman of Ohio as his running mate, to replace Vice President Thomas A. Hendricks, who had died in 1885. When the Republican National Convention began in late June the front-runner was Sen. John Sherman of Ohio, who led the voting on the first six ballots but lacked the necessary votes to secure the nomination. With the fourth ballot, however, a groundswell of support began for a grandson of President William H. Harrison, a little-known Indiana lawyer and former senator named Benjamin Harrison. After supporters of James G. Blaine gave up hope that he would recant his refusal to run again, they shifted their votes to Harrison on the seventh ballot. Harrison took the lead in the voting and won the nomination easily on the next roll call. Former congressman Levi P. Morton of New York won the vice-presidential nomination easily on the first round of balloting. Both Harrison and Cleveland were equally uncharismatic and relied on their respective party organizations for voter appeals. The Republicans scored points by attacking Cleveland for his advocacy of lower tariffs, his veto of veterans' pension bills, and his signing of an order to return Confederate battle flags to the South. Rumors also circulated that he was a drunkard and a wife beater. Cleveland won in the popular voting by a margin of less than one hundred thousand votes (48.62 percent to 47.82 percent), but Harrison took most of the heavily populated northern and midwestern states, including the key states of Indiana and New York, winning the election in the electoral college by a vote of 233–168.

The Election of 1892. Despite opposition within their own parties Harrison and Cleveland easily won the nominations of their respective parties on the first ballots. The Republicans replaced incumbent vice president Levi P. Morton on the ticket with Whitelaw Reid, ambassador to France and former editor of *The New York Tribune*. Adlai Ewing Stevenson of Illinois (grandfather of the Democratic presidential candidate in 1952 and 1956) won the second spot on the Democratic ticket. With Populist candidate Weaver waging the most successful third-party campaign of the nineteenth century, Cleveland defeated Harrison by more than 370,000

popular votes (46.05 percent to 42.96 percent) and 132 electoral votes (277–145).

The Election of 1896. Discontent with the Bourbon Democrats in general, and particularly Cleveland and the depressed economy over which he presided, culminated in the emergence of a different Democratic Party in 1896. No one shaped this new direction more than Illinois governor John Peter Altgeld, who seized control of the party platform and attempted to cut the party free of Bourbon Democrat machines and the gold standard.

William Jennings Bryan. While Altgeld shaped the platform for the upcoming election, William Jennings Bryan was the spokesman for the new Democrats. A charismatic Nebraska lawyer, Bryan earned a national reputation in the early 1890s with an assault on the McKinley Tariff of 1890, which set import duties at an all-time high. Skillfully responding to the growing agrarian discontent, Bryan took up the free-silver issue with a vengeance, and by 1896 he was the leading champion of farmers. Adopting the populist slogan "Equal Rights to All and Special Privileges to None," Bryan brought some of the vitality of the Populist Party to the divided Democratic Party. His capacity to draw crucial support from both Populists and "Silver Democrats" made him a powerful player in the 1896 political season.

"Cross of Gold." At the 1896 party convention, the thirty-six-year-old Bryan regaled Democrats with his famous "Cross of Gold" speech during the floor debate on the currency plank in the platform. Announcing that the country could not exist without farmers, Bryan called for an end to the single gold standard and unrestricted coinage of silver and gold, saying: "You shall not press down upon the brow of labor this crown of thorns. You shall not crucify mankind upon a cross of gold." The speech electrified the convention and was instrumental in winning him the presidential nomination on the fifth ballot at the divided convention. Arthur Sewall of Maine was the Democrats' choice for the second slot on the ticket.

New Divisions. Bryan's position on silver divided the party, and some Democrats who favored the gold standard bolted for the Republican Party while others organized the National Democratic Party, which nominated John M. Palmer of Illinois and Simon B. Buckner of Kentucky to run on a platform that supported the gold standard. Western Republicans who supported free silver formed the National Silver Party and endorsed Bryan and Sewall. The Populists were divided as well. To avoid splitting the free-silver vote between two candidates, they eventually gave their presidential nomination to Bryan. Yet some Populists feared that the free-silver issue would overshadow their broader reform goals. Western Populists supported joining with Silver Democrats while southern Populists held out for a third-party campaign. The Populists chose Thomas E. Watson of Georgia rather than Sewall as their vice-presidential candidate.

The Republicans. Under the leadership of Mark Hanna, an Ohio businessman-turned-politician, the GOP also set a new course, becoming the party of industrial capitalism. As campaign manager for Gov. William McKinley of Ohio, Hanna had spent more than a year before the convention courting delegates for his candidate, especially in the South. His hard work paid off when McKinley won the presidential nomination handily on the first ballot. McKinley supporter Garret A. Hobart of New Jersey won the vice-presidential nomination almost as easily. Lacking Bryan's charisma, McKinley had quiet dignity and an impressive record of service in the Civil War. Running on the promise of the "full dinner pail," McKinley argued that high tariffs and adherence to the gold standard protected American companies as well as the jobs and wages of their employees.

The Campaign. Both Bryan and McKinley set new records for campaigning. Bryan's speaking tours covered an unprecedented twenty-seven states. He traveled some eighteen thousand miles by train, speaking up to thirty-six times a day and reaching about five million people. Bryan took on a messianic aura with crowds of people pressing close to him just to touch his clothes. His opponents tried to depict him as a radical antichrist who would plunge the nation into anarchy. McKinley did not travel but also reached substantial numbers of voters. Hanna ran an organized, efficient campaign, using opinion polls to pinpoint areas in which to concentrate campaign efforts and producing hundreds of millions of pamphlets, fliers, and books depicting McKinley as an exemplar of solid middle-class and working-class values.

Republican Dominance. McKinley became the first presidential candidate since Ulysses S. Grant in 1872 to win a majority of the popular vote (51.01 percent to 46.73 percent for Bryan). Bryan did well in the West and the South, but with a strong showing in the more populous Northeast and Midwest McKinley defeated Bryan in the electoral college by a vote of 271–176. The election solidified Republican gains in the 1894 congressional elections, assured the national supremacy of the party for a generation, and established its position as the voice of industrial, middle-class America. Until 1912 Bryan remained nearly unchallenged as the leader of the Democratic Party, an uneasy coalition of his western and southern populist and agrarian supporters and Altgeld's northern liberals. With the exception of Woodrow Wilson's two terms in 1913–1921, Republicans controlled the White House until 1933.

Sources:

Richard Hofstadter, *The Age of Reform: From Bryan to F.D.R.* (New York: Knopf, 1955);

Stanley Llewellyn Jones, *The Presidential Election of 1896* (Madison: University of Wisconsin Press, 1964);

Morton Keller, *Affairs of State: Public Life in Late Nineteenth Century America* (Cambridge, Mass.: Harvard University Press, 1977);

Gil Troy, *See How They Run: The Changing Role of the Presidential Candidate* (New York: Free Press, 1991).

HEADLINE MAKERS

CHESTER A. ARTHUR

1829-1886

PRESIDENT OF THE UNITED STATES,

1881-1885

Stalwart Turned Reformer. A member of the Stalwart faction of the Republican Party, Chester A. Arthur was elected vice president in 1880 and became president on 19 September 1881, after the death of President James A. Garfield from wounds inflicted by an assassin. As president, Arthur surprised his Stalwart allies, who expected him to uphold political patronage and their conservative agenda on major issues, by working to reform the civil-service system and to lower protective tariffs.

Background. Born in Fairfield, Vermont, on 5 October 1829, Chester Alan Arthur was the fifth child of a Baptist clergyman and abolitionist. The family moved often as the Reverend William Arthur was assigned to different churches. By 1844 they were living in Schenectady, New York, where the following year Chester Arthur entered Union College as a sophomore and graduated in 1848. After teaching school and studying law in his spare time for several years, Arthur became a clerk in a New York law firm, where he continued his legal studies and passed the bar examination in May 1854.

Early Career. Two of the cases on which Arthur worked during his early years as an attorney involved the rights of African Americans; one ensured the freedom of a group of slaves who had been brought to New York by their owner while the other led to the integration of the New York streetcar system. In 1859 he married Ellen Lewis Herndon, a native of Virginia. Having become involved with local Republican politics shortly after his arrival in New York City, Arthur was appointed to Gov. Edwin D. Morgan's general staff in January 1861. During the Civil War he worked with the governor in organizing state volunteers for the Union cause. He was given

the rank of brigadier general, and by July 1862 he had been named quartermaster general of New York State. The job ended when a Democratic governor took office in January 1863. Arthur returned to his law practice while continuing to be active in Republican politics, remaining a loyal member of the Stalwart, or conservative, wing of the party.

Federal Appointee. In 1871, during the administration of President Ulysses S. Grant, Arthur was appointed collector of the Port of New York, where about 75 percent of U.S. customs duties were collected. In that lucrative post, which earned him roughly $50,000 a year, he controlled more than one thousand federal employees, organizing their political activity for the New York Republican Party. In 1878 President Rutherford B. Hayes tried to inaugurate a merit system for government employees. After a federal investigation of customs houses in several major port cities, Hayes ordered all federal employees to refrain from managing "political organizations, caucuses, conventions, or election campaigns." When Arthur and an associate, Alonzo Cornell, refused to cease political activity, Hayes replaced them.

National Office. Two years later, when Arthur arrived at the Republican National Convention, the intraparty battle between the conservative Stalwarts and the reformers was still raging. James Garfield, who represented the reform wing, won the presidential nomination, and Arthur was chosen as his running mate to provide some satisfaction to the Stalwarts of New York. After the Republican ticket was elected, Garfield served for fewer than four months before he was felled by an assassin's bullet on 2 July 1881 and lingered for just over two months before he died. Garfield's assassin, a deranged office seeker named Charles Guiteau, claimed that he was a Stalwart and had shot Garfield because he wanted Arthur to be president.

President Arthur. His wife having died in January 1881, Arthur was one of a handful of unmarried U.S. presidents. He was a large man, six feet two inches tall and heavily built, and he dressed impeccably, looking the part of a dignified leader. Although he never sought the presidency, he did his best to administer the government fairly. During his administration the federal government showed a regular surplus of revenue over expenditure, and several steps were taken to modernize the U.S. Navy. Stung by Guiteau's remarks, Arthur distanced himself from the Stalwarts, and he tried to clean up government corruption. He investigated frauds and abuses in the civil service, especially in the granting of post-office contracts, and helped to pass the Pendleton Civil Service Act (1883). As a consequence, he lost the support of many Stalwarts, without winning the support of reformers. In 1882 his vetoes of an $18 million "pork barrel" rivers and harbors bill and the Chinese Exclusion Act on the grounds that it violated the Burlingame Treaty of 1868 did little to endear him to Congress, which overrode both vetoes. He did not win his party's nomination for the presidency in 1884. He died of Bright's disease on 18 November 1886.

Sources:

Justus D. Doenecke, *The Presidencies of James A. Garfield and Chester A. Arthur* (Lawrence: Regents Press of Kansas, 1981);

Thomas C. Reeves, *Gentleman Boss: The Life of Chester Alan Arthur* (New York: Knopf, 1975).

WILLIAM JENNINGS BRYAN

1860-1925
DEMOCRATIC PRESIDENTIAL CANDI-DATE, 1896, 1900, 1908

The Great Commoner. Known as the "Boy Orator of the Platte" for his stirring oratory and as the Great Commoner for his representation of the poor, the working class, and the farmer, William Jennings Bryan based his political strength in the South and West of the United States. Yet his widespread appeal showed that national politics at the end of the nineteenth century had begun to move away from a focus on regional interests and toward representing class interests and developing a national economic and monetary policy.

Background. Born in Salem, Illinois, on 19 March 1860, William Jennings Bryan earned an A.B. (1881) and A.M. (1884) from Illinois College and a law degree (1884) at Union Law School in Chicago. After practicing law and becoming active in Democratic Party politics in Illinois, he moved to Lincoln, Nebraska, and opened a law office in 1888. In 1890 he ran for Congress as a Democrat, winning in a normally Republican district. In 1892 and again in 1895 he sought election to the Senate, but failed to win enough support in the Nebraska legislature, which was controlled by the Republicans. In the House of Representatives Bryan spoke out against high tariffs and in favor of the free coinage of silver, winning a reputation as a spellbinding orator. After his second term ended in March 1896, Bryan, who had already decided to run for president, became editor of the *Omaha World Herald*.

Presidential Candidate. As a delegate to the 1896 Democratic National Convention, he took an active part in the free-silver movement, causing a sensation with his "Cross of Gold" speech. The Democrats chose him as their presidential candidate, despite the opposition of the New York wing of the party, which remained conservative and probusiness. His opponents and some of his supporters began to call him the "Boy Orator of the Platte." Bryan conducted a vigorous speaking campaign, arguing for "bimetallism"—the free coinage of silver and gold—and fighting for the working man against big business and financial interests. He also received the nomination of the Populist Party. Breaking with the tradition holding that presidential candidates should say little and be seen even less, Bryan made more than six hundred speeches in twenty-nine states, covering more than thirteen thousand miles in a hard campaign. The Republicans, who had nominated William McKinley, depicted Bryan as an anarchist and revolutionist. In the end Bryan won almost 6.5 million votes of the nearly 14 million cast, but lost to McKinley. Perhaps more than any other election in the period, the election of 1896 demonstrated the national division that pitted the poor, the debtors, and the farmers of the South and West—who supported Bryan—against the industrialists, much of the middle class, professionals, and the rich of the Northeast—who supported McKinley.

Later Career. Bryan served briefly as colonel of the Third Nebraska Regiment, which became known as the "Silver Regiment," during the Spanish-American War, but he became ill and received a medical discharge before the regiment was shipped out for occupation duty in Cuba. He won the Democratic presidential nomination again in 1900 and 1908, each time losing by a wider margin than he had in 1896. As secretary of state under President Woodrow Wilson in 1913–1915, Bryan opposed American involvement in World War I, resigning in protest when it became clear that Wilson was moving away from neutrality. Bryan's final time in the public spotlight came in 1925, when he served as attorney for the prosecution in the so-called Scopes Monkey Trial, opposing the teaching of Charles Darwin's theory of evolution. The aging Bryan was no match for defense attorney Clarence Darrow, and the Great Commoner died on 25 July 1925, soon after the conclusion of the trial.

Sources:

David D. Anderson, *William Jennings Bryan* (Boston: Twayne, 1981);

Robert W. Cheney, *A Righteous Cause: The Life of William Jennings Bryan* (Boston: Little, Brown, 1985);

Lawrence W. Levine, *Defender of the Faith* (Cambridge, Mass.: Harvard University Press, 1965).

GROVER CLEVELAND

1837-1908

PRESIDENT OF THE UNITED STATES, 1885-1889, 1893-1897

Reformer and Fiscal Conservative. The only president to serve two nonconsecutive terms, Grover Cleveland was also the only Democrat to serve in the White House between 1861 and 1913. Willing to take unpopular stands on the issues of his day, he endorsed civil-service reform, while opposing U.S. imperialism, currency inflation, and militant labor unionism. His refusal to distribute positions to loyal party members hurt him politically, as did his opposition to the free-silver movement and the railway unions.

Background. Born on 18 March 1837 in Caldwell, New Jersey, Stephen Grover Cleveland was the son of a Presbyterian clergyman, and spent much of his childhood in Fayetteville, New York, outside Syracuse. The family had intended that Grover Cleveland would attend Hamilton College, in Clinton, New York, like his older brother, but the death of their father in 1853, when Grover was sixteen, forced him to take a job as an assistant teacher at a school for the blind in New York City so he could help to support his mother and younger siblings. By the end of 1854 he was back in upstate New York, where an uncle in Buffalo hired him to assist in compiling a herd book of shorthorn cattle. In December 1855 Cleveland began clerking and reading law with a Buffalo attorney.

Entering Politics. By the time he was admitted to the bar in 1859 he had become involved in local Democratic politics and was appointed assistant district attorney by the newly elected Democratic district attorney of Erie County in November 1862. During the Civil War—with one brother a newly married, poorly paid clergyman and the other two in the army—Cleveland was solely responsible for supporting his mother and sisters, and rather than enter the military he borrowed money to pay a substitute to take his place. After losing an election for district attorney of Erie County in 1865, he became a popular and successful attorney in private practice and served three years as sheriff of Erie County (1871–1873). Known for his honesty and impartiality, he was elected mayor of Buffalo in 1881 on a platform that promised to clean up a corrupt city government controlled by a Republican machine. During the political scandals that swept the New York State Republican Party in the 1880s, Democrats realized they could win over many dissatisfied Republicans if they put forward young, reform-minded Democrats for office. Thus the forty-five-year-old Cleveland was elected governor of New York State in 1882.

Running for President. In 1884 the Democratic Party selected Cleveland as its candidate for the presidency. After the publication of letters implicating Republican candidate James G. Blaine in corruption, Republicans tried to find some scandal associated with Cleveland, who had never used political office for personal gain or to grant favors. They found, however, that the unmarried Cleveland had fathered an illegitimate child, whom he supported financially. When asked by his campaign managers what to say about the revelation, Cleveland said to tell the truth. After a bitter campaign, Cleveland was elected to the presidency. He was inaugurated on 4 March 1885, just two weeks before his forty-eighth birthday.

First Term. Cleveland married Frances Folsom, who was more than twenty-five years his junior, at the White House in 1886, and his personal life continued to be a subject of great interest to the press and his political opponents, who tried to implicate him in a variety of personal scandals. Besieged by Democratic job-seekers expecting patronage appointments from the first member of their party to serve as president since before the Civil War, Cleveland nonetheless continued the civil-service reform started under Presidents Rutherford B. Hayes, James A. Garfield, and Chester A. Arthur. He also fought for lower tariffs and was conservative in his views on federal spending.

Losing in 1888. Cleveland's civil-service reforms and his veto of a bill that would vastly expand the number of Civil War veterans eligible for federal pension hurt him in the election of 1888, which he lost to Republican Benjamin Harrison. He garnered more popular votes than Harrison but lost in the electoral college. Cleveland returned to New York and the practice of law. Opposition to Benjamin Harrison mounted after the passage of the McKinley Tariff of 1890, which raised import duties, and in 1892 the Democrats once again chose Cleveland as their presidential candidate. He beat Harrison in the election, using against his opponent not only the tariff issue but also the drain of the new pensions on the federal budget.

Second Term. Like the Populists of the 1890s, many Democrats supported the idea of inflating the currency through coinage of silver. Cleveland, however, opposed this movement and alienated the Silver Democrats by calling Congress into special session in 1893 to abolish the issuance of silver-backed notes redeemable in silver. The repeal helped to end the drain on the gold reserve that caused the Panic of 1893, but it alienated an influential faction in Cleveland's own party. Many Democrats were also angry in 1894, when Cleveland sent federal troops to Chicago to break up the Pullman railroad strike, on the grounds that the strikers had interfered with the delivery of the mails. In 1895, when he made an arrangement with J. P. Morgan and other financiers to help shore up the gold reserve, Cleveland appeared to be working hand-in-hand with big business and lost still more support within the Democratic Party. At a time when public sentiment seemed to lean toward overseas involvement, Cleveland remained a staunch anti-imperialist. He opposed and put a stop to U.S. involvement in both Cuba and Hawaii, and he negotiated a settlement with Great Britain regarding British claims against Venezuela. Cleveland died on 24 June 1908.

Source:

Richard E. Welch Jr., *The Presidency of Grover Cleveland* (Lawrence: University Press of Kansas, 1988).

GEORGE DEWEY

1837-1917

ADMIRAL, U.S. NAVY, 1899-1917

The Making of a World Power. The success of Commodore George Dewey's squadron in the Battle of Manila Bay on 1 May 1898 not only ensured U.S. victory in the Spanish-American War and made Dewey a popular American hero, but it also echoed through history, laying the groundwork for the continued role of the United States in that region of the world for the next century.

Background. Born in Montpelier, Vermont, on 26 December 1837, George Dewey graduated from the U.S. Naval Academy in 1858, and during the Civil War he served as a Union naval officer aboard the *Mississippi,* one of the ships under the command of Capt. (later admiral) David Farragut in the Battle of New Orleans in 1862. During the naval expansion of the 1880s and 1890s Dewey became chief of the Bureau of Equipment in 1889, president of the Lighthouse Board in 1893, and president of the Board of Inspection and Survey in 1895. The following year he was promoted to the rank of commodore. In 1897 he assumed command of the Asiatic Squadron in the Pacific.

The Spanish-American War. In February 1898 he received orders from Undersecretary of the Navy Theodore Roosevelt that in the event of war with Spain he should take his fleet to the Philippines and engage the Spanish navy. In the early morning hours of 1 May, less than two weeks after war was declared, Dewey moved his fleet into Manila Bay. At dawn he attacked the Spanish fleet at anchor. Dewey's squadron consisted of only four cruisers and two gunboats, but they were all more modern than were the seven Spanish ships. The Spanish fleet, however, was moored behind a minefield and protected by heavy guns mounted on shore. Following a strategy he had learned under Farragut, Dewey kept his ships in a column and steamed back and forth across the Spanish anchorage, always presenting a moving target. After seven hours of fighting, all the Spanish ships were burned, sunk, or abandoned, while Dewey's fleet escaped practically without damage. With the capture of the naval base at Cavite and the city of Manila under the guns of his ships, he accepted the surrender of the Spanish forces. The stunning victory ended forever Spanish power in the Far East. Two weeks later Congress passed a special resolution increasing by one the number of rear admirals so that Dewey could be promoted.

Naval Hero. Dewey was hailed as a national hero, and in March 1899 Congress created a new rank, Admiral of the Navy, especially for Dewey with the provision that he could choose to remain on active duty for the rest of his life or retire at full pay. When he returned to the United States in September 1899 he was honored with huge parades and other celebrations in New York and Washington, D.C., and the following April some Democrats began a campaign to win him their party's presidential nomination. Dewey, who had little interest in politics, briefly considered running but withdrew his name from consideration in mid May. From 1900 until his death on 11 January 1917, Dewey, as the highest ranking uniformed officer of the U.S. Navy, served as president of the General Board of the Navy.

Justifying the New Navy. Dewey's victory at Manila Bay justified, in the eyes of pro-navy advocates, the seventeen-year program of building the New Navy, a fleet of modern steel, steam-powered warships. The short naval war with Spain gave immense confidence to the American people regarding the ability of the nation to be a power on the world scene, and at the same time it provided an argument for military readiness. Suddenly the United States had Pacific bases and had become a major power in the Far East.

Source:

Ronald Spector, *Admiral of the New Empire: The Life and Career of George Dewey* (Baton Rouge: Louisiana State University Press, 1974).

JAMES A. GARFIELD

1831-1881

PRESIDENT OF THE UNITED STATES,

1881

The Brief Presidency of a Reform Republican. James A. Garfield's short presidency was dominated by the continuing fight over political patronage and attempts to institute a series of reforms, reflecting the extent to which corruption in federal employment and contracts had nearly immobilized the federal government by the early 1880s.

Background. The last American president to be born in a log cabin, James Abram Garfield was born on 19 November 1831 in a remote area of northern Ohio, near the communities of North Union and Kirkland. For a brief time in 1848 he worked as a canal boy, trudging along towpaths with the horses that pulled the barges. After Garfield, who could not swim, had to be rescued from the canal fourteen times in the space of six weeks, he decided to enroll in Geauga Academy in Chester, Ohio. In November 1849 Garfield left the academy and began teaching at rural schools and working as a carpenter, earning money while continuing his education at the Western Reserve Eclectic Institute in Hiram, Ohio (later Hiram College). A devout member of the Disciples of Christ, he also honed his oratorical skills as a preacher in local churches. Admitted to the junior class of Williams College in Williamstown, Massachusetts, in 1854, Garfield worked his way through school, graduating in 1856.

Early Career. Returning to Ohio, Garfield worked as a teacher and later president at the Eclectic Institute and became involved in local Republican politics. On 11 November 1858 he married Lucretia Randolph, and in October 1859 he was elected to the Ohio state senate on the Republican ticket. Garfield joined the Union army after the outbreak of the Civil War and was made lieutenant colonel of the Forty-second Ohio Regiment. Although he had no military training, he studied military texts and served with distinction at the battles of Shiloh and Chickamauga. He was elected to Congress in 1862 as a Lincoln Republican and was mustered out of the army as major general before Congress convened in December 1863. Serving in the House of Representatives through 1880, he continued to gain recognition, emerging as a Republican leader in the House.

Republican Presidential Candidate. In 1880 the Ohio legislature elected Garfield to the U.S. Senate, but he never served in that body. During the Republican National Convention of 1880, Garfield, who was campaign manager for presidential hopeful John Sherman, emerged as a dark-horse candidate in his own right and won the nomination. To satisfy the New York Stalwart faction, which opposed Garfield and Sherman, the party selected Chester A. Arthur of New York for his running mate. In November Garfield defeated Gen. Winfield Scott Hancock, another veteran of the Civil War, in a close election.

Presidency. During the winter of 1880–1881 Garfield put together a list of appointees for his new administration. The Stalwarts were outraged to discover that—like Rutherford B. Hayes before him—Garfield had ignored the recommendations of the New York Republican Party, especially in his choice of James G. Blaine for secretary of state and Wayne MacVeagh as attorney general, but he assuaged some of their ire by appointing Stalwart Thomas James to the position of postmaster-general. During the early months of his administration he vigorously prosecuted the Star Route Frauds, a scheme involving an assistant postmaster-general, through which excessive government charges were funneled to contractors for western mail-delivery routes.

Assassination. On 2 July 1881 Garfield set out for a vacation in New England. At the train station in Washington, D.C., he was shot by Charles J. Guiteau, a deranged, disappointed office seeker who had been plotting the assassination of the president for more than a month. Garfield was seriously wounded. For about three weeks his condition seemed to improve, but then he went into a slow decline, lingering on, confined to his bed, until his death on 19 September 1881.

Sources:

Justus D. Doenecke, *The Presidencies of James A. Garfield and Chester A. Arthur* (Lawrence: Regents Press of Kansas, 1981);

Allan Peskin, *Garfield* (Kent, Ohio: Kent State University Press, 1978).

MARK HANNA

1837-1904

REPUBLICAN POLITICAL LEADER

Changing the G.O.P. Mark Hanna, an Ohio industrialist turned politician, modernized the Republican Party and helped to win the presidency for fellow Ohioan William McKinley in 1896.

Background. Marcus Alonzo Hanna was born on 24 September 1837 in New Lisbon (later Lisbon), Ohio. When he was fifteen Hanna and his family moved to Cleveland, where Hanna entered Western Reserve College in 1857. In spring 1858 he dropped out of school to work in the family's wholesale-grocery business. During the Civil War Hanna served a few months of 1864 as a lieutenant in an Ohio militia company. In September 1864 a few weeks after he returned to Cleveland, he married C. Augusta Rhodes, daughter of a successful coal and iron merchant and became a partner in the Rhodes family business, Rhodes & Co., which diversified into shipbuilding and became M. A. Hanna & Co. in 1885. Hanna became a wealthy man with civic and commercial interests that included the ownership of streetcar franchises, the Cleveland Opera House, and the *Cleveland Herald*, directorships of two railroads, and the presidency of the Union National Bank.

Career in Politics. Hanna became involved in local Republican politics in the early 1870s. A fierce supporter of Republican causes such as protective tariffs and the gold standard, he used the *Cleveland Herald*, which he bought in May 1880, to further the successful campaign of Republican presidential nominee James A. Garfield. In 1884 Hanna was a delegate to the Republican National Convention. He supported Ohio favorite son Sen. John Sherman, who garnered only minimal support at a convention dominated by forces loyal to James G. Blaine, who won the nomination. Though his candidate was unsuccessful, Hanna formed important political associations with fellow Ohio delegates Congressman William McKinley and Joseph B. Foraker, who was elected governor of Ohio in 1885 with Hanna serving on his executive election committee. Although initially closer to Foraker, who supported Sherman, than to McKinley, who supported Blaine, Hanna had a disagreement about political patronage with Foraker in 1887 and eventually drew closer to McKinley. After supporting Sherman's strong but ultimately unsuccessful bid for the Republican presidential nomination in 1888, Hanna turned to McKinley, who, like Hanna, supported a high tariff and had a friendly view of labor. Hanna's ability to raise campaign money contributed greatly to McKinley's election as governor of Ohio in 1891. Hanna and McKinley planned to bring McKinley forward as a presidential candidate if President Benjamin Harrison failed in his bid to run for a second term at the Republican National Convention of 1892, and right after the convention McKinley and Hanna began to set their sights on the White House for 1896. In 1895 Hanna withdrew from active involvement in business to devote himself to politics full time.

The Election of 1896. After demonstrating his ability to attract delegates nationwide to win the presidential nomination for McKinley at the Republican National Convention of 1896, Hanna became chairman of the Republican National Committee, managing fund-raising and propaganda with particular zeal. Under Hanna's leadership the campaign broke new ground and established a model followed in later presidential bids. He flooded newspapers and journals all over the country with stories about McKinley's virtues and his heroism in the Civil War, creating an image of McKinley as a solid middle-class man of the people. While McKinley's opponent, William Jennings Bryan, traveled an unprecedented number of miles to take his message to voters, Hanna arranged for McKinley to conduct his campaign from the front porch of his house in Canton, Ohio; on 18 September alone McKinley received as many as eighty thousand people. Hanna recruited fourteen hundred speakers to extol McKinley's virtues nationwide, and he was one of the earliest political operatives to use opinion polls to pinpoint campaign weak spots. The national campaign committee reported spending about $4 million on McKinley's campaign, but far more money was actually spent to take the candidate's message to the voters. Thanks in large part to Hanna's meticulous campaign organization, McKinley won the election.

The Spanish-American War. Following the election and the appointment of Sen. John Sherman as secretary of state, Hanna was appointed to complete Sherman's term in the Senate, where he continued to serve until his death in 1904, despite charges that he tried to buy the vote of an Ohio legislator in 1898. When the rebellion in Cuba reached a crisis point in 1898, Hanna, like McKinley and other Republicans, was reluctant to involve the United States in Cuban affairs, fearing that hostilities would disrupt business. Nonetheless, they backed war in April 1898. Like most conflicts, the Spanish-American War (1898) initiated an upsurge of popular support for the president, and, in fact, it proved to be good for business, contributing to the sense that Republicans were indeed the party of prosperity.

The Election of 1900. The good times that followed the war made Republicans confident that the election of 1900 was theirs. Touting "Republican Prosperity" and reusing the theme of the "full dinner pail," Hanna again ran a massive campaign for McKinley. Hanna would have preferred a more predictable vice-presidential candidate than war hero Theodore Roosevelt, but Roosevelt's military record and his successful campaign for the New York governorship made him an important asset. McKinley beat Bryan by a wider margin than he had in 1896. The Republicans also strengthened their control over both houses of Congress. Again Hanna had proved himself a master political campaigner.

Later Years. After McKinley's assassination in September 1901, Hanna maintained close connections to President Roosevelt. To conservative Republicans who viewed Roosevelt as a "radical," Hanna seemed a logical choice for president. In the midst of speculation about whether he was considering a bid for the Republican presidential nomination; Hanna became ill and died on 15 February 1904 without making his intentions public.

Sources:

Herbert Croly, *Marcus Alonzo Hanna: His Life and Work* (New York: Macmillan, 1912);

Clarence Ames Stern, *Resurgent Republicanism: The Handiwork of Hanna* (Ann Arbor: University of Michigan Press, 1963).

BENJAMIN HARRISON

1833-1901

PRESIDENT OF THE UNITED STATES,

1889-1893

A One-Term President. The grandson of President William Henry Harrison(1773–1841) and the great-great grandson of Benjamin Harrison (1726–1791), who signed the Declaration of Independence, Benjamin Harrison was little known outside Indiana before he ran for president in 1888. During his one term in office he was often overshadowed by his well-known secretary of state, James G. Blaine, and he lacked the political clout to hold his own in the sharply divided battles over tariffs and civil-service reform that dominated American politics in the 1880s and 1890s.

Background. Benjamin Harrison was born on 20 August 1833 in North Bend, Ohio, and grew up on his family's nearby farm. Graduating from Miami University in Oxford, Ohio, in 1852, Harrison began reading law in Cincinnati and married Caroline Scott on 20 October 1853. After he was admitted to the Ohio bar in 1854, the couple settled in Indianapolis, where he established a law practice and became involved in local Republican politics. He was elected city attorney in 1857, secretary to the Indiana Republican Central Committee in 1858, and reporter to the state supreme court in 1860. He served in the Civil War, fighting in Gen. William Sherman's Atlanta campaign and the Union victory at Nashville and rising to the rank of brigadier general. In 1864, while still serving in the military, he was reelected to the lucrative post of supreme court reporter. After the war he continued law practice.

Political Career. Harrison ran for governor of Indiana in 1876 and lost. He continued to be active in the national Republican Party, and President Rutherford B. Hayes appointed him to the Mississippi River Commission in 1879. In 1880 the Indiana legislature elected him to the U.S. Senate, where he established a reputation for favoring civil-service reform, pensions for Civil War veterans, and regulation of railroads. After the Democrats gained control of the Indiana legislature, Harrison was not elected to a second term in the Senate. In 1888 he won the Republican presidential nomination. He conducted a campaign from his front porch, granting extensive interviews to visitors. Although the incumbent president, Grover Cleveland, earned more popular votes, Harrison won the election in the electoral college.

Harrison's Presidency. Harrison supported the modernization of the navy and U.S. expansion overseas, backing the establishment of a U.S.-German-British protectorate in Samoa and the treaty for the annexation of Hawaii. In 1891 he took a vigorous stand after a mob in Valparaíso, Chile, killed two American sailors on shore leave and injured several others. Secretary of State Blaine demanded and got an official apology and a $75,000 indemnity after Harrison sent a message to Congress that came close to asking for a declaration of war. Although Harrison favored civil-service reform, he appointed many of his Republican backers to office, losing support among reformers in his own party. In 1890 he supported the Sherman Anti-Trust Act, which lay the groundwork for government regulation of big business; the McKinley Tariff Act, which raised import duties; and the Dependent Pension Act, which greatly increased the number of Civil War veterans who were eligible for pensions. When he ran for reelection in 1892, he was hurt by his stands in favor of raising tariffs, which had led to higher retail prices, and veterans' pensions, which were popular among former soldiers but had proved a drain on the federal budget. His civil-service appointments had also lost him support from a significant segment of his own party. Like other presidents of his the period, Harrison was caught in a dilemma: support civil-service reform and alienate his own party structure or appoint followers and lose the support of reformers.

Later Years. After losing the 1892 presidential election to Cleveland, Harrison returned to an active law practice. He also remained active in politics, campaigning for candidates in 1894 and 1896. He died on 13 March 1901.

Sources:

Harry J. Sievers, *Benjamin Harrison, Hoosier Warrior, 1833–1865* (Chicago: Regnery, 1952); *Benjamin Harrison, Hoosier Statesman, From the Civil War to the White House, 1865–1888* (New York: University Publishers, 1959); *Benjamin Harrison, Hoosier President: The White House and After* (Indianapolis: Bobbs-Merrill, 1968);

Homer E. Socolofsky and Allan B. Spetter, *The Presidency of Benjamin Harrison* (Lawrence: University Press of Kansas, 1987).

RUTHERFORD B. HAYES

1822-1893
PRESIDENT OF THE UNITED STATES, 1877-1881

Controversy. The presidency of Rutherford B. Hayes started in public controversy and ended with his having alienated the major factions of his own party. Winning the election of 1876 because of what many considered a corrupt political bargain, Hayes made his reputation by fighting the corrupt spoils system in which federal employees paid for their appointments by giving political support and cash donations to the politicians who selected them.

Early Years. Hayes was born on 4 October 1822 on a farm near Delaware, Ohio, and graduated first in the class of 1842 from Kenyon College. After attending Harvard Law School (1843–1845), he passed the Ohio bar examination and practiced law in Lower Sandusky (later renamed Fremont) until 1850, when he moved to Cincinnati. On 30 December 1852 he married Lucy Webb, whose strong abolitionist and anti-alcohol sentiments influenced his own views on those issues. In 1855 he helped to organize the Ohio Republican Party, and he served as city solicitor of Cincinnati in 1858–1860. During the Civil War he joined an Ohio regiment as a major. He was wounded in the Union victory at South Mountain, Virginia, in 1862 but continued to command his troops until the end of the war, serving with distinction under Generals George Crook and Philip Sheridan in the crucial Virginia campaigns of 1864 and rising to the rank of brigadier general. After he was mustered out in June 1865 he was breveted major general for his "gallant and distinguished services during the campaign of 1864."

Political Career. In October 1864, while still serving in the military, Hayes was elected to the House of Representatives. After serving one term in the House, he was elected governor of Ohio, winning a second two-year term in 1869. He ran again for the governorship in 1875. His victories in this "swing state" that sometimes voted Democratic and sometimes Republican made him a good candidate for the presidency in 1876.

The Election of 1876. After emerging as a compromise candidate for various factions of the party opposed to James G. Blaine, Hayes won the Republican presidential nomination on the seventh ballot. Running against Democrat Samuel J. Tilden in the fall, Hayes won some 250,000 fewer popular votes than his opponent, but because of some disputed electoral votes in three southern states the election was still up for grabs. After a bargain with southern congressmen, Hayes received a bare electoral-college majority and won the election. As president he kept the bargain that had gained him the presidency by removing the remaining federal troops from the South and by appointing a southern Democrat to his cabinet. After encountering fierce and successful opposition to his naming Confederate general Joseph E. Johnston as secretary of war, he selected Sen. David M. Key of Tennessee to serve as postmaster-general. Already in ill repute with GOP reformers, Hayes angered Stalwart Republicans, especially those from New York State, by giving jobs to members of the opposition party and by attempting to reform the civil service.

Civil-Service Reform. Hayes believed that federal employees should not be expected or forced to contribute to the political party in power and that they should be selected and promoted on merit, regardless of party. Led by Interior Secretary Carl Schurz, who would lead the Mugwump faction of the Republican Party in 1884, Hayes's cabinet began to cut back on political activity among appointees, further enraging the Stalwarts. In 1878 Hayes took on the Stalwarts in New York, their stronghold of power, asking for the resignation of Chester A. Arthur, the collector of customs for the Port of New York, because he would not follow orders to institute the same reforms there. When Arthur refused to resign, Hayes replaced him. Hayes's victory in this battle, however, earned him the lasting enmity of the Stalwarts, who successfully blocked his attempts to get Congress to pass a civil-service reform act. He left the civil-service question to his successor, James A. Garfield, whose vice president was Chester A. Arthur, the customs officer Hayes had fired.

Later Years. Holding to a promise that he would be a one-term president, Hayes did not seek the Republican

presidential nomination in 1880. He returned to Ohio, where he practiced law and played an active role in the temperance campaign and movements for civil-service and prison reform. He died on 17 January 1893.

Sources:
Ari Hoogenboom, *The Presidency of Rutherford B. Hayes* (Lawrence: University Press of Kansas, 1968);

Hoogenboom, *Rutherford B. Hayes: Warrior and President* (Lawrence: University Press of Kansas, 1995).

WILLIAM McKINLEY

1843-1901

PRESIDENT OF THE UNITED STATES, 1897-1901

Early Life. Born in Niles, Ohio, on 29 January 1843, McKinley lived for much of his childhood in Poland, Ohio. He entered Allegheny College when he was seventeen but soon left because of illness and worked as a teacher and a post-office clerk before the outbreak of the Civil War. After the war he read law and studied at the Albany Law School (1866–1867) before passing the Ohio bar examination and establishing a law office in Canton, Ohio. On 25 January 1871 he married Ida Saxton, the daughter of a prominent Canton banker and businessman.

Political Career. Elected to the House of Representatives on the Republican ticket in 1876, McKinley served in Congress until 1891, after a Democratic gerrymandering of the Ohio House districts cost him the 1890 election. As a congressman McKinley developed a reputation for favoring civil-service reform and a high tariff. In 1890, as chairman of the House Ways and Means Committee, he secured the passage of the protectionist McKinley Tariff, which raised duties on most imports. Returning to Ohio, McKinley was elected governor in November 1891 and served in that office until January 1896. During the 1890s, as the issue of monetary reform became more and more crucial, McKinley appeared at first to favor increased silver coinage. In 1896, however, backed by millionaire Marcus Hanna, McKinley ran for president on a Republican platform that emphasized the gold standard and high protectionist tariffs, defeating free-silver Democrat William Jennings Bryan, who called for lowered tariffs.

The Presidency. After McKinley took office on 4 March 1897 Congress passed the Dingley Act, once again raising tariffs, which had been lowered during the administration of McKinley's predecessor, Democrat Grover Cleveland. Although Cleveland had tried to maintain U.S. neutrality in the Cuban uprising against Spain, McKinley had won the election on a platform that endorsed Cuban independence, and he soon faced a mounting cry for U.S. military aid to the Cuban rebels. Forced into war with Spain by an upsurge of public sentiment after the explosion of the U.S. warship *Maine* in Havana harbor on 15 February 1898, the United States emerged from that brief conflict with new possessions in the Caribbean and the Pacific. The issue of how the United States should administer these territories immediately gripped the country, with Democrats and many reform-minded Republicans advocating independence for all the territories and some expansionist (mostly western) Republicans advocating keeping them as U.S. possessions. McKinley's own views were a mix of the "imperialist" and "anti-imperialist" positions and eventually became: independence for Cuba, with the United States maintaining the right to intervene in its internal affairs; U.S. control over the Philippines until it was deemed ready for self-government; and territory status for Guam, Hawaii, and Puerto Rico.

Assassination. Reelected in 1900 with the popular Theodore Roosevelt of New York as his vice president, McKinley was shot by an assassin while visiting the Pan-American Exhibition in Buffalo, New York, on 6 September 1901, almost exactly six months after his second inauguration. He died on 14 September and was succeeded by Vice President Roosevelt.

Sources:
Lewis L. Gould, *The Presidency of William McKinley* (Lawrence: University Press of Kansas, 1980);

Charles S. Olcott, *The Life of William McKinley*, 2 volumes (Boston & New York: Houghton Mifflin, 1916).

PUBLICATIONS

Edward Bellamy, *Looking Backward* (1888)—a popular utopian novel that depicts Boston in the year 2000, transformed into an orderly and just society by the nationalization of industry and the organization of the work force into an industrial army;

James Bryce, *American Commonwealth* (London & New York: Macmillan, 1888)—a British lord's government in the Gilded Age;

Ignatius Donnelly, *Caesar's Column* (Chicago: F. J. Schulte, 1890)—a dark futuristic, Populist novel set in New York during 1988 and depicting rule by the wealthy class over a race of brutal serfs and downtrodden laborers;

Richard T. Ely, *An Introduction to Political Economy* (New York: Chautauqua Press, 1989)—a groundbreaking text by one of the most important and social scientists of the Progressive;

Henry George, *Progress and Poverty* (New York: Appleton, 1880)—a book popularizing the notion that social inequality resulted from unearned profits on land and that a "single tax" on this increased value would produce a more egalitarian social order;

Albert Bushnell Hart, *Practical Essays on American Government* (New York: Longmans, Green, 1893)—a primer on politics by a well-known nineteenth-century American author;

William Hope Harvey, *Coin's Financial School* (Chicago: Coin Publishing, 1894)—a Populist attack on the gold standard and the political elites who defended it;

Harvey, *A Tale of Two Nations* (Chicago: Coin Publishing, 1894)—a melodramatic novel of political intrigue and corruption featuring a free-silver hero bearing an uncanny resemblance to William Jennings Bryan;

Henry Demarest Lloyd, *Wealth Against Commonwealth* (New York: Harper, 1894)—an influential attack on the dangers of monopoly and the corrupting influence of the captains of industry on the American state;

Theodore Roosevelt, *American Ideals and Other Essays, Social and Political* (New York: Putnam, 1897)—popular essays on politics and society by a future vice president and president of the United States.

Josiah Strong, *Our Country: Its Possible Future and Present Crisis* (New York: Baker & Taylor, The American Home Missionary Society, 1885)—an evangelical Protestant tract, which sold more than half a million copies, warning of the dangers of immigrants and Catholics to the American commonwealth;

Lester Frank Ward, *Dynamic Sociology* (New York: Appleton, 1883)—an important salvo against Social Darwinism and the political philosophy of laissez-faire, this book provided the intellectual underpinnings of the progressive movement;

Woodrow Wilson, *Congressional Government: A Study in American Politics* (Boston: Houghton Mifflin, 1885)—an early, enduring work in American political science by a future president of the United States of America.

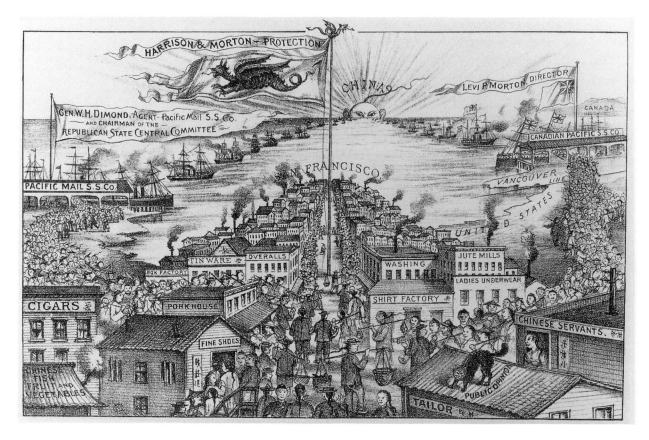

Political cartoon accusing the Republicans of favoring an all-Chinese California, 1889

LAW AND JUSTICE

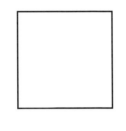

By ROBERT J. ALLISON

CONTENTS

Sidebars and tables are listed in italics.

1878

- Massachusetts authorizes a paid probation officer for Boston criminal courts.

- Deputy Customs Inspector Isaac D. Dennis in Wrangell, Alaska, prohibits the liquor trade.

- Congress establishes the Light Horse, a Native American police force, in Indian Territory, or what is today the state of Oklahoma.

- The Supreme Court in *Hall* v. *DeCuir* overturned a Louisiana court decision that awarded damages to a black woman who had been refused admission to a steamship's stateroom reserved for whites. Since the ship had traveled between Louisiana and Mississippi, the Supreme Court held that the state of Louisiana had no right to regulate interstate commerce.

- In *Harkness* v. *Hyde* the Supreme Court declares that the state of Idaho cannot serve warrants on a Shoshone Indian reservation.

- The Ku Klux Klan terrorizes Swedish immigrants in Iowa.

11 Feb. Ann Restell-Lohman, a New York abortionist, is arrested at the behest of moral reformer Anthony Comstock. Arraigned on 30 March, Restell-Lohman commits suicide on 1 April.

25 Mar. Three leaders of the "Molly Maguires," a secret labor terrorist organization, are executed in Pennsylvania for murdering a political opponent. In the next few months two other leaders of the movement will be executed for similar crimes.

18 June Congress forbids soldiers to act as *posse comitatus* except in cases of armed insurrection.

21 Aug. The American Bar Association has its first meeting in Saratoga, New York.

7 Oct. President Rutherford B. Hayes warns citizens of Lincoln County in New Mexico Territory not to prevent the execution of laws, or he will impose martial law as of 13 October.

1879

- The Michigan legislature defeats a prohibition bill but puts a heavy tax on liquor. The Kansas legislature endorses prohibition. Meanwhile the U.S. House of Representatives creates the Committee on Alcoholic Liquor Traffic.

- Dr. T. V. McGillicudy, Indian agent at the Rosebud (Sioux) Reservation, creates an Indian police force.

- The West Publishing Company publishes *Northwest Reporter*, the first compendium of state court decisions.

- The Supreme Court declares that federal patent power does not cover trademarks.

- New York City considers a proposal to regulate prostitution.

5 May The Supreme Court upholds an antipolygamy statute in *Reynolds* v. *U.S.* One month later George Reynolds is convicted of polygamy.

31 May The circuit court of New York upholds the conviction of Derogier M. Bennett for mailing a tract, "Cupid's Yokes," in violation of federal antiobscenity laws.

7 July	A federal circuit court in San Francisco awards $10,000 to Ho Ah Kow, whose queue was cut off while in police custody (an anti-Chinese ordinance required male prisoners to have their hair cut to within one inch of the scalp).
8 Oct.	Jesse James and his gang rob a Chicago & Alton Railroad train at Glendale, Missouri, making off with $6,000.
9 Dec.	Samuel Singleton, doorkeeper at New York's Grand Opera House, is indicted under the Civil Rights Act of 1875 for refusing to admit William Davis Jr. to the theater on account of Davis's color.

1880

- Nebraska repeals a prohibition law.

- A New York legislative committee investigates Standard Oil Company.

- In *Strauder* v. *West Virginia* the Supreme Court strikes down the conviction of a black man because only whites had served on the jury.

- In *Densmore* v. *Scofield* Justice Noah Swayne asserts that a valid patent must display originality or a "flash of thought."

20 May	San Francisco requires laundries in wooden buildings to have city permits to operate.
13 Oct.	Anti-Chinese rioting in Denver kills one person and destroys $50,000 in property.
2 Nov.	Voters in Kansas approve prohibition, 92,302 votes to 84,304.

1881

- Nebraska passes the first "high license" law, imposing a large fee on liquor licenses. Massachusetts adopts a local option, allowing towns to decide whether or not alcohol can be sold.

- The U.S. Treasury Department permits beer and wine to be imported into Alaska.

- Theodore Woolsey, president of Yale University, forms the New England Divorce Reform League in order to toughen divorce laws.

- New York replaces unwritten common law with a written legal code setting penalties for criminal offenses.

24 Jan.	Supreme Court Justice Noah Swayne retires.
22 Feb.	President Hayes bans the sale of intoxicating liquors at army posts and forts.
2 July	Charles J. Guiteau shoots President James A. Garfield, who succumbs to his wound on 19 September.
14 July	At Fort Sumner, New Mexico, Sheriff Patrick F. Garrett shoots William H. Bonney, popularly known as Billy the Kid.
15 July	The Jesse James gang robs a Chicago, Rock Island, & Pacific train near Winston, Missouri, killing the conductor and a passenger.

26 July	Missouri governor Thomas J. Crittenden meets with railroad leaders, who agree to give a $5,000 reward for the capture of any member of the James gang, with an additional $5,000 each for Jesse and Frank.
4 Aug.	A North Carolina referendum overturns the prohibition law previously adopted by the legislature, 166,325 votes to 48,370.
7 Sept.	Jesse James and his gang rob a Chicago & Alton train at Blue Cut, Missouri. Before leaving the scene James gives the engineer two silver dollars and says, "Here is two dollars for you to drink the health of Jesse James tomorrow morning."
26 Oct.	In Tombstone, Arizona Territory, the famous gunfight at the O. K. Corral occurs when Marshal Virgil Earp and his brothers Wyatt and Morgan, along with John "Doc" Holliday, confront the Clanton-McLaury gang. Tom and Frank McLaury and Billy Clanton are killed. In the wake of the shooting Virgil is suspended as city marshal, and public opinion turns against the Earps.
14 Nov.	The trial of Guiteau begins in Washington.
20 Dec.	The Senate confirms Horace Gray's appointment to the Supreme Court.

1882

•	A New York law prohibits cigar manufacturing in tenements.
•	The Nebraska legislature revokes prohibition.
•	California requires separate schools for Chinese children.
•	Justice Ward Hunt retires from the Supreme Court.
•	Voters in sixty-two of Arkansas's seventy-four counties support prohibition.
2 Jan.	John D. Rockefeller reorganizes Standard Oil Company as a trust.
5 Jan.	Guiteau is found guilty in the murder of President Garfield.
2 Mar.	The Senate confirms former New York senator Roscoe Conkling's nomination to the Supreme Court, thirty-nine votes to twelve. Conkling declines the appointment.
22 Mar.	Congress bans polygamy in federal territories.
27 Mar.	The Senate confirms Samuel Blatchford's nomination to the Supreme Court.
3 Apr.	Robert Ford, a member of the James gang, shoots and kills Jesse James at his home in Saint Joseph, Missouri.
3 May	President Chester Arthur threatens to impose martial law in the Arizona Territory to prevent outlaws from rustling Mexican cattle.
6 May	The first Exclusion Act bars further Chinese immigration for ten years.
27 June	Iowa passes prohibition by a vote of 155,436 to 125,677. The state supreme court will later strike down the measure.
30 June	Guiteau is executed.
5 Oct.	Frank James surrenders himself to the governor of Missouri.

1883

- Congress establishes the Courts of Indian Offences, consisting of judges drawn from tribal police forces, to arrest and convict Native Americans practicing polygamy and traditional religions.

- Isaac Vincent, Alabama state treasurer, flees to Mexico with over $200,000 in state funds.

- An investigation in Arkansas reveals that the former state treasurer and future governor Thomas J. Churchill had left a shortage of $294,876 in the state treasury.

18 Jan. Tennessee state treasurer Marshall T. Polk, adopted son of former president James K. Polk, disappears with $400,000 in state funds. Polk will eventually be apprehended and sentenced to twenty years in prison.

16 Apr. The Supreme Court rules that a man injured in a railroad accident was not negligent in placing his arm on an open window sill.

7 May In *U. S.* v. *43 Gallons of Whiskey,* the Supreme Court rules that paying an internal revenue tax in a collection district that includes an Indian reservation does not authorize the sale of whiskey on Indian lands.

21 July Frank James is tried and acquitted in Gallatin, Missouri, for the 1881 murder of a train passenger.

25 July In Fulton County, Georgia, Klansmen attack Berry Saunders, a black man who had registered to vote.

12 Oct. Eight Georgia Klansmen are indicted for violating Saunders's civil rights.

15 Oct. The Supreme Court strikes down the Civil Rights Act of 1875.

5 Nov. In *Manhattan Life Insurance Co.* v. *Broughton* the Supreme Court maintains that a widow can collect on the insurance policy of her late husband. His death is not a suicide because he was deemed insane when he took his own life.

17 Dec. The Supreme Court rules that Lakota spiritual leader Crow Dog cannot be charged in territorial court for a murder committed on the reservation where Sioux law prevails.

1884

- In *Hurtado* v. *California* the Supreme Court rules that "due process of law" does not guarantee a grand jury indictment in state prosecution for murder.

3 Mar. The Supreme Court upholds the federal government's power to punish Klansmen who had tried to intimidate Berry Saunders, asserting that the United States must protect citizens' voting rights.

17 Mar. In *Stevens* v. *Griffith* the Supreme Court rules that a former Confederate court's judgment confiscating a claim due a U.S. citizen and payment made to a Confederate agent are not barred from recovery claims.

10 May A statue of Chief Justice John Marshall (1801–1835) is unveiled outside the Capitol building.

3 Nov. In *Elk* v. *Wilkins* the Supreme Court rules that John Elk, a Native American who has separated from his tribe and no longer lives on the reservation, is not a citizen of the United States because he has not been naturalized.

1885

- The National Divorce Reform League is formed to make divorce more difficult.

20 Jan. In *In re Jacobs* the New York court of appeals strikes down a ban on tenement manufacture of cigars as an infringement on an individual's liberty to make contracts.

3 Mar. In response to *Ex parte Crow Dog*, the Major Crimes Act gives federal and territorial courts jurisdiction over serious crimes committed by Indians on Indian lands.

2 Apr. Under pressure from moral reformer Josiah Leeds, Philadelphia district attorney George Graham approves the arrest of heavyweight boxer John L. Sullivan, thus prohibiting him from fighting. After further legal challenges Sullivan and his opponent will fight on 3 September in New York City.

15 June The Supreme Court strikes down a New York law prohibiting the manufacture of oleomargarine.

2 Sept. A white mob in Rock Springs, Wyoming, kills twenty-eight Chinese miners.

24 Oct. A Seattle mob burns Chinese homes and drives Chinese residents out of the city.

8 Nov. President Grover Cleveland uses federal troops to restore order in the Washington Territory as anti-Chinese violence continues.

23 Nov. The Supreme Court asks that models, diagrams, and exhibits introduced as evidence in patent cases be submitted one month before the case is argued and removed one month after a verdict is rendered.

7 Dec. The Supreme Court maintains that the contract between Pullman Palace Car Company and St. Louis, Iron Mountain, & Southern Railway is still valid even though the railway is bought out by Missouri Pacific Railroad.

1886

- The Supreme Court bars cameras from the courtroom after Justice Gray is photographed napping on the bench.

- New York State launches an unsuccessful campaign to regulate prostitution.

- In *U. S.* v. *Kagama* the Supreme Court upholds the Major Crimes Act of 1885.

- Fourteenth Amendment protection of citizens is extended to corporations with *Santa Clara County* v. *Southern Pacific Railroad Co.*

4 Jan. In *Stone* v. *Farmer's Loan & Trust* the Supreme Court allows courts to review the reasonableness of railroad rates set by state regulatory commissions.

5 Apr. Iowa prohibits common carriers from bringing liquor into the state without a permit.

4 May Striking workers hold a rally in Haymarket Square, Chicago, to demand shorter hours and to protest police brutality. A bomb is thrown into the crowd by an unidentified assailant, and in the ensuing confusion the police open fire.

10 May In *Yick Wo* v. *Hopkins* the Supreme Court revokes the right of the city of San Francisco to require laundries to have operating licenses.

20 Aug.	Eight anarchists accused in the Haymarket bombing are convicted of conspiracy to commit murder. Seven receive the death penalty while the eighth is sentenced to fifteen years in prison.
25 Oct.	The Supreme Court rules that an Illinois law prohibiting railroads from discriminating between long-haul and short-haul freight rates interferes with Congress's power to regulate interstate commerce.
24 Nov.	A Missouri court admits a telephone conversation as evidence in a civil case.

1887

•	Former Alabama treasurer Isaac Vincent is apprehended, tried, and sentenced to fifteen years in prison for embezzlement.
•	Supreme Court Justice William Woods dies.
4 Feb.	Congress passes the Interstate Commerce Act.
7 Feb.	The Supreme Court rules that a federal law against "cohabiting with more than one woman" forbids a continuous act of polygamy; a man, therefore, cannot be indicted for separate acts committed with the same woman.
8 Feb.	Congress passes the General Allotment or Dawes Severalty Act to distribute reservation land among individual Indians.
15 Apr.	The first issue of *Harvard Law Review* is published.
2 Nov.	A writ of error is denied to the Haymarket anarchists by the Supreme Court.
4 Nov.	A federal judge in West Virginia dismisses the conviction of Elmina Slenker, accused of sending a manuscript, "The Girl and the Dog," in the mail, contrary to antiobscenity laws.
10 Nov.	Louis Lingg, one of the Haymarket anarchists, commits suicide. The next day August Spies, Albert Parsons, George Engel, and Adolph Fischer are executed for the bombing.
5 Dec.	*Mugler* v. *Kansas* upholds a Kansas prohibition law.

1888

•	Kentucky state treasurer James W. Tate embezzles $229,000 in state funds.
16 Jan.	The Senate confirms (thirty-two votes to twenty-eight) Lucius Quintus Cincinnatus Lamar's appointment to the Supreme Court, making Lamar the first former secessionist to serve on the Court.
19 Mar.	The Supreme Court upholds Alexander Graham Bell's patents of different parts of the telephone.
20 Mar.	In *Bowman* v. *Chicago & Northwestern Railroad* the Supreme Court strikes down an Iowa prohibition law.
12 Apr.	Iowa passes a new license law to regulate alcohol sales.
18 May	The Michigan Supreme Court rules that an act "to regulate the manufacture and sale of intoxicating liquors" is invalid as it actually prohibits the manufacture and sale of alcohol.

13 Sept.	The Scott Act bars twenty thousand Chinese who had left the United States from reentering the country.
22 Oct.	The Supreme Court upholds the constitutionality of Iowa's prohibition law.

1889

•	New Jersey passes new laws on incorporation, giving corporations broad powers free of state regulation.
1 Jan.	New York replaces hanging with electrocution as the manner of execution in capital crime cases.
6 Feb.	Congress passes the Criminal Appeals Act, allowing the Supreme Court to hear appeals in capital cases coming from federal courts.
1 Mar.	Congress creates a federal judgeship and court at Muscogee with jursidiction over all the Indian Territory.
22 Mar.	Supreme Court Justice Thomas Matthews dies.
22 Apr.	Homesteaders rush into Oklahoma after Congress buys land from the Five Civilized Tribes.
4 May	Chicago doctor Patrick H. Cronin is murdered by opponents in Clan-na-Gael, an Irish American political organization.
14 May	The Supreme Court upholds the Scott Act and refuses to admit Chae Chan Ping into the United States.
14 Aug.	David Neagle, bodyguard to Supreme Court Justice Stephen Field, shoots and kills former California chief justice David S. Terry when he strikes Field in a Lathrop, California, restaurant.
16 Dec.	The murderers of Dr. Cronin are convicted.
18 Dec.	David J. Brewer, the nephew of Justice Field, joins the Supreme Court.

1890

•	Henry B. Brown joins the Supreme Court.
4 Feb.	The celebration of the Supreme Court Centennial occurs at the Metropolitan Opera House, New York.
24 Mar.	In a series of cases the Supreme Court strikes down railroad rates set by a Minnesota state legislative commission.
28 Apr.	In *Leisy* v. *Hardin* the Supreme Court rules that licensing power does not allow states to prohibit the sale of alcohol in original containers, thus overturning an 1847 precedent.
2 May	Congress incorporates unoccupied areas of Indian Territory as Oklahoma, thus allowing for white settlement.
23 May	The Supreme Court denies that electrocution constitutes "cruel and unusual punishment."
10 June	The McKinley Tariff, which reduces duties on steel and iron and eliminates duties on raw sugar, becomes law.

2 July The Sherman Anti-Trust Act becomes law.

10 July Louisiana passes a law requiring separation of races on railroad cars.

6 Aug. William Kemmler, convicted of murdering his wife with a hatchet, becomes the first person in the United States to die in the electric chair. The execution occurs at Auburn Prison in Auburn, New York, and is botched. George Westinghouse Jr. reports: "It has been a brutal affair. They could have done better with an axe."

8 Aug. Congress responds to *Leisy* v. *Hardin* with the Wilson Act, subjecting alcohol to laws of the state into which it is sent.

6 Oct. The Mormon Church agrees not to sanction plural marriage and calls on all members to obey federal laws on marriage. It also removes its objection to Utah's statehood.

13 Oct. Supreme Court Justice Samuel F. Miller dies.

15 Oct. New Orleans police commissioner David Hennessy is murdered.

1891

- Massachusetts creates a statewide probation system.

- Georgia requires separate railroad cars for whites and blacks.

- The first issue of *Yale Law Journal* appears.

1 Feb. Helen Neilson Potts dies of a morphine overdose. Carlyle Harris, a New York medical student, is charged and eventually convicted of her murder.

3 Mar. Congress creates a new federal appellate court to relieve the Supreme Court of its overwhelming number of cases.

12 Mar. A New Orleans jury acquits three defendants, but cannot agree on verdicts for three others, in the murder trial of police chief David Hennessy. Two days later a mob storms the jailhouse and lynches eleven prisoners accused in the Hennessy murder.

23 Dec. Altena Davis, twenty-three, a shopkeeper from Everett, Massachusetts, drowns in the Mystic River after falling or being pushed off a bridge. James A. Trefethen is later charged with her murder.

1892

- Violence occurs in Johnson County, Wyoming, between cattle ranchers and rustlers. President Benjamin Harrison sends troops to restore order.

22 Jan. Supreme Court Justice Joseph P. Bradley dies.

14 Feb. Rev. Charles Parkhurst delivers a sermon blasting the New York City police for supporting gambling, prostitution, and saloons through selective enforcement of laws.

2 Mar. The supreme court of Ohio dissolves Standard Oil Company; Rockefeller recharters it in New Jersey.

9 Mar. Three black businessmen are lynched in Memphis, Tennessee, prompting Ida B. Wells, editor of *Free Speech,* to launch a crusade against lynching.

4 May	Trefethen is convicted of murdering Davis. He appeals the conviction and is granted a new trial.
5 May	Congress suspends Chinese immigration for another ten years and requires each Chinese resident to apply within one year to an internal revenue collector for a certificate of residence. Failure to obtain a certificate would be cause for deportation.
7 June	Homer Plessy is arrested on a train in New Orleans, Louisiana, for refusing to move into a car reserved for nonwhites.
6 July	A battle occurs in Homestead, Pennsylvania, between steelworkers striking against the Carnegie Company and nonunion workers brought in by the Pinkerton Detective Agency. Nine workers and seven Pinkerton agents are killed.
18 July	Seven leaders of the Homestead strike are indicted for murder but are never convicted.
23 July	Anarchist Alexander Berkman stabs the managing head of the Carnegie Company, Henry Clay Frick. The latter survives, and Berkman spends fourteen years in prison.
26 July	The Senate confirms George Shiras Jr. to the Supreme Court.
4 Aug.	Andrew J. and Abbie Borden are murdered in Fall River, Massachusetts. Andrew Borden's daughter from a previous marriage, Lizzie, is arrested.
5 Oct.	The Dalton gang is gunned down by the residents of Coffeyville, Kansas, when it attempts to rob two banks simultaneously. The sole survivor, Emmett Dalton, is sentenced to life imprisonment.
26 Oct.	Pennsylvania Chief Justice Edward Paxson unsuccessfully calls for indictments of treason against 176 leaders of the Homestead strike.
4 Dec.	The Pinkerton Detective Agency decides not to provide protection to businesses in industrial disputes.

1893

•	Harvard professor James Bradley Thayer writes "The Origin and Scope of the American Doctrine of Constitutional Law." This was one of the first scholarly reconsiderations of judicial review, or the power of the Supreme Court to determine what the Constitution means.
4 Jan.	President Harrison pardons all persons accused of polygamy who have obeyed the law since 1 November 1890.
23 Jan.	Supreme Court Justice Lamar dies.
4 Mar.	Howell Jackson takes his seat on the Supreme Court.
15 May	In *Fong Yue Ting* v. *U.S.* the Supreme Court upholds the residency requirements for Chinese immigrants.
20 June	Lizzie Borden is acquitted of murdering her father and stepmother.
26 June	Illinois governor John Peter Altgeld pardons the three remaining Haymarket prisoners.
7 July	Supreme Court Justice Blatchford dies.

27 Sept.	In his second trial Trefethen is acquitted of murdering Davis.
23 Oct.	Chicago mayor Carter Harrison is shot and killed by Patrick Eugene John Prendergrast. Despite attorney Clarence Darrow's effort to prove Prendergrast insane, he is convicted and later hanged on 23 March 1894.
3 Nov.	Congress requires Chinese residents who had previously been in the United States to have two non-Chinese witnesses swear to their legality before being allowed to reenter.

1894

•	The Supreme Court permits a Chinese merchant to reenter the United States. Meanwhile, Congress forbids the courts from interfering with the exclusion of Chinese.
12 Mar.	Edward D. White joins the Supreme Court.
30 Apr.	A march of unemployed men led by Jacob Coxey reaches Washington, D.C., demanding that the federal government provide jobs and improve transportation by building highways.
26 May	The Supreme Court rules that Virginia did not violate the federal rights of Belva Lockwood, the first woman allowed to argue before that court, when it refused to admit her to the state bar.
22 June	A New York court dismisses an attempt by Anthony Comstock to prevent the sale of books he deems obscene, but which sellers argue have literary merit.
29 June	The American Railway Union calls for a boycott of trains hauling Pullman cars.
2 July	The United States files a complaint against Eugene V. Debs, leader of the American Railway Union. The government charges that a boycott of trains is a violation of the Sherman Anti-Trust Act because it is a conspiracy in restraint of trade.
15 Aug.	Congress authorizes the nation's first peacetime income tax, a flat 2 percent rate on all incomes over $4,000.
24 Oct.	The Supreme Court hears the federal government's argument that the sugar trust has violated the Sherman Anti-Trust Act through control of all the sugar refined in the United States.

1895

•	South Carolina requires all voters to have $300 in real estate and be able to read and understand the state constitution.
•	John J. Crawford drafts the Negotiable Instruments Law, which governs promissory notes. It is one of the first and most successful "uniform laws."
•	New York's Lexow Commission issues a report on corruption and patronage in the New York City police department.
3 Jan.	A Michigan court dismisses the case against Catherine Ketchum, a woman accused of hiring a photographer to take nude pictures of her.

8 Jan.	The trial of Debs and other leaders of the American Railway Union charged with conspiring to restrain interstate commerce opens in Chicago. After four days Judge Peter S. Grosscup discontinues the trial until May, but it never resumes.
21 Jan.	A decision in *U.S.* v. *E. C. Knight Company* is rendered. The Supreme Court rules that the sugar trust did not violate the Sherman Anti-Trust Act.
7 Mar.	Arguments begin in *Pollock* v. *Farmer's Loan and Trust Co.*, a case concerning the income-tax law of 1894.
25 Mar.	Clarence Darrow and former senator Lyman Trumbull argue Eugene Debs's case in the U.S. Supreme Court. Attorney General Richard Olney argues against Debs.
6 May	Theodore Roosevelt becomes chairman of the New York City board of police commissioners.
20 May	In the *Pollock* case the Supreme Court determines that a tax on income from real property is unconstitutional because it is a direct tax. An income tax is not adopted in this country until the Sixteenth Amendment in 1913.
27 May	The Supreme Court upholds an injunction against Debs.
7 June	Roosevelt and journalist Jacob Riis take their first "midnight stroll" to inspect police activity in Manhattan. One of the reforms Roosevelt recommends is to arrest both prostitutes and their customers.
8 Aug.	Supreme Court Justice Howell Jackson dies.
22 Nov.	Debs is released from McHenry County Jail in Woodstock, Illinois, after serving six months for violating a court injunction.

1896

•	Reformers press Congress to bar pictures or descriptions of prizefights from the mail or interstate commerce.
•	Louisiana imposes a "grandfather clause," requiring that a prospective voter be the grandson of an eligible voter. By 1900 this will reduce the number of black voters from 127,000 to 3,300.
6 Jan.	Rufus Peckham takes a seat on the Supreme Court.
30 Mar.	Utah forbids miners to work more than eight hours a day.
13 Apr.	The Supreme Court hears arguments in *Plessy* v. *Ferguson.*
18 May	In *Plessy* v. *Ferguson* the Supreme Court decides that states can require separation of races on railroad cars. This is a landmark decision, and the doctrine of "separate but equal" remains in effect in this country until 1954.
8 Aug.	Three Italians — Salvatore Arena, Giuseppe Venturelia, and Lorenzo Salardino — are lynched in Hanville, Louisiana. On 3 May 1897 President William McKinley will recommend $6,000 in indemnity to the Italian government.
1 Sept.	Congress removes criminal jurisdiction over the Indian Territory from a Fort Smith court.

1897

- Nevada licenses prizefights.

- The Pinkerton Detective Agency and the American Bankers Association block a move to pardon Jesse James accomplices Cole and Jim Younger, convicted with their brother Bob in an 1876 Northfield, Minnesota, robbery. (Bob Younger died from tuberculosis in 1889.) The two surviving Youngers are released from prison in 1901.

19 Apr. Theodore Roosevelt resigns as New York City police commissioner.

10 May The Supreme Court upholds the conviction and fine of a man who gave a speech on Boston Common without a license from the mayor.

7 June Congress declares that after 1 January 1898 all offenses in Indian Territory will fall under the laws of the United States and the state of Arkansas, not Indian nations.

10 Sept. In Lattimer, Pennsylvania, a sheriff and some deputies kill twenty-two and injure forty-four striking miners. The sheriff and deputies will be tried and acquitted of murder.

12 Oct. Justice Field retires, setting a Supreme Court tenure record (thirty-four years, eight months, and twenty days).

8 Nov. The Supreme Court strikes down the Interstate Commerce Commission's prohibition on long-haul/short-haul discrimination.

1898

26 Jan. Joseph McKenna joins the Supreme Court.

28 Feb. In *Holden* v. *Hardy* the Supreme Court upholds a Utah law that limits miners to eight-hour workdays.

7 Mar. In *Smyth* v. *Ames* the Supreme Court strikes down railroad rates set by the Nebraska legislature because they deprive railroads of property without due process of law.

28 Mar. The Supreme Court in *Wong Kim Ark* v. *U. S.* rules that a child born in the United States to Chinese parents is an American citizen.

25 Apr. The Supreme Court upholds the murder conviction of Henry Williams, a black man living in Mississippi, despite the fact that the state keeps blacks from voting and thus off juries. The Court rules that the literacy test and poll tax in Mississippi are constitutional.

31 May A circuit court in Wisconsin strikes down an 1896 Milwaukee ordinance setting trolley fares at six tickets for twenty-five cents, or twenty-five tickets for one dollar, because such rates deprive Milwaukee Electric Railway & Light Company of property without due process of law.

7 July Congress extends the exclusion of Chinese to the Hawaiian Islands.

10 Nov. Race riots occur in Wilmington, North Carolina, where white mobs destroy a black-owned hospital and newspaper.

17 Dec. A federal court in California refuses to allow Jew Wong Loy, born in America of Chinese parents, to reenter the country.

1899

• The state of Illinois instructs prison wardens to pay more attention to early social influences on convicts.

6 Mar. A circuit court orders two Chinese boys, aged eleven and thirteen and the sons of a legal resident in Portland, Oregon, deported to China.

15 May The Supreme Court rules that Congress had power to establish the Dawes Commission to allot lands of Cherokees, Creeks, Choctaws, and Chickasaws and to sell lands deemed vacant to white settlers.

2 June Butch Cassidy and the Sundance Kid along with the Wild Bunch rob a Union Pacific train near Wilcox, Wyoming. The outlaws detach the express car and dynamite the safe within, making off with approximately $30,000.

1 July Illinois establishes the first juvenile court in the country.

OVERVIEW

Technological Change. During the last three decades of the nineteenth century, the railroad, telegraph, telephone, electric light, and other technological innovations had a large impact upon the American legal system. In order to secure the exclusive right to make, use, or sell an invention, an inventor had to obtain a patent, or written document, conferring that privilege. With thirteen thousand patents issued every year during this period, patent law became a source of controversy. If two inventors claimed credit for the same innovation, a judge had to decide the merits of each one's claim. When a state claimed the power to regulate public transportation, a judge had to determine if reasonable prices were being charged. Lawyers, legal scholars, and law enforcement officials attempted to reform the legal system by instituting written codes to guide judges and to keep their decisions more consistent. The role of the Supreme Court changed dramatically, as the justices spent much of their time listening to cases rising from changing economic or social conditions. The membership of the court changed more in these decades than at any other time in the nation's history.

Regulation and Police Power. Between 1878 and 1899 the courts were overwhelmed with increasingly complicated lawsuits. Some judges relied on the principles of English common law, the unwritten legal precedents handed down by English courts since the thirteenth century. For example, the state of Illinois in the 1870s attempted to regulate the storage rates charged by railroads and grain-elevator operators. The railroads and elevator operators opposed such a measure, but in 1877 the U.S. Supreme Court, relying on an English common law principle that allowed for the state regulation of ferries and taverns, determined that a state could regulate businesses in which the public had a legitimate interest. Nevertheless, local courts would not allow the states to impose "unreasonable" rates because that would deprive the railroads and elevator operators of property without due process of law.

Corporate Law. States and the federal government both tried to regulate corporate activity, attempts that corporations challenged vigorously. In 1888 Congress established the Interstate Commerce Commission to regulate commerce between the states. The

commission's first chairman, Judge Thomas Cooley of Michigan, firmly opposed state regulation of business. Under Cooley's leadership the ICC generally adhered to the wishes of railroads in setting guidelines for rates. Nevertheless, the railroads challenged this minimal regulation, and the Supreme Court restricted the ICC's power in a series of cases. In order to control the growth of business "trusts," or monopolies, Congress passed the Sherman Anti-Trust Act (1890), which prohibited conspiracies and combinations in restraint of trade. In 1895 the Supreme Court ruled that the E. C. Knight Company, a sugar trust that controlled more than 90 percent of all refined sugar in the country, was not subject to the Sherman Act. The court maintained that this trust did not violate the 1890 law because it was a monopoly in manufacturing, not trade.

Patent Law. Conflicts over contracts and patents not only absorbed much time and attention, but also led to a proliferation of new lawyers. George Harding, whose first patent case involved Samuel F. B. Morse's telegraph, brought working models of inventions into the courtroom to demonstrate his clients' originality. Justice Noah Swayne ruled in 1880 that to qualify as a valid patent an invention had to display an original "flash of thought," and as a result lawyers hired by inventors flooded the Supreme Court with models and blueprints. The Court's working space, which consisted of the old Senate chamber in the Capitol building, became so crowded that the justices requested that all patent models not be sent until one month before the case was argued, and that they be collected a month after the case was decided. The Court calendar also became full. For two weeks in early 1888 the court heard arguments involving Alexander Graham Bell's patents for different parts of the telephone. The Court's decision in the case (resolved in favor of Bell) took up an entire volume of the Court's records. In 1891 Congress created a new court of appeals that had final jurisdiction in all patent cases, thus relieving the Supreme Court of some of its burden.

The New Lawyer. A growing number of lawyers in the country helped to protect the expanding corporate world. In 1850 there had been one lawyer for every 1,000 Americans; by the 1880s this ratio had changed to one lawyer for every 780 people. The lawyers of the 1880s were different from their 1850 counterparts. Many new lawyers in 1880 had been trained in professional schools as opposed to "reading law" in the office of a practicing attorney. Instead of handling general practices and a wide variety of cases, lawyers began working for corporations where the pay was better and the work more consistent. Some leading lawyers, such as James C. Carter or Joseph Choate, even maintained successful private practices while handling corporate cases. In addition lawyers tended to work more in their offices and less in the courtrooms.

American Bar Association. Lawyers were one of many groups to form professional associations in this period. Local bar associations had already existed in various cities and states before 1878. In that year lawyers met in Saratoga, New York, to form the American Bar Association. Its 201 members came from twenty-nine states, mainly in the East. Although the American Bar Association did not represent all of the nation's 64,137 lawyers, it tried to address issues of concern to all counselors. Connecticut lawyer Simeon Baldwin drafted its constitution and said that the purpose of the ABA was "to advance the science of jurisprudence, promote the administration of justice and uniformity of legislation throughout the union, uphold the honor of the profession of the law, and encourage cordial intercourse among the members of the American Bar." Through annual meetings at Saratoga the ABA tried to accomplish these goals. It established committees to work toward uniform laws and legal reforms. In 1890 the ABA proposed giving an annual gold medal to a person making a significant contribution to the law; two medals were given in 1891 and then the idea was abandoned until 1929.

Codification. In the 1880s the American Bar Association proposed model legal codes to cover various aspects of American life. For instance, the Negotiable Instruments Law set standards governing the issuance of promissory notes, making them uniform in every state. Many state legislatures adopted legal codes to replace the confusing and often conflicting past decisions of judges. David Dudley Field, a New York lawyer (the brother of Supreme Court Justice Stephen Johnson Field and financier Cyrus West Field), had proposed a civil code for the states in 1848. The Field Code of Civil Procedure was most readily adopted in Western states, which were eager to have a code of laws and did not have time to allow the law to evolve through precedence. Many legal scholars opposed the codification movement, arguing that codes of laws drawn up by legislatures would lack the fundamental principle of justice that common law judges needed to determine individual cases. Nonetheless, as the twentieth century neared, states moved to make laws more uniform.

Labor and the Law. In the late nineteenth century the courts viewed the liberty to make contracts as a fundamental American right. When states tried to adjust working hours or regulate unsafe or unhealthy conditions, the courts usually found these attempts to be violations of liberty of contract. The law became increasingly an ally of business, rather than a neutral force designed to resolve disputes. In this era workers began to organize into unions to win higher wages and shorter hours. Businesses tended not to recognize unions, which had only one weapon, a strike, to force employers to negotiate. In the 1880s when laborers threatened to walk out, many employers petitioned a judge to grant an injunction or a writ forbidding the strike. If the union then struck, the leaders could be jailed for violating a court order. In 1894 when the American Railway Union struck against the Pullman Palace Car Company, the leaders of the strike were put on trial for violating the Sherman Act, because by blocking trains the workers were in fact conspiring to obstruct interstate commerce. The case itself was dismissed, but in 1895 the strike's leader, Eugene V. Debs, received a prison sentence of six months for violating the Supreme Court's injunction not to strike. Organized labor leaders decried the decision of *In re Debs* as "government by injunction."

Indians and the Law. The U.S. Army suppressed the last remnants of Native American resistance in the West between 1876 and 1890. The Indians were moved onto reservations and made dependent on the United States. However, they had an ambiguous legal status: they were not citizens of the United States, or of the state in which they lived, but their tribes were not independent nations, either. In the case *Ex parte Crow Dog* (1883), the Supreme Court freed a Sioux leader who had killed another Sioux. The laws of the United States against murder, the Court maintained, did not apply on Indian land. (The crime happened on the Pine Ridge Reservation in the Dakota Territory.) Congress quickly acted to allow U.S. courts to punish Indian murderers and passed the Major Crimes Act in 1885. Indian agents, federal officers assigned to distribute rations and to supervise the reservations, recruited Native Americans as policemen to apprehend criminals and to suppress traditional religious ceremonies. In 1887 Congress passed the Dawes Severalty or General Allotment Act to introduce the Native Americans to individual land ownership and farming. The reservations were divided into individual tracts of land, and the "surplus" acreage was given to white settlers.

Chinese and the Law. In the late nineteenth century China's growing population forced many of its inhabitants to go abroad for work. Thousands came to the American West and worked in laundries, mines, and mills and on the railroads. By the late 1870s, California alone had seventy-five thousand Chinese laborers, about one-ninth of the population. Racism and economic depression made them a handy scapegoat for the frustrations of the times. The 1879 state constitution of California forbade the hiring of Chinese on public works projects and allowed towns to ban Chinese residents. In 1882 Congress barred Chinese from entering the United States for ten years, and other federal legislation made it difficult for Chinese immigrants to stay in the country. By responding to public pressure, Congress helped exacerbate racial tension. In Denver, Seattle, and Los Angeles and in mining camps throughout the West, white mobs burned Chinese homes and killed their residents. The courts generally supported the anti-Chinese legislation; the only real exception was an 1898 case, *Wong Kim Ark* v. *United States,* when the Supreme Court asserted that a child of Chinese immigrants born in the United States was an American citizen.

African Americans and the Law. The Fourteenth Amendment (1868) to the Constitution granted to all persons born or naturalized in the United States citizenship both of the United States and of the state in which they lived. In conjunction with this amendment Congress passed the Civil Rights Act (1875), forbidding discrimination in public accommodations on the basis of race. In 1883 the Supreme Court declared this law unconstitutional, arguing that it only prohibited state discrimination, not individual or corporate action. Furthermore, eighteen years after slavery had ended, the Court asserted that it was time for black Americans to cease being "the special favorite of the laws." In response to this decision, many Southern states kept blacks off juries, out of the voting booth, and in separate railroad cars. This campaign to restrict black citizenship encouraged a crusade of lynching: in the 1880s an average of 116 African Americans were lynched every year in the United States. Although many state governments passed laws against lynching, these statutes were almost impossible to enforce: local law-enforcement officers often supported the mobs, and white juries would not convict accused lynchers.

Conclusion. Judges were perhaps not the best prepared individuals to deal with the profound changes occurring in the legal system. The courts themselves were changing in this period, under pressure from legislatures, the public, and the growing economy. In the 1880s the membership of the Court changed more than it has during any other decade in its history. Only one justice, John Marshall Harlan, served on the Court during this entire period (1877–1911). Harlan is remembered today as a dissenter in some of the most pivotal Supreme Court decisions ever made, including two cases on civil rights and one each on income tax and trusts. Harlan criticized his colleagues for making political decisions, but he was criticized in turn for turning his dissents into political speeches. Ironically Harlan's dissenting opinions eventually became law, not because Harlan was wiser than his colleagues or a better judge, but because he understood that the Court's province was not just law, but justice.

TOPICS IN THE NEWS

CHINESE EXCLUSION

Chinese Immigrants. In the 1870s Chinese immigrants in California, Oregon, and Washington suffered legal discrimination as well as physical intimidation. Chinese immigrants represented cheap labor and competed with native-born Americans for jobs. When a major depression struck in 1873, many Americans blamed the foreigners for contributing to the massive unemployment rate. Racism also played a role in popular attitudes toward the newcomers. To protect themselves Chinese immigrants formed Zhongua Huiguan, or Six Benevolent Companies, which lobbied against restrictive laws and tried to protect Chinese from physical violence. In 1870 California passed a "Cubic Air Law," aimed at lodging houses that crowded Chinese laborers into small rooms. Each adult had to have at least five hundred cubic feet of clear air, and both landlords and tenants could be jailed for violations. The Clear Air Board, created to enforce this law, also mandated that prisoners in the city jail have their hair cut to within one inch of the scalp, thus requiring Chinese prisoners to have their queues, or long, braided ponytails, cut off.

State and Federal Law. In October 1876 a Congressional committee held hearings in San Francisco to determine what, if anything, Congress should do about Chinese immigration. Two years later Congress passed the "Fifteen Passenger Bill," limiting to fifteen the number of immigrants one ship could bring to the United States from China. President Rutherford B. Hayes vetoed the bill on 1 March 1879 as a violation of

Damaged Chinese storefront in Seattle, Washington, after an anti-Chinese riot of the late 1870s

the Burlingame Treaty (1868), which guaranteed free travel to Chinese and Americans in each other's country. Nonetheless, Hayes noted in his diary that the "Chinese labor invasion was pernicious and should be discouraged." In May of the same year California officials responded to public pressure by revising the state constitution and prohibiting all county and municipal governments from hiring Chinese laborers. The legislature was also given the power to ban Chinese immigration and to let towns or cities deport Chinese. During this time the Supreme Court ruled that mandatory haircutting was unconstitutional and awarded Ho Ah Kow $10,000 for the loss of his queue.

The Exclusion Act. In 1880 American diplomats in Peking signed a treaty to "regulate, limit, or suspend" but not to exclude completely the entry of Chinese nationals into the United States. The need for cheap labor on the railroads had waned, and China was willing to accommodate the United States, especially since its friendship would be needed to counter growing Japanese influence in the Pacific. The new president, Chester A. Arthur, vetoed a bill in April 1882 that barred Chinese immigration for twenty years, but on 6 May he signed a

bill with a ten-year suspension. At the time 102,991 immigrants from Great Britain and 250,630 from Germany came to the United States; in contrast, only 39,579 Chinese immigrated to American shores. In the year after the first Chinese Exclusion Act was passed, 10,000 Chinese left the United States, and over the next ten years the Chinese immigrant population dropped by nearly 80,000.

Tightening the Exclusion Order. With the federal government supporting exclusion, the state of California went further to restrict Chinese activities. In June 1882 San Francisco passed an ordinance requiring laundries to be licensed by a board of supervisors. In order to receive a license, the proprietor had to have the approval of twelve neighbors. In August the Supreme Court struck down this ordinance. In October 1888, hoping to use immigration as an election issue, Democratic chairman William Scott pushed through Congress a bill with stringent stipulations. The Scott Act held that a Chinese laborer who had left the country and did not return before passage of the act could not return in the future. Some twenty thousand Chinese previously eligible to return to America now were denied admittance. Because

As the federal government and various state legislatures restricted Chinese immigration in the 1880s, Chinese throughout the United States were brutally attacked. In Denver, Colorado, on 13 December 1880, a mob of three thousand whites surrounded the homes of four hundred Chinese on Blake Street, rampaging for eight hours before police dispersed the mob with fire hoses. One Chinese man was killed; the rest were put in the city jail for their own protection. Unfortunately, while they were in jail, the mob looted their homes. When Chinese minister Chen Lanpin asked Secretary of State James G. Blaine to compensate the immigrants for their destroyed property, Blaine responded that the federal government was not liable because it had no jurisdiction over the state of Colorado.

This federal policy encouraged further attacks. In September 1885 mobs in Rock Springs, Wyoming, and Coal Creek, Washington, attacked Chinese miners. Twenty-eight Chinese died in Rock Springs, and $150,000 worth of property was destroyed. A grand jury dominated by the Knights of Labor refused to indict any of the rioters. President Grover Cleveland, under pressure from the Chinese government, agreed to compensate the immigrants for their losses. The formation of an "Anti-Chinese Congress" in the state of Washington soon followed. On 24 October a Seattle mob burned Chinese homes to the ground, and on 3 November white residents in Tacoma drove all the Chinese from that city. Chinese laborers were warned to leave Washington by 5 November. Federal troops did not restore order until three days later.

the Scott Act exempted merchants and teachers, many Chinese took advantage of this loophole and created new identities in order to return. In 1892 Congress passed a second exclusionary act. Aside from excluding laborers for another ten years, the Geary Act denied bail to Chinese in certain cases and gave all Chinese one year to apply for a residence certificate or face deportation. The McCreary Act (1893) amended the time period needed to obtain a certificate to six months and further defined laborers to include merchants, laundry owners, miners, and fishermen.

Challenges to Exclusion. The Six Benevolent Companies challenged the exclusion acts in court. One case concerned Chae Chan Ping, who had been a legal resident of the United States from 1874 to 1887. Attempting to return to America after the Scott Act had become law, Chan Ping was detained and then turned away. He argued that the Scott Act was unconstitutional because it violated provisions of the 1882 treaty with China. In May 1889 the Supreme Court ruled that the Scott Act was indeed constitutional and that Congress alone had the power to interpret treaty stipulations. On behalf of three detained Chinese laborers, the Six Benevolent Companies in 1893 engaged America's leading constitutional lawyers — William Maxwell Evarts, J. Hubley Ashton, and Joseph Choate — to challenge the Geary Act. Fong Yue Ting of New York had lived in the United States since 1879. Arrested without a writ or warrant, Fong admitted through an interpreter to being a laborer and to never applying for a residence certificate. Wong Quan was arrested and ordered deported after it was discovered that he too lacked the proper documentation. When Lee Joe made an application he was denied a certificate because his only witnesses to permanent residence in the United States were Chinese. (Under the law only whites were credible witnesses for residency.) All three cases were argued before the Supreme Court in May 1893. Government lawyers maintained that the United States had the authority to exclude whomever it pleased; the plaintiffs argued that the Bill of Rights guaranteed to all "persons," not just all "citizens," due process of law, including the rights to trial by jury and to have witnesses on their behalf. On 15 May the Court upheld the Geary Act as constitutional. Justice Horace Gray, for a majority of the Court, said sovereignty included the power of admitting or excluding immigrants. In dissent, Justice David Brewer, joined by Chief Justice Melville W. Fuller and Justice Stephen Field, argued that Congress had gone too far. "It is true," Brewer wrote, "this statute is directed only against the obnoxious Chinese; but if the power exists, who shall say it will not be exercised to-morrow against other classes and other people? . . . . In view of this enactment of the highest legislative body of the foremost Christian nation, may not the thoughtful Chinese disciple of Confucius fairly ask, Why do they send missionaries here?"

Conclusion. In 1894 the United States and China negotiated a new treaty which rescinded the Scott Act but still banned immigration for ten years and denied American citizenship to Chinese workers. In 1896 the Supreme Court ruled that Congress had gone too far in prescribing imprisonment and hard labor to Chinese found in violation of the exclusion orders. However, the courts in general upheld the government's power to deport Chinese. After the United States acquired Hawaii and the Philippines in 1898, Congress barred Chinese in either of those places from entering the mainland. Even Chinese born in the United States were subject to exclusion. Jew Wong Loy, born in San Francisco in 1877, went to China the following year with his parents. In August 1898 he tried to return to California but was refused. His uncle, who had remained in America, testified that Jew Wong Loy was an American by birth, but his testimony was discounted because he could not remember where Loy's parents lived in China. On the other hand, in the same year Loy was denied entry, the Supreme Court ruled that Wong Kim Ark was an American citizen, as he was born in the United States to parents who were permanent residents. Meanwhile, a legal immigrant working in an Oregon laundry sent for his two sons, aged eleven and thirteen. The boys came from Hong Kong in 1896 and were enrolled in school. The federal government moved against the two boys, Chu Hee and Chu How. Though a district court in Oregon decided that the boys could stay, the federal government appealed the decision, and in 1899 a circuit court ordered the boys deported. The discrimination against Chinese culminated with the Chinese Exclusion Act of 1902, which put an indefinite ban on all Chinese immigration. This act was not repealed until 1920.

Source:
Shih-shan Henry Tsai, *The Chinese Experience in America* (Bloomington & Indianapolis: Indiana University Press, 1986).

CIVIL RIGHTS CASES, 1883

Civil Rights Act of 1875. Race remained a contentious issue in America after the Civil War, and racial discrimination a fact of life for minorities. Sen. Charles Sumner of Massachusetts sponsored the Civil Rights Act of 1875, which prohibited racial discrimination in public accommodations. Sumner said that "It is essential to just government that we recognize the equality of all men before the law, and, it is the duty of government in its dealings with the people to mete out equal and exact justice to all, of whatever nativity, race, color, or persuasion, religious or political." The act guaranteed that "all persons within the jurisdiction of the United States shall be entitled to the full and equal enjoyment of the accommodations, of inns, public conveyances on land and water, theaters and other places of amusement, subject only to the conditions and limitations established by law, and applicable alike to citizens of every race and color." Violators could be fined up to $1,000, and/or be sent to jail for a year.

Reaction to the Act. The public response to this federal legislation varied from place to place. Some hotels closed rather than comply, while certain theaters interpreted "equal enjoyment" to mean that blacks could be seated in the balcony. A Louisville, Kentucky, theater restricted African Americans to the balcony, while the theater across the street allowed them to sit anywhere. Federal judges, like the hotel and theater owners, also disagreed about the exact meaning of the Civil Rights Act. Some dismissed cases of discrimination because they believed the Civil Rights Act was an unconstitutional infringement on state or local power. Others ruled the Civil Rights Act a legitimate exercise of power. Federal judges in Texas, Maryland, Pennsylvania, and Kentucky found the act constitutional, while judges in New Jersey, California, and North Carolina did not.

Joseph Bradley, associate justice of the Supreme Court, who wrote the majority opinion in the 1883 ruling that declared the Civil Rights Act of 1875 unconstitutional

In New York, Missouri, Kansas, and Tennessee panels of federal judges divided on the issue, calling for the Supreme Court to clarify the law.

The Civil Rights Cases. Five cases came before the Supreme Court in November 1882. Two of them involved hotels in Missouri; two concerned theaters in San Francisco and in New York City; and the fifth involved a railroad. In each case the plaintiff had been denied service because of color. The defendants had clearly and consciously based their refusals on the complainant's race; but sometimes the person's ethnicity was not obvious. For example, a husband and wife sued the Memphis and Charleston Railroad when the conductor forbade the woman from entering the women's car. She was dark, but her husband was so light-skinned that the conductor thought he was white. Based on that assumption, the conductor deduced that the woman must be an "improper person," and that her relationship with this white man was inappropriate. In the New York case, William Davis (an African American) and his lady friend (an octoroon, or a person of one-eighth black ancestry) bought two tickets to the Grand Opera House. When they appeared at the entrance, doorkeeper John Singleton told them their tickets were not valid. Davis and his friend then found a white boy who agreed to buy two more tickets, which the couple then presented to Singleton. The tickets were valid, Singleton admitted, but the theater managers did not admit "colored people." "Perhaps the managers do not," Davis said, "but the laws of the country do." He refused to leave, was arrested, and then filed a civil suit in federal court.

The Supreme Court. When the five cases reached the Supreme Court, it was not clear how the Court would rule. The U.S. government argued that Congress had the power to pass the Civil Rights Act by virtue of the Thirteenth Amendment (1865), which forbade slavery, and the Fourteenth Amendment (1868), which barred states from denying any person the equal protection of the laws. Racial discrimination was a badge of servitude, the government maintained, and Congress had the power to eliminate it. On the other hand, the defendants argued that Congress did not have the power to tell individuals how to run their businesses, and that only certain kinds of state action were banned under the Fourteenth Amendment. For example in the *Slaughterhouse Cases* (1873) the Court determined that the Fourteenth Amendment forbade the abridgment of those rights associated with United States, not state, citizenship. In *United States* v. *Cruikshank* (1876) the Court said Congress could forbid states from discriminating, but not individual citizens.

The Court Rules. On 15 October 1883 Justice Joseph Bradley wrote the majority opinion of the Supreme Court, which held that the Civil Rights Act of 1875 was unconstitutional. The Thirteenth Amendment, according to eight of the nine justices, did not give Congress the broad authority claimed by the U.S. government. Private discrimination was neither slavery nor involuntary servitude. "It would be running the slavery argument into the ground to make it apply to every act of discrimination. When a man has emerged from slavery, there must be some stage in the progress of his elevation when he takes the rank of a mere citizen, and ceases to be the special favorite of the laws." Bradley clearly thought that this stage had been reached. In addition the Fourteenth Amendment prohibited state actions of a certain character — for example, depriving citizens of the right to vote or serve on juries or hold property. The kinds of discrimination banned by the Civil Rights Act, Bradley said, could not be touched by congressional action because they dealt with individual businesses.

Reaction. At a protest meeting in Lincoln Hall in Washington, African American leader Frederick Douglass said the Court had left his people "naked and defenseless against . . . malignant, vulgar, and pitiless prejudice." Douglass recalled that before the Civil War the Supreme Court had ruled that states and individuals could not interfere with the Fugitive Slave Act. "When slavery was the base-line of the Republic," Douglass charged, Congress's power was unlimited. Now that freedom was the issue, the Court restricted Congress's power and said individuals could deprive one another of liberty. Orator Robert Ingersoll said that "From the moment of the adoption of the thirteenth amendment the law became color-blind." John Finnel of Kentucky wrote to his friend Justice John M. Harlan: "Now the patriotic vagabonds of the South will feel called upon to vindicate the Supreme Court by `jumping on' the poor darkey. . . ."

Harlan's Dissent. Harlan was the only former slave-owner on the Supreme Court; he was also the only dissenter in these cases. The Thirteenth Amendment, Harlan wrote, was intended to abolish slavery. The institution of slavery rested on an assumption of racial inferiority, and in order to do away with slavery this notion of inferiority had to go as well. The second clause of the amendment, Harlan wrote, gave Congress the power to enforce the act through "appropriate legislation." He observed that his colleagues on the Court had declined to decide in 1877 whether it was appropriate for states to regulate grain elevators, but now the Court would decide what kind of laws were "appropriate" to remove racial barriers. In addition, Harlan noted that aside from granting all Americans' citizenship, the Fourteenth Amendment gave Congress further power to remove racial distinctions. As for Bradley's contention that the Civil Rights Act made blacks "the special favorite of the laws," Harlan said the Act merely extended to blacks the same rights as other citizens enjoyed. "The one underlying principle of congressional legislation has been to enable the black race to take the rank of mere citizen. The difficulty has been to compel a recognition of their legal right to take that rank. . . . Today, it is the colored race which is denied, by corporations and individuals wielding public authority, rights fundamental in their freedom and citizenship. At some future time, it may be that some other race will fall under the ban of race discrimination. If the constitutional amendments be enforced, according to the intent with which, as I conceive, they were adopted, there cannot be in this republic, any class of human beings in practical subjection to another class, with power . . . to dole out . . . just such privileges as they may choose to grant." Harlan's forceful dissent was widely published and is one of the classic statements in the Supreme Court's history. One hundred years later his position would be accepted as the legitimate one. However, at the time, the majority of the Court allowed certain persons to be treated as second-class citizens.

Sources:

Alan F. Westin, "The Case of the Prejudiced Doorkeeper," in *Quarrels That Have Shaped the Constitution*, edited by John A. Garraty (New York: Harper & Row, 1962), pp. 128–144;

Tinsley E. Yarbrough, *Judicial Enigma: The First Justice Harlan* (New York: Oxford University Press, 1995).

THE DAWES ACT

The Indian Problem. Richard Henry Pratt, an army officer on the southern Plains, made an interesting observation in the late nineteenth century. He noted that between 1880 and 1890 five million people had immigrated to the United States, where they found

The Lakota leader Sitting Bull's camp on the Missouri River near Fort Yates, Dakota Territory, circa 1883. The Dawes Act attempted to replace such traditional tribal villages with a system of individual land ownership.

work, raised their children, and abandoned "their language, their Arabia, their Turkey, their Italy, their Russia, their Spain, with all their former habits, and have become American citizens in ten years." Yet at the same time, it proved to be nearly impossible for 250,000 Indians to become incorporated into American society. In his first annual message to Congress, President Chester A. Arthur noted the same vexing problem: "We have to deal with the appalling fact that though thousands of lives have been sacrificed and hundreds of millions of dollars expended in the attempt to solve the Indian problem, it has until within the past few years seemed scarcely nearer a solution than it was half a century ago."

Solutions. President Arthur and most sympathetic whites viewed the "Indian problem" in the same way. They maintained that the Indians could overcome the disease and poverty afflicting them by embracing the idea of private property. Many Americans accepted the idea that private property stimulated social progress; that an individual's desire to improve his property and his urge to compete with his neighbors had driven America since the colonial era. In order to help Indians compete with white Americans, reformers believed Indians needed to adopt these ideas of property and progress. Indian commissioner Merrill Gates stated: "We must make the Indian more intelligently selfish before we can make him unselfishly intelligent. We need to *awaken in him wants.* In his dull savagery he must be touched by the wings of the divine angel of discontent. Then he begins to look forward, to reach out. The desire for property of his own may become an intense educating force. The wish for a home of his own awakens him to new efforts. Discontent with the teepee and the starving rations of the Indian camp in winter is needed to get the Indian out of the blanket and into trousers — and trousers with a pocket in them, and with a *pocket that aches to be filled with dollars!* " President Arthur called on Congress to

educate the Indians and to find ways to divide land held by tribes into small plots owned by individuals. The fact that Native Americans had no sense of individual ownership of land and were unwilling to accept that concept was not important; it was essential that Indians learn the ways of whites in order to survive.

Indian Citizenship. In 1884 the Supreme Court checked advocates of Indian citizenship with its decision in *Elk* v. *Wilkins.* Four years beforehand the registrar in Omaha, Nebraska, refused to allow John Elk to vote because he was an Indian. Elk insisted that he could vote because he no longer lived on an Indian reservation and had fully assimilated into white American society. He was, he claimed, no longer an Indian. The Supreme Court, however, ruled that Elk was indeed an Indian and did not have citizenship because that required specific recognition by the federal government. In dissent Justice John M. Harlan noted that the U.S. Constitution referred to "Indians not taxed," which suggested that when the document was written in 1787 some Indians had been taxed and therefore were citizens. This complicated issue would not be fully resolved until 1924 when American citizenship was extended to all Indians.

The Dawes Act. Partly in response to this legal ambiguity and in order to speed up the process of Indian citizenship, Sen. Henry Dawes of Massachusetts proposed the General Allotment or Dawes Severalty Act of 1887. Under the Dawes Act, the federal government would survey all Indian reservations. Each head of an Indian family would choose 160 acres, while single people and orphans would receive eighty acres each. If the Indians failed to choose plots within four years, an Indian agent would designate land for them. In 1888 Congress appropriated $30,000 for seeds and agricultural equipment for the new landowning individuals. The allotted land could not be sold or leased for twenty-five years and was held in trust by the federal government. The object was for Native Americans to learn to be farmers and at the same time to protect them from land speculators. Once an Indian successfully completed the twenty-five-year apprenticeship, he would be given title to his land and be recognized as an American citizen.

The New Law at Work. Despite the best of intentions, the Dawes Act had a negative impact upon Native Americans. It created an opportunity for unscrupulous individuals to hoard the best plots of land, and it disrupted what remained of traditional cultures. More important, it dramatically reduced the amount of land Indians owned. The acreage not distributed to Indian families was sold to white settlers, while land speculators flocked to the reservations and took advantage of the Indians' inexperience with private ownership. In 1887 Indian tribes in the United States owned approximately 138 million acres of land. On the first reservation to be allotted, the Sisseton and Wahpeton Sioux Reservation on the Red River in the Dakota Territory, two thousand Indians had their holdings reduced from one million acres to 340,000 acres; the rest was declared surplus and opened to white settlement. Within four years of the act's passage, fifteen million acres nationwide were turned over to whites. By 1900 Indian holdings fell to about 80 million acres, and when the federal government ended the policy in 1934, Indians held only 48 million acres of land.

Reaction. While some tribes willingly had their land divided, others resisted allotment. In 1887 a delegation from nineteen tribes gathered to oppose allotment. The Five Civilized Tribes of Oklahoma (forcibly moved there in the 1830s) were the most opposed to allotment but also suffered the most pressure to turn their land over to whites. Senator Dawes was appointed to head a commission to investigate conditions in Oklahoma and was appalled at what he discovered. The Dawes commission found that traditional chiefs had been bribed by cattlemen to oppose allotment. The cattlemen were benefiting from open-range land and did not want this territory to be fenced in by small farms. In 1896 the Dawes commission criticized the Indians of Oklahoma for the mismanagement of their own affairs: "The U.S. granted to these tribes the power of self-government . . . . They have demonstrated their incapacity to so govern themselves, and no higher duty can rest upon the government that granted this authority than to revoke it when it has so lamentably failed." The Dawes commission then set about allotting the lands of Oklahoma.

Faith of Believers. Senator Dawes told the Lake Mohonk Conference, an annual gathering of white Indian supporters in New York, in 1897: "Remember that your work is not for the regeneration of a locality, but for a race. And until in every Indian home, wherever situated, the wife shall sit by her hearthstone clothed in the habiliments of true womanhood, and the husband shall stand sentinel at the threshold panoplied in the armor of a self-supporting citizen of the United States, then, and not till then, will your work be done." Dawes and his allies called the General Allotment Act the "Indian Magna Carta," firmly believing that private property would save the Indians. By forcing the Indians to live on individual plots of land, sponsors of the Dawes Act believed the Indians would become property-owning citizens. They were wrong, partly because Indians would not accept the notion of private ownership, but also because the lands allotted were almost completely unsuited to small farms.

Sources:

Janet A. McDonnell, *The Dispossession of the American Indian, 1887–1934* (Bloomington & Indianapolis: Indiana University Press, 1991);

Francis Paul Prucha, ed., *Americanizing the American Indians: Writings by the "Friends of the Indian," 1880–1900* (Cambridge, Mass.: Harvard University Press, 1973).

EX PARTE CROW DOG

Crow Dog and Spotted Tail. Native Americans and white Americans had fundamentally different legal systems and ideas. This dichotomy was borne out in the 1880s when Crow Dog, a Brule Sioux medicine man, murdered a chief named Spotted Tail on a reservation in the Dakota Territory. While Crow Dog maintained traditional Sioux values, Spotted Tail had argued for peace and cooperation with the whites. The federal government built a house for Spotted Tail in appreciation of his friendship, allowed him to distribute rations, and even named an Indian agency for him. Spotted Tail's prominence antagonized other Sioux, particularly when he began taking the wives of more-traditional chiefs.

Indian Law and American Law. Under the unwritten law of the Sioux, a murderer could be exiled from the tribe or the victim's family could kill him unless it agreed to restitution. To avoid further bloodshed, the families of Spotted Tail and Crow Dog agreed on a settlement: Crow Dog gave Spotted Tail's family fifty dollars, eight horses, and a blanket to "cover" the crime. This settled the case for the Sioux, but when white settlers in South Dakota learned that their friend Spotted Tail had been murdered, they summoned a grand jury. Crow Dog was tried for murder in the territorial court at Deadwood, South Dakota. Not surprisingly, he was convicted and sentenced to death.

Return of the Condemned. The convicted medicine man asked permission to return home in Rosebud to settle his personal affairs before his execution. The court allowed him to leave and set a date for him to surrender. On the day he was to return, a snowstorm raged in Deadwood. Court officials, knowing that no white man would walk several hundred miles in a blizzard to be executed, were certain Crow Dog would not appear. They waited at the courthouse, betting with one another on the likelihood of his arrival. On schedule Crow Dog emerged from the blizzard to surrender himself to the authorities. He instantly was transformed from a local villain into a celebrity, and newspapers celebrated his courage and stoic nobility. Lawyers volunteered to appeal his case, and in 1883 they brought it to the U.S. Supreme Court.

A New Verdict. The lawyers argued that because he had killed Spotted Tail on a reservation, Crow Dog was subject to tribal, not United States, law. In *Ex parte Crow Dog* (*ex parte* is Latin for "on behalf of"), the Supreme Court upheld this argument and ruled that the Dakota territorial court was without jurisdiction. All nine justices agreed that the Sioux Treaty of 1868, which established the reservation in the Dakota Territory, did not explicitly limit tribal self-government. As a result the Sioux tribe retained exclusive judicial jurisdiction over all reservation affairs.

Reaction. The fact that Crow Dog could not be executed for murder disturbed many members of Congress as well as their constituents. A concentrated effort soon developed to outlaw the Indians' "heathenish" laws and customs. In response to this case, Congress appended to the Appropriation Act of 3 March 1885 a section known as the Major Crimes Act, which gave the federal government jurisdiction over seven major crimes — murder, kidnapping, rape, assault, incest, arson, and burglary — committed by Indians on reservations. By limiting the jurisdiction of Indian courts, the Major Crimes Act removed an element of tribal sovereignty. The new law also clarified the legal standing of Native American tribes as wards of the federal government. The first test of the Major Crimes Act came in 1886. When two Hoopa Indians were found guilty of a murder committed on a California reservation, the Supreme Court upheld their convictions.

Source:
Vine Deloria Jr. and Clifford M. Lytle, *American Indians, American Justice* (Austin: University of Texas Press, 1983).

GARFIELD AND GUITEAU

The Election of 1880. Republican campaign workers in 1880 were both annoyed and amused by an eccentric character named Charles Julius Guiteau. A former Chicago lawyer, more recently a self-proclaimed theologian, Guiteau, aged thirty-nine, considered himself central to the Republican campaign. He wrote a long, convoluted speech, "Garfield versus Hancock," which he offered to the campaign. Guiteau was certain his arguments would sway the American people to vote for the Republican presidential candidate James A. Garfield and not the Democratic nominee, Winfield S. Hancock. When Garfield was elected, no one rejoiced more than Guiteau, and no one more firmly credited himself with the victory.

The Office Seeker. In January 1881 Guiteau moved

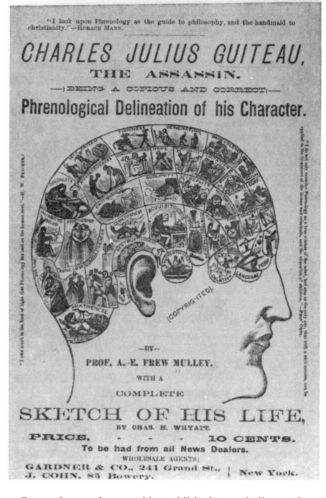

Cover of a popular pamphlet published to capitalize on the notoriety of the assassin Charles Guiteau

to Washington and bombarded president-elect Garfield with applications for consulships in Vienna, Paris, and Liverpool. Guiteau explained that his impending wedding to a wealthy heiress made him a suitable candidate for such positions. After Garfield took office on 4 March, Guiteau became both more determined and desperate. He could not pay his boardinghouse bill but left a note for the landlady promising her payment when he received his consulship, which paid $6,000 a year. With no friends in Washington, his clothes tattered and worn, Guiteau wrote more frequently and at greater length to the only people he thought he knew, the president and secretary of state. He advised the president on matters of policy and politics, encouraging him to seek reelection in four years. He did not meet Garfield, but a meeting with Secretary of State James G. Blaine on 14 May could not have been encouraging: "Never bother me again about the Paris consulship as long as you live," Blaine told him.

Guiteau's Plans. The lack of response on the part of the administration to his advice and proposals greatly angered Guiteau. Moreover, President Garfield's policies alienated a faction of the Republican Party that

Circus poster advertising a reenactment of President James A. Garfield's assassination

Guiteau supported. (The Stalwarts advocated the spoils system and a punitive policy toward the former Confederate states.) Alone and friendless, Guiteau decided that President Garfield had to be "removed" from office. He prayed for four weeks to ensure that the voice telling him to remove Garfield was God, not Satan. Once convinced, Guiteau borrowed fifteen dollars from a relative on 8 June, telling him that he needed to pay his landlord; instead he bought a .45-caliber revolver. For several weeks Guiteau divided his time observing the president's routine, practicing with his pistol, and drafting an "Address to the American People," explaining that Garfield's death "was a political necessity, because he proved a traitor to the men who made him, and thereby imperiled the life of the Republic." At 9:30 on the morning of Saturday, 2 July 1881, Guiteau approached Garfield as the president prepared to board a train at the Baltimore and Potomac Station. Garfield planned to attend a college commencement and then to take a much-needed vacation on the New Jersey shore. Guiteau shot Garfield twice, wounding him in the back and arm, before trying to flee. A District of Columbia police officer apprehended the assassin at the entrance to the train station. Guiteau said mildly: "I did it. I will go to jail for it . . . and I am a Stalwart."

Death and Arraignment. Guiteau was taken to the District of Columbia jail. President Garfield, badly wounded, was taken to the White House. He lingered for two long, hot months. His suffering was eased somewhat by a crude air conditioner — navy engineers rigged a blower to pass air over a vault of ice and into the president's sickroom. In September he was taken by special train to his oceanside cottage at Elberon, New Jersey, where doctors hoped the sea breezes would provide greater comfort; he died on 19 September. Meanwhile, Guiteau saw the president's death as a sign that he had indeed acted as an emissary of God. He fully expected the American people, aside from those officeholders who owed their positions to Garfield, to thank him. However, with the president dead, Guiteau was indicted for murder. The District of Columbia prosecutor called in Judge John Porter of New York, a distinguished lawyer, to help in the prosecution. Guiteau was represented by his brother-in-law, George Scoville.

Defense Strategy. Scoville knew the only way to save his brother-in-law from the gallows was to argue that he was insane, and thus not criminally responsible for his actions. Guiteau always maintained that he acted as God's agent and had no free will in the matter. "The responsibility lies on the Deity, and not on me, and that, in law, is insanity." This would be Scoville's main point, though he also argued at first that the doctors treating Garfield, not Guiteau's bullets, had actually killed the president. In addition, Scoville noted that Garfield had died in New Jersey and claimed that the Washington court did not have jurisdiction. Eventually Scoville dropped the last two points and focused instead on the insanity plea.

Insanity and Criminal Responsibility. Scoville's defense strategy posed two problems. First, the law on insanity was changing in the late nineteenth century, as doctors and scientists debated the causes of mental illness. The modern science of psychiatry was then called alienism and had its origins during this time. Most Americans regarded the outward signs of mental illness as evidence of sin, rather than disease. Laws to protect the innocent did so by punishing sinners, not by curing them. Most American courts followed the M'Naghten rule, developed in England in 1843. Under this rule, the jury would presume a man sane until the defense demonstrated otherwise. The defense had to prove clearly that at the time the accused committed the crime he was suffering from a mental disease that made him either not "know the nature and quality of the act he was doing, or, if he did know it, that he did not know he was doing what was wrong." American courts had modified this rule somewhat. In 1868 an Iowa judge had suggested that a man would not be criminally responsible if he were driven by an irresistible impulse rooted in some mental disorder. The "irresistible impulse" theory had many critics. Then-congressman Garfield had supposedly written in 1871: "All that a man would need to secure immunity from murder would be to tear his hair and rave a little, and then kill his man." A New York judge remarked: "If a man has an irresistible impulse to commit murder, the law should have an irresistible impulse to hang him." In New Hampshire, Justice Charles Doe had suggested that the accused's mental state was a matter of fact, not law, and that it would thus be up to the jury to determine criminal responsibility.

Guiteau as Defendant and Counsel. In this case it appeared that Guiteau clearly knew what he was doing and also understood the difference between right and wrong. However, the burden of proof was only part of Scoville's problem; more fundamental was the problem of Guiteau himself. He regarded himself as his own counsel and claimed that he was clinically, if not legally, sane. During Scoville's opening statement, Guiteau argued with the main point his counsel tried to make. When a defense witness, a Washington editor, characterized Guiteau's "Garfield versus Hancock" speech as incomprehensible, Guiteau objected: "Mr. Scoville had no business to put you on the stand . . . he must not put any more of this expert fool business on the stand. . . . I am not a fool. I would rather be hung as a man than acquitted as a fool." Throughout the trial Guiteau harassed witnesses, insulted the judge, jury, and lawyers, compared himself to the apostle Paul, and signed autographs. Guiteau had become a celebrity, enjoyed receiving visitors and mail in jail, and believed that God, who had made him kill President Garfield, and the American people, who benefited from his action, would never let him be executed.

Expert Witnesses. Guiteau and the prosecution both argued for his sanity. Both the prosecution and defense called a succession of prominent doctors to examine Guiteau. The most famous was John P. Gray, superintendent of the New York Asylum for the Insane at Utica, editor of the *American Journal of Insanity,* and a firm believer in the M'Naghten rule. Gray interviewed Guiteau for three days in November 1881 and was convinced the assassin was sane. Guiteau was depraved, Gray concluded, and intensely egotistic, swayed completely by his uncontrolled passions and self-indulgence, and his life therefore had been one of "moral degradation, moral obliquity, profound selfishness and disregard for the rights of others." On the other hand, Charles Folsom of McLean Hospital in Boston found Guiteau to be insane. Folsom noted that Guiteau was coherent, had a quick memory in subjects that interested him, and on some matters could converse "calmly and amiably," but Folsom was struck by Guiteau's inability to connect his thoughts, his weak judgment, reason, and reflection and his maniacal excitement when challenged or contradicted. Gray and other traditional physicians saw a difference between true mental illness and simple immoral behavior. Others, like Folsom, and a growing number of doctors trained in Europe, were influenced by the work of Italian criminologist Cesare Lombroso, believing that criminal behavior and insanity were the result of heredity, that they represented a degeneration from a contemporary moral order. Edward Spitzka, a New York neuroanatomist who had trained in Europe, argued that the brains of criminals and the insane would have characteristic structural patterns, demonstrating a hereditary degeneration. Spitzka, who had severely criticized Gray in medical journals, testified that Guiteau was completely unable to evaluate the world realistically, as evidenced by Guiteau's plan to tour Europe and America as a lecturer once he was acquitted.

Conviction and Sentence. On 5 January 1882 the jury deliberated for just over one hour before agreeing that Guiteau was guilty of first-degree murder. A month later, when the judge denied a motion for a new trial, Guiteau exploded at Scoville that his "jackass theory" had convicted him. The convicted murderer was sentenced to hang on 30 June. He remained convinced that President Chester A. Arthur, owing his position to Guiteau's act, would pardon him. In late June a group of neurologists unsuccessfully petitioned Arthur to spare Guiteau's life, not out of gratitude, but because they believed he was insane. Meanwhile, Guiteau published his autobiography, *The Truth and the Removal,* the first half a religious tract he had written earlier and the second half a collection of documents and commentaries on Garfield's assassination and the trial. On the

Illustration of the aftermath of the Haymarket bombing from a contemporary magazine

appointed day Guiteau was led to the gallows. Before dying he sang a song he had written at ten o'clock that morning: "I am going to the Lordy, I am so glad, I am going to the Lordy, I am so glad."

Aftermath. Guiteau's bizarre behavior at his execution convinced some who had thought him sane that he truly was not. His autopsy suggested, but did not conclusively demonstrate, abnormality. The gray cells of his brain had degenerated, and a modern pathologist looking at the results noted evidence of "syphilitic involvement" with the brain, as well as evidence of chronic malaria. Four months after Guiteau's execution, his sister, Frances Scoville, was judged insane, evidence perhaps of hereditary insanity. No jury in 1882 would have acquitted the man who murdered the president. However, three years later a *Student's Guide to Medical Jurisprudence* claimed that if Guiteau's victim had been less prominent, he would not have been put on trial.

Source:
Charles E. Rosenberg, *The Trial of the Assassin Guiteau: Psychiatry and Law in the Gilded Age* (Chicago & London: University of Chicago Press, 1968).

HAYMARKET

Strike for an Eight-Hour Day. On 1 May 1886 more than 190,000 American workers went on strike, demanding an eight-hour workday. Railroads and factories stopped, and by the end of the day 150,000 workers had earned a guarantee of shorter working hours. This was one of the greatest victories for organized labor, but it quickly turned into one of the most bitter defeats. At the McCormick Harvester Company plant in Chicago, which produced machinery to harvest wheat, fourteen hundred strikers demanding an eight-hour workday and daily wages of two dollars had been locked out since February. The Illinois state courts, supporting the company's right to negotiate contracts with its employees, turned a deaf ear to the pleas of the striking workers. In March the company brought in three hundred nonunion workers, protected by the police and Pinkerton detectives. On 3 May the strikers clashed with these "scab" workers and the police fired into the crowd, killing one protester and seriously wounding six others.

Haymarket Rally. The strike leaders called for a mass meeting on the evening of 4 May in Haymarket Square to protest this episode of police brutality. Only three thousand of an expected twenty-five thousand protesters showed up. Mayor Carter Harrison not only gave the protesters permission to hold their rally, but he attended the gathering himself. Harrison left shortly after 10 P.M. when rain threatened. He had already heard socialists Albert Parsons and August Spies denounce Chicago's police for provoking the previous day's violence. The police, as well as the business leaders of Chicago, had already marked Parsons and Spies as the most dangerous radicals in the city's labor movement. After most of the crowd had gone home, labor leader Samuel Fielden spoke. Mayor Harrison stopped at a nearby police station to inform the officers that the peaceful rally was nearly over.

The Riot. Shortly after the mayor left, 180 police appeared at the rally and ordered the remaining twelve hundred to thirteen hundred people to disperse. Fielden shouted "We are peaceable" at the very moment a bomb exploded among the police ranks. Policeman Matthias Degan died instantly, and seventy-six others were wounded, six of them fatally. The surviving police opened fire, killing one and wounding at least twelve of the crowd, some of whom later died. In the wake of the riot, the police arrested several hundred labor leaders. Thirty-one people were indicted for the bombing, but the state decided to press charges against eight leaders of the strike: Parsons, Spies, Fielden, Michael Schwab, Adolph Fischer, George Engel, Louis Lingg, and Oscar Neebe. (A ninth individual, Rudolph Schnaubelt, reportedly threw the bomb, but he fled to his native Germany immediately after the incident.) Although only Fielden had been at the rally when the bomb exploded, all were accused of murder. None was actually charged with throwing the bomb, but Spies, Parsons, and others had urged the workers to arm themselves against police violence. Judge Joseph E. Gary of the Cook County Criminal Court declared that a person inciting a bombing was at least as responsible as the person throwing the bomb. It would be enough for the prosecution to show that the accused were anarchists, individuals who advocate the use of force to overthrow all government, and that police officers had died as a result of a conspiracy. The grand jury found that the accused "had in their abuse of [free speech] been more or less instrumental in causing the riot and bloodshed in Haymarket Square."

The Trial. The trial began on 21 June, and finding an impartial jury was difficult since most of Chicago's newspapers had savagely denounced the anarchist leaders for the bombing. The state never made an effort to find impartial jurors: special bailiff Henry L. Ryce, charged with finding jurors, said, "I am managing this case and I know what I am about. Those fellows are going to be hanged as certain as death." The jurors he found shared Ryce's belief: one was related to one of the dead policemen; another was a close friend; and a third stated that the court probably could not "bring proof enough to change my opinion." Judge Gary would not allow defense lawyers to contest the selection of jury members, insisting instead that even men with prejudices might give a fair verdict. In closing the state's case, prosecutor Julius Grinnell told the jury, "Law is on trial. Anarchy is on trial. These men have been selected, picked out by the grand jury and indicted because they were leaders. They are no more guilty than the thousands who follow them. Gentlemen of the jury; convict these men, make examples of them, hang them and you save our institutions, our society."

The Verdict. The jury deliberated for three hours on 20 August and found seven of the defendants guilty of first-degree murder; the eighth, Oscar Neebe, was guilty of a lesser charge. While Neebe was sentenced to fifteen years in prison, the others received death sentences. Most Americans had welcomed the indictments as a means to suppress dangerous radicals, and no newspaper in the country criticized Judge Gary's handling of the case (he sometimes let ladies visiting the court sit with him on the bench, and during one lawyer's argument Gary and a guest were busy working on a puzzle). However, once the trial was over, many people had second thoughts. In speaking to the court after the verdict, Spies said, "You may pronounce the sentence upon me, honorable judge, but let the world know that in A.D. 1886, in the state of Illinois, [seven] men were sentenced to death because they believed in a better future." Neebe asked to join his comrades on the gallows, "for I think it is more honorable to die suddenly than to be killed by inches. I have a family and children; and if they know their father is dead, they will bury him. They can go to the grave and kneel down by the side of it; but they can't go to the penitentiary and see their father, who was convicted of a crime that he hasn't anything to do with." Parsons suggested that Chicago's business leaders had themselves planted the bomb.

Move to Appeal. Judge Gary refused a request for a new trial, and the Illinois Supreme Court upheld the verdicts. The Massachusetts politician Benjamin Butler joined noted lawyer Roger Pryor in appealing to the U.S. Supreme Court, which refused to grant the anarchists a writ of error. From Europe came calls for clemency, and in America mass meetings called for a review of the trial and pressured Gov. Richard Oglesby for clemency. Some Chicago businessmen thought Schwab and Fielden should be spared, but powerful department-store magnate Marshall Field squelched a move to pardon them. Lingg, Fischer, Engel, and Parsons denounced all efforts to save their lives. Parsons sarcastically asked the governor to delay his execution until his wife and children could be tried and convicted of attending the rally; if he was being hung for his attendance, then his family was also guilty, and they should all die together. On 10 November 1887 Lingg committed suicide in his jail cell by placing a dynamite cap in his mouth. Later that day Governor Oglesby commuted Schwab's and Fielden's sentences to life in prison.

Execution. On 11 November Engel, Fischer, Parsons, and Spies went to the gallows. Before the trapdoor swung open, each man was allowed to speak. "There will come a time when our silence will be more powerful than the voices you strangle today," Spies shouted. "Hurrah for anarchy" were Fischer's last words, and Engel said, "This is the happiest moment of my life!" Parsons shouted, "Let the voice of the people be heard!"

Reactions. The Haymarket trial wounded the credibility of the American legal system. The Chicago police, it was learned, had planted incriminating evidence in the suspects' homes and had provoked some of the violence with striking workers. The Knights of Labor, which had been at the forefront of improving labor conditions throughout the country, threatened to expel any affiliate union which supported the move for clemency. Samuel Gompers, leader of the more conservative American Federation of Labor, supported the call for fair trials, and after the verdict and executions Gompers and the AFL gained new legitimacy, while the Knights of Labor lost much support. On 25 June 1893 in Waldheim Cemetery in Chicago, a bronze monument to the executed Haymarket leaders was unveiled. The next morning, the new Illinois governor, John Peter Altgeld, pardoned the three men still in prison.

The Pardon. A former prosecutor and judge, Altgeld examined the case in detail and was appalled by the bias of the jury, the lack of substantial evidence, and Judge Gary's incompetency. Altgeld pardoned the Haymarket leaders because they had not received a fair trial and also because he saw a golden opportunity to restore the integrity of the judicial system. While Altgeld's action satisfied those who thought the trial a miscarriage of justice, and the executions judicial murder, the majority of Americans still thought the anarchists were guilty to some extent. In the long run Altgeld's decision hurt his political career. While Judge Gary was overwhelmingly reelected to his position on the Cook County Court, Altgeld was defeated for reelection as governor in 1896.

Sources:

Philip S. Foner, *History of the Labor Movement in the United States*, vol. 2 of *From the Founding of the A.F. of L. to the Emergence of American Imperialism* (New York: International Publishers, 1975);

Ray Ginger, *Altgeld's America: The Lincoln Ideal versus Changing Realities* (New York: Funk & Wagnalls, 1958);

Page Smith, *The Rise of Industrial America*, vol. 6 of *A People's History of the Post-Reconstruction Era* (New York: McGraw-Hill, 1984).

INCOME TAX CASE, 1895

Taxes in History. The Constitution forbade Congress to tax land or people unless the taxes were apportioned according to the population of each state. Before 1913 all federal revenue came from tariffs on imports, excise taxes, or selling of public land. In the 1790s Congress had taxed carriages, but the Supreme Court ruled that it was not a direct tax, but an excise tax. During the Civil War, the United States government needed to raise money and taxed the incomes of professionals, such as lawyers, who earned over $1,000 each year. This tax lasted until 1872, and in 1881 the Supreme Court ruled that it had been constitutional.

Changing Circumstances. In the 1870s and 1880s agitation grew for a new tax on incomes. In the 1780s most Americans lived on farms and could not measure annual income in dollars. One hundred years later the economy had changed. The disparities of wealth between the rich and poor had grown, and it became obvious to some that while land had been the real source of wealth in the 1780s, by the 1880s wealth was measured in other ways, for instance in stocks or bonds. In 1894, with the nation's economy ruined by a depression, Congress passed the Wilson-Gorman Tariff, which placed a 2 percent tax on incomes from stocks, bonds, and rents of more than $4,000.

Proponents of the Tax. The Populist Party made an income tax central to its platform. Sen. William Wilson sponsored such a tax after the sugar trust blocked his proposal to lower the tariff on sugar. Wilson was dismayed that his fellow senators speculated in sugar company stocks while they debated the sugar tariff, and he argued that "the question is now, whether this is a government by the American people for the American people, or a government of the sugar trust for the benefit of the sugar trust." Alabama congressman Milford Howard denounced this kind of corruption and warned of a coming war between large capitalists and the people. "If constitutional methods will not avail, this continent will be shaken by a mighty revolution . . . The spirit of avarice is devouring the heart of this nation."

Arguments Against the Tax. On the one side, proponents of the tax saw it as a weapon against concentrated wealth. On the other side, opponents saw it as the first step toward communism. President Grover Cleveland, who thought a small tax on corporate investments might not be harmful, did not want to associate himself with this tax and so let the Wilson-Gorman Act become law without signing it. Almost immediately opponents of the tax challenged the law. Charles Pollock, a Massachusetts investor, sued the Farmers' Loan & Trust Company, claiming that the company should not have paid the tax out of money he had invested in it. Joseph Choate, a leading constitutional lawyer, joined former senator George Edmunds in arguing against the tax, claiming that it was "communistic in its purposes and tendencies." Their main arguments were:

1. The tax was actually a land tax because it taxed income from real estate. Therefore it could not be levied unless it was apportioned among the states;

2. It was not a uniform tax because it was only on incomes above $4,000;

3. The taxing of income from state and municipal bonds was the same as the federal government taxing states or towns.

Counterarguments. In response, Attorney General Richard Olney and lawyer James C. Carter argued that the tax had not been levied on land, and so was not a land tax, though it was a tax on income from real estate. It was no different from the tax on carriages that the Court had affirmed in 1796. The tax did not destroy wealth but was an attempt by the majority to get wealthier people to pay their fair share. The 2 percent of the people being taxed derived about 50 percent of the income. The tax was not an assault on them but merely an attempt by 98 percent of the people to stop the minority's assault on them.

The Two Decisions. The Supreme Court handed down two decisions in *Pollock* v. *Farmers' Loan & Trust Company.* Justice Howell Jackson had been too ill to listen to the arguments or participate in the decision in April 1895, when six justices found the real estate portion of the tax unconstitutional and two found it constitutional. The eight members of the Court could not reach an agreement on the taxes on personal property. Jackson recovered enough to listen to arguments, and the Court heard the case again in May. This time, five judges found all aspects of the tax unconstitutional. Chief Justice Melville Fuller spoke for the majority in both cases. Fuller hoped to avoid the political question of whether an income tax was desirable and merely focus on the constitutional question of whether Congress could levy such a tax. Fuller thought the answer to each question was "no," but he tried to make clear he was only answering the second question. Other justices were not so careful to separate their political views from their constitutional interpretations. "Where is the course of usurpation to end?" Justice Stephen Field asked. "The present assault upon capital is but the beginning. It will be but the steppingstone to others, larger and more sweeping, till our political contests will become a war of the poor against the rich."

The Dissenters. No member of the court was in favor of a class war pitting the poor against the rich. But four members dissented from the majority's decision. Justice John Harlan warned that the majority's decision threw the country back to its condition in the 1780s, before the Constitution was adopted, when the federal government relied on the goodwill of the states for its revenue. "I cannot assent to an interpretation of the Constitution that impairs and cripples the just powers of the national government in the essential matter of taxation, and at the same time discriminates against the greater part of the people of our country." Justice Jackson called the decision "the most disastrous blow ever struck at the constitutional power of Congress." Justice Edward White deplored the decision as a return of "a long repudiated and rejected theory of the Constitution" that deprived the government of its necessary power to tax. Justice Henry Brown said that the charges of socialism raised by the tax's opponents were a smokescreen, since socialism would not be established by taxing "people in proportion to their ability to pay." Seeing the case "fraught with immeasurable danger to the future of the country," White concluded, "I hope it may not prove the first step toward the submergence of the liberty of the people in a sordid despotism of wealth." Congress continued to rely on tariffs for revenue until 1913, when the Sixteenth Amendment to the Constitution was

William H. Bonney, "Billy the Kid," who first gained notoriety in the Lincoln County War by shooting two unarmed men

ratified, giving Congress the power to levy taxes on incomes.

Sources:

James W. Ely Jr., *The Chief Justiceship of Melville W. Fuller, 1888-1910* (Columbia: University of South Carolina Press, 1995);

Lawrence M. Friedman, *A History of American Law* (New York: Simon & Schuster, 1985);

Tinsley E. Yarbrough, *Judicial Enigma: The First Justice Harlan* (New York: Oxford University Press, 1995).

LAW ON THE FRONTIER: THE LINCOLN COUNTY WAR

The Lincoln County War. In 1878 a "war" erupted in Lincoln County, New Mexico Territory. Gen. Philip Sheridan, a Civil War hero, observed that "the population of that section is divided into two parties, who have an intense desire to exterminate each other . . . It is said that one of these parties is made up of cattle and horse thieves, and the other party of persons who have retired from that business." In Lincoln County, as in other western areas during this period, the legal system ceased to function because impartial authority could not

The Daltons of Coffeyville, Kansas, were one of the most notorious outlaw groups in the American West; they were cousins of the Younger brothers, who rode with Frank and Jesse James. Ironically four of the Dalton brothers had experience in law enforcement before turning to crime. Frank Dalton was one of Judge Isaac Parker's deputy marshals in the Indian Territory. In 1887 he was shot and killed trying to arrest three whiskey peddlers. Parker then appointed Frank's brothers Bob and Gratton as deputy marshals. Emmett Dalton worked on a ranch but sometimes would help his brothers by serving on a posse. As law enforcement officers the Dalton brothers were known for being ruthless and fast with their weapons: having lost a brother to outlaws made them wary of giving chances.

The pay for deputies was abysmal: two dollars for arresting a suspect and bringing him in to Fort Smith, and, if the deputy kept his receipts, six cents a mile for expenses. A successful arrest might earn a deputy forty dollars; and unsuccessful one, as the Daltons knew, could cost him his life. Disenchanted with the legal system, the Daltons decided to switch sides. They stole some horses and then headed for California.

In California the three Dalton boys joined their brother Bill, and in February 1891 they robbed a train in Tulare County, killing a fireman. While Bob and Emmett fled to Oklahoma, Bill and Gratton were caught. Bill was acquitted, but Gratton received a twenty-year jail sentence. He quickly escaped from the prison train and joined Bob and Emmett in Oklahoma, where they planned one of the most daring robberies in American history. Along with two henchmen, the Daltons planned to rob two banks simultaneously, and in their own hometown.

The people of Coffeyville recognized the Daltons and suspected the worst when they rode into town on 5 October 1892. While the brothers and their accomplices were robbing the banks, getting $11,000 from one and $20,000 from the other, armed citizens gathered outside. When the gang emerged, the citizens and sheriff's deputies began firing. In the ensuing ten-minute gun battle, eight people died, four on each side. Among the dead in front of the bank were Marshal Charles Connelly and Bob Dalton. Gratton Dalton escaped, badly wounded, but died a mile outside of town. Emmett Dalton was the sole survivor of the gang. He was captured and sentenced to life in prison. In 1906 he was paroled, and he lived the rest of his life quietly, dying in 1937.

Source: Paul Trachtman, *The Gunfighters* (New York: Time-Life Books, 1974).

be maintained; it seemed that nearly everyone had a vested interest in whatever dispute plagued the community. The area was perfect cattle country, and in 1866 John Chisum, a Texas cattleman, found a ready market for his beef: the federal government, having placed the Navajo and Apache on reservations, needed to feed them, as well as the soldiers fighting on the northern plains. Chisum became the undisputed cattle king of New Mexico, and some said he had the largest single cattle herd in the country.

Competitors. Chisum's cattle herd was the county's largest economic enterprise. (Some said that rustling from Chisum was the second largest.) His most important competition came from the trading house of L. G. Murphy & Company, popularly known as The House. Lawrence Murphy founded his company in 1873 and sold land and goods to small ranchers and farmers and then bought their produce, including cattle. He also had a government contract to supply the nearby Mescalero Apache reservation with foodstuffs and farm equipment. This was a lucrative arrangement for Murphy and the Indian agent on the reservation because they connived to overbill the federal government and

pocket the difference; moreover, the supplies they sold to the Indians were second-rate. Murphy used his economic position for political leverage and was elected a probate judge. However, he was forced to resign in 1875 when it was learned he had used the county's taxes to pay personal debts. Two years later Murphy sold his share of The House to James J. Dolan and John Riley, who did not realize that the company was nearly bankrupt.

The War Begins. Alexander McSween had been Murphy's lawyer and knew about the precarious financial status of The House. He decided to compete and contacted Chisum, who was looking for investments, as well as John J. Tunstall, a twenty-four-year-old Englishman full of romantic notions about the American West. The three men pooled their resources and opened a general merchandise store under Tunstall's management in Lincoln, the county seat. In the ensuing conflict, many farmers and small ranchers became caught in the middle. While some resented Chisum for his monopoly on cattle, others detested The House for its harsh credit terms. The spark that ignited the war occurred when "the Boys," a group of rustlers led by Jesse Evans and allied to the Murphy-Dolan-Riley faction, stole some of Tunstall's horses. Sheriff William Brady, a House ally, reluctantly arrested Evans and his gang, but they quickly "escaped" from the county jail.

The Murder of Tunstall. The House faction controlled Lincoln County's political and legal structure and arranged for McSween to be indicted for embezzling $10,000 from one of Murphy's business associates. In January 1878 Sheriff Brady arrested McSween and seized his home. Meanwhile, Brady sent a posse, or a group of armed citizens, to Tunstall's ranch on the pretense of recovering stolen horses and cattle. They found the Englishman alone on the range and killed him; among the posse members was Jesse Evans.

The Law. In Lincoln, Justice of the Peace John B. Wilson issued warrants for the arrest of Brady and the posse. A group of Tunstall supporters, armed with these warrants and supported by troops from Fort Stanton, rode into town and tried to serve the warrants. Brady refused to recognize the legality of the Tunstall posse and arrested three of its members, including a young drifter named William H. Bonney, soon to be known as Billy the Kid. On 1 March, Justice Wilson made Dick Brewer, a former Tunstall employee, a constable with the authority to arrest Tunstall's murderers. Brewer's posse included Bonney and nine other men who called themselves the "Regulators." Meanwhile, Gov. Samuel Axtell paid a brief visit to Lincoln after receiving alarming reports about the disorder there. He issued a proclamation revoking Wilson's commission as justice of the peace. This meant that Brewer's commission as constable was void, and the Regulators were not a legitimate law enforcement group. Only Sheriff Brady was considered to be the legal authority in the county. Nevertheless, the Regulators managed to capture two of Tunstall's murderers. Rather than turn them over to Brady, who would let them escape, Bonney shot both men.

International Pressure. In Washington, D.C., British minister Sir Edward Thornton wrote to American secretary of State William Evarts, demanding to know what had happened to Tunstall. Thornton had learned that warrants for the arrest of Tunstall's killers had been given to a constable rather than to the sheriff because the sheriff was "indirectly connected with the murder" and had in fact arrested members of the posse who had tried to serve the warrants. Two weeks later Thornton wrote that the murder "was incited by the District Attorney . . . and that the murderers are being screened or attempted to be screened by the Governor of the Territory and the Judge of the District." The British minister wanted to know what the U.S. government would do about this. Secretary of State Evarts referred the matter to the Justice Department, which sent a special investigator to New Mexico to look into this web of corruption and murder.

Grand Jury. On 1 April a grand jury was to meet in Lincoln to look into Tunstall's murder and the embezzlement charges against McSween. All of the principals were in Lincoln, including the Regulators and the Brady posse. As Brady walked to the courthouse, Bonney shot and killed him and then fled with the other Regulators before troops from Fort Stanton could arrest them. The court hearing was postponed until 13 April when the presiding judge, an ally of The House faction, pressed the panel to indict McSween. The grand jury, nonetheless, dismissed the charges against McSween but indicted Evans and four others in Tunstall's death. The grand jury also indicted Bonney and three other Regulators for Brady's murder.

Dudley's Actions. On 17 April a group of ranchers killed Brewer and captured two other Regulators. The new sheriff in Lincoln, John Copeland, then asked the commander of Fort Stanton, Lt. Col. Nathan A. M. Dudley, for military protection of his prisoners. Dudley refused to help until warrants had been issued for all the Regulators. Though Dudley credited himself with restoring order, in fact he had undermined the existing legal structure. The sheriff had been made subservient to the military, and a justice of the peace was forced to issue warrants in violation of the Fourth Amendment to the U.S. Constitution. A military lawyer examining the matter determined that Dudley had acted improperly, and in summer 1878 Congress passed a law forbidding soldiers from acting as *posse comitatus* (a body of persons summoned by a sheriff to assist in preserving the public peace.) In Lincoln County, Sheriff Copeland released his prisoners, telling everyone to go home. Governor Axtell then replaced the sheriff with George Peppin, a former meat cutter for the Murphy store.

A New Sheriff. Peppin promptly moved against the Regulators. Many questioned his authority because the office of sheriff was an elected post and Peppin had been appointed by the governor. Peppin hired a group of Texas vigilantes who ransacked the town of San Patricio. The ranks of the Regulators swelled, as they seemed to be the only protection against the ravages of the Texas posse and other outlaws. On 14 June fifty Regulators returned to Lincoln and occupied the McSween residence. Peppin and his posse besieged the house, eventually setting it on fire. All the men inside then surrendered, except Bonney and two other Regulators who escaped under heavy gunfire. The Texas posse then killed McSween and four others.

End of the War. The deaths of Tunstall and McSween ended the war but did not bring peace to the area. Instead, with the law enforcement apparatus thoroughly discredited, new groups of outlaws moved into the county. In October 1878 *The New York Times* reported on disorders in the area, attributing the violence to "a handful of uneasy, wandering, and lawless people . . . mostly Mexicans and other mixed races." In the same month Governor Axtell was replaced by Lew Wallace, a Civil War general and novelist, who called on

President Rutherford B. Hayes to declare martial law. Wallace then issued an amnesty order for all citizens who would lay down their arms. The Regulators, meanwhile, had begun living near Fort Sumner, where the local population embraced them as heroes, especially William Bonney. In February 1879 Bonney, Jesse Evans, and James Dolan agreed to a truce.

The Legend. Bonney quickly found that the amnesty did not apply to him. He was indicted for murdering Sheriff Brady and the man who killed Dick Brewer. He met secretly with the governor, believing Wallace would pardon him in exchange for his testimony in another murder case. On 23 March Bonney was arrested but allowed to stay on his ranch near Fort Sumner. He apparently continued to steal cattle. In the fall of 1880 a federal official named Azaraiah Wild came to New Mexico to investigate counterfeiting. He appointed as deputies two men who had been involved with The House faction during the Lincoln County War. They quickly convinced Wild that Bonney was the most dangerous criminal in New Mexico. Local newspapers called him "Billy the Kid" because of his boyish appearance and described him as a "desperate cuss" who killed a man for every year of his life. (At the time he was twenty-one years old.) Governor Wallace pledged a $1,000 reward for his capture. Most murders in the territory were attributed to the Kid, who found himself both a hero and a wanted criminal.

Trial, Escape, and Death. In December 1880 newly elected Lincoln County sheriff Pat Garrett pledged to finally bring Bonney to justice. Garrett and a posse of Texans captured Bonney and his men near Stinking Springs. In April 1881 he was convicted of killing Sheriff Brady and sentenced to death. The old L. G. Murphy & Company building had become the new county courthouse, and Bonney was held there under heavy guard. Nevertheless, on 28 April Bonney killed one of his guards, cut his shackles with a miner's pick, stole a horse, and escaped. This dramatic escape made the "outlaw king of the frontier" into even more of a legend. The Santa Fe *Daily New Mexican* reported that "Billy, the Kid has got more friends . . . than anybody." Garrett, anxious both for the reward money and to demonstrate that he could not be outwitted, devoted all his time to the capture of Billy the Kid. On 13 July the sheriff and two deputies went to the ranch of Pete Maxwell because the Kid had been sighted nearby. The deputies waited on the veranda while Garrett talked with Maxwell, who lay in bed. In the orchard outside, a group of men, presumably ranch hands, conversed in Spanish. One of them came to the house to cut a steak for dinner. Seeing the strangers, he quietly entered the darkened house, whispering to Maxwell "Quién es?" ("Who is it?"). Unfortunately for the stranger he did not see Garrett, who promptly shot him in the heart; Billy the Kid was dead.

THE COMMON LAW

Oliver Wendell Holmes Jr. (1841–1935), son of a prominent Boston family, veteran of the Civil War, and one of the most influential Supreme Court justices in American history, argued that experience was as important as legal principle in the life of the law.

The life of the law has not been logic; it has been experience. The felt necessities of the time, the prevalent moral and political theories, intuitions of public policy, avowed or unconscious, even the prejudices which judges share with their fellow-men, have had a good deal more to do than the syllogism in determining the rules by which men should be governed. The law embodies the story of a nation's development through many centuries, and it cannot be dealt with as if it contained only the axioms and corollaries of a book of mathematics. In order to know what it is, we must know what it has been, and what it tends to become. We must alternately consult history and existing theories of legislation. . . . The substance of the law at any given time pretty nearly corresponds, so far as it goes, with what is then understood to be convenient; but its form and machinery, and the degree to which it is able to work out desired results, depend very much upon its past.

Source: Oliver Wendell Holmes Jr., *The Common Law* (Boston: Little, Brown, 1881).

Sources:

Pat F. Garrett, *The Authentic Life of Billy the Kid* (Norman: University of Oklahoma Press, 1954);

Joel Jacobsen, *Such Men as Billy the Kid: The Lincoln County War Reconsidered* (Lincoln: University of Nebraska Press, 1992);

Frederick W. Nolan, *The Lincoln County War: A Documentary History* (Norman: University of Oklahoma Press, 1992).

LEGAL EDUCATION AND PROFESSIONALISM

Law School. The nature of legal education in the last decades of the nineteenth century changed significantly. In 1878 there were over three thousand students in American law schools; only 703 of them had college degrees. The law was viewed by many as a practical trade, not a learned profession. Justice Samuel Miller stated in 1879 that with "the accelerated pace at which modern human beings are propelled, under the influence of railroads, telegraphs, and the press, it is . . . absurd to spend . . . four collegiate years in the study of dead languages and theoretical mathematics." Most law schools did not require a college degree, and most had less stringent requirements than colleges. In 1899 Cornell required that students in its law school meet the same admission standards as students in its undergraduate college, requesting a high-school diploma for admission. Because of this reform, the entering class for that year shrank from 125 to sixty-two pupils. Many law schools required twelve to eighteen months of study, with the expectation that students would then apprentice themselves to a practicing lawyer.

The Harvard Method. Harvard University instituted the most fundamental changes in legal training. Traditionally law teachers would be practicing attorneys who would lecture on various legal principles. Under the leadership of Christopher Columbus Langdell, dean of Harvard Law School from 1870 to 1895, gradually implemented longer periods of study, eventually requiring three years to earn a degree. Langdell also replaced the teaching lawyers with full-time law professors. Instead of legal textbooks, students would read cases, and from them try to understand the underlying legal principles. Professors would not lecture but would question the students, using a Socratic dialogue to draw out the principles of the law. For Langdell and proponents of the Harvard case method, the law was a science, not a trade or "a species of handicraft." As Harvard president Charles Eliot explained, "Langdell's method resembled the laboratory method of teaching physical science, although he believed that the only laboratory the Law School needed was a library of printed books."

The American Bar Association. At the same time as the case method defined law as a science, some lawyers began a move to raise the standards of their profession. In 1876 Lewis Delafield, president of the American Social Science Association, called for the formation of a professional association of lawyers. He believed that the law was a public calling, and that lawyers should have both a good character and learning. His ideal was for a student to attend law school, followed by a year of work in a law office, and finally a public examination by impartial judges before admission to the bar. In January 1878 Connecticut judge Simeon Baldwin, who taught at Yale, also proposed the establishment of a national bar organization, and on 21 August the American Bar Association was formed at Saratoga, New York. About one hundred lawyers, mainly from the eastern states, attended the first meeting, and by the end of the year the ABA had 201 members from twenty-nine states. Baldwin drafted the group's constitution, with its object "to advance the science of jurisprudence, promote the administration of justice and uniformity of legislation throughout the union, uphold the honor of the profession of the law, and encourage cordial intercourse among the members of the American Bar." Prospective candidates had to be nominated by full members and had to have at least five years of good standing with their respective state bar associations.

Controversy. In 1891 the ABA charged that the case method introduced by Harvard University made young lawyers focus too much on what happened in court, not enough on keeping clients out of court. To the ABA, the case method encouraged litigation, rather than settlement, of cases. By the middle of the decade, ten American law schools used the case method, while fifty-seven continued to rely on lectures and textbooks. Yale University most vigorously opposed the case method. Theodore Dwight of the Yale Law School believed that reading cases "in a haphazard way leads to mental dissipation . . . . Law decisions are but a labyrinth. Woe to the man who busies himself with them without a clue . . . to guide him." It would be better, opponents of the case method argued, to present the legal principles first, and turn to the cases, if necessary, as supporting evidence.

Triumph of the Case Method. The Harvard method of studying law gradually converted the skeptics. In 1886 Oliver Wendell Holmes Jr., whose criticism of the old method of teaching had helped bring on the changes at Harvard, reported that he had tried the case method with great skepticism, but "after a week or two, when the first confusing novelty was over, I found that my class examined the question proposed with an accuracy of view which they never could have learned from textbooks, and which often exceeded that to be found in the textbooks. I, at least, if no one else, gained a good deal from our daily encounter." By 1895 Harvard had replaced Columbia as the largest American law school, with over four hundred students and ten professors. By 1920 virtually every law school in the country used the case method.

Source:
Robert Stevens, *Law School: Legal Education in America from the 1850s to the 1980s* (Chapel Hill: University of North Carolina Press, 1983).

THE LIZZIE BORDEN CASE

The Borden Family. Andrew Jackson Borden was one of the leading businessmen in Fall River, Massachusetts. Senior partner in Borden, Almy, and Company, he had been president of the Fall River Savings Bank and owned textile mills and other real estate. Despite his wealth, estimated at $500,000 in 1891, Borden lived simply with his wife, Abbie Durfee Gray Borden (his first wife had died in 1863), and his two grown daughters from his first marriage: Emma, aged forty, and Lizzie, aged thirty-one. The aging Mr. Borden may have lived simply, but his life was far from peaceful. His daughters grew jealous of their stepmother, especially in the 1880s when Mr. Borden gave his sister-in-law some property for a home. The father tried to soothe his children with gifts of money and rental property, but afterward they called their stepmother "Mrs. Borden" instead of "Mother," as they had done for twenty years.

Murder of Andrew and Abbie Borden. After dinner on 3 August 1892 the senior Bordens were ill. The next morning Bridget Sullivan, the housekeeper, also became sick. Mrs. Borden thought someone was trying to poison

The murder scene at the Borden house on 4 August 1892: the bodies of Andrew Borden (left) and his wife, Abbie (right)

them. While Mr. Borden went downtown to his office, his wife went upstairs to clean the guest room. Meanwhile, Lizzie suggested to Bridget, whom she always called "Maggie," that she go downtown to a department store, which was having a sale. Bridget did not feel up to it, and instead cleaned the windows before taking a nap. At around 10:30 A.M. Mr. Borden returned home. When he asked for his wife, Lizzie told him that she had gone to visit a sick friend. Mr. Borden then lay down on a sofa in the parlor. Shortly after 11 A.M. Lizzie woke up Bridget, telling her an intruder had come into the house and killed her father. Bridget and Lizzie went downstairs where Mr. Borden's body lay on the sofa, his head hacked to pieces. Bridget quickly left to summon a doctor. When they returned they searched the house and found Mrs. Borden's body in the guest bedroom, also with her head horribly mangled. Mrs. Borden was found to have been struck nineteen times on the head with an axe; Mr. Borden had been hit ten times.

Lizzie's Arrest. The youngest daughter of Andrew and Abbie Borden quickly became a suspect. (Emma had been at a friend's house at the time of the murders.) Lizzie told Bridget that she had been in the barn when the intruder had killed her father. There was neither sign of forced entry nor evidence of robbery; no weapon was ever found. However, the circumstantial evidence against Lizzie was very strong. A few days before the murders, Lizzie bought prussic acid, a poison, saying she

needed to kill rats. A friend reportedly found Lizzie burning a dress at the kitchen stove a few days after the slayings; she said she had spilled paint on it. The police arrested Lizzie on 13 August. Neighbors who were shocked at the crime were not stunned by Lizzie's arrest. Lizzie engaged in charitable causes, but, like her mother, she had a reputation for being hot tempered, "worse than insane." Moreover, she was "known to be ugly" and jealous of her stepmother. Nonetheless, the prosecutor doubted that he could convict Lizzie without a weapon. The brutal murder of the elderly couple generated national publicity, and people from all over the country wrote to the police with theories and suggestions. Some said Mr. Borden had an illegitimate son who committed the murders or that Bridget Sullivan was somehow involved.

The Trial. Lizzie Borden went on trial in Taunton in June 1893. Prosecutor Hosea M. Knowlton was assisted by William H. Moody, later attorney general of the United States and justice of the Supreme Court. George D. Robinson, former congressman and governor of Massachusetts, defended Borden, arguing that the case against her was circumstantial. His argument was strengthened on the day the trial opened, when a Portuguese servant committed a similar murder in a nearby town. Though this killer was not in the United States when the Bordens were killed, his crime cast doubts on the case against Lizzie. Robinson played upon appearances; during his closing argument he pointed to his prim client and asked the jury: "To find her guilty, you must believe she is a fiend. Gentlemen, does she look it?" On 20 June the jury deliberated for an hour before finding Lizzie Borden not guilty.

Reaction to the Borden Case. Public opinion seemed to support Lizzie's innocence, but her neighbors shunned her after the trial. Some thought Lizzie had escaped conviction because her lawyers had skillfully cast doubts on the case of the prosecution and because news reporters had come to like Lizzie. Boston lawyer N. Sumner Myrick wrote, "Miss Borden seems to have 'hoodooed' the Court and jury, not forgetting the newspaper men. Had Bridget Sullivan been on trial, I venture to say she would at this moment be confined in a convict's cell." A year after the trial Lizzie and Emma moved from their home, where the neighbors did not speak to them, to a more fashionable Fall River address. Free from the constraints of her father and stepmother, Lizzie called herself Lizbeth A. Borden and took an interest in the theater, entertaining friends from the stage and traveling to performances in New York and Boston. In 1905 Emma moved to New Hampshire, spending the rest of her life under an assumed name. She avoided the public eye and any further contact with her sister. Emma and Lizzie Borden died within a few days of one another in 1927.

Source:
Michael Martins and Dennis A. Binnette, eds.,. *The Commonwealth of Massachusetts vs. Lizzie A. Borden: The Knowlton Papers, 1892–1893* (Fall River, Mass.: Fall River Historical Society, 1994).

LYNCHING AND THE LAW

Lynching in America. By the 1880s nearly 90 percent of all lynchings in the United States occurred in the southern states; most of the victims were black. In the last decade of the nineteenth century an average of 187 black men, women, and children were lynched every year; in contrast, there were an average of 130 legal executions per year in this period. Lynch mobs were motivated by a variety of factors. Some defended their conduct by claiming that the executed individuals had raped white women (the perception of the African American male as a sexual predator was common during this era). Many times white crowds took the law into their own hands in order to keep African Americans in their "place." F. B. Baker of Lake City, South Carolina, was lynched in the 1890s for accepting the office of town postmaster. Economic competition played a role in some incidents. For example, Calvin McDowell, Thomas Moss, and Wil Stewart opened a grocery store outside of Memphis, Tennessee, in 1891. Their store, the People's Grocery, was just across the street from a white-owned store. The white grocer did not like the competition, and one evening in March 1892 he went into the People's Grocery carrying a gun. McDowell disarmed the man and soundly thrashed him. The white grocer left the

---

EDWARD COY BURNED ALIVE

In February 1892 Edward Coy of Texarkana, Arkansas, was accused of assaulting a white woman. A lynch mob tied him to a tree, cut flesh from his body, and poured coal oil over him. The woman then applied a match as fifteen thousand people watched. According to writer and magazine publisher Albion W. Tourgée:

1. The woman who was paraded as victim of his violence was of bad character; her husband was a drunkard and a gambler.

2. She was publicly reported and generally known to have been criminally intimate with Coy for more than a year previous.

3. She was compelled by threats, if not by violence, to make the charge against the victim.

4. When she came to apply the match Coy asked her if she would burn him after they had "been sweethearting" so long.

5. A large majority of the "superior" white men prominent in the affair are the reputed fathers of mulatto children.

These are not pleasant facts, but they are illustrative of the vital phase of the so-called race question which should be properly designated an earnest inquiry as to the best methods by which religion, science, law and political power may be employed to excuse injustice, barbarity, and crime done to a people because of race and color. There can be no possible belief that these people were inspired by any consuming zeal to vindicate God's law against miscegenationists of the most practical sort. The woman was a willing partner in the victim's guilt, and being of the "superior" race must naturally have been more guilty.

Source: Ida B. Wells, "A Red Record," in *Southern Horrors and Other Writings: The Anti-Lynching Campaign of Ida B. Wells, 1892–1900*, edited by Jacqueline Jones Royster (Boston: Bedford Books, 1996).

---

store vowing to "clean them out" and returned with twelve men identifying themselves as sheriff's deputies. A gun battle ensued before the defenders of the store fled. The authorities eventually arrested the three black owners and twenty-eight other people for resisting arrest and for wounding three officers. Two days after the attack, a mob stormed the jail, took McDowell, Stewart, and Moss out of their cells, and shot them to death.

Lynching and the Law. African Americans were not the only victims of such violence. Native Americans as well as Chinese, Japanese, and Italian immigrants all suffered at the hands of angry white crowds. When the victim of a lynching was a newly arrived immigrant, the

A lynching in Clanton, Alabama, circa 1891

matter. Unfortunately, state governments were firmly in the hands of white politicians who often used race to justify their hold on power. For example, Gov. Benjamin Tillman of South Carolina was elected in 1890 by promising to see "justice" done to black criminals. During his tenure a white woman was raped, and John Peterson, a black man, was accused of the crime. He fled to Columbia where he put himself under Governor Tillman's protection. Peterson pleaded innocence and was able to produce witnesses to support his alibi. A white reporter confirmed Peterson's story, but a white mob still demanded that the governor deliver Peterson. Tillman turned him over to the mob. Even though the white victim testified that Peterson was not the rapist, the mob decided that "the crime had been committed and somebody had to hang for it, and if he, Peterson, was not guilty of that he was of some other crime." Peterson was then hung from a tree and one thousand bullets fired into his body.

McKinley. Governors did not always cave in to public pressure. In October 1894 a mob surrounded the Fayette County Courthouse in Ohio and demanded a prisoner. Instead of allowing the mob to administer its own form of justice, Gov. William McKinley sent the state militia to protect the prisoner. Five men were killed and twenty wounded in a battle which was fought, McKinley said, not to spare a prisoner but to maintain "the principle that the law must be upheld." When McKinley became president of the United States in 1897, he said in his

federal government could only pay an indemnity to the victim's country and issue an official apology because lynching was a crime that fell under the jurisdiction of the states. Some states tried to control lynching. A Georgia law in 1893 allowed a sheriff to form a posse to fight a lynch mob, and two years later the state made it a criminal offense to interfere with a law enforcement official trying to disperse such a gathering. North Carolina in 1893 passed a law against breaking into a prison and killing or injuring a prisoner, with a penalty of a $500 fine and fifteen years in jail. South Carolina's state constitution of 1895 forbade mobs to take prisoners from a sheriff's custody. In 1897 Tennessee, Kentucky, and Texas passed laws against lynching, and Indiana and Michigan did so in 1899. Though the states passed laws, no one was indicted under any of these laws before the twentieth century, and no jury would convict accused members of a lynch mob. When members of one lynch mob were held in a Tennessee jail, another group stormed the jail and freed them.

What To Do About Lynching? In the 1890s Congressman Henry Blair of New Hampshire proposed that Congress investigate lynching, but the measure was blocked because Congress viewed that activity as a state

SOUTHERN LYNCHINGS, 1882-1903

	Whites	Blacks
Mississippi	39	294
Texas	114	199
Louisiana	34	232
Georgia	28	241
Alabama	46	198
Arkansas	60	139
Tennessee	49	150
Kentucky	64	103
Florida	19	115
South Carolina	8	109
Missouri	49	42
Virginia	21	70
North Carolina	15	48
West Virginia	19	27
Maryland	2	18
Total	567	1,985

Source: James Elbert Cutler, *Lynch Law: An Investigation into the History of Lynching in the United States,* revised edition (New York: Negro Universities Press, 1969), p. 181.

From a Photograph taken just before the Murder.

Dr. Patrick Henry Cronin, who was murdered in 1889 by political opponents in the Clan-na-Gael

inaugural address that "Courts, not mobs, must execute the penalties of the laws." Despite McKinley's support, and the public campaign against lynching led by Ida B. Wells-Barnett, lynching remained a brutal reminder that the laws cannot always restrain the tyranny of the majority.

Source:
James Elbert Cutler, *Lynch Law: An Investigation into the History of Lynching in the United States,* revised edition (New York: Negro Universities Press, 1969).

THE MURDER OF DR. PATRICK HENRY CRONIN

The Good Doctor. Born in County Cork, Ireland, in 1846, Patrick Henry Cronin came to the United States as an infant, and, with his family, traveled from New York to Baltimore and Ontario, Canada, before settling in the mining areas of Pennsylvania. Moving to Missouri after the Civil War, he studied medicine, served in the militia during the strikes of 1877, then spent much of the following year in Ireland. In 1882, having earned a medical degree as well as a Ph.D., he moved to Chicago, where he practiced medicine and involved himself in Irish American politics.

The Clan-na-Gael. One of the largest Irish American political organizations, the United Brotherhood or Clan-na-Gael, was established in 1869 and espoused loyalty to Ireland and independence of the island from British rule. The estimated ten thousand members of the Clan-na-Gael were organized into local chapters, or "camps," which supported a central Executive Board by donating 10 percent of their revenues. At a national convention in Chicago in 1881, the board warned that the Irish movement would soon have extraordinary expenses, and that the camps needed to contribute more to the cause. The convention voted to submit all revenues, nearly $100,000 each year, to the board, whose five members were led by Chicago lawyer Alexander Sullivan. The board did not define the extraordinary new expenses of the Irish movement, though the money seems to have been used to finance a terrorist campaign in England. Over the next few years dynamite explosions occurred at the Tower of London, London Bridge, and Whitehall Palace. Between 1881 and 1885 twenty-nine Irish revolutionists connected with these terrorist attacks were extradited from America.

Charges of Embezzlement. The Clan-na-Gael Executive Board denied any possible link to the explosions. However, when the board called for more money in 1885, some camps protested. The protesters were then expelled from the organization. As a leading member of Clan-na-Gael, Cronin came forward criticizing the secret operations of the board. The board responded by accusing Cronin of treason against the Irish cause and voted to expel him from Clan-na-Gael. Nonetheless, he continued to charge Sullivan and the board with misappropriating funds. An exasperated Sullivan was reportedly heard to say that he wished Cronin could be "removed." On 8 February 1889 Clan-na-Gael Camp 20 appointed a secret committee that charged Cronin with being a British agent.

Abduction. On 4 May 1889, as Cronin prepared for a meeting of the Celto-American Society, a man in a carriage came to ask his assistance; an employee of Patrick O'Sullivan's icehouse had been injured. Cronin jumped into the carriage and sped off, never to be seen alive again. Cronin's friends were worried when he failed to return. They believed he had been killed, and their suspicions were confirmed when a bloody trunk was discovered north of the city. But while they suspected he was dead, a friend of Cronin's named Anna Murphy reported seeing him on a streetcar late at night on 4 May, and streetcar conductor William Dwyer also reported seeing Cronin. On 10 May, nearly a week after Cronin had disappeared, Chicago's papers received dispatches from Toronto, filed by reporter Charles Long, reporting that Cronin was in Canada, on his way to England to testify against the Clan-na-Gael. He admitted, the dispatches said, to being a British spy, and he had arranged his own disappearance.

Cronin's Body Found. On 22 May the public works department in Lake View received complaints about the sewer at Evanston Avenue and North 59th street. The sewer was apparently jammed, and a horrible stench was permeating the neighborhood. The men sent to clear the pipes found Cronin's decomposing body wedged into the catch basin. Cronin had not disappeared; he had been murdered. Now that the body had been discovered, Cronin's friends pushed the police to find the killers. There were few leads. The owner of a livery stable, though, recognized the horse and carriage described as taking Cronin away on the night of the murder. It belonged to his stable, he reported, and had been reserved on 4 May by Chicago police detective Daniel Coughlin. The stable owner reported this to Coughlin's superior officer, Capt. Michael Schaack, who had become famous for his investigation into the Haymarket bombing. Confronted with evidence that one of his officers was involved in a murder, Schaack called in Coughlin for an explanation. Coughlin admitted reserving a carriage for a friend. Schaack promptly ordered Coughlin to find the friend. Coughlin and another policeman spent a week walking the streets of Chicago, looking for the mysterious friend; they never found him.

The Murder Scene. The police found a small cottage behind Patrick O'Sullivan's icehouse where the murder apparently occurred. It had been rented from its owner, a Swede named Jonas Carlson, by a mysterious man named Frank Williams in late March, who was scarcely seen at the cottage. On the evening of 4 May Carlson recalled seeing Williams on the porch and later heard two men talking in loud voices. On 13 May a man identifying himself as a friend of Williams came to pay the rent. Five days later a suspicious Carlson checked the cottage and found its front room covered in blood.

Prosecution. Alexander Sullivan, known to have a great personal hatred for Cronin, was arrested but was soon released. Though he clearly wanted Cronin silenced, no evidence linked him to the murder. The police also arrested O'Sullivan and Detective Coughlin. The mysterious Frank Williams turned out to be Martin Burke and was discovered hiding in Winnipeg, Canada, trying to flee to England. He was soon extradited to the United States and, along with O'Sullivan and Coughlin, indicted for murder. Two others were also placed on trial: John Beggs was a senior member of Camp 20 accused of conspiring to commit murder while John Kunze was a common laborer accused of being an accessory.

Conspiracy. Cronin's murder was the result of a conspiracy motivated by both personal and political reasons. The Irish patriots, having undertaken a series of bombings in England, were under investigation by the British government. The bombings had discredited the Irish movement in the eyes of many potential supporters. Charges that Sullivan, leader of the American supporters of Irish independence, had embezzled Clan-na-Gael funds could not have been more damaging. It was essential to silence Cronin. Because some members of Clan-na-Gael held positions of power and influence in the municipal government of Chicago, they may have believed they could escape detection. Even when the conspiracy was unveiled, the Clan-na-Gael still hoped its members could influence the trial's outcome. A bailiff unsuccessfully tried to bribe jurors. On 16 December the jury returned with verdicts after seventy hours of deliberation. Coughlin, O'Sullivan, and Burke were convicted of murder and sent to prison for life. Beggs was acquitted while Kunze was convicted of manslaughter and sent to prison for three years. The police department came under heavy criticism as a result of these verdicts. Captain Schaack, whom some had charged with planting incriminating evidence in the homes of Haymarket suspects, was suspended from the police force for his failure to investigate Coughlin's complicity.

Source:
Henry M. Hunt, *The Crime of the Century: Or, the Assassination of Dr. Patrick Henry Cronin* (Chicago: H. L. & D. H. Kochersperger, 1889).

THE MURDER OF POLICE CHIEF DAVID HENNESSY

Death of David Hennessy. On 15 October 1890 New Orleans police chief David Hennessy was shot as he walked home in a light drizzle. He died the next morning. Deeply shocked, the people of New Orleans paid their respects (more filed past his casket at City Hall than had paid similar respects to former Confederate president Jefferson Davis, whose body lay in state there a few months earlier). City officials vowed to punish his killers.

Who Killed Hennessy? Shortly before he died, Hennessy whispered to a bystander, "The Dagos did it." Hennessy was involved in a dispute between two rival groups of Italian immigrants working on the New Orleans docks. For years, Joseph Provenzano had a monopoly on the fruit trade from Central America. Provenzano owned ships that brought bananas, coconuts, and pineapples to New Orleans, where longshoremen in his pay unloaded the produce and then sold it. In 1886 Carlo Matranga had started a rival company. When city merchants gave Matranga a monopoly on their trade, Provenzano decided to retaliate against the competition. On 6 May 1890 Provenzano gunmen opened fire on seven Matranga longshoremen; several people died on both sides. In August seven Provenzano loyalists were convicted of attempted murder. They were granted a new trial, which was scheduled for 22 October. Chief Hennessy planned to testify on behalf of the Provenzano faction. He told the press he had uncovered the existence of a crime syndicate known as the Mafia. He believed that

Illustration from the New Orleans *Times-Picayune* of the street where Police Chief David Hennessy was murdered. *A* marks the spot where the shooting occurred, *B,* where the murderers hid.

the Matrangas were bringing Italian and Sicilian criminals to New Orleans and warned that as many as one hundred such criminals were at work on the docks. He was gunned down one week before the trial, and his dying declaration raised suspicion that the Matrangas had arranged his killing.

Public Reaction. Hennessy's murder came at a time of great antiforeign sentiment in the United States. Many Americans feared Italian immigrants and perceived them as common thugs. In December 1890 *Popular Science Monthly* ran an article, "What Shall We Do with the Dago?" The author haughtily suggested that laws were inadequate to prevent immigrant criminals from terrorizing Americans because the immigrants would find an American jail a great improvement over life at home. The police quickly arrested scores of Italians in the wake of Hennessy's death. Nineteen men described as Mafia members were indicted as principals and conspirators in the Hennessy murder; most of them were allied with the Matrangas. Mayor Joseph Shakespeare vowed that "We must teach these people a lesson they will not forget for all time." Perhaps with this in mind, Thomas Duffy, the son of a prominent businessman, went to the prison on the day of Hennessy's funeral and shot one of the prisoners in the neck. "I'm willing to hang if one of those Dagoes

dies. . . ," Duffy said as he was sentenced to six months in jail.

Arraignment and Trial. On 16 February 1891 the nineteen accused appeared in court. The trial was viewed by most people as a farce. Many of the sixty witnesses were threatened, and several jury members took bribes from the Mafia. Lionel Adams, former district attorney appointed to defend the accused, forced the state to drop charges against Matranga and Bastian Incardona, as it had no evidence against either. The charges against Asperi Marchesi were also dismissed in exchange for his cooperation with the prosecutors. Despite overwhelming evidence against eleven of the defendants, all but three were acquitted (Antonio Scaffidi, Manuel Politz, and Pietro Monasterio), and the jury could not reach a verdict on these men. The judge remanded all the defendants to jail for their own protection. As the men were led from the courtroom a stunned and angry crowd taunted them, shouting in mock-Italian accents, "Who killa da chief?"

Reaction to Verdict. Unwilling to accept the court's verdict, a prominent New Orleans lawyer named W. S. Parkerson formed a "movement to correct justice." On 14 March, two days after the verdicts, Parkerson led an angry mob to an arsenal, where every man grabbed a weapon. "When courts fail the people must act!"

Parkerson shouted as the mob marched on the prison. In a frenzy of violence, the crowd shot nine of the defendants and hanged two from lampposts. The crowd released the other prisoners because evidence against them was weak. The armed citizens then searched for Detective Dominic O'Malley, suspected of aiding and abetting the defendants.

New Orleans Congratulates Itself. Parkerson dismissed the mob after the day of carnage. "I have performed the most painful duty of my life today. Now let us go home, and God bless you and our community." Mayor Shakespeare, when asked if he was sorry to see a mob usurping the role of the courts, said, "No sir. I am an American citizen and I am not afraid of the Devil. These men deserved killing and they were punished by peaceful, law abiding citizens. They [the accused] took the law in their own hands and we were forced to do the same." The New Orleans Chamber of Commerce congratulated the citizens of New Orleans for restoring order. On 6 May a grand jury indicted Detective O'Malley and several others, including two jurors, for obstructing justice by allowing the accused Italians to be acquitted. The grand jury also considered evidence against the lynch mob, but in the end praised Parkerson and the other leaders.

Repercussions. The acquittal and lynching of the suspects had repercussions far beyond New Orleans. The Italian government recalled its ambassador to the United States and demanded that the American government compensate the lynched men's families. Secretary of State James G. Blaine telegraphed Louisiana governor Francis Nichols: "The President deeply regrets that the citizens of New Orleans should have disparaged the purity and adequacy of their own judicial tribunals as to transfer to the passionate judgment of a mob, a question that should have been adjudged dispassionately and by settled rules of the law." Most Americans supported the New Orleans mob. In West Virginia coal miners went on strike when their foreman refused to fire two Italians. Many called for a stronger navy to prevent Italian criminals from entering the United States and to guard against a Catholic army the Pope was supposedly planning to raise. The United States government, unable to restrain the lawlessness of its own citizens, decided to compensate the Italians for the death of theirs. Ironically eight of the eleven murdered men were American citizens. Congress appropriated $25,000 for the families of all the victims. No one else was charged in the death of Hennessy.

Sources:

James D. Horan, *The Pinkertons: The Detective Dynasty that Made History* (New York: Crown, 1967);

Luciano J. Iorizzo and Salvatore Mondello, *The Italian-Americans*, revised edition (Boston: Twayne, 1980).

OBSCENITY AND THE LAW

Lucifer, the Light-Bearer. In the later half of the

The seal used by the Society for the Suppression of Vice — on the left, a purveyor of obscenity is being put in jail; on the right, obscene volumes are burned.

nineteenth century, conservative moral crusaders such as Anthony Comstock, who had lobbied for the 1873 "Comstock Law" barring obscene material from the U.S. mail, struggled against purveyors of obscenity and a growing cadre of men and women who advocated frank discussion of sex, birth control, woman's rights in marriage, and other controversial issues. The 1873 law was very strict and defined any mention of sexual relations as obscenity. It was, therefore, simply impossible to address sexual issues without breaking the law. The struggle between moral reformers such as Comstock and more-libertarian individuals can be seen in a case involving a citizen of Valley Falls, Kansas, who published a weekly newspaper called *Lucifer, the Light-Bearer.* The newspaper had for a motto "Perfect freedom of thought and action for every individual within the limits of his own personality. Self-government is the only true government. Liberty and responsibility the only basis of morality."

The Case. In 1891 the publisher of *Lucifer,* a quiet, sixty-year-old man named Moses Harmon, was indicted for violating the 1873 law by placing an obscene publication in the mail. Harmon maintained that he published his paper in order to educate people. For example, he attacked the prevailing sexual ethics that subjected women to the brutal lusts of their husbands. Though *Lucifer* contained some general news and political commentary, much of it discussed sexual relations. Harmon's lawyer tried to have the court consider all of *Lucifer,* not just the passages the prosecutor selected out as obscene. By seeing these passages in their proper context, Harmon's lawyer reasoned, the court would understand that his client's purpose was to improve and not corrupt morals. Judge John F. Phillips of the federal district court of western Missouri rejected this strategy and dismissed Harmon's argument that he printed his paper as a public service, not to gratify men's baser lusts. In fact, Harmon's argument reminded the judge of Charles Guiteau's reasons for killing President James Garfield. "Guiteau stoutly maintained to the end his sanity, and that he felt he had a patriotic mission to fulfill in taking off President Garfield, to the salvation of a political party. The Hindu mother cast her babe to the adoring Ganges to appease the gods. But civilized society says both are murders."

Obscenity in the Mail. Having equated Harmon with presidential assassin Guiteau, Phillips discussed the role of courts in upholding public morality. "Where vituperation or licentiousness begins, liberty of the press ends." In determining obscenity, the court had to decide how the language in question would be received by a man or woman of average intelligence and sensibility. "The subjects discussed and the language employed are too coarse and indecent for the man of average education and refinement to recapitulate." The court warned that "the appetite for such literature increases with the feeding. The more it is pandered to, the more insatiable its craving for something yet more vicious in taste. And while it may be conceded . . . that the federal government, under its constitutional limitation, ought not to take upon itself the office of *censor morum*, nor undertake to legislate . . . the private morals of the people, yet Congress may, as the basis of legislation of this character, have regard to the common *consensus* of the people that a thing is *malum in se* — is hurtful to the public morals, — endangering the public welfare, and therefore deny to it as a vehicle of dissemination the use of its post-offices and post-roads, devised and maintained by the government at the public expense for the purpose of promoting the public welfare and common good."

Intention and Knowledge. The decision in the Harmon case gave sanction to the idea that prevailing community standards should define obscenity while Congress could prevent the public circulation of all offensive material. In some cases, however, this approach actually aided the distribution of such literature. For example, when Elmina Slenker of Snowville, Virginia, was convicted in 1887 for mailing some writings, including the essay "The Girl and the Dog," her conviction was overturned. While Slenker had placed the pamphlets in the mail, the prosecution had not shown that she knew their content, or knew they would be considered obscene. In an 1894 case a New York court rejected Comstock's contention that certain books were obscene after it compared them with standard works of literature. However, these cases were exceptions; men or women who knowingly distributed material that the community regarded as obscene were usually punished in the late nineteenth century.

Source:
Heywood Broun and Margaret Leech, *Anthony Comstock: Roundsman of the Lord* (New York: Albert & Charles Boni, 1927).

PLESSY V. FERGUSON

Jim Crow. Following the end of Reconstruction in 1877, Southern states made racial discrimination a matter of public policy by passing Jim Crow laws. Named after a 1830s minstrel-show character, these statutes maintained racial segregation and varied from state to state. In 1887 Florida became the first state to require whites and blacks to ride separately in railroad cars. Other states followed: Mississippi (1888), Texas (1889), Louisiana (1890), Alabama, Arkansas, Georgia, and Tennessee (1891), and Kentucky (1892). The Louisiana law, "An Act to Promote the Comfort of Passengers," required equal but separate accommodations for people of each race.

Homer Plessy's Train Ride. On 7 June 1892 Homer A. Plessy bought a ticket and boarded an East Louisiana Railway train bound from New Orleans to Covington, Louisiana. Plessy was an octoroon, a person of one-eighth black ancestry (one of his great-grandparents was African American). Someone told the conductor that Plessy was "colored," who then instructed him to sit in the "colored coach." Plessy refused and was arrested. Brought before John H. Ferguson of the New Orleans district criminal court, Plessy was found guilty of violating the 1890 law. Plessy's lawyers, Albion Tourgée and James Walker, filed a writ of certiorari that allowed the case to be taken to the state supreme court. In November 1892 state chief justice Francis Nichols, who had been governor in 1890, upheld the state law but granted a writ of error that brought Plessy's case, now *Plessy* v. *Ferguson*, to the U.S. Supreme Court in April 1896.

Tourgée's Argument. Tourgée served as a judge in North Carolina during Reconstruction. His novel about his experiences, *A Fool's Errand* (1879), remains one of the classic accounts of that difficult period. In arguing for Plessy, Tourgée developed two arguments. First, the law was unconstitutional because it violated the Thirteenth Amendment , which abolished slavery. Second, the state had deprived Plessy of his property, a violation of the Fourteenth Amendment. Plessy's property, in this case, was the "reputation of being white." Tourgée noted that Plessy appeared white, but the conductor had made the judgment that he was black and thus deprived him of "the master-key that unlocks the golden door of opportunity." Race prejudice barred any man labeled a Negro from the opportunity to succeed. Because Plessy, and many others labeled as "black," were visibly white, the state had no reason to segregate them because of their race. Tourgée noted that the state law exempted black women hired to care for white children, who were permitted to travel with their charges. This exemption, Tourgée told the Court, "shows that the real evil lies not in the color of the skin but in the relation the colored person sustains to the white. If he is a dependent, it may be endured: if he is not, his presence is insufferable." Instead of promoting the general comfort of passengers, as the law's title suggested, it instead was "intended to promote the happiness of one class by asserting its supremacy and the inferiority of another class. Justice is pictured blind and her step-daughter, the Law, ought at least to be color-blind." Tourgée speculated that the state would next require whites and blacks to walk on different sides of the street and to paint their houses different colors. He mockingly asked the Court if people with different hair or eye colors should also be segregated.

The Court's Opinion. The court did not accept Tourgée's argument. On 18 May 1896 Justice Henry Brown wrote for the majority that the state had the power to pass segregation laws. According to the Court, the Thirteenth Amendment only applied to actions whose purpose was to reintroduce slavery itself. The Fourteenth Amendment had extended legal rights to all citizens but had not abolished distinctions based on color. The law could not abolish these distinctions, anyway, Brown wrote, and social prejudices could not be overcome by legislation. Plessy may have been deprived of his reputation, but the laws requiring him to sit in a separate car did not really stigmatize him as inferior. If he felt stigmatized, Brown said, "it is not by reason of anything found in the act, but solely because the colored race chooses to put that construction upon it." If blacks subjected whites to segregation, Brown was sure whites would not see it as proof of white inferiority.

Harlan's Dissent. Justice John Harlan, who had dissented in the 1883 *Civil Rights Cases*, found himself alone in dissent again in 1896. "In my opinion, the judgment this day rendered will, in time, prove to be quite as pernicious as the decision made by this tribunal in the *Dred Scott* case." He reasoned that the Court's decision would encourage lawless attacks on citizens and would encourage states to continue challenging the Thirteenth and Fourteenth amendments. Harlan dismissed the idea advanced by proponents of segregation that separating the races prevented racial conflict. Instead of establishing racial harmony, the decision allowed states "under the sanction of law" to plant the "seeds of hate." "What can more certainly arouse race hate, what can more certainly create and perpetuate a feeling of distrust between the races, than state enactments, which, in fact, proceed on the ground that colored citizens are so inferior and degraded that they cannot be allowed to sit in public coaches occupied by white citizens?"

Second-Class Citizens. Harlan concluded his dissenting opinion with one of the ringing statements for which he is best known. "In the view of the Constitution, in the eyes of the law, there is in this country no superior, dominant, ruling class of citizens. There is no caste here.

Theodore Roosevelt during his tenure as president of the New York City Police Board

Our constitution is color-blind, and neither knows nor tolerates classes among citizens. In respect of civil rights, all citizens are equal before the law. The humblest is the peer of the most powerful. The law regards man as man, and takes no account of his surroundings, or of his color when his civil rights as guaranteed by the supreme law of the land are involved." In 1896 the Court affirmed the right of states to enshrine private prejudices in public law. Four years later a Richmond, Virginia, newspaper editor insisted that "God Almighty drew the color line and it cannot be obliterated. The negro must stay on his side of the line and the white man must stay on his side," and the sooner both accepted this the better it would be for them. States drew the line, mandating not only separate railroad cars, but separate schools, hotels, theaters, parks, drinking fountains, and restrooms. The doctrine of "separate but equal" would remain in place until 1954.

Sources:
Plessy v. *Ferguson*, 163 U.S. 537-564 (1895);

John E. Semonche, *Charting the Future: The Supreme Court Responds to a Changing Society 1890-1920* (Westport, Conn.: Greenwood Press, 1978);

C. Vann Woodward, "The Case of the Louisiana Traveler," in *Quarrels That Have Shaped the Constitution*, edited by John A. Garraty (New York: Harper & Row, 1964);

Tinsley E. Yarbrough, *Judicial Enigma: The First Justice Harlan* (New York: Oxford University Press, 1995).

REFORMING THE NEW YORK POLICE

Parkhurst and Graft. As chairman of the Society for the Prevention of Crime, Rev. Charles Parkhurst of Madison Square Presbyterian Church knew that illegal gambling and prostitution flourished in New York City in the 1890s. He suspected that the city's police were paid to "look the other way." The reverend was justified in his accusations: taverns paid the police $10,000 to open on Sunday; gambling dens set aside between $15 and $300 each month as insurance against raids; and a successful brothel would contribute $30,000 each year to a precinct captain. This kind of graft was so lucrative that there were two applicants for every one position on the thirty-eight-thousand-man police force. It was commonplace to buy rank, as in the case of one officer who paid his superiors $15,000 in order to receive a captain's badge. Police Chief Thomas Byrnes presided over this network of extortion and was said to be worth $350,000.

Parkhurst's Proof. On 14 February 1892 Parkhurst delivered a sermon on graft and corruption, charging New York's police with allowing gambling, prostitution, and other illegal activities to flourish. A reporter happened to be in the church that day, and the next morning Parkhurst's allegations were in the newspaper. City officials demanded that the clergyman prove his charges or face a libel suit. On 13 March he delivered another sermon on vice, this time with 284 affidavits that alleged that the New York police department permitted gambling and prostitution to prosper. Furthermore, Parkhurst claimed that police officials had the approval of Tammany Hall, the Democratic Party organization of New York.

The Lexow Commission. In Albany, Republicans in the state legislature saw this as an opportunity to embarrass the Democrats in New York City and appointed a senate committee to investigate Parkhurst's charges. Chaired by Republican Sen. Clarence Lexow, the committee was more eager to expose Democratic corruption than police misconduct. It produced a 10,576-page report that estimated that the police extorted over $10 million each year. The public learned enough from the Lexow investigation to call for a change, and in 1894 they elected social reformer William Strong as mayor of New York City. The next year Strong appointed Theodore Roosevelt to the New York City Board of Police Commissioners. Roosevelt was the well-known son of a social reformer and philanthropist, and in the early 1880s he had been a member of the state legislature. In 1886 Roosevelt had been the Republican candidate for mayor of New York. Appointed to the Civil Service Commission by President Benjamin Harrison, Roosevelt investigated corruption in the U.S. Post Office. The other members of the police commission elected Roosevelt as chairman because of his past experience and charismatic personality.

Roosevelt's Strategy. Before meeting with his fellow commissioners, Roosevelt met with newspaper reporters Lincoln Steffens and Jacob Riis. He asked, "Now then, what'll we do?" Roosevelt's first action was to force out Chief Byrnes, who promptly resigned, and to begin formal investigations of other officers. During Roosevelt's tenure as chairman, the city police department adopted a written civil service exam, placed a limit on the number of years an officer could work, and raised the physical requirements for applicants above those set for soldiers. These reforms forced senior officers out at triple the previous attrition, and hundreds of new recruits, who no longer had to pay bribes, joined the force at four times the prior rate. The police force was younger, healthier, and less political than it had ever been before. Bicycle patrols were also introduced and allowed the officers to move more quickly and efficiently than they could on horseback.

The Midnight Strolls. Riis described Roosevelt's strategy as "publicity/publicity/publicity." At two in the morning on 7 June 1895 Roosevelt and Riis strolled through Manhattan to check on how well the police were working. They did not see a single officer in a fifteen-block area and discovered some patrolmen quietly napping. One officer found relaxing in a restaurant did not recognize the commissioner and threatened to arrest him for vagrancy; fortunately for the policeman the restaurant owner knew Roosevelt. This surprise inspection had the desired effect. One newspaper reported that the police began watching for Roosevelt's glasses and huge teeth coming through the darkness; another reported that "He Makes the Night Hideous for Sleeping Patrolmen." On 14 June Roosevelt made his second night patrol and found a big improvement. He went to one station house to congratulate the captain for his well-patrolled precinct and was delighted to find on the bathroom wall a caricature of himself, with a warning that Roosevelt was watching.

The Sunday Excise Law. By 1895 the Sunday Excise Law, which forbade the sale of intoxicating liquors on the Sabbath, had become a lucrative source of graft for the New York City police department. Saloons that paid a "fee" to the local police precinct could remain open on Sunday. Roosevelt knew that when people ignored one law, it was hard for them to obey others; he was therefore determined to enforce the Sunday Excise Law. Unlike the midnight strolls and the investigation into corrupt police officers, which promised safer streets for all citizens, Roosevelt's adherence to the Sunday Excise Law caused him many enemies. In July a judge ruled that the law forbade the sale of all drinks, not just alcoholic ones, in saloons on Sunday; therefore the police would have to prevent New Yorkers from drinking lemonade and iced tea. As the summer of 1895 stretched on, New Yorkers wondered why Roosevelt was punishing them for the corruption of the police. Many began speculating about when the commissioner would be shot, and on 5 August he received a letter bomb.

Roosevelt Defends His Policy. The police commissioner defended the Sunday closings in a meeting of the Good Government Club, a civic organization made up of German Americans. He could not have found a more hostile audience: Sunday at the beer garden was a German tradition, and these citizens, otherwise law-abiding, resented being told they were breaking the law. Roosevelt explained that the only purpose of the law was to provide graft and to keep the saloons as "subservient allies to Tammany Hall." He noted that the law had previously been enforced only against saloon keepers who could not pay off the police or those too honest to do so. Roosevelt warned that the real problem was not the sale of liquor, but corruption of the municipal government. "Where justice is bought, where favor is the price of money or political influence, the rich man held his own and the poor man went to the wall. Now all are treated exactly alike." Moreover, he declared that if the law was unpopular the legislature should repeal it. Otherwise, "it is the plain duty of a public officer to stand steadfastly for the honest enforcement of the law." Later in the summer when the Liquor Sellers Association came out in support of strict enforcement of the law and vowed to expel any member who violated it, Roosevelt knew he had won the battle.

Roosevelt's Reputation. Roosevelt's stand did not win him warm personal support, but his integrity was beyond question. British novelist Bram Stoker, author of *Dracula,* wrote that Roosevelt "must be President some day. A man you can't cajole, can't frighten, can't buy." Others were less impressed. The *New York Herald* reprinted Roosevelt's speeches, putting every "I" in bold type, emphasizing how often Roosevelt referred to himself. Lawyer Abraham Hummel, of the criminal defense team Howe and Hummel, said "Roosevelt, Roosevelt — when they bury him, they can write on his tombstone, `Here lies all the civic virtue there every was.'" Roosevelt himself enjoyed the controversy. In September the United Societies for Liberal Sunday Laws held a protest rally and parade, to which they jokingly invited Roosevelt, whom they planned to burn in effigy. Roosevelt, to their surprise, attended the rally and thoroughly enjoyed the spectacle. He left with two souvenir banners: "Send the Police Czar to Russia" and "Roosevelt's Razzle-Dazzle Reform Racket."

Greener Pastures. Roosevelt, a man of great restless energy, turned his attention elsewhere once he had "cleaned house" at the New York City Police Department. He campaigned for presidential candidate William McKinley in 1896 and in 1897 resigned as police commissioner to become undersecretary of the navy. Years later, after Roosevelt had served as governor of New York, vice president, and president of the United States, former police commissioner Avery Andrews stated: "It may truthfully be said that Theodore

Roscoe Conkling, who argued before the Supreme Court that corporations needed to be protected from excessive state taxation

Roosevelt at no time in his career fought more effectively for the basic principles of free government than he fought for them as New York City Police Commissioner."

Source:
Edmund Morris, *The Rise of Theodore Roosevelt* (New York: Coward, McCann & Geoghegan, 1979).

RIGHTS OF CORPORATIONS

The California Constitution. In 1879 the state of California drew up a new constitution that tried to bring corporations, particularly railroads, under the control of the state. A Board of Equalization was established to set tax rates for railroads, ensuring that large businesses paid their fair share in taxes. A new Railroad Commission also set rates and investigated business practices. Lawyers representing the railroad companies thought that both measures were unconstitutional under the Fourteenth Amendment to the Constitution.

The Fourteenth Amendment. In 1868 the Fourteenth Amendment was adopted. Its first section reads:

All persons born or naturalized in the United States, and

In the late nineteenth century Stephen J. Field (1816-1899) was the Supreme Court's intellectual giant and one of its most controversial figures. Appointed by Abraham Lincoln in 1863, Stephen Field was promoted as a Democratic presidential candidate in 1880. In 1889 he was assaulted by David Terry, the former chief justice of the California Supreme Court. In the ensuing scuffle Field's bodyguard shot and killed Terry. The next year Field's nephew, David Brewer, joined him on the court.

Field dominated his colleagues through his powerful mind and sometimes explosive temper. However, in the 1890s Field began to exhibit signs of senility; he dozed during arguments and sometimes did not understand the case at hand. Chief Justice Melville Fuller stopped assigning cases to Field, who could not understand why. His periods of confusion alternated with moments of lucidity. Nevertheless, in 1896 the other members of the court decided to approach Field and to convince him to resign. (As a Supreme Court justice, Field was entitled to serve for life.) Justice John M. Harlan, the most senior justice after Field, was delegated to discuss the matter with Field. Finding him dozing in the justices' robing room, apparently unaware of his surroundings, Harlan gradually approached the question. He noted that in 1869 Field, as the most junior judge, had been sent by his colleagues to convince the elderly Justice Robert Grier to retire. He recalled that Grier's resignation was in the Court's best interest. At first Field showed no sign of understanding, but gradually became more alert and concentrated. When Harlan asked if Field recalled what he had said to Grier that day, the old justice retorted, "Yes! And a dirtier day's work I never did in my life!"

The justices made no more attempts to persuade Field to retire. In April 1897 Field notified President William McKinley that he would retire in December. Field's term of 34 years, 8 months, and 20 days eclipsed by three months the record set by Chief Justice John Marshall in 1835 (34 years, 5 months, 9 days). It would eventually be broken in 1975 by Justice William O. Douglas (36 years, 7 months, 8 days).

Source: Kermit L. Hall, ed., *The Oxford Companion to the Supreme Court of the United States* (New York & Oxford: Oxford University Press, 1992).

subject to the jurisdiction thereof, are citizens of the United States and of the State wherein they reside. No State shall make or enforce any law which shall abridge the privileges or immunities of citizens of the United States; nor shall any State deprive any person of life, liberty, or property, without due process of law; nor deny to any person within its jurisdiction the equal protection of the laws.

The *Slaughterhouse Cases.* In 1873 the Supreme Court restricted this broad protection of citizens against state encroachment in a series of three suits known as the *Slaughterhouse Cases,* which involved a Louisiana law regulating a livestock company. The Court said that people held most of their rights as citizens of the states, that the "privileges or immunities" people possessed as citizens of the United States were limited to participating in elections, seeking redress from the federal government, and using seaports and navigable rivers. Fundamental rights, the Court maintained, came to individuals as citizens of the states, and the states could limit these rights. Justice Stephen Field and three other justices dissented in this case, arguing for a broad interpretation of the amendment. Among the fundamental rights of citizens of the United States were the right to travel and pursue a profession, and, according to Field, a state could not limit these rights.

San Mateo v. *Southern Pacific Railroad Company.* When the California Supreme Court ruled against the railroads in *San Mateo* v. *Southern Pacific Railroad Company* (1882), they transferred their case to the federal circuit court. (Aside from being a Supreme Court justice, Field was also chief judge for the circuit court in California.) The railroad companies argued that they had been deprived of equal protection under the law, since California allowed most taxpayers the right to deduct mortgage payments from their tax bills, but did not allow railroads to do so. The Equalization Board of the state set tax rates without consulting the railroads, thus depriving them of property without due process of law. The state argued that it had an unlimited power to tax, that corporations it chartered were subject to state regulation, and that the Fourteenth Amendment was designed to protect former slaves, not railroads.

The Rights of Railroads. On 25 September 1882 Justice Field agreed with the Southern Pacific Railroad Company. "Whatever acts may be imputed justly or unjustly to the corporations," Field wrote, "they are entitled when they enter the tribunals of the nation to have the same justice meted out to them which is meted out to the humblest citizen. There cannot be one law for them and another law for others." Field acknowledged that the Fourteenth Amendment meant to guarantee civil rights of freed people, but its broad language made it more than a civil rights act. After the verdict Field received much criticism for attending a banquet given by Central Pacific president Leland Stanford to thank the lawyers who had argued the case. Although Field and

"The Bosses of the Senate," an editorial cartoon mocking the influence of corporate trusts on American politics (from *Puck*, 1889)

Stanford were old friends, it is doubtful that the banquet influenced the judge's decision.

Conkling. California appealed the case to the United States Supreme Court, which heard arguments on 19 December. Roscoe Conkling, a former senator from New York who had declined an appointment to the Supreme Court earlier in the year, argued the case for the railroads. Conkling had helped to write the Fourteenth Amendment and insisted that the framers had intended to protect railroads and other corporations from oppressive state taxation. "At the time when the Fourteenth Amendment was ratified," he told the Court, "as the records of the two houses will show, individuals and joint stock companies were appealing for congressional and administrative protection against invidious and discriminating state and local taxes. One instance was that of an express company, whose stock was owned largely by citizens of the State of New York, who came with petitions and bills seeking acts of Congress to aid them in resisting what they deemed oppressive taxation in two states, and oppressive and ruinous rules of damages applied under state laws. . . . That complaints of oppression, in respect of property and other rights, made by citizens of the Northern states who took up residence in the South, were rife in and out of Congress, none of us can forget." According to Conkling the status of the freed people had made the amendment necessary, but the real reasons behind the legislation were oppressive state laws.

The Supreme Court Responds. The railroads and

California agreed to settle the San Mateo suit out of court, but argued the same points in a new case, *Santa Clara County* v. *Southern Pacific Railroad Company*

Source:
Carl Brent Swisher, *Stephen J. Field: Craftsman of the Law* (1930; Chicago & London: University of Chicago Press, 1969).

SHERMAN ANTI-TRUST ACT

Rise of the Trusts. By 1878 the Standard Oil Company of Ohio owned seventy-four refineries and controlled 90 percent of the country's oil. One year later John D. Rockefeller was indicted for creating a monopoly. Though he was not convicted, Rockefeller sensed the danger of creating monopolies. In late December 1881 he decided to turned the ownership of his empire over to nine "trustees," who held all the stock from the different companies under Rockefeller's control. Thus, Rockefeller, and the trustees, could escape prosecution for creating a monopoly. Soon other industries followed Rockefeller's example in creating "trusts." Between 1884 and 1887 manufacturers and distributors of cotton oil, linseed oil, whiskey, envelopes, school slate, sugar, meat, and natural gas all formed trusts.

State Antitrust Action. The general public could not see the difference between a trust and a monopoly. Reformers called for regulation of the trusts, and some states complied. In 1889 Michigan, Nebraska, and Kansas passed antitrust laws, and by 1900 twenty-seven states prohibited or regulated trusts. These antitrust laws followed a principle of common law, that combinations which restrained trade unreasonably or monopolies that were hostile to the public good were illegal. States could regulate some trusts, but many were too big to be controlled or intimidated by the laws of any one state. When the state of Ohio moved against the Standard Oil Company in 1892, Rockefeller simply reformed the company under the more business-friendly laws of New Jersey.

The Sherman Anti-Trust Act. In 1887 President Grover Cleveland told Congress, "As we view the achievements of aggregated capital we discover the existence of trusts, combinations, and monopolies, while the citizen is struggling far in the rear or is trampled to death beneath an iron heel. Corporations which should be carefully restrained creatures of the law and servants of the people, are fast becoming the people's masters." In 1888, in response to public demands to do something about trusts but conscious of the importance of trusts to business organization, Sen. John Sherman of Ohio introduced an antitrust measure in the Senate. In 1890, after considerable revisions by Massachusetts senator George Hoar and Vermont senator George Edmunds, Congress passed a national antitrust law. The law barred any "contract, combination in the form of trust or otherwise, or conspiracy, in restraint of trade" and made it a federal crime "to monopolize or attempt to monopolize, or combine or conspire . . . to monopolize any part of the trade or commerce among the several states."

Enforcing the Sherman Act. Unlike the Interstate Commerce Act, which established a commission to investigate violations of the law, the Sherman Act left enforcement up to the U.S. attorney general. Most attorneys general did not think it necessary to move against trusts. Richard Olney, a corporate lawyer who served as attorney general in the Cleveland administration, took "the responsibility of not prosecuting under a law I believed to be no good." The presidential administrations of Benjamin Harrison, Cleveland, and William McKinley filed a total of eighteen antitrust suits. More combinations and trusts were formed between 1897 and 1901 than at any other time in American history.

United States v. *E. C. Knight.* In 1894 the E. C. Knight Company, part of the sugar trust, had tried to buy four Pennsylvania refiners, the last remaining competitors to the American Sugar Refining Company.

The national government moved to enforce the Sherman Act and asked a federal court to grant an injunction against this buyout; the court refused. In October the Supreme Court heard the case of *United States* v. *E. C. Knight.* In January 1895 Chief Justice Melville Fuller declared that the sugar trust was not subject to the Sherman Act. The chief justice noted that the trust refined 98 percent of the sugar sold in the United States, but it did not sell the sugar. Under the Constitution, Congress can regulate commerce between states, but could not regulate manufacturing. The Sherman Act, therefore, could not apply to a manufacturing monopoly. The trust could restrain the sugar trade only in an indirect manner; Congress could only prevent direct restraints on interstate trade.

In re Debs. The Court's decision revealed that it would be difficult to enforce the Sherman Act against trusts. Six months after deciding the sugar case, the Court used the Sherman Act against labor leader Eugene V. Debs. In May 1894 the American Railway Union struck against the Pullman Palace Car Company, which had cut workers' wages by 20 percent, while raising executive salaries and paying the dividends to stockholders. The union called for a boycott of Pullman cars, and workers refused to move trains hauling Pullmans. Attorney General Olney said the union was obstructing interstate commerce, and he sought an injunction against Debs and the union under the Sherman Act. Debs refused to call off the strike, and was sentenced to six months in jail for contempt of court. In March 1895 Clarence Darrow and former Illinois senator Lyman Trumbull defended Debs in the Supreme Court. In June the Court upheld the injunction. Justice David Brewer wrote that "The strong arm of the national government may be put forth to brush away all obstructions to the freedom of interstate commerce or the transportation of the mails." Debs served his six-month prison sentence at Woodstock, Illinois. Passed to control the abuses of business, the Sherman Act became a weapon against organized labor.

Sources:

James W. Ely Jr., *The Chief Justiceship of Melville W. Fuller, 1888–1910* (Columbia: University of South Carolina Press, 1995);

Lawrence M. Friedman, *A History of American Law* (New York: Simon & Schuster, 1985);

John E. Semonche, *Charting the Future: The Supreme Court Responds to a Changing Society 1890–1920* (Westport, Conn.: Greenwood Press, 1978);

Tinsley E. Yarbrough, *Judicial Enigma: The First Justice Harlan* (New York: Oxford University Press, 1995).

HEADLINE MAKERS

JAMES COOLIDGE CARTER

1827-1905
LAWYER

Reflecting on the Century. James C. Carter, one of the leading lawyers of the nineteenth century, asked his college classmates at their fifty year class reunion in 1900, "What has become of the spirit, the philosophy, the ideals, which held such firm control at the middle of the century?" These ideals had been discredited, if not dismissed, and replaced by "an enormous pressure of material interests which hold in disdain any appeals to the universal principles of truth and right." These material interests had not been established by appealing to reason, truth, science, or history, but by asserting that this impending materialism was an irresistible force. Anyone who questioned these trends were seen as either "impracticable theorists, or traitors to the interests of humanity."

Background and Training. Born in Lancaster, Massachusetts, and educated at Harvard College, Carter tutored in New York and clerked occasionally in the Wall Street law office of Judge William Kent and Henry E. Davies. He graduated from the Harvard law school in 1853 and was critical of its teaching methods. Until the 1870s Harvard trained men for the law by lecturing to them, giving them abstract principles, and having them read Sir William Blackstone and other commentators on the law. These "abstract statements of teachers and text books," Carter wrote, "even the best, make little impression upon the mind," and a lawyer's attention was not really concentrated "until he turns to the actual *cases* . . . and finds in them the *living* law as it has been actually developed by the real transactions of men."

Legal Practice and Political Involvement. In 1853 Carter became managing clerk in the Kent and Davies office. The following year Carter formed his own firm, Scudder and Carter, and by the end of the Civil War Car-

ter was one of the city's leading lawyers. In the 1870s he was one of the prosecuting attorneys in the case against the Tweed Ring and helped recover for the city more than $6 million pilfered by corrupt politicians. Following this, Carter was named by Gov. Samuel Tilden to a commission to investigate municipal governments. Carter's two suggestions, that city elections be closely monitored and that all municipal funds be handled by a Board of Finance chosen only by voters who met certain property qualifications, were little heeded at the time. Twenty years later, though, when Carter was president of the National Municipal League, he reasserted his proposals, warning that municipal corruption "is the subject of purchase by the great monied interests, and of corrupt bargains with party interests."

The Field Code. Carter was one of the founders of New York City's Bar Association, and served as its president five times. He led that organization in a campaign against enacting the proposed civil code of David Dudley Field. An eminent New York lawyer, Field had proposed a code of civil procedure in 1847, and New York had adopted it the following year. The code simplified legal practice and explained common law principles on personal rights, property, and legal obligations. In 1849 Missouri adopted the Field Code, and California, where David Field's brother Stephen (later a justice of the U.S. Supreme Court) was a prominent lawyer and state legislator, adopted the code in 1851. Field produced a revised civil code in 1865 and over the next twenty years worked to have New York, and other states, adopt it.

Opposition to the Code. Carter saw the move to adopt Field's civil code in the 1880s as an attempt by "a few men," or more properly one man, to "discard the principles and methods" of the law "and to substitute in its place a scheme of codification borrowed from the systems of despotic nations." More to the point, Carter worried that the Field Code would turn over to the legislature the power to govern relations between people, rather than leaving this kind of "private law" under the jurisdiction of judges. Field was influenced by Jeremy Bentham and other legal reformers, who wanted to rationalize a chaotic world. Carter's philosophy saw the law as more than a list of rules; the law was a system of justice derived from the unwritten folk wisdom of the people. A legal code was a statute frozen in a particular time, while the common law could be changed and adapted through practice. By 1883 there were six thousand cases in New York State involving disputes about the meaning of various provisions in Field's 1848 Code. While the code promised to make the law simpler and more rational, Carter maintained that it was beyond the scope of human reason to make a firm set of rules that would cover all cases and situations. In 1889 Carter wrote *The Provinces of the Written and the Unwritten Law,* which influenced the New York State legislature to reject the Field Civil Code of 1865.

Other Activities. Carter argued many cases before the U.S. Supreme Court and became an expert in constitutional and maritime law. He also represented the United States at an international court of arbitration in March 1893 to resolve a dispute with England over seal fishing in the Bering Sea. In the income-tax case of 1895, Carter rejected the notion of the tax as a dangerous, communistic attempt to overthrow the established order. He warned the court: "Nothing could be more unwise and dangerous — nothing more foreign to the spirit of the Constitution — than an attempt to baffle and defeat a popular determination by a judgment in a lawsuit. When the opposing forces of sixty millions of people have become arrayed in hostile political ranks upon a question which all men feel is not a question of law, but of legislation, the only path of safety is to accept the voice of the majority as final." Carter was condemned by his client, the Continental Trust Company, as a class traitor for accepting the wisdom of the masses. This was in keeping with his belief in common law, and of the necessity to change. However, as his Harvard class reunion address suggests, Carter did not accept change blindly or with unlimited approval.

Sources:

Lawrence M. Friedman, *A History of American Law* (New York: Simon & Schuster, 1985);

George Alfred Miller, "James Coolidge Carter," in *Great American Lawyers,* edited by William Draper Lewis (Philadelphia: John C. Winston, 1909).

CHARLES W. CHESNUTT

1858-1932
LAWYER, NOVELIST

Chesnutt's Parents. Aside from being a noted attorney, Charles Waddell Chesnutt was America's first important black writer of fiction. He was born in Cleveland, Ohio, to Andrew J. and Maria Sampson Chesnutt, free people of color from North Carolina. His father joined the Union army during the Civil War, serving as a teamster. After the war he returned to North Carolina and settled with his wife and children. Within a few years Andrew Chesnutt was elected a county commissioner and a justice of the peace.

Education and Experience in North Carolina. Charles Chesnutt enjoyed school, and by the time he was a teenager he was a pupil-teacher. In his travels through North Carolina looking for summer teaching positions, Chesnutt learned firsthand what it meant to be an African American. He was so light-skinned that he could pass for white. He recalled one white man calling to a friend, "Look here, Tom. Here's a black as white as you are," when introduced to Chesnutt. He decided not to pass for white, but to work hard enough to be accepted anywhere. In 1877 he was made the assistant principal of a new state normal school for "colored" teachers at Fayetteville, and three years later he became the school's principal, earning $75 a month. By this time he was married, and in his spare time he studied Greek, Latin, French, and German as well as shorthand. He was also active in the Prohibition movement in North Carolina, working alongside whites to stop the sale of alcohol. At this time Chesnutt read Albion Tourgée's novel on Reconstruction, *A Fool's Errand* (1879). Tourgée, who had been a judge and Freedmen's Bureau agent, wrote of the racial barriers faced by freed people. Chesnutt admired Tourgée's ability to describe people and situations realistically; he was ambitious to write fiction and do the same.

Stenography and Law. In 1883 Chesnutt, who now could write two hundred words a minute in shorthand, set out for the North. He worked for the Dow Jones & Company in New York and wrote a Wall Street gossip column for the *New York Mail and Express.* He then moved to Cleveland, where he found work in the legal department of the Nickel Plate Railroad. His supervisor, former judge Samuel E. Williamson, encouraged Chesnutt to study law. In 1887 Chesnutt received the highest score on the Ohio bar exam. Though he was hardworking and well qualified, no law firms or corporations offered him a position. He continued to work as a stenographer and court reporter while he waited for a legal practice to blossom. His stenography, which he had taken up to feed and house his family while he learned the law, became a business in itself, earning Chesnutt $2,000 to $3,000 each year. Chesnutt also began to write fiction, selling his sketches and short stories to popular magazines. When he sold a story to the prestigious *Atlantic Monthly,* Chesnutt's literary career was launched.

Chesnutt and Race. Chesnutt's stories were set in New York, Cleveland, and North Carolina, and though they cover the range of human experiences, the most popular and enduring ones detail the relationships between people of different races. Racial identity itself was a problem for Chesnutt; in an 1889 essay, "What is a

White Man?," he examined laws on racial identity. An Ohio statute, for example, declared anyone who was more than half white to be a white person, while a Georgia law maintained that anyone with any Negro blood was black. The state of Mississippi in 1885 declared that anyone with three-quarters white blood (three white grandparents) was white, then in 1890 made it seven-eighths white blood (seven white great-grandparents). In South Carolina the law left the matter up to juries to decide, establishing the criteria by which to determine one's race: reputation, reception in the white community, and the exercise of white privileges. For Chesnutt the variety of laws showed how ridiculous it was for states to try to separate people of different races. The people of America, Chesnutt wrote, shared many things, and only the fiction of race was allowed to keep them apart. "There can manifestly be no such thing as peaceful and progressive civilization in a nation divided by two warring races, and homogeneity of type, at least in externals, is a necessary condition of harmonious social progress."

Subsequent Career. In 1899 Chesnutt published *The Conjure Woman, The Wife of His Youth and Other Stories of the Color Line,* and a biography of Frederick Douglass. He then retired from stenography to write fiction full-time. *The House Behind the Cedars* (1900) again focused on the impossibility of racial definition. Chesnutt wrote two more novels, but after 1902 he returned to his business of legal stenography because he could no longer support his family by writing fiction. Nevertheless, he continued to be a spokesman for African American rights and corresponded with both Booker T. Washington and W. E. B. Du Bois. His novels did not receive critical acclaim until the 1960s.

Sources:

Helen M. Chesnutt, *Charles Waddell Chesnutt: Pioneer of the Color Line* (Chapel Hill: University of North Carolina Press, 1952);

Frances Richardson Keller, *An American Crusade: The Life of Charles Waddell Chesnutt* (Provo, Utah: Brigham Young University Press, 1978).

JOHN MARSHALL HARLAN

1833-1911
SUPREME COURT JUSTICE

Supreme Court. John Marshall Harlan was one of the most influential Supreme Court justices in history, partly because he disagreed with his colleagues on some of the most pivotal cases to appear before the court. "He could lead but he could not follow. . . . His was not the temper of a negotiator," Attorney General George Wickersham said of Harlan. In his thirty-four years on the court, Harlan wrote opinions on 703 cases, but he was more noted for his 316 vigorous dissents. Harlan disagreed profoundly with Justice Stephen Field, the court's intellectual giant, for whom liberty of contract and natural rights became almost sacred, untouchable by state of federal law. Harlan was more willing to let state legislatures regulate business enterprise and working conditions and did not think judges should base decisions on their own political philosophy.

Political Background. Harlan was born in Boyle County, Kentucky. During the Civil War Harlan and his father were staunch unionists. President Abraham Lincoln rewarded the elder Harlan by appointing him federal prosecutor of the state; the younger Harlan, who unsuccessfully ran for Congress in 1861, became a colonel in the state's volunteer infantry. Though he supported the Union, Harlan was a harsh critic of the Lincoln administration. He supported the Constitutional Union presidential nominee in 1860 and in 1864 campaigned actively for Democratic candidate George McClellan. Harlan opposed the Thirteenth Amendment to end slavery as a "flagrant invasion of the right of self government" that he would oppose even "if there were not a dozen slaves in Kentucky." After the war Harlan became reconciled to the importance of Reconstruction, the federal policy that emancipated African Americans and extended full citizenship rights to them. At the 1876 Republican convention he supported Rutherford B. Hayes. When Hayes became president, he sent Harlan to Louisiana to resolve a dispute between white Democrats and black Republicans. In October 1877 Hayes appointed Harlan to the Supreme Court. Harlan was confirmed despite opposition from southerners for his support of Reconstruction and from Republicans for his criticism of Lincoln.

Civil Rights Cases. Harlan's first major dissent was in the *Civil Rights Cases* (1883), when the court struck down the 1875 Civil Rights Act. The court found this law, which forbade racial discrimination in public accommodations, to be beyond the power of Congress. Harlan, who had seen the racial turmoil of the 1860s and 1870s, recognized what would happen if private prejudices were codified into law. According to Harlan racial discrimination in public accommodations was a "badge of servitude" that Congress had to prohibit under the provisions of the Thirteenth Amendment. He also evoked the Fourteenth Amendment, which granted the federal government the affirmative power to protect U.S. citizens.

Judicial Restraint. Harlan consistently admonished his fellow justices to show judicial restraint in their renderings. He opposed the court's substitution of its own opinion for that of the Congress or a state's legislature. When the court struck down the income-tax law in *Pollock* v. *Farmers' Loan & Trust Company* (1895), Harlan dissented and warned the other justices that they were not judging the law but were entering into a political debate in which they had no part. He affirmed that Congress had a right to levy taxes. As for the argument that giving Congress the power to levy a tax on income or to protect the civil rights of American citizens would destroy the rights of the states, Harlan responded that "the best friends of states rights . . . are those who recognize the Union as possessing all the powers granted to it in the Constitution, whether expressly or by implication."

Legacy. Though Harlan was often a lone voice, his vitriolic dissents have fared much better than many of his colleagues' majority opinions. In *United States* v. *E. C. Knight Company* (1895) Harlan advocated a broader role for the federal government in regulating the economy, and in *Plessy* v. *Ferguson* (1896) he rejected the doctrine of "separate but equal." In both of these cases, as well as in *Civil Rights* and *Pollock*, his dissenting opinions later became law. Harlan lectured on constitutional law at Columbian (now George Washington) University from 1889 until his death. In 1893 he served on the Bering Sea Arbitration Tribunal, which settled a dispute between the United States and Great Britain over Alaskan fisheries. His grandson, John Marshall Harlan II, was also a Supreme Court justice and noted dissenter.

Sources:

John E. Semonche, *Charting the Future: The Supreme Court Responds to a Changing Society, 1890–1920* (Westport, Conn.: Greenwood Press, 1978);

Tinsley E. Yarbrough, *Judicial Enigma: The First Justice Harlan* (New York: Oxford University Press, 1995).

WILLIAM C. HOWE

1828?-1902

ABRAHAM HUMMEL

1849-1926
CRIMINAL LAWYERS

Background. William F. Howe, called "the father of the criminal bar in America," was British or American by birth. At about the age of thirty he arrived in New York, where by 1861 he was practicing law. During the Civil War he was very successful in getting men out of the Union Army. He would argue that they had enlisted when drunk, or that family circumstances exempted them from service. At one time Howe was credited with having an entire company (seventy men) discharged. In one criminal case Howe argued that his client had not received a fair trial, as only two of the three judges on the court had sat through the entire trial. Though other lawyers thought the argument a joke, a higher court sustained Howe, and his client went free. In 1863 Abraham Hummel, a fourteen-year-old son of Jewish emigrants from Germany, came to work as an office boy for the renowned lawyer. Howe took Hummel under his tutelage, and in 1869 the two formed a partnership, Howe & Hummel, one of the most successful, and notorious, law firms in the country. Until its demise in 1907, Howe & Hummel defended more than one thousand people charged with murder or manslaughter; Howe himself handled 650 of these cases. At one time all but two of the twenty-five men awaiting trial in New York's Tombs, the prison across the street from the law office, were Howe & Hummel clients.

Drama and Brains. Howe was a big man, fond of diamonds and flashy clothes, a brilliant defense lawyer with a great flare for drama. In defending Ella Nelson, Howe tried to convince the jury that Miss Nelson had found her lover despondent and on the verge of suicide. She tried to wrestle his gun away from him, and in doing so accidentally shot him six times. At the end of his closing argument, which happened after a long day of testimony, Howe paced behind his client, who sat dressed in black, her hands over her face. He suddenly reached around her, grabbed both her arms and forced them in front of her, all the while digging his fingernails into her wrists. She screamed "as that jury and everyone else in the courtroom had never heard a human being scream before." The prosecutor became so rattled by the scream that he could barely sum up the case against Nelson, and the jury deliberated ten minutes before acquitting her. While Howe was flashy, Hummel was a short man who gave the impression of being a hunchback. Nonetheless, he was extremely smart. When an opposing lawyer boasted that he had Hummel "in his pocket," Hummel responded, "Then he's got more brains in his pocket than he ever had in his head." Hummel observed that there were two kinds of lawyers: those who knew the law, and those who knew the judge.

Technicalities and Loopholes. One lawyer said of Howe & Hummel: "The firm had a perfect setup. You might say that Hummel was the man you saw when you wanted to commit a crime without getting caught. He could tell you if the ice was thick enough to hold you up. If you went ahead on his advice and got into trouble anyway, or if you got over where the ice was too thin, Howe was there to get you out. He would see that nothing very serious happened if you did get caught." Howe and Hummel were adept at finding technicalities and loopholes for their clients. In 1888 "Handsome Harry" Carlton murdered New York policeman Joseph Brennan. Howe defended Carlton unsuccessfully, and he was convicted. However, as the court prepared to sentence Carlton to hang, Howe objected. Under New York statutes, Howe declared, murder was no longer a crime. The legislature had passed the Electrical Death Penalty Law, which abolished hanging as of 4 June 1888 and instituted electrocution on 1 January 1889. The law did not specifically state that murderers convicted after 4 June would be electrocuted as of 1 January, although that was the intention of the legislature. Howe pointed out that execution was the only punishment for first-degree murder, and since the legislature forbade executions during a seven-month period, the state did not consider murder to be a crime. The judge agreed, and Carlton briefly was spared. However, a higher court closed the loophole, and shortly before the new year Carlton became the last man to be hanged in the Tombs.

Other Business. In 1888 the lawyers published *In Danger, or Life in New York*, which pretended to be a guide to the dangers of the city. Actually it advertised Howe & Hummel's clients, their gambling houses and brothels, as well as the legal services of the firm. By the 1880s the firm took on more civil cases, which were Hummel's particular interest, and arranged with lawyers in states where divorces were easy (Indiana, Illinois, and South Dakota) to handle those cases. When New York prosecuted heavyweight boxer John L. Sullivan and British champion Alf Greenfield for "fighting without weapons" at Madison Square Garden, Howe successfully defended the fighters. Sullivan lost all his winnings in order to pay for Howe's legal services, but the court decision helped to establish boxing as a legitimate sport. Hummel helped establish theatrical contracts as binding business agreements. As lawyer for P. T. Barnum and the Hutchinson & Bailey Circus, Hummel handled the merger that created the Barnum & Bailey Circus.

Blackmail. As a theatrical lawyer Hummel also pioneered the breach-of-promise suit. If Hummel learned that a young actress had had a romantic engagement with a rich married man, he would convince the woman to file an affidavit, testifying that her former lover had promised marriage. Hummel would contact the man's lawyer, offering to settle the matter quietly. The alternative, a breach-of-promise suit, would be a public spectacle that would ruin the man's reputation. (No one ever opted for a public lawsuit.) Hummel would meet with the defendant's lawyer; the two would negotiate a payment of between $5,000 and $10,000; and then they would burn the affidavit. The woman received half the settlement, though first she would swear out a new affidavit vowing that she had never had an affair with the man in question. For Hummel it was a point of honor not to let his client blackmail the same man twice. Some men did pay twice: architect Stanford White finally gave the firm a retainer so he would not be victimized again.

The End. Howe died of a heart attack in 1902. Hummel continued to run the firm for a few more years. He spent a year in prison for forging an affidavit. After his release in 1908, Hummel left the United States for England, where he died in 1926.

Source:

Richard H. Rovere, *Howe & Hummel: Their True and Scandalous History* (London: Michael Joseph, 1948).

CHRISTOPHER COLUMBUS LANGDELL

1826-1906

LAW PROFESSOR

Background. Christopher Columbus Langdell was born on a farm in New Boston, New Hampshire, in 1826. He went to work in the textile mills of Manchester, New Hampshire, then worked his way through Exeter Academy before entering Harvard at the age of twenty-two. He left Harvard without a degree, returned to Exeter to read law, and then at the age of twenty-five entered Harvard Law School. Langdell stayed at the law school for three years, twice as long as most law students at the time. He supported himself by working in the college library and doing occasional editorial work for professors. After graduating in 1853, he practiced law in New York for sixteen years before returning to Harvard in 1870 as Dane Professor of Law and dean of the law school.

Changing the Law School. Langdell changed the law school and the role of the dean. He saw the dean as a leader, not just an administrator. Langdell raised the standards for admission to the law school, requiring prospective students to translate a long passage of Latin (without a dictionary) and answer questions drawn from Sir William Blackstone's *Commentaries on the Laws of England* (1765–1769). At the end of the first year students were examined to determine if they could continue. In 1871 Harvard extended from eighteen months to two years the course of study to earn a law degree and by 1899 required three years to complete a degree. Langdell also began to draw on legal scholars rather than lawyers to teach in the school, creating the idea of a law professor as someone who taught, rather than practiced, law. James Barr Ames, appointed to teach at Harvard in 1873, was the first of these academic lawyers. University administrators were reluctant at first to accept the appointments, wanting instead to find practicing attorneys to teach law. However, Langdell and Harvard president Charles Eliot, wanted the law school to train not only lawyers, but prospective law teachers. By 1895, when Ames succeeded Langdell as dean, Harvard graduates were teaching at influential law schools across the country.

The Case Method. Under Langdell's supervision the law courses at Harvard did not require memorization of facts, but the ability to reason and think. In 1870 Langdell introduced the case method of teaching. Instead of professors lecturing on abstract principles of law, students would read collections of cases and court decisions and from them gather the underlying principles. Roscoe Pound, later dean of the law school himself, recalled, "Langdell was always worried about 'Why?' and 'How? He didn't care particularly whether you knew a rule or could state the rule or not, but how did the court do this, and why did it do it?" Pound recalled that Langdell's class on equity pleading bored him at times, but that when he went back to Nebraska to practice law he looked over his notes from the course and discovered he "knew an awful lot about it."

Challenges to the Case Method. Not all lawyers or law schools readily embraced the case method. In 1891 the American Bar Association's Committee on Legal Education's Committee on Legal Education attacked the case method for not teaching lawyers the law. The case method, the ABA committee warned, was producing lawyers too eager to litigate, too willing to support clients in bad cases, able to cite opinions without fully comprehending underlying ideas of justice, and, like eager college students, leaving it to the judge to make a ruling. Lawyers, the ABA argued, should know the rules and should try to resolve questions before they came to court. In 1892 the ABA further attacked the case method. "The result of this elaborate study of actual disputes, . . . ignoring . . . the settled doctrines that have grown out of past ones, is a class of graduates admirably calculated to argue any side of any controversy, . . . but quite unable to advise a client when he is safe from litigation." Trained in the case method, the lawyer saw himself as a "hired gladiator" ready to argue any case.

Success of the Case Method. By the time Langdell retired in 1895, the case method was established not only at Harvard, but at Northwestern, the University of Wisconsin, and the University of Cincinnati, where dean and future U.S. president William Howard Taft reorganized the law school. In the early twentieth century some law schools still rejected the case method as being too unconventional. However, by the 1940s virtually every law school in the country followed the case method.

Sources:

James Barr Ames, "Christopher Columbus Langdell," in *Great American Lawyers,* edited by William Draper Lewis (Philadelphia: Winston, 1909);

Arthur E. Sutherland, *The Law at Harvard: A History of Men and Ideas, 1817–1967* (Cambridge, Mass.: Harvard University Press, 1967).

ISAAC PARKER

1838-1896

FEDERAL JUDGE, FORT SMITH, ARKANSAS

Background. Isaac Parker was born in Belmont County, Ohio. After studying and teaching school, Parker was admitted to the bar in Ohio when he was twenty-one. He moved to Saint Joseph, Missouri, where he practiced law and worked for the Republican Party. In 1864 he was elected district attorney and served as a presidential elector for Abraham Lincoln. Four years later he was elected to a judgeship, and in 1870 to Congress. In 1875 President Ulysses S. Grant nominated Parker to be chief justice of the Utah Territory. After the Senate had confirmed Parker, though, Grant decided to send him instead to Fort Smith, where the federal circuit court for the Western District of Arkansas had jurisdiction over thirty counties in Arkansas and the entire Indian Territory (modern-day Oklahoma). Parker, at thirty-six, was the country's youngest federal judge.

The Indian Territory. The Western District of Arkansas had approximately seventy-four thousand square miles of land and eighty-five thousand people. The trouble spot of the district proved to be the Indian Territory, where five Native American tribes lived — Cherokee, Creek, Seminole, Choctaw, and Chickasaw. (They had been forcibly moved there in the 1830s by the federal government). Federal and state law did not apply to them, and their laws did not apply to the twenty-six thousand non-Indians who had illegally migrated to the region. Plains Indians not living on the reservation hunted in the western areas of the territory, and Texas cattlemen used vacant lands to graze their herds before taking them to the slaughterhouses and railroads in Kansas. Renegades fled the law in their own states to take up residence in the territory, where there was little chance of capture. It was said that "There is no Sunday west of St. Louis — no God west of Fort Smith."

The Hanging Judge. Parker's predecessor, Judge William Story, had resigned after only fourteen months in Fort Smith rather than face impeachment. Parker arrived to find the court in disrepute and outlaws in control of the territory. On 10 May 1875 Parker's court opened for business in the two-story brick federal courthouse, which had two jail cells in the basement. Eighteen people came before Parker that day charged with murder; fifteen were convicted. On 3 September, six of these men were executed in a public display of the law's power. Five thousand people, including reporters from as far away as New York, came to watch. Parker was quickly given the name "the hanging judge"; in the next twenty-one years he would sentence 160 people to death; seventy-nine would hang on the gallows at Fort Smith.

Parker's Posse. Parker hired two hundred deputy marshals to assist in the "fight between the court and the lawless element" in the Indian Territory. This force, though, was hardly enough to do more than chase after known criminals. A marshal received two dollars for arresting and bringing a suspect into Fort Smith. In addition, the government would pay the deputy six cents per mile and expenses when he traveled on official business and could present the proper receipts. Capturing a suspect and successfully bringing him to Fort Smith might earn a deputy marshal thirty or forty dollars. The deputy would not be paid if the suspect was not returned to the fort. For the suspect, resisting a federal officer would mean one year in prison: for a man facing execution if found guilty, this was not a severe penalty. If a suspect resisted and the deputy killed him, the deputy was responsible for paying burial expenses and would not receive any compensation from the federal government. During Parker's judgeship sixty-five deputy marshals died trying to apprehend suspects. Parker petitioned the federal government for more manpower and money, but the Indian Territory had no representation in Congress and his pleas went unheard. Congress did remove the western half of the Indian Territory from Parker's jurisdiction and divide it between the federal courts in Kansas and Texas.

Parker and Indians. In 1881 David Payne led a group of whites called "Boomers" onto lands that had never been assigned to any specific tribe. The white settlers began homesteading and were driven out by the U.S. Army, but they kept coming back. Finally Payne was brought to Fort Smith and charged with intruding in the Indian Territory. The Five Tribes and the cattlemen who grazed their herds on the vacant lands joined the suit, paying lawyers to assist the prosecutor at Fort Smith. Though most whites supported the Boomers, arguing that they had a right to vacant land, Parker ruled that the land rightfully belonged to the Cherokee and fined Payne $1,000. Though the Cherokee regarded Parker as their ally, in this case, as in others, he merely followed the letter of the law. When the Cherokee tried to stop the Southern and Kansas Railroad from building a line through their lands, Parker refused to grant an injunction to stop the railroad. The Cherokee tribe,

Parker ruled, was not a sovereign entity and so could not claim the right of eminent domain against the superior claim of the United States. In 1888 the Supreme Court affirmed Parker's ruling, and the following year Congress opened portions of the Indian Territory to white settlers.

Parker and the Supreme Court. Since Parker's court was both a district court and a circuit court, his decisions were final. The only recourse for a person convicted in Parker's court before 1889 was a presidential pardon. In that year Congress passed the Criminal Appeals Act, giving the Supreme Court jurisdiction to hear appeals in federal criminal cases. Between 1890 and 1897 the Supreme Court reviewed forty-four cases from Fort Smith; it reviewed only nineteen cases from all the other federal courts in the country. Of the forty-four cases from Fort Smith, the Supreme Court reversed thirty-one convictions. An average of more than four men each year were hanged at Fort Smith between 1875 and 1890, with Parker generally favoring large group hangings. The average fell to two each year after 1890. The Supreme Court chastised Parker, sarcastically calling him the "learned judge," for his emotional and inflammatory charges to the jury. Parker retorted that if a jury was guided it would render justice, which was the greatest pillar of society."

Parker's Death. With the Indian Territory opened to white settlement, and the Supreme Court and Justice Department almost routinely correcting him, Judge Parker grew ill in the summer of 1896. Ada Patterson, reporter for the *St. Louis Republic,* interviewed the dying judge, who had grown famous in the press as a blood-thirsty monster. Patterson was deeply moved by Parker's fundamental decency. "I am glad to have the honor of knowing this alleged cruel judge," he wrote. According to the reporter, he was a hero, "worthy of the fame of the most just of Romans." On 17 November 1896 Parker died. Prisoners in the Fort Smith jail tried to celebrate, but throughout the Indian Territory there was mourning.

Sources:
John E. Semonche, *Charting the Future: The Supreme Court Responds to a Changing Society, 1890–1920* (Westport, Conn.: Greenwood Press, 1978);

Glenn Shirley, *Law West of Fort Smith: A History of Frontier Justice in the Indian Territory, 1834–1896* (Lincoln: University of Nebraska Press, 1957).

PUBLICATIONS

John Peter Altgeld, *Our Penal Machinery and Its Victims* (Chicago: McClurg, 1886);

Altgeld, *Reasons for Pardoning Fielden, Neebe, and Schwab* (Chicago: s.n., 1893) — Altgeld, a critic of the American legal system, was elected governor of Illinois in 1893. He pardoned the surviving men convicted of the 1886 Haymarket bombing;

Hampton L. Carson, *The Supreme Court of the United States: Its History*, 2 volumes (Philadelphia: A. R. Keller, 1892);

James C. Carter, *The Proposed Codification of Our Common Law* (New York: M. D. Brown, 1884) — New York lawyer Carter was a harsh critic of attempts to replace common law with legal codes adopted by legislatures;

Carter, *The Provinces of the Written and the Unwritten Law* (New York: Banks & Brothers, 1889);

R. Floyd Clarke, *The Science of Law and Lawmaking: Being an Introduction to Law, a General View of its Forms and Substance and a Discussion of the Question of Codification* (New York: Macmillan, 1898);

William W. Cook, *Treatise on the Law of Corporations Having a Capital Stock* (Chicago: Callaghan, 1898);

Cook, *Treatise on Stock and Stockholders, Bonds, Mortgates, and General Corporation Law* (Chicago: Callaghan, 1889);

Cook, *"Trusts." The Recent Combinations in Trade, Their Character, Legality and Mode of Organization* (New York: L. K. Strouse, 1888);

Thomas M. Cooley, *The Elements of Torts* (Chicago: Callaghan, 1895);

Cooley, *The General Principles of Constitutional Law in the United States* (Boston: Little, Brown, 1880) — Cooley, first chairman of ICC Believed federal regulatory power was limited;

Cooley, *A Treatise on the Law of Torts: or the Wrongs which Arise Independent of Contract* (Chicago: Callaghan, 1879);

Henry M. Field, *The Life of David Dudley Field* (New York: Scribners, 1898) — Biography of proponent of uniform legal code, and brother of Justice Stephen Field;

Ernst Freund, *The Legal Nature of Corporations* (Chicago: University of Chicago Press, 1897);

John Chipman Gray, *Restraints on the Alienation of Property* (Boston: C. C. Soule, 1883) — Boston lawyer, Harvard law professor, and brother of Justice Horace Gray believed states had only limited power over private property;

Gray, *The Rule Against Perpetuities* (Boston: Little, Brown, 1886);

Gray, *Select Cases and Other Authorities on the Law of Property* (Cambridge, Mass.: C. W. Sever, 1888–1892) — six volumes of cases on property for Professor Gray's law students;

Charles M. Hepburn, *The Historical Development of Code Pleading in American and England* (Cincinnati: W. H. Anderson, 1897);

Oliver Wendell Holmes Jr., *The Common Law* (Boston: Little, Brown, 1881) — Holmes's treatise on nature of law and society;

William F. Howe and Abraham Hummel, *In Danger, or Life in New York: A True History of the Great City's Wiles and Temptations: True Facts and Disclosures* (New York: J. S. Ogilvie, 1888) — New York criminal lawyers wrote this exposé to show folly of hiring lawyers other than themselves, and to advertise their clients' brothels, gambling dens, and other businesses;

J. H. Hubbell, ed., *Hubbell's Legal Director for Lawyers and Businessmen* (New York: Hubbell, 1870–) — guide to the legal profession;

William Kent, *Memoirs and Letters of James Kent* (Boston: Little, Brown, 1898) — biography of Kent, leading judge in New York early in the nineteenth century;

Cesare Lombroso, *The Man of Genius* (New York: Scribners, 1891) — Lombroso, an Italian criminologist, probed links between psychology and criminal behavior, trying to find alternative solutions to imprisonment;

Lombroso and William Ferrero, *The Female Offender*, introduction by W. Douglas Morrison (New York: Appleton, 1895);

David McAdam, ed., *The Act to Abolish Imprisonment for Debt, and to Punish Fraudulent Debtors, Commonly Called the "Stilwell Act"* (New York: E. G. Ward, 1880);

McAdam, *The Rights, Duties, Remedies, and Incidents Belonging to and Growing out of the Relation of Landlord and Tenant* (New York: G. S. Diossy, 1882);

Victor Morawetz, *The Law of Private Corporations*, 2 volumes (Boston: Little, Brown, 1886);

Aaron M. Powell, *State Regulation of Vice: Regulation Efforts in America* (New York: Wood & Holbrook, 1878) — account of attempts to regulate prostitution, pornography, and gambling;

Henry Taylor Terry, *Some Leading Principles of Anglo-American Law Expounded with a View to its Arrangement and Codification* (Philadelphia: T. & J. W. John Johnson, 1884);

James B. Thayer, *Cases on Constitutional Law. With Notes* (Cambridge, Mass.: C. W. Sever, 1894–1895) — Harvard law professor assembled this "case book" for law students;

Thayer, *The Dawes Bill and the Indians* (Boston: Reprinted from the *Atlantic Monthly*, 1888) — Thayer was critical of Dawes Bill and its alienation of Indian land;

Thayer, *A Preliminary Treatise on Evidence at the Common Law*, 2 volumes (Boston: Little, Brown, 1896–1898);

Christopher G. Tiedeman, *An Elementary Treatise on the American Law of Real Property* (Saint Louis: F. H. Thomas, 1884);

Tiedeman, *The Income Tax Decisions as an Object Lesson in Constitutional Construction* (Philadelphia: American Academy of Political and Social Sciences, 1895);

Tiedeman, *A Treatise on the Limitations of Police Power in the United States* (Saint Louis: F. H. Thomas, 1886);

Theodore D. Woolsey, *Divorce and Divorce Legislation*, second edition revised (New York: Scribners, 1882) — Woolsey founded a divorce-reform league, fearing that easy divorces contributed to moral decline and social decay.

The saloon-courthouse of Justice Roy Bean in Langtry, Texas, circa 1882

LIFESTYLES, SOCIAL TRENDS, AND FASHION

by JANE GERHARD

CONTENTS

Sidebars and tables are listed in italics.

1878

- Native Americans continue their struggles against confinement on reservations.

- The first American-made bicycle goes on the market. Bicycling becomes a fad. Cycling clubs hold parades and meets, and by 1882 there are some twenty thousand cyclists in the United States.

10 Jan. Sen. Aaron A. Sargent (R-Cal.) introduces a woman suffrage amendment to the Constitution on the floor of the U.S. Senate, where it is defeated by a vote of 34–16. The amendment is reintroduced in each succeeding Congress until it is finally ratified in 1920.

28 Jan. The first commercial telephone exchange begins operation in New Haven, Connecticut. It serves twenty-one telephones.

15 Oct. The first electric-power company, the Edison Electric Light Company, is formed to serve Fifth Avenue in New York City.

1879

- Fox hunting in the British manner is a popular recreational activity among the upper classes of Long Island, New England, the Philadelphia suburbs, Virginia, and Maryland.

- The first system of public electric street lights is installed in Cleveland, Ohio.

- The Boston Cooking School opens.

- Frank W. Woolworth opens his first five-and-ten-cent store in Lancaster, Pennsylvania. By 1895 he has a chain of twenty-eight stores and by 1911 more than one thousand.

14 Jan. Chief Joseph, called the "Indian Napoleon" by the U.S. press, eloquently addresses cabinet members, congressmen, and diplomats about the war with the Nez Percé and his people's suffering. "The earth is the mother of all people, and all people should have equal rights upon it," he admonishes.

15 Feb. Female attorneys win the right to argue cases before the U.S. Supreme Court.

7 May California adopts a new constitution, which includes a provision forbidding employment of Chinese laborers. Between 1850 and 1882 some three hundred thousand Chinese immigrate to the United States, settling mostly on the West Coast.

1880

- The 1880 census lists the U.S. population at 50,155,783. New York is the first state to reach a population of more than 5 million people.

- Approximately 17 percent of the U.S. population is illiterate, a decrease of 3 percent since 1870.

- Social critic Henry George's *Progress and Poverty,* an analysis of urban life, becomes a best-seller.

- Founded in Great Britain in 1865, the Salvation Army opens its first American branch in Philadelphia.

1 Mar. The Supreme Court rules that it is unconstitutional to exclude African Americans from jury duty.

31 Mar.	Wabash, Indiana, becomes the first U.S. city to be entirely lighted by electricity.
17 Nov.	The United States and China sign the Chinese Exclusion Treaty, which gives the United States the right to limit or suspend the immigration of Chinese but not to exclude them entirely.

1881

- Suffragists and women's rights advocates Elizabeth Cady Stanton, Susan B. Anthony, and Matilda Joselyn Gage publish the first two volumes of their *History of Woman Suffrage.*

- The first central electric-power plant is constructed on Pearl Street in New York City.

21 May	Clara Barton founds an American branch of the International Red Cross, established in Europe in 1863, and serves as its president until 1904.

1882

- When a reporter for the *Chicago Daily News* asks William H. Vanderbilt, owner of the New York Central Railroad, whether he is operating his railroad for the good of the public or his stockholders, Vanderbilt responds, "The public be damned!" For many the phrase comes to typify the arrogance of the "barons" of industry during the so-called Gilded Age of the late nineteenth century.

2 Feb.	The Reverend Michael Joseph McGivney founds the Knights of Columbus, a fraternal benefit society of Roman Catholic men, in New Haven, Connecticut. The group is chartered on 29 March.
6 May	Congress passes the first Exclusion Act, banning for ten years all further Chinese immigration, including immigrant workers' wives, thus driving many of the Chinese living in western states to return to China.

1883

- *Demorest's* magazine reminds its readers, "Many a man's heart has been kept from wandering by the bow on his wife's slipper." During the 1880s, "experts" explain that a woman's feminine appearance helps to tame a man's roaming eyes and "baser passions."

24 May	The Brooklyn Bridge, connecting Manhattan and Long Island, is officially opened.
4 July	In North Platte, Nebraska, William Cody's Buffalo Bill's Wild West Show gives its first performance. A former buffalo hunter, Pony Express rider, and army scout, Cody tours with the popular show in the United States and abroad. Hunkpapa leader Sitting Bull, who has returned to Dakota country in 1883, travels for a time with the show.
15 Oct.	The Supreme Court overturns the Civil Rights Act of 1875, which forbade segregation or discrimination in public accommodations, ruling that the government can outlaw state-imposed discrimination but not that of individuals or private businesses.
18 Nov.	U.S. and Canadian railroads adopt a system of standard time zones to solve schedule problems caused by the unsystematic setting of local times.

1884

- Delegates at an international conference in Washington, D.C., establish a worldwide system of standard time zones with the prime meridian passing through the British Royal Observatory in Greenwich, England.

- In the United States some fifty thousand people own bicycles, and racing and touring clubs flourish in every major city.

- A group of suffragists founds the National Equal Rights Party and nominates Mrs. Belva A. Lockwood of Washington, D.C., as its presidential candidate. The first woman to run for president, Lockwood is nominated again in 1888.

- Anti-Catholicism figures in presidential politics as Protestants accuse Catholics of plotting against secular schooling. By 1880 the Catholic Church was the largest religious body in the United States, with more than 6 million communicants.

- At the annual Knights of Labor convention the first Monday in September is designated as Labor Day. In the late 1880s several states make the day an official holiday, and in 1894 it becomes a legal holiday for federal employees.

5 Aug. The cornerstone for the pedestal of the Statue of Liberty is laid on Bedloe's Island (later Liberty Island) in New York Harbor.

1885

- In *Our Country,* an attack on immigration, Josiah Strong gives voice to the nativism that is on the rise across the United States.

24 Jan. The New Orleans Exposition opens. A third larger that the Centennial Exposition held in Philadelphia in 1876, it is the largest world's fair yet held in the United States, but it is later eclipsed by the still-larger World's Columbian Exposition held in Chicago in 1893.

21 Feb. The Washington Monument is dedicated in Washington, D.C. It is opened to the public on 9 October 1888.

25 Feb. Congress outlaws the fencing of public lands in the West to prevent special interests from expanding their holdings by restricting access to water sources.

26 Feb. Under pressure from the Knights of Labor, which charges that American employers are bringing in foreign workers as strikebreakers, Congress passes the Contract Labor Act (also called the Foran Act), outlawing alien contract labor.

3 Mar. The U.S. Post Office inaugurates special-delivery service.

1886

- Coca-Cola is introduced in Atlanta, Georgia.

1 Jan. The first Tournament of Roses parade is held in Pasadena, California, organized by Charles Frederick Holder, a naturalist and the founder of the Valley Hunt Club. Club members decorate their carriages with flowers for the parade, and a variety of athletic events round out the day.

4 Sept. Geronimo of the Chiricahua Apaches surrenders at Skeleton Canyon, Arizona, signaling the end of armed resistance in the American Southwest.

28 Oct. President Grover Cleveland unveils and dedicates the Statue of Liberty.

1887

- The U.S. Postal Service begins free mail delivery in communities of ten thousand or more people.

- The General Allotment Act, or Dawes Act, passes in Congress, dividing reservation lands into family parcels and allowing the sale of lands deemed "surplus" to non-Indians.

- Congress passes the Hatch Act, which provides annual funding for the establishment and operation of an agricultural research and experimentational office in each state that has a land-grant college.

- The American Protective Association, which becomes the largest anti-Catholic organization in the United States, is founded, consolidating a rising wave of nativism in the wake of massive immigration from southern Europe. At its height its membership reaches one hundred thousand.

- Theodore Roosevelt calls for the formation of a Boone and Crockett Club to further the protection of American wildlife.

1888

- The electrified street railway is perfected in Richmond, Virginia, revolutionizing mass transportation within cities and to suburbs.

12 Mar. Four hundred people die during a thirty-six-hour blizzard that shuts down New York City and its environs, destroys millions of dollars worth of property, and virtually cuts off the city from the outside world. Messages to Boston are relayed via London.

1889

- The Sons of the American Revolution, an exclusive society of white descendants of Revolutionary War soldiers, is founded. The Daughters of the American Revolution is formed the following year.

- Americans smoke 2.1 billion cigarettes a year, a tenfold increase from 1881.

- Frances Willard, president of the Woman's Christian Temperance Union, publishes her autobiography, *Glimpses of Fifty Years.*

- Jane Addams founds Hull-House, a settlement house in a Chicago slum neighborhood.

- The Singer Manufacturing Company becomes the first company to market an electric sewing machine in the United States.

22 Apr. Thousands of people participate in the Oklahoma land rush to establish claims on 1.9 million acres of land that the federal government bought from the Creeks and Seminoles.

31 May In Pennsylvania the rain-swollen Conemaugh River breaks through a dam above Johnstown, destroying four valley towns, covering Johnstown in thirty feet of water, and killing nearly twenty-three hundred people.

1890

- The 1890 U.S. Census puts the population of the United States at 62,947,714. Nearly 17 million people live west of the Mississippi, three times the U.S. population in 1803, the year the Louisiana Purchase made a large portion of that western land part of the United States.

- About 13.3 percent of Americans are illiterate, a decrease of 3.7 percent since 1880.

- Roughly twenty-three thousand children work in southern factories.

- Journalist Jacob Riis educates the American public about life in urban slums in his groundbreaking book *How the Other Half Lives.*

- Smoking cigarettes in public becomes socially acceptable for men during the 1890s, but it is still unacceptable for women.

- The two-step becomes the most popular dance, replacing dances such as the polka, the galop, the reel, and the quadrille.

10 Feb. About 11 million acres of Lakota land ceded to the United States in 1889 is opened for general settlement.

15 Dec. Sitting Bull is shot and killed in a scuffle with tribal policemen who are trying to arrest him for leading the Ghost Dance movement, a religious revival founded on the belief that a deliverer from the spirit world will restore the Lakotas' dominance over the plains and make them impervious to whites' rifle bullets.

29 Dec. More than three hundred Ghost Dancers led by Chief Big Foot are massacred at Wounded Knee Creek in western South Dakota.

1891

- In 1891 alone 560,319 immigrants arrive in the United States; more than 3.6 million arrive during the decade.

16 Jan. The Lakotas surrender, ending the last American Indian war.

22 Sept. Nine hundred thousand acres of Oklahoma land ceded to the federal government by the Sauk, Fox, and Potawatomi tribes are opened for general settlement.

1892

- *The Chicago Tribune* reports that mobs have lynched 241 African Americans in 1892 alone.

- Ida B. Wells-Barnett publishes *Southern Horrors,* her first separately published exposé of lynching in the American South.

- The boll weevil arrives in Texas, probably from Mexico or Central America, and spreads throughout the South, causing severe damage to U.S. cotton crops.

- The term *The 400* comes into use as a description of the New York elite after social arbiter Ward McAllister is asked to shorten an invitations list to match the four-hundred-person capacity of the Astor ballroom and comments that there are "only four hundred persons in New York society."

- George W. G. Ferris designs the Ferris wheel and builds the first one for the 1893 World's Columbian Exposition in Chicago.

1 Jan.	The federal government opens its immigrant receiving station on Ellis Island in New York Bay; it closes on 12 November 1954, after processing some 20 million immigrants.
15 Oct.	The 1.8-million-acre Crow Indian reservation in Montana is opened for general settlement.
20–23 Oct.	Dedication ceremonies are held for the World's Columbian Exposition in Chicago.

1893

•	Frederick Jackson Turner delivers his famous speech on "The Significance of the American Frontier" to the American Historical Association.
•	Whitcomb L. Judson secures a patent for his zipper, a series of hooks and eyes fastened with a slider. The modern mesh-toothed zipper is patented in 1913.
1 May	The World's Columbian Exposition is opened to the public.
24 Aug.	A cyclone kills about one thousand people and causes major damage in Savannah, Georgia, and Charleston, South Carolina.
16 Oct.	More than one hundred thousand people take part in the Cherokee Strip land rush in Oklahoma, staking claims to 6 million acres of land that the federal government bought from the Cherokees.
18 Oct.	Lucy Stone, abolitionist and president of the American Woman Suffrage Association, dies at age seventy-five.
7 Nov.	Women are granted the vote in Colorado.

1894

8 Jan.	A fire at the World's Columbian Exposition destroys several major buildings. A fire on 7 February virtually destroys another building, and a third, on 5 July, consumes many remaining buildings.
27 Aug.	Congress authorizes the first graduated income tax, which the Supreme Court declares unconstitutional in 1895.

1895

•	Jane Addams's *Hull-House Maps and Papers,* a sociological report on the living conditions of the poor in Chicago, is published.
•	Ida B. Wells-Barnett publishes *A Red Record,* an exposé of three years of lynchings in the southern states.
•	Magazine illustrator Charles Dana Gibson's depictions of slim, small-waisted women with pompadour hairstyles begin to have a major influence on women's fashions.
•	Women's bicycling skirts are shortened to one or two inches above the ankle.

1896

- The first of many bills to impose a literacy test on immigrants is introduced in the Congress. Such a test, wrote the congressional committee that recommended it, would "shut out those classes of immigrants which . . . contribute most heavily to pauperism and crime and juvenile delinquents."

- Fannie Farmer publishes *The Boston Cooking-School Cook Book,* which becomes popular nationwide because of Farmer's no-nonsense approach to food preparation, including exact measurement of ingredients.

- Bicycle manufacturing is a $60 million business in the United States.

4 Jan. Utah becomes a state, with a constitution making it the second state to allow women to vote.

18 May In its ruling on *Plessy* v. *Ferguson* the Supreme Court establishes the "separate but equal" doctrine, which holds that segregation is legal if equal facilities are provided for both races.

1 Oct. The U.S. Postal Service establishes rural free delivery.

1897

- Chief Joseph again travels to Washington, D.C., to complain about white encroachment on reservation lands. He then goes on to New York City, where he participates in the dedication of Grant's Tomb and has a place of honor in the parade.

- The Tremont Street subway opens in Boston. The first practical and successful underground railway line, it is completed in 1898 and runs for 1.8 miles. (The Boston subway system eventually extends to twenty-two miles.)

- Mr. and Mrs. Bradley Martin of New York City host a lavish party, turning the Waldorf-Astoria ballroom into a replica of the Palace of Versailles. Mrs. Martin attends the ball dressed as Mary, Queen of Scots and wearing a necklace once owned by Marie Antoinette. Although conspicuous consumption has characterized the Gilded Age, the Martins' spending is judged excessive even by those standards, and the Martins are the focus of so much disapproval in the press that they go to live in England.

1898

- Fannie Farmer publishes *Chafing Dish Possibilities,* another popular cookbook.

18 Feb. Frances Willard, president of the Woman's Christian Temperance Union, dies at age fifty-nine.

1899

- The movement to bring science into the American home adopts the name *home economics.*

- Manhattan has 1,140 acres of parkland, mostly in Central Park. Social reformers nationwide are working to create parks and playgrounds that are accessible to all city dwellers.

OVERVIEW

The Gilded Age. The years between 1878 and 1899 were a soul-searching time for Americans, as they examined the basic values they lived by. Middle-class white women became interested in social causes such as helping the urban poor, promoting temperance or prohibition of alcohol, and winning suffrage, or the right to vote, for themselves. Racial tensions worsened in the South, and the ongoing bloody conflict with Native Americans ended with the surrender of the Lakotas in 1891. Millions of immigrants arrived in the United States. Bringing with them new customs, foods, and points of view, they contributed to the political and social conflict of the day. Despite great hostility from whites, Chinese immigrants in the West built the railroad system that linked the East and the West, and then they stood by powerless as new immigration restrictions prevented them from bringing their families to America. Racial, ethnic, and class conflict prompted widely discussed books claiming with authority that nonwhites were genetically inferior. Insecure whites were frightened that the social gains they had managed after the Civil War would be lost if nonwhites were treated as equals. The result was a society rushing into an uncertain future with fearful, yet hopeful, anticipation.

Nationalization. During the last two decades of the nineteenth century Americans began to think of themselves as having a national identity, with their own distinct culture and institutions. The national rail system allowed people and goods to move freely from region to region; mass-circulation magazines and professionally edited newspapers kept their readers informed of what other Americans were thinking and doing; changing methods of business and manufacturing brought similar foods, clothing, and furniture to Americans throughout the country. The newly emerging field of advertising encouraged Americans to seek similar lifestyles, and mail-order houses such as Montgomery Ward (founded in 1872) and Sears, Roebuck (founded in 1886) offered them the opportunity to fulfill their dreams with the same goods at the same prices no matter where they lived. Americans began to think more alike too, as voluntary and professional associations fostered a sense of belonging beyond the local community, and editorial writers helped to forge national points of view on issues. Before the Civil War the noun *United States* took a plural verb; by the end of the nineteenth century the United States *was*.

Public Transportation. The urban population soared after the Civil War. Generally, an urban territory was defined by the census bureau as a city or town with more than eight thousand residents. Between 1860 and 1890 the number of urban territories in the United States more than tripled, and the number of cities with more than fifty thousand residents increased from sixteen to fifty-eight. Cities could be very unpleasant places to live. Plumbing was primitive; transportation was nonmotorized before about 1880, when the largest cities began installing in-city trains and trolleys; and electricity was scarcely available before 1890. The development of steam and electric public transportation offered a solution to the problems of city living for many Americans. As public transportation enabled more people to live farther away from where they worked, suburbs sprouted up along trolley lines.

Everyday Life. Homeowners in cities and suburbs were introduced to running water, gas, electricity, and sewer systems. Public places such as schools, stores, restaurants, and government offices were the first lighted by electricity, a service that became increasingly available in the 1890s. There were only 120 electric generating plants in the entire country in 1890, but they increased tenfold during the decade. The benefits of electricity were especially evident in the new department stores and five-and-ten-cent stores. These stores offered Americans an entirely new way to shop and introduced them to a dizzying array of gadgets that could take advantage of the new utilities available to them. Practicality gave way to material fascination as consumerism became an increasingly powerful force in American life.

More Food, More Variety. The cross-country railroads played a large role in the development of a national food market. Thanks to refrigeration cars, first used in the 1870s, Florida grapefruits and California avocados could be bought anywhere in the country that was connected to the rail system. New Yorkers ate fruit from California and meat slaughtered in Chicago. Scheduling deliveries was a nightmare, though, because there were eighty different time zones throughout the nation. In 1883 U.S. railroad interests petitioned the federal government to establish four standard U.S. time zones to help ensure that goods could get to market predictably. Despite the emergence of a reliable, national food delivery system and national marketing of brand-name products, people refused to abandon regional and ethnic food preferences. For instance, southerners still enjoyed their traditional fried chicken, cornbread, and black-eyed peas, but they also began to eat Armour smoked sausage from Chicago.

Gold Fever. No event epitomized the American dream of wealth like the Klondike gold rush of 1898 and 1899. Men from all over the country left their jobs in droves, spending their last dollar on supplies for the long trip to the gold fields in the Klondike region of the Yukon Territory of northwestern Canada, where they expected to strike it rich. So many Americans set out for the trip that roads leading to San Francisco, the jumping-off point for the long trip north, were gridlocked for months at a time. The long journey, which usually involved taking a ship from San Francisco to the Alaskan panhandle and then embarking on a long, overland trek through the mountains to Dawson in the Yukon Territory, took the better part of a year. The journey to Dawson, the epicenter of the gold fever, was harder than most had dared to imagine. The harsh weather, swindlers, robbers, bad luck, and mental anguish proved too much for many, who died in their quest or despaired of realizing their dream. Yet, for some there was a pot of gold at the end of the trail, and, surprisingly, others found reward enough in the adventure of living in a wilderness outpost.

Redefining Women's Work. Between 1878 and 1899 educated white women invented new roles for themselves. As colleges and universities opened their doors to women, they helped to create a new generation of professional women. When many of these female college graduates had difficulty finding employment in traditional jobs, they created meaningful careers for themselves addressing the needs of the new society. The settlement houses that sprang up in lower-class urban neighborhoods during the 1880s were staffed almost exclusively by educated white women attempting to address the human toll of industrialization through direct aid and education. The Woman's Christian Temperance Union (WCTU), established in 1874, campaigned to end the ill affects of alcohol on families, lobbying for a prohibition on the sale of alcoholic beverages nationwide. With president Frances Willard's "Do Everything" philosophy, WCTU activists branched out to address other pressing social issues, including poverty, child abuse, and unsafe labor conditions. Activist women also fought for a voice in electoral politics, applying methods learned in other movements in the battle for woman suffrage, which was finally won with the ratification of the Nineteenth Amendment in 1920.

Fashion. As women began to work outside the home and both men and women became more active, clothing styles were simplified. While middle- and upper-class American men and women continued to take fashion cues from London and Paris, men's fashions were more distinctively American than those worn by American women. Appearing to be fit became equated with masculinity, and men's clothing was designed to emphasize the masculine silhouette. By the 1890s women were becoming increasingly concerned with practical dress, and they gave up the uncomfortable, awkward styles that characterized high fashion immediately after the Civil War. With the increased availability of ready-made, machine-manufactured clothing, people began to dress with more similarity than before the Civil War, when homemade garments were common. Department stores and mail-order catalogues marketed garments nationally, and Americans of all regions and social classes bought them. Reasonably priced ready-made clothing also helped new immigrants to "blend in" and "look American."

Racism and Nativism. Racism and xenophobia, or fear of foreigners, plagued the country in the years between 1878 and 1899. As more and more immigrants arrived, American anxieties and animosities increased. Hate groups mushroomed as many blamed foreigners and nonwhites for economic hard times. People found comfort with others who looked and believed as they did, and they feared outsiders. Religious prejudice was common, especially against Jews and Catholics, and ethnic groups bound together to resist their "enemies." Though the Ku Klux Klan was formally disbanded in 1869, local groups continued to be active. When the Democrats resumed their political control over the South after Reconstruction ended in 1877, there was an upsurge in the lynching of blacks, to the horror of many. African American journalist Ida B. Wells-Barnett inaugurated a campaign to stop lynching. She wrote and spoke so movingly about the problem that she made people around the world aware of it, and as a result reformers from other countries added their voices to the campaign against racial prejudice in America. During the same period the federal government pursued a policy of stripping all property rights from Native Americans, first herding them onto reservations and then chipping away at those lands until they were all but ravaged.

The American Character. Americans suffered from growing pains in the last two decades of the nineteenth century. It was a time when national ideals were questioned, when the ringing pronouncements of the Declaration of Independence and the preamble to the Constitution were put to the test. The Gilded Age is characterized as a time of excess, when wealthy and powerful industrialists reigned without limits and created modern society after patterns of their own design. But it was also a time when Americans developed a social conscience. Led by women seeking to fulfill their role in modern life, people came to terms with the problems of racial injustice, child abuse, immigration, alcoholism, and suffrage. By the end of the century the everyday life of almost every person in the country had been changed dramatically by new gadgets and inventions, but so had the character of the nation changed as people began to face up to the responsibilities of prosperity and power.

TOPICS IN THE NEWS

EVERYDAY LIFE: CONSUMERISM

Palaces of Consumption. In the mid nineteenth century most American city dwellers bought the goods they needed to conduct their lives at small shops. General stores stocked a variety of items, including food, a small offering of clothing, and hardware items, but the selection was small and the available goods were limited to the necessities. Late in the century a new type of store, called the department store, began to flourish in large cities. Such stores as A. T. Stewart, Lord & Taylor, and R. H. Macy's in New York City; the John Wanamaker store in Philadelphia; and the Jordan Marsh department store in Boston offered a selection of dry goods that astonished the shopper of the day. These large, centrally located retail establishments offered merchandise such as clothing for women and children, small household wares, home furnishings, and often dry goods such as fabrics and notions—all in one huge, often palatial, building. Department-store managers were merchandisers. They displayed their goods attractively in large, street-level glass windows, which gave rise to a new and popular pastime, "window shopping," and showed passersby what they were missing. Central light and heat, glass display cases, high ceilings, ornate decorations, and the new electric passenger elevators (installed in Macy's and Wanamaker's department stores in 1889 and elsewhere soon thereafter) distinguished these stores from the dim and dusty little "general" stores in which most people had shopped before the Civil War. The atmosphere made shoppers feel special, offering distractions from "ordinary life," intended to encourage impulse buying. Department stores further removed themselves from "ordinary life" by providing various cultural events throughout the day, including organ music, fashion shows, and lectures. Some also offered baby-sitting. Department stores had become so enormously popular by the final decade of the century that when Siegel-Cooper opened in New York City in 1896, more than one hundred thousand people attended its opening festivities. The store joined B. Altman and Lord & Taylor on the "Ladies' Mile," known as the place where the Gilded Age elite bought their finery.

The Five-and-Ten-Cent Store. The poor man's department store was the five-and-ten-cent store, a sort of consumers' bazaar. Like the department store, the five-and-ten-cent store appealed to consumer fantasies by displaying a wide and tempting array of goods, but while department-store prices varied according to the quality of goods offered, five-and-ten-cent stores offered only items that could be bought for small units of cash. If the price of an attractive item was low enough, the sellers reasoned, the customer would buy it on a whim, even if he or she did not need it After succeeding with a dry-goods store in Watertown, New York, and failing with a five-cent store in Utica, New York, F. W. Woolworth opened his first five-and-ten-cent store in Lancaster, Pennsylvania, in 1879. By 1895 he had twenty-eight stores; by 1900 he had fifty-nine; ten years later, he had a thousand.

Mail-Order Houses. Farmers and other rural dwellers partook of the new consumerism through mail-order houses, or catalogue buying. Montgomery Ward and Sears, Roebuck and Company began to reach thousands of consumers for whom no Macy's or Woolworth store

Perhaps, as Henry Adams observed, the lives of the very rich were no more worth living than those of their cooks, but wealthy people paid a lot more trying to improve their lot. New York was the center of the nation's wealth at the end of the nineteenth century, and to the status-conscious it seemed that everyone who mattered lived on Fifth Avenue between Fifty-first and Ninety-fifth Streets, where there were some eighty mansions by the end of the century. The Vanderbilts set the standard. By 1882 they owned four dwellings on what was know as Millionaires' Row, including the Twin Mansions, adjoining three-story homes of classical architecture built that year by William Henry Vanderbilt, son of the famous commodore, at a cost of $3 million. (He could afford it; he inherited $60 million when his father died and invested well.) Vanderbilt and his wife lived in one of the buildings; his married daughters shared the other. Both homes had forty-seven rooms and were decorated with Vanderbilt's million-dollar art collection, the finest of the day.

A dollar in 1880 bought about the same as fifteen dollars in 1990. It was estimated that a fortune of about $50 million in the mid 1880s was required to live on Millionaires' Row, and William C. Whitney estimated that it cost about $300,000 a year simply to maintain his home — in 1880 dollars, that is. When his daughter Pauline got married in 1895, Whitney spent $1 million on the wedding party, which President Grover Cleveland attended. Mrs. William Astor did not move to Millionaires' Row at Sixty-fifth Street until 1896; before that she lived on Fifth Avenue, but thirty-one blocks south. She was a social maven and liked to entertain. She had a house designed with sliding doors on one wall of her ballroom that accommodated five hundred. The doors were opened for large parties to form a room that held as many as fifteen hundred rich revelers. Her dinners were served by male servants in court livery of green velvet with gold buttons sporting the Astor coat of arms.

The rich had opulent tastes. In his book *The Robber Barons* (1934) Matthew Josephson reported on the parties of the very rich in New York:

"At Delmonic'os [restaurant] the Silver, Gold and Diamond dinners of the socially prominent succeeded each other unfailingly. At one, each lady present, opening her napkin, found a gold bracelet with the monogram of the host. At another, cigarettes rolled in hundred-dollar-bills were passed around after the coffee and consumed with an authentic thrill. . . . One man gave a dinner to his dog and presented him with a diamond collar worth $15,000. . . . This was at a time when saleswomen made between $2 and $4.50 per week.

was easily accessible. As a traveling salesman for a dry-goods wholesaler, Aaron Montgomery Ward learned the problems farmers and their families faced when their only source of consumer goods was a single, small general store. In 1872 he published an unillustrated list of items, their prices, and ordering information. By buying goods in large quantities from manufacturers and selling them directly to consumers he eliminated the middleman and was able to promise his customers savings of 40 percent. In a matter of years, the booklet grew to a 72-page illustrated catalogue, and by the 1880s it had enticing woodcut pictures with nearly all the listings—which included fans, parasols, writing paper, needles, stereoscopes, cutlery, trunks, harnesses, and many other goods. In 1884 the catalogue had 240 pages and listed nearly ten thousand items. Richard Warren Sears set up a mail-order house for watches in 1886. The following year he moved to Chicago and joined forces with watchmaker Alvah Curtis Roebuck, who also owned a job-printing shop. Sears soon demonstrated a flair for advertising. By the time the pair had incorporated as Sears, Roebuck and Company in 1893, they were publishing a 196-page catalogue that included such items as clothes, furniture, sewing machines, baby carriages, and musical instruments. Marketing innovations like Ward's and Sears and Roebuck's linked rural Americans to the same trends and styles found in large and mid-sized cities and helped to break the isolation felt by many Americans who lived far outside city limits.

Source:
Daniel J. Boorstin, *The Americans: The Democratic Experience* (New York: Random House, 1973).

EVERYDAY LIFE: FASHION

The Clothing Industry. Before the 1870s most Americans women made clothes. Only the wealthy could afford to have their garments custom-made, and to them clothing was the mark of their success. Manufacturers began to make some inexpensive, ready-made clothing in the early nineteenth century, but it was of poor quality and was worn mainly as work clothes by sailors and southern slaves. New technology in the textile industry—especially the invention of practical, workable sewing machines around 1850—and an influx of cheap immigrant labor produced cloth goods that were cheap, du-

John Wanamaker's department store in Philadelphia, early 1880s

rable, and fashionable. The demand for uniforms during the Civil War forced manufacturers to develop an efficient model for the ready-to-wear clothing. Northern garment makers geared up to fill orders for hundreds of thousands of Union army uniforms, creating standard sizing based on government statistics that identified the most commonly occurring human measurements. After the war these same garment makers converted their expanded manufacturing capacity to civilian needs and tastes. Between 1880 and 1890 sales of machine-made, ready-to-wear clothing increased by 75 percent, to well over $1 billion. Yet despite this remarkable growth, more than half of American men still wore hand-sewn shirts in 1880.

Sweatshops. The high level of immigration from Germany, Russia, Poland, and Italy during the last quarter of the century stimulated the textile industry. Many of these new arrivals had tailoring skills and provided clothing manufacturers with an abundance of cheap labor. Sewing machines were so easy to operate that the cheapest laborers in the workforce, immigrant women and children, could be hired to sew. The result was the "sweatshop," where women and children worked long hours at piecework for low wages. In the textile industry the average workday was more than ten hours, and the average wage was ten cents an hour in 1890. Workers in the sewing sweatshops often made less and worked more. Garment makers worked in large, crowded, stuffy rooms with few amenities, and thus the cost of ready-to-wear clothes was very cheap. In 1896 a man's suit could be bought for as little as three dollars, though discriminating shoppers at such trendsetting stores as Brooks Brothers in New York City might pay as much as twenty dollars. A woman's blouse in the early 1890s cost between fifty cents and two dollars, depending on the quality of the fabric, and an all-wool evening suit cost six dollars. Wealthy shoppers still tended to patronize small local dress and tailoring shops where clothes were custom-made, and thrifty women spent their money on their own sewing machines, which could be purchased for as little as nine dollars from Singer in 1896.

The Strenuous Ideal. In the 1880s and 1890s fashionable men adopted a new image. Instead of favoring leanness and a stylized genteel weakness as signs of mental prowess and a safe distance from menial labor, men began to value muscles and physical strength as the outward signs of manliness. The images of the cowboy, the boxer, and the football player linked masculinity and muscularity for men of all classes. At the end of the century Theodore Roosevelt, an active outdoorsman and the hero of San Juan Hill during the Spanish-American War, symbolized the "strenuous ideal" of vitality, strength, and courage. Men flocked to gymnasiums to engage in vigorous exercise, including weight lifting and calisthenics. While exercising, men wore loose-fitting trousers and, because of the privacy of all-male clubs, did without shirts altogether. By the end of the century garments designed for specific sports such as baseball, football, or gymnastics allowed men a fuller range of motion than did street clothes.

A three-piece sack suit, 1881

The Sack Suit. The strenuous ideal influenced how men dressed in public and at work as well. The "elegant gentleman" with his monocle, gloves, and gold-headed cane disappeared, ridiculed as foppish, effeminate, un-American, and incapable of hard work. Men who spent their days in offices felt compelled to prove that "mental" work had not made them "sissies." By the 1880s the formal suit all respectable men wore in public had been largely replaced by a new, distinctively American, casual-looking sack suit. This new business suit dropped the pleated "skirt" of the frock coat; it was streamlined and had "masculine" detailing. Men wore softer shirts and lower collars under their unadorned suit jackets, which had narrow lapels, and a smooth bottom hem that fell just below the hips. These jackets gave men the appearance of having solid, muscular bodies. The pants were similarly narrow. Worn with a vest, a bow tie, and a bowler hat, the sack suit soon became the standard costume for middle-class, white-collar men, while wealthy men still wore frock coats on some occasions. East or West, men who worked in banks, post offices, and governmental offices, as well as farmers and ranchers doing business in town, all donned the sack suit. During this same period many men shaved off their beards, preferring a clean-shaven look that they hoped would give them a youthful, "go-getter" appearance. Mustaches remained popular, and some men, particularly older men in rural areas, still wore beards.

High Style for Women. Ready-made clothing for women became popular and readily available later than men's ready-made suits and shirts. Wealthy women spent hours with their dressmakers discussing engravings of the latest French designs as they were depicted in popular magazines such as *Godey's Lady's Book,* selecting fabrics, and having fittings for custom-made clothing. A woman with a generous clothing allowance bought her clothing from American designers who followed European fashion trends. The most influential American designers—including Mme Harris and Sons, James Gray and Company, Mrs. Cripp, Clark & McLoghan, and Mme Demorest—worked in small shops on major thoroughfares in Philadelphia, Chicago, or New York, three cities that were equally central to setting American fashion trends. As the period wore on, these designers competed with designers who worked in large department stores. Department-store dressmakers, who tended to be more democratic in their pricing, also contributed innovative design changes.

The Sewing Machine. By the 1870s sewing machines were widely available for home sewers, as were precut printed patterns based on the latest fashions, making it possible for middle-class women to dress more like society women. The precut paper pattern was invented by Ellen Curtis Demorest, who was also one of the designers favored by wealthy women. She marketed her patterns by publishing *Mme Demorest's Mirror of Fashion* (founded in 1865), a magazine that featured illustrations of the clothing women could make using Mme Demorest's patterns. A Demorest pattern for a a "Chelsea jacket for child, ornamented with the favorite Capuchin hood, turned down collar, and reverse on the double-breasted fronts; sizes for 12-16 years" cost twenty cents in 1881. Demorest was eventually beaten out by the Butterick company, which started advertising its patterns by publishing two magazines, *The Ladies' Quarterly Report of Broadway Fashions* (founded in 1867) and the monthly *Metropolitan* (founded in 1868), which merged in 1874 as *The Delineator.* In 1896 *The Delineator* offered a pattern for a "lady's basque waist with a waist decoration; in thirteen sizes for ladies from 28" to 46" bust measure" for thirty cents.

Foundations. Women who could afford to do so dressed in elegant full-length dresses that required elaborate underwear. A woman first donned a tight corset, a torturous device worn around the midsection that could mold most bellies into hourglass figures. Corsets were girdles with vertical strips of curved bone or steel embedded in the fabric. They normally laced up the back, and they could exert as much as eighty pounds of compacting pressure, forcing a woman's waistline bulk into her chest cavity, thus enlarging her bustline while pinching her middle. Some models extended well below the waist to contain flabbly backsides. A linen corset cover protected delicate dresses from being damaged by the corset's functional strings and eyelets. Petticoats, which gave shape to dress skirts, were often very frilly and cumbersome, consisting of yards of fabric. During the 1870s the stylish woman wore a bustle at the small of the back. Made of horsehair or a special spring, the bustle enabled fashion designers to drape layers of fine fabrics of various textures across the full skirt. In a gesture toward simplicity women in the 1880s and 1890s wore only one petticoat instead of the five to seven worn earlier.

High Style in the Late 1870s. Women's dresses most typically had pointed necklines with lavishly trimmed collars. It was thought generally unhealthy and unvirtuous for women to expose their chests. Blouses were also layered, with full wrist-length sleeves. Hairstyles varied, but many women wore their hair up, in some sort of bun. Curls were popular either in bangs or cascading down the back of the neck. Favorite accessories were fans and lace-trimmed parasols.

The Narrow Dress. In the early 1880s the narrow look came into vogue for women. From neck to knee the dress was straight. Below the knees the skirt flared out and formed a shallow train. Many women actually tied their knees together, making anything but small steps impossible. These narrow dresses still required a bustle, but it was moved to a lower position. Later, as these skirts shortened to the ankle so that feet became visible, women wore elegant shoes with high heels. The narrow dress demanded a correspondingly small hat.

The Hourglass Shape. By the late 1880s and early 1890s women were emphasizing the hourglass shape, with its narrow waist, by wearing flared skirts with bigger-than-ever bustles moved back to the small of the back. An 1890 article in *Ladies' Home Journal* estimated that a fashionable evening dress of the time might be fourteen to fifteen feet across the bottom, and all of that gathering of material draped to the floor. Men who were less than gentlemen called such dresses street-sweeper fashions because women wearing them could not help brushing up dirt as they walked. They also had the effect of limiting close contact. Blouses had sleeves puffed high at the shoulder. These "leg-of-mutton" sleeves grew steadily in size for the first half of the 1890s. The blouse of the 1890s was more ornamental than in the 1880s, with bands of ribbon tied in bows, ruffles of lace, and other decorative effects following the line of the sleeve across the bodice. By the end of the century the bustle had disappeared, but women were still attempting to achieve the hourglass shape by wearing corsets, full sleeves, and flared, toe-length skirts.

THE GIBSON GIRL

During the 1890s a new feminine role model appeared in the pages of the popular humor magazine *Life*. The Gibson Girl, as she was soon called, was stylishly dressed, assertive, and independent, but not wicked. Her creator, artist Charles Dana Gibson, perfectly captured the promise of the New Woman who pushed the boundaries of acceptable female behavior and the American definition of feminine charm. In Gibson's drawings the Gibson Girl wore her hair piled softly on her head, a shirtwaist blouse, and a full skirt with a wide, stiff belt that accented a tiny, corseted waistline. She finished her look with dark boots and a straw boater hat. She was witty without being threatening, charming without being submissive, exciting without being bad. The real-life Gibson Girl was most likely to be a telephone operator or clerical worker in a large city, taking advantage of the new work opportunities for women, and she dated without a chaperon.

Source: Barbara Clark Smith and Kathy Peiss, *Men and Women: A History of Costume, Gender, and Power* (Washington, D.C.: Smithsonian Institution, 1989).

Clothes for Housework. In the late nineteenth century, women's primary labor continued to be housework and child rearing. Poor women often raised their families in unsanitary, crowded conditions, and many took in boarders or piecework sewing to supplement the family income. Wealthy women, or "ladies of leisure," employed working-class women to cook, clean, and care for children. While upper-class women dressed in elaborate clothes and jewels, following fashion trends set in London and Paris and becoming living symbols of their husband's wealth and social status, the middle-class woman handled her household chores in a housedress of sturdy, washable fabric that withstood dirt and sweat day after day. Many middle-class women hired a female helper for heavy housework. Only for dinner, social calls, or church did the middle-class women change into what was called a "day dress" made of finer materials.

The New Woman. In the years following the Civil War, more and more women of all classes lived lives outside the domestic sphere, as opportunities in education, work, and politics increased. Women joined clubs, charity organizations, temperance societies, labor unions, and consumer-protection societies. No longer restricted to work as domestic servants, mill workers, or farm wives, some women became typists, secretaries, salesclerks, or waitresses. Such changes in women's lifestyles directly affected fashion. Their need for work clothes motivated the women's ready-to-wear industry to offer more items at reasonable prices, and practicality became an important quality. The first popular ready-made women's garment was the shirtwaist, modeled after a

Clothing of the Gilded Age: (top left) a silk gown with a pleated skirt and a fabric-draped bustle, a style popular in the late 1870s and into the 1880s; (top right) a suit with the straight skirt that came into fashion in the early 1880s; (bottom left) age-appropriate clothing for men, women, and children in the early 1890s; and (bottom right) the "Gibson Girl" look of the late 1890s

Beachwear of the late 1890s

"Gibson Girls" at the beach, by Charles Dana Gibson (from *Life,* 25 August 1897)

man's shirt. Widely available by the 1890s, it buttoned down the front, or appeared to, and had a small collar, full sleeves, and narrow cuffs. Women in many occupations—secretaries, teachers, settlement-house workers, housewives, or factory workers—wore the shirtwaist, which came in inexpensive versions for working-class women and more elaborate styles decorated with lace, pleats, and large sleeves for those who had public contact. By the late 1890s the full-sleeved, tailored shirtwaist was worn by women of all classes with full skirts that emphasized their tiny corseted waists. This look, complete with upswept hair, was popularized by magazine illustrator Charles Dana Gibson. Young women all over the United States tried to look like the Gibson Girl, and many succeeded thanks to the availability of ready-made skirts and blouses in stores and mail-order catalogues. By the end of the century, a well-dressed woman could buy her entire wardrobe in a department store or from a mail-order catalogue.

The Strenuous Ideal for Women. During the late nineteenth century a new generation of health experts rejected the traditional view that exercise was dangerous for the so-called weaker sex. Instead they asserted that exercise increased women's physical and mental health, gearing women's physical activities toward health, beauty, and grace rather than strength and competition. Women's colleges encouraged their students to participate in fitness programs and sports teams. While exercising, women wore bloomers, short skirts, or other loose-fitting dresses with dark tights. When riding bicycles, women wore shortened skirts over knickerbockers, or divided skirts (some of which were pleated to look like a full skirt when the woman stood still). A few daring souls wore "Syrian trousers," loose slacks that reached to the ankle. In many parts of the country, women who bicycled in pants caused a scandal. Female bicyclists rode astride, breaking a rule that "proper" women horseback riders, who rode sidesaddle, had followed for generations. On the beach and at the lake or river, women wore full dresses with short sleeves and black tights; their legs had to be covered. These garments got so heavy in the water that swimming any distance proved impossible for all but the fittest. By the turn of the century, a trend toward practical swimwear helped change the standards for what constituted feminine modesty.

Sources:

Daniel J. Boorstin, *The Americans: The Democratic Experience* (New York: Random House, 1973);

Lee Hall, *Common Threads: A Parade of American Clothing* (Boston, Toronto & London: Little, Brown, 1992);

Ludmila Kybalova, Olga Herbenova, and Milena Lamarova, *The Pictorial Encyclopedia of Fashion* (New York: Crown, 1968);

Barbara Clark Smith and Kathy Peiss, *Men and Women: A History of Costume, Gender, and Power* (Washington, D.C.: Smithsonian Institution, 1989);

EATING OUT

While most nineteenth-century Americans ate simply, the upper classes dined lavishly at elegant "French" restaurants where menus often listed 70 to 120 items. Established in 1832, Delmonico's Restaurant in New York City set the standard for elegant dining during the 1880s and 1890s, a time when eight-to-ten-course banquets featuring vast amounts of food were typical among wealthy diners. In 1880 a Delmonico's dinner honoring Gen. Winfield Scott Hancock, soon to become the Democratic presidential candidate, began with raw oysters, a choice of two soups, an hors d'oeuvre, and a fish course. The next course — saddle of lamb and filet of beef — was followed by chicken wings with green peas and lamb chops with beans and mushroom-stuffed artichokes. After terrapin *en casserole à la Maryland,* the diners were served sorbet to "cleanse the palate" before tackling on the "roast" course of canvasback duck and quail. Desserts included timbale Madison, various kinds of ice cream, whipped creams, jellied dishes, banana mousse, and various elaborate pastry dishes. The dinner ended with coffee and liqueurs served with fruit and petits fours. As this menu suggests, "plumpness" was fashionable in the 1880s.

Source: Harvey A. Levenstein, *Revolution at the Table: The Transformation of the American Diet* (New York & Oxford: Oxford University Press, 1988).

Estelle Ansley Worrell, *American Costume, 1840–1920* (Harrisburg, Pa.: Stackpole, 1979).

EVERYDAY LIFE: FOOD

Ethnic Tastes in a National Market. During the 1870s, 1880s, and 1890s two opposing trends were visible in American eating habits. Regional and ethnic differences powerfully influenced selection and preparation of food. Where they lived—the western frontier, the rural South, the East, the Midwest, the Southwest—and where they left—Greece, Italy, Central Europe, or Africa—shaped what a family ate. Their style of food preparation linked people to their pasts and to their ethnic, regional histories. The second and competing trend in the United States was a move toward standardization, as improvements in transportation and preservation helped to create national markets for brand-name foods. Favorites from one region could be transported to others without spoiling, giving rise to a distinctive "American" diet.

Southern Food. The American South produced some of the most enduringly popular dishes in the United States, many of them influenced by the cooking practices slaves brought with them from Africa. For centuries many poor southerners subsided on the three M's—meat

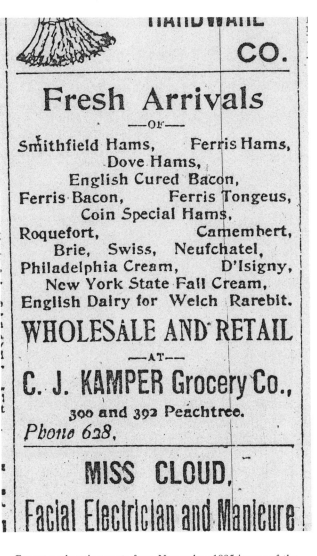

Grocery advertisements from November 1895 issues of the Atlanta Constitution

(sowbelly), meal (corn), and molasses. Goobers, or peanuts, and yams were major fare in the South as were corn products such as hominy, grits, cornmeal mush, hush puppies, and cornbread, as well as cowpeas, collards, and turnip greens. Chicken was the favorite food for special occasions with pork a close second. Louisiana Creole and Cajun cuisine introduced gumbo with celery, tomatoes, and bell peppers, and soups or stews thickened with okra into the national diet. New Orleans developed a unique mix of French, Spanish, African, and Native American foods that relied heavily on spices, crawfish, and redfish.

Western and Midwestern Food. As they traveled west settlers survived on a limited, monotonous diet of heavy, greasy foods, mainly fatback (meat from the back of a hog), cornbread, and perhaps a handful of seasonal vegetables. With the establishment of family farms the diet of westerners and midwesterners improved. By the 1890s a typical day's diet included two kinds of meats, eggs, cheese, butter, cream, bread, corn, several other vegetables, jellies, preserves, relishes, cake, pie, milk, coffee, and tea. Because cattle were more widely available, midwesterners and westerners also consumed more beef than did southerners.

Immigrant and Ethnic Foods. Central and eastern Europeans brought with them foods that became widely popular in the United States: Polish kielbasa (sausage); Hungarian *gulyas* (goulash); Italian pasta with tomato-based sauces, including spaghetti and lasagna; and Greek moussaka, *pastitsio*, and other lamb dishes. Greek and Italian immigrants were especially influential on American food tastes because of their tendency to enter the restaurant business. A distinctive Greek American contribution was Cincinnati "five-way" chili, made from

A Connecticut Family in the Textile Industry

Nine family members: husband, age 56, is a cloth inspector; wife, age 52, works at home; children — male 21, male 18, male 17, female 14, female 12 — three work, two are at school; two are boarders.

Annual family income:

Husband's salary:	188.00
Children's wages:	710.00
Boarder's rent:	40.00
	$938.00

Annual expenses:

Rent	49.44
Food	482.31
Other	317.40
	$849.15

Annual food expenditures

Beef	$108.75
Hog products	99.25
Other meat	3.30
Eggs	19.50
Lard	6.40
Butter	58.24
Tea	12.00
Coffee	6.00
Sugar	36.00
Molasses	1.80
Potatoes	9.60
Poultry	0.00
Fish	3.00
Milk	21.90
Flour/meal	30.00
Bread	27.20
Rice	.60
Cheese	8.32
Fruit	0.00
Vinegar/pickles	1.00
Vegetables	1.20
Other	28.25
	$ 482.31

The family of nine lives in a rented house with six rooms heated with wood. The house has one carpet. The light for the house is provided with oil lamps. The family uses twenty-four gallons of oil a year, costing $3.60. The husband spent $13.25 on clothing; the wife spent $7.00, and the children spent $130.00. The family spent $10.25 on furniture and paid $1.38 in taxes. The family paid no life insurance or labor dues. They contributed $30.00 to the church and $2.50 to charity. They spent $4.00 on vacations, $4.00 on alcohol, and $10.40 on tobacco. At the end of the year the family had a surplus of $88.85.

A Georgia Family in the Textile Industry

Four family members: husband, age 54, is a card rinder; wife, age 25, works at home; one child — female, age 4; one boarder.

Annual family income:

Husband's income:	312.00
Boarder's rent:	10.00
	$322.00

The family does not own its home.

Annual expenses

Rent	21.00
Food	119.70
Other	241.70
	382.40

Annual food expenditures

Beef	$0.00
Hog products	17.00
Other meat	13.00
Eggs	5.20
Lard	6.50
Butter	5.00
Tea	0.00
Coffee	4.50
Sugar	4.00
Molasses	2.00
Potatoes	6.40
Poultry	2.00
Fish	1.50
Milk	3.60
Flour/meal	25.00
Rice	.50
Cheese	1.00
Fruit	4.00
Vinegar/pickles	2.00
Vegetables	13.00
Other	3.50
	$119.70

This family rents a two-room apartment. Heat is provided with wood. The home is lighted by oil, of which the family uses thirteen gallons at $1.95 annually. The home is comfortably furnished, and the family owns a sewing machine. The husband spent $20.00 on clothing; the wife, $20.00 and the child's clothing cost $6.00. The family spent $46.90 for furniture. The family gave $2.60 to the Woodsmen of the World, $3.00 to the church, and $.50 to other charities. They spent $3.25 on alcohol, $3.00 on tobacco, and $65 on medical expenses. Their vacations cost $3,25.

Source: Bulletin of the Department of Labor (1890).

A Minneapolis parlor with a typical decorative stove of the 1890s

ground beef and a complex combination of flavorings and served over pasta with grated cheese, kidney beans, and onions. Jewish immigrants were well represented in the delicatessen business, which introduced foods from Germany, Romania, Hungary, and various Slavic countries, including pastrami, corned beef, latkes (potato pancakes), and borscht (beet soup). Spanish-speaking immigrants introduced tortillas, salsa, chilis, and *posole*. Mexican and Anglo food sensibilities eventually blended in such "American" foods as barbecue and various Tex-Mex dishes.

Standardization. During the 1870s, 1880s, and 1890s the expansion of railroad networks enabled foods to be transported farther and faster. The refrigerated railroad car allowed foods grown only in one part of the country to be shipped safely and cheaply to shoppers all over the nation. Californians began shipping fresh fruits to the East Coast in 1869, but the practice of shipping fruits and vegetables by rail did not become widespread for another decade. Improvements in refrigeration also allowed meats to be shipped long distances without the threat of spoiling. Businessmen such as Gustavus Franklin Swift and Philip Danforth Armour made fortunes in the burgeoning meatpacking industry centered in Chicago. Swift and Armour worked separately on perfecting the refrigerated train car in the early 1880s, and each supplied the railroad lines with his own cars. Swift's system of transporting beef, which he began to develop in 1879, became a model for the industry. Cattle were slaughtered in Chicago, and large slabs of meat were loaded on overhead hanging racks in refrigerated train cars. To avoid spoilage when refrigerated cars arrived at their destinations, the cars were brought to a stop directly opposite the doors of cold-storage buildings. The overhead racks in the cars were connected to those in the buildings, and the meat was quickly moved inside. From there butchers cut and packaged the meat before it was transported to stores.

Competition. Almost immediately after they had invested enormous amounts of money in refrigerator cars, Swift and Armour faced competition from a rapidly growing canned-meat industry. Canned meat, from which gristle and bones had been removed, weighed only one-third as much as regular meat. As canned meat became more popular, Swift and Armour found that their meat-shipping revenues were slipping, and they were forced to find some way to fill their expensive railroad cars. Armour sent his agents to the South to encourage farmers there to raise large quantities of perishable fruits and berries that would require refrigerated shipping to northern cities. Soon Armour was making a fortune transporting fresh fruits from Florida and California across the country, helping to further diversify the American diet. In 1880 vegetables for all but the wealthiest Americans tended to mean potatoes and cabbage. By 1910, thanks in part to advertising by the big companies that processed and shipped fruits and vegetables, Americans were eating a much wider variety of these foods.

Canning. In the 1870s city dwellers preserved their own summer perishables for winter use. The housewife would buy local strawberries or peaches in season and use them to make preserves and jams. Apples, potatoes, and other fruits and vegetables of local origin were stored in the family cellar. By the 1880s and 1890s, however, the central heating installed in more and more houses had made some cellars too warm for winter storage. Many

A middle-class family's kitchen in New York City during the 1890s

city dwellers, particularly immigrants and working-class families, lived in apartments and had no cellars in which to store food. Families without cold-storage facilities had to buy whatever perishables were available daily and to rely on commercially canned foods. Improvements in technology during the 1860s and 1870s helped the canning industry to meet growing demands. While the industry produced only five million cans of food in 1860, it put up thirty million by 1870, and over the next decade the value of its output increased by 200 percent. Farmers in Florida and California started to grow new strains of fruits, including the navel orange from Brazil and the Valencia orange from Europe, precisely for canning. A half-dozen new kinds of potatoes, as well as new varieties of tomatoes that were better suited for canning, were cultivated by farmers eager to sell their crops to canning factories.

"Scientific Housekeeping." Another contribution to food standardization came from the scientific-housekeeping movement popular among middle-class women. Becoming known as home economics in 1899, scientific housekeeping sought to bring modern science into the home by introducing improved cleaning and sanitation methods and nutritious recipes that used standardized measurements. Women involved in the movement became instructors at colleges and universities that admitted women and in cooking schools such as the Boston Cooking School, founded in 1879 by members of the movement. The most famous graduate of this school was Fannie Farmer, whose *The Boston Cooking-School Cook Book* (1896) became a best-seller. Farmer approached food preparation with practicality, enthusiasm, and an emphasis on nutrition. She was the first cookbook author to use the spoon-and-cup measurements that had recently become available. The overall effect of the movement of which Farmer was a member was the promotion of a nationally standardized cuisine prepared from identical recipes with identical equipment.

Sources:

Daniel J. Boorstin, *The Americans: The Democratic Experience* (New York: Random House, 1973);

Richard Osborn Cummings, *The American and His Food: A History of American Eating Habits in the United States* (Chicago: University of Chicago Press, 1941);

Richard J. Hooker, *Food and Drink in the United States: A History* (Indianapolis: Bobbs-Merrill, 1981);

Harvey A. Levenstein, *Revolution at the Table: The Transformation of the American Diet* (New York & Oxford: Oxford University Press, 1988).

EVERYDAY LIFE: HOME IMPROVEMENTS

Utilities. Between 1880 and 1899 technological innovations made it possible for more and more middle-class homes to be connected to city services supplying water, heat, light, and sewerage. The new utilities came to wealthy people and city dwellers before poor people and farmers. Easterners tended to get them before southerners and westerners. Homeowners enjoyed the new services; yet they also brought a host of new expenses and worries.

Water. During the 1870s hauling fresh water into the house and carrying wastewater out was a daily chore for many women and children. In the country they filled buckets at cisterns, rain barrels, wells, or springs and other natural water sources. Some houses had a kitchen

The development of plumbing was a high-priority concern in the late 1800s, especially in large cities. Indoor plumbing of any description was a novelty, and bathrooms were rare except in the mansions of the rich.

The phrase "going to the bathroom" was meaningless then. People took care of their personal needs in outhouses, where weather and sensibilities permitted, or in chamberpots, containers usually made of porcelain that were stored in a closet or underneath a bed and were dumped after use; fashion-minded people kept a commode, which was a wood case with a lid for the chamber pot. When separate outhouses were provided for men and women, they were distinguished by a crescent shape on the door of the women's facility; and a full moon on the man's door. Inside was a wooden bench with a hole in the center; newspapers or mail-order catalogues were provided to serve the purpose of toilet paper. Outhouses were smelly, uncomfortable, and usually far enough away from a family's living quarters to make a midnight nature call a dreaded occurrence. The odor was controlled (but not very well) by spreading lime or dirt over the waste.

Baths were also different a hundred years ago. Tubs were free-standing containers, usually made of iron, or sometimes porcelain, that were round or oval-shaped. Water had to be carried to fill them, and unless the bather was content with a cold bath, the water had to be heated on a stove. Store-bought soap was a luxury associated with city life. More often homemade lye soap was used as a cleanser. Because baths were so much trouble, people took them less often than they did after running water was introduced. People thought that good hygiene required a weekly bath and a hair washing at least every two weeks for women.

pump located over a well, or they had their own water tanks with windmill-powered pumps. In small cities water-hauling trucks filled outdoor water barrels. By 1880 most cities of more than ten thousand people had some sort of municipal water supply for some neighborhoods. People in tenements might get water from street hydrants or water taps in hallways. Some individual families had house plumbing systems hooked up to public water mains. Small towns also assumed some responsibility for providing a regular supply of water for their residents by building water towers or hilltop reservoirs, but in rural areas families still had to find their own water supply.

Heat. Most American homes relied on stoves for heat. In frontier communities almost anything that could be burned was used as fuel. Homesteaders in west Texas during the 1880s used mesquite, shinnery (a dwarf oak), corncobs, and cow chips (dried cow manure). Even after railroads brought coal to this region, settlers continued to maintain chip sheds to ensure a regular supply of heat. Urban dwellers fueled their stoves with coal. By the end of the nineteenth century middle-class Americans had begun to install central, coal-burning furnaces in their cellars to provide heat through a system of ducts and vents to the entire house. Often cheaper furnace systems provided heat through one large grate located on the first floor directly above the furnace. While middle-class families could afford furnaces, working-class families continued to heat with stoves, which brought with them a host of problems. The most serious was the leaking of deadly carbon monoxide caused from burning the wrong kind of fuel. Most houses heated this way had only one stove centrally located. In the winter the room with the stove tended to be too hot for comfort while adjoining rooms were frigid. Many Americans believed that waking up cold on winter mornings was simply part of life.

Light. After the Civil War artificial light from a variety of sources extended the hours of productive activity in American households. Rural homes still used candles and oil lamps; kerosene lamps were gradually improved. In 1870 they provided light equivalent to that of six to twenty candles; by 1910 their light had been increased to sixty to eighty candlepower. In middle-class homes during the 1880s and 1890s, first in urban areas and later in the country, kerosene lamps began to give way to gas and electrical lighting. Most Americans first experienced gaslights at midcentury in public spaces such as city streets, department stores, schools, hospitals, and government buildings. If the homeowner could afford it and lived close to a gas supply, gaslighting offered a welcome alternative to the dirt and odor of the kerosene lamp. After Thomas Edison perfected the incandescent electric lightbulb in 1879 and developed the delivery system, gas gradually lost out to electricity. Electrical power appeared to have many advantages over gas. It provided more regular light; and it was clean and odorless. In 1899 about 75 percent of the gas produced in the United States was used for lighting; in 1919 that figure had dropped to 21 percent (while more than half the gas produced was used for heating). In 1881 the first central electric power plant in the world was constructed in New York City; it became operational the following year. Two years later about five hundred households and one thousand businesses in the city had electricity. By 1907 about 8 percent of households nationwide had electric lighting. Electricity also made telephone systems possible. The first commercial exchange, serving twenty-one telephones, opened in New Haven, Connecticut, in 1878, the same year in which a telephone was installed in the

A house in a suburb of Philadelphia, 1885

White House. By 1900 Americans had nearly 1.5 million telephones.

The Bathroom. Not until the 1910s did the modern bathroom with a tub, sink, and toilet become a standard part of the American house. For most Americans the toilet was an outdoor privy or a chamberpot tucked under a bed when it was not in use. People washed using a bowl and pitcher in a bedroom and took baths in a portable tub. In 1876 only wealthy homes had a room designated only for the toilet. Most indoor toilets were located in closets or storage areas, not in "rooms." By the 1880s and 1890s some wealthy Americans had modern flush toilets, an invention developed in England during the 1870s. Toilets were usually connected to individual cesspools, which were not practical in heavily populated urban areas. Various patents for different kinds of water closets, as bathrooms were called, had been issued in the United States since the 1830s, but the water closet did not come into general use until after the development of sewerage systems, which lagged behind water provision in most cities. Before 1880 drainage was managed by open ditches. Some cities began building sewerage systems during the 1880s, but they were mostly for draining storm water not wastewater. The result was that unpaved areas were likely to be muddy slogs dotted with foul-smelling and unhealthy puddles. It took decades before sewers were built to carry waste from individual homes. Even then it was difficult to convince landlords to install indoor plumbing and sewer connections. At the end of the century thousands of city dwellers living in tenements on streets with sewer lines were still using old-fashioned outdoor privies.

Sources:

Daniel J. Boorstin, *The Americans: The Democratic Experience* (New York: Random House, 1973);

Thomas J. Schlereth, "Conduits and Conduct: Home Utilities in Victorian America, 1876–1915," in *American Home Life, 1880–1930,*

edited by Jessica H. Foy and Schlereth (Knoxville: University of Tennessee Press, 1992), pp. 225–241.

EVERYDAY LIFE: SUBURBS

Growth of Suburbs. During the first part of the nineteenth century Americans thought of a suburban home as an isolated country house to which a wealthy family retired. As railroads began to extend farther from cities, as the cable car was put into use in the 1870s, and as the electric streetcar was developed in the 1880s, however, more and more city dwellers were able to move outside the city limits to more rural areas. Such changes permanently refashioned the image of suburbia in the United States as more and more suburbs grew up along rail lines. These "streetcar" or "railroad suburbs" placed suburban living within the reach of middle-class Americans. Suburbs fulfilled the desire of many late-nineteenth-century Americans for the beauty and serenity of the country without the isolation of truly rural areas. Convenient and affordable, suburbs offered many a compelling reason to commute.

City Services for the Suburbs. Throughout the 1880s many early suburbs tried to provide residents urban-style amenities—including parks, schools, and cultural associations—and services such as running water and sewer connections. These additions took time and money. Community associations and real-estate developers met some of these needs, but residents also turned to local governments. By the 1890s the best suburban communities advertised their paved streets, schools, good transportation, and other services formerly available only in cities. As suburbs grew, rural life also changed. In many regions agricultural villages became suburbs.

Industrial Suburbs. By the turn of the century factory owners took advantage of the services suburban homeowners had obtained from their local governments.

Klondike gold prospectors, 1897

Drawn away from urban areas by less expensive lands, industrialists build large suburban factories supported by good roads, mass transportation, sewerage, and water services. The first to take advantage of business opportunities in the suburbs was George Pullman, who built his Pullman car works and the model town Pullman in a southern suburb of Chicago in 1882. Such an arrangement, where workers lived in a single-industry suburb, provided them access to good services but left them vulnerable to the dictates of their employer and landlord.

Sources:

Daniel J. Boorstin, *The Americans: The Democratic Experience* (New York: Random House, 1973);

Kenneth T. Jackson, *Crabgrass Frontier: The Suburbanization of the United States* (New York & Oxford: Oxford University Press, 1985).

THE KLONDIKE GOLD RUSH

Finding Gold. In the summer of 1897 Americans caught gold fever. Nothing captured the American male's search for manly adventure, rugged individualism, and money as the Klondike gold rush. In July the first tattered gold-laden millionaires landed on a San Francisco wharf, dragging suitcases, canvas sacks, and old cartons heavy with gold. Within a matter of minutes the Klondike stampede began. At the height of the gold rush in 1898 and 1899, more than one million people made plans to go to the Klondike region of the Yukon Territory of 1898 and 1899 in northwestern Canada, and one hundred thousand actually set off. The prospect of ad-

venture and wealth appealed to many American men who found themselves doing repetitive, dull, and low-paying work day in and day out. For those men who wanted to mine gold and for those businessmen and -women who saw opportunity in supplying services to prospectors, the 1898 and 1899 gold rush seemed to promise great wealth for little more than hard work and the application of "Yankee ingenuity."

Setting Out. By mid July 1897 vessels that had been deemed unseaworthy in June were in service transporting men, horses, dogs, and supplies to Alaska, to begin the long overland journey to the Yukon Territory. Crushed together onboard ship would-be miners slept in crowded berths or on the open deck, sometimes waiting seven hours for a meal and suffering storms, explosions, starvation, shipwreck, and even mutiny. Once on dry land, prospectors faced swindlers and shopkeepers eager to make a profit in the tent towns of Skagway and Dyer. Saloons, houses of prostitution, and land offices were among the businesses that prospered. Food sold at ridiculous prices in these tent towns because they were the last places to buy supplies for the trek into the Yukon interior, and each prospector had to take with him a year's supply of food.

The Journey to Dawson. Within a few miles of Skagway the road became a narrow winding path. The forty-five-mile trail wound around and over a steep mountain. Weakened by infected hooves, heavy loads, relentless beatings, and the icy-cold weather, pack animals died by a frontier boating village amazingly well supplied with drills, nails, and tools. When the ice on the lakes and rivers finally melted, 7,124 kayaks, scows, and canoes traveled the five hundred miles through canyons and rapids. The first boats landed at Dawson, the center of the Yukon mining activity, on 8 June 1898, and boats continued to arrive without a break for more than a month.

Dawson. The boom town of Dawson stood in stark contrast to the rest of the empty Yukon Territory. As the boom continued big steamers brought wood, liquor, food, horses, and more and more people into a city filled with stores, hotels, dance halls, post offices, and newspapers. Many of the men who struggled to reach Dawson ended up never staking claims for themselves and worked instead at mining other men's gold. Others found work in town. As the city grew, thousands of gold seekers indulged themselves in the festive and dramatic atmosphere as gambling, theater, and prostitution expanded to meet the demands of the population. On 26 April 1899 a fire completely destroyed the town, but by the end of the summer a new Dawson had been built, fancier and more Victorian than the rugged frontier town it replaced. By then gold had been discovered in Nome, Alaska, and the golden party prepared to move on. In a single week in August, eight thousand people left Dawson for Nome and Fairbanks, Alaska. The gold fever continued for restless American men hoping for adventure and money.

Sources:

Pierre Berton, *The Klondike Quest: A Photographic Essay, 1897–1899* (Boston: Little, Brown, 1983);

David B. Wharton, *The Alaska Gold Rush* (Bloomington: Indiana University Press, 1972).

Chief Joseph and his family during their confinement on a reservation in Oklahoma, early 1880s

the thousands. Their bodies littered the path and inspired American writer Jack London, who went to the Yukon in the fall of 1897, to call it the "Dead Horse Trail." Despite such harsh conditions, the prospectors continued to climb the mountain, each carrying more than sixty-five pounds of supplies. The line of men was spaced so tightly that the queue could pass a given point for five hours straight without a break.

The Golden Stairs. Just below the summit of the coastal mountain range, prospectors had to abandon their pack animals and climb on foot through the Chilkoot Pass over the mountains. The mountains were covered with thick icy snow all year long. The feet of the seemingly endless trail of men cut "steps" into the ice of the pass that become known as the Golden Stairs. Because of the difficulty of reaching the summit, men divided their supplies into smaller loads and made several trips from the base camp to the summit. It took many prospectors three months to move their supplies to the top of the mountain. Those who survived the Golden Stairs had to wait on the other side of the mountains for the ice to melt on the lakes and rivers of the Yukon Valley. As they waited, they built boats of all kinds, forming

RACE AND ETHNICITY: GOVERNMENT POLICY TOWARD NATIVE AMERICANS

Indian Wars. With more and more whites moving west, Indians had little hope of stopping the invasion of their lands. Despite great odds, however, many tribes fought back. During the 1860s and 1870s, Indian wars were almost constant, and they continued intermittently in the 1880s. The deaths of Gen. George A. Custer and more than two hundred of his men in a battle with Sioux and Cheyenne warriors at Little Bighorn in 1876, the resistance and flight of the Nez Percé in 1877, and the long fight with Chiricahua Apaches led by Geronimo, whose capture in 1886 brought the Indian wars to a virtual end, vividly demonstrated to white Americans that the subjugation of Native Americans would not be easy.

Indian Policy. Racism against Native Americans continued to shape government policy toward them during the 1870s, 1880s, and 1890s, just as it had since the early days of the republic. The Indian Appropriation Act of 1871 made all Native Americans wards of the federal government and nullified all treaties with them. By declaring that the government would no longer sign treaties with Indian tribes, Congress effectively erased the remaining traces of the Native Americans' national sovereignty. Beginning in the 1850s and intensifying efforts in the West after the Civil War, the government created reservations, tracts of land on which tribes agreed to settle in return for a restricted amount of cultural and legal freedom. Yet even the reservation system started to crumble as white settlers eagerly pressed against the borders of reservations in Oklahoma, Arizona, South Dakota, and Idaho. Many Native Americans worked in good faith with the government to secure their lands and homes within the reservation structure. Yet many states believed that the Indians had more land than they needed, and Arizona was the only state that actually added to reservation lands during the period.

The Dawes Act. The Dawes Act of 1887 decreed that reservation lands, previously held in common by a tribe, should be divided into 160-acre plots for families, 80-acre parcels for single men, and 40-acre pieces for orphans. Any land left over was defined as "surplus," and tribes were required to sell all surplus land to the government for resale to non-Indians. Sen. Henry M. Dawes of Massachusetts, who sponsored the bill, intended the legislation as a "reform" measure to introduce Native Americans to the concepts of individual ownership and agricultural life—white beliefs about the "proper" way for Indians to live. The new policy proved devastating to the Native Americans, many of whom did not live in traditional family units or fully understand the concept of private property.

Repercussions. For every three acres owned by Native Americans in the 1880s, two were no longer under their control by the 1920s as a result of the Dawes Act. Socially, the act encouraged individualism over traditional ideas of communalism. It upheld the sanctity of the family rather than emphasizing the importance of community. The land allotments were rarely large enough to sustain a family, and divisions of the parcels among heirs created smaller and smaller sections. Such situations encouraged Native Americans to lease or sell their land to whites and increased their displacement.

Indian Schools. Another component of the Indian policy during this period was the establishment of Indian boarding schools, which brought children from many nations together and discouraged them from speaking anything but English. "The language of the white man and the black man ought to be good enough for the red man," a commissioner of Indian affairs announced in 1887. Schools established in Kansas, Oklahoma, Oregon, and California emphasized vocational and technical training and taught their pupils that future success lay in blending into white society. In such settings Indian youths suffered. Many caught diseases for which they had no immunity, and all were deprived of education in their nations' traditions and ceremonies. The schools encouraged youths to embrace Christianity and to leave behind the old religion of their people. Many resisted enrollment or ran away.

Chief Joseph's War. The consequences of the Indian policy were dramatically demonstrated by the plight of the Nez Percé tribe of the Northwest, a tribe with a long history of friendship to whites. The Nez Percé homeland was located in northern Idaho, southeastern Washington, and northeastern Oregon. Numbering about thirty-six hundred, the Nez Percé had a reputation for breeding superior horses. Their society considered all tribesmen equal, with villages in close proximity loosely organized into separate bands, each directed in peacetime by a civil chief and in battle by a war leader. While white Americans singled out Chief Joseph as the head chief of the Nez Percé, he was one of many tribal leaders. In 1876 the federal government sent Gen. Oliver Otis Howard and four other commissioners to convince the Nez Percé of the Wallowa Valley in eastern Oregon to sell their ancestral land and move to the Lapwai Reservation in Idaho, where other Nez Percé had relocated.

The Long Flight. Realizing that resistance would be futile Chief Joseph convinced his people to yield, but in June 1877, days before they were going to enter the reservation, three young warriors avenged the death of a friend by killing four whites who were known to have mistreated Indians. Inspired by this act of defiance, other warriors formed a raiding party that killed more than a dozen more whites. Hoping to avoid war, Chief Joseph led his people into the hills for protection. Government troops pursued the retreating Nez Percé. In the battle that followed on 17 June, some seventy Nez Percé warriors armed with bows and arrows gave the ninety-nine cavalrymen one of the worst defeats of the Indian wars: thirty-four whites and not a single Nez Percé were killed. News of the "massacre" spread across the country. Looking Glass, chief of another Nez Percé band, had urged his people to remain neutral, but after white soldiers destroyed his village on 1 July in the mistaken belief that he planned to take up arms as well, he and his band joined with Chief Joseph, increasing the number of warriors to about three hundred. Nearly eight hundred Nez Percé men, women, and children fled through Idaho, Wyoming, and Montana, doing battle with government troops along the way. Their defeat was assured when rival tribes, the Bannock and Crow, joined the government. From 30 September to 5 October the Nez Percé fought their last battle at the Milk River in Montana, some forty miles from the Canadian border. With Chiefs Toohoolzote, Looking Glass, and other leaders killed, Joseph surrendered, saying: "It is cold, and we have no blankets. . . . My heart is sick and sad. From where the sun now stands I will fight no more, forever." Some four hundred Nez Percé, less than one hundred of them warriors, surrendered with him. Some three hundred, roughly a third of them warriors, slipped into Canada, where they joined the Lakotas led by Sitting Bull, who had fled there in spring 1877, after the end of the Sioux Wars the previous year.

Exile. Chief Joseph believed that he and his people would be allowed to settle on the Lapwai Reservation in Idaho, but instead he and his people were sent into exile on reservations in Kansas and then Oklahoma, where many died in the unfamiliar and inhospitable climate. Conditions were terrible, with little fresh water or food. The climate was harsh and dry, a far cry from their green homeland. Chief Joseph's pleas for better treatment won him national celebrity but little in the form of relief.

The "Indian Napoleon." During the summer of 1877 the nation had read about the plight the Nez Percé with rapt attention, and many Americans felt sympathy and respect for the heroism of the Nez Percé and their commitment to freedom. Even in defeat Chief Joseph came to symbolize all that was brave and good in the Native American tradition. Heralded as the "Indian Napoleon," he became a spokesman not only for the Nez Percé but for all Native Americans who had been pushed off their lands. In January 1879 he traveled to Washington, D.C., where he met with President Rutherford B. Hayes and addressed a group of cabinet members, congressmen, and businessmen, imploring for better treatment and asking that his people be allowed to return home. By the 1880s Chief Joseph and the Nez Percé had become a national cause célèbre. Despite Chief Joseph's fame, securing reservation lands in the Northwest for the Nez Percé proved difficult. The government dragged its feet on granting his request because of resistance from many of the white residents of the Northwest, but in May 1885 he and his followers were allowed to return to that region but not to the Wallowa Valley. Instead they were placed on the Colville Reservation in Washington, while other Nez Percé peoples who had taken part in the long flight were allowed to settle at Lapwai. After the passage of the Dawes Act, Chief Joseph agreed to take an allotment but only if it was located on his ancestral land in the Wallowa Valley. His request was refused. In 1897 he returned to Washington, D.C., to plead his case. While he was invited to participate in the dedication of Grant's Tomb in New York City and enjoyed the attention of press and politicians, his requests were again denied. He never returned to the Wallowa Valley, dying at the Colville Reservation in 1904, and his people were increasingly at the mercy of an uncaring government. In 1895, after the Nez Percé reservation land in Idaho was allotted to tribe members, some half million acres were declared surplus and eagerly claimed by white settlers. By 1910 there were thirty thousand whites and only fifteen hundred Nez Percé on what was once a Nez Percé reservation.

The Rise of the Ghost Dancers. In 1890, as Native Americans all over the West experienced the loss of their lands and traditions, a religious revival spread across the Plains, led by a Paiute prophet named Wovoka, who preached a religion combining traditional and Christian elements:

IMMIGRANTS' WORK

A survey of 1,348 Italian families living in Chicago in 1896 listed the occupations most frequently followed:

Under the general industry heading of agriculture, fisheries and mining, 28 worked as quarrymen; under professional, musicians and organ grinders numbered 62; under domestic and personal service were found 797 laborers, 126 street sweepers, 73 bootblacks, 45 barbers, 32 sewer diggers, 23 pavers, 22 saloon keepers, and 18 scissors grinders; under trade and transportation, 186 worked as rag and paper pickers, 154 as small peddlers, 119 as railroad laborers, 78 as newspaper boys, news dealers, 32 as small merchants or dealers in various lines, 20 as salesmen, 15 as teamsters, and 14 wood pickers; under manufacturers were found 60 hod carriers, 38 candy makers and candy factory employees, 26 pant makers and finishers, 22 mosaic layers, 19 tailors and 16 shoemakers and 14 tinkers.

I bring you the promise of a day in which there will be no white man to lay his hand on the bridle of the Indians' horse, when the red men of the prairie will rule the world. . . . I bring you word from your fathers the ghosts, that they are marching now to join you, led by the Messiah who came once to live on earth with the white man but was killed by them.

He called on his followers to give up alcohol and violence and to dance in a circle calling on the spirits of their ancestors to grant them a vision of this new world to come, where they would rejoin the ancestors who had died before them.

The Wounded Knee Massacre. Among the participants in the Ghost Dance were the Lakotas of South Dakota, whose lands were the only Indian lands left to be allotted, thanks to a unified, peaceful resistance led by Sitting Bull. The Lakota Ghost Dancers interpreted Wovoka's message as meaning the Indians' dominance of the Plains could come in this world rather than the next, and they wore shirts painted with symbols that they believed would protect them from the white man's bullets. As more and more Lakotas joined the Ghost Dance, some Indian agents became frightened, and in November one of them wired the army for help. On 15 December 1890 Sitting Bull and eight of his followers were killed in a scuffle that occurred when tribal policemen attempted to arrest him. Other followers, led by Chief Big Foot, joined a group of Ghost Dancers at the Cheyenne River reservation. Believing that the Indians were getting ready to provide armed resistance, the cavalry followed. Big Foot surrendered, and soldiers led his band to Wounded Knee Creek to camp for the night. There, frightened by the dancing of a medicine man and a scuffle with a deaf Indian over a rifle, troops opened fire on the Lakotas, who fought back as best they could. Some 250 Lakota men, women, and children and twenty-five

An immigrant family in New York City, 1889

soldiers were killed. Many others were wounded. Fighting continued sporadically until 15 January 1891, when the last of the Lakota Ghost Dancers surrendered. The final Indian War was over.

Sources:

John Carroll, *The Indian Removals* (New York: AMS Press, 1974);

Alvin M. Josephy Jr., *The Nez Percé Indians and the Opening of the Northwest* (New Haven: Yale University Press, 1965);

Robert M. Utley, *Frontier Regulars: The United States Army and the Indian, 1866–1891* (New York: Macmillan / London: Collier Macmillan, 1973);

Geoffrey C. Ward and others, *The West: An Illustrated History* (Boston, New York, Toronto & London: Little, Brown, 1996);

Murray Lionel Wax, *Indian Americans: Unity and Diversity* (Englewood Cliffs, N.J.: Prentice-Hall, 1971).

RACE AND ETHNICITY: IMMIGRATION

The "Old" Immigration. During the first half of the nineteenth century German, Irish, Chinese, Mexican, Scandinavian, and French Canadian immigrants poured into the United States in search of a better life or better work opportunities. The largest groups were by far the Germans, Irish, and Mexicans. Each settled in different regions of the country. Germans settled in the Northeast and Midwest and the Irish in eastern cities such as Boston, Philadelphia, and New York. Many Mexican immigrants had not moved into the United States; instead, they found themselves living in the United States after it annexed Texas in 1845 and the Southwest and California in 1848. Chinese immigration to the United States was not large during this period, but it played a significant role in the economic development of California, particularly in building the cross-country railroads. No matter where they settled, new immigrants made their mark on American society. Their labor contributed to the building of railroads and canals, the outpouring of goods from factories and mills, and the increased production of food on farms. Whole city neighborhoods of immigrants thrived, introducing new customs, new foods, and new sounds. Foreign-language newspapers sprang up across the country. Many native-born Americans worried that their country was being "overrun by foreigners." Such sentiment fueled the growth of hate groups and racism.

The "New" Immigration. A new wave of immigration began in the late 1880s as hundreds of thousands of immigrants from eastern European and Mediterranean countries entered the United States. They were joined by a growing number of Japanese, Indians, and Koreans. Irish, German, and Mexican immigrants continued to arrive as well. This second wave of immigration peaked in 1907. From the 1880s through the 1920s more than twenty-two million immigrants entered the United States. In 1892 the government opened a new processing center on Ellis Island in New York Harbor to handle the huge waves of newcomers. Most left their countries of origin because they were poor and they hoped to better their lot in life. They arrived in American cities with dreams of economic security and better living conditions for their children. Italians, numbering almost five million between 1880 and 1930, were the largest group of new immigrants. Jews from Poland, Russia, and Romania constituted the second largest group. Large numbers of Slavs—such as Ukrainians, Poles, Croatians, Czechs, and Serbs—as well as Greeks and Portuguese also arrived in the United States.

Tenements and street vendors on Hester Street, in the Lower East Side of New York City, home to many new immigrants during the 1880s and 1890s

Finding Work. Most new immigrants started in the least desirable jobs available. Introduced to employers by relatives or friends from their homelands, certain ethnic groups dominated specific industries. For instance, Slavs worked in steel factories, meatpacking, and other heavy industries. Greeks opened small businesses selling fruit, flowers, ice cream, and food. Italians worked construction. Mexicans worked at agricultural jobs in the West. Many Jews settled in New York City, where large numbers of them applied their tailoring skills in the growing garment industry; others opened restaurants and delicatessens.

Hard Work and Poverty. Immigrants had difficult lives in their new country. They lived in crowded, unsanitary tenements, sometimes sleeping four or five to a room. To help pay the rent, many families took in boarders, which made their apartments still more cramped. Many men and women, old and young, worked at home making paper flowers, wrapping cigars, or sewing garments. Children worked alongside parents or grandparents doing piecework. With little aid from cities or states, immigrants turned to settlement houses, ethnic societies, labor unions, and churches for help.

Adjusting. Conditions slowly improved for those who remained healthy and could move into skilled positions. By pooling resources, families moved out of foul tenements and into their own modest homes. Some became active in the labor movement and politics. In cities such as Boston, New York, and Chicago, the Irish, Jews, and Germans dominated city jobs and political machines. Even as immigrants assimilated into American life, they retained many customs and traditions of their homelands.

Source:
Roger Daniels, *Coming to America: A History of Immigration and Ethnicity in American Life* (New York: HarperCollins, 1990).

RACE AND ETHNICITY: LIFE IN THE MELTING POT

The Rise of Hate Groups. As more and more people with different customs, religious beliefs, and languages filled American cities, people worried that there would

A CALL FOR BLACK POWER

Ida B. Wells was effective in her crusade against what she called "the last relic of barbarism and savagery" — lynching of African Americans — because she was a good journalist who did not mince words. And she supported her stories with facts. In *A Red Record* she printed the name of every one of the 197 lynched black men in America in 1894, the date of his murder, the reason, and the place. One-third more blacks were killed that year by lynch mobs than were legally executed. It was assumed, she pointed out, that sex crimes against white women most often aroused lynch mobs, but in fact only about one-third of all lynchings were for alleged sexual indiscretion. Moreover, she said, many white women enjoyed the sexual attentions of black men and made false accusations of rape to save their own reputations. She followed that statement with examples of white women who, after an attack of conscience, had recanted their charges of rape against black men. That was an inflammatory assertion at a time when modesty was considered the primary virtue of respectable women, and it was intended to attract readers' attentions and make them angry.

Wells offered solutions to lynching. She said it was up to blacks to take the offensive against such outrageous mistreatment. In *Southern Horrors: Lynch Law in All Its Phases* (1892) she observed that

The only times an Afro-American who was assaulted got away has been when he had a gun and used it in self-defense.

The lesson this teaches and which every Afro-American should ponder well, is that a Winchester rifle should have a place of honor in every black home, and it should be used for that protection which the law refuses to give. When the white man who is always the aggressor knows he runs as great a risk of biting the dust every time his Afro-American victim does, he will have greater respect for Afro-American life. The more the Afro-American yields and cringes and begs, the more he has to do so, the more he is insulted, outraged and lynched.

not be enough jobs or housing for the immigrants and that newcomers would take the jobs and overrun the neighborhoods of established citizens. People worried, too, that the beliefs and customs they cherished would be undermined by outsiders determined radically to alter the American way of life. These fears evolved into a hatred of racial, ethnic, and religious differences. Militant hate groups were formed, typically under the guise of protecting American values, to deny rights to racial, religious, and ethnic minorities. African Americans, Asian immigrants, and Native Americans were especially vulnerable to prejudice from white Protestants, who also re-

sented Catholics and Jews because of their religious beliefs. Hate groups flourished after Reconstruction.

Nativism. Nativism, a generalized prejudice against foreigners and outsiders, and xenophobia, a fear of foreigners, mushroomed as immigration increased. Native-born whites argued that this new wave of immigrants, unlike earlier generations, was unworthy of American liberty, dangerous to American order, and incapable of assimilation. They encouraged politicans to place quotas on immigration and vigorously upheld traditional social values. Flash points included conflicts over bilingual education in public schools, the required observance of the Christian Sabbath, and restriction in the use of alcoholic beverages. In the face of mounting hostility, ostracized groups turned to each other for strength. Such group solidarity translated into voting blocs that gave new immigrants a strong political voice, inflaming traditionalists all the more because they believed that minority voters who belonged to such groups were controlled by foreign forces who sought to subvert Americanism. Some of the new immigrants were outspoken political or social radicals on whom nativists were quick to blame the labor unrest of the period.

Anti-Catholicism. Catholics in America had faced prejudice against their religious views since the colonial period. Increases in southern European immigration in the 1880s brought a new wave of Catholics to the country, reviving hate-group charges that Catholics were unworthy citizens because they pledged their allegiance to the Pope in Rome and not to the U.S. government. During the 1884 presidential campaign native-born Protestants voiced fears of a Catholic conspiracy against public schools and republican government. A host of secret anti-Catholic groups was formed, each with an elaborate initiation procedure and a code secrecy deemed necessary to fight what they saw as the ruthless, secretive Catholic enemy. In 1887 the American Protective Association (APA) absorbed several small, local nativist groups to become the largest anti-Catholic association in the country. The APA adopted the secrecy of the Know-Nothings of the 1840s, including written and verbal codes to safeguard the secrecy of its communications. The APA was neither anti-immigrant nor racist and accepted African American and immigrant Protestant members. It also supported the woman suffrage movement as a way to mobilize Protestant women to protect public schools.

Anti-Semitism. Hostility to members of the Jewish faith had a much longer history than anti-Catholicism. Throughout Western history Christians blamed the Jews for the Crucifixion and characterized them as a prideful, bigoted, money-hungry people. In popular folklore Jews were often blamed for disasters such as famines, epidemics, and even wars. Many Protestant Americans viewed Jews as excessively self-protective and tribalistic and thus unworthy of participating in a democracy that called for individuals to transcend group identity. During the

WHAT IS A TENEMENT?

In his exposé *How the Other Half Lives* (1890) Jacob Riis defined the tenement as follows:

The law defines it as a house "occupied by three or more families, living independently and doing their cooking on the premises; or by more than two families on a door, so living and cooking and having a common right in the halls, stairways, yards, etc." That is the legal meaning, and includes flats and apartment-houses, with which we have nothing to do. In its narrower sense the typical tenement was thus described when last arraigned before the bar of justice: "It is generally a brick building from four to six stories high on the street, frequently with a store on the first floor which, when used for the sale of liquor, has a side opening for the benefit of the inmates and to evade the Sunday law; four families occupy each floor, and a set of rooms consists of one or two dark closets, used as bedrooms, with a living room twelve feet by ten. The staircase is too often a dark well in the centre of the house, and no direct through ventilation is possible, each family being separated from the other by partitions. Frequently the rear of the lot is occupied by another building of three stories high with two families on a floor." The picture is nearly as true to-day as ten years ago, and will be for a long time to come. The dim light admitted by the air-shaft shines upon greater crowds than ever. Tenements are still "good property," and the poverty of the poor man his destruction. A barracks down town where he *has to live* because he is poor brings in a third more rent than a decent flat house in Harlem. The statement once made a sensation that between seventy and eighty children had been found in one tenement. It no longer excites even passing attention, when the sanitary police report counting 101 adults and 91 children in a Crosby Street house, one of twins, built together. The children in the other, if I am not mistaken, numbered 89, a total of 180 for two tenements! Or when a midnight inspection in Mulberry Street unearths a hundred and fifty "lodgers" sleeping on filthy floors in two buildings. Spite of brown-stone trimmings, plate-glass and mosaic vestibule floors, the water does not rise in summer to the second story, while the beer flows unchecked to the all-night picnics on the roof. The saloon with the side-door and the landlord divide the prosperity of the place between them, and the tenant, in sullen submission, foots the bill.

Source: Jacob Riis, *How the Other Half Lives* (New York: Scribners, 1890).

1870s, 1880s, and 1890s nativists viewed Jews as a menace to civilization, as unable to assimilate, and as conspirators to subvert Christianity and Gentile society. Prejudice against Jews became a prime example of American xenophobia in the 1880s, symbolizing for the hate groups the dangers posed by open immigration.

Social Darwinism. In the mid nineteenth century a new theory of social evolution supported the belief that African Americans, Native Americans, and Asians—as well as poor people of all races—were unworthy of full citizenship and unequipped to participate in the democratic process. This new kind of prejudice had its roots in Charles Darwin's *On the Origin of Species* (1859), which put forth the theory that all species evolved from less complex life forms through a process of natural selection that gave the greatest chance of survival to those species most capable of adapting to their environments. His fellow Englishman Herbert Spencer applied Darwin's theory to society, coining the phrase "survival of the fittest" to argue that human society and institutions were progressively evolving toward "the establishment of the greatest perfection and the most complete happiness." In this view the wealthiest individuals had proved their superior capacity for survival, while the poor were the least fit. Efforts to help the poor would impede the greater good of progress toward social perfection, which would benefit humanity as a whole. Social Darwinism also had racial implications. Groups long described as "biologically" inferior were now identified as victims of incomplete evolution—they were less than fully human. On both sides of the Atlantic whites believed that they represented the most advanced expression of human evolution.

Social Darwinism in the United States. In the United States one of the foremost academic spokesmen for Social Darwinism was William Graham Sumner, a professor at Yale University who argued in favor of letting natural selection take its own course in human society in *What Social Classes Owe to Each Other* (1883) and other works. His chief opponent was Lester Frank Ward, who argued against applying Darwin's theory on the social level. In his *Dynamic Sociology* (1883) Ward pointed out that the human mind was capable of purposeful decision making, which allowed people to reflect on situations and then act to change them, thus influencing the course of evolution. Rather than viewing humankind as helpless pawns of the evolutionary process, Ward believed that individuals and government could shape the future through eradication of poverty and education of the masses.

Eugenics. In 1869 Darwin's cousin Francis Galton founded the science of eugenics, the study of ways to improve hereditary physical and mental characteristics of a race or breed. Concluding that the races could be ranked and that higher and lower grades of people existed within each race, nineteenth-century eugenicists talked of social engineering that would eliminate feeblemindedness, criminality, and poverty through selective breeding. Eugenicists favored immigration barriers, social segregation, stricter marriage laws, and even sterilization of individuals considered physically or mentally inferior. In the United States racial theorists argued that African Americans were the least developed race and that as a people they were "unfit" to assume full political and social equality. Similarly, they argued that Native Americans were an "inferior," childlike race that required white protection. Reservations were cast as the only way to ensure that Indian populations would survive.

The "Yellow Peril." The California gold rush of 1849 and new discoveries of gold in Colorado and Nevada in

Delegates from the Woman's Christian Temperance Union, the National-American Woman Suffrage Association, and other women's groups at the founding conference of the National Council of Women, formed in 1893 to coordinate reform efforts

the late 1850s attracted a large number of Asians to the American West. In the 1860s others came to work on the cross-country railroad, and some were shipped east to break strikes in the 1870s. Denigrated as the "Yellow Peril," Asians became the target of racist attacks. Anti-Chinese riots erupted in San Francisco in 1877, leading President Rutherford Hayes to write in his diary in 1879, "I would consider with favor any suitable measures to discourage the Chinese from coming to our shores." In 1882 Congress passed the Chinese Exclusion Act, which suspended all immigration from China for ten years. The act was extended periodically until 1904, when Congress made it permanent.

Racism in the South. After the end of Reconstruction white state governments in the South stripped former slaves of their newly established rights. Throughout the 1880s whites forcibly removed black officeholders and through intimidation, poll taxes, literacy tests, and even murder effectively robbed black majorities in the Deep South of their rights as citizens. A series of Supreme Court rulings between 1882 and 1888 upheld segregation based on race. The Ku Klux Klan, a secret organiza-

tion of whites devoted to terrorizing and intimidating African Americans and their white Republican allies, was founded during Reconstruction. The Klan exerted a powerful presence in nearly every southern state, acting as a guerrilla military force to reassert white supremacy. The national organization was formally disbanded in 1869, but local Klan groups continued to be active into the 1870s, killing hundreds of Africans Americans during the first three years of the decade and terrorizing thousands.

Responses to Racism. Southern Republicans, who supported the goals of Reconstruction, turned to Washington to stem the violence. The Ku Klux Klan Act of 1871 made the violent infringement of civil and political rights a federal crime, and hundreds of Klansmen in North Carolina and Mississippi were prosecuted. Other federal laws asserted the sanctity of voting for all eligible citizens and pledged government support for the freedoms of African Americans, but the laws proved more an assertion of principle than a direct federal intervention. Though many Americans felt outraged at the violence inflicted on African Americans, political options failed

MODESTY IN DRESS

Julia Ward Howe was a prudish woman. The famous reformer, women's rights advocate, and author of the "Battle Hymn of the Republic" was sixty-eight when she wrote "Dress and Undress," an article in *Forum Magazine* in 1887 that showed how narrow her view of women's rights was when measured by the standards of the 1990s.

The object of Mrs. Howe's irritation was the fashion current among young socialites of wearing evening dresses that bared their arms and their chests. Just as shocking, in her view, were what she called tranparencies — dresses that featured sheer fabric, often beeded, around the upper arms and bodice, allowing titillating glimpses of unshielded skin.

Mrs. Howe's argument that such attire was scandalous had four parts. First, she submitted, it was unhealthy. "The female slaves of a Turkish harem are obliged to leave the bosom so much exposed that pulmonary disease is frequently the result," she warned.

Second, such dress invited subjugation; "The girl who sits beside the young man at college, the woman who meets men at the lecture or in the clinic, meets them as an equal. She is bound to abstain from all that could subject them to that slavery of the senses from which she herself claims to be free."

Third, because such dress is uncomfortable, it is impolite: By failing to wear proper undergarments that cover her body to the neck she risks chafing her skin, and the resulting discomfort would create tension among those around her, proving her to be inconsiderate of the feeling of others.

Finally, bare skin is immodest, Mrs. Howe declared, and thus unattractive: "Good women are bound to maintain the best traditions of their sex. Refinement and good sense are foremost among these and neither of them will permit either the dressing or the acting down to a low level of attraction."

to stop it. The federal government justified its inaction by calling lynching a southern practice that must be addressed by the individual southern states. African Americans organized to fight back. Journalist Ida B. Wells-Barnett began a national and international campaign to end lynching. Using the language of Social Darwinism, but turning its logic on its head, she argued that white society could not be as civilized as it claimed if it relied on violence and murder to maintain its so-called superiority. Wells-Barnett and others aroused public sentiment against lynching, but the practice continued well into the twentieth century.

Sources:

Gail Bederman, "Civilization, The Decline of Middle-Class Manliness, and Ida B. Wells' Anti-Lynching Campaign (1892–1894)," in *Gender and American History Since 1890*, edited by Barbara Melosh (New York: Routledge, 1993), pp. 207–239;

Rogers Daniels and Harry Kitano, *American Racism: Exploration of the Nature of Prejudice* (Englewood Cliffs, N.J.: Prentice-Hall, 1970);

Carl N. Degler, *In Search of Human Nature: The Decline and Revival of Darwinism in American Social Thought* (New York: Oxford University Press, 1991);

Michael Dobkowski, *The Tarnished Dream: The Basis of American Anti-Semitism* (Westport, Conn.: Greenwood Press, 1979);

John Higham, *Strangers in the Land: Patterns of American Nativism, 1860–1925*, revised edition (New York: Atheneum, 1963).

THE SETTLEMENT-HOUSE MOVEMENT

Settling in Urban Neighborhoods. During the 1880s and 1890s newly arrived immigrants faced a difficult struggle to earn a living wage, and cities offered little in the way of tangible aid. The urban neighborhoods in which these immigrants lived were filled with overcrowded tenements that lacked kitchens and bathrooms. Tenants drew water at a sink or pump in the hallway and used unsanitary privies in the basement. The settlement-house movement was established to help immigrants and the working poor. Settlement houses helped newcomers adapt to American life and customs by providing job placement and training, citizenship classes, legal aid, health services, child care, public kitchens, cultural programs, and classes on subjects such as nutrition and parenting. Springing up in most major cities, settlement houses were staffed mainly by educated middle-class white women who "settled" among the people they helped. The movement was not financed by government funds and depended solely on the labor of charitable women and men. The first settlement house in the United States was Jane Addams's Hull-House, founded in 1889. Many others quickly followed. In 1893 Lillian Wald opened the Henry Street Settlement in New York City, and graduates of Wellesley College opened Denison House in Boston. By 1900 there were some one hundred settlement houses nationwide.

Activist Women. At the same time that new immigrants were flooding into American cities, more and more American colleges and universities were beginning to open their doors to women. In 1870 about eleven thousand women, mostly middle-class and white, were enrolled in institutions of higher education; by 1880 there were roughly forty thousand. Female graduates pioneered the field of social work. Many women in this field started their professional careers as staff members at settlement houses, forming professional networks within the movement. The movement also drew in less-educated middle-class women who were concerned about the poor and felt a personal need to help them.

Becoming Political. The settlement-house movement was part widespread political impulse for national self-improvement, or progressivism. Whereas settlement-house workers at first believed that introducing art, music, and the humanities to the poor would uplift them from their degradation, the hardships of the economic crisis of 1893 and 1894 caused the workers to seek more practical ways to end suffering. For example, Hull-House joined with the Illinois Women's Alliance, an organization of working-class and middle-class women, to convince the Illinois legislature to pass protective legislation for working women and children. Many women who were clients or staff members at settlement houses gained a political education there and went on to participate in the labor movement, civic-reform organizations, and national party politics.

Sources:
Dolores Hayden, *The Grand Domestic Revolution: A History of Feminist Designs for American Homes, Neighborhoods, and Cities* (Cambridge, Mass.: MIT Press, 1981);

Barbara Solomon, *In the Company of Educated Women: A History of Women and Higher Education in America* (New Haven: Yale University Press, 1985).

THE SUFFRAGE MOVEMENT

Fighting for Voting Rights. Among women's rights activists, the most hotly debated topic of the day was suffrage—the right to vote. The suffrage movement was a quarter of a century old by the end of Reconstruction, and women such as Susan B. Anthony and Elizabeth Cady Stanton were having a difficult time understanding how African American men could be extended the right to vote by the Fifteenth Amendment to the Constitution (1870) and yet women could be regarded as unfit to vote. The increase in college programs to educate women and their success in such social and political efforts as the settlement-house movement only exaggerated the outrage of activist women that they lacked the basic rights of an American citizen. In 1869 two national organizations were formed to attack the problem: Stanton and Anthony formed the National Woman Suffrage Association to work for a constitutional amendment to give women the vote. Julia Ward Howe and Lucy Stone, both of whom favored the Fifteenth Amendment, formed the American Woman Suffrage Association to focus on state referenda.

Forging a Single Association. The two national associations combined into the National-American Woman Suffrage Association in 1890, but many issues, especially Prohibition, continued to make unity difficult. The eastern wing of the new association associated immigration with alcoholism, and they felt that by opposing the sale of alcohol they could garner the support of conservative men. Many women in the western states, on the other hand, argued that they could never get the support of men in their region if they advocated closing bars. Despite such tensions, suffragists agreed that women needed the ballot to clean up corrupt governments, to

FRANCES WILLARD'S BICYCLE

Like many female reformers of the 1890s, Frances Willard, president of the Woman's Christian Temperance Union (WCTU), believed in healthy diet and exercise. In fall 1893 Willard, who was in her fifties, took up the popular new sport of bicycle riding, attracting the attention of the *New York World*, which described her cycling costume as "a navy blue blazer, a shirt waist and a skirt, 5 1/2 inches from the floor, alpine hat and bicycle boots." Willard later described how she learned to ride her bicycle, which she named Gladys, in a popular book, *A Wheel within a Wheel* (1895):

The bicycle is like the world. When it had thrown me painfully once, and more especially when it threw one of my dearest friends, then for a time Gladys had gladsome ways for me no longer, but seemed the embodiment of misfortune and dread. . . . I finally concluded that all failure was from a wobbling will rather than a wobbling wheel. . . . January 20 will always be a red-letter bicycle day because, summoning all my force, I mounted and started off alone. Gladys was no more a mystery. Amid the delightful surroundings of the great outdoors. . . . I had made myself master of the most remarkable, ingenious, and inspiring motor ever yet devised upon this planet. Moral: Go thou and do likewise!

protect their own interests, and to enhance their capacity to carry out their traditional roles. Only a mother who exercised her right to vote, they argued, could truly teach her children how to be an upstanding citizen.

Female Reformers. Calling for "city housekeeping," women active in temperance, the settlement-house movement, and suffrage created a new kind of women's reform movement. All these movements argued that they were protecting and enhancing home life and contributing a valuable new perspective to justify women's involvement in public life. The WCTU campaigned on the promise that prohibition of alcohol would protect home life. Suffragists argued that women voters would bring compassion and charity to politics and end the pervasive corruption in local, state, and national governments. Settlement-house workers argued that city and state authorities must assume a maternal responsibility for the most vulnerable members of society. By politicizing such "feminine" characteristics as nurturing, domesticity, and purity late-nineteenth-century female reformers offered a new view of women and a new vision of government.

Racism. Racism continued to haunt the woman suffrage movement until the ratification of the Nineteenth Amendment in 1920. As more white southern women joined the movement at the end of the century, they voiced deep reluctance to be a part of any organization which had African American members. Remaining allied with their husbands, brothers, and fathers, white women upheld the racist policies of the "Jim Crow" laws in the South. As the push for ratification of the Nineteenth Amendment strengthened after the turn of the century, the national suffrage movement accepted the views of its southern members in an effort to win the support of southern states.

Sources:

Ellen Carol DuBois, *Feminism and Suffrage: The Emergence of an Independent Women's Movement in America, 1848–1869* (Ithaca, N.Y.: Cornell University Press, 1978);

Eleanor Flexner, *Century of Struggle: The Woman's Rights Movement in America,* revised edition (Cambridge, Mass.: Harvard University Press, 1975);

Paula Giddings, *Where and When I Enter: The Impact of Black Women on Race and Sex in America* (New York: Morrow, 1984).

THE WOMAN'S CHRISTIAN TEMPERANCE UNION

Forging a National Movement. In 1874 women concerned with the adverse effects of alcohol consumption on American family life formed the Woman's Christian-Temperance Union (WCTU), an organization devoted to limiting Americans' consumption of alcohol and the influence of the liquor business in city, state, and national politics. With its roots in Protestant reform, the WCTU grew throughout the 1870s and 1880s. By the end of the century the WCTU had become the single largest organization of women in the nation and its leader, Frances Willard, one of the most influential women in the United States. In 1892 the WCTU membership of 150,000 far outstripped that of other activist groups, including the National-American Woman Suffrage Association, with 13,000 dues-paying members, and the General Federation of Women's Clubs, with some 20,000 members.

Alcohol Consumption. Since the early days of the republic, alcohol had played an important role in the American diet, including that of children. Parents regularly quieted crying babies with sweetened liquor. Alcohol was a main ingredient in many medicines; it was part of military rations; and it was often the only beverage available at work sites. Many factors contributed to the popularity of beer, wine, and liquor. Clean water was hard to find in urban areas, and fresh milk was expensive and frequently tainted with tuberculosis and other diseases. In contrast alcohol was cheap and plentiful. Furthermore, many Americans believed that alcohol was beneficial, supplying the necessary energy for hard physical labor and the internal warmth that enabled men to work in cold conditions.

The Liquor Business. By 1900 the liquor industry employed one out of 116 Americans. The nation spent more than $1 billion on alcoholic beverages, as compared to $900 million on meat, $150 million on contributions to churches, and less than $200 million on public education. In Chicago, where the WCTU established its national office, the number of saloons in 1899 equaled the

A southern temperance poster

number of grocery stores, meat markets, and dry-goods stores combined. A survey in 1895 reported that on an average day the number of saloon customers was equal to one-half of the Chicago population.

Saloons. Saloons figured centrally into the lives of city dwellers. For the price of a drink a poor workingman could also get a free lunch. Bars served as public meeting areas and places for men to relax away from their work and from their families. Of the 1,002 political meetings held in New York City in 1886, 800 of them were held in saloons. Critics worried that the liquor industry corrupted the political process through buying votes, bribing officials, and fostering crime. In many cities the liquor business controlled a disproportionate number of public offices, especially on the local level. For example one-third of the aldermen of Detroit and Milwaukee in the 1890s were saloon keepers, as were half the Democratic precinct workers in Chicago at the turn of the century.

The "Drunkard Husband." Alcohol use and abuse created both personal and social problems, many of which affected the lives of women and children. During the 1870s and 1880s most Americans viewed alcohol as a male prerogative and the saloon as a male institution where only "fallen" women went. The husband who drank had a reputation for beating his wife and children, spending his family's meager income on drink, and driving his wife and children into destitution. Statistically this reputation was well founded. If women worked outside the home, they were expected to turn over their wages to their husbands, and wives had no legal claims on their husbands' earnings. When the WCTU was formed in 1874, no woman in the United States possessed full suffrage. In thirty-seven states women possessed no legal rights to their children, and all their possessions became their husbands' property when they married. Given women's restricted legal rights and social customs that discouraged divorce, the drunken husband came to be seen by temperance workers as a woman's true oppressor.

The WCTU. Because alcohol was an accepted part of family and social lives of Catholic and Jewish immigrants, the WCTU attracted mainly Protestant women from "old" American families during the 1870s and 1880s. For many it was their first organizational experience outside church. For others it was an extension of their missionary work. Members demonstrated in front of saloons, pressuring them to close and trying to convince their patrons to sign abstinence pledges. A few demonstrations resulted in the destruction of saloon property. Although they themselves could not vote, WCTU members nationwide worked to convince voters in local elections to turn their communities from "wet" to "dry." Under the leadership of the dynamic Frances Willard, who assumed the presidency in 1879, the WCTU abandoned its claim that alcohol was the cause of poverty and misery and instead emphasized that poverty and social injustice were the causes of many social ailments, including alcohol abuse.

"Home Protection." As the WCTU grew, it came to embody women's changing relationships to the public world of work and politics. It drew women out of the home and into the public life. Under the banner of "Home Protection," the WCTU expanded political discourse by offering a new concept of "the home" as the entire community, leading many women to call for equal suffrage so that women could strengthen their efforts to protect families. As the first organization controlled exclusively by women, the WCTU gave women new experiences in leadership roles. Although women had long been active members of abolitionist and church movements, they had never had leadership or institutional control. From its beginnings the WCTU excluded men from voting. Women ran the organization on local, state, and national levels. The WCTU cut across regional, racial, and ethnic boundaries, with seamstresses, artisans, teachers and clerks, housewives, and career women working side by side.

"Do Everything." As the movement grew, its focus expanded to include issues that were not directly related to alcohol. Willard's "do everything" program encouraged local branches to address issues that members defined as pressing. Politically diverse women found places in the WCTU as the organization turned to prison reform and labor reform, supporting the eight-hour workday and child-protection laws. In Chicago the local branch sponsored two day nurseries, two Sunday schools, an industrial school, a mission that sheltered four thousand homeless or destitute women a year, a free medical dispensary, a lodging house for homeless men, and a low-cost restaurant. By defining the community as an extension of women's maternal responsibilities, the WCTU enabled thousands of women to become active outside the home without threatening the men in their traditional roles.

The WCTU in the 1890s. Despite its considerable successes, the WCTU became less influential in the 1890s than it had been during the 1880s. Willard died in 1898, and she became less involved in running the WCTU during the final years of her life. As her influence waned, the organization turned away from her "do everything" philosophy and became a single-issue movement. The economic crisis of 1893 left the organization strapped for funds for the first time, placing severe restrictions on the activities of its national and state organizations, its publishing house, and its paid leaders. The WCTU also faced competition from other major women's organizations, particularly the General Federation of Women's Clubs, which concentrated on education, self-improvement, and sociability rather than an activist program. Unlike the WCTU, the Women's Clubs comprised white middle-class women, rendering them more attractive to women of means than the racially and ethnically mixed WCTU. The National-American Woman Suffrage Association grew rapidly in the 1890s, drawing away many younger women from the WCTU. Jane Addams's settlement-house movement, with its emphasis on helping poor and immigrant populations directly, also pulled many activist women away from temperance. By the turn of the century many young women concluded that temperance was old-fashioned and out of date. While the WCTU continued into the twentieth century, it never again reached the heights of popularity and influence it held in the 1870s and 1880s.

Sources:
Ruth Bordin, *Women and Temperance* (New Brunswick, N.J.: Rutgers University Press, 1990).

HEADLINE MAKERS

JANE ADDAMS

1860-1935
SOCIAL REFORMER

Early Life. Jane Addams was born on 6 September 1860 at Clearville, Illinois, the eighth of nine children. Her father was a prosperous miller, banker, abolitionist, and community leader who served eight terms as a state senator. Her mother died when Jane was two, and young Jane became devoted to her father, who remarried about two years later. In 1877 Addams entered the Rockford Female Seminary, in nearby Rockford, Illinois, where she became a student leader, graduating in 1881. The seminary encouraged young women to become Christian missionaries in foreign lands, but Addams resisted pressure to enter service abroad. As she wrote in *Twenty Years at Hull-House* (1910), "I was quite settled in my mind that I should study medicine and live with the poor."

Finding Her Way. After her father's death during the summer after her graduation from Rockford, Addams entered a difficult period. She left Women's Medical College in Philadelphia after only a few months, and, suffering from various physical ailments that left her bedridden for months at a stretch, she was frequently depressed. Travels in Europe in 1883–1885 and 1887–1888 introduced her to urban poverty and blight, experiences that left lasting impressions on her. In 1888 she and Ellen Gates Starr, a close friend and former Rockford classmate, enthusiastically adopted a plan to settle in an urban neighborhood and work directly to relieve the ill effects of poverty. Interested in tearing down divisions between the classes, Starr and Addams insisted that the upper classes must take responsibility for the adverse effects of rapid industrialization on the poor. In 1889 the two bought Hull-House in a Chicago neighborhood populated with Greek, Italian, Russian, German, and Sicilian immigrants. Addams lived at Hull-House for the remaining forty-six years of her life.

Hull-House. Addams's settlement house provided a new generation of educated white women with a place in which to do meaningful work. Many of Addams's peers were eager to apply their knowledge and talents in settings where human suffering was the greatest. As Starr wrote to a friend, Addams considered settlement-house work "more for the benefit of the people who do it than for the other class." Bringing these two groups together was by any measure brilliant. By 1893 the Hull-House complex was the center of neighborhood activity, offering day care for children, a gymnasium, a dispensary, a playground, courses in cooking and sewing, and a cooperative boardinghouse for working girls. Two thousand people entered Hull-House each week. As was typical of other nineteenth-century progressives, Addams believed in the relationship between art and social justice, and Hull-House supported a range of artistic activities, such as a gallery, a theater company, and a music school. By 1907 the Hull-House complex included thirteen buildings spread over a large city block.

City Politics. By 1895 Addams and her group of settlement-house workers had realized that neighborhood services and cultural uplift alone could not solve the deep-seated problems associated with urban poverty. The staff published their views in *Hull-House Maps and Papers,* which called attention to unsafe and unsanitary conditions in urban tenements and sweatshops and to widespread child-labor practices. Pressure from Hull-House on the Chicago city government had already resulted in the passage in 1893 of the first Illinois factory-inspection act, and in 1894 the Hull-House staff had mounted an ambitious campaign to improve the lives of the working poor. They proposed to end child labor, shorten hours for working women, improve welfare procedures, convince the city to recognize labor unions, provide protection for immigrants from unscrupulous landlords and employers, institute compulsory schooling, and improve industrial safety. In 1899 the establishment in Chicago of the first juvenile court in the United

States was largely the result of the efforts of the Hull-House staff.

National Fame, Local Suspicion. Addams's efforts in Chicago brought her national fame. Much sought after as a lecturer, she served on the Chicago school board in 1905–1909 and became involved in the movement for world peace. Her articles appeared in many periodicals, and she published four books during the years 1900–1910: *Democracy and Social Ethics* (1902), *Newer Ideals of Peace* (1907), *The Spirit of Youth in the City Streets* (1909), and *Twenty Years at Hull-House* (1910). She was awarded an honorary degree by Yale University in 1910, becoming the first woman to receive such an honor, and in 1911 she became the first head of the National Federation of Settlements. Celebrities regularly visited her at Hull-House, and Theodore Roosevelt made several tours. While Addams had become a national hero, in Chicago her support for labor unions made her unpopular among the wealthy classes. She often managed to offend patrons with her open-minded approach to politics, believing as she did that every person deserved to be heard. Despite criticism, Hull-House continued to support unpopular causes and Addams enjoyed a long public career. In 1931 she and Columbia University president Nicholas Murray Butler shared the Nobel Peace Prize for their efforts to bring about worldwide disarmament and international peace. She died on 21 May 1935. Her funeral at Hull-House brought thousands of mourners, reportedly as many as two thousand an hour.

Sources:

Allen F. Davis, *American Heroine: The Life and Legend of Jane Addams* (New York: Oxford University Press, 1973);

Cornelia Meigs, *Jane Addams, Pioneer for Social Justice: A Biography* (Boston: Little, Brown, 1970).

SUSAN B. ANTHONY

1820-1906
WOMAN'S RIGHTS ACTIVIST

Early Life. Born on 15 February 1820 in Adams, Massachusetts, Susan Brownell Anthony was a descendant of early settlers of Rhode Island. She grew up in Battenville, New York, a small village about thirty-five miles north of Albany and about ten miles east of the Hudson River, where the family settled in 1832. In 1838 her father enrolled her at Deborah Moulson's Female Seminary, a Quaker school in Hamilton, Pennsylvania, outside Philadelphia, where Anthony was taught that women and men were equal in the eyes of God. After only one term she left school to work as a teacher so that she could help to pay debts her father had incurred during the Panic of 1837, and at the age of nineteen she moved away from home to take a better position at a Quaker boarding school in New Rochelle, New York. In 1846, after moving with her family to a new farm near Rochester, New York, she was hired as headmistress of the female department of Canajoharie Academy, on the Mohawk River between Schenectady and Utica. She resigned her position in 1849 and returned to her family's Rochester farm.

Forming a Women's Movement. Anthony's family had been active in abolitionism, which had strong Quaker roots, and by 1849 Anthony herself had become involved in that movement as well as in the temperance crusade. She soon learned that women did not enjoy full equality in those movements—a discovery that motivated her to campaign for woman's rights. Until the Civil War she focused on improving married women's property rights. In 1860 she succeeded in convincing the New York State legislature to pass a law granting married women the rights to own property, conduct business, enter into legal contracts, retain their own earnings, sue or be sued, and be joint guardians of their children. Throughout the Civil War, even as she worked for the emancipation of slaves, she strongly opposed giving the vote to illiterate males ahead of educated white women.

Suffrage. After the war Anthony's fears were confirmed. The American Equal Rights Association, of which she became a founding member in 1866, considered women's rights to be secondary to those of former slaves. In 1869 Anthony and Elizabeth Cady Stanton formed the National Woman Suffrage Association (NWSA) and opposed the Fifteenth Amendment, which enfranchised male former slaves. Many of her abolitionist friends saw Anthony's position as elitist, and in the same year they formed an alternative suffrage organization, the American Woman Suffrage Association (AWSA), headed by Lucy Stone. Anthony at first argued for woman suffrage on the basis of the Fourteenth and Fifteenth Amendments to the Constitution, which made former slaves citizens and gave them the right to vote. The Fourteenth Amendment states in part, "All persons born or naturalized in the United States. . . are citizens," while the Fifteenth forbids the denial of citizens' right to vote "on account of race, color, or previous servitude." Since neither amendment assigns a gender to "persons" or "citizens," she contended, they also applied to women. In 1872 she tested this assumption by casting a ballot in Rochester, New York. She was promptly arrested. While the city pressed no charges against Anthony, she dramatically proved that the Constitution did not mean women when it said "citizens."

Unifying the Suffrage Movement. Throughout the 1870s and 1880s Anthony tirelessly worked for woman suffrage by writing and speaking across the country. In 1890 the NWSA and AWSA resolved their differences and merged as the National-American Woman Suffrage Association. In 1892 Anthony became its second president and served until 1900. During the 1890s Anthony traveled throughout the United States and Europe promoting woman suffrage. She lived to see women granted the vote in two nations, New Zealand (1893) and Australia (1902). She died on 13 March 1906 at eighty-six. While she did not live to see the passage of the Nineteenth Amendment, which gave American women the vote in 1920, she died believing that failure to reach this goal was impossible.

Source:
Kathleen Barry, *Susan B. Anthony: A Biography of a Singular Feminist* (New York: New York University Press, 1988).

FANNIE FARMER

1857-1915

COOKBOOK AUTHOR, NUTRITIONIST

Early Life. Born on 23 March 1857 in Boston, Massachusetts, Fannie Farmer was the eldest of four daughters. At the age of sixteen Farmer contracted polio, which caused her left leg to become paralyzed. Her illness prevented her from pursuing her education after graduating from Medford High School. During a period of financial difficulty in the 1880s, Farmer worked as a mother's helper in the home of a family friend, Mrs. Charles Shaw. The job changed Farmer's life. Never having done any cooking at home, she took an interest in preparing meals and became a good cook. In 1887, encouraged by her employer, Farmer enrolled in the Boston Cooking School, which had been started in 1879 as part of the scientific-housekeeping movement. By the time Farmer graduated in 1889 at the age of thirty-two, the school had become so impressed by her talent that it hired her as assistant principal. She became principal in 1894, and in 1902 she resigned to open her own school, Miss Farmer's School of Cookery.

Gaining a National Voice. Throughout the 1890s Farmer offered weekly cooking demonstrations for homemakers and professional cooks. Her popular lectures were regularly reprinted in the *Boston Transcript* and were soon syndicated in other papers. By the time she published *The Boston Cooking-School Cook Book* in 1896, she had already established a national reputation. The cookbook made her famous. It has since gone through eleven revised editions, sold nearly four million copies, and been translated into French, Spanish, and Japanese. Her emphasis on nutrition and diet as preventive health measures was unique at that time. Her specific directions and standardized, level measurements, such as teaspoons, tablespoons, and cups, made cooking easier for women, who had previously relied on cookbooks that used measurements such as "pinches" or "handfuls" in their recipes.

Writing and Speaking. Farmer reached many thousands of women with her cookbooks. In addition to the *Boston Cooking-School Cook Book* she also published books such as *Chafing Dish Possibilities* (1898) and *What to Have for Dinner* (1905). For ten years she and her sister, Cora Dexter Farmer Perkins, wrote a column for *Woman's Home Companion*. Farmer believed her most important work was *Food and Cookery for the Sick and Convalescent* (1904), in which she emphasized the importance of diet for good health. She gave lectures for nurses and at various New England hospitals, trained hospital dieticians, and once taught a yearlong course on cooking for invalids at the Harvard Medical School.

Later Life. Farmer continued to lecture even after losing the ability to walk. She died on 15 January 1915 at age fifty-seven, but her school continued until World War II food rationing caused it to shut down.

Source:
Richard J. Hooker, *Food and Drink in the United States: A History* (Indianapolis: Bobbs-Merrill, 1981).

GERONIMO

1829-1909

APACHE WAR LEADER

A Living Legend. Geronimo was one of the most famous Native American leaders of the late nineteenth century. He has earned a reputation in American history as the ultimate holdout, a renegade willing to fight for his freedom long after many of his people had accepted defeat. His tribe, the Apache, lived in present-day Arizona and New Mexico. A group of nomadic bands that relied upon hunting for their subsistence, they were considered one of the most warlike tribes in the Southwest. In fact, the tribe's name was derived from the Zuni word *apachu,* meaning "enemy."

Early Life. Geronimo was born near present-day Clifton, Arizona, in 1829. His Indian name was Gokhlayeh or "One Who Yawns." Why the Mexicans called him Geronimo (Spanish for Jerome) is not certain. Some believe it was a Spanish attempt to pronounce the name

Gokhlayeh. Others maintain that his enemies prayed aloud to Saint Jerome whenever the Apache leader struck. In 1846 he gained admittance into the warriors' council of the Chiricahua Apache and started to lead raids on Mexican and American settlers, stealing their horses. He quickly became known for his cunning and ferocity. A fellow warrior observed that "Geronimo seemed to be the most intelligent and resourceful as well as the most vigorous and farsighted. In times of danger he was a man to be relied upon." When Mexican soldiers killed his mother, wife, and three children in 1858, Geronimo swore vengeance and for the next nineteen years conducted many raids into Mexico. In April 1877 American authorities apprehended the Apache leader and placed him on the San Carlos Indian Reservation.

Reservation Life. The United States had acquired the Apache homeland by treaties with Mexico in 1848 and 1853. In 1872 the federal government established the San Carlos Reservation on the banks of the Gila River in eastern Arizona. The five-thousand-square-mile tract became known as "Hell's Forty Acres" by all who resided there. Sandstorms blew frequently across a landscape of cactus, mesquite, and cottonwood trees. The temperature in the summer regularly reached 110 degrees. By the 1880s the government had forcibly placed on this barren wasteland approximately five thousand Apache, hoping to turn these people into self-sufficient farmers. The Apache, however, refused to plow the fields or to dig irrigation trenches. Instead, they relied on weekly food rations of flour and beef from the U.S. Army and the Office of Indian Affairs. Civilian contractors who distributed beef for the government cheated the Indians out of fifteen hundred pounds per week. Reservation authorities made the Apache organize a police force and set up courts. Traditional ceremonies and practices were banned, including the brewing of *tiswin*, a beer made from corn. The greatest hardship on the reservation, however, proved to be boredom. Women and children tried to keep busy by gathering bundles of hay that they sold at a penny a pound for cavalry horses. The men, meanwhile, had little to do except play traditional games and brood.

Flight. In 1880 white squatters and miners started to appear on reservation lands, where deposits of copper, coal, and silver had been discovered. The next year an Apache shaman named Noch-ay-del-klinne began to preach that dead Apache leaders would arise and reassert the tribe's greatness. When reservation police tried to arrest the mystic, he was shot and killed in a scuffle. Fearing that he, too, would be arrested, Geronimo fled to Mexico with seventy-four followers. For the next two years his band eluded capture and raided American territory. In March 1883 the renegades killed three white men outside of Tombstone, Arizona; a few days later they killed a federal judge and his wife. Meanwhile, the American and Mexican governments negotiated an agreement whereby soldiers of either nation could cross the border when pursuing the renegades. Be-

lieving that he needed an Apache to capture an Apache, American Gen. George Crook enlisted 193 Apache scouts who tracked down Geronimo in May. Crook convinced him to return to San Carlos, but the Apache leader again became disenchanted with reservation life. In May 1885 he went on a spree of drinking corn beer in direct defiance of reservation policy and then decamped with forty-two men and ninety-two women and children. Throughout the winter 1885–1886 Crook gave chase with three thousand troops. In March 1886 he found the fugitives, but this time they were not so willing to return to the reservation. Crook observed that "they were in superb physical condition, armed to the teeth, fierce as so many tigers." On a dark and rainy night Geronimo slipped away with twenty warriors and eighteen women and children.

An Emissary. After an immense public outcry against him, Crook resigned. His replacement, Gen. Nelson Miles, had orders to "capture or destroy." Miles had five thousand troops and built thirty heliograph stations consisting of large mirrors to flash Morse code messages across southeastern Arizona and into northern Sonora, Mexico. Troops guarded the springs and passes of the Sierra Madre to prevent the renegades from moving about. Miles, like Crook, found his Apache adversary to be an elusive foe. (An Apache warrior could travel as far as seventy miles per day over rough terrain.) In April 1886 the renegades killed some ranchers and ambushed an army detachment. Miles became so exasperated that he tried a different strategy. He dispatched Lt. Charles Gatewood by himself to find Geronimo and convince him to return to the reservation. Gatewood, who had served at San Carlos for two years, had met Geronimo on several occasions. In late August Gatewood found Geronimo, who was impressed by the officer's poise and courage. When Gatewood told the Apache war leader that his remaining family members had been exiled to Florida, Geronimo lost all heart and surrendered.

Exile. Geronimo never saw his homeland again. From 1886 until 1888 he was imprisoned in Pensacola, Florida. In 1894 federal authorities allowed him to take up residence at Fort Sill, Oklahoma, where he spent his time making and selling bows and arrows and peddling photographs of himself. In 1901 Geronimo marched in the parade of President Theodore Roosevelt's inauguration, and three years later he appeared at the World's Fair in Saint Louis. In 1906 he dictated his autobiography. Following a drinking spree in 1909, Geronimo fell from his horse, lay on the chilled ground all night, and died of pneumonia shortly thereafter.

Sources:
S. M. Barrett, ed., *Geronimo's Story of His Life* (New York: Duffield, 1906);

Benjamin Capps, *The Great Chiefs* (Alexandria, Va.: Time-Life Books, 1975);

Robert M. Utley, *Frontier Regulars: The United States Army and the Indian, 1866–1891* (New York: Macmillan, 1973).

IDA B. WELLS-BARNETT

1862-1931

JOURNALIST, FOUNDER OF THE ANTILYNCHING CAMPAIGN

Early Life. Ida Bell Wells, the oldest of eight siblings, was born into slavery in Holly Springs, Mississippi, on 16 July 1862, during the Civil War. Her mother, Lizzie Wells, had been sold away from her mother at age seven and belonged to several owners before she arrived at Holly Springs to work as a cook for a carpenter named Bolling. While in Holly Springs, she met and married James Wells, who had been apprenticed to Bolling by his master, who was also his acknowledged father. After Lizzie and James Wells became free, they continued to work as cook and carpenter to Bolling.

Education. Wells was educated at Shaw University (later Rust College), a freedman's school established in Holly Springs in 1866. After her parents and three siblings died of yellow fever in 1878, sixteen-year-old Ida Wells assumed responsibility for her family, attaining a teaching position in Holly Springs by claiming to be eighteen. In 1880 she moved to Memphis, Tennessee, where she taught in Negro schools while attending summer-school classes at Fisk University.

Journalism and Activism. During the 1880s Wells began writing for the Negro Press Association. Soon after arriving in Memphis, she became editor of a weekly literary paper called the *Evening Star* and shortly thereafter became editor of another weekly, the *Living Way,* as well. By the end of the decade her articles for the *Living Way,* published under the pen name Iola, were being republished in African American newspapers nationwide. She had become well known in part because of her 1884 challenge to segregation. In that year she had taken a seat in the ladies' coach on a train. When the conductor informed her that she had to ride in the smoking car, where other blacks were seated, she refused to move and was removed from the train. Wells sued the railroad and won in a circuit court, but the decision was overturned in the Tennessee Supreme Court in 1887. In 1889 Wells bought a one-third interest in the *Memphis Free Speech and Headlight,* becoming editor of the paper and concentrating her efforts on criticism of inadequate funding, run-down school buildings, and poor training of teachers for Negro schools. By 1891 she had so angered the Memphis school board that they refused to renew her teaching contract. Subsequently Wells gave her full attention to journalism, becoming half owner of the *Free Speech* the following year.

Antilynching Campaign. In March 1892 Wells launched a one-woman crusade against lynching after three black male friends were lynched in Memphis. She lectured in Boston, New York, and other major cities, founding many antilynching societies and Negro women's clubs. Under her editorial banner, the *Free Speech* led the charge against the loss of liberties that African Americans had been granted during Reconstruction. She urged Memphis blacks to fight back, not with violence but with economic pressure, by boycotting city streetcars. She also encouraged her readers to move west to the newly opened Indian territories in Oklahoma, suggesting there was "only one thing left that we can do; save our money and leave a town which will neither protect our lives and property, nor give us a fair trial in the courts, but takes us out and murders us in cold blood when accused by white persons." Wells further drew the ire of Memphis whites by attacking the myth of the black rapist, asserting: "Nobody in this section of the country believes the old thread bare lie that Negro men rape white women." Black men who were lynched were rarely accused rapists, she wrote; rather, she concluded, lynching was a racist attempt to rid a community of prosperous black men. On 27 May, while she was out of town, a mob destroyed the *Free Speech* office and threatened to kill her if she tried to publish the paper again. After this incident Wells moved to New York, where she became an employee and part owner of the *New York Age,* a weekly newspaper edited by T. Thomas Fortune. The following October the paper published Wells's feature story on lynching, which was subsequently published as a pamphlet, *Southern Horrors: Lynch Law in All Its Phases* (1892).

Taking the Antilynching Campaign Abroad. Wells left the *New York Age* in April 1893. She took her cause to Great Britain in 1893 and again in 1894, claiming to audiences that tolerance of lynching in the United States proved that white American society was not civilized but rather was primitive and violent. British society fell under the spell of Wells's considerable rhetorical force, and her visits were instrumental to the creation of a British antilynching committee formed with the intention of swaying American opinion on racial violence. British citizens threatened a boycott on cotton from the American South if lynching did not stop. Wells also spoke out against American racism in general. After returning from her first trip abroad she went to live in Chicago, where she published a pamphlet protesting the virtual exclusion of African Americans from any meaningful role in the World's Columbian Exposition.

Publishing and Politics. In Chicago Wells began writing for the *Chicago Conservator,* an African American weekly, and the *Chicago Inter Ocean,* a white paper where she was the first black employee. On 27 June 1895 Wells married a widower, Ferdinand Lee Barnett, a Chicago lawyer and founder of the *Conservator.* While rearing Barnett's two children by his first marriage and four children of her own,

Wells-Barnett traveled and turned her attention to local race relations. During that time she wrote *A Red Record: Tabulated Statistics and Alleged Causes of Lynchings in the United States, 1892–1893–1894* (1895). In 1898 Wells-Barnett was part of the committee that met with President William McKinley to demand government action in the case of an African American postman who had been lynched in South Carolina.

Isolation. Wells-Barnett played a major role in publicizing the horrors of lynching, but she received little attention or appreciation for her work. She wrote less after 1897 and devoted her efforts to improving race relations in Chicago. She established the Negro Fellowship League in 1910. She also became involved in the women's rights movement, founding he Alpha Suffrage Club in 1915, becoming chair of the Chicago Equal Rights League in 1915, and playing an active role in the National-American Woman Suffrage Association. She died on 25 March 1931.

Sources:

Gail Bederman, "Civilization, The Decline of Middle-Class Manliness, and Ida B. Wells' Anti-Lynching Campaign (1892–1894)," in *Gender and American History Since 1890*, edited by Barbara Melosh (New York: Routledge, 1993), pp. 207–239;

Nora Hall, "Ida B. Wells-Barnett," in *Dictionary of Literary Biography*, volume 23: *American Newspaper Journalists, 1873–1900*, edited by Perry Ashley (Detroit: Gale Research, 1983).

FRANCES WILLARD

1839-1898

TEMPERANCE LEADER, SUFFRAGIST

Early Life. Born in September 1839 in Churchville, New York, Frances Elizabeth Caroline Willard, the fourth of five children, was the daughter of Mary Hill Willard and Josiah Flint Flint Willard, a farmer and cabinet maker. Willard's first ancestor in the New World was Simon Willard, who arrived in the Massachusetts Bay Colony in 1634 and made a name for himself as an Indian fighter and as a founder of Concord, Massachusetts. When Frances was two, her family moved to Ohio, where her father enrolled at Oberlin College to study for the ministry. Her unconventional mother also took courses until Josiah Willard was diagnosed with tuberculosis in 1845. The following year, on the advice of his doctor, her father moved the family to a large farm in Janesville, Wisconsin. Frances Willard grew up on the western prairie. For years she was a tomboy, preferring the nickname Frank and wearing her hair short like her brothers. She longed for an education and chafed under her father's strict discipline.

Education. Educated at home while her brothers attended the district school, Frances Willard finally went to school at age fifteen, when a private school opened in Janesville. In spring 1857 she studied for one term at Milwaukee Normal Institute, founded by Catharine Beecher, sister of novelist Harriet Beecher Stowe and a pioneer in women's education. The next year she entered North Western Female College in Evanston, Illinois, graduating in 1860. Throughout the 1860s Willard taught in Methodist schools in Illinois, New York, and Pennsylvania. After touring Europe and the Middle East with a wealthy friend during 1868–1870, Willard was appointed president of the Evanston Ladies College in 1871. Two years later the college was absorbed by the all-male Northwestern University, becoming the Woman's College of Northwestern University, and Willard was made dean of women, with an increase in salary and authority. Willard was one of the first female administrators of a major coeducational university. In 1873 she helped to found the Association for the Advancement of Women.

The WCTU. In 1874, after a year as dean, Willard resigned her post and began what became her true life-work, when she took the position of corresponding secretary for the newly organized Woman's Christian Temperance Union (WCTU). She acted as an organizer and traveled the country giving lectures. Willard's commitment to woman suffrage did not threaten midwestern supporters of temperance as much as it did easterners, many of whom viewed woman suffrage as a means of achieving full prohibition of alcohol. In 1879 Willard combined her two commitments when she led a campaign in Evanston that lobbied the Illinois legislature for the right of women to vote in local referendums on the sale of liquor. Her efforts in Illinois were unsuccessful, but they gained her a national reputation, and she was elected president of the national WCTU that same year.

Master Politician. Assuming the leadership of the WCTU at the age of forty, Willard headed the organization for the next twenty years. Because she was also linked to the woman suffrage movement, Willard became one of the best known and most influential women of the late nineteenth century. Her energy was renowned. By 1883 she had lectured in every state of the union. She was a master organizer and a speaker with a reputation for wit. A member of many organizations—including the International Council of Women, the Universal Peace Union, and the General Federation of Women's Clubs—Willard made the WCTU an international organization, becoming president of the World WCTU.

Supporting Woman Suffrage. Willard appreciated the power of the ballot and was a lifelong supporter of suffrage for women. Yet her organization proved more conservative than Willard on this issue, so she moved cautiously by protecting the rights of local WCTU branches to set their own agendas. Thus, southern women, who tended to be skeptical about suffrage, and western women, who tended to support suffrage, could share the same banner. Willard herself continued to favor suffrage, arguing that having the right to vote would further enable women to protect their homes and families. In 1887 she presented to the U.S. Congress a petition for woman suffrage signed by two hundred thousand WCTU members. The following year she testified before a Senate committee, presenting herself as a conservative woman devoted to the idea of the ballot.

Later Life. Willard suffered from chronic anemia and other ailments and spent much of the 1890s in England trying to regain her health. After she died on 17 February 1898, at age fifty-eight, more than twenty thousand people paid their last respects at services in New York City and Chicago.

Sources:

Ruth Bordin, *Frances Willard: A Biography* (Chapel Hill & London: University of North Carolina Press, 1986);

Bordin, *Women and Temperance: The Quest for Power and Liberty, 1873–1900* (New Brunswick, N.J.: Rutgers University Press, 1990).

PUBLICATIONS

Jane Addams, *Hull-House Maps and Papers* (New York & Boston: Crowell, 1895)—an extensive study of tenement conditions, sweatshops, child labor, and other problems in the Nineteenth Ward of Chicago;

Charles Carroll, *"The Negro a Beast": or, "In the Image of God"* (Saint Louis: American Book & Bible House, 1900)—one of the most racist books of the period, hich Carroll declared that Africans, Native Americans, and "Mongolians" were subhuman;

Fannie Farmer, *The Boston Cooking-School Cook Book* (Boston: Little, Brown, 1896)—a best-selling cookbook that emphasized nutrition and introduced the use of standard measurements to many American households;

Henry George, *Progress and Poverty: An Inquiry into the Cause of Industrial Depressions and of Increase of Want with Increase of Wealth* (New York: Appleton, 1880)—a famous argument for a "single tax" on wealthy landholders that would relieve the burdens of the working man and end cyclical economic depressions;

Jacob Riis, *How the Other Half Lives* (New York: Scribners, 1890)—an influential exposé of substandard living conditions among immigrants living in the tenement houses of New York City;

Elizabeth Cady Stanton, Susan B. Anthony, and Matilda Joselyn Gage, *History of Woman Suffrage*, volumes 1–3 (volume 1, New York: Fowler & Wells, 1881; volumes 2 and 3, Rochester: Susan B. Anthony, 1881, 1886)—three of six volumes documenting the campaign to win voting rights for women by leaders of that struggle; volumes 4–6, completed by Ida Harper, were published between 1906 and 1922;

Josiah Strong, *Our Country: Its Possible Future and Its Present Crisis* (New York: Baker & Taylor for the American Home Missionary Society, 1885)—a nativist book that argued against immigration and argued that the Anglo-Saxon "is divinely commissioned to be. . . his brother's keeper";

Adna Ferrin Weber, *Growth of Cities in the Nineteenth Century* (New York: Published for Columbia University by Macmillan, 1899)—one of the first descriptions of the suburb and urban growth;

Ida B. Wells-Barnett, *A Red Record: Tabulated Statistics and Alleged Causes of Lynchings in the United States, 1892–1893–1894* (Chicago: Donohue & Henneberry, 1895)—an account of lynchings in the South during the years 1892–1894, with a preface by Frederick Douglass;

Wells-Barnett, *Southern Horrors: Lynch Law in All Its Phases* (New York: New Age Print, 1892)—Wells's first separately published analysis of lynching in the southern United States;

Frances Willard, *Glimpses of Fifty Years* (Boston: G. M. Smith, 1889)—the autobiography of the influential longtime president of the Woman's Christian Temperance Union;

George Washington Williams, *A History of the Negro Race in America from 1619 to 1880: Negroes as Slaves, as Soldiers, and as Citizens*, 2 volumes (New York: Putnam, 1882)—one of the first histories of African Americans in the United States.

RELIGION

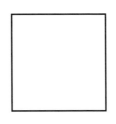

by   ANDREW WALSH

CONTENTS

Sidebars and tables are listed in italics.

1878

- Vanderbilt University fires professor Alexander Winchell for using Darwinian ideas in teaching zoology and geology.

- Methodists and Baptists account for 90 percent of southern church membership, almost twice the strength (47 percent) of these two denominations in the nation as a whole.

- Washington Gladden publishes *Working People and Their Employers* and maintains that the idea of true Christianity lies not in rituals or dogmas but in the principle of "Thou shalt love thy neighbor as thyself."

1879

- The U.S. Supreme Court upholds an 1862 federal law banning polygamy. In Utah the Church of Jesus Christ of Latter-Day Saints, or Mormons, defends the doctrine of plural marriage.

- Mary Baker Eddy incorporates the Church of Christ, Scientist in Boston, Massachusetts.

- Nestor Zakkis is appointed Russian Orthodox bishop of the Aleutian Islands and Alaska.

1880

- The Salvation Army, an English evangelical and philanthropic organization, forms a chapter in Pennsylvania under the leadership of Commissioner George Railton.

- The American Jewish community has approximately 250,000 members.

- Daniel Sidney Warner organizes the Church of God in Anderson, Indiana, one of the first Protestant denominations to stress the need for a second baptism.

- Russell Conwell, a Baptist minister, delivers a lecture titled "Acres of Diamonds" for the first time in Philadelphia. Conwell insists that to "make money honestly is to preach the gospel."

- Henry Steele Olcott, a cofounder of the Theosophical Society in New York in 1875, moves to Ceylon and converts to Buddhism.

1881

- Spelman College, the first college for African American women in the nation, is founded in Atlanta through the assistance of the American Baptist Home Mission Society.

- Francis Clark, a Congregationalist minister in Maine, founds the Young People's Society of Christian Endeavor. Within a few years it becomes a national Protestant youth movement with five hundred thousand members.

- Frances Willard is elected president of the Woman's Christian Temperance Union (WCTU) and commits the organization to a broad program of social and political reform.

- Archibald Alexander Charles Hodge and Benjamin Warfield of Princeton Theological Seminary publish an article entitled "Inspiration," which asserts the infallibility of biblical Scripture.

30 June   Henry Highland Garnet, an African American Presbyterian minister and former abolitionist, is appointed ambassador to Liberia.

1882

- Congress strips the vote from all practitioners of polygamy. This controversy over plural marriage blocks Utah's entrance into the union because many residents of the territory are Mormons.

29 Mar.   The Knights of Columbus, a fraternal benefit society of Catholic men, is chartered by Father Michael Joseph McGivney in New Haven, Connecticut.

1883

- Tumult ensues when shrimp cocktail is served at a banquet honoring the first class of graduates at Hebrew Union College in Cincinnati (under Mosaic law Jews are forbidden to eat shellfish).

- St. Benedict the Moor becomes the first African American Roman Catholic Church in New York City.

1884

- The Third Plenary Council of American Catholic Bishops meets in Baltimore and endorses proposals including a system of parochial education and the establishment of the Catholic University of America.

- Benjamin Tucker Tanner founds the African Methodist Episcopal (AME) *Church Review,* a leading magazine of the day.

1885

- Congregationalist minister Josiah Strong writes *Our Country: Its Possible Future and Its Present Crisis.* According to Strong, the Anglo-Saxon exhibits "a pure spiritual Christianity" and is "divinely commissioned to be, in a peculiar sense, his brother's keeper."

Nov.   A group of fifteen rabbis led by Kaufmann Kohler meets in Pittsburgh to discuss the adjustments Jews need to make in order to fit into American life. The resolutions passed by the group become known as the Pittsburgh Platform.

1886

- Washington Gladden publishes *Applied Christianity.*

- James Gibbons, Roman Catholic cardinal of Baltimore, forestalls official condemnation of the Knights of Labor. He also prevents the listing of Henry George's *Progress and Poverty* (1879) on the *Index of Forbidden Books.*

- Augustine Tolton is the first full-blooded African American to be ordained a Catholic priest.

- Protestant urban mission workers form the International Christian Workers Association.

- Josiah Strong becomes secretary of the Evangelical Alliance and develops it into an influential Protestant movement oriented toward urban evangelism and social service.

Aug.   In Northfield, Massachusetts, one hundred students, later called the "Mt. Hermon One Hundred," dedicate themselves to serve as foreign missionaries.

1887

- Under provisions of the Dawes Severalty Act Protestant and Catholic missionary groups are placed in charge of education on Indian reservations.

- Orthodox synagogues in New York City join to form the Association of American Hebrew Congregations, the first major organization of its kind in the nation. Jacob Joseph of Vilnius, Lithuania, is made the chief rabbi.

- Protestant nativists form the American Protective Association (APA) in Clinton, Iowa, in reaction to European, and especially Catholic, immigration. Members of the APA swear never to vote for a Catholic and, if possible, never to hire or strike with one.

2 Jan.   Rabbi Sabato Morais opens the Jewish Theological Seminary in New York, a traditionalist institution meant to counter the Hebrew Union College in Cincinnati.

1888

- The Student Volunteer Movement (SVM) organizes under the leadership of John R. Mott of the Young Men's Christian Association (YMCA) in Northfield, Massachusetts. The SVM commits itself "to the evangelization of the world in this generation."

1889

- The American Catholic Church celebrates its one hundredth anniversary. Its nearly nine million members are found primarily in northern cities.

- The Ghost Dance religion, an ecstatic, visionary, and prophetic movement, originates among the Northern Paiutes of Nevada and quickly spreads to other tribes. The religion and its rituals promise to revive traditional Indian cultures, forms of sustenance, and independence in the face of white encroachment.

- Christian Socialism is founded by a group of Protestants in reaction to the problems caused by rapid industrialization. Known as the Social Gospel movement, it advocates the abolition of child labor, better working conditions for women, and a living wage for all workers.

- The Society of Christian Socialists meets in Boston. The leaders include Josiah Strong, David Jayne Hill, and E. Benjamin Andrews.

- The settlement house known as Hull-House is founded by Jane Addams in Chicago.

- Wisconsin passes a law that does not allow a parochial school to be accredited unless it teaches the basic subjects in English.

- Andrew Carnegie's article "Wealth" appears in the *North American Review* and emphasizes the moral obligation of the rich to aid the poor.

- Charles Augustus Briggs publishes *Whither? A Theological Question for the Times,* a groundbreaking exposition on the "higher criticism" of Scripture.

1890

- In the South, Methodists and Baptists together have 4.5 million to 5 million members (approximately one-half are African Americans). The Southern Presbyterian Church has 190,000 members.

- Washington Gladden's *Burning Questions* is published.

- William James writes *Principles of Psychology,* which advances pragmatism, a belief that truth is found not in theoretical speculation but in the practical outcome of ideas.

- A. C. Dixon calls the first Holy Spirit Conference in Baltimore, a precursor of the Pentecostal movement. He tells the gathering that "Faith is the connecting power between the battery of God's power and the hearts of men."

6 Oct. The sanctioning of polygamy is discontinued by Wilford Woodruff, president of the Mormon Church.

15 Dec. Sitting Bull, a Lakota leader of the Ghost Dance movement, is killed by Indian police when they try to arrest him along the Grand River in South Dakota.

29 Dec. A band of Ghost Dance practitioners is massacred by the U.S. Seventh Cavalry at Wounded Knee Creek, South Dakota.

1891

- Eastern Rite Catholics under Father Alexis Toth unite with the Russian Orthodox Church. Eventually more than 120 Eastern Rite parishes, mostly in Ohio and Pennsylvania, break with the Catholic Church in protest over restrictions placed on their traditional practices by American Catholic bishops.

- Professor Charles Augustus Briggs delivers an aggressive inaugural address, "The Authority of Holy Scripture," to mark his installation in a newly created chair in biblical theology at the Union Theological Seminary in New York. The lecture rejects the doctrine that God provided verbal inspiration for the precise text of the Bible and triggers a powerful conservative backlash among Presbyterians.

- Pope Leo XIII issues his encyclical *Rerum novarum* (Of Modern Things). This new expression of Catholic social doctrine upholds private property as a natural right but condemns capitalism where it has imposed poverty and the degradation of workers.

1892

- The Catholic Church estimates that at least 1.5 million out of 2.2 million Catholics of school age are attending public schools.

- In the wake of the massacre at Wounded Knee, the federal Courts of Indian Offenses investigate, convict, and punish Native Americans who persist in following their ancient tribal religions, including the Sun Dance.

- The Presbyterian General Assembly supports the Princeton Theological Seminary's version of biblical inerrancy, declaring that "the inspired Word, as it came from God, is without error."

1893

- The World's Parliament of Religions takes place in Chicago as part of the world's fair. The parliament is an unprecedented gathering of Protestant, Catholic, and Eastern Orthodox leaders, as well as representatives of other world faiths.

- The Southern Presbyterian Assembly makes dancing a valid ground for excommunication.

- The Catholic University of America opens its doors in Washington, D.C. Bishop John Lancaster Spalding's "Cornerstone Address" claims a place for Catholic thought in American intellectual life.

- Josiah Strong publishes *The New Era; or the Coming Kingdom*, which predicts that Anglo-Saxons will win the worldwide struggle for racial dominance, partly on the basis of their Protestantism.

4 Jan. Violators of the Anti-Polygamy Act of 1882 are granted amnesty by President Grover Cleveland with the stipulation that they observe the law henceforward.

1894

- The Central Conference of American Rabbis publishes the *Union Prayer Book*, a radical simplification and revision of inherited Hebrew-language prayer books.

- Old Testament scholar Henry Preserved Smith of Lane Presbyterian Seminary in Cincinnati is dismissed from the Presbyterian ministry for heresy.

- The Open and Institutional Church League is formed to promote the construction of church gymnasiums, libraries, lecture rooms, and other facilities for social programs.

1895

- Pope Leo XIII's encyclical letter *Longinqua Oceani* lauds the growing strength and freedom of the American Catholic Church but rejects the proposition that American-style separation of church and state is desirable worldwide.

- The Anti-Saloon League, which draws on close church ties, organizes as a national movement to stop the manufacture and sale of alcoholic beverages in the United States.

28 Sept. The National Baptist Convention, the last and largest of the post–Civil War African American Protestant denominations, is founded in Atlanta.

1896

- William Ashley "Billy" Sunday, a former professional baseball player, ends his career with the Chicago YMCA. During his five years there, Sunday promoted Prohibition and Bible fundamentalism.

- Bishop John Keane is removed as rector of the Catholic University of America as part of a papal drive against "Americanism."

- The Rabbi Isaac Elchanan Theological Seminary is founded in New York City by Eastern European immigrants who wish to make a traditional Orthodox Jewish education available in the United States.

4 Jan.   Utah is admitted into the Union.

1897

- The American Society for Church History is founded.

- W. E. B. Du Bois publishes *The Souls of Black Folk,* an important interpretation of African American life describing the centrality of religion in black communities.

- African American Baptists in Mississippi led by Charles Prince Jones and Charles H. Mason organize the Church of God in Christ, the first black Pentecostal church in the nation.

1898

15 Sept.   Bishop Alexander Walters of the AME Zion Church is elected president of the National Afro-American Council in Rochester, New York.

1899

- Tikhon Belavin, Russian Orthodox bishop of the Aleutians and Alaska, petitions the Holy Synod of Russia to change the name of his diocese to that of North America and Alaska in order to reflect its growing focus on Eastern European immigrants to Canada and the United States.

- Pope Leo XIII issues his encyclical, *Testem Benevolentiae,* which explicitly condemns Americanism as a heresy.

1 July   The Christian Commercial Men's Association of America, a group of traveling salesmen, meets in Boscobel, Wisconsin. The group is better known as the Gideons International and begins to place Bibles in hotel rooms.

OVERVIEW

New Outlooks. In the last quarter of the nineteenth century industrialization and urbanization profoundly affected the manner in which Americans viewed their society. Great cities arose and industrialization proceeded so quickly that within two generations the United States emerged as the world's supreme economic power. Massive waves of European immigrants arrived to find jobs in factories, mines, farms, and transportation networks. Meanwhile bold new ideas circulated faster and farther than ever before, and, as the prestige of the natural sciences rose, evolutionary themes reshaped the ways in which educated men and women thought about the world and the future. Optimism and even confidence about humanity's new capacity to solve ancient and intractable problems began to take hold in many quarters. American religious life shared fully in this sense of growth and rapid change. Protestantism continued to hold a central, although unofficial, place in the nation's life. Formal membership in churches and other local religious organizations continued along the upward-arching path set during the early nineteenth century, reaching the highest levels yet known in the history of the nation. In sharp contrast to the situation in Europe, the proportion of the population that claimed formal religious membership was growing faster than the rate of increase in the population at large. Along with this growth, however, came a sense of the increasing diversity in American religious life. Cities in particular exhibited religious, ethnic, and racial complexity. New intellectual currents also stirred religious life. For more than two centuries Calvinism (the theological system of John Calvin [1509–1564] marked by a strong emphasis on the sovereignty of God, the depravity of mankind, and the doctrine of predestination) had dominated American theology. However, it began to weaken in many quarters, and during the 1870s and 1880s liberal voices held the initiative among Protestants, Catholics, and Jews. In general, these liberals sought to soften dogmas that seemed outdated or insupportable in the light of the scientific and intellectual advances of the day. A sense of optimism about the human future also permeated much of the "New Theology." Liberal theologians increasingly emphasized God's love and presence in the world rather than human sinfulness. By the late 1880s, however, strong conservative reactions against liberalism were developing in many religious communities. A series of highly publicized heresy trials occurred, and, especially among Protestants and Jews, a strong polarization of religious attitudes and outlooks became increasingly evident during the 1890s.

Regional Variation and Division. The United States was a religious patchwork with remarkable variances in religious demography: evangelical Protestantism, for example, held sway in the South and in much of the Midwest, while Catholicism dominated many new metropolitan centers in the North. New waves of immigration were also creating a larger and more religiously conservative Jewish community in northeastern cities. The regional diversity of religion was also reinforced by the failure of many Protestant denominations to heal the breaches caused by the Civil War and the struggle over slavery. Of the major Protestant denominations, only the Episcopal Church was able to reintegrate its organizational life after the Civil War. The Baptist, Methodist, and Presbyterian churches, which had set the pace in the rapid expansion of American church life during the early decades of the nineteenth century, remained divided into separate Northern and Southern denominations for many decades.

Protestantism. Protestant churches continued to play a privileged and dominant role in American religious life. Approximately 60 percent of the population viewed itself as Protestant, and the major Protestant denominations all grew faster than the rate of population throughout the last three decades of the nineteenth century. Indeed, in many communities Protestantism seemed all but formally established as the state religion, with Protestants playing a leading role in public education, charitable activities, and the Republican Party and among the rising middle and upper classes. Many Protestant denominations and congregations experienced a remarkable burst of energy during these decades. They mobilized large cadres of volunteers and donors to support missionaries at home and abroad and advocated social reform movements such as temperance and relief for the poor. Strong elements of continuity also flavored Protestant life. Revivalism, which had shaped Protestant church life in the early nineteenth century, continued to play a central role, with celebrated preachers such as Dwight Moody carrying the evangelical message into the cities with energy and success. The nation's public school system reflected a Protestant ethos, and popular education movements such as the Chautauqua also tapped deep Protestant attitudes and values. Although a small proportion of immigrants who arrived during the period 1878–1899 were Protestants, these new arrivals adjusted readily to American patterns—even the Lutherans, who preferred to maintain both ethnic and denominational distinctions in their church life.

An Uneasy Dominance. In many ways, however, it was also becoming clear that American Protestant dominance was not completely solid. Protestantism remained an amazingly diverse and, in moments of stress, fragmented phenomenon. At the end of the century most Protestant groups still shared some elements of the evangelical revivalist tradition and Calvinist heritage, but they were divided by significant theological, regional, class, ethnic, and racial divisions. Viewed from a Catholic or Jewish perspective, American Protestantism seemed well organized and determined. But from within, the Protestant church was often beset by rivalries, tensions, and a small but unquenchable sense of foreboding about the increasing religious diversity of the nation.

Protestant Liberalism. Perhaps the most significant internal tension in American Protestantism was the growing debate over theological liberalism. During the late 1870s and the 1880s a new school of theologians and clergy worked to weaken and even dismantle the nation's longstanding Calvinist theological consensus. Scholars such as Charles Augustus Briggs of Union Theological Seminary in New York and Newman Smythe, a Congregational pastor and seminary instructor, introduced American schools to new methods of biblical studies that had been pioneered in German universities. These methods emphasized attitudes of scientific rigor, historical research, the mobilization of linguistic and archaeological evidence, and an attitude of skepticism about inherited doctrines and creeds. Liberal scholars saw themselves as seekers of the truth whose task was to purify Protestantism by exploding myths and revealing errors that had crept into sacred texts and teachings over the course of centuries. They sought, in particular, to refute the rigid literalism that had governed American Calvinist interpretations of Scripture and theology earlier in the century. The work of these "New Theologians" reflected the optimism about the human condition and the broad popular impact of evolutionary thinking, which convinced many late-nineteenth-century thinkers that human progress was an unbreakable law of history.

Conservative Response. The work of these liberals stirred up both enormous enthusiasm and growing opposition. Princeton Theological Seminary, in particular, asserted itself as the great bastion of conservative Calvinist literalism. A wave of heresy accusations and trials punctuated the late 1880s and the 1890s, contributing to a growing sense of polarization within American Protestantism. The Presbyterian Church, which was firmly committed to Calvinist creeds and traditions, emerged as a particular battleground. Conservatives worried that liberal innovations were gutting the Bible of basic Christian doctrines. Liberals, on the other hand, believed that if Christianity refused to test itself against the most rigorous standards of truth and intellectual honesty, it would, in the age of science, appear morally and intellectually bankrupt. The clear division of mainstream Protestantism into modernist and fundamentalist camps would take place, however, only in the twentieth century.

The City. Protestants of all theological stripes also began to worry that their faith was not faring well in the anonymous world of the modern industrial city. American cities seemed to be dominated by strange new groups: a swelling and seemingly permanent and impoverished working class; millions of foreigners with alien religions, customs, and languages; and a new business culture that seemed to dismiss traditional moral imperatives and to lure successful churches and prosperous "Princes of the Pulpit" into the uncritical affirmation of wealth and success. Protestant thinkers such as the Reverend Josiah Strong began to treat the situation in the cities as a pressing moral and religious challenge for Protestants. In *Our Country: Its Possible Future and Its Present Crisis* (1885), Strong confidently predicted the worldwide triumph of "Anglo-Saxon" political, economic and religious values in the Darwinian struggle of races, religions, and cultures for dominance—but only if America could resolve the challenge of its cities, which presented the threats of unchecked capitalism, dehumanizing poverty, the explosion of non-Protestant populations, and the specter of socialism. Evangelists such as Dwight Moody targeted the growing cities with some success, aided by militant and highly organized support from the Salvation Army, which arrived in the United States from Britain in 1880 to spearhead conservative Protestant responses to urban poverty and diversity.

Catholicism. After decades on the margins of American life, Catholicism came into its own as a major, and in many places dominant, force during the last quarter of the nineteenth century. Millions of Catholic immigrants flooded into the United States after 1880. Discrimination and prejudice against Catholics remained common and was often virulent, but the sheer size and increasing acculturation of their community made it harder for Protestants to ignore or exclude Catholics. Much of the church's leadership persuasively articulated the case for Catholic participation in American life. But the dominant trend in American Catholic life was the creation of a distinct Catholic subculture with its own religious practices, institutions, rich community life, and boundaries. The Third Plenary Council of America's Catholic Bishops, held in Baltimore, Maryland, in 1884, helped set strong tones of unity and solidarity. Sitting under the chairmanship of the charismatic James Cardinal Gibbons of Baltimore, the council produced a uniform administrative code for the church, called for the creation of a parish-based system of education in response to Protestant control of public schools, and planned the establishment of a national Catholic university. The bishops also approved the text of a standard catechism that proved to be the touchstone of Catholic religious education in America for more than a century. The call for a parochial school system was not new, but it caught hold in an unprecedented manner in the late 1880s. The millions of Catholic immigrants who arrived after 1880 embraced the parochial-school movement and made the creation of a Catholic subculture possible.

Catholic Diversity. The accelerating diversity of the American Catholic Church also made it extremely difficult to secure harmony and unity. It was the internal experience of diversity that troubled American Catholics most during the Gilded Age, not anti-Catholic discrimination. Irishmen and Germans had dominated the stream of Catholic immigration earlier in the nineteenth century. By the 1890s, however, at least a dozen major Catholic ethnic groups were establishing themselves in the United States, particularly in the cities. Tensions erupted between immigrants who wished to preserve their own ethnic and religious customs and autonomy and the followers of American bishops, most of whom were of Irish origin and tended to insist on the goal of creating a unified, English-speaking Catholic community in the United States. While theological liberalism was never a major issue in the American Catholic community, a group of bishops, priests, and lay leaders did stake out a new kind of liberalism characterized by optimism about the possibility of Catholic assimilation in the United States and an emphasis on the compatibility of Catholicism and American traditions of democratic politics, especially the separation of church and state. Cardinal Gibbons of Baltimore and bishops such as John Ireland of Saint Paul, Minnesota; John Keane of Richmond, Virginia; and John Lancaster Spalding of Peoria, Illinois, shared a vision of a unified Catholic culture in America, one that would be open to the possibilities and promises of the United States. More recently arrived European immigrants, however, often resisted the Americanist platform, preferring that parishes be organized by ethnicity and centered around the preservation of homeland languages, cultures, and religious traditions.

Internal Tensions. Clashes between Irish American bishops and German, Slav, and French Canadian Catholics were common. During the 1890s Catholic emigrants from Poland and other eastern European nations who practiced Eastern Rite Catholicism broke with the American church in protest over the demands of bishops for uniformity and obedience. Restless Catholic immigrants often received support from their home countries, especially Germany, where church activists and politicians such as Peter Paul Cahensly lobbied the Vatican

and continuously voiced their concerns that the policies of Americanist bishops were causing millions of Catholic immigrants to drift away from the faith. Cahensly in particular sought the creation of ethnic dioceses as well as ethnic parishes in the United States. Liberal bishops, shielded by the effective diplomacy of Gibbons, received a large measure of papal support until the mid 1890s. After that point, papal authorities began to grow concerned about the effect that American arguments for the separation of church and state were having in Europe. Papal disapproval of the Americanist position was stated clearly in two papal encyclicals: *Longinqua Oceani* (1895) and *Testem Benevolentiae* (1899). The latter branded Americanism as a specific heresy for allegedly suggesting that the Catholic Church should alter its historic and foundational religious teachings in order to accommodate itself to the modern world. Gibbons and other bishops hotly denied that any such heretics existed in America. The papal crackdown had a marked and lasting conservative impact on American Catholicism. "National" parishes, which were organized on the basis of immigrant identity, became increasingly common in the United States after 1890; however, all of them continued under the authority of local—and usually Irish American—bishops. Nevertheless a universal Catholic identity prevailed, and the church did not suffer the lasting organizational divisions that affected so many other American religious denominations in the late nineteenth century.

Reform Judaism. Religious liberalism advanced further in the American Jewish community than in virtually any other American religious group. By the early 1880s the Reform movement in Judaism, which was committed to the modernization of the faith and its reconciliation with the modern world, had captured virtually the entire American Jewish community. In 1880 American Jewry totaled about 250,000 members scattered thinly across the nation. The Reform movement rose along with German Jewish immigration in the late 1840s and 1850s. Rabbi Isaac Mayer Wise of Cincinnati, Ohio, was the movement's organizing genius, but its intellectual leader was Rabbi David Einhorn, who emigrated from Germany in 1855. He was an uncompromising religious radical who demanded a restructuring of Judaism, defining it as a monotheistic and ethically oriented religion, and rejected the teaching that Jews formed a separate people. Einhorn's attacks on Jewish law and ritual profoundly influenced the rabbis who gathered to draft the "Pittsburgh Platform" of 1885, the theological manifesto for Reform Judaism for the following five decades. Within a few years, however, the Reform movement's dominance was being drastically eroded by massive Jewish migration from eastern Europe. This influx brought to the United States hundreds of thousands of observant Orthodox Jews who bitterly rejected liberalism. Orthodox synagogues and periodicals proliferated during the late 1880s and 1890s, especially in the northeastern cities where large Jewish populations settled. While both the Reform and Orthodox movements had their origins in Europe, the 1880s also produced a distinctively American movement within Judaism, Conservatism, which offered a middle way between the radical experimentalism of Reform and the unyielding traditionalism of Orthodoxy. By 1900 the Reform movement was far outnumbered by its more conservative competitors. It remained, however, a powerful voice in the Jewish debate over adjustment to both the United States and modernity.

African Americans. The failure of Reconstruction deeply affected African American religious life between 1878 and 1899. As white supremacy reasserted itself in the South, where 90 percent of the nation's blacks lived, religious institutions persisted as the most influential and independent African American entities. The clearest religious trend among freed slaves was withdrawal from white-dominated denominations into black churches. Only a small percentage of black Christians remained affiliated with the Episcopal, Presbyterian, and Congregational denominations; the overwhelming majority affiliated with one of three black Methodist denominations or with Baptist groups. These black denominations followed the general patterns of theology and organization. The largest black church, the National Baptist Convention, U.S.A., Inc. was organized in 1895 under the leadership of E. C. Morris. For most African Americans the Protestant religious life fostered by these churches provided a sheltered space free from racism and relatively independent of white control. Ministers, who derived their livelihoods from their congregations, were often the most independent figures in black communities. The black denominations also struggled to preserve the networks of schools, colleges, and seminaries that had been created after the Civil War. These schools produced successive generations of black leaders in many fields. Black denominational publications focused on racism, and church meetings provided a forum for religious, cultural, and political discourse. During the last quarter of the nineteenth century, the first generation of formally educated black theologians emerged into prominence. Theologians such as Theophilus Steward of Wilberforce University in Ohio produced pioneering theological texts that offered fundamental critiques of white Christianity. Steward, for example, offered a scathing analysis of the shortcoming and sinfulness of white Protestantism and called for the evangelization of Africa by black Christians rather than white ones.

Native Americans. During the 1870s and 1880s Native American opposition to white expansion in the West was crushed. As had been the case since the early seventeenth century, relations between the Indians and whites reflected mutual incomprehension and suspicion. In the realm of religious life, the period featured both white attempts to settle the Indian problem conclusively and Indian efforts to formulate a religious response to white encroachment. The Dawes Severalty Act of 1887, besides mandating the gradual elimination of most tribal lands and their allotment to individual families, also provided for the systematic introduction of both Catholic and Protestant missionaries on the reservations. These missionaries had the responsibility of educating the Native Americans, an effort whose chief goal was to eradicate Indian identity, often by sending Indian children to boarding schools where they were forbidden to speak their native languages or practice their tribal religions. Soldiers and officials of the Bureau of Indian Affairs also attempted to eradicate traditional religious and cultural practices, including the annual Sun Dance held by the Lakota. This ritual was suppressed by the federal Office of Indian Affairs in 1883, causing a profound crisis among the Lakota, whose religion taught them that the return of the bison herds was dependent on petitions to the natural powers that sustained all life. In this period of crisis, an extensive series of religious movements swept through the surviving Plains Indian tribes. The most famous of these was the Ghost Dance religion, which, like many of these spiritual movements, was characterized by attempts to use rituals and prophecy to roll back white encroachment and restore the physical and cultural conditions of the early nineteenth century. The Ghost Dance religion, which originated in a vision given to a Northern Paiute named Wovoka during an eclipse of the sun on 1 January 1889, spread rapidly across the plains. Practitioners danced in a circle to achieve an ecstatic state and open communications with the dead. Those returning from the trance state reported that the "old ways" would soon return. The Ghost Dance spread despite the many significant variations and differences in tribal religions and had to be reinterpreted by Indian teachers and prophets to make sense in the context of local religious systems. Among the Lakota, who were extremely responsive, the Ghost Dance offered a means to revive ritual forms banned by the government and missionaries, thus defeating the whites and creating the circumstances for the return of the buffalo. Practitioners of the religion were actively persecuted by federal troops, culminating in the tragic massacre of a band of Lakota Ghost Dancers at Wounded Knee Creek in South Dakota on 29 December 1890. The massacre of Wounded Knee ended Indian resistance to white control, although some groups continued to practice elements of the Ghost Dance religion well into the twentieth century.

TOPICS IN THE NEWS

CATHOLIC AMERICA

Melting Pot. Catholic immigration to the United States rose steadily in the late nineteenth century, increasing the number of Catholics from approximately three million in 1860 to twelve million by 1900. The resulting changes in the scope and composition of the Catholic population had a significant impact both within and outside the Catholic community. Before 1870 Catholicism was a strong but regional presence in a Protestant America. Recent Irish immigrants dominated the institutional life of the church, while a German Catholic minority exercised great strength in the Midwest. Hispanic Catholics held sway in the newly acquired Southwest, and Creole Catholicism had a strong presence along the Gulf of Mexico. But soon after 1880 a remarkably diverse stream of immigrants began arriving, and within a few years large communities of French, Canadian, Portuguese, Spanish, Belgian, Slovak, Croatian, and Hungarian Catholics settled in the United States. Overshadowing these groups were massive numbers of Italians and Poles—more than three million of each group arrived in the United States between 1880 and 1920. Catholic immigrants concentrated their settlements in the rising industrial settlements of the Northeast, often transforming local demography. Many New England towns and cities, for example, had entirely homogeneous Protestant populations at the beginning of the nineteenth century and almost entirely immigrant Catholic populations by the early twentieth century.

Uniformity. Within the American Catholic Church this great migration created a diversity that was almost bewildering—and not particularly welcome among the longer-established Irish Americans. American Catholics experienced their own version of the perennial American problem of diversity and unity and had the added task of relating the many subtraditions of European Catholicism to a united, hierarchical church. This challenge was deepened by complex divisions of loyalty among many of the new ethnic groups and often significant differences of ritual and customary pious practice. The problem of uniformity was addressed directly at the Third Plenary Council of American Catholic Bishops in Baltimore, Maryland, in 1884, which produced a uniform set of parish and diocesan procedures, a catechism for Catholic

John Ireland, the archbishop of Saint Paul, Minnesota, and Monsignor Denis O'Connell, the rector of the North American College, Rome

youth, and a plan to require all Catholic parishes to operate their own parochial schools. Sentiment varied among Catholic bishops, but during the 1880s the dominant approach emphasized the formation of a united and uniform American Catholic culture, which was to be created and reinforced by uniting Catholics of all backgrounds in panethnic parishes that would emphasize the English language and acculturation to the United States. This position was particularly identified with Americanist bishops such as John Ireland of Saint Paul, Minnesota; John Lancaster Spalding of Peoria, Illinois; and James Cardinal Gibbons of Baltimore, the leader of the American hierarchy.

Ethnic Concerns. Non-Irish immigrants tended to oppose this orientation, seeking to gather the church in a loosely connected set of ethnic networks that could meet the cultural and religious needs of particular immigrant groups. In the cities and towns populated by new immigrants, religion often played a larger role than it had in their homelands, since Catholic churches and practices could provide tangible ways of retaining ethnic identities. The Catholic religion provided a powerful framework for the observance of individual and collective turning points from birth to death, and parishes often provided the key social organizations that facilitated urban life. One typical parish in Chicago in the 1890s sponsored religion classes, athletic events, and twenty-three other programs for its ten thousand members. (Catholic parishes of the period tended to be amazingly vast by Protestant standards.) The parish network was doubly important among immigrants who did not speak English. Although interethnic conflict strained American Catholicism and provided a strong undercurrent to the debates of Americanists and conservatives during the 1890s, immigrants brought with them some important common traditions and attitudes that functioned over the longer term to support the development of a new Catholic subculture.

Acceptant of Church Authority. Most Catholic immigrants of the period were shaped by common peasant and conservative origins, and they proved to be open to the influence of Catholic authorities. They were also willing, along with Irish American Catholics, to accept papal authority as definitive. In addition the Catholic ritual system, which was promoted energetically, provided a common set of religious experiences and ideas that reinforced Catholic distinctiveness in a Protestant-dominated country. The parochial-school system that emerged in the 1880s and 1890s proved to be a powerful force for Catholic cohesion. While Protestant institutions tended to shed their distinctive religious identities after 1880, the growing American Catholic subculture fortified its religious character. And although anti-Catholic discrimination remained a powerful reality, the tendency toward neighborhood segregation reinforced the distinctive sense of Catholic identity.

Sources:

Jay P. Dolan, *American Catholic Experience: A History from Colonial Times to the Present* (Garden City, N.Y.: Doubleday, 1985);

Dolan, *Catholic Revivalism: The American Experience, 1830–1900* (South Bend, Ind.: University of Notre Dame Press, 1978);

James Hennessey, *A History of the Roman Catholic Community in the United States* (New York: Oxford University Press, 1981);

Ann Taves, *The Household of Faith: Roman Catholic Devotions in Mid-Nineteenth Century America* (South Bend, Ind.: University of Notre Dame Press, 1986).

POPISH PLOTS

Anti-Catholicism, a sentiment developed over the centuries since the Protestant Reformation, was deep-seated in many American Protestants. Nativist, anti-Catholic views welled up several times during the nineteenth century and enjoyed considerable social respectability. Under the leadership of Henry Francis Bowers, the American Protective Association (APA) gained support during the depression that began in 1893. John L. Brandt's 1895 work, *America or Rome, Christ or the Pope?*, expressed the exaggerated fears of the APA. "The United States is Rome's favorite missionary field. . . . Our country is a paradise for Rome. She has, without being disputed, introduced into our beautiful and fair land, many dogmas, founded upon pretended visions and fabulous tales, more fit for pagan darkness than for evangelical light; she has burdened millions of our people with masses, auricular confessions, priestly celibacy, and fears of purgatory; she has attacked our public schools; she has denounced our Bible; she has favored the union of church and state; she has thrust her hands into our treasury; she has monopolized the funds donated to the religious bodies for Indian education; she controls our telegraphic system; she censures and subsidizes the public presses; she manipulates many of our political conventions; she rules many of our large cities. . . . she has put judges on the bench and muzzled the mouths of many of our ablest statesmen and editors; she has plotted to destroy our government; she has made her subjects swear allegiance to a foreign power."

Source: John L. Brandt, *America or Rome, Christ or the Pope?* (Toledo, Ohio: Loyal, 1895), pp. 4–8.

CHRISTIAN SCIENCE

Spiritualism. The religious imagination of Americans had never been contained fully by inherited or orthodox religious organizations and dogmas. Throughout the nineteenth century many popular religious movements crystallized around new leaders and ideas. Spiritualism, for example, appealed powerfully throughout the nineteenth century to many Americans, even though it was widely condemned by established Christian denominations. Spiritualism maintained that the spirit was the prime element of reality and that spirits of the dead could communicate with the living, usually through a medium. It cut across denominational and religious lines, in part because it offered relief for many people yearning for contact with dead relations, often either children or other relatives killed in the Civil War.

The first Christian Science church, built in 1886 in Oconto, Wisconsin

Eddy. Interest in Spiritualism was often particularly strong among women. One of the most famous female religious thinkers was Mary Baker Eddy, the founder of Christian Science. Eddy, a native of New Hampshire, experienced the intense sense of loss felt by many New Englanders as Calvinism declined as the central force that gave the region's dominant culture its meaning and direction. Throughout her early life, like many middle-class Victorian women, Eddy suffered chronic, debilitating, and unexplained ailments and turned to religion for comfort. In 1862 she experienced a dramatic "mind cure" at the hands of an itinerant healer and mesmerist. Phineas Parkhurst Quimby strongly influenced Eddy, suggesting that all disease and suffering originated in mental phenomena and could be resolved without medicine. He also used a vocabulary that included the phrases "Christian science" and "science of health." Soon after Quimby died in 1866, Eddy underwent a powerful spiritual experience. After a wrenching fall on ice, Eddy cured her injured back by mobilizing her spirit and the mind. Over the next several years she worked to reinterpret Quimby's teachings in terms of Christian language and correlated them with biblical teachings. She developed a distinctive religious argument, which she believed was both an act of human discovery and a divine revelation. She taught that God constituted all reality, and that all reality was ultimately spiritual. Human regeneration came from recognizing that the empirical evidence of the material world was an illusion and by subsequently allowing God through Christ to transform one's being. This recognition of the illusory character of the material world also led to physical health without resorting to doctors or conventional medicine. Eddy held her first public religious service in her home in Lynn, Massachusetts in 1875. She published the first edition of *Science and Health* the same year (later she would add the subtitle *With a Key to the Scriptures*). Eddy incorporated the Christian Scientists' Association in 1876 and the Church of Christ, Scientist in 1879. Over the next several decades, Eddy led the church from a small band into a sophisticated international organization that claimed one hundred thousand members at the time of her death in 1910.

Sources:

Stephen Gottschalk, *The Emergence of Christian Science in American Religious Life* (Berkeley: University of California Press, 1973);

Robert Peel, *Mary Baker Eddy: The Years of Discovery* (New York: Holt, Rinehart & Winston, 1996);

The Female Almshouse on Blackwell's Island, New York, circa 1885–1890, at which Protestant clergymen aggressively attempted to convert the predominantly Irish Catholic inmates

Peel, *Mary Baker Eddy: The Years of Trial* (New York: Holt, Rinehart & Winston, 1971).

CONSERVATIVE PROTESTANTISM

Inerrancy. Liberal Protestants committed to progressive orthodoxy came into increasingly open conflict with the dominant conservative theological system of the day, a form of Calvinism that stressed the binding nature of creeds and the inerrancy and infallibility of Scripture. The center of conservative orthodoxy in late-nineteenth-century America was Princeton Theological Seminary, where Calvinist faculty had been building a sharply focused and unyielding school of theology for several decades. The Princeton faculty, who viewed the early-nineteenth-century theologian Archibald Alexander Charles Hodge as the founder and chief inspiration of their school, defended a series of propositions that they believed expressed the historic teachings of Protestantism. Princeton theology focused on two key matters, the centrality and permanence of doctrinal statements and the inerrancy of Scripture. While liberals increasingly viewed creedal statements as limited, imperfect, and transient documents, Princeton conservatives stressed that truth could be captured in precisely stated propositions, expressed in written language that could, in turn, convey the same message at all times. For American Calvinists, the most authoritative written summary of Christian doctrine had been the Westminster Confession of 1648, a creedal statement that Princeton theologians insisted would always remain the governing expression of Calvinist belief. Conservatives rejected the liberal claim that doctrines must be restated in different eras to express God's continuing revelation and to reflect the interests and the growing intellectual sophistication of humanity. Hodge's proudest boast was that "a new idea had never originated" at Princeton Theological Seminary. The conservative insistence on the inerrancy of Scripture, while it upheld longstanding Protestant ideas, also contained important elements of distinctly nineteenth-century thinking. Since the Protestant Reformation of the sixteenth century, virtually all

With each religious sect advertising its own special road to salvation, camp meetings served an important role in the indoctrination of the laity. Gatherings of the faithful became even more popular with the post–Civil War moral slump and the rising tide of skepticism. Rural areas featured most of the camp meetings, which lasted on an average of seven to ten days. All services were held in a large tent, or "brush arbor." Families camped around the tent and lived out of their wagons or lean-tos. The day began at 6 A.M. with a prayer meeting; breakfast followed, and then the morning sermon. The afternoon was free for people to visit and to do camp chores. In the evening the big service occurred, with three or four ministers speaking in rotation. The service usually ended with the call for repentance and the walk to the mourner's bench by those seeking salvation. In towns, camp meetings were known as annual revivals, or "protracted" meetings. Stores closed, and farmers came into town to hear the visiting evangelist and song leader. Services frequently lasted all day, with dinner being served to the listeners. In both the camp meeting and annual revival it was common for the audience to become supercharged with emotion and to shout and speak in unknown tongues.

Source: John Samuel Ezell, *The South Since 1865* (New York: Macmillan, 1963), p. 347.

Protestants had held that the Bible was true and that most passages were meant to be interpreted literally. The American Calvinist defense of biblical inerrancy developed early in the nineteenth century but espoused a more aggressive and unequivocal doctrine that advanced the claim that *every* statement in the Scriptures was a statement of literal, scientific fact. Hodge, for example, asserted in the early 1870s that the Bible was "a storehouse of facts."

Modern Science. Before the publication of Charles Darwin's *On the Origin of Species* in 1859, few American Protestants, including the Princeton theologians, had found much conflict between scientific and religious truth. Most simply assumed that Christian faith, the human intellect, and science were harmonious. By the 1880s, however, most theological liberals had accepted Darwin's evolutionary theory (with its implied rejection of the biblical story of creation as told in Genesis) and increasingly regarded the Bible as a collection of religious and ethical teachings, not as a uniform volume of historical and scientific facts. The inerrantists, however, refused to accommodate modern science. In 1881 Hodge and Benjamin Warfield published a critical essay called "Inspiration," which reemphasized the absolute trustworthiness of the plain reading of Scripture and asked Christians to stand on the unshakable ground of a Bible that was literally true in every detail. In Presbyterianism, in particular, the inerrantists reasserted their dominance in the 1890s, and the Princeton formulation of inerrancy became a major component of the theological outlook of twentieth-century fundamentalism.

Heresy. As the conservative reaction against liberal innovations grew in strength, accusations of heresy cropped up in most Protestant denominations, although controversy centered on northern groups, particularly the Presbyterian Church. Formal church proceedings against liberal ministers, theologians, and biblical scholars on seminary faculties started in the late 1870s and peaked in the 1890s. In 1878 Alexander Winchell was forced from the faculty of Vanderbilt University after being accused of contradicting the biblical account of creation in Genesis. Winchell refused to resign, so the university's trustees simply abolished his position. The next year Crawford H. Toy was forced to resign from the Southern Baptist Theological Seminary in Louisville after he was charged with undercutting the absolute authority of Scripture. The hottest disputation occurred, however, within the denominations most clearly committed to the Calvinist tradition: Congregationalism and Presbyterianism. In the late 1880s the Board of Overseers of Andover Theological Seminary, Massachusetts, the oldest American seminary and the most prestigious Congregational training facility for ministers, grew increasing disenchanted with the faculty, which had developed and popularized progressive orthodoxy. The board accused Egbert Smythe and three others of failing to keep their promise to teach within the boundaries of the seminary's creedal statement of 1808. The four men were dismissed from the faculty, but in 1892 the Massachusetts Supreme Court ruled against the board and reinstated the professors.

Presbyterians. Conservative critics, however, were much more successful within the Presbyterian Church, where three prominent theologians were accused of heresy. The Presbyterian General Assembly's decision in 1893 to overturn Charles Augustus Briggs's acquittal by the Presbytery of New York and to suspend Briggs from the Presbyterian ministry was the most famous heresy action of the period. The next year Henry Preserved Smith of Lane Presbyterian Seminary in Cincinnati was convicted of charges similar to those laid against Briggs and was dismissed. In 1896 the church historian Arthur Cushman McGiffert of Union Theological Seminary, New York, resigned from the Presbyterian ministry rather than contest heresy charges against him. While the influence of theological liberalism continued to grow in the 1890s, the heresy trials were a powerful symptom of conservative reaction, and they accelerated the process of polarization that would lead to more clear and decisive

Group of boys in front of the Children's Aid Society in New York City,
circa 1890

divisions within Protestantism in the early decades of the twentieth century.

Sources:

William R. Hutchison, *The Modernist Impulse in American Protestantism* (New York: Oxford University Press, 1976);

George M. Marsden, *Fundamentalism and American Culture: The Shaping of Twentieth Century Evangelicalism, 1870–1925* (New York: Oxford University Press, 1980);

Mark Stephen Massa, *Charles Augustus Briggs and the Crisis of Historical Criticism* (Minneapolis: Fortress Press, 1990);

Jack B. Rogers and Donald K. McKim, *The Authority and Interpretation of Scripture* (San Francisco: Harper & Row, 1970).

EVANGELICAL RESPONSES TO THE CITY

Salvation Army. Religious liberals held no monopoly on concern for the poor in the swelling industrial cities. Missions and voluntary societies that focused on individual conversion were extremely active in late-nineteenth-century urban centers. Among the most distinctive and comprehensive of these groups was the Salvation Army, which was introduced by its English founders to the United States in 1880. Its military style of organization and aggressive approach were unfamiliar at first in the United States, but by 1890 the Salvation Army was an accepted and increasingly visible presence in urban life. The Army was founded in London in 1865 by the Methodist preachers William and Catherine Booth. The Booths wanted to carry evangelism into the streets, and they developed a colorful and entertaining style of ministry that included bombarding poor neighborhoods with brass bands, preachers, and "Hallelujah Lasses" (female evangelists). The group adopted its military name and style of organization in 1878. Its primary religious focus was on converting individuals to faith in Jesus Christ and then guiding them through the experience of sanctification. While the Army's theological focus was individual and not social, it shared many of the techniques and theories used in emerging liberal movements. The Booths believed that acts of social relief symbolized the New Testament's command to believers to care for the poor in Jesus' name and demonstrated the sincerity with which the Salvationists regarded both the spiritual and social aspects of Christianity. The Army sought to provide the poor with at least the three things the Booths believed even a cart horse had a right to expect: "shelter for the night, food for its stomach, [and] work allotted to it by which it can earn its own corn." Aside from rescue missions, the Army's programs included legal assistance,

Arapaho braves resting during a Ghost Dance ceremony, circa 1890

nurseries, visiting nurses, and educational and job-training programs.

Social Gospel. The Social Gospel movement emerged from evangelical Protestant attempts to address the poverty and confusion of the nation's growing industrial cities. Although the movement did not take clear shape until the twentieth century, its stirrings were discernible in the late 1870s. Adherents of the movement worked to apply Christian principles to the new circumstances of life in a fast-paced, impersonal, industrial order. They tended to shift theological emphasis from the salvation of individual sinners to an imperative that stressed love of neighbor and the communal nature of salvation. Socially oriented theologians, such as Walter Rauschenbusch of Rochester Seminary, argued that the church needed to rouse itself and reverse "the spiritual domination of the commercial and professional classes." The economist Richard Ely summarized the dominant liberal side of the Social Gospel message this way in 1899:

> Christianity is primarily concerned with this world and it is the mission of Christianity to bring to pass here a kingdom of righteousness and to rescue from the evil one and redeem all our social relations. . . . The 'Church militant' is something more than a phrase, or the Church itself is a mockery. . . . It means a never-ceasing attack on every wrong institution, until the earth become a new earth, and all its cities of God. It is as truly a religious work to pass good laws, as it is to preach sermons; as holy a work to lead a crusade against filth, vice and disease in slums of cities, and to seek the abolition of the disgraceful tenement-houses of American cities, as it is to send missionaries to the heathen. Even to hoe potatoes and plant corn ought to be regarded, and must be regarded by true Christians as religious acts; and all legislators, magistrates, and governors are as truly ministers of God's Church as any bishop or archbishop.

Sources:

Richard T. Ely, *Social Aspects of Christianity* (New York: Crowell, 1899);

George M. Marsden, *Fundamentalism and American Culture: The Shaping of Twentieth Century American Evangelicalism, 1870–1925* (New York: Oxford University Press, 1980);

Norman H. Murdoch, *Origins of the Salvation Army* (Knoxville: University of Tennessee Press, 1995).

THE GHOST DANCE

Wovoka. Spreading rapidly from it origins among the Northern Paiutes of Nevada, the Ghost Dance became the major pan-Indian religious movement of the late nineteenth century. The movement was based on responses to visions recounted by a Paiute holy man named Wovoka, who claimed to have inherited his father's powers as a dreamer. Wovoka's visions, which promised an imminent end to the world to be followed by a renewal of life for Indians in a lush and plentiful land, struck a powerful chord among Plains Indians traumatized by white expansion and yearning for a restoration of their traditional and independent life. As a child, Wovoka learned from his father both the traditional Paiute creation story, which emphasized the renewal of human life and a blooming of the desert, and the teachings of other Indian spiritual leaders, perhaps including the Squaxin prophet John Slocum. Wovoka experienced other visions, including being taken into heaven, and he claimed miraculous powers, such as the ability to predict and control the weather. His health was seriously affected by scarlet fever until he made a dramatic recovery on 1 January 1889, a day that coincided with a total eclipse. The prophet announced that he had had a vision in which he had talked with the Great Spirit. During the vision Wovoka had seen the dead of his tribe in a pleasant land, looking youthful and living according to Paiute traditions. The Great Spirit promised Wovoka that the world would be renewed—the dead would rise again, and game would be restored in plenty. In turn, Wovoka was asked to prepare his people to love one another, to avoid war with the whites and fights among themselves, and to be ethical and diligent. The Great Spirit then gave the Paiutes a dance that would hasten the time of the renewal of the world and put families in touch with their dead relatives. The people were to perform the dance, which was similar to a traditional Paiute round dance, each month for four consecutive nights and on the morning of the fifth day.

Word Spreads. Reports of the vision spread rapidly among the Indians of the West, many of whom were starved of hope. Most Plains and West Coast Indians sent representatives to Nevada, and many delegates returned as initiates into the Ghost Dance. The Ghost Dance fit closely into the context of traditional Paiute religion, opening the people to spiritual influence and enabling dancers to share in Wovoka's vision. The movement offered a powerfully attractive alternative to the religious options offered by white missionaries. The dance and its promise of Indian revival appealed powerfully to many Indian groups, even though few of them shared in the specific religious worldview of the Paiutes. Ghost Dance teachers, therefore, had to select elements from Wovoka's teaching that could be connected to their own spiritual traditions.

Lakota. Among the Lakota people, who were still seeking to resist white control, the Ghost Dance recalled the tribe's Sun Dance ritual, which had been suppressed by whites in 1883. The Lakota viewed the Sun Dance as an essential rite of purification that led to the annual return of the buffalo, the main source of food on the Plains. Many Lakota also believed that the Ghost Dance would make them invincible against whites, providing them with magic talismans, such as "ghost shirts," which would stop army bullets. The movement aroused fear among whites, and then persecution. The conflict peaked in late 1890. On 15 December Sitting Bull, a Lakota leader of the movement, was killed in a scuffle with Indian police. Fourteen days later a band of about two hundred Lakota practitioners under the leadership of Big Foot was massacred by federal troops at Wounded Knee in South Dakota. After the massacre at Wounded Knee Wovoka urged Indians to stop the dancing and attend to the pacifist message of his original vision. The movement did subside, but some groups carried on the dance well into the twentieth century.

Sources:

Alice Beck Kehoe, *The Ghost Dance: Ethnohistory and Revitalization* (New York: Holt, Rinehart & Winston, 1989);

James Mooney, *The Ghost-Dance Religion and the Sioux Outbreak of 1890* (Chicago: University of Chicago Press, 1965).

THE GOSPEL OF WEALTH

Working Hard. Industrialization created amazing disparities between rich and poor in the United States, and the rapid pace of change concerned many American Protestants. One early, but prominent, stream of Protestant reaction emphasized acquiescence to the social consequences of industrialization. Many regarded this tendency as an unexpected result of the growing liberal practice of loosening the doctrinal restrictions that had bound preceding generations. Prominent liberal Protestant clergymen followed the lead of Henry Ward Beecher in blessing the new industrial order. Protestantism carried over from the eighteenth century the Calvinistic belief that God created the world with an intrinsic system of rewards and punishments. Under the divine scheme, those who worked and lived ethically prospered, while the lazy or irresponsible poor suffered deservedly from poverty. Beecher insisted that "even in the most compact and closely-populated portions of the East, he that will be frugal and save continuously, living every day within the bounds of his means, can scarcely help accumulating." This doctrine made sense to middle-class Protestants, who were prospering as a group, but it ignored the reality that the wages of most working-class families fell far short of sufficiency. In the view of the emerging Protestant middle class and elite, the key to both success and holiness was for individuals to help themselves. This strong cultural preference often led to the assumption that wealth was a sign of spiritual attainment. As William Lawrence, an Episcopal bishop, put it, "Godliness is in league with riches." This was comforting news to the Protestant elite as they sat in the pews of the magnificent new urban churches and listened to sermons by Beecher and other "princes of the pulpit."

Opportunity. The reverence for worldly success was widely accepted outside the boundaries of the new industrial elite, in part because it resonated so strongly with values inherited from an earlier period of American history. The Baptist minister Russell Conwell emerged as a celebrated proponent of the gospel of opportunity. Conwell delivered his famous sermon, "Acres of Diamonds," an estimated six thousand times to audiences estimated at thirteen million in the closing decades of the century. The sermon recounted the allegedly factual case of a farmer who lived in destitution until he began to work his land conscientiously. In the course of plowing vigorously, the farmer discovered "acres of diamonds" on the land. Conwell rejected suggestions that pursuit of wealth was spiritually corrupting. "To make money honestly is to preach the gospel," he claimed. In modern America, he asserted, any upright and hardworking individual could discover success "in his own backyard."

Responsibility. Conwell and others in the tradition also emphasized honesty, charity, and civic responsibility. Because of his vast wealth and willingness to write and speak publicly about his moral, economic, and political ideas, the steel magnate Andrew Carnegie was one of the best-known religious skeptics of the era. In 1889 he wrote a book called *The Gospel of Wealth*, which espoused Conwell's beliefs. (A British editor writing a headline for Carnegie's 1889 essay titled "Wealth" actually coined the phrase "Gospel of Wealth.") Carnegie believed in the central moral and economic role of moneymaking: "Don't shoot the millionaire, for he is the bee that makes the honey." He stressed, however, that the rich had both the moral right to complete control of their wealth and a moral obligation to use their wealth for the public good. "This then is the duty of the man of wealth," Carnegie wrote, "to set an example of modest, unostentatious living, shunning display or extravagance; to provide moderately for the legitimate wants of those dependent on him; and after doing so, to consider all surplus revenues which come to him simply as trust funds, which he is called upon to administer, and strictly bound as a matter of duty to administer in the manner which, in his judgment, is best calculated to produce the most beneficial results for the community." As American industry expanded, however, the individualistic Protestant ethic supporting unrestrained expansion to maximize profits tended to overwhelm such moral restraints. In practice, this approach meant that many Protestants absolved the economic sphere of life from the moral and religious constraints they still sought to apply to personal relationships.

Sources:

Agnes Rush Burr, *Russell H. Conwell and His Work: One Man's Interpretation of Life* (Philadelphia: Winston, 1926);

Joseph Frazier Wall, *The Andrew Carnegie Reader* (Pittsburgh: University of Pittsburgh Press, 1992).

LIBERAL PROTESTANTISM

A New Approach. The most dramatic and fastest-growing intellectual movement of the late nineteenth century originated as a response to two European trends: the rise of evolutionary science and the development of biblical criticism. By the early 1870s a section of American Protestant leadership was beginning to advocate the reconstruction of Christian theology in response to the rapid changes and developments of the period. Several key factors played a role. One of the most important was the overpowering sense of progress and liberation felt by many people as the nineteenth century closed. Progress seemed more and more inevitable as science and technology were harnessed to solve ancient problems. Some people even thought that humanity was evolving into the millennial Kingdom of God. Adaptation was the watchword. As early as 1871 Henry Ward Beecher, the most famous American minister of the period, warned divinity students at Yale Theological Seminary that the Protestant ministry was "in danger, and in great danger, of going under, and of working effectively only among the relatively less informed and intelligent of the community; of being borne with, in a kind of contemptuous charity, or altogether neglected, by the men of culture who have been strongly developed on their moral side—not their moral side as connected with revealed religion, but as connected with human knowledge and worldly wisdom."

IN THE HOUSE OF THE LORD

One of the most significant and permanent social changes that occurred in the South after 1878 was the establishment of separate African American churches and the growth of independent black denominational organizations. The most important denominations with African American membership were the Baptist, African Methodist Episcopal, African Methodist Episcopal Zion, Colored Methodist Episcopal, Reformed Episcopal, Presbyterian, and Protestant Episcopal. By 1900 the Baptists outnumbered all other black denominations combined. The typical African American church was a small, unpainted or whitewashed wooden structure. Its interior was sparse, with a few wooden benches and a homemade pulpit. The cemetery flanked the building and had either wooden boards or small stone markers. In contrast to the drab appearance of the church, its services were lively and enthusiastic, featuring participation of the congregation in songs, prayers, and sermons. Preachers focused on sin, the Devil, loose sex, and drink. The Reverend Alexander Bettis said that "excitement, shouting, and hallelujahs" were a regular part of his services. A white observer in 1898 noted that black congregations would "sing and shout, and dance the holy dance, and jump over the benches, and have a regular jubilee time."

Source: George Brown Tindall, *South Carolina Negroes 1877–1900* (Columbia: University of South Carolina Press, 1952).

Staying with the Times. One of the most basic traits of the emerging liberal movement in theology was its willingness to concede the accuracy of Charles Darwin's principle of evolution that only the fittest survive. Liberals began to stress that Christians throughout history had to address the conditions and realities of their own time. They conceded that the Bible and the historic Christian creeds were cast in the language and worldview of their times and had to be interpreted critically in that light. The purpose of modern theology was to excavate below relative truths in order to discover what was pure, true, and eternal. Theological "orthodoxy, so far as man is concerned, is relative and defective; it is measured by the knowledge he has of the truth," the leading liberal theologian and Old Testament scholar Charles Augustus Briggs wrote in 1889. "It varies in different men, in different nations and societies, and still more in different epochs of time."

German Tradition. The chief centers of the liberal movement in theology were the nation's Protestant seminaries, seats of learning where the complex developments of the higher critical movement in scriptural studies could take hold. Many professors were recent gradu-

Temple Emanuel, the oldest Reform synagogue in New York City, in 1896

ates of German universities, known throughout the world for both the rigorous academic study of religion and their theological liberalism. The Congregational theologian Newman Smythe, for example, had studied at the universities of Berlin and Halle in the late 1860s and early 1870s. Smythe was deeply influenced by the teaching of Isaak Dorner, whose ideas about the development of Christian doctrine made historical criticism one of the foundations for theological discussion. Like many thinkers influenced by evolutionary thought, Dorner argued that religious truth evolved over centuries and that knowledge of God was possible through the scientific study of historical records.

Beliefs. Although the liberal Protestantism of the late nineteenth century was far from uniform, liberals as a group shared basic beliefs. Perhaps the most significant belief was the need to modify the insistence on Scripture as the sole source of Protestant religious authority and teaching. "The sacred Scriptures do not decide for us all questions of orthodoxy," Briggs argued.

> They do not answer the problems of science, of philosophy or history. They do not cover the whole ground of theology. There are important matters in which the

Christian religion enters into the spheres of science, philosophy, and history where the divine revelation given in these departments of knowledge is either presupposed by the sacred Scriptures, or else has been left by them for mankind to investigate and use in successive constructions of Christian theology, which have gone on since the apostolic age and which will continue until the end of the world.

Liberals also rejected biblical literalism and embraced scientific tools of investigation. They put considerable faith in human ability, rejecting the inherited Calvinist insistence on humanity's sinfulness and depravity. Few believed that a loving God would damn anyone to eternal punishment. Liberals typically portrayed sin as a limitation or error that might be remedied by education and, most of all, by the moral example of the life of Jesus. While few liberals of this period denied the divinity of Christ, many of them virtually ignored it in favor of an emphasis on Christ's accomplishments as the man who best revealed God's will for humanity. They preferred titles like "Master" or "Teacher" when speaking of Christ. For them the most important aspect of God's activity was his immanence, or involvement in the world, not the majestic, judgmental transcendence emphasized by Calvinism. Ethics emerged as the central theological concern. Liberals, especially those who stressed the historical continuity of Christian doctrinal and institutional experience, insisted that Christianity had to meet the challenge of demonstrating that it was true by the standards of its own day. Most Gilded Age liberals aimed to adapt Christian doctrine, but to do so as little as possible and with as strong a sense of the historical experience of the church as possible. Captured in the phrase "progressive orthodoxy," this group formed the liberal mainstream, and its optimism attracted an enormous popular following. A smaller group, often described as modernists, took an uncompromising stand on modern science and culture. They took the scientific method, scholarly detachment, empirical reasoning, and the prevailing philosophical skepticism of the day as their necessary starting point. The most advanced of them viewed the Bible as only one of many human religious documents and Christianity as one religious and ethical tradition among many.

Sources:

Sydney Ahlstrom, *Theology in America: The Major Protestant Voices from Puritanism to Neoorthodoxy* (Indianapolis: Bobbs-Merrill, 1967);

William R. Hutchison, *American Protestant Thought in the Liberal Era* (Lanham, Md.: University Press of America, 1981).

REFORM JUDAISM

Origins. Reform Judaism emerged from the experience of European Jews and made its first major impact in the United States when German immigrants began to arrive in the mid 1840s. The tiny American Jewish population of the time identified with traditional Judaism, but it had little trained leadership and scant contact with European Jewry. Demands for reform accelerated as

German Jewish immigrants began to form new synagogues all across the country. At the heart of the movement was an emphasis on rationality and the moral aspects of religion and a deemphasis on the supernatural and inherited ritual. Two major figures dominated the Reform movement, Rabbi Isaac Mayer Wise and Rabbi David Einhorn. Wise was the movement's main organizer, while Einhorn was its radical theoretician. Wise's agenda for reform focused on those dietary restrictions and ritual practices that visibly set Jews apart from their neighbors. Judaism, he wrote, did not center "on victuals," but rather "in fear of the Lord and the love of many in harmony with the dicta of reason." He argued that Judaism should be trimmed of layers of outdated law and ritual, leaving "only such observances and practices which might and should become universal because they would be beneficial to all men." His prayer book, *Minhag America* (translated as *American Ritual*), published initially in 1857, abbreviated many of the prayers for the daily and Sabbath services and eliminated others entirely.

Radical Reform. Einhorn, who never felt at home in America, was largely responsible for formulating the distinctive central currents in Reform thought. Einhorn argued for a radical restructuring of Jewish life and thought. His goal, like that of many religious radicals at midcentury, was to locate and preserve the eternal essence of Judaism and to purge all that was "temporary," by which he meant the traditional Jewish ritual obligations that had developed at particular times and places in the past. Einhorn also argued that Judaism was a religion, a pure and ethical faith in monotheism, and not an ethnic identity. Jews were not a distinct or chosen people; instead they were distinguished by their mission as the bearers of a newly clarified religious goal, "to lead the nations to the true knowledge and worship of God." Einhorn was the moving spirit behind a document produced in 1869 by a group of rabbis meeting in Philadelphia, Pennsylvania, which produced the first explicit group statement of Reform ideas. By 1880 perhaps only a dozen of the two hundred of the largest American Jewish congregations had refused to adopt Reform ritual and doctrine.

The Pittsburgh Platform. The liberal theological platform of Reform Judaism was refined in 1885 at a meeting of fifteen rabbis in Pittsburgh, Pennsylvania. The "Pittsburgh Platform," which Wise called "The Jewish Declaration of Independence," advocated for the rejection of a sweeping array of elements of Mosaic law and ritual judged "not in keeping with the views and habits of modern civilization." Organized by Rabbi Kaufmann Kohler of New York, who drafted the manifesto, the meeting culminated several decades of disputation about how to modernize traditional Judaism. The platform's ideology reflected the intellectual leadership of Kohler's late father-in-law, Einhorn. It asserted that Judaism was "a progressive religion, ever striving to be in accord with

NO JEWS ALLOWED

Anti-Semitism was deeply rooted in the attitudes of most European Christians, but the Jewish population of the United States was so small that overt anti-Semitism was far less common than anti-Catholicism or antiblack sentiments. It did exist, however, and in many states Jews could not exercise full citizenship rights until the second half of the nineteenth century. Well into the century many New England states carried colonial-era laws on their statute books that forbade non-Christians from holding office or conducting public worship. These laws, however, were often not enforced. Between the 1840s and 1880s the small American Jewish community was largely composed of German immigrants, and there was a large overlap in social and cultural life between German Jews and Christians. Anti-Semitism never developed into the sort of passionate mass political and cultural movements that took energy from anti-Catholicism. As the Jewish community began to grow and to become more visible in the 1880s, the easy acceptance of Jews by members of the American upper class, which had characterized most of the century, began to harden. Rabbi Gustav Gottheil of Temple Emanu-El in New York complained that in the 1880s "private schools began to be closed to Jewish children. . . . Advertisements of summer hotels, refusing admittance to Jewish guests, commenced to appear in the newspapers." By the 1890s restrictions and quotas on Jewish participation were common in institutions that served the Protestant upper class. They were especially strong in the schools, colleges, and universities that served the children of the American elite. Among poorer Jewish immigrants anti-Semitism was more likely to be experienced as intense competition among immigrant groups and on the borders of ethnic neighborhoods.

Source: Nathan Glazer, *American Judaism* (Chicago: University of Chicago Press, 1972).

the postulates of reason." The central purpose of the religion, the rabbis argued, was spiritual elevation—a process that they stated was no longer served by adherence to "such Mosaic and Rabbinic laws as regulated diet, priestly purity, and dress." These outmoded customs should be eliminated, the platform stressed, because "they fail to impress the modern Jew with a spirit of priestly holiness." One particularly momentous change was the platform's decisive assertion that Judaism is a religion and not an expression of "national" character. Judaism, the platform asserted, was "no longer a nation, but a religious community, and therefore expects neither a return to Palestine, nor sacrificial worship under the sons of Aaron, nor the restoration of any of the laws concerning the Jewish state." The document was the most radical produced by the Reform movement. In Pittsburgh discussion about adaptation to American life ran so far as to weigh the advisability of moving the Sabbath to Sunday to conform to the larger society's patterns. In 1889 the Pittsburgh Platform served as the founding document of the Central Conference of American Rabbis, the denominational organization that still gives institutional shape to Reform Judaism in America.

Shrimp Cocktail. The first significant attempt to reverse the tide of Reform Judaism came in 1883, after a banquet held to honor the first graduates of the Hebrew Union College in Cincinnati, Ohio. The school was intended to train religious leaders for the entire Jewish community, which at that point seemed to be converging unanimously toward Reform. Guests from across the nation attended the banquet, including many who observed traditional Mosaic dietary laws. The seminary had hired a Jewish caterer, but when the first course was served, waiters brought shrimp cocktail to the tables. As shellfish, shrimp is considered ritually unclean, or *terefa*. Several guests raced from the room, and the "terefa banquet" became the center of a long controversy in the Jewish press. The publication of the Pittsburgh Platform of 1885 underlined the break of the Reform movement with Mosaic law even more clearly. Conservatives gathered around Rabbi Sabato Morais of Philadelphia, who founded the Jewish Theological Seminary Association in 1885 to represent Jews "faithful to Mosaic Law and ancestral tradition." The seminary, and the Conservative movement that would grow up around it, did not, however, flourish immediately. It was only the emigration of hundreds of thousands of observant Jews from eastern Europe, which began at full force in the late 1880s, that led to strong institutional responses to Reform Judaism and facilitated the spread of conservative theology. In 1896 the first major Orthodox yeshiva, or school for rabbinical studies, the Rabbi Isaac Elchanan Theological Seminary, opened in New York. In 1898 the Union of Orthodox Jewish Congregations was formed and began to organize the rapidly growing Orthodox synagogue movement.

Sources:

Joseph L. Blau, *Judaism in America* (Chicago: University of Chicago Press, 1976);

Nathan Glazer, *American Judaism* (Chicago: University of Chicago Press, 1972);

Howard M. Sachar, *A History of the Jews in America* (New York: Knopf, 1992);

Jonathan D. Sarna, ed., *The American Jewish Experience* (New York: Holmes & Meier, 1986).

SKEPTICISM

Ingersoll. As modern scientific thought percolated through American society, religious belief became genuinely optional for the first time in American history. Before 1878 religious skepticism made little impact on American life. Under the influence of both Darwinian biology and popular evolutionary thought, however, it became possible for Americans to reject religion forthrightly without negative consequences in genteel society. One popular strain of the new agnosticism (a belief that neither accepts nor denies the existence of God) moved beyond religion in the name of higher moral evolution. Robert Green Ingersoll, whom one admirer called "the Dwight L. Moody of Free Religion," was loosely associated with this movement. In a public career that spanned the closing decades of the nineteenth century, Ingersoll traveled the country promoting agnosticism as a morally superior replacement to conventional Christianity and attacking the hypocrisy of organized religion. A veteran of the Civil War and an accomplished trial lawyer, Ingersoll was a well-known figure in Republican politics. On the lecture circuit Ingersoll caused waves of sensation by forthrightly attacking the clergy and comparing organized religion to the institution of slavery. He described agnosticism as mental abolitionism. Ingersoll emphasized modern science, which he viewed as a surer form of faith in the modern world. He advocated reliance on rational science, the irresistible nature of human progress, and the potential for human moral perfection with the fervor of an itinerant evangelist. He looked forward to a day when organized religion would wither away. "Humanity is the sky, and these religions and dogmas and theories are but mists and clouds continually changing, destined finally to melt away," he wrote.

Other Skeptics. To the rage of Protestant leaders, Ingersoll successfully presented agnosticism in a socially impeccable and conventional form. Religious skepticism was also increasingly common among the growing group of university-educated Americans and became the norm among scientists. A few American intellectuals went so far as to portray the relationship between science and religion in military terms. Andrew White, the first president of Cornell University, captured this spirit in the title of his polemical work published in 1896, *The History of the Warfare of Science with Theology in Christendom*. William Graham Sumner of Yale University, a prominent social Darwinist, was also a critic of organized religion. More representative of the trend of university thought about religion was the philosopher John Dewey, who abandoned Christianity in the 1890s. Dewey grounded his search for meaning on naturalistic and evolutionary principles. He came to view abstract questions about God or the nature of ultimate reality as unanswerable and therefore futile. As a result, he built a philosophical system based on the confidence that science can observe and describe how the human mind and society work.

Feminist Skepticism. Feminist leaders also advanced arguments critical of institutional religion. Elizabeth Cady Stanton, one of the leaders of the women's suffrage movement in the United States, came to view Christianity as an instrument of female enslavement. She organized and edited the controversial *Woman's Bible,* which was published in two volumes in 1895 and 1898. The volumes focused criticism on biblical passages in both Hebrew and Christian Scriptures in which women figure. Stanton and her collaborators criticized what they regarded as the degradation of women in key biblical texts and offered alternative readings of some passages that affirmed women and their equality. Stanton recruited women scholars with advanced training in the historical-critical methods, and the book was well informed about the most advanced biblical scholarship. But although Stanton endorsed the tools of modern biblical criticism, she was chiefly interested in using them to undermine American popular values and social conventions that rooted the restriction of women in the sacred texts of the Bible. The project led Stanton to deny the divine inspiration of the Hebrew and Christian Scriptures on the grounds that God would not inspire inequality. Like many women of her social class and Protestant background, Stanton looked more favorably on the Spiritualist movement, a belief that the spirit is a prime element of reality and that the dead can communicate with the living through a medium.

Sources:

David R. Anderson, *Robert Ingersoll* (Boston: Twayne, 1972);

Carol A. Newsome and Sharon H. Ringe, eds., *The Women's Bible Commentary* (Louisville, Ky.: Westminster/John Knox Press, 1992);

James Turner, *Without God, Without Creed: The Origins of Unbelief in America* (Baltimore: Johns Hopkins University Press, 1985).

WORLD'S PARLIAMENT OF RELIGIONS

Gathering. The liberal religious temper of the 1880s and early 1890s was reflected in a meeting of the leaders of all the world's major religions at the World's Columbian Exposition in Chicago. The World's Parliament of Religions was inspired by Charles C. Bonney, a Chicago attorney, and organized by John Henry Barrows, pastor of Chicago's First Presbyterian Church. They promoted the event as an unparalleled opportunity for ecumenical discussion, and it attracted hundreds of delegates and thousands of observers to solemn meetings in the "White City" fairgrounds during September 1893. Many Christian religious groups were represented, as were small but unprecedented delegations of Hindus, Buddhists, Muslims, Zoroastrians, Shintoists, Confucians, Taoists, and Jains.

Impact. The parliament was an essentially liberal project—conservative Protestants, Catholics, and Orthodox Jews all objected vigorously to a meeting that seemed to place all religions on an equal plane. Indeed, the conference's motto, "Have we not all one Father? Hath not one God created us?," did suggest the movement of liberal Protestantism toward broad toleration of non-Christian religious groups. Discussion at the parliament tended to focus on the commonalities, rather than the differences, between the world's religions, which tended to reinforce the notion of the equality, or at least the broadly shared fundamental character of world religions. Barrows and other Protestant organizers simply assumed that open discussion would show that Christianity was the most highly evolved of all the world's religions and that other religions were evolving toward the spiritual and ethical norms of liberal Protestantism. In fact, the event served largely to highlight and lend legitimacy to non-Christian religion. The parliament attracted several charismatic and well-trained spokesman for Asian religions, who were the first representatives of these traditions ever to speak before American audiences. As an unintended consequence the parliament produced several celebrities, most notably the Hindu reformer Swami Vivekenanda and the Buddhist Angarika Dharmapala, both of whom lectured widely in the United States after the parliament and established convert groups.

Sources:

Richard H. Seager, *The World's Parliament of Religions: The East/West Encounter* (Bloomington: Indiana University Press, 1994);

Thomas Tweed, *The American Encounter with Buddhism, 1844–1912: Victorian Culture and the Limits of Dissent* (Bloomington: Indiana University Press, 1992).

HEADLINE MAKERS

CHARLES AUGUSTUS BRIGGS

1841-1913
BIBLICAL SCHOLAR

A Modernist Champion. Charles Augustus Briggs was a Presbyterian minister and seminary professor who was among the first Americans to master historical-critical approaches to Scripture. He placed himself at the center of the struggles that led to the polarization of mainline and fundamentalist Protestants. His 1893 trial for heresy, perhaps the most celebrated in the history of the United States, revealed the depth of division between liberals and conservatives in the nation's dominant Protestant religious tradition. For almost four decades Briggs was an Old Testament scholar of international stature and an intellectual leader at Union Theological Seminary, the leading center of liberal scholarship.

Education. The son of a barrel maker, Briggs was born in New York City on 15 January 1841. He graduated from the University of Virginia, where he was converted during a college revival and decided to enter the Presbyterian ministry. He was studying for the ministry when the Civil War broke out in April 1861; he answered President Abraham Lincoln's call for ninety-day volunteers and joined the Seventh New York Regiment. Briggs returned to New York from military service in the summer of 1861 and entered Union Theological Seminary, where he studied until 1863. After working for several years in the family business while his father was ill, Briggs traveled to Germany, where he enrolled as a graduate student in Old Testament and theology at the University of Berlin.

Scientific Study. Briggs was among the first generation of Americans to receive an advanced graduate education in Germany, where universities used the emerging scientific mode of teaching. At Berlin, Briggs worked to develop a scientific approach to biblical scholarship, one driven by the open and fearless search for truthful interpretation of Scripture. This search, he argued, should not be governed by inherited doctrine but through the use of linguistic, historical, and archaeological tools. In 1869 Briggs returned to the United States and became pastor of the First Presbyterian Church in Roselle, New Jersey, where he served until 1874. He was then appointed professor of Hebrew at Union Theological Seminary in New York. The course of Briggs's career changed decisively in 1881, when he was appointed coeditor of a new scholarly journal, *The Presbyterian Review*. He worked with another editor, Archibald Alexander Charles Hodge of Princeton Theological Seminary, who upheld a vigorous and unyielding conservative position. The two men clashed, and the journal became an instrument of conflict within Presbyterianism.

Aggressive Liberal. Briggs's increasingly advanced views on scriptural interpretation caused friction with the literal view of the Bible espoused at Princeton. Throughout the 1880s Briggs produced scholarly articles attacking the Princeton schools and explaining the methods of scholarship emerging from German universities. In 1889 he published *Whither?*, which emphasized the evolution of divine revelation over time. The book argued that liberals were, in fact, far more orthodox, than conservatives. "The absolute standard of human orthodoxy is the sum of the total truth revealed by God—a sum which continued to grow and unfold in history," he argued. "Any man or church that refuses to accept the discoveries of science or the truths of philosophy or the facts of history or the new light that breaks forth from the Word of God to the devout student on the pretense that it conflicts with his orthodoxy or the orthodox standards of his church, prefers the traditions of man to the truth," Briggs wrote.

Heresy. In 1891 Briggs was promoted to a new endowed chair in biblical theology, and his inaugural lecture, "The Authority of Holy Scripture," was a conscious challenge to doctrinal conservatives. In the lecture Briggs rejected the nineteenth-century Presbyterian doctrine of God's verbal inspiration of the Bible and that the text of the Bible was inerrant. "We have to undermine the breastworks of traditionalism," he said in the lecture. "Let us blast them to atoms. We have forced our way through the obstructions; let us remove them from the face of the earth, that no man hereafter may be kept from the Bible." In response to this address, the Presbyterian General Assembly refused to approve Briggs's appointment at Union, and conservatives demanded that he be tried for heresy. He was acquitted by the Presbytery of New York in 1892, but the acquittal was reversed by the Presbyterian General Assembly, which suspended Briggs from the ministry in 1893. The seminary responded by severing its ties with the Presbyterian Church, and Briggs remained a leading faculty member for the rest of his life. He left the Presbyterian Church in 1898 and was ordained as an Episcopal priest the same year.

Ecumenism. As an Episcopalian Briggs remained controversial, although not in exactly the same ways he had been as a Presbyterian. His attention was shifting to the cause of ecumenism, or worldwide Christian unity and cooperation. In 1903 he called for the "re-catholicization" of Christianity, which many Protestants interpreted incorrectly as a prelude to Briggs's conversion to Roman Catholicism. Briggs's twentieth book, *Church Unity*, was published in 1909, just before his retirement from active teaching. He died in his rooms at Union Theological Seminary on 8 June 1913.

Sources:

Paul Carter, *The Spiritual Crisis of the Gilded Age* (DeKalb: Northern Illinois University Press, 1972);

Mark Stephen Massa, *Charles Augustus Briggs and the Crisis of Historical Criticism* (Minneapolis: Fortress Press, 1990).

JAMES GIBBONS

1834-1921

ROMAN CATHOLIC CARDINAL

Helmsman. The son of Irish immigrants, James Gibbons was the most visible and influential figure in American Catholicism during his sixty years as a clergyman. He guided the church through the tumultuous years of massive Catholic migration to the United States from 1880 to World War I. Gibbons's tact, diplomatic skill, and enthusiasm made him the most respected Catholic in the United States. While he did not always achieve his goals, he was an inspired liaison between Rome and Catholics in the United States. President Theodore Roosevelt praised him as "the most re-

spected and venerated and useful citizen of our country."

Early Life. James Gibbons was born in Baltimore on 23 July 1834, but because of his father's poor health the family returned to Ireland in 1837. (Gibbons's American birth would later be a mark of distinction that set him apart from the majority of his fellow Catholic bishops.) Gibbons returned to America with his mother in 1853, settling in New Orleans. The course of his life changed dramatically in January 1854, when he heard a mission sermon and discovered a calling for the priesthood. In 1855 he entered St. Charles College in Maryland and later continued his studies for the priesthood at St. Mary's Seminary in Baltimore. He was ordained on 30 June 1861 in Baltimore, a city divided by the Civil War. Gibbons served as a chaplain to Union troops stationed in the city and as pastor of a church with a congregation predominantly composed of Confederate sympathizers. He demonstrated great pastoral, organizational, and diplomatic skill in his first assignment as a priest. Archbishop Martin Spalding recognized his talents quickly and asked the young priest to serve as his secretary. Gibbons's first task was to coordinate preparations for the Second Plenary Council of American Catholic Bishops in Baltimore in 1866. As assistant chancellor of the council, he made many contacts with church leaders. When the papacy established the Vicariate Apostolic of North Carolina in 1868, Gibbons was named the first Catholic bishop of that state.

Catholic Apologist. The thirty-two-year-old Gibbons was the youngest bishop in the Catholic Church when he was consecrated on 16 August 1868. His diocese in North Carolina had fewer than seven hundred Catholics and only three priests. Nevertheless Gibbons demonstrated the talents that would make him a Catholic leader of the front rank: a capacity to mount articulate, forceful, and diplomatic defenses of Catholic teaching; an attitude of openness and warmth to non-Catholics; and a bedrock confidence that American political institutions were beneficial to church interests. In 1872 Gibbons became bishop of the diocese of Richmond. Once again he led a tiny Catholic population living in the midst of an overwhelmingly Protestant society. He drew on this experience while writing his most important published work, *The Faith of Our Fathers* (1877). A vigorous and engaging apologetic for Catholicism in America, the book became a best-seller among Catholics. (By the time of Gibbons's death two million copies were in circulation, and it had been translated into six foreign languages.) Gibbons's effective defense of the Catholic faith rapidly made him the most widely known spokesman for Catholicism in America.

Baltimore. The archdiocese of Baltimore was the senior Catholic diocese in the United States, and its bishop was acknowledged by his peers as the leader of the American church. In the late 1870s the archbishop was James Bayley, whose poor health often caused him to call on Gibbons for assistance. Concerned about the smooth transition of authority in his diocese, Bayley asked Gibbons in 1877 to serve as his coadjutor archbishop (an assistant with the automatic right of succession). Gibbons hesitated for months but finally agreed to serve with Bayley. In October Bayley died, and Gibbons sat on the most important diocesan throne in America. As archbishop of Baltimore, Gibbons corresponded frequently with the Vatican and was deeply involved in formulating the church's response to the massive surge of Catholic migration to the United States. Gibbons epitomized the American Catholic hierarchy, an Irish American with little personal exposure to Catholics from eastern and southern Europe. Indeed his own pastoral experience was gained in circumstances where Catholics of any sort were an overwhelming minority of the population. Like many Irish American bishops, he was not always sensitive to the concerns of immigrants. Gibbons, however, proved to be an effective administrator, presiding over the Third Plenary Council of Baltimore in late 1884. That council set in place the framework for an extensive system of Catholic parochial schools and reorganized the routine operations of the Catholic Church in America. Pope Leo XIII rewarded Gibbons in June 1886 by naming him a cardinal of the church.

Decades of Struggle. The next two decades were exceedingly taxing, as Gibbons was called upon to mediate repeated and complex disputes about how simultaneously to meet the needs of immigrants and establish the Catholic Church as an American institution. Gibbons also advised Rome about American realities, a difficult task in a period when the political and social changes taking place in Europe, particularly in France and Italy, preoccupied Vatican authorities. To Rome it often looked like the United States was a source of political doctrines that emphasized revolution and the separation of church and state. During the 1880s Gibbons interceded with papal officials often, working successfully to prevent condemnations of the Knights of Labor and the writings of the economic reformer Henry George.

"Americanists." Gibbons also lent substantial support to a group of bishops who eagerly embraced American culture and the political system. This group, led by Archbishop John Ireland of Saint Paul, Minnesota, argued that all Catholics in the United States should conform to a single Catholic culture, firmly American in ethos, language, and political commitment. The group, known in Europe as the "Americanists," believed that the growing ethnic diversity of the American Catholic Church and the passionate loyalty of many immigrants to old-world identities threatened both the unity of Catholicism and the authority of the bishops. American bishops who opposed the Americanists frequently complained to Rome that concessions to American culture would lead to

widespread abandonment of the Catholic faith by immigrants.

Ecumenical Outlook. Gibbons himself was optimistic about Catholic success in America and willing to make public ecumenical gestures. He and Ireland, for example, attended the World's Parliament of Religions in Chicago in 1893, an event organized and dominated by liberal Protestants. Gibbons even agreed to lead the parliament's opening session in a recitation of a Protestant translation of the Lord's Prayer. That and similar gestures scandalized many conservative Catholics. Throughout his career, Gibbons was also a highly vocal supporter of American political institutions and of the nation's increasingly aggressive foreign policy.

Papal Intervention. The papacy's growing concern about the influence of American society on the American Catholic Church became evident in the mid 1890s. In 1895 Pope Leo XIII's encyclical *Longinqua Oceani* praised the progress of the Catholic Church in America but explicitly rejected the view that the American model of separation of church and state should be universally adopted. In 1899 the Americanist conflict culminated when Pope Leo addressed an apostolic letter to Gibbons called *Testem Benevolentiae*. It stated that reports had reached Rome that some American Catholic clerics held the heretical view that the Catholic Church should alter both its external forms and traditional doctrine to respond to the pressures of the modern world. Gibbons hurriedly condemned those views, too, assuring the pope that no American bishops or priests supported those ideas.

A Record of Successes. The shift in papal policy left a decisive conservative mark on American Catholicism that lasted for decades. In the final decades of his life, Gibbons witnessed the easing of ethnic tensions within the church. He also served as an unofficial adviser to several presidents on Catholic matters, conveying, among other things, the view of the papacy to American leaders. His greatest public success, however, was cumulative. Over the course of decades he succeeded in reassuring millions of American Protestants and other non-Catholics that Catholicism was ultimately compatible with the American political and cultural system.

Catholic and American. Gibbons died on 21 March 1921, and his passing was widely mourned. Although he remained firmly in the Irish American camp, Catholics of many ethnic identities gave him credit for guiding the American church through the peak years of internal ethnic tension. During Gibbons's tenure the Catholic Church could well have been marginalized in America because of its association with reactionary European political currents. Instead, the Catholic community was grudgingly and gradually accepted into the American mainstream. This was, in some considerable measure, because of Gibbons's deft leadership and sincere American patriotism.

Sources:

John Tracy Ellis, *The Life of James Cardinal Gibbons: Archbishop of Baltimore, 1834–1921* (Milwaukee: Bruce, 1963);

James Gibbons, *Faith of Our Fathers* (Baltimore: J. Murphy, 1904).

DWIGHT LYMAN MOODY

1837-1899
URBAN EVANGELIST

Era of the Evangelist. Dwight Lyman Moody was the most famous and widely admired Protestant evangelist of his day, and perhaps the last great itinerant evangelist to receive the wholehearted support of both liberal and conservative Protestants. His greatest successes came in a series of urban revivals in the United States and Great Britain that began in London in 1872. More than any other religious leader of his era, Moody found effective ways to repackage the "old-time religion" in an increasingly urban and industrial world. Moody remained a layman throughout his life and never presented himself as an expert in theology. He had a great talent for delivering simple and straightforward sermons that reflected personal warmth. In fact his style could not have been more different from his predecessor Charles Grandison Finney, the "father of modern revivalism," whose sermons were more direct, tough, and forceful.

Humble Beginnings. Born in Northfield, Massachusetts, on 5 February 1837, Moody received little formal education or religious instruction. In 1854 he went to Boston to work for an uncle who was a cobbler, and two years later he started selling shoes. During a revival organized by the Young Men's Christian Association (YMCA), Moody underwent a profound evangelical conversion experience and began to attend church regularly. Soon he joined the Plymouth Congregational Church. At the time most Protestant churches relied on the sale or rental of pews to generate operating income. Moody rented four pews at Plymouth, and each Sunday morning he walked through the city's streets and knocked on boardinghouse doors to find men and women who would join him for the Sabbath service. In 1858 he became the superintendent of a Sunday school in a slum neighborhood. By 1860 Moody had left his shoe-selling business to devote himself entirely to missionary work. During the Civil War Moody worked as an agent of the U.S. Christian Commission, which offered religious and practical support to Union troops. Returning to Chicago after the war, he became president of the city's branch of the YMCA. Moody was a gifted executive and fund-raiser. He guided the YMCA through a rapid expansion to serve the needs of young men who were flocking to Chicago to find work in the city's offices and factories. When his YMCA building was destroyed in the great Chicago fire of 1871, Moody went on national and international assignments for the YMCA.

Finding a Role. Moody's life took a definitive turn in the spring of 1872, when he was called upon to preach at a London church while on a business trip for the YMCA. Moody was startled after he closed his sermon with the customary evangelical invitation to his hearers to dedicate their lives to Christ. Four hundred people answered the altar call. Reflecting on the experience, Moody felt that he had found his vocation as an evangelist. Returning briefly to the United States, he asked the musician Ira Sankey to join him as an itinerant evangelist. The team returned to Britain for an experimental evangelistic tour. Between 1873 and 1875 they spoke and sang to audiences that exceeded a cumulative total of approximately three million. Moody and Sankey's British revivals attracted attention around the world. Success abroad catapulted them to immense fame and popularity in America. They capitalized on their celebrity by mounting a long series of revivals during the 1870s and 1880s that involved virtually every major American city. Moody perfected the art of organizing urban revivals, blending careful preparation and elaborate efforts to unify local Protestant leadership. He often committed months to a particular revival, preaching nightly for weeks at a time. The meetings combined sermon and music in a simple, stirring, and effective way. Sankey himself popularized a new religious musical form, the gospel hymn, which blended pious and emotional lyrics with tunes adapted from dance and march music.

Salvation Alone. In the pulpit Moody focused on God's offer of salvation through rebirth in Christ. He consistently declined to discuss all other topics, including doctrinal, social, or political matters. His social platform was based on his conviction that the only effective means of solving human problems was individual salvation. At the end of each revival sermon Moody would hold up his Bible and assure his listeners that eternal salvation was available if only they would accept it. "I look upon the world as a wrecked vessel," Moody frequently told journalists. "God has given me a lifeboat and said to me 'Moody, save all you can.' "

In the Middle. Moody's personable disposition, avoidance of conflict, and lack of interest in formal theological disputation combined to leave him comfortably out of reach of the sharpening dispute between Protestant liberals and conservatives. Moody himself was unquestionably conservative and a biblical literalist. In fact his evangelism helped to encourage the militantly conservative movement that would come to be called Fundamentalism. Nevertheless Moody always maintained cordial personal relations with liberals and often emphasized the importance of Christian activism to relieve poverty and other social ills, themes that warmed liberal imaginations.

A New Era. Almost single-handedly Moody revitalized the American religious tradition of revivalism and made it popular in the industrial age. His legacy, however, has been even greater. Moody founded several educational institutions that have had significant impact on American religious life. In 1879 he established the Northfield Seminary for Girls and the Mount Hermon School for boys in 1881. He also began holding summer conferences in which he invited hundreds of laymen and laywomen for discussions, worship, and training sessions. These conferences proved to be influential in the development of both the early Fundamentalist movement and the Holiness movement that prepared the way for Pentecostalism. College students participating in the 1886 Northfield Conference conceived the Student Volunteer Movement two years later. The movement, led by the "Mount Hermon One Hundred," eventually mobilized thousands of American missionaries to "convert the world in a single generation." Moody also founded a Bible training school in Chicago in 1889 that set the pattern for a conservative Protestant educational movement; after the evangelist's death, the school was renamed the Moody Bible Institute in his honor.

Twilight. Moody began to curtail his activities in 1892 in response to a heart ailment. No figure of equal stature or equivalent appeal across the spectrum of Protestant belief and opinion has ever appeared on the urban religious scene. Moody died at Northfield on 22 December 1899.

Sources:
James F. Findlay, *Dwight L. Moody: American Evangelist, 1837–1899* (Chicago: University of Chicago Press, 1969);

William G. McLoughlin, *Modern Revivalism: Charles Grandison Finney to Billy Graham* (New York: Ronald Press, 1959).

PUBLICATIONS

Charles Augustus Briggs, *The Authority of Holy Scripture: An Inaugural Address* (New York: Scribners, 1891)—this vigorous defense of historical criticism of the Bible triggered a Presbyterian heresy trial and one of the most significant defenses of academic freedom in American history;

Briggs, *Biblical Study: Its Principles, Methods and History* (New York: Scribners, 1883)—a defense of the new historical and literary criticism of the Bible;

Briggs, *Whither? A Theological Question for the Times* (New York: Scribners, 1889)—a controversial defense of scientific and historical criticism of Scripture;

James Freeman Clarke, *Ten Great Religions: An Essay in Comparative Theology* (Boston & New York: Houghton, Mifflin, 1883)—a widely read work, which reflects both the late-nineteenth-century fascination for Asian religions and confidence in the superiority of Christianity;

William Newton Clarke, *An Outline of Christian Theology* (New York: Scribners, 1898)—the most influential scholarly attempt to synthesize and represent a systematic theology from a modernist Protestant perspective;

Daniel Dorchester, *Christianity in the United States from the First Settlement down to the Present Time* (New York: Hunt & Eaton, 1895)—a Methodist historian's account asserting the pervasive, formative, and continuing influence of Protestantism on American culture;

Richard T. Ely, *Social Aspects of Christianity* (New York: Crowell, 1889)—an influential treatise by a leading American economist and theorist of the Social Gospel movement;

James Cardinal Gibbons, *The Faith of Our Fathers: Being a Plain Exposition and Vindication of the Church Founded by Our Lord Jesus Christ* (Baltimore: Murphy, 1877)—an immensely influential popular apologetic for the Roman Catholic faith by the leading American Catholic hierarch of the late nineteenth century, this work had many editions and was the most widely read Catholic book in America;

Washington Gladden, *How Much Is Left of the Old Doctrines?* (Boston & New York: Houghton, Mifflin, 1899)—a popular and nontechnical assessment of the profound impact of modernist revisions to theology, biblical studies, and church history;

Gladden, *Who Wrote the Bible? A Book for the People* (Boston & New York: Houghton, Mifflin, 1891)—a general survey of modernist biblical studies by the most widely known liberal Protestant clergyman of the 1890s, Gladden's book introduced historical criticism to a mass audience;

Robert Ingersoll, *Some Mistakes of Moses* (New York: Farrell, 1879)—penned by America's most celebrated agnostic and critic of organized religion, this is a detailed, rationalistic, and scathing attack on the proposition that the Bible was divinely inspired;

Theodore Munger, *The Freedom of Faith* (Boston & New York: Houghton, Mifflin, 1883)—an optimistic essay on the "New Theology" developing among modernist theologians whose goal was to modify evangelical Calvinism and bring it into conformity with modern science;

Charles Sheldon, *In His Steps* (Chicago: Advance, 1897)—a Kansas minister's melodramatic novel, novel that spoke for a conservative strain of the Social Gospel movement;

Egbert Smythe, ed., *Progressive Orthodoxy* (Boston: Houghton, Mifflin, 1885)—a series of essays with strong modernist leanings by professors at Andover Theological Seminary, this book provided the grounds for a storm of heresy accusations and legal actions that would rock one of the nation's elite Protestant seminaries in the late 1880s and early 1890s;

Newman Smythe, *Christian Ethics* (New York: Scribners, 1897)—Smythe's most important work, this book exemplifies the growing emphasis by theological modernists on ethics, rather than on personal salvation, as the central theme in Christianity;

Smythe, *Old Faiths in a New Light* (New York: Scribners, 1879)—a New England theologian's influential introductory discussion of the main themes and findings of the historical-critical school of scholarship evolving in Protestant universities and seminaries in Europe;

Elizabeth Cady Stanton, ed., *The Woman's Bible*, 2 volumes (New York: European Publishing, 1895, 1898)—a withering critique of the repression of women in the Hebrew and Christian Scriptures and of conventional organized religion edited by a leading feminist;

Josiah Strong, *Our Country: Its Possible Future and Its Present Crisis* (New York: American Home Missionary Society, 1885)—a Cincinnati minister's national best-seller mixing optimistic predictions of the eventual global triumph of American forms of democratic capitalism and Protestantism with considerable nervousness about the present impact of mass immigration, Mormonism, and socialism on American society;

Lewis Wallace, *Ben-Hur: A Tale of Christ* (New York: Harper, 1880)—a Civil War general's best-selling popular novel capitalizes on widespread American curiosity about the historical setting of the life of Christ.

SCIENCE AND MEDICINE

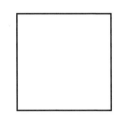

by THOMAS GLICK

CONTENTS

Sidebars and tables are listed in italics.

1878

- The first meeting of the International Union of Geological Sciences is held in Paris.

- James J. Sylvester founds the *American Journal of Mathematics.*

- William Henry Welch of Bellevue Hospital Medical College in New York City opens the first pathology laboratory in the United States.

- A yellow-fever epidemic in the Gulf states and Tennessee kills some fourteen thousand people.

1879

- Thomas A. Edison demonstrates a practical incandescent electric light bulb.

- Elmer Ambrose Sperry improves the dynamo, increasing the flow of electric current for generators and thus making electric-power plants more efficient.

- George B. Selden applies for a patent on a "road locomotive" with an internal-combustion engine. A patent is granted in 1895.

- Leroy B. Firman invents the multiple-telephone switchboard.

1880

- The U.S. Coast Survey, which is involved in mapping the United States, is renamed the Coast and Geodetic Survey.

- Charles Sanders Peirce lectures to the Paris Academy of Sciences on his measurements of the acceleration of gravity.

- George Eastman receives a patent on roll film for cameras.

1881

- Samuel Pierpont Langley invents the bolometer, a precision thermometer.

- U.S. Army doctor George Miller Sternberg isolates the bacillus that causes bacterial pneumonia.

- New York, New Jersey, Michigan, and Illinois are the first states to pass pure-food laws.

21 May   Clara Barton founds the American Red Cross.

1882

- Edward C. Pickering invents a prism device for photographing simultaneously the spectra of several stars — the colors that become visible when light from the stars is separated according to wavelength.

- Henry Rowland invents a machine to make difraction gratings, another means of separating light beams, for spectroscopy.

- Johns Hopkins University professor G. Stanley Hall establishes the first experimental psychology laboratory in the United States.

1883

4 Sept.   The Edison Electric Light Company is established in the Pearl Street district of lower Manhattan, providing electric light to eighty-five buildings and heralding the beginning of a major new industry.

•   Alexander Graham Bell and his father-in-law, G. G. Hubbard, found *Science* magazine, which becomes the official organ of the American Association for the Advancement of Science.

17 May   Lydia Pinkham, inventor of the best-selling patent medicine Lydia Pinkham's Vegetable Compound, dies.

1884

•   Dr. Edward Livingston Trudeau opens a sanatorium for tuberculosis patients in Saranac, New York, introducing the idea of treating the disease by exposing patients to clear mountain air.

•   Dr. William Halsted, a New York surgeon, discovers the anesthetic properties of cocaine and subsequently becomes addicted to it.

•   Lewis Edson Waterman invents the first practical fountain pen with a capillary feed.

•   At an international conference in Washington, D.C., delegates establish standard, international time zones with the prime meridian passing through Greenwich, England.

•   Physiologist Philip Smith discovers that the pituitary gland exerts a controlling effect on other endocrine glands.

1885

•   Veterinarian Daniel Elmer Salmon, head of the U.S. Bureau of Animal Husbandry, delivers a paper that describes a bacterium that causes food poisoning in humans. Although Salmon is reporting on research conducted by Theobald Smith, the bacterium is later named salmonella in Salmon's honor.

4 Jan.   Dr. William West Grant of Davenport, Iowa, performs what is believed to be the first successful appendectomy in the United States.

1886

•   Henry Rowland uses diffraction gratings to map the spectrum of sunlight.

•   Johnson & Johnson markets the first ready-to-use sterile surgical dressings.

Feb.   Charles Martin Hall invents an inexpensive electrolytic process for extracting aluminum from bauxite ore (aluminum oxide).

1887

- An experiment conducted by Albert A. Michelson and Edward W. Morley fails to establish the existence of "the ether," thought to be an invisible substance that fills space and allows light rays to pass from one point to another.

- A thirty-six-inch telescope is mounted at the Lick Observatory on Mount Hamilton in California.

- Louis J. Girard, Baylor College of Medicine, invents a contact lens. (The first plastic lens is invented in 1938, and the first practical lens, the corneal contact, is introduced in 1950).

- G. Stanley Hall founds the *American Journal of Psychology.*

2 Mar. Congress passes the Hatch Act, establishing agricultural experiment stations in states with land-grant colleges.

1888

- Croatian American Nikola Tesla invents an alternating-current (AC) electric motor, which runs more efficiently than the direct-current (DC) motor favored by Thomas Edison.

- To measure the intensity of California earthquakes, the first seismograph in the United States is installed at Lick Observatory on Mount Hamilton.

- The New York Mathematical Society (later the American Mathematical Society) is founded.

Oct. Clinton H. Merriam publishes the first issue of *National Geographic.*

1889

- A worldwide influenza epidemic infects 40 percent of the world's population over the next two years.

- St. Mary's Hospital opens in Rochester, Minnesota, with Dr. William Worrall Mayo and his physician sons William James Mayo and Charles Horace Mayo on the medical staff. The hospital later becomes the Mayo Clinic.

1890

- Edward Pickering and Williamina Fleming introduce the "Harvard Classification" of stars, a system based on alphabetical arrangement.

- *The Principles of Psychology*, by William James, is published.

- The National Carbon Company markets the first commercial dry-cell battery under the brand name Ever Ready.

- New York State passes the Howe Law, requiring physicians to put silver nitrate drops in newborn babies' eyes to prevent blindness from gonorrheal infection. Most other states later pass similar laws.

- Despite opposition from some dairy interests, many American communities pass laws requiring that milk be pasteurized.

30 Aug. Congress passes the Morrill Act of 1890, establishing more research programs to help farmers.

1891

- Astronomer George Ellery Hale invents the spectroheliograph to photograph the surface of the Sun.

- Edward Goodrich Acheson perfects a method for manufacturing carborundum (silicon carbide), a strong, abrasive compound used to control the flow of current in electrical circuits.

- The U.S. Weather Bureau, formerly a military bureau, becomes a civilian agency of the federal government.

- Samuel Pierpont Langley publishes *Experiments in Aerodynamics*.

- African American surgeon Daniel Hale Williams establishes Provident Hospital in Chicago. It is the first interracial hospital in the United States.

- Charles and James Duryea design a gasoline engine that can power a road vehicle.

24 Aug.   Thomas Alva Edison applies for a patent on the first American motion-picture camera.

29 Dec.   Edison receives a patent for a "wireless telegraph."

1892

- The American Psychology Association is founded.

- Thomas Corwin Mendenhall directs the Alaska border survey.

- Albert Abraham Michelson detects the fine spectral lines of hydrogen.

- Edward Emerson Barnard at the Lick Observatory discovers the fifth moon of Jupiter.

- Thomas J. Jackson propounds a theory of the origin of the binary star, a system of two stars that revolve around one another.

- Theobald Smith identifies the tick as the carrier of Texas cattle fever, an important advance in epidemiology.

- Charles and James Duryea produce what is believed to be the first American motor car.

1893

- The Johns Hopkins Medical School is founded in Baltimore, Maryland.

- Dr. Daniel Hale Williams of Chicago performs the world's first open-heart surgery, saving the life of a man with a knife wound to an artery near his heart.

- Charles Proteus Steinmetz devises a method of calculating alternating current that makes the use of AC motors commercially feasible.

1894

- Percival Lowell establishes an observatory at Flagstaff, Arizona, to search for a ninth planet.

- Dr. Hermann Michael Biggs of New York becomes first American physician to inoculate his patients with the diphtheria antitoxin developed by German physician Emil von Behring in 1890.

1895

- Astronomer James Keeler suggests that Saturn's rings are not solid, as is generally believed, but are made of particles.

- Simon Newcomb publishes his influential *Astronomical Constants.*

1896

- Lick Observatory publishes the first photographic atlas of the Moon.

- The first diagnostic X ray in the United States is taken at Columbia University by Michael Pupin.

6 May At the Smithsonian Institution in Washington, D.C., astronomer Samuel Pierpont Langley achieves the first flight of a mechanically propelled flying machine by sending a steam-powered model airplane on a three-thousand-foot flight.

1897

- The Yerkes Observatory at Williams Bay, Wisconsin, installs a forty-inch refracting telescope, the largest of its kind in the world.

- James T. Morehead produces the first commercial high-carbon ferrochrome for plating steel in the United States.

1898

- Contaminated meat kills more U.S. troops than do bullets during the Spanish-American War, prompting a public outcry for government regulation of the meatpacking industry.

1899

- Jacques Loeb conducts experiments on parthenogenesis in sea-urchin eggs, causing unfertilized eggs to develop into new organisms.

- The American Physical Society is founded.

- Astronomer William Wallace Campbell demonstrates that Polaris (the "North Star") is in fact a cluster of three stars.

- William Henry Pickering discovers the ninth moon of Saturn.

- A pure-food bill is defeated in the U.S. Senate.

- Assistant surgeon Bailey Kelly Ashford of the U.S. Army Medical Corps discovers an effective treatment for hookworm.

- A cholera epidemic begins, spreading through much of the world and continuing until 1923.

OVERVIEW

An Era of Optimism. The scientific trends in the United States during the late nineteenth century were representative of a sense of optimism fed by western expansion, new successes in treating disease, technological advances, and the progressive belief that society was evolving in a positive direction. This association with progress linked science to the social and political goals of society and promised even more gains in the future.

Government Funding. During the last quarter of the nineteenth century the federal government funded several important scientific projects, putting into motion a transition away from military control of scientific research at the beginning of the period to civilian control by the end. This shift partly involved shedding a model borrowed from Europe, where countries that were constantly at war concentrated many strategic scientific activities in army bureaus. American civilian agencies such as the U.S. Coast Survey (later the Coast and Geodetic Survey), the Geological Survey, and the Naval Observatory were able to command the services of the best scientists, such as Charles Sanders Peirce, later one of the greatest American philosophers, who began his career as a talented physicist with the Coast Survey. The ability of the U.S. government to fund laboratories and research programs requiring extensive fieldwork was important in an era when universities had limited funds for research and foundations with scientific and educational programs had not yet been established.

Exploring the West. Western exploration was the scientific keynote of the period. The vast areas opened to settlement by the railroads were unmapped and unexplored, particularly from a geological perspective. Settlers, land speculators, railroads, miners, and timber interests had a stake in the successful completion of such surveys. In this monumental mapping project John Wesley Powell was the dominant figure, not only because his surveys produced high-quality work but also because of his broad perspective on land use in general and his dynamism as a scientific administrator.

European Models in Medicine. In medicine Americans followed the lead of the Europeans. There was the steady shift in American medical education from purely clinical training to the European model in which clinic and laboratory were co-equal. The new science of bacteriology—especially the discoveries of the Frenchman Louis Pasteur and the German Robert Koch—had a major impact on both the organization of medicine itself and how diseases were treated. The drive to identify the microbes that caused specific diseases and then to develop effective vaccines against them was a powerful stimulus for making experimental research a part of the curriculum in American medical schools, along the lines of the German laboratories where many Americans sought postdoctoral experience throughout this period. Experimental medicine had been developed by Claude Bernard (1813–1878), but during the 1860s and 1870s, the period of his greatest influence, American medical schools were too small, too attuned to the dire need for clinicians, and too poor to take up Bernard's call for the transformation of medicine into a laboratory-based science.

The Popularization of Science. Exploration was the topic that most engaged the American public's imagination during the late nineteenth century. Another subject of interest was the debate over evolution, which was the centerpiece in the popular conception of the "warfare between science and religion"—or the "military metaphor," as it has been called. American evolutionary science was enjoying a kind of golden epoch, with paleontologists attached to the great geological surveys making major fossil finds in the West. While dinosaur bones caught the public eye, the most enduring monuments of evolutionary science were Othniel Marsh's reconstruction of the evolution of the horse and Edward Drinker Cope's discoveries of previously unknown extinct species. Much of the public looked at science from a religious perspective and was uncertain about evolution. Yet Christian liberals and others who had already distanced themselves from traditional religious beliefs were comfortable with the notion that an improved environment would offer its inhabitants benefits that could be passed on to the next generation.

TOPICS IN THE NEWS

BELL AND THE TELEPHONE

The Idea. Alexander Graham Bell (1847–1922), who suffered from deafness, was interested in devising a form of "visible speech" for the deaf, first in the form of a universal alphabet and later by mechanical means. The telephone is scientifically uncomplicated: when the sound of a voice vibrates through an iron diaphragm, it changes the electromagnetic field in such a way as to reproduce the vibrations in an electric current. These vibrations are then transformed back into sound through a receiving diaphragm.

The Inventors. Several inventors were aware of how to make a telephone. By the time Bell applied for a patent on his "harmonic multiple telegraph" (as he called it), other inventors, including Thomas Alva Edison, Elisha Gray, and Amos Dolbeare, were also close to producing functioning instruments. To head off Edison, whom Western Union had engaged to proceed at full speed on his "speaking telegraph," Gray agreed not to contest Bell's patent, which was granted on 7 March 1876.

Three days later Bell spoke the first intelligible telephone message to his assistant: "Mr. Watson, come here!" Bell then tinkered with the basic model and caused a sensation at the Centennial Exposition in Philadelphia in June 1876, when Emperor Dom Pedro of Brazil and other dignitaries tried it out. On the advice of a surgeon Bell had modeled the receiver on the anatomy of human ear; by January 1877 he had created a reliable working model.

Competition. In 1877 Bell founded the Bell Telephone Company and faced tough competition from Edison, who had developed a transmitter that was as good as or better than Bell's. Over an eighteen-year period other inventors challenged Bell's patents in court on six hundred different occasions, with Bell winning all the cases. In Great Britain Bell and Edison started out in competition, with Edison's telephone company taking the lead, and forcing a merger of Bell and Edison interests in England. (It is interesting to note that Edison and Bell both suffered from varying degrees of deafness and considered

The first successful flight of a mechanically propelled flying machine, a steam-powered model airplane flown by astronomer Samuel Pierpont Langley along the banks of the Potomac River in Washington, D.C., on 6 May 1896 (from *McClure's Magazine,* June 1897

Alexander Graham Bell conducting one of his airplane experiments

the invention of the telephone to be especially important.)

The Success of the Telephone. The speed with which people accepted the telephone was remarkably quick, and Bell turned to new interests, including airplanes. He left the Bell Company a wealthy man in 1881. The social effects of the telephone were startling and immediate: it changed the way business was conducted, encouraging decentralization and allowing managers and salespeople to carry out their functions on a regional, and later a national, scale. According to twentieth-century communications expert Marshall McLuhan, telephone introduced "a seamless web of interlaced patterns in management and decision making," making an older style of rigidly delegated authority impossible. The telephone also changed the way doctors practiced medicine, linking patient to physician to pharmacy almost instantaneously. Its effects on interpersonal and family relations were so profound that people today have great difficulty conceiving of how people ever carried on their day-to-day lives without it.

Sources:
Robert V. Bruce, *Alexander Graham Bell and the Conquest of Solitude* (London: Gollancz, 1973);

Matthew Josephson, *Edison: A Biography* (New York: McGraw-Hill, 1959);

Marshall McLuhan, *Understanding Media: The Extensions of Man* (New York: McGraw-Hill, 1965).

THE COAST AND GEODETIC SURVEY

Measuring the United States. Established in 1807 and known as the United States Coast Survey until 1880, the Coast and Geodetic Survey was primarily involved in geodesy, or geodetic measurement, the survey of large land areas in which mathematical corrections are made to take into account the curvature of the earth's surface. In 1871, at the urging of Coast Survey supervisor Benjamin Peirce, Congress appropriated funds to make a "geodetic connection" between the two coasts. They used an astronomical method recently devised by American engineer Andrew Talcott for determining latitude and employed the electric telegraph for finding longitude—taking advantage of new technology to improve the accuracy of their measurements. (Old methods of calculating longitude were accurate to one thousand feet; with the electric telegraph the margin of error was only one hundred feet.) The survey proceeded slowly from east to west using triangulation. In this process, once the exact longitudes and latitudes of two places are determined and the exact distance between them is measured, the location of a third place can be determined by the angles that lines drawn from it make with a line drawn between the first two places.

Studying Gravity. During the 1880s the Coast Survey studied the acceleration of gravity to establish the degree to which it varied with latitude. Since the earth is not a perfect sphere, gravitational pull is greater at the North and South Poles, which are flattened, than it is at the equator. Thus, measuring gravity at various points on the globe could help geodesists to determine the actual shape of the earth and lead to greater accuracy of mapping. (Although the earth is now known to be somewhat pear-shaped, bulging in the Southern Hemisphere, scientists in the late nineteenth century theorized that it bulged at the equator.) The force of gravity was measured with a pendulum, which swings at slower and slower rates of speed the closer it gets to the equator. This project was mainly the work of Benjamin Peirce's son, Charles Sanders Peirce. In 1880 he demonstrated to the Paris Academy of Sciences that his measurement of the acceleration of gravity was superior to those of distinguished French scientists. The worldwide reputation of the Coast and Geodetic Survey for gravity studies came to an end in 1891, when Charles Peirce resigned after arguing with the director, Thomas C. Mendenhall, over methods of measurement.

The Battle for Civilian Control. Throughout the last quarter of the century, the Coast and Geodetic Survey had to compete for funding and for the definition of its scientific mission with the U.S. Naval Hydrographic Office, established in 1866. The original distinction between the two government entities was that the Coast Survey would map the domestic shoreline while the naval office was responsible for mapping foreign coasts. In practice, however, there was considerable overlap, as naval officers were appointed to the Coast Service. The battle for civilian control of science occupied the Congress throughout the 1880s and resulted in the restriction of naval scientific efforts to oceanographic projects.

Source:

Thomas G. Manning, *U.S. Coast Survey vs. Naval Hydrographic Office. A 19th-Century Rivalry in Science and Politics* (Tuscaloosa & London: University of Alabama Press, 1988).

ELECTRICITY AND THE ELECTRIC LIGHT

Illuminating Possibilities. The possibility of creating artificial light with electricity was established as early as 1808, when the English chemist Sir Humphry Davy demonstrated that current from batteries can create light either by heating some substance until it glows or by causing an arc of electricity to jump over a gap between two conductors. Arc lighting uses a lot of current and creates a brilliant light and it was limited to the outdoors or large interior spaces. The problem of lighting smaller spaces—which technicians of the nineteenth century called subdividing the light—was to find a lighting material that would not burn or melt when the current ran through it. Carbon and platinum seemed most promising but not ideal: the first does not melt, but it burns easily, while the second resists chemical changes at high temperatures (oxidation) but catches fire if the temperature becomes too high. All of the early lighting experiments were with low-resistance lamps, that is, lamps in which very little of the electrical energy passing through them is dissipated as heat. These lamps used a great deal of low-voltage current.

Edison's Experiments. When Thomas Alva Edison (1847–1931) began his experiments at his laboratory in Menlo Park, New Jersey, in 1878, he realized that he could prevent the platinum filament from burning if he could put it in a glass bulb with all the air removed from it. At the same time he was trying to conceptualize an extensive system of lighting powered by generators. It occurred to him that a system of several hundred low-resistance lamps would require huge generators and large conducting wires in order to accommodate the current required. But, he reasoned, high-resistance, high-voltage lamps would need much less current to produce the same amount of light. (According to Ohm's law, which Edison applied but did not completely understand, the electric current flowing through a given resistance is equal to the applied voltage divided by the resistance.) This new system could distribute current efficiently from a central station through reasonably sized lines.

The Invention of the Light Bulb. Having solved the conceptual problem, Edison next had to find a material for a light-bulb filament that would glow for a long time without burning up. Finally, on the night of 22 October 1879, his famous bulb number 9, with a carbon filament,

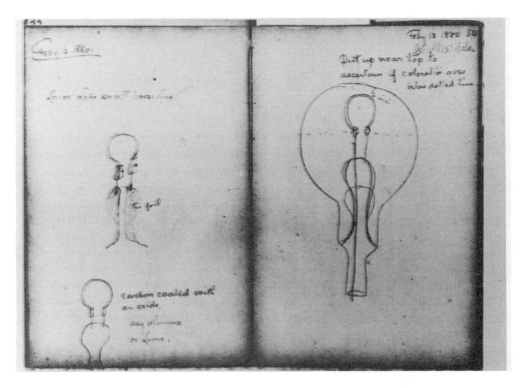

Notes on the electric light bulb in Thomas Edison's laboratory notebook, February 1880

stayed lit for almost fifteen hours. The following week he patented a bulb with a carbon filament. He then applied this technology by illuminating the town of Menlo Park, causing such a sensation that special trains ran from New York City so that people could view the spectacle at night.

From Bulb to System. Having made his earlier experiments with electricity from batteries, Edison next had to develop a dynamo, or generator, to produce a steady current capable of sustaining a large, integrated electrical system. The Menlo Park system ran on a series of small generators. At the Paris Electrical Exposition in 1881 he exhibited a large steam-run dynamo, causing great excitement. The following year he unveiled a small generator-driven electrical plant at the famous Crystal Park Exhibition in London. In December 1880 the Brush Electric Light Company began operation in New York City, illuminating Broadway with arc lights, thus creating the "Great White Way" of theatrical legend. Although it was not in direct competition with Edison, the beginning of the Brush electric service impelled Edison to push even harder to complete an underground electric-wire system for a generating station with a machine works and a lamp works in the Pearl Street district of lower Manhattan. Almost a year passed before the underground wire system was complete. Meanwhile he established free-standing "isolated" systems, mainly for factories, which allowed him to test most of his components. Finally, on 4 September 1882, the Pearl Street electrical station came on line, beginning a new era of urban life.

Source:
Robert Friedel and Paul Israel, *Edison's Electric Light: Biography of an Invention* (New Brunswick, N.J. : Rutgers University Press, 1987).

EXPLORATION OF THE WEST: THE GEOLOGICAL SURVEYS

Mapping the West. From 1867 practically to the end of the nineteenth century a series of geological surveys led by Clarence King (1842–1901), Ferdinand V. Hayden (1829–1887), and John Wesley Powell (1834–1902) explored and mapped the West. Carried out under the aegis of the U.S. Army Corps of Engineers, King's survey of the Fortieth Parallel (the "Great Basin" between the middle Rockies and the Sierra Nevada) in 1867 was mainly utilitarian in its objectives: King had justified the survey by claiming it would stimulate the discovery of mineral deposits. His books *The Mining Industry* (1870) and *Systematic Geology* (1878) were products of this survey.

Searching for Dinosaurs. Hayden, who joined the Interior Department in 1867, organized a survey of the western territories, pushed for the establishment of Yellowstone Park (which was authorized in 1872), and became first director of what was then called the U.S. Geological and Geographical Survey of the Territories. Hayden established the tradition of attaching paleontologists to geological surveys, his best ones being Edward Drinker Cope, well known for his studies of dinosaurs, and the great paleobotanist Leo Lesquereux. Insofar as geology was concerned, the results of both the King and Hayden surveys were stratigraphic, mapping layers of

Clarence King, the first head of the U.S. Geological Survey, established in 1879

the steeper it will be; and conversely, the farther it is from the divide the gentler it will be.

Establishment of the U.S. Geological Survey. The U.S. Army also mapped the West during the 1870s, mainly to supply its need for accurate maps in waging Indian campaigns. Hayden and Powell opposed the army mapping projects because of inevitable duplication of efforts and because a new generation of American scientists did not want to serve under army officers who had no scientific education. Powell also felt that maps drawn by civilian scientists would display both the topographical features that the army needed as well as scientifically interesting geological features. Finally the National Academy of Sciences recommended that a U.S. Geological Survey be established within the Interior Department to provide economically useful data, a strategy designed to appeal to western congressmen, while the Coast Survey would remain in charge of geodesy and topography. As a result, the Geological Survey, with King as director, was established in 1879.

Powell's Leadership. From his earlier studies of the West, Powell came to believe that the laws regulating the settlement of the arid regions of the West were environmentally destructive. He opposed the provision in the Homestead Act (1862) of 160 acres per settler, favoring grants of smaller parcels that could be irrigated. Western grazing interests defeated Powell's attempts to convince Congress to act on his suggestions. When King resigned as director of the Geological Survey in 1881, Powell became director. In 1884, when Congress investigated the federal government's role in scientific research, Powell responded to representatives who wanted to restrict the scientific activity of government bureaus to applied problems and described what these agencies had accomplished:

> The scientific works prosecuted under the General Government of the United States, and in like manner prosecuted by other nations, may broadly but with sufficient accuracy be classed under two heads: In the first class are constructive works, such as the erection of public buildings, the improvement of rivers and harbors, and the construction of light-houses. In all of the operations of this class, in order that the work may be properly executed, scientific principles and methods must be observed: but such works chiefly involve problems of applied science. The second class of operations in which the government of the United States, like all other civilized nations, is engaged, involve in their nature original investigation. They are designed in large part to furnish needed information to the people, and they involve not only questions of applied science, but, that the purpose for which they are prosecuted may be properly accomplished, new facts and principles must be discovered. Such an institution is the Geological Survey, the Coast and Geodetic Survey, the Signal Service or Meteorological Bureau, the Fish Commission, the National Museum, the Hydrographic Bureau, and the National Observatory. The functions of such bureaus cannot properly

rock following the terminology established by James Dwight Dana in his influential *Manual of Geology* (1863).

Powell and Geomorphology. During the 1870s Powell established his own survey in the Colorado River basin. His brand of earth science was quite different from that of his predecessors. While King and Hayden had been classical stratigraphers, Powell and his staff were more interested in geomorphology, that is, the historical processes that had created the major topographical features of the region. Thus one of Powell's principal interests was in the force of erosion that had carved out the canyons of the West. In 1875 Powell hired Grove Karl Gilbert to study the Henry Mountains in Utah. Gilbert's 1877 report includes an important chapter on the principles of earth sculpture by water and rain. In addition to climate Gilbert found two other conditions that influence the way water erodes rock. According to the law of structure, soft rock washes away faster than hard rock, which remains in prominent formations. The law of declivities, Gilbert's most important contribution to modern geology, deals with the slopes of drainage lines: the closer a slope lies to the divide between two watersheds

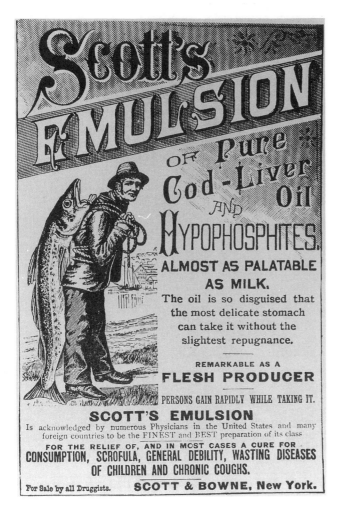

A patent-medicine advertisement from the 1890s

William H. Goetzmann, *Exploration and Empire: The Explorer and the Scientist in the Winning of the American West* (New York: Knopf, 1966);

Thomas G. Manning, *Government in Science: The U.S. Geological Survey, 1867–1894* (Lexington: University of Kentucky Press, 1967);

Wallace Stegner, *Beyond the Hundredth Meridian: John Wesley Powell and the Opening of the West* (Boston: Houghton Mifflin, 1954).

THE GERM THEORY

The Germ Theory. Scientists developed the modern approach to understanding and controlling epidemic diseases during the last quarter of the nineteenth century. In 1862 French scientist Louis Pasteur (1822–1895) showed that airborne bacteria were the cause of fermentation, thus giving rise to the "germ theory," which replaced an older theory that attributed diseases to environmental causes. In 1876 German scientist Robert Koch (1843–1910)—who was studying anthrax, a disease of sheep and cattle—demonstrated that specific diseases were caused by specific pathogens (the agents, such as bacteria or viruses, that cause disease), and in 1879 Pasteur found that he could use the bacilli (rod-shaped bacteria) that caused various diseases to vaccinate people against them, generalizing from the discovery of the smallpox vaccine by British physician Edward Jenner (1749–1823) in the late eighteenth century. During the 1880s and 1890s scientists identified the pathogens responsible for many diseases, including cholera, diphtheria, tetanus, tuberculosis, and typhoid.

Medical Technology. The discoveries leading to modern bacteriology were based on a series of technological innovations. The first was the development in the 1860s and 1870s of aniline stains, dyes that could be applied to cultures of bacteria to make them visible under a microscope. The second was the introduction of microscopes that could yield images of bacteria at high magnification without distortion. All of Koch's discoveries during the 1880s were dependent on the development of oil-immersion lenses.

Vaccines. In 1882 Koch identified the tuberculosis bacillus, and eight years later he developed tuberculin, a vaccination that proved more or less ineffective. Once it was recognized that tuberculosis was a communicable disease, it became possible to adopt public-health methods to combat it, such as disinfecting the homes of the afflicted and isolating them in sanatoriums. Diphtheria represented a more complex problem because its symptoms overlapped with those of other common diseases. One of Koch's assistants isolated the diphtheria bacillus in 1884, but the disease was not fully understood until the next decade. An investigation of 5,611 suspected cases reported in New York City during 1893–1894 revealed that only 60 percent were really diphtheria. By the middle 1890s an antitoxin had been developed, making diphtheria the first of the epidemic diseases to be fully studied and then prevented by a vaccine. As a result the diphtheria death rate for Illinois—a state with highly accurate medical records—dropped from 113 per 100,000

be performed without scientific research, and their value depends upon the wisdom and efficiency of the methods of investigation pursued.

Powell knew that advances in science were frequently made unexpectedly, and therefore he argued against strict legislative control of scientific research programs. In this instance Congress heeded Powell's advice.

Western Irrigation Studies. In 1888–1894 some western senators—spurred to rethink Powell's recommendations regarding irrigation by a severe western drought that lasted from 1886 until 1897—let him conduct an irrigation survey of the West. Powell called for long-term planning, including the resolution of federal versus state jurisdiction over large rivers and a rational program of building dams for irrigation and flood control. Congress, however, looked to short-term gain and refused to fund the programs necessary to implement Powell's plans. This difference of opinion led to another struggle and ultimately to Powell's resignation from the Geological Survey in 1892.

Sources:
William Culp Darrah, *Powell of the Colorado* (Princeton, N.J.: Princeton University Press, 1951);

in 1886 to 22 per 100,000 in 1902. More than any other event, the success of the diphtheria antitoxin is responsible for initiating a phase of "bacteriomania" in American medicine.

Source:
William G. Rothstein, *American Physicians in the Nineteenth Century* (Baltimore: Johns Hopkins University Press, 1972).

THE GERM THEORY AND PATENT MEDICINE

Unregulated Medicines. In the days before the germ theory was established, many different substances were used to treat specific disorders. Indeed physicians so despaired of finding effective cures that many subscribed to a doctrine of "therapeutic nihilism," prescribing as little as possible and making no claims that the available remedies would work. Since governments did not regulate medicines, anyone could invent one and try to sell it. Patent medicines got their name because their manufacturers had secured or applied for government patents, granting them exclusive rights to make and sell particular remedies. Such a patent protected the seller, not the buyer, and attested to a product's originality, not its curative powers.

Marketing the "Cure-All." Manufacturers of patent medicines typically claimed that they cured many ailments, sometimes a very long list of them. Many had scientific-sounding names, such as Lithiated Hydrangea, Extract of Pinus Canadensis, or Syrup of the Hypophosphites. Some stressed the chemical apparatus supposedly used to make them, such as Dr. Judge's Hydrogenated Air. Many included a foreign or exotic element in their names. Oriental associations were particularly favored, such as Dr. Lin's Celestial Balm of China, Carey's Chinese Catarrh Cure, or Japanese Life Pills, but there were also Crimean Bitters, Mecca Compound, and Mexican Mustang Liniment. Patent medicine manufacturers were pioneers in mass marketing and in making psychological appeals through advertising. Frequently the name of a product stressed its beneficial nature, as with Swift's Sure Specific, Dr. Sweet's Infallible Liniment, and Dr. Warner's Safe Cure.

Changing with the Times. When the germ theory became widely known in the 1880s and 1890s, patent-medicine makers jumped on that bandwagon too. William Radam, inventor of Radam's Microbe Killer, went so far as to devise an elaborate, but absurd, theory that he expounded in his book *Microbes and Microbe Killer* (1890). Picking up on Pasteur's experiments on fermentation, he said microbes cause decay and fermentation, which is the basic underlying disease, and he asserted that microbes are all the same, causing ailments that only appear different when they infect different people. Thus, he billed his product as a "universal non-poisonous antiseptic," which in addition to its curative powers also preserved fruit and meat. He manufactured the potion, whose main ingredient was water, in seventeen factories.

THE COPE-MARSH POLEMIC

In 1885 Edward Drinker Cope was enraged by the appointment of his rival Othniel Charles Marsh as president of the National Academy of Sciences — proof, Cope thought, of his opponent's political machinations. In October of that year Cope aired some of his beliefs about Marsh in a letter to a former student, passing on information given to him by some of Marsh's former assistants:

> The four men who have left Marsh wish to place themselves and him right before the Scientific public. They have found M. to be more a pretender than even I had supposed him to be. I have recently seen a statement in [manuscript] which sets forth a number of things which are worse than I had supposed. It is now clear to me that Marsh is simply a scientifico-political adventurer who has succeeded, in ways other than those proceeding from scientific merit, in placing himself in the leading scientific position in the country. It is now perfectly certain that he, M., has not written either of the quarto books that bear his name, and it is doubtful whether he has written much or any of his 800 papers.
>
> I consider that his career is a disgrace to our scientific community, and one that we ought to wipe out. The American National Academy of Sciences "will stink" in the noses of corresponding bodies in other countries.

Source: Nathan Reingold, *Science in Twentieth-Century America: A Documentary History* (New York: Hill & Wang, 1964).

Toward Government Regulation. The greatest enemy of patent medicines was Harvey Washington Riley, who was appointed chief chemist of the U.S. Department of Agriculture in 1883. He launched Bulletin 13 (with ten parts published over a period of sixteen years and totaling fourteen hundred pages), describing and analyzing chemical modifications of foodstuffs, including medicines, that were commonly available to the consumer. As a result of his efforts the first Pure Food Bill was introduced in the Senate in 1899. It did not pass, but momentum continued to grow until a similar bill became law in 1906, giving government the tools to make patent-medicine manufacturers prove their claims.

Source:
James Harvey Young, *The Toadstool Millionaires: A Social History of Patent Medicines in America Before Federal Regulation* (Princeton, N.J.: Princeton University Press, 1961).

THE GREAT FOSSIL WAR

Cope versus Marsh. For most of the last three decades of the nineteenth century paleontologists Edward Drinker Cope (1840–1897) and Othniel C. Marsh (1831–1899) engaged in a running battle over dinosaur discoveries in the American West. Cope, a professor at the University of Pennsylvania, was the paleontologist attached to Ferdinand V. Hayden's geological survey, with which he spent eight months of every year unearth-

One of Edward Drinker Cope's prize discoveries, the fossil from the *Phenacodus* genus, ancestors of modern hoofed mammals

ing fossil vertebrates (animals with spinal columns). He discovered more than twelve hundred previously unknown genera or species, and *The Vertebrata of the Tertiary Formations of the West* (1883), his report on the Hayden survey, was soon baptized "Cope's Bible." (In geological time the Tertiary period, from five million to sixty-five million years before the present, begins with the extinction of the dinosaurs and ends before the appearance of the earliest humans; it is the first period of the Cenozoic era.) Marsh, who named some five hundred new vertebrates, was vertebrate paleontologist at the Peabody Museum in New Haven. He is best known for tracing the evolution of the horse from the tiny *Eohippus* to its modern descendant and for having described a group of extinct birds with teeth, proving their reptilian ancestry.

Fighting over Fossils. Difficult and eccentric individuals, Cope and Marsh adopted aggressive entrepreneurial styles in amassing their considerable fossil collections, and each feared being undermined by the other. The dispute between the two paleontologists erupted in 1872, when Marsh attacked the validity of some of Cope's specimens. Cope's fears of being overshadowed by Marsh were realized in 1879, when Marsh became chief paleontologist of the U.S. Geological Survey. Cope had always suspected the head of the survey, John Wesley Powell, of conspiring with Marsh against him. Powell had indeed refused to publish Cope's writings on the Hayden survey. The feud burst into the national news in 1889–1890, when the government attempted to

force Cope to relinquish the fossils he had collected on the Hayden survey to the National Museum, on the assumption that these specimens were government property. Cope claimed that Marsh, who was president of the National Academy of Sciences, was packing that organization with his allies from the U.S. Geological Survey. Congressmen who wanted to reduce Powell's budget welcomed Cope's allegations, cutting government appropriations for Powell's agency from the $720,000 he requested in 1890 to $162,500. A key chapter in the emergence of government science, the Cope-Marsh episode also contributed significantly to Powell's resignation in 1892.

Sources:

William Culp Darrah, *Powell of the Colorado* (Princeton: Princeton University Press, 1969);

Nathan Reingold, *Science in Nineteenth-Century America: A Documentary History* (New York: Hill & Wang, 1964);

Wallace Stegner, *Beyond the Hundredth Meridian: John Wesley Powell and the Opening of the West* (Boston: Houghton Mifflin, 1954).

MARINE BIOLOGY

Origins of Modern Marine Biology. During the last quarter of the nineteenth century, several leading American biologists became interested in establishing a marine station capable of promoting and sustaining advanced research and instruction in marine biology along the lines of successful and influential European biological stations, such as Anton Dorrn's marine-biology station in Naples (in which four American universities officially participated) or Henri Lacaze-Duthier's laboratory at

The Marine Biology Laboratory in Woods Hole, Massachusetts, 1888

Woods Hole researchers leaving on an expedition to collect marine specimens, 1895

"THE END OF SCIENCE"

By the time he delivered the Lowell Lectures on *Light Waves and Their Uses* at Harvard University in 1899, Albert A. Michelson had come to believe that the age of great scientific discoveries had come to an end and that the physicist's future role would be in the realm of refining previously established laws through precise measurement:

What would be the use of such extreme refinement in the science of measurement? Very briefly and in general terms the answer would be that in this direction the greater part of all future discovery must lie. The more fundamental laws and facts of physical science have all been discovered, and these are now so firmly established that the possibility of their ever being supplanted in consequence of new discoveries is exceedingly remote.

Six years after Michelson spoke these words Albert Einstein published his special theory of relativity, overturning all of Michelson's assumptions about the nature of the universe.

Source: Albert A. Michelson, *Light Waves and Their Uses* (Chicago: University of Chicago Press, 1903).

Banyuls-sur-Mer, France. Louis Agassiz, a Swiss-born zoologist, (1807–1873) mounted the first such endeavor at Penikese Island, Massachusetts, in 1873, and during the same period his students Alpheus Hyatt (1838–1902) and Alpheus Packard (1839–1905) established summer programs at the Massachusetts seaports of Annisquam and Salem, respectively. These programs were all short-lived.

The Woods Hole Laboratory. The most influential early research station was the U.S. Fish Commission laboratory, at Woods Hole, Massachusetts, directed by Spencer Fullerton Baird between 1871 and 1887. Created to survey and study the offshore fish populations and to manage a hatchery, this laboratory contributed to scientific knowledge mainly in the classification of fish species and marine ecology.

The Marine Biology Laboratory. Hoping to expand the scope of his laboratory in concert with a coalition of research-oriented universities, Baird drew up a plan that was the basis for the establishment of the Marine Biological Laboratory (MBL) at Woods Hole in 1888, the year after Baird's death. Under its first director, Charles O. Whitman (1842–1910), who ran the laboratory until 1908, the MBL established a summer program with instruction in invertebrate zoology in 1888, adding marine botany in 1890, general physiology in 1892, and embryology in 1893. The courses were designed to address problems of marine biology but also employ the specific advantages offered by marine biology in order to push ahead the research perspectives of biology generally. The

general-physiology course taught at Woods Hole was the first of its kind in the world. Everywhere else physiology was limited to the study of mammals. At Woods Hole in 1899–1900 German-born physiologist Jacques Loeb (1859–1924), conducted his famous experiments on artificial parthenogenesis of sea-urchin eggs, causing unfertilized eggs to develop into new organisms. Embryology courses at Woods Hole took advantage of the specific characteristics of marine eggs, many of which (including those of the sea urchin) have no outer shell and are transparent.

A Pioneering Institution. By giving the study of marine biology the broadest possible focus, the MBL became a leader in experimental biology. Until universities developed their own research facilities, institutions such as the MBL functioned as centers for scientific research and discovery. Following Dorrn's model, the MBL allocated benches in its laboratory to participating universities, which sent their most promising students to Woods Hole. In addition to Loeb, the earliest researchers at the MBL included geneticists T. H. Morgan (1866–1945), who won a Nobel Prize in Physiology and Medicine in 1933, and E. B. Wilson (1856–1939)—who, like Morgan, had earlier worked in the U.S. Fish Commission laboratory—as well as embryologist Frank R. Lillie (1870–1947) and geneticist Nettie Stevens (1861–1912).

Sources:

Dean C. Allard, "The Fish Commission Laboratory and Its Influence on the Founding of the Marine Biological Laboratory," *Journal of the History of Biology*, 23 (1990): 251–270;

Frank R. Lillie, *The Woods Hole Marine Biological Laboratory* (Chicago: University of Chicago Press, 1944).

THE MICHELSON-MORLEY EXPERIMENT

Measuring Light. American physicist Albert Abraham Michelson (1852–1931) was interested in precise measurement, particularly of the velocity of light. According to the theory current during the second half of the nineteenth century, light traveled in waves through an invisible and imponderable medium called "the ether," and there were several theories concerning how observations of the velocity of light might be affected by the movement of the Earth, which was thought to drag the ether along with it by gravity through its orbit. Michelson believed that since the ether is at rest and the Earth moves through it, the speed of light as observed on the Earth's surface should depend on whether it is traveling in the same direction as the Earth's orbital motion or against it. In 1881, while studying in the physics laboratory of Hermann von Helmholtz in Berlin, Michelson designed an instrument called the interferometer, which used a mirror to split a light beam into two halves traveling in opposite directions. He used it to test his hypothesis with a null result in 1881, but working in partnership with Edward W. Morley (1838–1923) in Cleveland, Ohio, in July 1887, he conducted another experiment with the interferometer that yielded results. He tried to measure the "ether drift," or effect of the Earth's motion

The interferometer that Albert A. Michelson and Edward W. Morley used in their unsuccessful 1887 attempt to prove the theory that light traveled through an invisible substance called "the ether"

through the ether on the speed of light, by observing the extent of the phase shift between the two beams as they rotated through ninety degrees. Although the instrument was highly sensitive, no difference could be detected in the velocity of the two halves of the split beam, thus disproving Michelson's hypothesis. Deciding that the entire solar system might be moving contrary to the Earth, Michelson decided to repeat the experiment at three-month intervals. In 1897 he even staged the experiment on a mountain top, trying to detect the "ether-wind" as far from Earth's surface as he could. Again he found no evidence of the ether influencing the speed of light.

The End of the Ether Theory. The Michelson-Morley experiment has been described as "the greatest negative experiment in the history of science" because, although Michelson refused to admit it, the experiment failed to prove that the ether existed. As Albert Einstein (1879–1955) showed in his special theory of relativity (1905), the velocity of light is constant, and, therefore, ether does not exist. Whether Einstein had the Michelson-Morley experiment in mind when he formulated his special theory of relativity, whether he had once heard of it but had forgotten, or whether he was completely unaware of it is still keenly debated by historians of science. Michelson and Morley's experiment clearly demonstrates how firmly physicists of the late nineteenth century were wedded to a mechanical view of nature that could not admit the existence of action at a distance or through a vacuum. They conceived of the ether only because they thought that light had to travel through a medium. During the first two decades of the twentieth century Einstein and other physicists dis-

proved this idea, developing the quantum theory to show that light is made up of particles, as Michelson believed, but also moves in waves.

Source:

Loyd S. Swenson Jr., *The Ethereal Aether: A History of the Michelson-Morley-Miller Aether Drift Experiments, 1880–1930* (Austin: University of Texas Press, 1972).

PHYSIOLOGY GERMAN STYLE

Moving Science into the Laboratory. Before the 1870s American physiology, the study of how living organisms function and maintain life, was not research based. The laboratory model was imported from Germany during the last quarter of the nineteenth century by American students who studied there. So strong was the German influence that of the thirty-one European-trained founding members of the American Physiological Society (1887), twenty-eight had been trained at German universities. Virtually all the leading American physiologists of the 1890s were trained at the Leipzig laboratory of Carl Ludwig (1816–1895), whose personable, friendly style was more attractive to young Americans than the more typical hard-nosed and imperious demeanor of other leading German scientists.

Following the German Model. All the American scientists who studied in Germany were greatly impressed by the well-appointed experimental facilities—"an endless array of machines, frogs, dogs"—as William James described a laboratory in Berlin. The first German-style laboratory in the United States was established in 1871 at Harvard University by Henry Pickering Bowditch (1840–1911). As Bowditch's student Frederick W. Ellis described it this laboratory was modest indeed:

AN AMERICAN IN GERMANY

Among the many Americans who studied with Carl Ludwig in Leipzig was Henry Pickering Bowditch, who imported the German research style to Harvard University. Ludwig was friendly and receptive to the inexperienced young Americans, for whom he fashioned research problems that would bring out their specific talents. In an 1870 letter to a Boston medical journal Bowditch described his experiences in Leipzig:

Prof. Ludwig directs personally all the work done in the laboratory, devoting his whole time to the superintendence of his pupils and making no independent investigations. Each of the pupils, at present nine in number, makes, under the direction of the Professor, a series of experiments with a view of settling some special point in physiology. The results arrived at are published at the end of the year, sometimes under the names of the Professor and pupil together, and sometimes under that of the pupil alone. The whole work of the laboratory forms every year a pamphlet of 150 to 250 pages.

It will thus be seen that abundant facilities are here offered, not only for learning the existing state of physiological science, but also for becoming familiar with the manner in which physiology is at present studied in Germany. The patient, methodical and faithful way in which the phenomena of life are investigated by the German physiologists not only inspires great confidence in their results, but encourages one in the hope that the day is not far distant when physiology will take its proper place as the only true foundation of medical science.

Source: Henry Pickering Bowditch, "Letter from Leipzig," *Boston Medical and Surgical Journal*, 82 (1870): 305–307.

Henry Pickering Bowditch, whose physiology laboratory at Harvard University was the first modern research facility in the United States

At the time that Bowditch became a professor of physiology it was a gracious Harvard custom to allow an incumbent of a new chair of science to furnish his own apparatus, and so he purchased and brought home from Europe instruments that he knew he would need. . . . The main room of the old laboratory, which was not a large one, had for its principal furniture a table for experiments, a sink, a workbench and foot lathe and a tub for frogs. A smaller room which was shared with Quincy, who had just been appointed an assistant in histology, contained cases for instruments and a few books. This was the laboratory and equipment that Bowditch used for twelve years.

Yet these facilities were substantially better than those of Bowditch's predecessors. According to Ellis, the first chemistry professor at Harvard, Josiah P. Cooke, who started teaching there in 1850, had "to illustrate his lectures with apparatus from a juvenile laboratory which he had established in his father's house, and his first laboratory in Harvard was in a cellar." Another professor found himself assigned "some subterranean locality" for laboratory space and "was fortunate if he did not need a ladder to get into it, and rubbers after he arrived at his destination." Other Ludwig students set up German-style labo-

ratories at Yale and Johns Hopkins Universities. By 1880 physiology research required not only a laboratory with elaborate, German-style apparatus and precision instruments but also an array of assistants and technicians. Operating such a laboratory was expensive and required sustained financial support, such as an endowment or some other means of providing the necessary funding. Furthermore, because of the newness of research-based science and the scarcity of laboratories in the United States, Bowditch and other early physiologists had trouble placing their students in jobs.

The Rise of Laboratory Science. The development of bacteriology in the wake of advances in germ theory provided the stimulus for laboratory training that set American physiology and laboratory science in general on its way in the United States during the 1880s and 1890s. The founding of the American Physiological Society in 1887 marked the emergence of a new scientific discipline. Laboratory science required educational reform as well as funding. In a period when professors of medicine typically made their livings from their clinical practices and were only part-time instructors, professors of labora-

A public-health nurse calling on a working-class family, circa 1890

tory sciences had to be employed full-time and pursue research as well as teaching.

Sources:

Frederick W. Ellis, "Henry Pickering Bowditch and the Development of the Harvard Laboratory of Physiology," *New England Journal of Medicine*, 219 (1938);

Robert G. Frank Jr., "American Physiologists in German Laboratories," in *Physiology in the American Context, 1850–1940*, edited by Gerald L. Geison (Bethesda, Md.: American Physiological Society, 1987), pp. 11–46;

W. Bruce Frye, "Growth of American Physiology, 1850–1900," in *Physiology in the American Context, 1850–1940*, pp. 47–65.

PUBLIC HEALTH

Slow Development of Public Medicine. The emergence of a modern public-health system in the United States began in the last quarter of the nineteenth century. During the first half of the century most doctors were poorly trained, and—like most Americans at the time—they lived in rural areas of the country. Because the population was widely scattered most people could not afford the indirect costs of arranging a doctor's visit: first a messenger would have to be sent to the doctor, who would then have to travel to the patient's home. Until the mid nineteenth century these indirect costs of medical service outweighed direct costs such as the doctor's fee or the price of medicine.

Medicine and the Technological Revolution. With the beginning of the great movement of the American population from the countryside to the city, more doctors moved than people with other callings. The building of the railroads was critical to this process. Doctors relocated at rail centers, and once having moved, they located their offices along streetcar lines. As a result, doctors came into closer contact with their patients and their colleagues. The invention of the telephone reduced the time it took to locate the doctor. In fact some early tele-

phone systems linked doctors' offices directly with pharmacies.

A New Economics for Medicine. In cities doctors also tended to locate their offices near hospitals. The modern hospital was a response to the large numbers of city people who lived alone and had no family members to care for them when they were ill. When doctors' offices were located near hospitals and could be reached by streetcar, the market for their medical services expanded, encouraging competition and lower fees, important at a time when medical insurance was largely unavailable. Insurance companies did not begin to offer general private coverage until the late 1890s. Some illness benefits were provided by some immigrant societies, other fraternal organizations, and labor unions.

The Impact of the Germ Theory. The discovery that diseases were caused by specific pathogens, or germs, and the development of different treatments for individual diseases made it possible to enact public-health measures that were disease-specific and thus more effective, cleaning up water supplies that carry cholera, for example, or pasteurizing milk to prevent the spread of diseases such as undulant fever. Many cities began educational campaigns to instruct citizens on how to avoid certain infectious diseases. During the 1890s tuberculosis testing showed that large numbers of people carried the disease in a latent form, suggesting that improved housing and working standards might be effective in holding off onset of the disease, which was then the most common cause of death in large cities.

The Surgical Revolution. Significant scientific and technical advances made surgery a more common treatment option during the 1890s than it had been in previous decades. Joseph Lister's antiseptic method (disinfecting the operating room to kill bacteria), developed in 1865, was soon followed by the more effective technique of asepsis (using sterile procedures to prevent microorganisms from entering the surgical field of operation). This advance made possible abdominal operations, which had earlier been highly dangerous. X rays were discovered in 1895 and used as a diagnostic tool for the first time in the United States in 1896, providing an impetus for more, and earlier, surgical intervention. The increase in surgery cases was another stimulus to the growth of hospitals.

Educational Reform. Before the second half of the nineteenth century there were no standards for medical education and no provisions for licensing doctors. The right of states to license medical doctors was affirmed for the first time by the Supreme Court in *Dent* v. *West Virginia* in 1888. After this court decision state boards of medical examiners were established. Beginning around 1870, medical education was reformed. Before that time American medical schools had no laboratories and no tradition of research. At reform-minded medical schools such as Harvard, the course of instruction was lengthened from two to three years. In 1883 the Johns Hopkins Medical

John William Draper and Andrew Dickson White, authors of influential books defending modern science against fundamentalists who charged that it violated religious orthodoxy

School initiated the four-year course that became standard and made an undergraduate college degree a prerequisite for admission.

Source:
Paul Starr, *The Social Transformation of American Medicine* (New York: Basic Books, 1982).

REFORMING PSYCHIATRY

Redefining the Psychiatrist's Role. A public outcry against the lamentable state of patient care in public and private mental asylums during the 1870s and 1880s led to the formation of a reform movement that eventually changed not only hospitals but the nature of psychiatric practice as well. Psychiatry had been progressively moving away from an environmental theory of mental disease that associated it with a degenerate moral environment toward a new German approach that centered on the pathology of the brain and nervous system. This change brought alienists (as asylum-based psychiatrists were called) within the compass of scientific medicine.

Changing the Asylum. The quality of patient care, however, lagged behind advances in medical theory. The movement to reform asylums was led in part by neurologists, whose discipline rivaled psychiatry. Neurologists charged

that asylum superintendents were outside the mainstream of American medicine, unable to engage in scientific research and refusing to turn to medical experts for patient care or to submit to public scrutiny. Part of a larger movement to improve medical education in general, critics of mental-health care charged that asylum superintendents had no special expertise but had just worked their way up through the ranks of physicians attached to a particular institution. Rather than being centers of research into emotional and mental disorders, the asylums did no research at all.

Government Regulation. Criticism of conditions in asylums led to a wave of legislative reform. In New York State, for example, candidates for all medical positions in asylums were required to take competitive examinations. The state asserted its prerogative to control treatment of the mentally ill in the counties where asylums were located. Piecemeal changes were codified in the New York Insanity Law of 1896, which established a complete, supervised system of care for the insane. Treatment of the insane everywhere was improved, with greater emphasis on the individual patient and a renewed interest in innovative treatment and research. Yet therapy remained largely ineffectual until the ideas of Sigmund Freud began to be disseminated in the United

When President Andrew Dickson White of Cornell University instituted the elective system, he enraged traditionalists who favored the single, classical curriculum that had remained essentially the same since the Middle Ages. For White, however, the elective system, which made it possible to introduce the study of natural science at the undergraduate level, would have the desirable effect of defusing the "warfare" between science and theology. He concluded his influential book *A History of the Warfare of Science with Theology* with a comment on the changing nature of American university education:

Under the old American system the whole body of students at a university were confined to a single course, for which the majority cared little and very many cared nothing, and, as a result, widespread idleness and dissipation were inevitable. Under the new system, presenting various courses, and especially courses in the various sciences, appealing to different tastes and aims, the great majority of students are interested, and consequently indolence and dissipation have steadily diminished. Moreover, in the majority of American institutions of learning down to the middle of the century, the main reliance for the religious culture of students was in the perfunctory presentation of sectarian theology, and the occasional stirring up of what were called "revivals," which, after a period of unhealthy stimulus, inevitably left the main body of students in a state of religious and moral reaction and collapse. This method is now discredited, and in the more important American universities it has become impossible. . . . Religious truth . . . is presented, not by "sensation preachers," but by thoughtful, sober minded scholars. Less and less avail sectarian arguments; more and more impressive becomes the presentation of fundamental religious truths.

Source: Andrew Dickson White, *A History of the Warfare of Science with Theology in Christendom* (New York: Appleton, 1896).

States during the early years of the twentieth century. Typical Therapies were usually based on the assumptions that emotional problems were caused by defects of the patient's physical constitution. They included bed rest, hydrotherapy and, toward the end of the century electro-shock therapy.

Source:
Ruth B. Caplan, *Psychiatry and Community in Nineteenth-Century America* (New York: Basic Books, 1969).

THE "WAR" OF SCIENCE AND THEOLOGY

The Military Metaphor. Throughout the nineteenth century, particularly after the publication of Charles Darwin's *On the Origin of Species* in 1859, the presumed contest between science and religion was characterized in terms of warfare. This "military metaphor," as it has been called, fanned hostility on both sides, creating the impression that scientists and theologians were split into two warring camps with the general public choosing one side or the other. The truth was considerably more complex. At best the military metaphor characterized the viewpoints of pro- and anti-Darwinian extremists, but it failed to describe the views of the vast majority in the middle. At the center of the war between science and religion were two influential books purporting to provide its history: John William Draper's *History of the Conflict between Religion and Science* (1874), which went through fifty printings by 1930, and *A History of the Warfare of Science with Theology in Christendom* (1896), by Andrew Dickson White. Both authors attempted to present cautionary tales of religious obtuseness with respect to scientific ideas.

Draper's Attack on Roman Catholicism. Draper (1811–1882), a professor of chemistry at New York University, reached a wide audience because his book was published in a popular-science series directed by Edward Livingston Youmans, editor of *Popular Science Monthly* and the most influential popularizer of science in the English-speaking world. In spite of the title of his book Draper narrowed "religion" to just one, the Roman Catholic Church: "Roman Christianity and science," he wrote, "are recognized by their respective adherents as being absolutely incompatible; they cannot exist together; one must yield to the other; mankind must make its choice—it cannot have both." As much concerned by the presumed political power of the Pope as he was by Catholic dogma, Draper was writing in response to Pope Pius IX's "Syllabus of Errors" (1864), a broadside against liberalism and all its works. Although Draper wrote his book just as the Pope's political power was being substantially reduced by the reunification of Italy under King Victor Emmanuel II, Draper's charge was accepted as fact by anticlerical forces around the world. Indeed, his viewpoint seemed to be confirmed when the Spanish translation of his book (1876) was placed on the Catholic Church's Index of Prohibited Books, placing Draper in the select company of his heroes, including Copernicus and Galileo.

White's History. Much more scholarly than Draper's book, White's *A History of the Warfare of Science with Theology in Christendom* is an important part of the late-nineteenth-century drive to legitimize secular higher education, as opposed to church-sponsored colleges. For White (1832–1918), who had served as the first president of Cornell University during the years 1867–1885, the warfare between science and theology was mainly the result of an out-of-date and authoritarian university system, which was overly dogmatic in regard to religion and shut off its students from access to scientific learning. With Charles W. Eliot, president of Harvard University, White had led the movement to include elective courses in the college curriculum, a reform that made it possible for undergraduates to study the natural sciences. Thus White viewed the "war" as less a political contest than an intellectual one in which those antagonistic to science had overreacted to a perceived threat and consequently overstepped their bounds. Rather than single out Catholicism as the enemy, White noted that the recent "theological war against a scientific method in geology was waged more fiercely in Protestant countries than Catholic," suggesting that the Catholic Church had learned a lesson from the mistake it made when it found Galileo guilty of heresy in 1633 for writing that the Earth revolved around the Sun.

Source:
James R. Moore, *The Post-Darwinian Controversies: A Study of the Protestant Struggle to Come to Terms with Darwin in Great Britain and America, 1870–1900* (Cambridge: Cambridge University Press, 1979).

HEADLINE MAKERS

WILLIAM JAMES

1842-1910
PSYCHOLOGIST

The Education of a Scientist. The elder brother of novelist Henry James, William James entered the Lawrence Scientific School at Harvard University in 1861 and transferred to Harvard Medical School in 1864 without having first obtained an undergraduate degree. In 1865–1866 he accompanied Harvard biology professor Louis Agassiz on the Thayer Expedition to Brazil, where he collected fish specimens. While there he contracted a severe physical ailment that apparently left him in a weakened condition for the rest of his life. Like so many other American scientists of his generation, James studied in Germany to perfect his laboratory technique and to become acquainted with the latest ideas in experimental physiology. In 1867–1868 he attended the University of Berlin, where he was enrolled in Emil Du Bois-Reymond's physiology course. Listening to this great physiologist convinced James that psychology—then a branch of philosophy—had to be recast in the mold of experimental physiology. Returning to the United States, he received an M.D. degree from Harvard in 1869.

Professor at Harvard. Joining the Harvard faculty as a lecturer on anatomy and physiology in 1872, James began teaching a course on the relations between physiology and psychology in 1875. As psychologist G. Stanley Hall later recalled, in 1876 James organized a rudimentary laboratory, later called the Laboratory for Psychophysics, "in a tiny room under the stairway of the Agassiz Museum," in which he had "a metronome, a device for

whirling a frog, a horopter chart and one or two bits of apparatus." James taught his first philosophy course in 1879, and the following year he moved to the Department of Psychology and Philosophy, where he began to develop the philosophical ideas that he would later label "pragmatism" and worked on a psychology textbook. James complained that he lacked a theory of cognition—how people know what they know—and that he did not see how he could write a comprehensive text without one. He finally concluded that he should omit metaphysical questions and treat psychology as if it were a natural science. The core of his approach was to describe the nervous system as if it were a kind of electrical network that receives stimuli and transmits them to the brain. He concluded that this process had been perfected through Darwinian natural selection, in which the mind develops in such a way as to aid organisms in adapting to their environments.

The Standard Psychology Text. James's great textbook, *Principles of Psychology,* was finally published in 1890 and remained the standard psychology text well into the twentieth century. The final product mixed physiological determinism with more subjective and creative observations on how the mind functions. James dissented from prior, mainly philosophical, commentators such as David Hume and Immanuel Kant who denied that the mind was capable of perceiving real time and space, both of which were abstract categories. According to James, human beings can feel duration and perceive through their senses the three dimensions of space. To describe this process James devised the famous metaphor "stream of consciousness," whereby human beings cumulatively build on their experience of the passage of time. His emphasis on experience linked him with the tradition of British empiricism, which held that observation was at the core of science. James broadened the concept to include the personal, subjective experiences of each individual.

Pragmatism. The philosophical school known as pragmatism has its origins in the Metaphysical Club, whose members, including James and Charles Sanders Peirce, met in Cambridge during the 1870s. The term itself was coined by Peirce. As later reformulated by James, pragmatism is a general philosophy that builds on his psychological concept of experience and restores the metaphysical dimension that he pruned from his *Principles of Psychology*. Truth, James believed, was not something to be discovered; rather it is invented from one's own experience.

Sources:

Gay Wilson Allen, *William James: A Biography* (New York: Viking, 1967);

Kim Townsend, *Manhood at Harvard: William James and Others* (New York: Norton, 1996).

CHARLES SANDERS PEIRCE

1839-1914
GEODESIST, PHILOSOPHER
OF SCIENCE

Background. Charles Sanders Peirce, one of the greatest of American philosophers, was the son of Benjamin Peirce (1809–1880), superintendent of the U.S. Coast Survey in 1867–1874 and a professor of mathematics and astronomy at Harvard University. Charles Peirce, who used to say he was raised in a laboratory, received his bachelor's degree in chemistry from Harvard in 1863, as a member of the first class to graduate from the Lawrence Scientific School. Having already joined the Coast Survey as a temporary aide in 1859, Peirce went to work for the Survey full-time in 1861 and as a result was exempted from military service during the Civil War. He remained a member of the Coast Survey until 1891. He specialized in gravity research, but the accuracy of his observations during the solar eclipses of 1869 and 1870 also identified him as a first-rate observational astronomer, and he went on to measure the magnitudes of the stars in the galactic cluster that includes the Sun.

Measuring Gravity. In 1875 Peirce learned how to use the new convertible pendulum to measure gravity. Comparing his results with those obtained in Europe, he found an error in European measurement caused by the pendulum stand. As a result the Repsold pendulum used by the Coast Survey was replaced by one Peirce invented in 1878. In 1879 Peirce determined the length of a meter from a wavelength of light, anticipating the later experiments of Albert Michelson. In 1882 he made a mathematical study of the relationship between the variation of gravity and the shape of the Earth.

Philosophy. From 1879 to 1884 Peirce was a lecturer in logic at Johns Hopkins University but devoted much of his time to mathematics, developing a philosophy of mathematics based on the notion that mathematicians are concerned with what is logically possible, but not with actual reality. During the 1880s and 1890s he devised a classification of knowledge. Mathematics was the first science, while normative science had three divisions: aestheticism, ethics, and logic. He called logic the science of how humans should obtain their objectives. After leaving the Coast and Geodetic Survey in 1891, Peirce devoted himself mainly to philosophy. He has been recognized as the founder of the distinctly American school of philosophy called pragmatism, whose adherents also included William James and John Dewey.

Evolution. Like virtually all other American scientists of his day, Peirce was an evolutionist and sought to formulate philosophical concepts in accord with evolutionary theories. He shared with the leading American scientists of his generation a belief in a theory first formulated by Jean-Baptiste Lamarck (1744–1829): the doctrine that characteristics acquired by an organism during its lifetime may be passed on genetically to its offspring. Peirce believed that humans were born with their minds already adapted to identify the laws of nature more readily than if they had attempted to guess them by chance. Thus, he believed that common sense would tell which scientific hypotheses are true and which are not. Because of these views, he was also convinced that the direction of evolution was toward ever-increasing order.

Source: Carolyn Eisele, "Charles Sanders Peirce," *Dictionary of Scientific Biography*, 18 volumes (New York: Scribners, 1970) X: 482–488;

Murray G. Murphey, *The Development of Peirce's Philosophy* (Cambridge, Mass.: Harvard University Press, 1961).

NATHANIEL SOUTHGATE SHALER

1841-1906
GEOLOGIST, GEOGRAPHER

Background. A native of Kentucky, Nathaniel Southgate Shaler was a student of Louis Agassiz at the Lawrence Scientific School at Harvard University. After graduating in 1862, Shaler served in Kentucky during the Civil War and returned to Harvard in 1864 as a professor of geology. He later became dean of the Lawrence Scientific School. He also directed the Kentucky Geological Survey from 1873 to 1880, when he joined the U.S. Geological Survey as a part-time geologist, heading its Atlantic Coast Division from 1884 to 1900. One of Shaler's contributions was the correct assertion that the Earth had a fluid substratum beneath its solid surface. Therefore, he said, the topography of the surface is produced in two ways: by a contraction of the Earth's nucleus (producing the continental folds) and a contraction of the outer shell only (producing mountain ranges).

Accepting Evolution. One of the first American geologists to confront and accept Darwin's theory of evolution by natural selection, Shaler made evolution a basic organizing concept in all of his mature work. In an article on the rattlesnake and natural selection (1893) he stated that organisms "adapt themselves in an immediate manner to the peculiarities of their environment." In this way an accumulation of influences is passed on to each creature's offspring, leading "organisms ever upward to higher planes of existence." The upward thrust of evolution was a common theme among those students of Agassiz who became evolutionists. All of them also believed the now generally unaccepted neo-Lamarckian theory that animals have an inner drive to adapt to environmental changes. In this way, Shaler wrote, "organisms are educated to their environment."

Reconciling Evolution and Religion. Shaler took pains to reconcile evolution with revelation by stressing that design was still the basis of human cosmology. He believed that a sense of purpose in nature was logical because the perception of such had always been present in human history: Nature's design could be perceived in the finely adjusted habitats of organic beings; ecological niches were not haphazardly adopted. Shaler also believed that religion had evolved, coming close to the progressive orthodoxy of the theologians associated with the *Andover Review.* His student William Morris Davis, one of the founders of American academic geography, basically translated religious ideals into the language of secular science.

Geography. As a human geographer Shaler believed that there were strong geographic and environmental controls over the development of human culture. Thus in his study of Kentucky he explained that there had taken place a "geological distribution of politics," in that areas with rich soils had been proslavery, while those with poor ones had opposed slavery. Shaler was also a pioneer in American soil science, stressing the function of soil as "the realm of mediation between the inorganic and the organic kingdom," and he trained Curtis Marbut, the first professional soil scientist in the United States.

Sources:

David N. Livingstone, *Nathaniel Southgate Shaler and the Culture of American Science* (Tuscaloosa: University of Alabama Press, 1987);

John E. Wolff, "Memoir of Nathaniel Southgate Shaler," *Bulletin of the Geological Society of America*, 18 (1908): 592–608.

PUBLICATIONS

Edward Drinker Cope, *The Primary Factors of Organic Evolution* (Chicago: Open Court, 1896)—a defense of the Lamarckian theory that acquired characteristics may passed on genetically to an organism's offsprings;

Cope, *The Vertebra of the Tertiary Formation of the West* (Washington, D.C.: U.S. Government Printing Office, 1883)—Cope's report on the fossils of extinct vertebrates that he found on Ferdinand V. Hayden's geological survey of the American West;

Elliot Coues, *Birds of the Colorado Valley* (Washington, D.C.: Government Printing Office, 1878)—an important treatise on bird life that draws on Coues's research as part of Hayden's survey of the Colorado River basin;

John Call Dalton Jr., *The Experimental Method in Medical Science* (New York: Putnam, 1882)—an early treatise on experimental physiology by one of the founders of modern medical science;

James Dwight Dana, *Manual of Geology*, third edition (New York: Ivison, Blakeman, Taylor, 1880)—a standard college geology textbook that remained in use well into the twentieth century;

Amos E. Dolbear, *First Principles of Natural Philosophy* (Boston: Ginn, 1897)—a summation of Dolbear's "atomic theory," in which he describes molecules as "minute vortex rings of ether";

John William Draper, *History of the Conflict Between Religion and Science*, eighth edition (New York: Appleton, 1884)—a discussion of the role of science in the secularizatiion of Western society in a book that remained popular and influential well into the twentieth century;

Henry H. Gorringe, *Coasts and Islands of the Mediterranean Sea,* 4 volumes (Washington, D. C.: U.S. Government Printing Office, 1875–1883)—a pioneering study of the physical geography of the Mediterranean region;

Ferdinand V. Hayden, *The Great West* (Philadelphia: Franklin / Bloomington, Ill.: C. R. Brodix, 1880)—a description of western geology and geography based on Hayden's observations during his survey of the West;

Clarence King, *Systematic Geology* (Washington, D.C.: U.S. Government Printing Office, 1878)—an important manual by one of the foremost government scientists and surveyors of the nineteenth century;

Samuel P. Langley, *The New Astronomy* (Boston: Ticknor, 1888)—an important work of nineteenth-century astrophysics by an American pioneer in the scientific study of astronomy;

Leo Lesquereux, *The Flora of the Dakota Group,* edited by F. H. Knowlton (Washington, D.C.: U.S. Government Printing Office, 1891)—a description of western plant life by a participant in the Hayden survey;

Simon Newcomb, *Popular Astronomy* (New York: Harper, 1878)—one of several popular books on astronomy by a leading nineteenth-century authority on the subject;

Charles Sanders Peirce, *Photometric Researches* (Leipzig: W. Englemann, 1878)—results of Peirce's measurements of the acceleration of gravity;

John Wesley Powell, *On the Organization of Scientific Work of the General Government* (Washington, D.C.: U.S. Government Printing Office, 1885)—observations on the role of government in organizing and setting policy for scientific research projects;

Powell, *Report on the Lands of the Arid Region of the United States* (Washington, D.C.: U.S. Government Printing Office, 1878)—an influential survey of irrigation in the western United States that opened the possibility of farming lands once thought inhospitable to agriculture;

Nathaniel Southgate Shaler, *Nature and Man in America* (New York: Scribners, 1891)—an environmental interpretation of history;

John B. Stallo, *The Concepts and Theories of Modern Physics* (New York: Appleton, 1882)—an influential popularization of the nineteenth-century mechanistic view of physics.

CHAPTER ELEVEN

SPORTS AND RECREATION

By ADAM HORNBUCKLE AND MARTIN MANNING

CONTENTS

Sidebars and tables are listed in italics.

1878

- The Chautauqua movement, organized in 1874, begins a literary and scientific circle for home study; some seven thousand persons enroll during its first year.

- The National Archery Association is founded at Crawfordsville, Indiana.

2 Apr. President Rutherford B. Hayes inaugurates the annual Easter egg roll on the White House lawn.

8 June The New York Athletic Club forms the National Association of Amateur Athletes of America, governing the organization of track and field in the United States.

10 Oct. Jimmy McLaughlin rides the winners in three horse races in Nashville, Tennessee.

1879

- Baseball owners introduce a reserve clause to control movement of players from team to team.

- Madison Square Garden opens to the public in New York City. The original structure was a railroad depot on Twenty-sixth Street.

2 Jan. The Northwestern League, a minor baseball league, is formed.

1880

- William Muldoon, inventor of the medicine ball, wins the heavyweight wrestling championship.

- Patrick "Paddy" Ryan becomes the world heavyweight bare-knuckle boxer after defeating the defender, Joe Goss of England, in an eighty-seven-round bout near Colliers Station, West Virginia.

- *Chautauquan,* the monthly magazine of the Chautauqua movement, begins publication.

29 May W. P. Wurtz of Yale University wins the first intercollegiate bicycle race, riding two miles in 7:57.

31 May The first National Meet of American Bicyclists is held in Newport, Rhode Island.

1881

- The United States Lawn Tennis Association (USLTA) is created. Rules of play are set and adopted worldwide.

- Richard D. Sears wins the first USLTA men's singles title. He holds the title for the next six consecutive years.

- The American Association of Base Ball Clubs forms as a rival to the National League in major league baseball.

5 Oct. The International Cotton Exposition opens in Atlanta.

15 Oct. The first American fishing journal, *American Angler,* owned and edited by William C. Harris, is published in Philadelphia.

9–10 Nov.	The U.S. yacht *Mischief* wins two straight races from the Canadian challenger *Atalanta* in the America's Cup.

1882

- The American Association of Base Ball Clubs agrees with the National League to mutual recognition of reserved baseball players and exclusive territorial rights.

- The National Croquet Association and U.S. Intercollegiate Lacrosse Association are formed to revise and to standardize rules of their respective games.

7 Feb.	Bare-knuckle boxer John L. Sullivan knocks out Patrick "Paddy" Ryan in nine rounds in Mississippi City, Mississippi.
24 June	Richard Higham, a baseball umpire, is expelled from the National League for dishonesty.
5 Sept.	The first Labor Day celebration and parade, sponsored by the Knights of Labor, is held in New York City.
25 Sept.	The Providence and Worcester teams play major league baseball's first doubleheader.

1883

- Yale University wins the first national college football championship. Yale's record is 8 wins, 0 losses, and 0 ties.

- Hugh H. Baxter of the New York Athletic Club sets a world record by pole vaulting 11 feet, 1/2 inch.

- The first recorded U.S. cycling championship occurs in Springfield, Massachusetts; G. M. Hendrie wins the title.

17 May	Buffalo Bill Cody's Wild West Show opens in Omaha, Nebraska, and features mock stagecoach robberies and Indian attacks.
2 June	The first baseball game played under electric lights occurs in Fort Wayne, Indiana. The Fort Wayne team beats Quincy 19–11 in seven innings.
7–8 June	Amherst, Brown, Harvard, Trinity, and Yale compete in the first intercollegiate tennis tournament; J. S. Clark (Harvard) wins the singles title.
16 June	The New York Giants hold the first Ladies' Day game, during which all women are allowed into the stadium free.
1 Aug.	The Southern Exposition opens in Louisville, Kentucky.
22 Oct.	The first New York Horse Show is held at Gilmore's Gardens and becomes an annual event.

1884

- LaMarcus Thompson builds his Switchback Railway Coaster at Coney Island, New York. This early roller coaster is so popular that Thompson's receipts exceed $600 a day.

- Charles H. Sherrill Jr., of Yale University and the New York Athletic Club, becomes the first sprinter to employ the crouch start.

- The National League follows the lead of the American Association of Base Ball Clubs and adopts the percentage system to determine pennant winners.

- Greyhound racing is introduced in Philadelphia.

- Moses Fleetwood Walker and Welday Walker are the first African Americans to play major league baseball. They play one season for Toledo in the American Association of Base Ball Clubs.

27 Nov. The University of Pennsylvania defeats Wesleyan College 16–10 in the first intercollegiate polo match.

1885

- Annie Oakley, famous for her marksmanship, joins Buffalo Bill's Wild West Show.

24 Jan. The World's Industrial and Cotton Centennial Exposition opens in New Orleans. It is the largest world's fair yet held in the United States.

22 May Tecumseh, ridden by Jimmy McLaughlin, wins the thirteenth annual Preakness Stakes in Maryland.

14–16 Sept. *Puritan* of the United States defeats *Genesta* of England in the America's Cup.

20 Dec. William B. Curtis accomplishes a weight-lifting feat of incredible proportions by reportedly lifting 3,239 pounds "with harness."

1886

- The first international polo match is held between England and the United States at Newport, Rhode Island; England wins, 10–4 and 14–2.

1 Jan. The Valley Hunt Club stages the first Tournament of Roses in Pasadena, California.

28 Oct. The Statue of Liberty is dedicated in New York Harbor amid great rejoicings; President Grover Cleveland presides over the celebrations.

1887

- Ellen F. Hansell wins the first USLTA women's singles title.

- The National Association of Amateur Athletes of America becomes the Amateur Athletic Union.

2 May The American Trotting Association organizes in Detroit, Michigan.

26 May Racetrack betting becomes legal in New York State.

17–30 Sept. The American yacht *Volunteer* successfully defends the America's Cup against the British challenger *Thistle*.

1888

- The Chautauqua College of Liberal Arts, New York, is established for gifted students of the Chautauqua movement.

- The St. Andrews Club, a prestigious golf club, is established in Yonkers, New York; other clubs soon open in Boston and Philadelphia.

21 Jan. The Amateur Athletic Union of the United States (AAU) forms, winning control over amateur athletics from unscrupulous promoters. The first AAU track and field championships are also held.

9 June Sir Dixon, ridden by Jimmy McLaughlin, wins the twenty-second Belmont Stakes. McLaughlin is the only jockey in the history of the Belmont to win the race three times in a row on two separate occasions (1882–1884, 1886–1888).

1889

- A safety bicycle is manufactured for the first time on a large scale.

- Walter Camp chooses the first All-American football team in *Collier's Weekly*. He selects eleven college football players as the best in the nation at their positions.

19 Jan. Georgia makes Robert E. Lee's birthday a state holiday; Virginia follows the next year.

8 July Bare-knuckle boxing holds its last and most memorable bout when John L. Sullivan knocks out Jake Kilrain in the seventy-fifth round for the U.S. heavyweight championship in Richburg, Mississippi.

1890

- The Players' (Brotherhood) League, with eight teams in Pittsburgh, Chicago, Cleveland, Buffalo, New York, Philadelphia, Boston, and Brooklyn, forms in order to protest the low salaries paid by the National League and American Association of Base Ball Clubs.

- The Daughters of the American Revolution is founded.

- John J. Owen, of the Detroit Athletic Club, becomes the first sprinter to run 100 yards in less than 10 seconds (9.8 seconds).

- George Train sets the around-the-world record in a balloon (67 days, 13:03:03).

- *Sporting Times,* the first publication devoted entirely to baseball, debuts.

- Sequoia and Yosemite National Parks in California are established.

- The University of Pennsylvania defeats Cornell in the first intercollegiate cross-country meet.

29 Nov. Navy defeats Army 24–0 in the first Army-Navy football game, played at West Point, New York.

1891

- The architectural firm McKim, Mead, and White completes renovations on Madison Square Garden. The new structure is more elegant and features a tower modeled after the Giralda in Seville, Spain.

- James Naismith, a physical-education instructor in Springfield, Massachusetts, invents the game of basketball, the only popular American game that does not have English origins.

- The American Association of Base Ball Clubs disbands.

| 13 May | Kingman, ridden by Isaac Murphy, wins the seventeenth annual Kentucky Derby; it is Murphy's second consecutive win. |
| 18 Oct. | The first international six-day bicycle race in the United States is held at Madison Square Garden. The winner is "Plugger Bill" Martin. Most of the other competitors end up in the hospital, suffering from exhaustion. |

1892

•	The National League increases from eight to eleven teams after the dissolution of the American Association of Base Ball Clubs: East consists of Boston, New York, Philadelphia, Baltimore, Brooklyn, and Washington, D.C.; West includes Chicago, Saint Louis, Cincinnati, Pittsburgh, and Louisville.
12 Feb.	The Illinois legislature declares Abraham Lincoln's birthday a state holiday; New Jersey, New York, Washington, and Minnesota follow suit four years later.
18 Mar.	Jockeys are prohibited from using anything but a regulation whip and spurs on a horse after a jockey uses an electric spur during a race at Guttenberg, New Jersey.
3 June	Jefferson Davis's birthday is observed for the first time as an official holiday in Florida.
7 Sept.	James J. "Gentleman Jim" Corbett knocks out John L. Sullivan in the twenty-first round at New Orleans in the first heavyweight title bout fought with gloves.

1893

•	Ice hockey is introduced in the United States from Canada. Games are played at Yale and at Johns Hopkins Universities.
•	The first intercollegiate relay race is held at the University of Pennsylvania in Philadelphia.
•	The Chicago Fly Casting Club holds the first national fly-casting tournament.
1 May	President Cleveland opens the World's Columbian Exposition in Chicago to commemorate the four hundredth anniversary of the discovery of America.
14 June	Flag Day is observed in Philadelphia by mayoral order.

1894

•	The United States Golf Association (USGA) is established.
•	Harvard and Penn withdraw from the American Intercollegiate Football Association. The University Athletic Club of New York forms a new rules committee with Harvard, Penn, Princeton, and Yale.
•	The Jockey Club is incorporated to encourage the care and training of thoroughbred horses.
•	Hugh Duffy of the Boston Nationals has the highest batting average for a season ever compiled by a major league baseball player (.438).
27 Jan.	The California Midwinter International Exposition in San Francisco opens, the first of its kind on the West Coast.

5 May	Harvard defeats Columbia in the first intercollegiate fencing match.
16 June	The squeeze play is first employed by players on the Yale baseball team in a game against Princeton.
28 June	Congress declares the first Monday in September to be national Labor Day.

1895

- Sea Lion Park, the first enclosed amusement park, opens at Coney Island.

- C. S. Brown wins the first USGA women's amateur title in Newport, Rhode Island.

- *Field and Stream* debuts as a magazine devoted entirely to outdoor sports and recreation, such as fishing, hunting, and camping.

- Brown defeats Harvard in the first intercollegiate ice hockey game.

- The American Intercollegiate Football Association disbands.

9 Feb.	The Minnesota State School of Agriculture and Mining defeats Hamline College 9–3 in the first intercollegiate basketball game.
31 Aug.	In a game against the Jeannette, Pennsylvania, football team, the Latrobe team pays substitute quarterback John Brallier ten dollars, making him the first professional football player.
9 Sept.	The American Bowling Congress (ABC) forms in Beethoven Hall, New York City, to revive waning interest in a once popular sport.
18 Sept.	The Cotton States and International Exposition opens in Atlanta, Georgia.
21 Sept.	The New York Athletic Club defeats the London Athletic Club in the first international track and field meet held in New York City.
4 Oct.	The USGA holds the first U.S. Open golf tournament in Newport, Rhode Island. It is won by Horace Rawlins, an English immigrant working at the Newport Golf Club.
28 Nov.	Brothers Charles E. and J. Frank Duryea win the first gasoline-powered automobile race in the United States, the Chicago to Evanston Thanksgiving Day Race.

1896

- The first national ice hockey league, the Amateur Hockey League, organizes in New York City.

6–15 Apr.	The first modern Olympic Games are held in Athens, Greece. American James B. Connolly wins a gold medal for the triple jump.
7 Nov.	Yale, by a margin of thirty-five strokes, defeats Columbia in the first intercollegiate golf tournament.

1897

- Steeplechase Park, an amusement park built and owned by George C. Tilyou, opens at Coney Island.

• The first Frontier Day is celebrated by citizens of Cheyenne, Wyoming, at the town's fairgrounds.

17 Mar. Bob "Ruby Robert" Fitzsimmons wins the world heavyweight boxing title by defeating James J. Corbett in a fourteen-round fight in Carson City, Nevada. This is the first boxing match photographed by a motion-picture camera.

19 Apr. John J. McDermott of New York City wins the first Boston Marathon, with a time of 2:55:10.

1 May The Tennessee Centennial and International Exposition begins in Nashville.

1898

• The National Basketball League, the first professional league of basketball players, begins with teams in Philadelphia, New York, Brooklyn, and southern New Jersey.

7 May Columbia, Cornell, Harvard, Pennsylvania, Princeton, and Yale compete in the first intercollegiate trapshoot.

1 June The Trans-Mississippi and International Exposition starts in Omaha, Nebraska.

1899

• University of Chicago social scientist Thorstein Bunde Veblen publishes *The Theory of the Leisure Class,* which claims social decorum and refined tastes can only be acquired with leisure.

• Mount Rainier National Park in Washington State joins the national park system.

7 Mar. Pennsylvania defeats Columbia 2–0 in the first intercollegiate water polo game.

8 Mar. Pennsylvania, Columbia, and Yale compete in the first intercollegiate swimming meet, which consists of a four-man 200-yard relay race won by Penn in 2:23.

24 Mar. Yale wins the first intercollegiate gymnastics tournament.

16–20 Oct. *Columbia* of the United States defeats *Shamrock I* of England in the America's Cup.

OVERVIEW

The New Leisure Society. In the late nineteenth century a new middle class emerged that had more leisure time and more disposable income than common people had ever enjoyed before in America. They were the employees and managers of corporations, who, because they were working for someone else, kept strict hours, had a dependable source of income, and had less personal interest in their work than was common in small business, where the owner had direct contact with his workers. Eager to spend their newfound time and money outside the workplace, the middle class turned to sports, either as spectators or participants. Those not interested in athletic competition found other forms of recreation and leisure-time activities. Prior to the Gilded Age (the name given to this era by novelist Mark Twain) organized leisure was a luxury enjoyed by the upper classes, who had idle hours to spend in sports and recreation. Now, however, the elite had to compete with commoners on the playing field and for a seat in the audience. Blue-collar workers and unskilled laborers still lacked the resources to engage in the same sports and recreational pursuits of the middle class. They found their own fun in ways often considered uncouth by people conscious of their social status. Barroom games and saloon-sponsored teams were popular in lower-class neighborhoods.

Outlets for Social Anxieties. Middle-class men felt challenged at the end of the nineteenth century. Those who worked for large corporations often felt that they had lost some of the control over their destinies that self-employed people had. The women's movement and other civil rights activists threatened the sense of power and self-importance white men had traditionally enjoyed, and many felt compelled to declare their masculinity, especially in sport. Many American women also enjoyed sporting events and engaged in various recreational pursuits, sometimes in sexually segregated settings, sometimes with their husbands and boyfriends. Energy, vitality, and muscularity had become marks of the national character, and the new middle class proclaimed their American-ness for new immigrants and for the world alike.

The Amateur Ideal in Sport. Sports participation and spectator interest during the Gilded Age was unprece-

dented, and there was no shortage of games to play, especially in the cities. Nineteenth-century people had a peculiar attitude toward amateur athletics inherited from England. There amateurism was an ideal that celebrated sports for its own sake and insulated wealthy, upper-class people from participating with the middle- and working-class sportsmen. The lower classes took pay for athletic endeavors as if they were working a job. Amateur sports, such as golf, tennis, track and field, basketball, and college football, for example, represented the last attempt of the elite class to retain their traditional status. While most amateur sportsmen adhered strictly to the amateur ideal throughout the period, others, especially members of urban athletic clubs, who held winning to be the most important part of a sports contest, secretly recruited paid athletes to enhance their teams' prestige. The reintroduction of the Olympic Games in 1896, in which only amateurs could compete, carried the amateur ideal into the twentieth century.

Sports Embrace the Business Ethic. Reflecting the business mood of the time, professional sports gained a foothold in America during the last quarter of the nineteenth century. Although prizefighting and horse-racing offered money to its participants in the antebellum era, the chief professional sport after the Civil War was major league baseball. By the late 1890s, however, basketball, football, and golf also offered professional opportunities. Baseball, more than any of the other professional sports, mirrored the entrepreneurial and managerial experience of the era, as team owners maximized profits and players organized for increased pay. Despite agitation by players, team owners maintained strict financial control of baseball. Professional baseball, which evolved out of the structure of amateur clubs that flourished in the 1850s, overshadowed amateur baseball in establishing the rules and conduct of the game. The rise of professional basketball and football, however, was a consequence of efforts to resist the control of the Amateur Athletic Union, the governing body of amateur sports established in the 1870s. Boxing, or bare-knuckle prizefighting, as the sport was known for much of the era, epitomized professional sport: it was rough; there were limited rules; and it was a favorite of the working class.

Collegiate Sport. In the late nineteenth century the nation's colleges and universities became hotbeds of sports activity, especially football. The first college sport, rowing, had its origins in the antebellum era. Although colleges organized baseball, basketball, tennis, and track and field competitions during the period, football provided a solid foundation for college sports that persisted into the next century. Football evolved from English rugby on the playing fields of elite American schools. Walter Camp of Yale University was responsible for the refinement of football, as well as for the promotion of the game, in American culture. College sports, including football, began as intramural activities but by the end of the century came under faculty control and supervision. Essentially amateur in nature, college athletes came from the ranks of those who could afford a university education. In the pursuit of victory, however, colleges hired professional coaches, recruited skillful but academically unqualified performers, and profited materially from the success of their teams. College sports received much criticism for these practices, which, some educators argued, worked against the academic mission of the university.

Sports and Social Stratification. College sports, especially those played on the campuses of Harvard, Yale, and similar universities, reflected the social stratification inherent in American sports at that time. In addition to college sports, the social elite attended and participated in yachting events, particularly the America's Cup, tennis and golf tournaments, horse races, and other country-club and athletic-club events. In their leisure time the urban middle class flocked to the baseball stadiums. Some middle-class urbanites formed their own baseball clubs. For their recreational and healthful pursuits, both middle class men and women cycled through the streets of the burgeoning suburbs and urban parks. The working classes, who had less free time, bowled and played billiards in the saloons they frequented. Largely blocked from participating in the urban sporting mainstream, unskilled laborers, particularly Irish Americans and other ethic groups, engaged in sports and recreational activities frowned upon by proper Victorians. For Irish Americans prizefighting had the greatest appeal, and they idolized successful boxers. By the end of the century their heroes, such as John L. Sullivan, became the nation's heroes.

Rise of the Amusement Parks. Amusement parks were a popular new source of entertainment for the masses. Often located at the end of new electric-trolley lines, on the perimeter of urban areas, amusement parks offered city dwellers a diversion from work and responsibility. While the most notable of the late-nineteenth-century amusement parks was Coney Island, New York, others included Paragon Park and Revere Beach, Boston; Willow Grove, Philadelphia; Palisades Park, New Jersey; Ponce de Leon Park, Atlanta; Euclid Beach, Cleveland; Cheltenham Beach,

Chicago; Forest Park Highlands, Saint Louis; Manhattan Beach, Denver; and The Chutes, San Francisco. Amusement parks gathered together a variety of popular attractions and pastimes, all of which reflected the cultural change of the era. What made the amusement park remarkable were new mechanical rides, exotic sideshows, and the excitement of crowds of pleasure seekers gathered together to have fun.

Age of the Big Top. Akin to the amusement park, the circus offered the city people the same escape from the ordered world of work. Popular since the antebellum era, the circus became more popular during the late nineteenth century. A boom in railroad construction enabled circuses to reach more of the country. Because circuses moved from city to city, they had to be carefully managed. The swift construction and dismantling of the huge tent city required by two- and three-ring circuses with sideshows, menageries, and private quarters was done with factorylike precision as workers scurried to meet the demanding schedule of the traveling show. The circus was big business, and the largest and most successful shows merged with one another until finally the Ringling Brothers and Barnum & Bailey Circus dominated the big-top field. Circuses offered so-called freaks of nature, both human and animal, and the temptation and conquest of death. They exposed audiences to nature's thrilling mysteries and perils. More important, however, was the sheer astonishment aroused by the daring and skill of trapeze artists, lion tamers, high-wire artists, acrobats, and clowns.

Colorful Drama of the Wild West. Closely allied with the circus was Buffalo Bill Cody's Wild West Show, which opened in 1883. For over thirty years it enjoyed a place as one of the most popular attractions in the land, and the show entertained Europeans as well as Americans. Ownership and the show's title changed over time, but the show always contained cowboys performing feats of skill and daring, mock robberies of stagecoaches, and well-staged battle scenes depicting the bravery of the U.S. Cavalry against Indian savagery. One of the star attractions from 1885 to 1901 was a young woman named Annie Oakley, who could shoot a coin tossed in the air at thirty paces. The Lakota tribal leader Sitting Bull also toured with Buffalo Bill (1885).

Fairs and Expositions. Along with spectator sports, amusement parks, and circuses, fairs and expositions provided cultural displays in a country that was increasingly diverse. At the New Orleans Exposition (1885) and the World's Columbian Exposition in Chicago (1893), Americans enjoyed the various rides, ate ethnic foods, and saw exhibitions on the "arts, industries, manufactures, and products of the soil, mine and sea." Fairs and expositions also played an invaluable role in the development of museums by displaying some of their artifacts, including those from the Smithsonian Institution in Washington, D.C., and the Field Museum of Natural History and the Museum of Science and

Industry, both in Chicago. Many Americans agreed with President William McKinley when he called world's fairs the "timekeepers of progress."

Holidays. As they had throughout their history, Americans celebrated holidays to commemorate landmark events in the nation's past, the birthdays of presidents and other notable Americans, and other special occasions. Holidays such as Arbor Day, Memorial Day, Flag Day, and Labor Day had their origins in the late nineteenth century. While these annual celebrations were observed nationally, others, such as the birthdays of Confederates Robert E. Lee and Jefferson Davis, were observed regionally. Ethnic and religious groups celebrated their own holidays as well. Sports and holidays became linked during this period, as people turned to athletic contests as a diverison on their days off work. Thanksgiving Day, for example, became known as a day for college football games played after a festive dinner. Civic holidays, perhaps more than any other leisure activity, bound Americans of different social classes, ethnic backgrounds, and religions around values of patriotism, heroism, self-reliance, and tolerance.

TOPICS IN THE NEWS

AMATEUR SPORT

The Amateur Ideal. Many of the sports played in late-nineteenth-century America were considered amateur, meaning that the contestants did not earn a living from their athletic pursuits. Individuals who earned a living from athletic competition, either in the form of a salary or prize money, were professionals, and they competed apart from the amateurs. Amateurism originated in England, where it operated to prevent the working classes from competing against the landed aristocratic elite. In England amateurism, practiced in its purest sense, meant that an individual who earned a living from competition was considered a professional and, therefore, ineligible for participation in amateur sport. English amateurism also carried a code of sportsmanship, in which winning was secondary to gentlemanly competition. America inherited the concept, if not the practice, of amateurism from England. In America amateurism operated to insulate sportsmen of wealthy Anglo-Saxon Protestant roots from not only the working class but from racial, ethnic, and religious minorities as well. Moreover, the amateur ideal evolved in America to embrace a "win at all costs" ethic, which encouraged the organizers and promoters of amateur sports to seek surreptitious ways to materially compensate winning athletic performances and subsidize champion athletes.

Rise of the Athletic Club. The locus of amateur sport in late-nineteenth-century America was the urban athletic club. The first and most influential of these organizations, the New York Athletic Club (NYAC), was established in 1868 by a small group of socially prominent sportsmen who wanted to engage in athletic, specifically track and field, competition, with individuals of similar social standing and congenial interests. The London Athletic Club, which held the first English amateur track and field championships in 1866, served as the model for the NYAC. Soon other athletic clubs organized throughout metropolitan New York, including the Staten Island, American, Manhattan, Pastime, University, and Crescent clubs, each fashioned after the NYAC. By 1879 Baltimore, Buffalo, Chicago, Detroit, and Saint Louis had established similar athletic clubs. Throughout the 1870s the NYAC became the leading promoter of amateur sport in America, sponsoring nationwide championships in track and field in 1876, swimming in 1877, boxing in 1878, and wrestling in 1879. To prevent professionals of any sort from participating in these national championships, the NYAC defined an amateur as "any person who has never competed in an open competition for public or admission money, or with professionals for a prize, nor has at any period in his life taught or assisted in the pursuit of athletic exercises as a means of livelihood." In 1879 when the newly formed National Association of Amateur Athletes of America (N4A) assumed control of track and field, it adopted the same definition of amateurism.

Amateurism Transformed. While upholding the amateur ideal, athletic clubs during the 1880s became more than centers simply for urban amateur sport; they became broader and more socially inclusive organizations. During these decades athletic clubs began

One of the oldest footraces in North America is the Boston Marathon. The race was inspired by the 1896 Olympic marathon, conceived by Michel Breal, a French classicist and historian, who insisted that the athletic program of the first modern Olympic Games must include an endurance footrace. He suggested a forty-kilometer race to celebrate the feat of Pheidippides, a Greek soldier who ran that distance from Marathon to Athens to announce the Greek triumph over Persia in 490 B.C. Spiridon Louis, a Greek shepherd, won the 1896 Olympic marathon in less than three hours. After the Olympic Games the Boston Athletic Association decided to hold a similar race to commemorate the famous ride of Paul Revere on the eve of the American Revolution. The first race was held on 19 April 1897, in conjunction with the BAA handicap track meet. The race followed a 24.7-mile course from Ashland to Boston. Fifteen runners competed in the inaugural event, with John J. McDermott, a Canadian, winning in 2:55:10. The year before, McDermott had won the New York Marathon, and while that race was an one-time affair, the Boston Marathon became an annual Patriot's Day sporting event. John C. Lorden, of Cambridge, Massachusetts, became the first local runner to win the Boston Marathon in 1903.

Sources: Stephen Hardy, *How Boston Played: Sport, Recreation, and Community, 1865–1915* (Boston: Northeastern University Press, 1982);

David E. Martin and Roger W. H. Gynn, *The Marathon Footrace: Performers and Performances* (Springfield, Ill.: C. C. Thomas, 1979).

to seek and select members with, in addition to athletic skill, credentials such as membership in other prestigious social or athletic clubs, a college degree, and wealth from either an inheritance or a lucrative profession. The NYAC, which boasted a membership of fifteen hundred in 1885, became such a club, as it carefully screened its applicants and charged a $100 initiation fee and $50 annual dues. Membership in the NYAC became an important link in a web of associations that constituted an exclusive status community. Athletic clubs such as the NYAC began as player-centered organizations, but became less so as they sought members who were not necessarily athletes, but representatives of the social elite. As in the case of the NYAC, many of the athletes who originally established the club resigned as their power was usurped by a growing nonathletic membership. The athletes became merely representatives of the club, there to bring home trophies and entertain the new social elite membership. To the social elite, sports became a means to enhance the prestige of the club, not something to be pursued for its own sake. The effortprestige to enhance the prestige of the athletic club eroded its amateurism, as the clubs charged admission fees to events and rewarded athletes materially for championship performances.

The Amateur Athletic Union. Throughout the 1880s rivalries between the clubs for athletic superiority resulted in the rise of professionalism within amateur athletics. prestige of the most blatant violations of amateurism involved Lon Myers, a champion runner from the Manhattan Athletic Club (MAC). Myers received payment for serving as the club's secretary and directing the construction of a new clubhouse. The MAC also permitted Myers to compete against a British professional runner and keep his winnings. Upon his triumphant return from England, the MAC held a benefit banquet for him, which garnered Myers $4,000. These events led the NYAC and several other clubs to leave the National Association of Amateur Athletes of America in 1886, and two years later they established the Amateur Athletic Union (AAU) to govern primarily track and field. Despite the formation of the AAU, the problems with professionalism did not cease, as clubs continued to steal each other's top athletes, luring them away with promises of better training facilities and lavish expense accounts. Abuses abounded, since many involved smaller clubs that had no recourse against the larger organizations, such as the NYAC, that dominated the decision-making levels of the AAU. During the 1890s the AAU gained broader control over amateur sports by becoming involved with college athletic competitions. By the turn of the century the AAU, the colleges, and the American Olympic Committee fought for influence over amateur sports, as each entity had a stake in its athletes and activities.

Rise of Track and Field. The chief amateur sport in late-nineteenth-century America was track and field, and under the control of the AAU from the late 1880s onward, the sport flourished. The NYAC, as well as other clubs throughout the nation, produced the nation's top track and field performers, the best of whom were brought together for the AAU national championships. The AAU maintained a strict amateur code, severely penalizing violators. Although the Intercollegiate Association of Amateur Athletes of America (IC4A) governed intercollegiate track and field, the AAU promoted it as well, permitting college performers to compete in club meets, and inviting the best to compete in the national championships. Many of the best track and field athletes of the late nineteenth century and early twentieth century, however, came from ethnic clubs, such as the Irish-American Athletic Club in New York, which regularly battled with the NYAC for track and field supremacy. In 1895 American performers defeated an international delegation of athletes in a track and field meet between the NYAC and the London Athletic Club. With the revival of the

The *Valkyrie III* and the *Defender* in the 1895 America's Cup Race

Olympic Games in 1896, track and field became the showcase sport, with Americans dominating nearly every event. James B. Connolly, who won the first event—the hop, step, and jump—was the first Olympic champion to be crowned in fifteen centuries.

Sources:

Benjamin G. Rader, *American Sports: From the Age of Folk Games to the Age of Spectators* (Englewood Cliffs, N.J.: Prentice-Hall, 1983);

Steven A. Riess, *City Games: The Evolution of American Urban Society and the Rise of Sports* (Urbana & Chicago: University of Illinois Press, 1989);

Richard Wettan and Joe W. Willis, "The Effect of New York Athletic Clubs on American Amateur Athletic Governance, 1870–1915," *Research Quarterly*, 47 (October 1976): 499–505.

AMERICA'S CUP

Origins. One of the oldest and most prestigious prizes awarded in international yacht racing, the America's Cup was originally an 100-guinea silver trophy offered by the Royal Yacht Squadron to the winner of a race around the Isle of Wight on 22 August 1851. John Cox Stevens, a wealthy New Jersey real estate broker and founder of the New York Yacht Club, won the race by defeating seventeen British yachts. He named the cup after his yacht *America* and put the trophy on display at his Annandale, New Jersey, estate. After his death in 1857, the cup became the trust of the New York Yacht Club "as a permanent challenge cup, open to competition by any organized yacht club of any foreign country."

Social Atmosphere. In the late nineteenth century yacht racing in the United States, as in England, was a pastime of the wealthy, and it attracted many spectators. The first challenge for the cup since 1857 occurred in 1870 and stimulated enormous interest in New York. On the day of the race, businesses closed down and the harbor swarmed with countless spectator craft festooned with ribbons and pendants. The race itself was the focus of intense rivalry on the part of the participants. The seemingly glamorous world of yachtsmen attracted international public attention and led to speculation in sporting journals as to the merits of particular captains and hull designs. Ship owners spent fortunes on sleek vessels and highly trained crews. Until 1920 the course for the America's Cup generally started in Upper New York Harbor, ranged out into the Atlantic Ocean for thirty miles, and ended off Staten Island. (An inside course, which was sailed within the confines of New York Harbor, was last used in 1887.)

Ashbury. There was no competition for the cup in the 1860s because the Civil War brought a temporary halt to pleasure boating and racing off the eastern seaboard. In 1870 James Ashbury, a wealthy British railroad entrepreneur, became the first contender for the cup. On 8 August the race featured seventeen New York Yacht Club schooners against *Cambria*, the British vessel. *Cambria* finished 42 minutes behind *Magic*, the winning vessel. Ashbury complained about the course and number of ships, maintaining it gave the New York Yacht Club an unfair advantage in defending its possession of the cup. In response to that complaint,

WATER TOBOGGAN
1890

A popular ride at Cedar Point Park, Sandusky, Ohio, an early amusement center

the New York Yacht Club announced that future challenges would be one-on-one matches rather than mass affairs. In the first one-on-one challenge in 1871, Ashbury entered the *Livonia*, but it lost two of the three races to the *Columbia* of the New York Yacht Club.

Challenges. The Canadians and British were consistent challengers to the cup in the late nineteenth century. In August 1876 the Canadian yacht *Countess of Dufferin* lost to the American *Madeleine*. Five years later Canada again made a bid for the cup. The Bay of Quinte Yacht Club of Belleville, Ontario, entered *Atalanta*, a boat designed and owned by Alexander Cuthbert. *Mischief,* designed by A. Cray Smith, defeated *Atalanta*. Cuthbert, who wanted to challenge for the cup again with *Atalanta* in 1882, was thwarted by a rule change that said the same boat could not challenge for two years. In 1885 the New York Yacht Club accepted the challenge of England's Royal Yacht Squadron on behalf of Sir Richard Sutton. In perhaps the best series of races in the history of the challenge, the English cutter *Genesta* lost to the American sloop *Puritan*, owned by a syndicate headed by J. Malcolm Forbes, the son of railroad and shipping magnate John Murray Forbes. The New York Yacht Club retained possession of the America's Cup with victories by *Mayflower* over the British *Galatea* in 1886 and by *Volunteer* over *Thistle* in 1887.

Dunraven and Lipton. After *Volunteer's* victory, the New York Yacht Club instituted a new rule stipulating that the challenger had to reveal the design of its boat before the race. In 1889 the Royal Yacht Squadron, on the behalf of the earl of Dunraven, issued a challenge for the cup. The challenge was withdrawn, however, when Dunraven refused to indicate the design of his

boat, only its dimensions; however, in 1893 Dunraven yielded to the demands of the New York Yacht Club and entered his boat, *Valkyrie II*. The American boat *Vigilant,* the first of several America's Cup champions designed by master boatbuilder Nat Herreshoff, defeated *Valkyrie II*. In 1895 Dunraven's *Valkyrie III* lost to *Defender,* another boat designed by Herreshoff and owned by J. P. Morgan. Dunraven's charge that the interference of spectator boats caused his boat to lose led to such acrimony that the New York Yacht Club did not expect to receive another British challenge for the cup until the next century. However, in 1899 the Yacht Club received a challenge from Sir Thomas Lipton, the Scottish-bred Irish tea merchant. His yacht, *Shamrock I,* lost to the American vessel, *Columbia*. Lipton's 1899 challenge was the first of five that the New York Yacht Club would accept from him during the next thirty-one years. Despite his determination, Lipton failed each time to wrest the cup away from the Americans.

Sources:

Ian Dear, *The America's Cup: An Informal History* (New York: Dodd, Mead, 1980);

John Rousmaniere, *America's Cup Book, 1851–1983* (New York: Norton, 1983);

A. B. C. Whipple, *The Racing Yachts* (Alexandria, Va.: Time-Life Books, 1980).

AMUSEMENT PARKS AND THE NATIONAL PARKS SYSTEM

Leisure Time. Amusement parks and national parks in the late nineteenth century represented two sharply different visions of the use of leisure time. Amusement parks were man-made environments that duplicated and distorted the urban experience, and did everything they could to prevent contemplation. Meanwhile, national parks were celebrated for their natural grandeur and the possibility of solitude and contemplation.

Early Developments. American amusement parks in the late nineteenth century began as wooded parks at the end of trolley lines and noisy avenues on the outskirts of cities. Their growth was the direct result of the development of streetcar and railway lines and, later, subway systems. Since electric power companies charged transit firms a flat monthly rate regardless of the amount of electricity used, city railway owners needed to increase the number of riders during slow weekends and evenings. The solution was pleasure parks located at the end of the line. They started as picnic groves, often near bodies of water, then added regular entertainments, mechanical amusements, dance halls, sports fields, boat rides, and restaurants. By 1919 there were approximately fifteen hundred to two thousand amusement parks in the United States that provided entertainment for the general public.

Impact of 1893 Fair. The World's Columbian Exposition had a major influence on the development of amusement centers in the 1890s. At this event George Washington Gale Ferris built and operated his namesake wheel. Aside from the Ferris wheel, the Chicago fair introduced the midway, an avenue for concessions and amusements that became the trademark of amusement parks, carnivals, expositions, and fairs thereafter. The midway was nearly a mile long and six hundred feet wide and linked the rowdy "entertainment" concessions with the more educational and cultural exhibitions at the fair. Every major city soon had at least one amusement park that followed this formula: Cleveland (Euclid Beach), Boston (Revere Beach), Chicago (Cheltenham Beach), Denver (Manhattan Beach), Pittsburgh (Kennywood Park), Saint Louis (Forest Park Highlands), San Francisco (The Chutes), and Philadelphia (Willow Grove). Each amusement park had a midway with a carousel, a Ferris wheel, a roller coaster, a penny arcade, and fireworks displays.

Coney Island. The biggest attraction that opened during this period was Coney Island, New York, the supreme example of the American amusement park until Disneyland opened in 1955. Located south of Brooklyn and nine miles from Manhattan, Coney Island had attracted visitors since 1829, when the first hotel was built there. During the antebellum period the area slowly acquired restaurants, bathhouses, saloons, and a steamboat service that linked the island to Manhattan. In 1884 LaMarcus Thompson built on the island the Switchback Railway Coaster, an early version of the roller coaster. Sea Lion Park, the first enclosed amusement park with an admission fee in the nation, opened on Coney Island in 1895. Two years later Steeplechase Park, a fifteen-acre attraction built and owned by George C. Tilyou, opened to the public. Tilyou's success was based on an understanding of the

---

THE FERRIS WHEEL

At the 1893 World's Columbian Exposition in Chicago, George Washington Gale Ferris, a railroad and bridge engineer, built an amusement ride that is now a mandatory feature at any fair or carnival. The Ferris wheel was an instant hit after its 21 June debut, the highlight of the exposition for most visitors, and undoubtedly helped the fair turn a profit. The Ferris wheel earned back its entire cost of $380,000 on 1 September when it forwarded to the exposition $25,000 as royalty on the first profits. At the fair's end in late October, 1,453,611 customers had ridden the wheel, with a gross intake of $726,805.50.

The axle of the Ferris wheel was considered a manufacturing accomplishment, the largest single piece of steel ever forged at that time. Produced by the Bethlehem Iron Company, the axle was 45 feet 6 inches long, 33 inches in diameter, and weighed more than 45 tons. The towers supporting the axle were 140 feet high and anchored in bedrock. The entire structure was 264 feet high and had two concentric wheels from which hung 36 pendulum cars, each capable of holding 60 passengers (for a total of 2,160 riders). The total weight of the structure was 1,200 tons, and it was powered by two 1,000-horsepower engines.

After the World's Columbian Exposition, Ferris dismantled his wheel and made an unsuccessful attempt to develop a small park around it. Ferris died broke in 1896, but the original Ferris wheel entertained visitors at the 1904 Louisiana Purchase Exposition before Saint Louis citizens condemned it as a rusting eyesore. On 11 May 1906 the "Great Wheel" was destroyed by a one-hundred-pound dynamite charge.

Source: Judith A. Adams, *The American Amusement Park Industry: A History of Technology and Thrills* (Boston: Twayne, 1991).

---

needs of common Americans. He explained that "what attracts the crowd is the wearied mind's demand for relief in unconsidered muscular action. . . . We Americans want either to be thrilled or amused, and we are ready to pay well for either sensation." Upon entering the park, patrons paid a twenty-five-cent admission fee that allowed them to enjoy all the rides as many times as desired during the day. The central attraction of the park was a ride known as the Steeplechase, eight wooden double-saddled horses that raced along an undulating track. (The double saddles allowed a man and woman to ride together with the man's arms snugly around the woman's waist.) By 1900 more than one million people had ridden the Steeplechase.

National Parks. Reformers in the late nineteenth century considered parks oases for the protection of plant and animal life, for natural wonders, and for public recreation. When western naturalists, such as John Muir and John Wesley Powell, described the breathtaking sights and sounds of Yosemite, the Grand Canyon, and other natural areas, they aroused the interest of eastern seaboard residents. In the beginning, national parks protected magnificent scenery from timbering, mining, and other industries; their use as places of recreation and of leisure came much later. With time, the glories of Yellowstone, the Grand Canyon, and the Sierra Nevada became well known, and the idea of a national park system took off. Yellowstone National Park (1872), covering 1,189 square miles of Idaho, Montana, and Wyoming, was the first national park to be created. Visitors were astounded by its ten thousand hot springs and two hundred geysers, including Old Faithful. Yosemite started as a California state park (1864) but was incorporated into the national park system in 1890; it has the highest waterfall in North America. Sequoia National Park, also in California, was established in 1890 with its Sierra redwoods and Mount Whitney, the highest mountain peak in the United States outside of Alaska. In 1899 Mount Rainier National Park in Washington State, with the largest one-peak glacial system in the United States, was created. Until 1916 these parks were administered by the army before being transferred to the National Park Service in the U.S. Department of the Interior.

Sources:

Judith A. Adams, *The American Amusement Park Industry: A History of Technology and Thrills* (Boston: Twayne, 1991);

John F. Kasson, *Amusing the Million: Coney Island at the Turn of the Century* (New York: Hill & Wang, 1978);

Roderick Nash, *Wilderness and the American Mind,* revised edition (New Haven, Conn.: Yale University Press, 1973).

BARE-KNUCKLE PRIZEFIGHTING

The Irish American Subculture. For much of the nineteenth century boxers fought under the London, or Broughton, Rules, with bare fists, battering each other through endless rounds, until only one combatant remained standing. Known as bare-knuckle prizefighting, this type of boxing had special appeal to the working-class Irish American male subculture. Often ostracized from respectable occupations and mainstream American culture, some Irish American males sought opportunities in occupations that required little education and could produce quick rewards in a society that placed a high value on material success. Since many of these activities, including prizefighting, were against the law, Irish Americans developed a certain political savvy, often entering the political arena themselves to establish the rules, and even enforce them, as many police officers were of Irish descent.

The Role of Fighting. The prizefighter, usually an Irish American himself, was the hero of the bachelor subculture, which held fighting ability in the highest esteem. Street fighting prepared young boys for careers as pugilists, criminals, and policemen. Irish political machines employed these young brawlers in their battles with other political factions. If a boy garnered success as a prizefighter, he furnished a role model for other urban, particularly Irish American, youth. In the prizefighter, youngsters, as well as adults, saw the successful display of survival skills, as well as the possibility of material reward. In the late nineteenth and early twentieth century, Irish Americans dominated the ring. Later champions would emerge from other ethnic and racial groups—Jews, Italians, African Americans, and Hispanics—as they joined the Irish in the American metropolis.

New Era of Prizefighting. The 1880s and 1890s represented a new era in prizefighting, characterized by direct promotion of the sport and the fighters and reforms to lessen the sport's violence. In the 1880s Richard Kyle Fox, publisher of the sensational tabloid *National Police Gazette,* promoted prizefighting and other sports. Fox, who defined sport broadly, offered championship belts and other prizes for, among other things, the world's heavyweight boxing championship, teeth lifting, hog butchering, female cycling, and female weightlifting. He pleaded for the legalization of prizefighting, his favorite sport, and brought the sport national attention by leading a campaign to find a challenger to unseat heavyweight champion John L. Sullivan. Fox also promoted the development of weight classifications by awarding belts and naming champions at weights other than heavyweight. Another force of change in prizefighting was Harry Hill, the owner of a notorious New York City saloon, which staged legal boxing exhibitions. In the early 1880s both the wrestler William Muldoon and boxer Sullivan trained and performed at the saloon. Hill was also recognized as the nation's best boxing referee. Athletic clubs led to the legalization of boxing; in 1896 the Horton Law in New York permitted boxing in athletic clubs. The Twentieth Century Athletic Club once leased Madison Square Garden in New York to hold public prizefights under the Horton Law. The athletic clubs also promoted the adoption of the Marquis of Queensberry rules, which required combatants to wear gloves, limited rounds to three minutes, required ten-second knockouts, and prohibited wrestling holds. In addition to the provisions of the Queensberry rules, the athletic clubs instituted round limitations and joined Fox in the development of weight divisions. In 1890 New Orleans, Louisiana, legalized boxing under the Queensberry rules.

Sullivan: The Last Bare-Knuckle Champion. The new era of prizefighting had a hero in John L. Sullivan. As a teenager he fought in exhibitions in saloons in Boston, developing a reputation as a slugger. In 1882

Children playing baseball in the streets of New York City, circa 1890

Sullivan knocked out the reigning champion, Patrick "Paddy" Ryan, in the ninth round at Mississippi City, Mississippi, for a stake of $5,000 and a side bet of $1,000. Sullivan, who added nineteen more knockouts to his record from 1882 to 1886, enjoyed broad celebrity status, as all levels of society were interested in his love for fighting and flamboyant lifestyle. Fox, who wanted to find a fighter to unseat Sullivan, wrote about his binges and uncontrollable temper in the *National Police Gazette*. Fox's stories made Sullivan a larger-than-life celebrity. In 1889 Sullivan defended his title against Jake Kilrain in what would be his last championship bout of the bare-knuckle era. Three years later James J. "Gentleman Jim" Corbett defeated Sullivan in the first world heavyweight championship fight under the Queensberry rules. In 1897 Corbett lost the title to Bob "Ruby Robert" Fitzsimmons, a lean but powerful Australian, who held the title until 1899, when James J. Jeffries, a former Ohio ironworker, knocked him out in eleven rounds at Coney Island, New York.

Sources:

Elliot J. Gorn, *The Manly Art: Bare-Knuckle Prize Fighting in America* (Ithaca, N.Y.: Cornell University Press, 1986);

Michael T. Isenberg, *John L. Sullivan and His America* (Urbana & Chicago: University of Illinois Press, 1988);

Donald J. Mrozek, *Sport and the American Mentality: 1880-1910* (Knoxville: University of Tennessee Press, 1983);

Jeffery T. Sammons, *Beyond the Ring: The Role of Boxing in American Society* (Urbana & Chicago: University of Illinois Press, 1988).

BASEBALL

Early Professionalism. Since its beginnings in the 1830s, baseball had been played by loosely organized amateur clubs in the Northeast. In 1858 these teams organized the National Association of Base Ball Players (NABBP). In 1869 Harry Wright, a transplanted Englishman and former cricket player, organized the Cincinnati Red Stockings, the first publicly proclaimed professional baseball team. Wright, who earned $1,200 as a player and team captain, recruited many of the best amateur players, paying them salaries of $600 to $1,400. After completing the 1869 season with a record of 58 wins and 1 tie, in 1870 the Red Stockings lost several games and experienced great financial strain from the salaries of their top players. The team disbanded after 1870, and Wright took his best players to Boston and organized a new team. In 1871 professional teams formed the National Association of Professional Base Ball Players (NAPBBP). The formation of the NAPBBP, following the demise of the NABBP in 1870, signaled the end of the influence of amateurism on baseball in the United States, as the NAPBBP set the rules of the game and established a selection process for a national champion. In 1871 the Philadelphia Athletics defeated the Chicago White Stockings for the NAPBBP pennant. The most dominant NAPBBP team was Harry Wright's Bostonians, who posted a record of 227 wins and 60 losses and won four consecutive pennants from 1872 to 1875.

NATIONAL LEAGUE PENNANT WINNERS

DATE	TEAM	MANAGER	WON-LOST	PERCENTAGE
1876	Chicago	Albert G. Spalding	52 - 14	.788
1877	Boston	Harry Wright	31 - 17	.646
1878	Boston	Harry Wright	41 - 19	.683
1879	Providence	George Wright	55 - 23	.705
1880	Chicago	Adrian C. Anson	67 - 17	.798
1881	Chicago	Adrian C. Anson	56 - 28	.667
1882	Chicago	Adrian C. Anson	55 - 29	.655
1883	Boston	John F. Morrill	63 - 35	.643
1884	Providence	Frank C. Bancroft	84 - 28	.750
1885	Chicago	Adrian C. Anson	87 - 25	.777
1886	Chicago	Adrian C. Anson	90 - 34	.726
1887	Detroit	William H. Watkins	79 - 45	.637
1888	New York	James Mutrie	84 - 47	.641
1889	New York	James Mutrie	83 - 43	.659
1890	Brooklyn	William McGunnigle	86 - 43	.667
1891	Boston	Frank Selee	87 - 51	.630
1892	Boston	Frank Selee	102 - 48	.680
1893	Boston	Frank Selee	86 - 44	.662
1894	Baltimore	Edward H. Hanlon	89 - 39	.695
1895	Baltimore	Edward H. Hanlon	87 - 43	.669
1896	Baltimore	Edward H. Hanlon	90 - 39	.705
1897	Boston	Frank Selee	93 - 39	.685
1898	Boston	Frank Selee	102 - 47	.677
1899	Brooklyn	Edward H. Hanlon	88 - 42	.603
1900	Brooklyn	Edward H. Hanlon	82 - 54	.647

The Rise of the National League. In 1876 William A. Hulbert, president of the Chicago White Stockings, founded the National League of Professional Base Ball Clubs. With the National League (NL) Hulbert established a profitable organization and pioneered the business and bureaucratic structures that would characterize professional team sports into the twentieth century. The NL, which consisted of teams from Boston, Chicago, Cincinnati, Hartford, Louisville, Philadelphia, Saint Louis, and Indianapolis, maximized owner profits by restricting each city to only one team and limiting the owners' ability to trade players freely through the "reserve clause." Originally a "gentlemen's agreement," the reserve clause became a set rule in 1879. The reserve clause permitted team owners to reserve their five best players from trade negotiations with other teams. By the 1880s the owners applied the reserve clause to their entire rosters. Hulbert, who served as president of the NL until his death in 1882, ruled the league with an iron hand, throwing out teams that threatened the integrity of the league and the moral image of professional baseball. He expelled Philadelphia and New York from the league for refusing to complete their final road tours in 1876, and Saint Louis and Cincinnati in 1880 for selling beer and playing games on Sunday. The top team in the NL was Hulbert's Chicago White Stockings, led by Albert Spalding and baseball's first superstar player, Adrian "Cap" Anson.

The Challenge of the American Association. Hulbert's NL had such a monopoly on baseball by the early 1880s that the only way new teams could emerge was through the formation of rival leagues. In 1881 sportswriters Alfred H. Spink from Saint Louis and Oliver P. Caylor from Cincinnati organized the American Association of Base Ball Clubs (AA) to challenge the National League for the baseball dollar. The American Association, with teams in Baltimore, Cincinnati, Louisville, Philadelphia, Pittsburgh, and

SEGREGATED BASEBALL

During the late nineteenth century major league baseball became racially segregated. In 1867 the National Association of Base Ball Players (NABBP), which governed amateur baseball, barred African Americans, maintaining that only whites could uphold baseball's "gentlemanly character." Owners of professional teams in pursuit of winning records, however, signed contracts with skilled African American players. While the first African American professional baseball player was John "Bud" Fowler in New Castle, Pennsylvania, in 1872, the first to play in the major league was Moses Fleetwood Walker, who joined Toledo of the International League in 1884. Unfortunately he and his brother Welday only played one season. Racial tensions hit baseball in 1887, when a white player for Syracuse (International League) refused to stand in the team picture with an African American teammate. Afterward International League owners decided to discontinue signing African Americans, but permitted existing players to remain on the teams. Also that year Adrian "Cap" Anson, manager of the Chicago White Stockings, refused to let his team play an exhibition game against Newark (International League) because its starting pitcher, George Stovey, was an African American. This event led major league owners to release their African American players and agree not to sign any more to contracts. African Americans formed their own professional baseball teams and leagues, with the first being the Cuban Giants in New York in 1885. The team chose the name Cuban Giants because they wanted the public to think they were Cuban rather than American. In 1887 the League of Colored Baseball Clubs organized, with teams in Boston, New York, Philadelphia, Washington, Pittsburgh, Norfolk, Cincinnati, Baltimore, and Louisville. The Cuban Giants defeated the Pittsburgh Keystones in the first Colored Championships of America in 1888.

Sources: Arthur R. Ashe Jr., *A Hard Road to Glory: A History of the African-American Athlete, 1619–1918* (New York: Amistad Press, 1988);

Benjamin G. Rader, *Baseball: A History of America's Game* (Urbana & Chicago: University of Illinois Press, 1992);

David Quentin Voigt, *American Baseball: From the Gentleman's Sport to the Commissioner System* (University Park & London: Pennsylvania State University Press, 1983).

Saint Louis, catered to the working class by charging a low admission price of twenty-five cents, playing games on Sunday (the only day off for most workers), and selling beer. In 1882, after the first year of play by the American Association, the National League recognized the threat to its baseball monopoly and quickly reestablished teams in New York and Philadelphia. More important, the National League worked out a truce, the National Agreement, with the American Association and the Northwestern League, a minor league that operated in Michigan, Ohio, and Illinois, to mutually recognize the reserve clause and territorial rights of each team. Internal problems, however, undermined the stability of the American Association. Brooklyn and Saint Louis not only battled for the American Association pennant but for administrative control of the league. After a Saint Louis representative became president of the American Association in 1890, Brooklyn and Cincinnati resigned from the Association and joined the National League. After a poorly attended 1891 season, the American Association disbanded, and four teams joined the National League.

Players Revolt. In the 1880s baseball players organized for increased salaries and reform of the reserve clause. Although the 1880s were a prosperous decade for major league baseball, team owners held salaries at the levels of the previous decade and, to further maximize their profits, imposed a salary cap. The salaries of baseball players averaged $1,750 annually, nearly three times the wages of typical industrial workers. However, unlike the industrial worker who could (in theory at least) freely market his skills, baseball players were bound to specific teams by the reserve clause, and were unable to freely sell their skills to the highest bidder. In response to the players' demands for higher salaries and reserve-clause reform, John Montgomery Ward, a star player with the New York Giants and a law graduate of Columbia University, founded the Brotherhood of Professional Base Ball Players, the first baseball players' union, in 1885. Within two years Ward presented the National League with a player contract, which the National League accepted, but without abandoning its salary structure. In 1889 the National League imposed a salary cap of $2,500, and angry players called for a strike, but Ward advised against it, presenting the league with the ultimatum that it abandon its salary cap or face competition from a brotherhood league in 1890. That year he formed the Players' League (PL), with teams in seven of the cities with National League teams. Players and owners shared the wealth in the Players' League. Despite limited success in luring some players away from the National League, including the entire Washington team, the Players' League collapsed after the 1890 season, with the National League buying back many of its former stars. Moreover, the National League assured the failure of the Players' League through threats and bribes to its financial backers.

National League Troubles. Despite the demise of both the Players' League in 1890 and the American Association in 1891, the 1890s brought more troubles to the National League. As a result of buying out many of the players and teams of the Players' League and the American Association, the National League accumulated great debts, which the league could not settle because of a national economic depression, poor attendance, public disillusionment with the game, and increased competition from other forms of public entertainment. Fans refused to attend games at home or on the road involving teams with poor records, such as Louisville and Saint Louis, which consistently occupied last place in the final standings. Even the New York Giants, the mainstay of the National League, failed to field a strong team in the 1890s. To increase fan interest and profitability, the team owners wrestled with the decision to reduce the number of teams or form two six-team divisions. In 1899 the league returned to an eight-team circuit comprising of Boston, Brooklyn, Chicago, Cincinnati, New York, Philadelphia, Pittsburgh, and Saint Louis. Moreover, the NL navigated the troubled 1890s without a leader, as Albert Spalding, who led the league against the Players' League in 1890, had retired as president of the Chicago White Stockings. Indeed the National League's troubles would continue into the twentieth century, until a new agreement in 1903 created a stable league structure.

Sources:

Benjamin G. Rader, *Baseball: A History of America's Game* (Urbana & Chicago: University of Illinois Press, 1992);

Harold Seymour, *Baseball: The Early Years* (New York: Oxford University Press, 1960);

David Quentin Voigt, *American Baseball: From the Gentleman's Sport to the Commissioner System* (University Park & London: Pennsylvania State University Press, 1983).

BASKETBALL

Origins of the Game. In the fall of 1891 James Naismith, a physical-education instructor at the Young Men's Christian Association Training School in Springfield, Massachusetts, developed basketball to re-place gymnastics and calisthenics routinely practiced during the winter months. After studying the attributes of lacrosse, football, rugby, and soccer, he created a game in which players would bounce and pass a soccer ball from one another and score points by tossing the ball into a suspended goal. The fundamental concept for the game came to him from watching rugby players spend the winter months throwing rugby balls into boxes. Instead of boxes for goals, Naismith used bottomless peach baskets hung at opposite ends of the railing surrounding the YMCA gymnasium, ten feet above the floor. On 21 December 1891 he introduced basketball to his students, who had tired of their instructor's experimentation with new games that fall. Naismith recalled that "I asked the boys to try it once as a favor to me, and after the ball was first thrown up, there was no need for further coaxing." Some students wanted to name the new game "Naismith Ball," but when the inventor demurred, they started calling it "basket ball."

From the YMCA to the AAU. Basketball quickly spread throughout the YMCAs of the Northeast. The organization used the game as a means to increase membership and promote spiritual growth through athletic competition. Rivalry between the YMCAs became so intense that the organization attempted to regulate the game through the establishment of separate leagues, but the organizations were soon undermined by professionalism, which, according to Luther Halsey Gulick, the director of the YMCA, "resulted in men of lower character going into the game, for men of serious purpose in life do not care to go into that kind of thing." In 1896 the YMCA turned to the Amateur Athletic Union (AAU) for help in regulating the extramural basketball leagues and curbing the growth of professionalism. The AAU gained control of the sport by exercising editorial control over the official rules of basketball, which had been published by the A. G. Spalding & Brothers Company in 1894. The AAU also established leagues and sanctioned regional and national championships. AAU leagues and championship play first emerged in New York City in 1898, and then spread to other cities across the nation. The first AAU national basketball championship, however, was not held until 1908.

Professional Basketball. Independent professional basketball teams, which resisted the control of the AAU, emerged in the late 1890s, particularly in Philadelphia, Pennsylvania. After gaining control of amateur basketball in 1896, the AAU attempted to standardize the game by eliminating rough play and requiring teams to pay registration fees. Philadelphia teams, which played a rough style of basketball, objected to paying registration fees and formed a rival organization, the Eastern Amateur Basketball Association (EABA), in 1898, to accomplish the same goals of the AAU without the registration fees. The EABA, however, promoted professionalism, as team managers and players devised various money-making schemes. In 1899 the EABA became the National League of Professional Basketball (NLPB), with the primary function of making sure that owners and players would honor team contracts. Before the establishment of the NLPB, owners would raid teams for the best players, and players would jump teams for better pay. The NLPB folded in 1903 because it could not force managers and players to honor team contracts.

College Basketball. Colleges and universities throughout the Midwest and Northeast quickly embraced basketball as the Minnesota State School of Agriculture and Mining defeated Hamline College, 9–3, in the first intercollegiate game on 9 February 1895. This game, however, was played with nine-man teams, and a month later the first game played between five-man teams resulted in the University of Chicago defeating the University of Iowa YMCA, 15–12. Northeast colleges and universities took the lead in the development of intercollegiate basketball leagues in the 1900s, with the establishment of the Eastern League, composed of Yale, Harvard, Columbia, Cornell, and Princeton. Basketball

Contestants at the start of an 1890 bicycle race

became the chief sport for college women after Senda Berenson, the director of physical training at Smith College in Northampton, Massachusetts, introduced the game to her students in 1892. Berenson and representatives of Radcliffe, Oberlin, and the Boston Normal School of Gymnastics formed the Women's Basketball Rules Committee, which codified women's basketball rules and had them published by the A. G. Spalding & Brothers Company in 1899. In the first intercollegiate women's basketball game, Smith defeated Bryn Mawr, 4–3, in 1901. Berenson, however, emphasized intramural over intercollegiate games because they facilitated greater student participation in physical training and stressed the social and cooperative rather competitive aspects of sports.

Sources:

Albert G. Applin II, "From Muscular Christianity to the Market Place: The History of Men's and Boys' Basketball in the United States, 1891–1957," dissertation, University of Massachusetts, 1982;

Neil D. Isaacs, *All the Moves: A History of College Basketball* (New York: Harper & Row, 1984).

BICYCLING

Cycling Crazes. In the late nineteenth century, especially in the 1890s, middle-class Americans embraced the bicycle as an instrument of transportation, recreation, and sport. After the Civil War the "boneshaker," a clumsy and uncomfortable machine upon which the rider sat and propelled himself by walking, was introduced to the nation. Since it interfered with pedestrian traffic, the boneshaker was soon banned from most city streets and parks. The second cycling craze followed the introduction of the "ordinary," a

British cycle, at the 1876 Centennial Exposition in Philadelphia. The ordinary was an odd-looking contraption with a huge front wheel, with a diameter measuring up to sixty inches, and small rear wheel. The ordinary was uncomfortable, dangerous to ride, and expensive to own, costing up to $100. Riders of the ordinary were usually daring middle-class and upper-middle-class young men who had mastered the difficult techniques of mounting, riding, and braking the vehicle.

Organization of Cycling Clubs. The ordinary promoted the development of the nation's first cycling clubs, the most prominent of which were the Boston Bicycle Club, organized in 1878, and the Chicago Cycling Club, organized in 1879. The Boston club, the first in the United States, grew from ten to one hundred members in four years. These clubs aimed to enhance the pleasurable and competitive aspects of bicycling by holding club meets, tours, and races. The clubs also acted as a pressure group to promote the sport and the rights of cyclists to share public roadways. In 1880 the League of American Wheelmen was formed, with local branches scattered throughout the nation. More so than the Boston or Chicago clubs, the League of American Wheelmen promoted competitive races and fought for improved roads and equal access with horses on public thoroughfares. Its *Bulletin,* one of eighty-five cycling journals in America, had a readership of nearly one hundred thousand by the turn of the century. In 1883 the League of American Wheelmen achieved an important victory when New York City opened Central Park and Riverside Drive for part of the day to cyclists. Within the next few years few city streets and parkways were off-limits to wheelmen.

The Standard Revolution. A new bicycle, the "standard," was responsible for the bicycle craze of the 1890s. The standard had equally sized pneumatic tires in front and back, a chain rear drive, a diamond-shaped frame, and more efficient coaster brakes. In addition, the standard was more affordable, with a cheap model costing about $50 and a better one close to $100. Purchasing a bicycle, even one of the expensive models, was easier with installment purchasing plans. Sales of secondhand bicycles made the vehicle available to the working classes, but even these purchasing options were out of reach for the unskilled laborer. Bicycling sometimes worsened class resentments, as the residents of poor neighborhoods resented middle-class folk using their streets as riding paths, interfering with street life, and endangering children at play and pedestrians. Angry city residents were known to pelt cyclists with rocks, glass, garbage, eggs, and vegetables, and blocked their paths with pushcarts. In 1896 anarchists and socialists led community opposition to the paving of streets in certain neighborhoods of New York because it would make the community open to speeding cyclists.

Height of the Cycling Craze. By 1895 there were five hundred cycling clubs in America. Each had its own distinctive uniform worn by members on their outings, which could go as far as one hundred miles at a time. Riders represented an important subcommunity of sportsmen, as they constituted significant voting blocs who would support politicians that advocated road and highway improvement and equal access to streets and parks for cyclists. In 1897, when Carter H. Harrison II ran for the first of his five terms as mayor of Chicago, he became an active cyclist and participated in one-hundred-mile tours in order to gain the support of the cycling fraternity. Cycling clubs also sponsored races, and cycling gained popularity as a spectator sport in the 1890s. One of the most popular races was the fifteen-mile race from Chicago to Pullman held each Memorial Day that attracted two hundred to four hundred contestants. Popular from the 1870s to the 1920s were indoor professional track races. The most outstanding racing cyclist of the era was Marshall "Major" Taylor, an African American, who captured the national sprint championships in 1898, 1899, and 1900 and broke many national and world records before retiring in 1910. In 1897 white racers tried to bar him from the tracks, but race promoters and bicycling manufacturers supported Taylor's entry into the events. The success of the cycling craze was due to the masses, as there numbered more than one million cyclists in 1893, a figure that more than quadrupled by 1896.

Bicycling and Health Reform. Bicycling received strong support from physicians and other health promoters as exercise for sedentary urban workers and women. Influenced by the cult of masculinity and the notion of the strenuous life, middle-class urbanites embraced the healthful benefits of cycling. Riding a bicycle provided exercise and fresh air and could be enjoyed alone or with friends. Bicycling was one of the few sports socially sanctioned for participation by women, who had traditionally viewed sports as physically taxing and unfeminine. Bicycling, moreover, promoted fashion changes in women's garments, as women cyclists opted for less restrictive clothes, reflecting the broader social freedom and independence provided them by the machine. Although most physicians encouraged people to use the bicycle for exercise, others were more cautious, warning that overexertion on the bicycle could lead to heart strain and breathlessness. These physicians also cautioned women of childbearing age from excessive cycling, believing that the seat might injure the reproductive organs.

Decline. By the turn of the century there were ten million bicycles in the United States, but the bicycle fad had passed. The market was saturated, and innovative manufacturers were turning to a more sophisticated vehicle, the automobile. While in other parts of the world the bicycle was still regarded as a means of transportation, Americans began to see it as a child's toy. The automobile replaced the bicycle in the hearts of Americans because it was more exciting and ownership conferred greater prestige. Also, the automobile rendered roadways less safe for cyclists. At its height, however, the bicycle epitomized the progress of civilization, symbolizing the victory of technology over the environment.

Sources:

Norman L. Dunham, "The Bicycle Era in American History," dissertation, Harvard University, 1956;

Richard Harmond, "Progress and Flight: An Interpretation of the American Cycle Craze of the 1890s," *Journal of Social History*, 5 (Winter 1971): 238–250;

Robert A. Smith, *A Social History of the Bicycle: Its Early Life and Times in America* (New York: American Heritage Publishing, 1972).

CHAUTAUQUA MOVEMENT

Sunday School Beginnings. The Chautauqua movement grew out of summer Sunday school institutes held by the Methodist Episcopal Church during the 1870s. At an 1873 camp meeting in upstate New York John Heyl Vincent, a minister and later bishop of the Methodist Episcopal Church, proposed that a secular as well as a religious education be offered at these institutes based on the earlier methods used by Josiah Holbrook and other educators. The Chautauqua Assembly started the following summer as a "Sunday School Teachers' Assembly," at Fair Point, New York, on Lake Chautauqua. It was organized by Vincent and Lewis Miller, a wealthy manufacturer and an inventor respectively, as an eight-week program in the arts, sciences, and humanities. In 1877 it became "Chautauqua" by legislative enactment of the Teachers' Assembly. The word came to mean different things:

The Chautauqua Literary and Scientific Circle class of 1889

Sunday schools, traveling tent shows, correspondence courses, educational innovation, lectures, plays, and musical performances.

Early Days. During the first sessions, participants lodged in leaky tents and endured bland foods. From the beginning, both Vincent and Lewis Miller tried to avoid the evangelism that was common to summer camp meetings; instead, Chautauqua was a place of "serious study" expanded to include more secular activities. Educational innovation was the hallmark of Chautauqua. There were extension programs (similiar to continuing-education courses), correspondence courses, and a quarter system in which students could choose any term to study or to work.

Chautauqua Literary and Scientific Circle. In 1878 Vincent started a course of home reading that spread the Chautauqua movement nationally. He organized the C.L.S.C. (Chautauqua Literary and Scientific Circle) as a four-year plan of home reading in American and world history and literature. This plan was considered the first basic program of coordinated instruction on a national level for men and women in the United States. (By 1887 the circle had more than eighty thousand enrolled members.) The C.L.S.C. circulated books and study materials supplemented by a monthly magazine called the *Chautauquan* (1880–1914). At Fair Point the first amphitheater and the Hall of Philosophy were dedicated in 1879. Nine years later the Chautauqua College of Liberal Arts was established under the leadership of William Rainey Harper, a future president of the University of Chicago. The college was created for ambitious students already enrolled in the summer programs of the Chautauqua movement. This unusual institution awarded a bachelor's degree with a four-year course of study that combined traditional classroom work with extension and correspondence courses.

Decline of the Movement. After the turn of the century, "traveling Chautauquas" were organized as tent shows, moving from town to town during the summer and offering lectures and entertainment to many isolated communities. Some traveling Chautauqua meetings, however, quickly became circuslike events with political and evangelical oratory and popular musical entertainment with no intellectual or cultural content. After World War I the programs began to lose audience interest, and the movement had almost entirely disappeared by the 1930s in part because of the growing influence of radio and films.

Sources:

Jesse Lyman Hurlbut, *The Story of Chautauqua* (New York & London: Putnam, 1921);

Theodore Morrison, *Chautauqua: A Center for Education, Religion, and the Arts in America* (Chicago & London: University of Chicago Press, 1974);

Rebecca Richmond, *Chautauqua: An American Place* (New York: Duell, Sloan & Pearce, 1943).

THE CIRCUS

Emergence of a Tradition. In 1792 the Englishman John Bill Ricketts produced the first real circus in the United States: a public display that combined trick horse riding, tumbling, juggling, ropedancing, trained animal performances, and the antics of clowns. Ricketts's circus was a great success and attracted many important visitors, including President George Washington. As the United States expanded, the circus moved westward with the expanding population. American showmen soon departed from the traditional European methods of circus presentation, where they were staged in large permanent buildings. American circus owners developed the traveling show to

Charles Sherwood Stratton was a midget born in Bridgeport, Connecticut, in 1838 (his parents were of normal height). Until he was in his teens, he was only two feet, one inch tall and weighed about fifteen pounds; at maturity he was three feet, four inches tall and weighed about seventy pounds. He joined P. T. Barnum's museum at the age of five. Barnum quickly advertised him as "General Tom Thumb — the smallest human being ever born." (Barnum observed that Americans had a fancy for European "exotics" and so named Stratton after Sir Thomas, one of King Arthur's knights.) In 1844 the showman took him to Europe where he entertained royalty and caused a sensation. Stratton toured the United States (1847–1852) and then went into semiretirement. He married Mercy Lavinia Warren Bumpus, another midget, in 1863; their one child, a daughter, died young. By the time of his death in 1883, he had squandered the fortune he had made. In addition to Jumbo the elephant, Stratton was one of Barnum's two most famous attractions.

Source: Marian Murray, *Circus: From Rome to Ringling* (New York: Appleton Century-Crofts, 1956).

reach a predominantly rural population. For years the circus was an important form of amusement to most Americans, especially in nonurban areas, and it had a rough-and-tumble character in which the quantity of performers and of animals was emphasized.

Barnum's Dominance. After the Civil War the number of circuses in the country grew, as did their size. However, no one dominated the circus world more during this time than Phineas T. Barnum. A correspondent for the London *Times* described him as a "showman on a grandiose scale, worthy to be professed by a man of genius. . . . To live on, by, and before the public was his ideal." Before he entered the circus business, he was a storekeeper and journalist noted for his collection of curiosities at the American Museum, New York. In 1871 Barnum and two associates pooled their resources to form a circus. Barnum's knack for showmanship made the resulting company a great success. The circus had a three-acre canvas tent and two rings. The attractions included six hundred horses, mechanical figures, a giraffe, and oddities, such as Esau, the Bearded Boy, and Anna Leake, the armless woman. A specially designed circus train not only allowed the circus to tour the country in a more efficient manner but helped to attract larger crowds.

Bailey. By the late 1870s Barnum's circus was the largest show touring the United States. However, serious competition emerged in the form of the Great London, Cooper & Bailey's Allied Show, owned by a group of

showmen led by James Anthony Bailey. Their show had elephants and used electricity rather than gas to illuminate the rings. When Barnum tried to buy a baby elephant from the Allied Show, Bailey had his telegram blown up to poster size and displayed in various towns. The headline read: "What Barnum Thinks of the Baby Elephant." Barnum was not in the least bit dismayed, responding that he had at last found a foe "worthy of my steel." He offered to merge the two circuses, and the combined shows were organized in 1881. On 18 March the new circus opened to an audience of nine thousand in Madison Square Garden, New York City. In an unprecedented move three rings were used. The show had 338 horses, 14 camels, 20 elephants, 370 costumed performers, 4 brass bands, and the midget couple, Tom Thumb and his wife, Lavinia, who came out of retirement to help launch the new enterprise.

A Team Effort. Bailey, who had traveled with circuses since he was a boy, hated personal publicity and became the perfect partner for the self-glorifying Barnum. While Bailey managed the show and kept the circus train running, his partner attracted the crowds with extravagant claims. (Barnum reportedly coined the phrase "There's a sucker born every minute.") In 1882 the circus bought Jumbo, the largest elephant in the world, from the London Zoo. Jumbo became a star attraction before dying in a train accident in 1885. Two years later Barnum and Bailey had a falling out over how the circus should be managed, and Barnum toured temporarily with Adam Forepaugh's circus. However, the two showmen reconciled their differences, and in October 1887 Barnum agreed to give Bailey control of the show and to add his name for the first time to the title of the circus. Beginning in 1888 it was officially called Barnum & Bailey's Greatest Show on Earth. When Barnum died in April 1891, Barnum & Bailey had sixty-five railroad cars, making it the largest show in the nation traveling by rail. Bailey continued to tour following his partner's demise, but he had to contend with the five Ringling brothers—Albert, Otto, Alfred, Charles, and John— who had formed a circus in 1884. Bailey took his circus on a five-year tour of Europe in 1897. When Bailey died in 1906, his widow sold the show to Ringling Brothers Circus.

Sources:

John Culhane, *The American Circus: An Illustrated History* (New York: Holt, 1990);

LaVahn G. Hoh and William H. Rough, *Step Right Up!: The Adventure of Circus in America* (White Hall, Va.: Betterway, 1990).

COLLEGE SPORTS

Rise of College Sport. In the last half of the nineteenth century, sports became an essential element of college life. Intercollegiate sport emerged before the Civil War, with rowing, or crew, being the first college sport. In the 1830s students at prestigous eastern colleges formed informal rowing clubs, and by 1846

Jumbo with Matthew Scott, his keeper, in 1882

Harvard and Yale clubs began to compete against noncollegiate organizations. In the ensuing decades rowing was joined by baseball, cricket, and football on college campuses. The first intercollegiate football game played to rugby rules was between McGill and Harvard on 15 May 1874, and ended in a scoreless tie. In the 1870s football grew into the leading college sport in the United States, and in 1876 Princeton, Rutgers, Columbia, Harvard, and Yale met in Springfield, Massachusetts, to form the American Intercollegiate Football Association. At that meeting the schools agreed on the Rugby Union rules for college football.

Society and College Football. In the last quarter of the nineteenth century, college football developed from a game played by the student to one played for the spectator. Changes within the university promoted the growth of football. Beginning in the 1870s universities sought to increase their enrollments, and college presidents quickly came to recognize that a winning football team brought the recognition needed to stimulate enrollments. College authorities also realized that successful football teams contributed more to developing alumni loyalty than fond memories of chapels, classrooms, professors, and ivy-covered buildings. By the close of the century alumni wanted a stake in the success of their college teams, and they participated in the recruitment of players, raising money for the team, and assisting in the administration of college athletics. Urban social climbers associated themselves with successful college football teams regardless of whether they were graduates of that institution or not. More important, the men who played college football, especially in northeastern colleges, were

the sons of the elite, and their participation on a winning team, coupled with a degree from an exclusive college, could assure their ascendancy.

From Rugby to Football. In 1876 the American Intercollegiate Football Association agreed to play football according to the Rugby Union rules. Rugby rules, unlike the soccer rules under which the 1869 Rutgers-Princeton games were played, permitted a more physical game in which a player could pick up the ball and run with it for a touchdown. Moreover, players could dropkick the ball to score as well. The transition from English rugby to American football occurred in the late 1870s under the direction of Walter Camp, who played halfback for Yale from 1876 to 1882. One of his first innovations was to reduce the number of players on the field for each team from fifteen to eleven. In 1880 Camp proposed replacing the rugby scrum with the scrimmage. Whereas the scrum led to constant turnover of the ball from team to team, the scrimmage encouraged the undisputed possession of the ball by one team. The scrimmage brought order to the game and encouraged the development of rational strategy and team formations. The scrimmage, however, made it possible for a team to control the ball for the entire game, so in 1882 Camp proposed the downs system, in which the team was given three downs to advance the ball five yards (now four downs to move the ball ten yards) or relinquish possession of the ball. Under the downs system, lines marking five-yard increments were chalked across the playing field, thus producing the gridiron effect upon the field. Camp, who permitted tackling below the waist, also instituted the point system for touchdowns (6), field

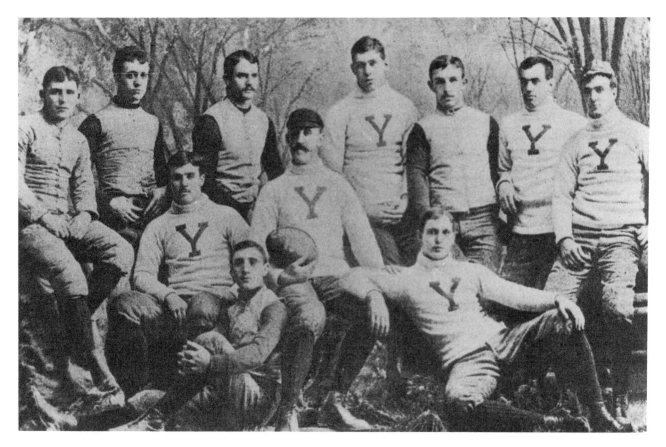

The Yale football team of 1889

goals (3), and safeties (2). In 1889 he promoted football by naming his first All-American team.

Dominance of the East. During the late nineteenth century, prestigous eastern universities dominated college football. Yale, coached by Camp, won the first national championship in 1883. In all Yale won eight national titles from 1883 to 1899. During the same period Princeton garnered four, Harvard three, and Pennsylvania two national titles. Players from these schools became the coaches who would spread football throughout the nation. Amos Alonzo Stagg, a Yale player and member of Camp's first All-American team in 1889, developed Chicago into one of early college football powers of the Midwest. One of the first athletic conferences established around football teams was the Western Conference, which would become known as the Big Ten. In 1896 Wisconsin won the first Western Conference championship and in 1897 retained that title. In 1898 Michigan won the Western Conference title, as did Chicago in 1899.

Sources:

Ivan N. Kaye, *Good Clean Violence: A History of College Football* (Philadelphia & New York: Lippincott, 1973);

Guy Maxton Lewis, "The American Intercollegiate Football Spectacle, 1869–1917," dissertation, University of Maryland, 1965;

Ronald A. Smith, *Sports and Freedom: The Rise of Big-Time College Athletics* (New York & Oxford: Oxford University Press, 1988).

1896 OLYMPIC GAMES

Revival. During the late nineteenth century, sports enthusiasts around the world called for the revival of the Olympic Games. Interest in the Olympic Games, which had been first contested in 776 B.C. and had continued until the fourth century A.D., increased significantly after German archaeologists, in the early 1880s, unearthed the ruins of Olympia the site of the ancient Greek athletic festival. The chief supporter for the revival of the Olympic Games was Baron Pierre de Coubertin, a wealthy French aristocrat, whose concern over the physical fitness of French youth following France's defeat in the Franco-Prussian War led to reform of physical education. The International Olympic Committee was organized in 1894, and Coubertin was selected as its secretary-general. IOC members also decided then that the games would be held in a different city every four years, that only modern sports would be contested, and that only amateur adult males would be allowed to compete. Although Coubertin wanted Paris to host the first Olympic Games, the IOC selected Athens to host the events in 1896.

Olympic Teams. Two hundred forty-five athletes from forty-three nations competed in forty-three events in the first modern Olympic Games, held 6–15 April 1896. Because of the novelty of the games, most of the nations did not send their best athletes, and many of those athletes who did compete paid for their own passage to Greece. The host country fielded the largest team—eighty-one athletes competing in Athens were Greek. France and Germany both sent nineteen-man teams. Thirteen athletes represented the United States and eight represented Great Britain. William M. Sloane, a professor of French history at Princeton University and the American representative in the IOC, organized the U.S. contingent, which consisted of ten track and field specialists, two marksmen, and one swimmer. Unable to persuade the New York Athletic Club, which had the most national track and field champions, to participate on the team, Sloane garnered the services of four Princeton students, including team captain Robert Garrett and six Harvard graduates who competed for the Boston Athletic Association (BAA). James B. Connolly, a Harvard undergraduate, joined the team despite threats from Harvard administrators to suspend him indefinitely for leaving during the middle of the spring semester. The marksmen, John and Sumner Paine, were brothers and captains in the U.S. Army.

Americans Dominate Track. Greek athletes dominated the competition, winning 49 of 133 medals awarded in the first Olympic Games. After the Greeks came the Americans with 19 medals, then the Germans with 16, the French with 11, and the British with 9. Sixteen of the medals won by the United States came in track and field. James B. Connolly, who won the triple jump, received the first gold medal awarded in the revived Olympic Games. In the long jump and high jump, Ellery Clark led U.S. sweeps of the gold, silver, and bronze medals. In addition to his triple jump gold, Connolly garnered silver in the high jump and bronze in the long jump. Pole vaulters William Hoyt and Albert Tyler won the gold and silver medals, respectively. Garrett, the team captain, won gold medals in both the shot put and the discus throw. Thomas Burke, of the BAA, won both the 100- and 400-meter dashes. In the 110-meter high hurdles, Thomas Curtis narrowly defeated Grantley Goulding of Britain by two inches for the gold medal. Marksman Sumner Paine won the free pistol competition. Gardner Williams, the lone American swimmer, withdrew from the 100-meter race because the temperature of the water was too cold.

Sources:

John Findling and Kim Pelle, eds., *The Historical Dictionary of the Olympic Games* (Westport, Conn.: Greenwood Press, 1996);

Allen Guttmann, *The Olympics: A History of the Modern Games* (Urbana & Chicago: University of Illinois Press, 1992);

Richard D. Mandell, *The First Modern Olympics* (Berkeley: University of California Press, 1976).

GOLF

Golf in America. Originating in Scotland around the fifteenth century, golf reached America during the colonial era, and Americans began playing the game after the American Revolution. The earliest clubs were established in Charleston, South Carolina, in 1786, and Savannah, Georgia, in 1795. Newspaper sources indicate that golf was regularly played at these clubs until the War of 1812. However Americans showed little interest in the game between the War of 1812 and the Civil War, one possible reason being that it was seen as an elitist sport and was therefore shunned.

Renewed Interest in Golf. The 1870s and 1880s witnessed a rekindled interest among Americans in golf. Charles Blair McDonald, a pioneer in the rejuvenation of the game, played golf in the Chicago area in 1875. Col. J. Hamilton Gillespie, a Scotsman who owned a lumber business in Sarasota, Florida, played golf there in 1883 or 1884. Andrew Bell of Burlington, Iowa, who attended the University of Edinburgh, set up a four-hole golf course in Burlington upon returning home and introduced the game to his friends. In 1884 Russell W. Montague, a New Englander, and four Scottish friends established a golf course near Montague's summer home in Oakhurst, West Virginia. U.S. Army soldiers stationed near the Rio Grande played golf in 1886, and Alex Findlay, a Scottish immigrant turned cowboy, played golf on the Nebraska prairies. Beginning in 1888 golf was played for three years at Rockwell's Woods, near Norwich, Connecticut. Members of the exclusive Tuxedo Club, in Tuxedo, New York, began playing golf in 1889, as did members of the Casino Club in Newport, Rhode Island, in 1890.

Establishment of St. Andrews. The first modern golfing club in the United States, St. Andrews, named after the historic Scottish club, was established in Yonkers, New York, in 1888. The idea for the club originated when John Reid, a Scottish immigrant and ironworks executive, invited some neighbors to a cow pasture across the street from his home to drive some golf balls. In 1887 Bob Lockhart, a friend of Reid, traveled to Scotland and brought back some clubs and the newly introduced gutta-percha golf ball. With the new equipment, Lockhart, Reid, and another friend, John B. Upham, gave an exhibition of the game on a three-hole course laid out on the cow pasture. Golf soon became so popular with Reid and his associates that by the end of 1888 they had formally organized the St. Andrews Golf Club, with Reid as president and Upham as secretary. Over the next three years St. Andrews moved twice: at Grey Oaks it held the first unofficial U.S. championship; and at its final location, Mount Hope at Hastings, the club constructed an eighteen-hole course, the first course of that length in the nation. (Although the Dorset Field Club in Dorset, Vermont, and the Foxburg Country Club in Foxburg, Pennsylvania, claim to be the oldest modern golf courses

James Park, Laurence Curtis, C. B. Macdonald, George Armstrong, and Louis Biddle at the first Amateur Championship in Yonkers, New York, 1894

in the United States, established in 1886 and 1887, respectively, they do not have the documentation to prove it, as does St. Andrews.)

Establishment of the United States Golf Association. Golf grew rapidly in the United States during the 1890s. In 1894 the Amateur Golf Association (AGA) was formed to administer and standardize the game. Later that year the AGA changed its name to the United States Golf Association (USGA). The five charter-member clubs were St. Andrews, Newport, Shinnecock Hills, the Chicago Golf Club, and the Brookline Country Club in Massachusetts. On 22 December 1894 Henry O. Tallmadge, the secretary of the St. Andrews Club, held a conference of USGA officials to establish a site for a single national championship. They decided to hold both an amateur and an open championship tournament at the Newport Club in October 1895. Charles Blair McDonald won the 1895 USGA amateur title over Laurence Curtis, who, according to the *New York Herald*, "was not in any way in the game against McDonald, for he a had low short drive compared to a long well directed drive of his opponent." The first U.S. Open was won by Horace Rawlins, the Newport assistant pro, against nine other professionals and an amateur. He won a $50 gold medal and $150 in cash. By 1895 there were seventy-five golf clubs in the United States. By the late 1890s golf had acquired such an elite following that *Outing* reported it as "a sport restricted to the richer classes of the country."

Rise of Women's Golf. Golf, like tennis, offered women the opportunity for high-level competition. In 1894 the British Ladies' Golf Union held the first women's golf championship. The USGA held the first women's amateur championship at the Meadowbrook Club on Long Island in November 1895. Mrs. Charles S. Brown won that inaugural event. The first player to dominate women's golf in the United States was Beatrix Hoyt, who won three consecutive amateur titles from 1896 to 1898. She won her first title at the age of sixteen and retired from competition at the age of twenty-one.

Sources:

Will Grimsley, *Golf: Its History, People and Events* (Englewood Cliffs, N.J.: Prentice-Hall, 1966);

John M. Ross, ed., *Golf Magazine's Encyclopedia of Golf* (New York: Harper & Row, 1979);

Herbert Warren Wind, *The Story of American Golf: Its Champions and Its Championships* (New York: Knopf, 1975).

HOLIDAYS

Importance. Americans began celebrating various new national and regional holidays in the late nineteenth century. National civic holidays assumed the importance they did because the United States lacked a state religion and was growing more ethnically diverse. In addition, the wounds inflicted by the Civil War were still healing, and national holidays helped blur sectional differences even as regional holidays preserved them. Celebrations of these holidays were marked by parades, picnics, fireworks, carnivals, and speeches. Workers had the day off depending on the business they worked for and whether or not the holiday was recognized by the state or federal government.

Arbor Day. A traditional tree-planting festival originating in Nebraska, Arbor Day was the work of conservationist Julius Sterling Morton, who encouraged fellow Nebraskans to take note of the beauty of trees as well as their practical uses. Morton, a member of the Nebraska State Board of Agriculture and later secretary of agriculture under President Grover Cleveland, introduced a resolution in 1872 that 10 April "be especially set apart and consecrated" for tree planting in the state. More than a million trees were planted that year. Two years later, Nebraska issued a proclamation to celebrate Arbor Day within the state as a holiday; later, the legislature passed a resolution calling Nebraska "The Tree Planters' State" (today it is better known as the Cornhusker or Beef State). In 1884 the state made it an annual event; the next year the state legislature passed an act designating 22 April, Morton's birthday, as the date on which Arbor Day would be celebrated as a legal holiday. Agricultural associations in other states soon petitioned their respective legislatures. At Ohio's first Arbor Day in 1882, Cincinnati schoolchildren started a new tradition by planting the trees themselves. By 1900 most states and territories in the United States, as well as several foreign countries, observed Arbor Day, usually on the last Friday in April.

Memorial Day. Formerly known as Decoration Day, Memorial Day was first observed on 25 April 1866 by the women of Columbus, Mississippi, to decorate the graves of both Confederate and Union soldiers. In 1868 Gen. John A. Logan, commander in chief of the Grand Army of the Republic, issued an order establishing 30 May for "strewing with flowers or otherwise decorating the graves of comrades who died in defense of their country during the late rebellion." Decorating graves quickly caught on in both the North and the South but on different days. For several years all commemorations remained unofficial, while ceremonies at Arlington National Cemetery provided a national focus to these events. Ceremonies were soon extended to honor the dead of all wars, and the day became known as Memorial Day. First official recognition of Memorial Day as a holiday came in 1873 when New York State designated it a legal holiday. Within the next six years four other states made similar decrees. In 1887 the U.S. Congress made it an official holiday for federal employees.

Flag Day. The official U.S. flag was adopted on 14 June 1777 by a joint resolution of the Continental Congress "that the flag of the thirteen states be thirteen stripes, alternate red and white" with thirteen stars, "white in a blue field." Tradition generally credits Betsy Ross with making the original Stars and Stripes at her Philadelphia home. The first Flag Day observance took place on 14 June 1861 when the people of Hartford, Connecticut, wanted to show their support for the Union during the opening days of the Civil War. These exercises were not repeated until 14 June 1877 when the celebration of Flag Day took place on the centennial of the flag's adoption. On that day Congress ordered the flag flown over all government buildings. It was not declared a legal holiday but was observed by presidential proclamation. On 14 June 1893 Flag Day was observed in Philadelphia by a mayoral order that ordered the flag displayed over every public building in the city. Four years later, the governor of New York commanded that the flag be flown over all public structures on 14 June.

Labor Day. By the end of the nineteenth century the United States had become an industrial nation with tens of thousands of laborers. The idea for a day to honor labor was first proposed by Peter J. McGuire, a New York City carpenter and general secretary of the new Brotherhood of Carpenters and Joiners, and Matthew Maguire, a machinist from Paterson, New Jersey. The Central Labor Union endorsed their idea, and the first Labor Day celebration and parade, sponsored by the Knights of Labor, was held on 5 September 1882 in New York City, a date chosen by McGuire to fill the time gap between 4 July and Thanksgiving. Two years later the Federation of Organized Trades and Labor Unions (later the American Federation of Labor) endorsed the idea of an annual Labor Day, scheduled for the first Monday in September. On that day parades of workers were held in most northeastern cities; the idea was quickly endorsed by the Knights of Labor. In 1887 Oregon became the first of several states that established the first Monday in September as Labor Day. On 28 June 1894 President Grover Cleveland signed legislation making the first Monday in September a legal holiday for federal employees and in the District of Columbia. All of the remaining states and Puerto Rico eventually legalized the day. With legal recognition of Labor Day, workers in the late 1890s and in the early 1900s used the holiday not only to honor their accomplishments but to proclaim their grievances. Labor Day celebrations were frequently marked not only by parades but by speeches and rallies in many industrial cities.

Other Observances. On New Year's Day 1886, the Valley Hunt Club, Pasadena, California, held the first Tournament of Roses parade followed by athletic events. The birthdays of several distinguished Americans were also observed during this period. Abraham Lincoln, born on 12 February 1809 in central Kentucky, was a much admired president of the United States, but there was no official designation of his birthday until almost thirty years after his death. The Illinois legislature made it a legal holiday which was first observed on 12 February 1892. The legislatures of four other states (New Jersey,

James Dwight, the founder of the United States National Lawn Tennis Association, and Richard Sears, the winner of the U.S. Singles Championship

LAWN TENNIS

British Origins. Tennis was one of the sports enjoyed mainly by the social elite and to a lesser degree by the middle class in late-nineteenth-century America. Although the origins of tennis can be traced to fourteenth-century France, the game, as was played in the nineteenth-century United States, developed in England during the 1870s. Maj. Walter Clopton Wingfield, a retired British army officer, developed the game, which was played on an hourglass-shaped grass court, and copyrighted the rules in 1873. Members of the All-England Croquet Club began playing tennis in 1874 on the croquet lawns, calling the game "lawn tennis." That year the club became known as the All-England Croquet and Lawn Tennis Club and one of its members, Julian Marshall, revised the rules of the game and had them published by the C. G. Heathcote publishing company. Marshall also promoted the new rules through *The Field,* the leading sports journal in Britain. John Moyer Heathcote developed a new ball for the game made of vulcanized rubber covered with white flannel. In 1877 the All-England Croquet and Lawn Tennis Club sponsored its first national tennis tournament.

American Beginnings. Although the first recorded tennis game in the United States occurred on 8 October 1874 at Camp Apache, near Tucson, Arizona, Mary Ewing Outerbridge, a New York socialite, is generally credited with introducing the game to the United States. In 1874, during her annual winter vacation in Bermuda, she observed British army officers hitting a rubber ball over a net stretched across a freshly mowed lawn with catgut-strung rackets. She purchased a box of tennis equipment and brought it back to the United States. Eugenius Outerbridge, brother of Mary and director of the Staten Island Cricket and Baseball Club, set up a tennis court in the corner of a cricket field. For nearly a year the Outerbridge family played tennis before other club members became interested in the game. As more members of the Staten Island Cricket and Baseball Club began playing tennis, the club devoted one day a week to the game.

Early Tournament Play. The first tennis tournament in the United States had fifteen players and was played at Nahant, Massachusetts, in 1876. William Appleton, James Dwight, and Fred R. Sears organized the event. Dwight and Sears met in the finals, with Dwight winning three sets to none. In 1880 the Outerbridge family held a tournament at Staten Island, which featured American and British players. The singles match was won by O. E. Woodson of Great Britain. The Americans and the English disagreed over the size of the ball used by the Staten Island Club. Dwight and Sears, who lost in second round of the doubles, disliked the ball as it differed from that used in New England. Disagreement over the ball led Dwight, a wealthy Bostonian, to organize a meeting of the leaders of tennis clubs from Philadelphia and New York to standardize

New York, Washington, and Minnesota) followed suit in 1896 with the rest of the country instituting their own observances, many held on the first Monday in February. In the South holidays arose to honor two Confederate leaders. The birthday of Jefferson Davis, president of the Confederacy, was officially observed for the first time on 3 June 1892 in Florida. Eight other southern states adopted similar legislation before the turn of the century. The birthday of Robert E. Lee, commander of the Army of Northern Virginia, was also honored in the South. Georgia made his birthday (19 January) a legal holiday in 1889; Virginia followed the next year.

Sources:

David Glassberg, *American Historical Pageantry: The Uses of Tradition in the Early Twentieth Century* (Chapel Hill: University of North Carolina Press, 1990);

Jane M. Hatch, *The American Book of Days,* third edition (New York: Wilson, 1978);

Sue E. Thompson and Barbara W. Carlson, *Holidays, Festivals, and Celebrations of the World Dictionary* (Detroit: Omnigraphics, 1994).

tennis play in the United States. This meeting, held 21 May 1881 in New York, led to the formation of the United States Lawn Tennis Association (USLTA). The USLTA, an amateur organization, adopted the rules developed by the All-England Croquet and Lawn Tennis Club. The first president of the organization was Robert Oliver of the Albany Tennis Club. In late 1881 the USLTA held its first men's singles and doubles national championship at Newport, Rhode Island. Richard D. Sears won the first of seven consecutive men's singles titles that year.

Influence of Dwight. Dwight, who served as president of the USLTA from 1882 to 1884 and 1893 to 1911, is recognized as the "father of American tennis" for his efforts to standardize the game's rules and equipment. Dwight also promoted competition between the United States and Great Britain. Younger players dominated tennis in the United States, while older players dominated the game in Britain. In the early years of Anglo-American competition, the aggressive play of the Americans was blunted by the skill and cunning of the older British players. In 1883 Dwight and Sears played the Clark brothers of Philadelphia for the right to play the Renshaw brothers, the top doubles team of Britain. After defeating Dwight and Sears, the Clarks were defeated by the Renshaws in England. In that same year Dwight, the second-best singles player in the United States, went overseas to play the best English singles players. Although he was beaten by Willie Renshaw, Dwight remained in England to hone his skills. Dwight's promotion of international play, especially between the United States and Britain, set the stage for the Davis Cup tournaments that would start in 1900.

Popularization of the Game. Tennis became very popular in the United States during the 1880s, but declined during the 1890s. Beginning with thirty-four clubs in 1881, the USLTA increased to seventy-five in 1890. Clubs in specific geographical regions formed separate tennis associations, and the USLTA granted these entire associations membership rather than run the risk of the organization of a separate association that would challenge the USLTA for supremacy in the sport. In 1895, 106 clubs and 10 associations belonged to the USLTA. However, a drop in membership occurred in the late 1890s, and by 1902 the total number of clubs and associations affiliated with the USLTA totaled forty-four. One reason for the decline in tennis clubs was the rise of golf during the 1890s; however, once interest in golf settled down, the USLTA realized that the two sports were compatible, especially in the country club setting, where the upper and upper middle classes enjoyed both activities. Many new golf clubs added tennis courts to their facilities and then became members of the USLTA. The middle and lower classes enjoyed the game. Prospect Park, in Brooklyn, New York, had more than one hundred clubs using its facilities by the turn of the century.

Women. Tennis was a popular game for women during the late nineteenth century, and the USLTA held the first women's singles championship in 1887, with Ellen F. Hansell claiming the title. Bertha L. Townsend became the first two-time singles champion in 1888 and 1889. Juliette P. Atkinson ranked as the top woman of the 1890s, winning the singles title in 1895, 1897, and 1898. An outstanding doubles player as well, Atkinson combined for the doubles championship with Helen R. Helwig (1894–1895), Elisabeth H. Moore (1896), Kathleen Atkinson (1897–1898), Myrtle McAteer (1901), and Marion Jones (1902). The USLTA introduced mixed doubles competition, teams of men and women, in 1892. The first champions were Mabel E. Cahill and Clarence Hobart. From 1894 to 1896 Juliette P. Atkinson, the top female player of the 1890s, teamed with Edwin P. Fischer for the doubles title.

Sources:

E. Digby Baltzell, *Sporting Gentlemen: Men's Tennis from the Age of Honor to the Cult of the Superstar* (New York: Free Press, 1995);

Allison Danzig and Peter Schwed, eds., *The Fireside Book of Tennis* (New York: Simon & Schuster, 1972);

Will Grimsley, *Tennis: Its History, People and Events* (Englewood Cliffs, N.J.: Prentice-Hall, 1971).

WILD WEST SHOWS

Colorful Effects. From 1883 to 1916 Buffalo Bill's Wild West Show enjoyed a place as the "National Entertainment." Ownership and the show's title changed several times, but the show always contained cowboys performing feats of skill and daring, stereotyped Indians attacking white settlers, and well-staged battle scenes between the U.S. Cavalry and Indian warriors. After seeing the show Mark Twain wrote: "It brought back to me the breezy, wild life of the Rocky Mountains, and stirred me like a war song."

Cody's Achievement. This type of entertainment started as a frontier celebration held in North Platte, Nebraska, in 1882 by William F. Cody. A former army scout and hunter, he claimed to have killed 4,280 buffalo in an eight-month period, thus earning the nickname "Buffalo Bill." The success of the 1882 performance encouraged Cody and Dr. W. F. Carver, a crack marksman, to organize a traveling show named the Wild West, Rocky Mountain and Prairie Exhibition. The first performance was given 17 May 1883 in Omaha, Nebraska, and featured Capt. A. H. Bogardus and his four sons as a sharpshooting family. By that summer the show was in Brooklyn, New York. The next year Buffalo Bill's Wild West Show was established as a permanent touring show that performed for extended periods in amusement parks, at world's fairs, and in similar places. In 1885 Annie Oakley joined Cody's show, as did Sitting Bull. During Queen Victoria's Golden Jubilee (1887) the queen and her family were thrilled by the performers; six

Phoebe Anne Oakley Moses was born on 13 August 1860 and was one of the most phenomenal shots in the history of firearms. She first gained national attention when she won a shooting match in Cincinnati against a crack shot named Frank E. Butler, whom she later married. Until 1884 she and her husband made tours of vaudeville shows and circuses. In that year Oakley auditioned for Buffalo Bill's Wild West Show. Buffalo Bill was immediately smitten with this pretty but shy twenty-four-year-old woman who could sight with a hand mirror and shoot backward as her husband threw glass balls in the air. (She could also shoot them from the back of a galloping pony.) At thirty paces she could shoot the thin edge of a playing card, a dime tossed in the air, or the lit end of a cigarette. She toured with the Wild West Show for seventeen years, with Buffalo Bill giving her top billing as "the Peerless Lady Wing-Shot." Buffalo Bill himself called her "Little Missy" while Sitting Bull, the Lakota tribal leader, adopted her as a member of his tribe, giving her the name Watanya Cicilla, or "Little Sure Shot." During the European tour of the Wild West Show in 1887, the Prince of Wales presented Oakley with a medal. In Berlin she obliged Crown Prince Wilhelm by shooting a cigarette from his lips. (After the prince became Kaiser Wilhelm II and World War I erupted in Europe, Annie was quoted as saying, "I wish I'd missed that day.") The holes punched into complimentary tickets reminded people of the bullet holes she fired into playing cards, and free tickets became known as "Annie Oakleys." In 1935, nine years after her death, Hollywood made a movie of her life, and in 1946 Irving Berlin made her the subject of a successful Broadway musical, *Annie Get Your Gun*.

Sources: John Culhane, *The American Circus: An Illustrated History* (New York: Holt, 1990);

Shirl Kasper, *Annie Oakley* (Norman: University of Oklahoma Press, 1992).

years later the show appeared successfully outside the World's Columbian Exposition in Chicago.

Makeup of the Show. For almost thirty years the show toured the United States and Europe. It featured horses and riders and held equal appeal for American crowds and European royalty. It was a logistical nightmare transporting, feeding, costuming, and organizing hordes of cowboys, Indians, sharpshooters, horses, buffalo, and hundreds of other elements necessary to evoke a world of parades, races, and reenactments such as stagecoach robberies and Custer's Last Stand. Later, the show dramatized such historical epics as the Charge at San Juan Hill and the creation of the Congress of Rough Riders of the World.

Western Propaganda. As a master showman, Cody displayed to his audiences that the West was a place of glory and adventure, an enormous territory reserved for the equestrian exercises of Indians, cowboys, and outlaws. As his own best publicist, Cody built on his life as a child of the West and as a genuine scout and hunter, adventures fictionalized in dime novels and in his own embellished autobiographies. His interpretations of the West were accepted as genuine and authentic, especially from audiences on the East Coast and in Europe. It is undeniable that Cody was a friend of the American Indian, but he devised his show to coincide with contemporary opinions of cowboys and Indians; the Wild West Show did little to raise the Indian's image in the public's esteem. It has even been argued among historians that the Wild West Show and its portrayal of the Western frontier shaped the American psyche since violence and the "white man's superiority" were constant themes of the show. This theory has weakened with time, but the stories and legends that Cody and his show perpetuated continue to be a part of the American myth.

Sources:
Buffalo Bill and the Wild West (Brooklyn, N.Y: Brooklyn Museum, 1981);

Rupert Croft-Cooke and W. S. Meadmore, *Buffalo Bill: The Legend, the Man of Action, the Showman* (London: Sampson Low, Marston, 1952);

The Cultures of Celebrations, edited by Ray B. Browne and Michael T. Marsden (Bowling Green, Ohio: Bowling Green University Popular Press, 1994).

WORLD'S FAIRS

Background. American world's fairs, also called international expositions, trace their beginnings to London's 1851 Crystal Palace Exhibition, the first world's fair. This exposition started a tradition of displaying agricultural and mechanical exhibits. The first American international fair was in New York (1853), but it was a financial failure. The success of the 1876 Philadelphia Centennial Exposition, put together by a group of Philadelphia civic leaders and the federal government, launched the first generation of American world's fairs.

World's Columbian Exposition. The Chicago world's fair of 1893 took place one year after the anniversary it was supposed to commemorate, the four hundredth anniversary of Columbus's voyage of discovery to America. It was the largest and most elaborate nineteenth-century exposition held in the United States. After leaving the fairgrounds, an old midwestern farmer reportedly told his wife that it was worth visiting the exposition "even if it did take all the burial money" to do so. The writer Hamlin Garland told his parents: "Sell the cook stove if necessary and come. You *must* see this fair." The fair was several years in the

Buffalo Bill Cody (front row, third from left) and other performers in the Wild West Show in
London, 1887

planning, beginning in 1889 when a corporation was established with professional and business leaders who raised more than $10 million in funds. An additional $2.5 million was generated through federally minted souvenir coins. Seven thousand workmen were employed in construction of the six-hundred-acre exposition.

Achievements. The exposition opened 1 May and the Pledge of Allegiance was written for the dedication ceremonies. The landscaping of the grounds and the design of the neoclassical buildings were supervised by a committee composed of the country's leading architects, especially Daniel Hudson Burnham. However, the architecture of the World's Columbian Exposition received mixed reviews. Its admirers found it innovative and original, but there were just as many critics who found it a horrible retrogression that turned its back on a distinctively American style. The 150 buildings of Greek, Romanesque, and Renaissance architectural styles became known as the White City; the buildings exhibited the talents of the foremost American architects and sculptors. Frederick Law Olmsted, designer of Central Park and a formidable influence on nineteenth-century landscape architecture, advised fair officials to construct lagoons on the grounds and "not rest content with a view of the lake from the shore." Another pioneering development was the unprecedented use

of electricity at the fair, which impressed upon the American people, for the first time, the importance of this new light source.

Attractions. A department of publicity and promotion established in 1890 advertised the event in eastern cities and Europe. Nineteen foreign countries, eighty-six non-American businesses, and thirty American state governments participated in the fair. The major exhibition buildings (holding approximately sixty-five thousand displays) were grouped by categories—agriculture, anthropology, electricity, fine arts, fisheries, forestry, horticulture, machinery, manufactures and liberal arts, mines and mining, transportation, U.S. government, and women. In an attempt to overcome contemporary prejudice against the Chinese, the Wah Mee Exposition Company built a theater, bazaar, and Chinese temple, or joss house. Special events included a World's Congress Auxiliary at which nationally known leaders, such as William Jennings Bryan, lectured; a Congress of Historians at which members heard Frederick Jackson Turner read a short version of his essay "The Significance of the Frontier in American History"; and the World's Parliament of Religions, at which a weeklong conference was held. Major attractions were the Court of Honor (the central area of the fairgrounds), the Ferris wheel, and Buffalo Bill's Wild West Show. In the Transportation Building there was an award-winning electric elevator, whose normal speed was 250 feet per minute, to carry visitors to the gallery.

Impact. The exposition closed on 30 October and added much to American life, including the mile-long entertainment strip (midway) which every subsequent fair has incorporated into its planning. Total attendance was 27,529,000, with a profit of $1.4 million. In writing about the event, a modern historian concluded: "For a summer's moment, White City had seemed the fruition of a nation, a culture, a whole society: the celestial city of man set upon a hill for all the world to behold."

Sources:

Norman Bolotin and Christine Laing, *The Chicago World's Fair of 1893: The World's Columbian Exposition* (Washington, D.C.: Preservation Press, 1992);

Robert L. Gale, *The Gay Nineties in America: A Cultural Dictionary of the 1890s* (Westport, Conn.: Greenwood Press, 1992).

HEADLINE MAKERS

ADRIAN CONSTANTINE "CAP" ANSON

1851-1922

BASEBALL PLAYER

Superstar. Adrian Constantine "Cap" Anson was baseball's first superstar. The first player to reach 3,000 career hits, he maintained a batting average of .300 or better for eighteen seasons and played twenty-seven seasons in the major leagues, more than any other player. In 1869 Anson played on the Marshalltown (Iowa) High School baseball team. After a year at Notre Dame University, he became the third baseman for the Rockford Forest Cities (Illinois) of the National Association in 1871 and led the club with a batting average of .352. In 1872 Anson joined the Philadelphia Athletics and batted over .350 for the next four seasons. When the National League formed in 1876, the Chicago White Stockings secretly signed him for $2,000, but Philadelphia counteroffered with $2,500, and he remained in Philadelphia.

The White Stockings. Anson joined the Chicago White Stockings in 1877 and remained with the team until 1897. A first baseman, he became team captain in 1878 and team manager in 1879. With Chicago, the six-foot-one-inch Anson achieved a career-high .399 in 1881. As National League batting champion in 1879, 1881, and 1888, he drove in more than 1,700 runs, hit 96 home runs, and led the league in runs batted in (RBIs) four times and in doubles twice. His season high of 21 home runs came in 1884. An inconsistent fielder, Anson still holds the record of 674 errors committed by a first baseman. As manager of the White Stockings from 1879 to 1897, he posted a record of 1,297 wins and 957 losses and led Chicago to five National League pennants between 1880 and 1886. Anson was on all-star teams that visited England in 1874 and later managed a team that toured the world.

Twilight. Anson's baseball career declined after 1883 when he canceled a game against Toledo (International League) because an African American, Moses Fleetwood Walker, was their catcher. In 1887 he refused to let Chicago play an exhibition game against Newark (IL) because its starting pitcher, George Stovey, was black. Later that year Anson prevented the New York Giants from signing Stovey and worked out a "gentleman's agreement" with New York's manager John Montgomery Ward to permanently bar African Americans from major league baseball. In 1891 Chicago's fortunes declined, and in 1897 James Hart, the president of the White Stockings, dismissed Anson as manager. After managing the New York Giants for twenty-five days in 1898, he retired from baseball. Anson was elected to the National Baseball Hall of Fame in 1939.

Sources:

Benjamin G. Rader, *Baseball: A History of America's Game* (Urbana & Chicago: University of Illinois Press, 1992);

PHINEAS TAYLOR BARNUM

1810-1891

CIRCUS PROMOTER

Early Successes. The circus promoter Phineas T. Barnum considered himself "the great American showman" and had an uncanny knack for knowing what the public wanted and how to promote it. He was born in a modest Bethel, Connecticut, home where he supported his family after his father's death. As a newspaper editor he was arrested for libel so he moved to New York City in 1834. He began his career as a showman by exhibiting a black woman, Joice Heth, claiming that she was the 161-year-old nurse of George Washington. In 1842 he opened the American Museum in New York, where for two decades visitors viewed "curiosities," including the diminutive "General Tom Thumb," whom Barnum took to meet Queen Victoria. In 1850 Barnum brought Jenny Lind, the famous Swedish singer, to America for a successful tour; five years later he published the first edition of his autobiography, *The Life of P. T. Barnum*, which he continued to revise and to republish.

Jumbo. Barnum, supposedly the originator of the phrase "There's a sucker born every minute," certainly lived by this rule when he began his three-ring circus that he transported by rail. Combining his resources with his keenest rival, James Anthony Bailey in 1881 (now the Ringling Bros. and Barnum & Bailey Circus), Barnum's circus featured exotic animals, including "the only mastodon on earth," Jumbo the elephant, the pride of the Royal Zoological Society in London. The British press who protested this "American vandalism." Barnum encouraged the protest for purposes of publicity and avoided custom duties on Jumbo by importing him "for breeding purposes." The animal earned its keep within its first few weeks and could feed from third-story windows as it walked the circus parade. Unfortunately Jumbo was killed by a locomotive on 15 September 1885.

Legacy. Barnum served in the Connecticut legislature (1865–1869); was elected mayor of Bridgeport, Connecticut (1875–1876); and was a benefactor of Tufts University, Medford, Massachusetts. However, his lasting memory will be as a circus promoter who knew the value of advertising and the effect it had on American marketing. He brazenly declared that the American public was "humbugged," or easily fooled (he called himself the "Prince of Humbugs"), and his hoaxes and other pranks were unlimited. For fifty years he gave the American public innocent diversion. Since his death in 1891, he has been the subject of children's books, sound recordings, and a Broadway musical, *Barnum*.

Source:
Alice M. Fleming, *P. T. Barnum: The World's Greatest Showman* (New York: Walker, 1993).

WALTER CAMP

1859-1925
FOOTBALL COACH

Father of American Football. Walter Camp, who was associated with football at Yale University from 1876 to 1910, first as a player and then as a coach, is considered the "Father of American Football." He played football at Yale from 1876 to 1882, four years as an undergraduate and the final two as a medical student. As the team captain, from 1877 to 1880, Camp developed rule changes that cast the foundation of modern American football; among his innovations were the scrimmage and the downs system. He also served as secretary of the intercollegiate football rules convention from 1877 to 1906.

Unofficial Coach. Although Camp started working for the Manhattan Watch Company in New Haven, Connecticut, in 1882, he served as Yale's unofficial advisory coach until 1910. Since he could not attend the team's daily practice sessions, he analyzed the team's progress from detailed notes taken by his wife. In the evenings Camp met with the team captain and other key players, suggesting improvements and formulating game-winning strategy. During Camp's association with the team, as a player and coach from 1876 to 1910, Yale established an astonishing record, losing only fourteen games. Camp vigorously promoted the commercialization of college football through the application of marketing techniques to boost spectator interest and promote the game to the public. His most successful device in generating broad spectator appeal was the selection of the All-American Team, which he first instituted in 1889. Camp developed a mass audience for college football by editing the annual *Spalding's Official Intercollegiate Football Guide* and writing hundreds of newspaper and magazine articles.

Response to Brutality. In the 1890s Camp led a crusade to reform the brutal and, at times, deadly play of college football. In 1891 he spearheaded an investigation of the brutality in college football. In 1894 he published his findings in *Football Facts and Figures*, maintaining that despite the game's hazards, football both physically and mentally benefited the men who had played it. The Intercollegiate Football Rules Committee in 1894, under Camp's direction, eliminated many of the dangerous mass plays, including the flying wedge, which resulted in injury and death. Further reform of college football, which led to the organization of the National Collegiate Athletic Association in 1906, marked the decline of Camp's influence over college football. He reluctantly withdrew from most aspects of Yale's athletic program in 1910. Camp died of a heart attack at the rules committee meeting that year.

Source:
Ronald A. Smith, *Sports and Freedom: The Rise of Big-Time College Athletics* (New York & Oxford: Oxford University Press, 1988).

WILLIAM FREDERICK CODY

1846-1917
SCOUT AND SHOWMAN

Varied Career. William Frederick Cody, known as "Buffalo Bill," was born in LeClaire, Iowa, but moved with his family to the Kansas Territory in 1854. He was a Pony Express rider (1860), served in the Union army with the Ninth Kansas

Cavalry (1863), and joined federal forces in Tennessee and Missouri (1864–1865) as a teamster. After the war he tried various jobs in the West until he became a buffalo hunter (1867–1868) to supply meat to the Kansas Pacific Railroad. Cody claimed he killed 4,280 buffalo by his own count and thus earned the nickname "Buffalo Bill." He scouted for the U.S. Cavalry (1868–1872), fighting against the Sioux and the Cheyenne. E. Z. C. Judson (Ned Buntline) soon began to write about Cody in a series of dime novels. Judson also encouraged him to appear in the author's popular play, *The Scouts of the Prairie,* a fictionalized account of Cody's exploits that opened in Chicago in 1872. Other dime novels starring Cody appeared, many by the lurid novelist Prentiss Ingraham, all of which kept Cody's name alive to the public imagination. Yet throughout his life Cody was always his own best publicist.

Personalizing the West. After these ventures Cody went back to the plains to raise cattle and to scout for the military; he allegedly killed and scalped the Cheyenne warrior Yellow Hand in a July 1876 duel. In 1883 he decided to profit from his fame by organizing "Buffalo Bill's Wild West Show" in Omaha, Nebraska, with himself as the star and with other talented marksmen and riders to support him. The show toured throughout the United States and Europe for thirty years. By 1902 it began to lose money and finally closed in 1916.

Active Decline. Cody continued performing almost until his death. During the unrest involving the U.S. Army and the American Indians after the 1890 murder of Sitting Bull, who had performed in the Wild West Show, Cody offered his services to Gen. Nelson A. Miles, commander of the Military Division of the Missouri. He spent much of his last years on a ranch he received from the state of Wyoming in the Bighorn Basin (later the site of the town of Cody). His various "autobiographies," many of them written by novelists, are not accurate. He died in Denver, Colorado, on 10 January 1917 and was buried on nearby Lookout Mountain. Dime novels on the life of Cody continued to appear as late as the 1950s.

Sources:

Buffalo Bill and the Wild West (Brooklyn, N.Y.: Brooklyn Museum, 1981);

Joseph G. Rosa and Robin May, *Buffalo Bill and the Wild West: A Pictorial Biography* (Lawrence: University Press of Kansas, 1989);

Henry B. Sell and Victor Waybright, *Buffalo Bill and the Wild West* (Basin, Wyo.: Big Horn Books, 1979).

LAWRENCE "LON" MYERS

1858-1899
TRACK AND FIELD CHAMPION

The Runner. The rise of track and field in the United States during the late nineteenth century was chiefly due to the accomplishments of Lawrence "Lon" Myers. As an amateur runner specializing in distances from 100 to 880 yards, he captured fifteen American, ten Canadian, and three British championships from 1879 to 1885. Myers also established nine American and eleven world records at distances of 50 yards to the mile. As a professional from 1886 to 1888, his races against Walter George of Great Britain established the United States as an international track and field power.

Early Start. Myers, a sickly child, started running after a physician suggested exercise to improve his health, and by the time he had graduated from high school in Richmond, Virginia, in 1876, he had developed into a good runner. In 1876 Myers began working as a bookkeeper in New York, where his father had become a successful businessman. He continued to run in his spare time and, in 1878, competed for the Knickerbocker Yacht Club in the New York Athletic Club's Election Day Games, winning the 440-yard dash in 55 seconds. This victory set the stage for Myers' domination of track over the next decade.

Champion. Representing the Manhattan Athletic Club in 1879, Myers captured the first of three consecutive national titles in the 220-yard dash, the first of six consecutive national titles in the 440-yard dash, and the first of two consecutive national titles in the 880-yard dash. As an amateur he remained undefeated in the quarter mile. In 1879 he became the first runner to cover that distance in less than 50 seconds, clocking 49.2 seconds. Myers also earned four consecutive Canadian titles from 1880 to 1883 and two British titles in 1881 and 1885. In the 1881 British 440 title race, he clocked 48.6 seconds, but the remarkable time was not recognized as an official world record because of the downward-sloping homestretch. That time, had it been accepted, would have earned Myers every U.S. championship through 1929. Upon retiring from amateur competition in 1885, Myers had established world records for 50 yards (5.5 seconds), 100 yards (10 seconds), 220 yards (22.5 seconds), 300 yards (31.6 seconds), 660 yards (1:22), 880 yards (1:55.4), 1,000 yards (2:13), and one mile (4:27.6).

Professional. Myers became a full-fledged professional runner in 1886. His amateur status had been questioned since 1884, when a sportswriter had accused him of accepting payment for various Manhattan Athletic Club services. His professional career was highlighted with several races against Walter George of Great Britain, who held every world record from one to ten miles. As an amateur, Myers had raced George the half-mile, three-quarter-mile, and one-mile distances. Despite winning the half, Myers lost the three-quarter and one-mile runs. In 1886, as professionals, they met for the "Middle Distance Championship of the World" at New York's Madison Square Garden. Myers defeated George at distances of 1,000 yards, 1,320 yards, and one mile and collected $3,000. They met again in Australia in 1887. After losing two straight races to Myers, George left the country before the end of the competition. Myers retired from competitive running to devote himself to raising horses and bookmaking, then a legal profession, in 1888. When he died in 1899, Myers still held five world records.

Sources:

D. H. Potts, *Lon* (Mountain View, Cal.: Tafnews Press, 1993);

Roberto Quercetani, *A World History of Track and Field Athletics, 1864–1964* (London: Oxford University Press, 1964);

Joe D. Willis and Richard G. Wetton, "L. E. Myers, 'World's Greatest Runner,'" *Journal of Sports History*, 2 (Fall 1975): 93–111.

FREDERICK LAW OLMSTED

1822-1903
LANDSCAPE ARCHITECT

Significance. Frederick Law Olmsted was America's foremost landscape architect in the late nineteenth century. More than any other American of his generation Olmsted represented a belief in the power of landscape to provide a refuge to urban residents and succeeded in planting the romantic ideal in the heart of some of the nation's largest cities. At a time when most urban land was in the hands of private speculators, he symbolized a belief in the civic good and the necessity of urban planning.

Restless Beginnings. Olmsted was born in Hartford, Connecticut, on 26 April 1822. When he was fourteen years old a severe case of sumac poisoning partially blinded him, and for several years thereafter he had poor eyesight. Doctors recommended that he do little reading, so he postponed entering college and traveled in the northeastern United States and Canada with his father, a wealthy merchant. He then worked for a New York importer (1840) and traveled to China (1843). Upon his return to the United States he briefly studied scientific farming at Yale University and did some publishing and editorial work. Between 1852 and 1854 he traveled through the South and wrote extensively on the region, submitting stories to the *New York Daily Tribune*. (The stories were compiled and published as *The Cotton Kingdom* in 1861.) Olmsted received an appointment as general secretary of the U.S. Sanitary Commission during part of the Civil War (1861–1863), then went to California as administrator of the forty-four-thousand-acre Mariposa Estate (1863–1865).

Landscaping Genius. Olmsted was an early American observer of British and of continental parks; he admired the eighteenth-century English garden and skillfully used open areas and natural watersheds in his designs. He developed his style of landscape design in response to urban needs; he was the first to call himself a landscape architect rather than a landscape gardener. With his partner, Calvert Vaux, he designed New York's 840-acre Central Park (1858–1861) and landscaped New York City north of 155th Street. Olmsted's style in turn inspired many city and national parks that followed. He also planned the Emerald Necklace (Boston), Prospect Park (Brooklyn), South Park (Chicago), Belle Isle Park (Detroit), Mount Royal Park (Montreal), the grounds of the U.S. Capitol, and the Boston and Buffalo park systems. His other projects included the Stanford University campus (1886) and the Biltmore Estate outside Asheville, North Carolina (1888). One of his last major projects was as chief landscape planner for the 1893 World's Columbian Exposition in Chicago. Olmsted died on 28 August 1903.

Sources:

Charles E. Beveridge and Paul Rocheleau, *Frederick Law Olmsted: Designing the American Landscape* (New York: Rizzoli, 1995);

Robert L. Gale, *The Gay Nineties in America: A Cultural Dictionary of the 1890s* (Westport: Conn.: Greenwood Press, 1992).

ALBERT GOODWILL "AL" SPALDING

1850-1915
BASEBALL PLAYER AND SPORTS ENTREPRENEUR

Baseball Pioneer. Albert Goodwill Spalding, the son of an Illinois farmer, is regarded as the "organizational genius of baseball's pioneer days" and the game's first great pitcher. He began playing baseball as a youngster and at age sixteen began pitching for the Rockford Forest Cities (Illinois), gaining a reputation for his fastball and exceptional batting. In 1871 Harry Wright recruited Spalding for the Boston Red Stockings of the National Association. Earning $1,500 annually, he led Boston to four consecutive pennants from 1872 to 1875. In that time Spalding won 207 and lost 56 games, becoming baseball's first 200-game winner. He also posted a batting average of .320. In 1876 he joined the Chicago White Stockings of the newly formed National League. As pitcher, captain, and manager of the team, Spalding earned $4,000. He also assisted William A. Hulbert, the owner of the White Stockings and president of the National League, in drafting the constitution for the league, in which he insisted that alcohol and gambling be barred from the game. Spalding pitched only one season for Chicago, winning 48 and losing 13 games, while leading his team to the pennant in 1876. After playing first and second base in 1877, he retired in 1878 but remained an advisor to the team.

Sporting Goods. In 1876 Spalding and his younger brother James Walter opened A. G. Spalding & Brothers, a sporting-goods store in Chicago that sold team uniforms and baseballs. In 1878 the Spalding baseballs became the official game ball (and continued to be the official game ball until 1976, when Rawlings became the official manufacturer). In late 1877 the Spalding brothers entered the publishing business, producing *Spalding's Official Baseball Guide*. Edited by Henry Chadwick, the *Baseball Guide* was the official source for the history of the game. Spalding published pamphlets and guides to other sports. After the death of Hulbert in 1882, Spalding became president of the Chicago White Stockings, which won five National League pennants during the 1880s. Following the 1888 season, he organized a world tour of the nation's best baseball players. In London Spalding opened a branch of his sporting-goods firm and began importing bicycles and golf clubs to the United States. In the 1890s he sold basketballs as that newly invented sport gained national popularity.

Later Career. Spalding resigned as president of the Chicago White Stockings in 1891 but remained the organization's principle stockholder. He went into real estate, founded the Chicago Athletic Club, and helped plan the Chicago World's Fair in 1893. After the death of his wife in 1899, he remarried and moved to Point Loma, California. In 1903 Spalding helped negotiate the National Agreement between the American and National Leagues and, in 1905, headed a special commission to determine the origins of baseball; the commission wrongly claimed that the game was uniquely American. Spalding ran unsuccessfully for the U.S. Senate in 1910 and died at age sixty-five in 1915. He was elected to the baseball Hall of Fame in 1939.

Sources:
Peter Levine, *A. G. Spalding and the Rise of Baseball: The Promise of American Sport* (New York & Oxford: Oxford University Press, 1985);

David Quentin Voigt, *American Baseball: From the Gentleman's Sport to the Commissioner System* (University Park & London: Pennsylvania State University Press, 1983).

JOHN LAWRENCE SULLIVAN

1858-1918

BARE-KNUCKLE PRIZEFIGHTING

CHAMPION

"The Strong Boy." John L. Sullivan, the last bare-knuckle prizefighting champion, was one of the first American sports heroes and contributed to the development of boxing. His father, Michael Sullivan, an Irish immigrant, encouraged his son to become a prizefighter because of his extraordinary strength. In his first recorded fight, Sullivan defeated John "Cockey" Woods in five rounds in Boston in 1879. By 1881 he was known in prizefighting circles as the "strong boy of Boston" because of his many victories by

knockouts. Sullivan captured the world bare-knuckle heavyweight championship on 7 February 1882 by defeating Patrick "Paddy" Ryan in nine rounds on a barge in the Mississippi River near Mississippi City, Mississippi. From 1882 to 1887 he fought in thirty-two matches, winning each time. During this period he also participated in exhibitions, offering $500 cash to anyone who could last three rounds with him. No one won the prize.

A Careless Champion. During his exhibition tours Sullivan neglected his training and slipped into poor physical condition. Many exhibitions were canceled because Sullivan was too drunk to perform. Always popular in Boston, however, his hometown lavished him with attention, including a diamond-studded championship belt. In his title defense bout on 10 March 1888 Sullivan fought to a thirty-nine-round draw with British champion Charlie Mitchell in Chantilly, France. Sullivan won the last bare-knuckle contest, defeating Jake Kilrain in seventy-five rounds at Richburg, Mississippi, on 8 July 1889. Lack of physical training as well as a change in fighting rules cost Sullivan his title. On 7 September 1892 he lost the world heavyweight title in a bout with James J. Corbett, who knocked out Sullivan in the twenty-first round. This fight, conducted under the Marquis of Queensberry rules, required the combatants to wear gloves and barred the wrestling holds so often employed by Sullivan.

Sullivan's Record. After his encounter with Corbett, Sullivan fought one more time; in 1905 he knocked out Jim McCormick in the second round in Grand Rapids, Michigan. Afterward Sullivan officially retired from the ring, but continued to appear in stage exhibitions. He also wrote an autobiography, *Life and Reminiscences of a 19th Century Gladiator* (1892), and toured the nation giving speeches on the evil of liquor. In a career that spanned twenty-five years, Sullivan participated in 47 prize bouts, which included 43 wins (of which 29 were knockouts), 1 loss, and 3 draws. Among his admirers were President Theodore Roosevelt and King Edward VII of Britain.

Sources:
Elliot J. Gorn, *The Manly Art: Bare-Knuckle Prize Fighting in America* (Ithaca, N.Y.: Cornell University Press, 1986);

GEORGE C. TILYOU

1862-1914

BUSINESSMAN

Junior Entrepreneur. George C. Tilyou was born in New York City on 3 February 1862. His father was a hotel proprietor at Coney Island. The younger Tilyou began his business career at age fourteen when he sold little boxes of sifted beach sand and bottles of seawater as souvenirs to visitors on Coney Island. In one day Tilyou made enough money to finance his own trip to the Philadelphia Centennial Exhibition (1876).

Coney Island Development. With an initial investment of only $2.50, Tilyou became one of the most successful businessmen on Coney Island. He laid out the famous Bowery, a carnival amusement street barred to wheeled vehicles, and built Tilyou's Surf Theatre, the first important show house at the resort. In 1897 he built Steeplechase Park, which quickly expanded to fifteen acres. It was wrecked by fire in 1907, but Tilyou restored it on a grander scale. He originated most of the rides used in his amusement enterprises to give patrons nervous thrills as they were whirled, tumbled, and shot down various dark chambers and hilly surfaces. Tilyou patented such rides as the Human Roulette Wheel, Human Pool Table, Earthquake Floor, Eccentric Fountain, Electric Seat, Funny Stairway, Barrel of Love, Aerial Thrill, and the Razzle Dazzle. All were clean, family-oriented amusements because Tilyou was opposed to the rowdy elements that frequently came to Coney Island. He became a reformer in politics and in 1893 helped to overthrow John Y. McKane, the infamous political boss who allowed Coney Island to become a corrupt haven for the type of crowd Tilyou disliked.

More Successes. Besides Coney Island, Tilyou operated amusement parks in New Jersey, New York, Massachusetts, Connecticut, Missouri, and California; many of these were also named Steeplechase Park. Tilyou is said to have been the inventor of the hot dog. He died on 30 November 1914, and his son Edward continued to manage his amusement empire.

Source:
Judith A. Adams, *The American Amusement Park Industry: A History of Technology and Thrills* (Boston: Twayne, 1991).

PUBLICATIONS

G. Mercer Adam, *Sandow on Physical Training* (New York: J. Selwin Tait, 1894)—a critique of current physical regimens and sports;

Alexander Bain, *Mind and Body* (New York: Appleton, 1873)—Bain examines the theories of the relationship between the mind and body;

Phineas T. Barnum, *Struggles and Triumphs: or, Forty Years' Recollections of P. T. Barnum* (Hartford, Conn.: J. B. Burr, 1869)—a self-serving account with many amusing stories;

Joel Benton, *Life of Hon. Phineas T. Barnum* (Philadelphia: Edgewood, 1891)—a routine biography of a larger-than-life showman;

Walter Camp and Lorin F. Deland, *Football* (Boston & New York: Houghton Mifflin, 1896)—a coaching guide by the father of American football;

Henry Chadwick, *The Art of Base Ball Batting* (New York & Chicago: A.G. Spalding & Brothers, 1885);

Chadwick, *The Game of Chess* (New York: American Sports Publishing, 1895)—a work designed for novices, with diagrams, explanations of selected problems, rules and technical terms;

F. W. Eldredge, *Camden, South Carolina, as a Winter Resort* (New York: Mook Brothers, 1880's)—a travel guide detailing field sports, fox hunting, and the luxuries of the Hobkirk Inn;

John H. Glenroy, *Ins and Outs of Circus Life* (Boston: M. M. Wing, 1885)—the interesting life of a circus bareback rider "through United States, Canada, South America and Cuba";

Frederick W. Janssen, *History of American Athletics* (New York: Charles R. Bourne, 1885)—a popular history of sports and their major figures;

Austin Fleming Jenkin, *Gymnastics* (New York: F. A. Stokes, 1891)—one of the more reliable coaching guides on the sport;

Louis F. Liesching, *Through Peril to Fortune; A Story and Adventure by Land and Sea* (London & New York: Cassell, 1880)—an illustrated narrative for young readers with a sports theme;

Richard A. Proctor, *Half-Hours with the Telescope* (London: Longmans, Green, 1896)—a popular guide to the use of the telescope as a means of amusement and instruction;

The Reason Why the Colored American Is Not in the World's Columbian Exposition, edited by Ida B. Wells (Chicago: Ida B. Wells, 1893)—Frederick Douglass wrote the introduction to this collection of essays by Wells. The focus is on race relations rather than the racial situation at the 1893 fair;

Matthew Scott, *Autobiography of Matthew Scott, Jumbo's Keeper* (Bridgeport, Conn.: Trows Printing and Bookbinding, 1885)—an amusing book with various stories about Jumbo;

John L. Sullivan, *Life and Reminiscences of a 19th Century Gladiator* (Boston: Jas. A. Hearn, 1892)—the boxing legend's autobiography that includes reports on his physical condition and measurements;

Benjamin C. Truman, *History of the World's Fair: Being a Complete and Authentic Description of the Columbian Exposition from Its Inception* (Philadelphia: H. W. Kelley, 1893)—a lavishly illustrated book with articles by prominent individuals connected with the exposition;

John H. Vincent, *The Chautauqua Movement* (Boston: Chautauqua Press, 1886)—a valuable account by the movement's founder;

Helen Cody Wetmore, *Last of the Great Scouts: The Life Story of Col. William F. Cody, "Buffalo Bill."* (Duluth, Minn.: Duluth Press, 1899)—a narrative by Cody's sister.

GENERAL REFERENCES

GENERAL

Edward L. Ayers, *The Promise of the New South: Life After Reconstruction* (New York: Oxford University Press, 1992);

Daniel J. Boorstin, *The Americans: The Democratic Experience* (New York: Random House, 1973);

Charles W. Calhoun, ed., *The Gilded Age: Essays on the Origins of Modern America* (Wilmington, Del.: Scholarly Resources, 1995);

Sean Dennis Cashman, *America in the Gilded Age: From the Death of Lincoln to the Rise of Theodore Roosevelt* (New York: New York University Press, 1993);

John Garraty, *The New Commonwealth, 1877-1890* (New York: harper and Row, 1968)

Samuel P. Hays, *The Response to Industrialism, 1885-1914*, second edition (Chicago: University of Chicago Press, 1995);

Richard Hofstadter, *The Age of Reform: From Bryan to F.D.R.* (New York: Vintage Books, 1955);

Gabriel Kolko, *Main Currents in Modern American History* (New York: Pantheon, 1984);

Vernon L. Parrington, *Main Currents in American Thought* , 3 Volumes (New York: Harcourt Brace, 1927);

Page Smith, *The Rise of Industrial America,* vol 6 of *A People's History of the Post-Reconstruction Era* (New York: McGraw-Hill, 1984);

Alan Trachtenberg, *The Incorporation of America: Culture and Society in the Gilded Age* (New York: Hill and Wang, 1982);

Robert Wiebe, *The Search For Order, 1877-1920* (New York: Hill and Wang, 1967)

ARTS

Alfred L. Bernheim and Sarah Harding, *The Business of the Theatre: An Economic History of the American Theatre, 1750-1932* (New York: Benjamin Blom, 1932);

Oscar G. Brockett and Robert R. Findlay, *Century of Innovation: A History of European and American Theatre and Drama Since 1870* (Englewood Cliffs, N.J.: Prentice-Hall, 1984);

Emory Elliot, ed., *Columbia Literary History of the United States* (New York: Columbia University Press, 1988);

William H. Gerdts, *American Impressionism* (New York: Abbeville Press, 1984);

Lawrence Levine, *Highbrow/Lowbrow: The Emergence of Cultural Hierarchy in America* (1988);

Russell Lynes, *The Lively Audience: A Social History of the Visual and Performing Arts in America, 1890-1950* (1985);

Lewis Mumford, *The Brown Decades: A Study of the Arts in America, 1865-1895* (New York: Dover Publications, 1959);

H. Barbara Weinberg et al., eds., *American Impressionism and Realism: The Painting of Modern Llife, 1885-1915* (New York: Metropolitan Museum of Art, 1994).

BUSINESS

Alfred Chandler, *The Visible Hand: The Managerial Revolution in American Business* (Cambridge, Mass.: Harvard University Press, 1977);

William Cronon, *Nature's Metropolis: Chicago and the Great West* (New York: Norton, 1991);

Milton Friedman and Anna J. Schwartz, *A Monetary History of the United States, 1867-1960* (Princeton, N.J.: Princeton University Press, 1963);

William Leach, *Land of Desire: Merchants, Power, and the Rise of a New American Culture* (New York: Pantheon Books, 1993);

David Montgomery, *The Fall of the House of Labor: The Workplace, the State, and American Labor Activism, 1865-1925* (Cambridge: Cambridge University Press, 1985);

Glenn Porter, *The Rise of Big Business, 1860-1910* (New York: Crowell, 1973).

COMMUNICATIONS

John Brooks, *Telephone: The First Hundred Years* (New York: Harper and Row, 1976);

Michael Emery and Edwin Emery, *The Press and America: An Interpretive History of the Mass Media*, seventh edition, revised and expanded (Englewood Cliffs, N.J.: Prentice Hall, 1992);

Sidney Kobre, *The Yellow Press and Gilded Age Journalism* (Tallahassee: Florida State University Press, 1964);

T. J. Jackson Lears, *Fables of Abundance: A Cultural History of Advertising in America* (New York: Basic Books, 1994);

Mitchell Stephens, *A History of News: From the Drum to the Satellite* (New York: Viking, 1988);

John Tebbel, *The American Magazine: A Compact History* (New York: Hawthorn Books, 1969);

EDUCATION

Burton J. Bledstein, *The Culture of Professionalism: The Middle Class and the Development of Higher Education in America* (New York: Norton, 1976);

Lawrence A. Cremin, *American Education: The Metropolitan Experience, 1876-1980* (New York: Harper and Row, 1988);

David Nasaw, *Schooled to Order: A Social History of Public Schooling in the United States* (New York: Oxford University Press, 1979);

William J. Reese, *The Origins of the American High School* (New Haven: Yale University Press, 1995);

Barbara Miller Solomon, *In the Company of Educated Women* (New Haven: Yale University Press, 1985);

Lawrence R. Veysey, *The Emergence of the American University* (Chicago: University of Chicago Press, 1965).

GOVERNMENT

Paul Boyer, *Urban Masses and Moral Order in America, 1820-1920* (Cambridge, Mass.: Harvard University Press 1978);

Morton Keller, *Affairs of State: Public Life in Late Nineteenth-Century America* (Cambridge, Mass.: Belknap Press of Harvard University Press, 1977)

Arthur M. Schlesinger, Jr., ed., *History of American Presidential Elections, 1789-1968* (New York: Chelsea House/McGraw-Hill, 1971);

Lawrence Goodwyn, *The Populist Moment: A Short History of the Agrarian Revolt in America* (New York: Oxford University Press, 1978)

Walter LaFeber, *The New Empire: An Interpretation of American Expansion, 1860-1898* (Ithaca: Cornell University Press, 1963)

Walter LaFeber, *American Age: United States Foreign Policy at Home and Abroad Since 1750* (New York: Norton, 1989);

Ernest R. May, *American Imperialism: A Speculative Essay* (Chicago Ill.: Impreint Publications, 1991);

Emily S. Rosenberg, *Spreading the American Dream: American Economic and Cultural Expansion, 1890-1945* (New York: Hill and Wang, 1982);

C. Vann Woodward, *The Strange Career of Jim Crow*, 3rd rev. edition (New York: Oxford University Press, 1974).

LAW

Lawrence M. Friedman, *A History of American Law* (New York: Simon and Schuster, 1985);

John A. Garraty, ed., *Quarrels that Have Shaped the Constitution* (New York: Harper and Row, 1964);

Morton Horwitz, *The Transformation of American Law, 1870-1960: The Crisis of Legal Orthodoxy* (New York: Oxford University Press, 1992);

Janet A. McDonnell, *The Dispossession of the American Indian, 1887-1934* (Bloomington: Indiana University Press, 1991);

Donald G. Nieman, ed., *The Constitution, Law, and American Life* (Athens: University of Georgia Press, 1992);

Robert Stevens, *Law School: Legal Education in America from the 1850s to the 1980s* (Chapel Hill: UNC Press, 1983);

LIFESTYLES

Roger Daniels, *Coming to America: A History of Immigration and Ethnicity in American Life* (New York: HarperCollins, 1990);

Eleanor Flexner, *A Century of Struggle: The Woman's Rights Movement in America*, rev. ed. (Cambridege, Mass.: Belknap Press, 1975);

Jessica H. Foy and Thomas Schlereth, eds., *American Home Life, 1880-1930* (Knoxville: University of Tennessee Press, 1992);

Lee Hall, *Common Threads: A Parade of American Clothing* (Boston: Little Brown, 1992);

John Higham, *Strangers in the Land: Patterns of American Nativism, 1860-1925*, rev. ed. (New York: Athenaeum, 1963);

Richard J. Hooker, *Food and Drink in the United States: A History* (Indianapolis: Bobbs-Merrill, 1981);

Kenneth T. Jackson, *Crabgrass Frontier: The Sububranization of the United States* (New York: Oxford University Press, 1985);

Alan M. Kraut, *The Huddled Masses: The Immigrant in American Society, 1880-1921* (1982);

Patricia Nelson Limerick, *Legacy of Conquest: The Unbroken Past of the American West* (New York: Norton, 1987);

Thomas J. Schlereth, *Victorian America: Transformations in Everyday Life, 1876-1915* (New York: HarperCollins, 1991);

Geoffrey C. Ward, et al, *The West: An Illustrated History* (Boston: Little Brown, 1996);

RELIGION

Sydney E. Ahlstrom, *A Religious History of the American People* (New Haven: Yale University Press, 1972);

Jay P. Dolan, *The American Catholic Experience: A History from Colonial Times to the Present* (Garden City, N.Y.: Doubleday, 1985);

William R. Hutchinson, *The Modernist Impulse in American Protestantism* (New York: Oxford University Press, 1976);

George M Marsden, *Fundamentalism and American Culture: The Shaping of Twentieth-Century Evangelicalism, 1870-1928* (New York: Oxford University Press, 1980);

Howard M. Sachar, *A History of the Jews in America* (New York: Alfred A. Knopf, 1992).

SCIENCE AND MEDICINE

Hamilton Cravens, Alan I. Marcus, David M. Katzman, eds., *Technical Knowledge in American Culture: Science, Technology, and Medicine since the Early 1800s* (Tuscaloosa: University of Alabama Press, 1996);

William Goetzmann, *Exploration and Empire: The Explorer and the Scientist in the Winning of the American West* (New York: Knopf, 1966);

David F. Noble, *America By Design: Science, Technology, and the Rise of Corporate Capitalism* (New York: Oxford University Press, 1977);

Leonard S. Reich, *The Making of American Industrial Research: Science and Business at GE and Bell, 1876-1926* (1985);

Nathan Reingold, *Science, American Style* (New Brunswick: Rutgers University Press, 1991);

William G. Rothstein, *American Physicians in the Nineteenth Century: From Sects to Science* (Baltimore: Johns Hopkins Press, 1972);

Hugh Richard Slotten, *Patronage, Practice, and the Culture of American Science* (New York: Cambridge University Press, 1994);

Paul Starr, *The Social Transformation of American Medicine* (New York: Basic Books, 1982).

SPORTS AND LEISURE

Warren Goldstein, *Playing for Keeps: A History of Early Baseball* (Ithaca, N.Y.:Cornell University Press, 1989);

Elliot J. Gorn, *The Manly Art: Bare-Knuckle Prize Fighting in America* (Ithaca, N.Y.:Cornell University Press, 1986);

Allen Guttmann, *A Whole New Ball Game: An Interpretation of American Sports* (Chapel Hill: University of North Carolina Press, 1988);

John F. Kasson, *Amusing the Million: Coney Island at the Turn of the Century* (New York: Hill and Wang, 1978);

Peter Levine, *A.G. Spaulding and the Rise of Baseball: The Promise of American Sport* (New York: Oxford University Press, 1985);

Peter Levine, *America Sport: A Documentary History* (Englewood Cliffs, N.J.: Prentice-Hall, 1989);

Theodore Morrison, *Chataqua: A Center for Education, Religion, and the Arts in America* (Chicago: University of Chicago Press, 1974);

Kathy Peiss, *Cheap Amusements: Working Women and Leisure in Turn-of-the-Century New York* (Philadelphia: Temple University Press, 1986);

James C. Whorton, *Crusaders for Fitness: The History of Health Reformers* (Princeton: Princeton University Press, 1984).

CONTRIBUTORS

THE ARTS

BUSINESS & THE ECONOMY

COMMUNICATIONS

EDUCATION

GOVERNMENT & POLITICS

LAW & JUSTICE

LIFESTYLES, SOCIAL TRENDS & FASHION

RELIGION

SCIENCE & MEDICINE

SPORTS & RECREATION

JESSICA DORMAN
Harvard University

FREDERICK DALZELL
*Maritime Studies Program of
Williams College & Mystic Seaport*

NANCY E. BERNHARD
Massachusetts School of Law at Andover

HARRIETT WILLIAMS
University of South Carolina

RODNEY P. CARLISLE
Rutgers University

JANE GERHARD
Brown University

ROBERT J. ALLISON
Suffolk University

JANE GERHARD
Brown University

ANDREW WALSH
Trinity College

THOMAS GLICK
Boston University

ADAM HORNBUCKLE
Alexandria, Va.

MARTIN MANNING
Woodbridge, Va.

INDEX

Bayard Building, New York City (Sullivan) 47, 81
Bayley, Archbishop James 350-351
Baylor College of Medicine 358
Bayou Folk (Chopin) 35
Beach, Mrs. H. H. A. 44
Beadle and Adams (publishing house) 53
Beautiful Joe (Saunders) 35-36, 54
Beaux, Cecilia 43
Beaux-Arts architecture 38, 40-41, 61, 74
Beecher, Catharine 323
Beecher, Henry Ward 34, 343-344
Beethoven Hall, New York City 387
Beethoven, Ludwig van 44
Beggs, John 261
Behring, Emil von 360
Belasco, David 30, 70-71
Belavin, Tikhon 331
Bell, Alexander Graham 119, 137, 229, 237, 357, 362-363
Bell, Andrew 407
Bell and the Telephone 362-363
Bell Telephone Company 137, 362, 363
Bellamy Clubs 32, 59
Bellamy, Edward 32, 54, 58-60, 205-206
Belle Isle Park, Detroit (Olmsted) 417
Bellevue Hospital Medical College 356
Belmont Stakes 385
Ben-Hur (play) 70
Ben-Hur: A Tale of Christ (Wallace) 27, 54-55, 70, 118
Bennett, Derogier M. 224
Bennett, James Gordon 135
Bennett, James Gordon Jr. 118, 133
Bentham, Jeremy 271
Berdan, Harry B. (Harry Braisted) 37-38
Berenson, Senda 400-401
Bering Sea Arbitration Tribunal 274
Berkman, Alexander 101, 232
Berlin, Irving 412
Berman, Nathan Barrett 105
Bernard, Claude 361
Bernhardt, Sarah 27
Beside the Bonnie Brier Bush (Maclaren) 54
Bessemer production process 111
Bethlehem Iron Company 395
Bettis, Rev. Alexander 344
Betty Alden: The First Born Daughter of the Pilgrims (Austin) 33
Bible 327, 329-331, 333, 337-338, 340, 344-345, 348-350, 352-353
"A Bicycle Built for Two" (Dacre) 34
Bidwell, John 208
Bierce, Ambrose 33-35, 39, 63
Bierstadt, Albert 32
Chief Big Foot 286, 308, 343
Biggs, Dr. Hermann Michael 360
Bijou Theater 29
Bill of Rights 241
Billboard 36
Billy Budd (Melville) 34
Billy the Kid. *See* Bonney, William H.
Biltmore Estate (Olmsted) 417
"A Bird from O'er the Sea" (White) 27
The Birth of Galahad (Hovey) 38
Bissell, Wilson 135
Black Beauty (Sewall) 54

Black Beetles in Amber (Bierce) 34
Black-Eyed Susan 70
The Black Riders (Crane) 36
Black Rock (Connor) 54
Blackface 56, 58
Blackstone, Sir William 271, 275
Blaine, James G. 132, 143, 179, 192-193, 208-210, 214, 216-219, 241, 246, 263
Blair Bill 148
Blair, Henry 259
Blake, James W. 36
Blakelock, Ralph Albert 46
Bland, James A. 26
Bland-Allison Act of 1878 195
Blatchford, Samuel 226, 232
The Bloody Chasm (De Forest) 27
Blooms of the Berry 31
Blount, James H. 202
Blow, Susan 162, 172
Bly, Nellie 122, 124, 128-129
Bogardus, Capt. A. H. 411
Bok, Edward W. 121, 130
Boll weevil 286
Bolton, Sarah 140
Bonner, Sherwood 29
Bonney, Charles C. 348
Bonney, William H. (Billy the Kid) 225, 254-255
Bonsack, James 108
Boodle 186, 188, 207
Boomers 277
Boone and Crockett Club 285
Booth, Catherine 341
Booth, Edwin 34
Booth, John Wilkes 34
Booth, Mary 140
Booth, William 341
Booth's Theater, New York City 27
Borden Milk Company 109
Borden, Abbie Durfee Gray 232, 256-257
Borden, Almy, and Company 256
Borden, Andrew Jackson 232, 256-257
Borden, Emma 256-258
Borden, Lizzie 232, 256-258
Borough Hall, Brooklyn 34
Boston 202
Boston and Albany Railroad 28
Boston Athletic Association (BAA) 392, 407
Boston Bicycle Club 401
Boston Classicism (music) 31
Boston Common 38
Boston Cooking School 148, 282, 302, 320
The Boston Cooking-School Cook Book 288, 302, 320
Boston Fruit Company 92
Boston Journal 120
Boston Latin School 171
Boston Marathon 388, 392
Boston Nationals 386
Boston Normal School of Gymnastics 401
Boston Public Library (McKim, Mead and White) 32, 61
Boston Red Stockings 417
Boston Transcript 320
The Bostonians (James) 30, 52, 64, 397

The Bow of Orange Ribbon (Barr) 30
Bowditch, Henry Pickering 372-373
Bowdoin College 79
Bowen, William Shaw 126
Bowers, Henry Francis 180, 337
"The Bowery" (Gaunt and Hoyt) 34
Bowery Theater, New York City 26
Bowery, Coney Island, New York 419
Bowman v. *Chicago & Northwestern Railroad* 229
Bowman, Euday Louis 57
Boyesen, Hjalmar Hjorth 26, 29, 33-35, 74
Boys' Club 148
Bradley, Joseph 231, 243
Brady, Matthew 37
Brady, William 254-255
Braham, David 26-27, 29-30, 33-34
A Branch of May (Reese) 31
Brandt, John L. 337
Brandt, Marianne 56
Bratton, John W. 36
Brave New World (Huxley) 60
The Bread-winners (Hay) 29
"Break the News to Mother" (Harris) 38, 69
The Breakers, Newport, Rhode Island 91
Breaking Down Barriers 128-129
Breal, Michel 392
Brearly, William 120
Brennan, Joseph 274
Brewer, David J. 230, 241
Brewer, Dick 254-255, 268, 270
Bricks Without Straw (Tourgée) 27, 73
Briggs, Charles A. 329, 333, 340, 344-345, 349-350
"Bring Back My Bonnie to Me" (Pratt) 28
Brisbane, Albert 141
Brisbane, Arthur 121, 126, 133, 139, 141, 144
British Ladies' Golf Union 408
British Royal Observatory 284
Brodie, Steve 34
Brook Farm, West Roxbury, Mass. 140-141
Brookline Country Club, Mass. 408
Brooklyn Bridge (Roebling) 29, 34, 41, 47-48, 49, 283
Brooks Brothers, New York City 293
Brotherhood of Carpenters and Joiners 409
Brotherhood of Locomotive Firemen 112
Brotherhood of Professional Base Ball Players 399
Broughton Rules (boxing) 396
"Brown October Ale" 33
Brown University 137, 383, 387
Brown, Alice 29, 31, 36-37, 39
Brown, C. S. 387
Brown, Henry 230, 252, 265
Brown, Henry Kirke 74
Brown, Mrs. Charles S. 408
Brown, William Hill 63
Brown, William Wells 73
Browne, Francis F. 27
The Brownies, Their Book (Cox) 31

F

"Factory Song" 70
Fagan, Barney 37
The Faith of Our Fathers (Gibbons) 350
Falconberg (Boyesen) 26
Fall River Savings Bank, Mass. 256
Fantastic Fables (Bierce) 39
Farmer, Fannie 288, 302, 320
Farmers' Loan and Trust Company 228, 234, 251-252
Farmers' Union 206
Farragut (Saint-Gaudens) 74
Farragut, David 215
"The Fatal Wedding" (Davis and Windom) 35
Father Goose: His Book (Baum) 39
Faust (Gounod) 29, 35, 55
Fayette County Courthouse, Ohio 259
Federal Elections Act of 1889–1890 194
Federal Penitentiary, Columbus, Ohio 138
Federal Steel Company 114
Federation of Organized Trades and Labor Unions 87, 409
Feminism 41, 59, 65, 68, 80, 347
Ferguson, John H. 264
Ferris Wheel 286, 395, 413
Ferris, George Washington Gale 286, 395
The Field 410
Field and Stream 387
Field Code of Civil Procedure 238, 271-272
Field Museum of Natural History 390
Field, Cyrus West 238
Field, David Dudley 238, 271
Field, Eugene 31, 76
Field, James G. 181, 208
Field, Marshall 250
Field, Stephen Johnson 230, 235, 238, 241, 252, 268-269, 271, 273
Fielden, Samuel 250
Fields, Annie Adams 80
Fields, James T. 80
Fifteen Passenger Bill 239
Figs and Thistles (Tourgée) 73
Filene, E. A. 162
Filene, William 87
Filene's store, Boston 162-163
Filson, Al W. 30
Financing the Federal Government 198
Findlay, Alex 407
Findlay's Hotel, Pine Ridge, S.D. 134
Finerty, John 133
Finley, James 48
Finnel, John 243
Finney, Charles Grandison 352
Firman, Leroy B. 356
First Modern Suite (McDowell) 28
First Presbyterian Church, Chicago 348
First Presbyterian Church, Roselle, N.J. 349
First Symphony (Ives) 38
Fischer, Adolph 229, 250
Fischer, Edwin P. 411
Fisk University 322
Fisk, Clinton 208

Fisk, James 113
Fiske, Harrison Grey 72
Fitzsimmons, Bob "Ruby Robert" 388, 397
"The Five-cent Shave" (Cannon) 27
Five Civilized Tribes 230, 245
The Five Little Peppers and How They Grew (Lothrop) 27, 54
Five-and-Ten-Cent Store 98, 291
Flag Day 386, 391, 409
Flaubert, Gustave 54, 67
Fleming, Williamina 358
Fletcher, Henry J. 94
"A Flower for Mother's Grave" (Kennedy) 26
Flower, Benjamin Orange 121
The Flying Dutchman (Ryder) 27
Folks from Dixie (Dunbar) 38
Folsom, Charles 248
Folsom, Oscar 199
Fong Yue Ting v. *U.S.* 232
Fong Yue Ting 241
A Fool's Errand (Tourgée) 26, 73, 264, 272
Fools of Nature (Brown) 31
Football Facts and Figures (Camp) 415
Foote, Arthur W. 31-33, 44
Foote, Mary Hallock 29, 34
For the Major (Woolson) 29
Foraker, Joseph B. 217
Foran Act 88, 284
Forbes, J. Malcolm 394
Forbes, John Murry 394
Ford Motor Car Company 92
Ford, Henry 91
Ford, Paul Leicester 35, 39
Ford, Robert 226
Ford, Walter H. 36
Foreman, Charles E. 38
Forepaugh, Adam 404
Forest Park Highlands, St. Louis 390, 395
Fort Smith 253, 276-277
Fort Stanton 254
Fort Sumner, New Mexico 225
Fortune, T. Thomas 119, 141-142, 322
Foster, Stephen 56, 128
Foster, William 135
"The Fountain in the Park" (Haley) 29
The 400 286
Fowler, John "Bud" 399
Fox tribe 286
Fox, John Jr. 37
Fox, Richard Kyle 396-397
Foxburg Country Club, Foxburg, Penn. 407
Franco-Prussian War 171, 406
Frank Merriwell series (Patten) 37
Frederic, Harold 31, 37
Free Joe and Other Georgian Sketches (Harris) 31
Free Masonry 102
Free Speech 231
Freedmen's Bureau 163, 272
Freeman, Mary E. Wilkins 31, 33, 35, 65
French Foreign Legion 143
French Impressionism 28, 43, 77
French, Alice (Octave Thanet) 31, 35
French, Daniel Chester 26, 30, 35, 74-75

Freud, Sigmund 172, 375
Frick, Henry C. 100-101, 111, 232
Froebel, Friedrich Wilhelm August 154-155, 162, 172
Froelich, John 90
From the New World (Dvorak) 35
Frontier Day 387
Fugitive Slave Act 243
"The Full Moon Union" (Braham and Harrigan) 27
Fuller, Henry Blake 35-36, 40, 49-50
Fuller, Melville W. 241, 252, 268, 270
Fuller, Sarah Margaret 141
Fundamentalism 331, 333, 340, 349, 352-353
Funny Stairway, Coney Island, New York 419
Furness, Frank 80

G

Gage, Matilda Joselyn 283
Gaines High School, Cincinnati 166
Galatea 394
Galileo 376-377
Gallegher and Other Stories (Davis) 33
The galop 286
Galton, Francis 312
Gardner Held by His Mother (Cassatt) 78
Gardner, William Henry 33
Garfield and Guiteau 246-249
"Garfield versus Hancock" (Guiteau) 246, 248
Garfield, James A. 178-179, 188, 205, 209, 212, 214-217, 219, 225-226, 246-249, 264
Garfield, Lucretia Randolph 216
A Garland for Girls (Alcott) 32
Garland, Hamlin 31, 33, 35-36, 42, 63, 65, 412
Garnet, Henry Highland 327
Garrett, Patrick F. 225, 255
Garrett, Robert 407
Garrick Theatre, New York City 37, 39
Garvey, Marcus 142
Gary, Joseph E. 250-251
Gates, Frederick T. 114
Gates, John "Bet-A-Million" 86
Gates, Merrill 244
Gaunt, Percy 34
Geary Act of 1892 241
Geauga Academy, Chester, Ohio 216
Geibel, Adam 37
General Allotment Act. See also Dawes Severalty Act 229, 285
General Appropriations Act of 1871 200
General Electric Company 90, 114
General Federation of Women's Clubs 316-317, 323
General Managers' Association 106
The General Method (McMurray) 154
Genesta 384, 394
The Gentleman from Indiana (Tarkington) 39
George of Greece (King) 127

George Peabody College for Teachers. *See*
Tennessee Normal College.
George, Henry   54, 205-207, 282, 327,
351
George, Walter   416
Georgia School of Technology   156
Germ theory   367-368, 373-374
Germ Theory and Patent Medicine   368
Geronimo   284, 306
Gerrymandering   186, 219
Gerster, Etelka   56
The Ghost Dance   342-343
Ghost Dance religion   286, 308, 328-329,
335, 342-343
Gibbons, James Cardinal   327, 334, 336,
350-351
Gibson Girl   295, 298
Gibson, Charles Dana   287, 295, 298
Gideons International   331
Gilbert and Sullivan   26, 29
Gilbert, Grove Karl   366
Gilbert, Mrs. George H.   31
The Gilded Age (Clemens and Warner)   79
Gilder, Richard Watson   28
Gillespie, Colonel J. Hamilton   407
Gillette, King   58
Gillette, William   37, 39, 71
Gilman, Charlotte Perkins   35, 41, 63, 68
Gilman, Daniel Coit   156
Gilman, G. F.   98
Gilman, George Houghton   68
Gilmore's Gardens, New York City   383
Gimbel's department store, New York City
96
The Giralda, Seville, Spain   385
Girard, Louis J.   358
"The Girl and the Dog" (Slenker)   229,
264
Gladden, Washington   326-327, 329
Glasgow, Ellen   37-38
"Gliding in the Rink"   69
Glimpses of Fifty Years (Willard)   285
Glimpses of Unfamiliar Japan (Hearn)   33
Globe   142
Goddard, Morrill   139, 144
Godey's Lady's Book   26, 126, 294
Godkin, E. L.   118, 123, 142-143
Gold Medal Flour   108
"Gold Will Buy Most Anything But a True
Girl's Heart" (Rosenfeld and Foreman)
38
*The Golden Argosy, Freighted With Treasures
for Boys and Girls* (later becomes just
Golden Argosy)   119, 138
The Golden Bowl (James)   64
The Golden Calf (Boyesen)   34, 74
The Golden House (Warner)   36
Golden Multitudes (Mott)   54
Gómez, Gen. Máximo   126, 128
Gompers, Samuel   101, 103, 106, 112,
200, 251
Gonorrhea   358
Good Government Club   267
Good Housekeeping   138
Good Roads Bill   104
"Good-By Old Stamp, Good-by"   69

The Goodness of St. Rocque and Other Stories
(Nelson)   39
Gorman, Arthur P.   189
Gospel of Wealth (Carnegie)   89, 343-344
Goss, Joe   382
Gothic architecture   49, 60
Gottheil, Rabbi Gustav   346
Goucher College. *See* Woman's College of
Baltimore.   161
Gould, Jay   88, 102, 107, 113, 132, 135
Goulding, Grantley   407
Gounod, Charles   29, 55
Government and Labor   199-200
Government Regulation of Big Business
99-100
Grady, Henry W.   97
Graham, Charles   31, 34-35
Graham, George   228
Grand Army of the Republic   409
Grand Canyon   396
Grand Central Terminal, New York City
(Warren and Wetmore)   61
Grand Depot department store,
Philadelphia   86
Grand Old Party (GOP). *See* Republican
Party.   190
Grand Opera House, New York City   225,
242
Grand Union grocery chain   98
Grand, Sarah   54
The Grandissimes (Cable)   27
The Grange   96, 197, 206
Grant, Ulysses S.   75, 192-193, 195, 209,
211-212, 276
Grant, William West   357
Grant's Tomb   288, 308
Gray, Alonzo   167
Gray, Elisha   137, 362
Gray, Horace   226, 228, 241
Gray, Dr. John P.   248
Gray, William B.   38
Great Atlantic and Pacific Tea Company
98
Great Chicago fire of 1871   65, 352
Great Depression   197
Great Five Cent Store, Utica, N.Y.   86, 98
Great Fossil War   368-369
Great London, Cooper & Bailey's Allied
Show   404
Great Northern Railroad   106, 112
Great Upheaval (1 May 1886)   102
The Greater Inclination (Wharton)   39
The Greek Slave (Powers)   74
Greeley, Horace   141, 143
Green, Anna Katharine   26, 54-55
Greenback Labor Party   86, 178-179, 195,
206-208
Greenfield, Alf   275
Greenough, Horatio   74
Greenstone Church, Pullman, Ill.   105
Grier, Robert   268
Grinnell, Julius   250
Grocery chains   98
The Gross Clinic (Eakins)   40, 46
Grosscup, Peter S.   234
Guaranty Building, Buffalo, New York   36,
47, 81

Guiteau, Charles Julius   178, 212-213,
216, 225-226, 246-249, 264
The Gulf Stream (Homer)   39, 46
Gulick, Luther Halsey   400
Gunter, A. C.   54
"Gypsy's Love Song" (Herbert and Smith)
38

H

H. J. Heinz and Company   109
Haggard, H. Rider   32, 54
Hailmann, Eudora   162
Hailmann, Dr. William   162
Haldeman, Eliza   77
Hale, Edward Everett   ·32, 34, 36, 138
Hale, George Ellery   359
Hale, Lucretia Peabody   27
Hale, Sarah Josepha   26
Halévy, Ludovic   54
Haley, Ed   29
Hall of Philosophy   403
Hall v. *DeCuir*   224
Hall, Charles Martin   357
Hall, Granville Stanley   149, 157, 159,
171-173, 356, 358, 377
Halley's Comet   78-79
Halpin, Mrs. Maria Crofts   199
Halsted, Dr. William   357
Hamilton College   214
Hamilton, Alexander   143
Hamlet (Shakespeare)   70, 160
Hamline College   387, 400
Hammond, George H.   87
Hampton Normal and Industrial Institute,
Va.   163-164
Hancock, Gen. Winfield Scott   178, 209,
216, 246, 248, 298
"A Handful of Earth from My Dear
Mother's Grave" (Murphy)   30
A Handful of Lavender (Reese)   33
Handley, John J.   30
Hanlon, Edward H.   398
Hanna, C. Augusta Rhodes   216
Hanna, Mark   189, 211, 216-217, 219
Hansell, Ellen F.   384, 411
"Happy Birds" (Holst and Steele)   31
Harbinger   141
Harding, George   237
Hardy, Thomas   138
Harkness v. *Hyde*   224
Harlan, John Marshall   239, 243-244, 252,
265, 268, 273-274
Harlan, John Marshall II   274
Harland, Marion   130
Harmon, Moses   263-264
Harney, Ben R.   36-37, 57
Harper, Florence   26
Harper, William Rainey   157, 403
Harper's Bazar   140
Harper's New Monthly Magazine   31,
62-63, 118, 126, 138
Harper's Weekly   45, 133, 138, 140
Harrigan, Edward   26-27, 29-30, 33-34,
71
Harris, Carlyle   231

Harris, Charles K.   34, 38, 69
Harris, George Washington   76
Harris, Joel Chandler   27, 29, 31, 34, 42,
    54, 65, 138
Harris, William C.   382
Harris, William Torrey   159, 162, 167, 172
Harrison, Benjamin   62, 134, 180-182,
    202, 205, 209-210, 214, 217-218,
    231-232, 266, 270
Harrison, Benjamin (1726–1791)   217
Harrison, Caroline Scott   205, 218
Harrison, Carter   233, 249-250
Harrison, Carter H. II   402
Harrison, William Henry   210, 217
Hart, James   414
Hart, John   167
Hart, Tony   71
Harte, Bret   76
Hartford, G. Huntington   98
Harvard Annex   171
Harvard Classics and Junior Classics   171
"Harvard Classification" of stars   358
Harvard College   171
Harvard Law Review   229
Harvard Law School   64, 218
Harvard Medical School   377
Harvard University   30, 60, 74-75, 141,
    149, 155, 159, 161, 171, 173, 232,
    271-272, 275, 371-374, 376-378, 383,
    386-388, 390, 400, 404-407
Harvard University — Boylston Prize   162
Harvard University — Laboratory for
    Psychophysics   377
Harvard University — Law School   256,
    271, 275-276
Harvard University — Lawrence Scientific
    School   377-378
Harvard University — Medical School
    162
Harvard University — Radcliffe College
    171
Harvard University — Summer School
    170
Harvard, John   30
Harvey, George   144
Harvey, William H.   54
Hassam, Childe   33, 41, 43
Hatch Act   89, 149, 285, 358
Havemayer, Henry O.   90
Hawaiian Constitution   181, 202
Hawkins, Sir Anthony Hope   36
Hawthorne, Julian   138
Hawthorne, Nathaniel   41, 62-63, 74, 80,
    141, 162
Hay, John   29, 184
Hayden, Ferdinand V.   365-366, 368-369
Hayden, Joe   37
Hayes, Lucy Webb   218
Hayes, Rutherford B.   178, 185, 193, 209,
    212, 214, 216, 218-219, 224-225,
    239-240, 255, 273, 308, 313, 382
Haymarket Riot (4 May 1886)   52, 70-71,
    88, 102, 200, 228-229, 232
Haymarket strike of 1886, Chicago   180,
    249-251, 261
A Hazard of New Fortunes (Howells)   33,
    63

Hazel Kirke (MacKaye)   27
"Hear Dem Bells" (McCosh)   27
Hearn, Lafcadio   32-33, 74
Hearst, Phoebe   162
Hearst, William Randolph   119, 122-123,
    125-127, 129, 133, 139, 141, 162, 203
Heathcote, John Moyer   410
The Heavenly Twins (Grand)   54
Hebrew Union College, Cincinnati
    327-328, 347
Heelan, Will A.   39
Heidi (Spyri)   54
Heintzemann Press   118
Heintzemann, Carl   118
Heinz company   162
Helene de Septeuil (Cassatt)   78
"Hello, Ma Baby" (Howard and Emerson)
    39
Helmholtz, Hermann von   371
Helwig, Helen R.   411
Hendricks, Thomas A.   179, 209-210
Hendrie, G. M.   383
Hennessy, David   231, 261-263
The Henrietta (Howard)   71
Henry Street Settlement, New York City
    52, 314
Henry, O. *See* Porter, William Sydney.   76
Herbart, Johann Friedrich   154, 172
Herbartian methods   150-151, 154
Herbert, B. B.   120
Herbert, Victor   38
Herland (Gilman)   68
Herne, James A.   33, 71
Herreshoff, Nat   394
Heth, Joice   415
Hewitt & Tuttle (mercantile firm)   114
"Hiawatha" (Longfellow)   28
"The High School Cadets" (Sousa)   44
Higham, Richard   383
"The Highway in the Air"   48
Hill, David Jayne   328
Hill, Harry   396
Hinduism   264, 348
Historical fiction   55
The History of Hungary and the Magyars
    (Godkin)   142
History of the City of New York (Booth)   140
*History of the Conflict between Religion and
    Science* (Draper)   376
*The History of the Warfare of Science with
    Theology in Christendom* (White)   347,
    376
History of Woman Suffrage   283
H. M. S. Pinafore (Gilbert and Sullivan)   26
Ho Ah Kow   225, 240
Hoar, George   190, 270
Hobart, Clarence   411
Hobart, Garret A.   183, 211
Hodge, Archibald Alexander Charles   327,
    339-340, 349
Hoe press   131
Hoffman House, New York City   139
Hogan, Ernest   37
"Hogan's Alley"   122, 139
Holabird, William   50
Holbrook, Josiah   402
Holden v. *Hardy*   235

Holder, Charles Frederick   284
Holiness movement   353
Holley, Marietta   27, 30-31, 34-35
Holliday, John "Doc"   226
Hollyhocks, Isles of Shoals (Hassam)   43
Holmes, Oliver Wendell   30, 63, 80
Holmes, Oliver Wendell Jr.   255-256
Holst, Edward   31
Holy Spirit Conference, Baltimore   329
Holy Synod of Russia   331
Home economics   152, 174, 288, 302
Home Insurance Building, Chicago (Jenney)
    30, 50
Homer, Winslow   30, 39, 42-43, 45-46
Homestead Act of 1862   366
Homestead steel plant. *See* Carnegie Steel,
    Homestead plant, Penn.   90, 94
Homestead Strike of 1892. *See also* Carnegie
    Steel, Homestead plant, Penn.   70, 90,
    100-101, 103, 111, 232
*The Honorable Peter Stirling and What People
    Thought of Him* (Ford)   35
Hoopa tribe   246
The Hoosier School-Boy (Eggleston)   29
The Hoosier Schoolmaster (Eggleston)   63
Hope, Anthony   32, 54
Hopkins University   157
Hopkins, Pauline   27, 41, 73
Hopper, DeWolf   32
Horgan, Stephen H.   123, 131, 135
Horton Law, New York   396
Hosmer, Harriet   74
"A Hot Time in the Old Town" (Metz and
    Hayden)   37
"Hottest Coon in Dixie" (Cook and
    Dunbar)   58
The House Behind the Cedars (Chesnutt)
    273
A Houseboat on the Styx (Bangs)   37
Hovey, Richard   33, 35, 39
How the Other Half Lives (Riis)   52, 121,
    144, 164, 286
Howard University   141
Howard, Bronson   71
Howard, Frank   29
Howard, Joe E.   39
Howard, Milford   251
Howard, Gen. Oliver Otis   307
Howe & Hummel (law firm)   274-275
Howe and Hummel (criminal defense team)
    267
Howe Law, New York State   358
Howe, E. W.   29, 65
Howe, Julia Ward   315
Howe, William F.   274-275
Howells, William Dean   26-28, 30-35, 42,
    52, 58, 60, 63-64, 76, 79, 119
Hoyt, Beatrix   408
Hoyt, Charles Hale   34, 71
Hoyt, William   407
Hubbard, Gardiner Greene   121, 357
*Huckleberries Gathered from New England
    Hills* (Cooke)   33, 65
Huckleberry Finn (Clemens)   122
Hudson River School   42, 45-46
Hugh Wynne, Free Quaker (Mitchell)   37
Hulbert, William A.   397-398, 417-418

John March, Southerner (Cable) 35
John Swinton's Paper 142
John Ward, Preacher (Deland) 32
"Johnny Get Your Gun" (Rosenfeld) 30
Johns Hopkins Medical School 359, 375
Johns Hopkins University 155-157, 171,
   356, 373, 378, 386
Johnson & Johnson 357
Johnson, Billy 38, 58
Johnston, Annie Fellows 37
Johnston, Joseph E. 219
Johnston, Mary 38
Johnston, Richard Malcolm 37
Jones, Charles Prince 331
Jones, Marion 411
Joplin, Scott 39-40, 42, 57
Jordan Marsh department store, Boston
   96, 291
Jordan, Joe 57
Jo's Boys (Alcott) 30
Chief Joseph 282, 288, 307-308
Joseph Seep Agency 110
Joseph, Jacob 328
Journal of the American Medical Association
   119
The Jucklins (Read) 54
Judaism 190, 311, 317, 326-327, 332-335,
   345-348
The Judge 118, 138
Judith and Holofernes (Aldrich) 37
Judson, E. Z. C. (Ned Buntline) 53, 416
Judson, Whitcomb L. 287
Jumbo (circus elephant) 404, 415
Jupiter Lights (Woolson) 32
"Just Tell Them That You Saw Me" 36,
   70

K

Kalakaua, King of Hawaii 180, 202
Kansas City Star 118
Kansas Exodus 178
Kansas Pacific Railroad 416
Kant, Immanuel 377
Keane, Bishop John 331, 334
Keeler, James 360
Keenan, Henry Francis 30
Keith, Benjamin Franklin 29
Keller's Roman Liniment. *See* St. Jacob's
   Oil. 125
Kelly, J. W. 33
Kemmler, William 231
Kennedy, Harry 26-27, 30-31, 34-35
Kennett, Karl 38-39
Kennywood Amusement Park, Pittsburgh
   395
Kent, William 271
"Kentucky Babe" (Geibel and Buck) 37
A Kentucky Cardinal (Allen) 36
Kentucky Derby 386
Kentucky Geological Survey 378
Kenyon College 218
Kerker, Gustave 38
Kersands, Billy 57
Ketchum, Catherine 233
Key, David M. 219

Kilrain, Jake 385, 397, 418
Kindergarten movement 149, 155, 159,
   161-162, 169, 172
The King in Yellow (Chambers) 36
The King of Folly Island and Other People (
   Jewett) 80
King Solomon's Mines (Haggard) 54
King, Clarence 365-366
King, Grace 32, 34
Kingman (racehorse) 386
The King's Missive and Other Poems
   (Whittier) 27
Kingsley, Charles 32
Kipling, Rudyard 54, 119, 130, 138
Kirkland, Joseph 31-33
"Kiss Me, Honey, Do" (Stromberg and
   Smith) 38
Klein, Charles 72
Klondike gold rush 128, 290, 305-306
Knickerbocker Yacht Club 416
Knights of Columbus 283, 327
Knights of Labor 87-88, 101-103, 187,
   199-200, 241, 251, 284, 327, 351, 383,
   409
Knitters in the Sun (French) 31
Knowlton, Hosea M. 257
Know-Nothings 190, 311
Koch, Robert 361, 367
Kodak box camera 32, 89, 109, 121
Kohler, Rabbi Kaufmann 327, 346
Koster and Bial's Music Hall, New York
   City 37
Kroger grocery chain 98
Ku Klux Klan 141, 224, 227, 290, 313
Ku Klux Klan Act of 1871 313
Kunze, John 261

L

L. G. Murphy, & Company (The House)
   253-255
Labor 101-103
Labor Day 91, 284, 383, 387, 391, 409
Lacaze-Duthier, Henri 369
Ladies' Home Journal 119, 121, 126,
   129-130, 138, 295
*Ladies' Home Journal and Practical
   Housekeeper* 129-130
Ladies' Journal 129
*The Ladies' Quarterly Report of Broadway
   Fashions* 294
The Lady of the Aroostook (Howells) 26
The Lady, or the Tiger? and Other Stories
   (Stockton) 29
La Farge, John 46, 61, 74
Lake Mohonk Conference 245
Lakota tribe 227, 286, 289, 307-308, 329,
   335, 343, 390, 412
Lamar, Lucius Quintus Cincinnatus 229,
   232
Lamarck, Jean-Baptiste 378
Lamb, Arthur J. 38
Lane Presbyterian Seminary, Cincinnati
   330
Lane Seminary, Cincinnati 340

Langdell, Christopher Columbus 256,
   275-276
Langley, Samuel Pierpont 356, 359-360
Lanier, Sidney 26
Lapwai Reservation, Idaho 307-308
The Last of the Buffalo (Bierstadt) 32
"The Last of the Hogans" (Braham and
   Harrigan) 34
Launcelot and Guenevere: A Poem in Dramas
   (Hovey) 33
Law on the Frontier: The Lincoln County
   War 252-255
Lawlor, Charles B. 33, 36
Lazarus, Emma 31
Lazenby, Robert F. 88
League of American Wheelmen *Bulletin*
   401
League of American Wheelmen 401
League of Colored Baseball Clubs 399
Leake, Anna (the armless woman) 404
The Leavenworth Case (Green) 26, 54-55
Leaves of Grass (Whitman) 28, 34
The Led-Horse Claim (Foote) 29
Lee, Robert E. 385, 391, 410
Leeds, Josiah 228
Legal Education and Professionalism
   255-256
Lehmann, Lilli 55-56
Leipzig laboratory 372-373
Leisy v. Hardin 230-231
L'Enfant, Pierre-Charles 52
Pope Leo XIII 127, 329-331, 351
Leslie's Illustrated 138
Lesquereux, Leo 365
"The Letter That Never Came" (Dresser)
   30
Letters from an American Farmer
   (Crèvecoeur) 72
Lewis, Alfred Henry 37
Lexow Commission, New York 233
Lexow, Clarence 266
Libbey, Laura Jean 53
Liberal Protestantism 339, 344-345
Lick Observatory, Mount Hamilton, Calif.
   358-360
Life 119, 138, 295
*Life and Reminiscences of a 19th Century
   Gladiator* (Sullivan) 418
Life in the Iron Mills (Davis) 63
The Life Line (Homer) 30
The Life of P. T. Barnum (Barnum) 415
Life on the Mississippi (Clemens) 29, 54, 79
The Light That Failed (Kipling) 54
Light Waves and their Uses (Michelson)
   371
Liliuokalani, Queen of Hawaii 181-182,
   202
Lillie, Frank R. 371
Lincoln (Saint-Gaudens) 31, 74
Lincoln County (New Mexico
   Territory) 252-255
Lincoln Hall, Washington D.C. 243
Lincoln Memorial, Washington, D.C.
   (French) 75
Lincoln Park, Chicago 31

Morris, E. C.   335
Morro Castle, Cuba   126
Morse, Samuel F. B.   237
A Mortal Antipathy (Holmes)   30
Morton, Hugh   38
Morton, Julius Sterling   409
Morton, Levi P.   180, 210
Mosaic laws   327, 346-347
Moses, Phoebe Anne Oakley. *See* Oakley, Annie.
Moss, Thomas   258
"The Moth and the Flame" (Witt and Taggart)   39
Mother and Child (Cassatt)   78
Mother and Children (Cassatt)   43
"Mother Was a Lady" (Stern and Marks)   37
Mother's Goodnight Kiss (Cassatt)   78
Motion pictures   32, 37
Mott, Frank Luther   54
Mott, John R.   328
"The Mottoes That Are Framed upon the Wall" (Mullaly and Devere)   32
Mount Hermon One Hundred   328, 353
Mount Hermon School for boys   353
Mount Rainier National Park, Washington   388, 396
Mount Royal Park, Montreal (Olmsted)   417
Movements for Change   204-208
Moving the Mountain (Gilman)   68
Mr. Barnes of New York (Gunter)   54
Mr. Dooley in Peace and War (Dunne)   38
Mr. Isaacs (Crawford)   28
Mr. Tangier's Vacations (Hale)   32
Mrs. Cassatt Reading to Her Gradchildren (Cassatt)   28, 78
Mrs. Joshua Montgomery Sears (Sargent)   43
Mrs. Cripp (fashion designer)   294
Muckraking   31, 52, 138, 144
Mugler v. *Kansas*   229
Mugwumps. *See* Republican Party — Mugwump faction   193
Muir, John   396
Muldoon, William   382, 396
Mullaly, W. S.   32
"The Mulligan Guard" (Harrigan)   71
The Mulligan Guard Picnic (Harrigan and Hart)   71
The Mulligan Guards' Ball (Harrigan)   26, 71
Mumford, Lewis   48, 61
Munn v. *Illinois*   197
Munro, Norman   53
Munsey, Frank A.   32, 119, 121
Munsey's Weekly   32, 121, 138
The Murder of Dr. Patrick Henry Cronin   260-261
The Murder of Police Chief David Hennessy   261-263
Murfree, Mary Noailles (Charles Egbert Craddock)   29-30, 33, 65
Murphy, Anna   260
Murphy, Isaac   386
Murphy, Joseph   30
Murphy, Lawrence   253-254
Museum of Art, Philadelphia   65

Museum of Fine Arts, Boston   65
Museum of Natural History, New York City (Cady)   55
Museum of Science and Industry, Chicago   391
Mutrie, James   398
"My Best Girl's a New Yorker" (Stromberg)   36
"My Dad's Dinner Pail" (Braham and Harrigan)   29
"My Gal Is a High Born Lady" (Fagan)   37
"My Gal Sal" (Dresser)   70
"My Love's a Rover" (White)   27
"My Old Kentucky Home" (Foster)   56
"My Old New Hampshire Home" (Tilzer and Sterling)   38
My Path Through Life (Lehmann)   55
"My Pedagogic Creed" (Parker)   173
My Wayward Pardner (Holley)   27
"My Wild Irish Rose" (Olcott)   39, 69
Myers, Lawrence "Lon"   392, 416
Myrick, N. Sumner   258
The Mysterious Stranger (Clemens)   79

N

Naismith, James   385, 400
Nana (Zola)   54
Napoleon   138, 308
The Narrative of the Life of Frederick Douglass (Douglass)   36
The Nation   118, 123, 142-143
National Academy of Design   46
National Academy of Sciences   366, 368-369
National Afro-American Council, Rochester, N.Y.   331
National Archery Association   382
National Association (baseball)   414, 417
National Association for the Advancement of Colored People (NAACP)   142
National Association of Amateur Athletes of America (N4A)   382, 391-392
National Association of Amateur Athletes. *See also* Amateur Athletic Union.   384
National Association of Base Ball Players (NABBP)   397, 399
National Association of Manufacturers   91
National Association of Professional Base Ball Players (NAPBBP)   397
National Association of Window Trimmers   92, 97
National Baptist Convention   330
National Baptist Convention, U.S.A., Inc.   335
National Baseball Hall of Fame   414
National Basketball League   388
National Carbon Company   358
National Cash Register Company   162
National Collegiate Athletic Association   415
National Colored Farmer's Alliance   206
National Cordage Company   103
National Croquet Association   383
National Divorce Reform League   228
National Editorial Association   120

National Education Association   149, 151, 172
National Education Association — Committee of Ten   151, 171
National Equal Rights Party   284
National Farmers Alliance of the Northwest   206
National Federation of Settlements   319
National Geographic Magazine   121, 358
National Geographic Society   121
National Grange   134
National Herbart Society for the Scientific Study of Education   152
National League (baseball)   382-386, 397
National League of Professional Base Ball Clubs (NL)   397-400, 414, 417-418
National League of Professional Basketball (NLPB)   400
National Meet of American Bicyclists   382
National Municipal League   271
National Museum   369
National Observatory   366
National Police Gazette   396-397
National Printer-Journalist   119
National Refiners Association   110
National Silver Party   210
National Woman Suffrage Association (NWSA)   315, 319-320
National-American Woman Suffrage Association   315-317, 320, 323
Nationalism   205
Nationalist Clubs   205, 207
Nationalist Party   59
Nativism   180, 190, 284-285, 290, 309, 311, 328, 337
Naturalism (literature)   42, 52, 55, 67-69
Navajo tribe   253
Neagle, David   230
Nebraska State Board of Agriculture   409
Neebe, Oscar   250
Negotiable Instruments Law   233, 238
Negro Fellowship League   323
Negro Press Association   322
Negro World   142
"Nellie Bly Guessing Match"   129
Nelson, Alice Moore Dunbar   36, 39
Nelson, Ella   274
Nelson, William Rockhill   118
Neoclassicism (architecture)   41-42
"Never Take No For an Answer" (Mitchell)   30
Nevin, Ethelbert   32, 38
New Atlantis (Bacon)   59
"The New Colossus" (Lazarus)   31
New Education   170-171
New England Divorce Reform League   225
New England Headlands (Hassam)   43
New England Magazine   35
A New England Nun (Freeman)   33, 65
New England Society of New York   97
The New Era or the Coming Kingdom (Strong)   330
New Journalism   124, 133, 141, 143
New Orleans Chamber of Commerce   263
New Orleans Exposition (1885)   284, 390
"The New South" (Grady)   97

Typhoid 367

U

U.S. v. 43 Gallons of Whiskey 227
Udall, Lyn 38-39
Ultima Thule (Longfellow) 27
The Uncalled (Dunbar) 39
Uncle Lisha's Shop (Robinson) 31
Uncle Remus 27, 34, 54, 65
Uncle Tom's Cabin (silent movie) 58, 79-80
Underground Railroad 73
Unguarded Gates and Other Poems (Aldrich) 36
Union army 53, 63, 72, 143, 172, 181, 189, 209, 215-216, 218, 272, 274, 293, 352, 409, 415
Union army — 42nd Ohio Regiment 216
Union army — Seventh New York Regiment 349
Union College 212
Union Labor Party 89, 180
Union Law School, Chicago 213
Union National Bank 216
Union Pacific Railroad 88, 113, 135, 236
Union Prayer Book 330
Union Theological Seminary, New York 329, 333, 340, 349-350
Union Trust Building, Saint Louis (Sullivan) 47
Unions 70, 87-88, 90-91, 95, 100-103, 106, 111-112, 132, 155, 180, 187, 199-200, 206, 214, 232, 238, 249, 251, 270, 295, 310, 374, 399
Unitarianism 141, 171
United Brotherhood of Carpenters and Joiners 70
United Brotherhood. *See* Clan-na-Gael 260
United Fruit Company 92
United Labor Party 89
United Mine Workers (UMW) 89, 91, 104
United Press 119, 124, 136
United Societies for Liberal Sunday Laws 267
United States Christian Commission 352
United States Golf Association (USGA) 386-387, 408
U.S. heavyweight championship 385
United States Intercollegiate Lacrosse Association 383
United States Lawn Tennis Association (USLTA) 382, 384, 410-411
U.S. Open golf tournament 387, 408
U.S. Steel 114
United States Type Founders Association 120
United States v. *Cruikshank* 243
United States v. *E. C. Knight* 270
United States v. *E. C. Knight Company* 91, 234, 274
U.S. v. *Kagama* 228
United States v. *Workmen's Amalgamated Council* 90
United Typothetae of America 120

Universal Peace Union 323
University Athletic Club of New York 386, 391
University of Berlin 349, 377
University of Chicago 50, 92, 114, 151-153, 155, 157, 161, 388, 400, 403
University of Chicago — School of Education 173
University of Cincinnati — Law School 276
University of Edinburgh 407
University of Iowa 150, 400
University of Pennsylvania 87, 151, 368, 384-386, 388
University of the South 35
University of Virginia 349
University of Wisconsin 151
—Law School 276
Upham, John B. 407
Urban League 142
Urbanization 40, 42, 47, 51-52, 67, 81, 93-95, 107, 124, 154-155, 159, 207, 332, 352
United States
  — Agriculture Department 13, 181, 189, 368, 409
  — Army 106, 128, 133, 158, 225, 238, 243, 277, 356, 366, 385, 396, 407, 411, 416
  — Army — Cavalry 390, 411, 416
  — Army — Seventh Cavalry 133, 329
  — Army — Third Nebraska Regiment (Silver Regiment) 213
  — Army Corps of Engineers 365
  — Army Medical Corps 360
  — Army Third Cavalry 133
  — Attorney General's Office 270
  — Board of Education 167, 172
  — Board of Health 172
  — Bureau of Animal Husbandry 357
  — Bureau of Education 150, 189
  — Bureau of Indian Affairs 189, 201, 335
  — Bureau & Labor 88
  — Capitol building, Washington D.C. 227, 237
  — Census 33
  — Census Board 282, 286
  — Census Bureau 189
  — Civil Service Commission 179, 189, 193, 266
  — Coast and Geodetic Survey 356, 361, 364, 366, 378
  — Coast Survey. *See* USG Coast and Geodetic Survey.
  — Committee on Alcoholic Liquor Traffic 224
  — Congress 62, 73, 86-91, 99-100, 114, 127, 134-135, 147, 148, 157, 178-185, 187-188, 192-197, 201-203, 205-206, 208, 211, 213-219, 224, 226-227, 229-231, 233-241, 243-244, 246, 248, 251-252, 254, 259, 263-264, 269-270, 273-274, 276-277, 282-285, 287-288, 306, 313, 324, 327, 358, 364, 366-367, 369, 387, 409
  — Constitution 62, 182, 185-186,

207, 230, 232, 234, 239-244, 251-252, 254, 264-265, 267, 270, 272, 274, 282, 287, 319; *Bill of Rights:* 241; *Eighteenth Amendment:* 207; *Fifteenth Amendment:* 187, 193, 319; *Fourteenth Amendment:* 88, 201, 228, 239, 243, 264-265, 267-269, 273, 319; *Fourth Amendment:* 254; *Nineteenth Amendment:* 187, 290, 315, 320; *Seventeenth Amendment:* 189; *Sixteenth Amendment:* 234, 252; *Thirteenth Amendment:* 243, 264-265, 273
  — Courts of Indian Offenses 330
  — Customs 224
  — Dawes Commission 245
  — Electoral College 180, 210
  — Fish Commission 366
  — Fish Commission laboratory, Woods Hole, Mass. 371
  — Geological and Geographical Survey of the Territories 365
  — Geological Survey 189, 361, 365-367, 369, 378
  — Geological Survey — Atlantic Coast Division 378
  — House Appropriations Committee 188
  — House of Representatives 62, 178-183, 185, 188-189, 193, 197, 200, 208-209, 213, 216, 219, 224
  — House of Representatives Rules Committee 188, 219
  — House Ways and Means Committee 188
  — Hydrographic Bureau 366
  — Interior Department 88, 189, 201, 365, 396
  — Interstate Commerce Commission 180, 189, 198
  — Interstate Commerce Commission (ICC) 237, 270
  — Justice Department 100, 254, 277
  — Labor Department 89, 180, 189
  — Land Office 189
  — Marine Band 44
  — Marines 182, 202
  — Meteorological Bureau 366
  — Mississippi River Commission 218
  — National Museum 366
  — National Park Service 396
  — Naval Academy 215
  — Naval Hydrographic Office 364
  — Naval Observatory 361
  — Naval War College 179
  — Navy 126-127, 179-180, 187, 202, 204, 207, 213, 215, 218, 263, 267, 385
  — Navy — Asiatic Squadron 215
  — Navy — Board of Inspection and Survey 215
  — Navy — Bureau of Equipment 215
  — Navy — General Board of the Navy 215
  — Navy — Lighthouse Board 215
  — Ninth Kansas Cavalry 415
  — Office of Indian Affairs 335
  — Pension Bureau 189
  — Post office 123, 128, 179, 266, 284

INDEX OF PHOTOGRAPHS